*Cutting Edges*

# Cutting Edges

## POSTMODERN CRITICAL ESSAYS
## ON EIGHTEENTH-CENTURY SATIRE

Tennessee Studies in Literature, Volume 37

**Edited by James E. Gill**

•

The University of Tennessee Press
Knoxville

**Library of Congress Cataloging-in-Publication Data**

Cutting edges: postmodern critical essays on eighteenth-century satire/
    edited by James E. Gill. —1st.
                    p.          cm.   —(Tennessee Studies in literature, v. 37)
        Includes bibliographical references and index.
        ISBN 0–87049–892–4 (cloth: alk. paper)
        1. Satire, English—History and criticism.
        2. English literature—18th century—History and criticism.
        3. Postmodernism (Literature)—Great Britain.
        4. Literature and society—Great Britain—History—18th century.
        I. Gill, James E., 1935-
        II. Series.
        PR935.C87    1995
        827'.509—dc20                                            95-4362
                                                                   CIP

*for Martha*

# Contents

# Preface

*James E. Gill*

The essays in this volume attempt in modest ways to discuss that most protean literary something—satire—in several of its manifestations in the great age of English satire. Some examine little-known works rendered especially interesting by postmodern concerns—the problems of authorship, the role of women, and modes of exchange; and some strive to think anew about well-known works in terms of contemporary critical issues. Nearly all of them have in some way or another come to see eighteenth-century satire and eighteenth-century issues within the framework of postmodern critical approaches—a mélange of sometimes ill-separated analytics such as Marxism, the new historicism, reader-reception theory, structuralism, deconstruction, dialogism and the special case of the carnivalesque, Foucaultian discourse analysis, Lacanian psychology, various kinds of feminist criticism, and the like. None of these approaches seem entirely able to exclude the others since they are related to one another in complex ways. What they have in common is a penchant for decentering interesting works of art and relating them to such intellectual material—philosophical, psychological, socioeconomic, semiological, and anthropological. They disperse the artwork across a range of interests and considerations rather than concentrating it or isolating and protecting it from all the worlds of contemporary thought and experience, and they tend to distrust exclusive moral or philosophical stances, especially those feigning embattled and lonely disinterestedness and objectivity. The disruption of the hegemonies of the New Criticism, phenomenology, and positivist historicisms by postmodernist critiques has sometimes led their practitioners bitterly to complain of the postmodernist as nihilistic and hypocritical. These are serious charges, but they are charges which can be leveled at certain individual practitioners of any movement or school of thought, as well as against those very stances themselves from which the charges have been hurled—stances which have achieved institutional power and status.

Most bona fide intellectual positions and practices in fact mark out "enemy territory" which includes the weaknesses of earlier attitudes and practices; and it seems to be an ineradicable truth that whenever critical positions receive "official sanction," their days are numbered. "New thought" derives much of its vitality and energy from its ability to point out the weaknesses of "old thought." Just as the Leavises sought to redeem culture from the Quiller-Couch school of criticism, so latter-day Marxists, among others, have sought to rescue literature from the growing isolation of the *Scrutiny* group. The New Critics attacked positivist historicism as a part of their revolt against modern industrial society and its values. Postmodern thinkers—who are, I repeat, not without their vanities, hypocrisies, and "roadblocks"—have developed in part through their ability to detect inconsistencies and the subtle violences in all of these earlier intellectual movements, and so they are in a manner continuing a vital part of the intellectual enterprises of their predecessors even in attacking them or revising their findings. As Linda Hucheon has pointed out, to participate in a special discourse is in some measure to contest it just as contesting it in some measure entails complicity with it. Indeed, perhaps the best justification for theory-based investigation of eighteenth-century satire is that both theory-based investigation and eighteenth-century satire are extremely skeptical; as James Thompson observed, both are characterized by what Paul Ricoeur calls the "hermeneutics of suspicion," and both are acutely aware that "language is always ironic—always pointing to the gap between signifier and signified" and hence "to the irreducible figuration of satire itself."

The authors of the essays in this volume express no contempt or impatience with their predecessors, and in many ways they continue their predecessors' work. At the very least, they bring to their enterprise a different view of the relation of language to reality and an expanded view of literature's subject matter and readership as well as a sense of the political relatedness of all intellectual disciplines and undertakings. No doubt, postmodernist approaches and attitudes have their blind sides, and this fact will doubtless have the real benefit of provoking (if it has not done so already) a post-post-modernism. At the very least, as Gerald Graff has persistently argued, we can confront and teach our differences. Indeed, we are obligated to do so.

This awareness of the multiple contexts of thought is one of the advantages of the approaches taken here. Just as the rise of formalist criticism in reaction to romanticism obscured its romantic origins and affinities in its isolation of the work of art and its application of the idea of "organic unity" or unitary truth (if nothing else), so the postmodern reactions to formalism, positivist historicism, and phenomenology have at least provided alternative models of reading by challenging their predecessors' cultural hegemony. And at the same time they have compelled sophisticated readers to acknowledge afresh the multiple contexts of reading through a general awareness of complex intertexts and intertextuality. If in looking at an "other" we cannot escape seeing ourselves in its reflective surfaces, there arises the question of whether that is all we can see or whether we can find a "crack in the mirror" which enables us to see something else—or if nothing else, to see ourselves as fractured and fragmented—"to explore our own critical and ideological blindspots," as one of the authors writing here comments, and to see ourselves differently than before. No one today would argue that awareness of differences insures "progress" or change (or, for that matter, even avoids a covert narcissism); but no one can argue that change of any kind in a not-too-perfect world can occur without such awareness.

The possibility of change is modestly served, I believe, in collections like this one in which a certain relatedness can be discerned in the matters, issues, and approaches which have often hitherto seemed obscure, different, or even irreconcilable. One of the essays included here deals, for example, with the issue of the grounds and "politics" of contemporary readings of Swift's *A Tale of a Tub*; and in a discussion of little-known political satires of the 1690s Robert Markley justifies his undertaking as being the kind of reassessment which enables readers to excavate the contradictions—contradictions arising from the crises of political economy in a time of war and scarcity—that such poems paradoxically foreground and mystify. Another general concern also appears here—the issue of the uses and abuses of satire, which John Zomchick shows here in his essay on Burney's *Evelina* to have become an element in the sexual maturing of the bourgeois subject. This same topic can be seen as a reflexive concern in earlier satirists—indeed, the issue may be inseparable from many satiric enterprises—as they have reflected on their motives and their ability or inability to correct, reform, or destroy the old, the unreal, and the corrupt. Indeed, one can see a neat reversal from early to late, as Jean Marsden reveals here, in Shadwell's drama, where the disruptiveness of satire is constantly allied with the disruptiveness—sometimes creative and sometimes destructive—of female sexuality. In other essays, Melinda Rabb deals with Mrs. Manley's struggle with the "masculine" mode of satire in two of her plays, and Mitzi Myers delineates Maria Edgeworth's satiric subversion of English cultural hegemony in her *Irish Bulls*.

A related topic treated here is the tendency of satire to become something else—to become an aspect of the novel, just as previously, according to Deborah Payne, it was assimilated into, but differed from, the comedy of the Restoration. In another case, in terms of Niklas Luhmann's systems theory, Jonathan Lamb gives a sensitive and recondite account of the metamorphosis of satire in Johnson's great formal verse satire *The*

*Vanity of Human Wishes*. In a little-known satire by the dramatist Thomas Otway, Jessica Munns also investigates the limitations of satire. Yet another essay, by Janice Thaddeus, studies subtle satiric ventriloquism in the now difficult-to-read constructive satire of Godwin by his admirer-critic Elizabeth Hamilton. In yet another case, Lindy Riley shows, through analyzing Mary Davys's mockery of traditional literary feminine inscriptions, how a minor novelist suggests the re-creation of honest relationships between the sexes.

There are other related insights also. Readers, for example, can trace herein through two independent studies—those of Braverman and Dunn—the issue of satiric "embodiment" in a range of texts—of literary practices and opinions—and by doing so compare and contrast in a fair-minded way their complementary methods and results, become aware of satiric embodiments' unexpected contributions to other kinds of thought, and assess the promise of further combination and development. One of these studies examines the sociohistorical construction of persons, places, and things in the context of the field "bodyworks," after Foucault, Scarry, and Stallybras and White. Against the "classical body"—which "projects its physicality but deflects its corporeality so as to sustain the aura rooted in the elevation not of just *any* body but of the *male* body" as "the public body par excellence, the measure of the world"—is juxtaposed with Bakhtin's grotesque body, which the "great champions of the classical body . . . ventriloquized," adopting its terms "whilst attempting to purify the language of the tribe," namely the "'body of classical writing.'" The other, related essay examines the collapse of epideictic literature in the seventeenth century into the imagery of abjection in satire and its incorporation in the Burkean sublime which in part arises from it. Writers considered include Butler, Rochester, Swift, Sterne, and Burke. This topic, I might add, also is related to the metamorphoses of satire as well as to satire's attempts to re-figure, or metamorphose, "realities."

This volume also includes a revised view of the satire of the Restoration—one which challenges the traditional view of all satire of the period 1660–1800 as criticisms "of the 'irrational' beliefs and 'dangerous dogmas' of the past" by contrasting abuses with positive norms. In short, it challenges the view that satire holds a mirror up to nature in order to lash knaves and fools. Rose Zimbardo sees in the satire of Rochester or Wycherley, for example, not parodies of real social types but "linguistic signs" and mental processes which force readers to "*create* the 'artifactuality of the real' and to embrace the 'fictiveness of truth.'" This "postmodern" view of satire as virtually a self-referential signifying system—one which Zimbardo interestingly grounds in the age's pervasive

Augustinianism—might be implicitly questioned in some essays, but it receives interesting partial corroboration from, among other sources, Dunn's scrutiny of the Restoration's assault on epideictic rhetoric through the imagery of abjection: "in rhetorical terms, abjection is not only a denial of epideictic amplification but of mimetic representation insofar as that it implies a process of generalization or the linguistic exchange of one term for another. The imagery of abjection," he observes, "supports a nominalist skepticism; it subverts linguistic equivalence with a deictic gesture toward a pure particularity." Some basic ambivalences of satire and aporia in the satiric structure of *Gulliver* IV are delineated in another approach through desconstructionist and sacrificial theory.

Another essay seeks to reconsider "Augustan" semiosis through Pope's view of the feminine in his satires. The question is transformed from one of whether Pope is "devaluing" women in a traditional way into one in which the feminine plays a somewhat different, even more fundamental role in the poet's signifying system. Yet other essays, as I note above, particularly examine the feminine as it is related to satire—both being dangerous, disruptive forces—in the plays of Thomas Shadwell and Mrs. Manley, and yet another considers feminine maturation in connection with the satiric impulse.

Other studies in very different ways seek to contextualize eighteenth-century satire. One of them, by David Wheeler, considers Pope's *Rape of the Lock* in the hands of a modern general reader, and another, by Nigel Wood, strenuously seeks to discover this "poem" amidst its many isotexts. Yet another defining "context" of the satirist's work is the use of the golden age—here studied in two minor poems of the late 1690s, one of them Whig and the other Tory, as they reflect "crises within what Jean-Joseph Goux calls the 'symbolic economies' of money and identity, the dynamics by which values are asserted, contested, subverted and rein-scribed." (In this scheme, in an economy of scarcity the genre of "renunciation" is satire—the "recognition of the Imaginary in crisis.") And Donna Landry's study consists of recognizing Pope's efforts to develop as context very special senses of the value of the countryside by combining the ideology of stewardship, especially its managerial relation to the rural and the natural world, with the suburban desire to substitute the country of the mind for the country as it is, which depends "upon a relation to the rural that is at once 'other,' primarily instrumental, and even coercively regulatory in its attitude." In another register, Claudia Thomas studies Pope's efforts to create a space for the bona fide "author," amidst grubstreet writers, in bourgeois society. J. Douglas Canfield sees pervasive, growing capitalism as the ground which Gay's and Fielding's dramatic satire in their separate ways join in rejecting.

The organization of the volume is roughly chronological, but it endeavors also to refine some issues and problems and to set some obviously related efforts together as well as to reveal a variety of approaches to literature which can be grouped under the heading "postmodern." All of these essays do what they were intended to do—they suggest fresh perspectives and relationships, and they provide hard-won knowledge about, intelligent approaches to, and vital insights into their subjects. If something less than a clear history and unified theory of eighteenth-century English satire emerges, that too was part of this project's modestly skeptical intention—to stimulate and provoke in thoughtful ways.

I would like to acknowledge the generous support of the John C. Hodges Better English Fund and the editorial board of *Tennessee Studies in Literature*. Especially heartening have been the help and encouragement of Allen Carroll and Norman Sanders. For suggestions about contributors, I am grateful to J. Douglas Canfield, Paula Bachscheider, James Turner, and Helen Burke, as well as to the essayists within. For help in assessing certain work I thank my colleagues and friends, especially Allen Dunn, John Zomchick, and Jack H. Wilson. For long-term, indispensable help, I am deeply thankful for my stalwart sons, Jonathan Gill and James Gill, and for my beloved wife, Martha Moore Gill.

# Comedy, Satire, or Farce?

## Or the Generic Difficulties
## of Restoration Dramatic Satire

*Deborah C. Payne*

## i. The Question at Issue

When it comes to Restoration plays, have we ever been able to distinguish between "comedies" and "satires"? And do our taxonomical difficulties indicate something vexed about the form itself, especially during the late seventeenth century?[1] This might seem an odd question to pose in the wake of postmodernism.[2] If a "text" results from the particular theoretical "lens" through which it is read, then it follows that critics deploying different theories will produce different classifications: some will see satire where others find comedy. While this seems incontrovertible, one is still struck by the unanimity of critical opinion when it comes to classifying other types of eighteenth-century literature, postmodernist clichés aside for the moment. Fielding may have described *Tom Jones* as a "history" (the same term Defoe used for his novels), but for some time now critics have called these texts "novels." The same generic boundaries hold firm for prose and verse satire. Is *A Tale of a Tub* ever called a "comedy"? *The Rape of the Lock* a farce? As much as critics might disagree locally about Swift's corpus, his name is virtually synonymous with the literary category we call satire.

When we turn to Restoration comedy these generic borders deliquesce. Classification proves equivocal, whether the object of scrutiny is a well-known play like Sir George Etherege's *The Man of Mode* or a lesser-known text like John Dryden's *The Kind Keeper or, Mr. Limberham.* Jocelyn Powell, for instance, considers *The Man of Mode* a "comedy of the classical tradition," which, like Etherege's other plays, shows "a subjective understanding and enjoyment of experience for its own sake, rather than a satirical awareness of the absurdity and pretentiousness of man's behavior" (63). This is not a definition that Laura Brown would recognize. By contrast, she sees this play as a "dramatic social satire . . . the formal expression of a peculiarly vexed and conflicted ideology, fundamentally conservative in its allegiance to traditional values and to the status quo, but daringly radical in its exposure of the hypocrisy, the immorality, and the material-ism of the society it must finally accept" (42). Robert Markley thinks the "social satire gives way to an ironic rendering of upper-class society that implicates the audience in the ambiguities of fashionable pretence and deception" (121).

Regarding *The Kind Keeper; Or, Mr. Limberham,* generic appellations are equally mixed. Robert D. Hume sees it as "a roaring, dirty farce" (34), a designation Richard W. Bevis also upholds: "a sex farce that out-trashes Durfey" (91). Susan Staves considers the play a "cynical comedy," a form "markedly more realistic than the romantic gay couple or cheerful in-trigue comedy that preceded it" (*Players' Scepters* 168). Laura Brown wants to classify it (and Dryden's other later comedies, such as *The Assignation* and *Amphitryon*) as "full social satires" (34). Eric Rothstein and Frances M. Kavenik, by contrast, regard *Mr. Limberham* as another instance of Dryden's habit of fusing generic "idioms"—in this case, comedy and farce—but with an important difference: ". . . Dryden does not counterpoint the two idioms, in accord with the technique of his double-plot plays of the 1660s or *Marriage A-la-Mode.* Rather, he sandwiches them together so that they say the 'same' thing" (205).

Even that most seemingly satiric of all Restoration plays, *The Plain Dealer,* by "manly" William Wycherley, slips through grasping critical fingers. Rose Zimbardo claims that Wycherley's "last two plays show the direct influence of Roman satire, particularly that of Juvenal" (124). While she pronounces Wycherley a satirist and his play a satire, this con-viction is by no means universally shared. Thomas H. Fujimura, writing some thirteen years earlier, says that "it is inferior as a play and also as a comedy of wit" (146). While admitting the presence of satiric elements, he nonetheless lists the play as a "wit comedy." Critics writing after Zimbardo are not quite certain what to make of it generically. Robert D. Hume, not one to eschew codification, says only that "its elements are an interesting mingling of 'domestic' social satire and 'foreign' intrigue and sword-play. The rape and sex motifs are a sign of the times. . . . Into this jumble of standard parts Wycherley's satiric fervour, however muddled, infuses exceptional vitality" (304). Robert Markley claims that *The Plain Dealer* is "structured on the premise that neither harsh satire nor festive comedy in and of itself adequately represents social reality" (178). And Eric Rothstein and Frances M. Kavenik alternate between "comedy," "satiric," and "moraliste wit" in describing the play (190–91).

In brief, critics cannot agree upon even the most basic of generic cat-egories. No one would call Swift's texts anything other than "satires"; however, the same cannot be said of Wycherley's plays, even though he is considered the most "satiric" of Restoration dramatists. This is not to suggest that other literary forms enjoy some sort of utopian critical consensus—far from it—but rather to propose that Restoration comedies (or even Augustan comedies, for that matter) present us with a fundamental difficulty in classification. New Critics, such as W. K. Wimsatt, spoke nearly thirty years ago of the "problem" of distinguishing satire from comedy; indeed, Wimsatt concluded that it was "insoluble" (88), as did Northrop Frye: "the distinction between an ironic comedy and a comic satire . . . is tenuous" (177).

Scholarly criticism of satire, be it the transhistorical examination of a genre or the historical study of a form, supports this claim; critics either ignore drama entirely or tiptoe around one lonely example. David Nokes, for instance, claims that "the literature of the early eighteenth century, indeed the literature of the entire century from the Restoration of Charles II to the accession of George III, is dominated by satire" (1). The drama, with the sole exception of John Gay's *The Beggar's Opera,* is exempt from this cultural domination, though. Nor does Nokes's one example even qualify as true satire, combining, as it were, "lightweight" entertainment and "serious social" satire (135), the same sort of generic mélange characteristic of the Restoration plays described previously.

A more recent study of eighteenth-century satire by Claude Rawson again registers the sense that, in the age prior to 1750, "satire was a dominant mode of literary expression" (xii). He is virtually silent on the subject of the drama, though. The same pattern holds true for studies of satire during the Renaissance; revealingly, Jonson's *Volpone* is the one play cited (if any are cited at all) and largely for reasons I describe below. Even a critical study upholding the idea of "dramatic satire"—Jean B. Kern's *Dramatic Satire in the Age of Walpole 1720–1750*—struggles mightily with classification: "What is dramatic satire? Obviously it is close to comedy because of the accepted importance of wit and humor in satire. This is why distinctions between comedy and satire are so often blurred and inconclusive" (4). Ultimately, this "blurring" becomes the form's greatest strength, allowing for "multiplicity and fluidity, borrowing and juxtaposing techniques to create new forms of drama" (4), making, as it were, an aesthetic virtue out of generic indeterminacy.

By now, it should be fairly evident that there *is* something about drama that resists—or makes difficult—the production of "pure" satire on the stage. Rather than pose this observation in terms of a generic "problem" to be solved (as though by arriving at the "right" category we can somehow prove that these plays are satires after all), I would like to examine the formal and historical conditions that make satire and comedy uneasy bedfellows. Simply put, the aims of satire differ from those of drama. The very semiotic texture of theatre makes dramatic satire almost impossible to realize utterly on the stage, while the narrative voice essential to satire tends to be absent in drama. Inevitably, dramatic satire drifts toward comedy, the genre more in keeping with the theatre's particular strengths, thus accounting for the hybridization of so many of these plays.

In making these claims, I can be accused of falling back on some rather un-postmodernist critical moves—specifically, my reliance on structuralism and semiotics to explain at least part of this phenomenon. If I believed— as I do not—that drama or satire existed prior to history, then the criticism would be apt. Rather, I am suggesting that comedy in the theatre is based (in a very Derridean sense) on a positive exclusion of the very thing necessary to satire—narration. It is in that sense that comedy operates as the determined exclusion of satire. Although critiques of Derrida often level accusations of nihilism or subjectivism, as Jonathan Loesberg has shown, Derrida's questioning of foundations—including the "science" of structuralism—shows "the necessary inclusion within foundational systems of elements they need to exclude in order to remain internally coherent" (91). The question then becomes: why must comedy exclude narration to function coherently as theatre? And why is narration so important to satiric meaning?

In another sense, then, my reading is "exorbitant" (to use another Derridean term), largely because it is based on the theme of supplementarity. As Derrida notes, any theme (even the theme of supplementarity) is simply one among many (163), and, indeed, other explanations could be substituted for the one I offer below. But in describing those formal properties that hold apart satire and comedy, I am not claiming for them an ontological status; instead, through a kind of pragmatic observation based on certain questions (Why do these patterns occur? Why don't we have a narrative theatre? Why can't criticism talk about dramatized satire?), I am following, as Derrida puts it, "a wandering thought on the possibility of itinerary and of method" (162). And, just as Derrida justifies his use of Rousseau "as an event that was too exorbitant to serve as an example even as that exorbitance itself was the only example possible" (Loesberg 131), similarly, the structural and semiotic themes noted below exceed as they suffice.

History, of course, always qualifies genre. And it is in this sense that formal considerations of a genre inevitably invoke history to explain origins, change, and exceptions. Thus, it should not surprise that the hybrid noted above, the play poised between comedy and satire, appears more frequently in some periods rather than others. Certain dramatic techniques, such as highly exaggerated characters and "closed" actions, can arrest a play's natural drift toward comedy, anchoring it more firmly in satiric waters. During the Restoration period, though, such "hypercorrective" techniques were difficult to sustain in the theatre. The architectural features of the playhouse, the customs governing performance, not to mention the sheer performative nature of social life complicated the culture's equally strong impulse toward verse satire. Additionally, censorship governing the theatre made it difficult for playwrights to transmit satire's normative values in as public a realm as the theatre. In effect, the phenomenon of the Restoration play, half comedy, half satire, can be explained culturally as well as structurally.

### ii. The Structure of Satire and the Structure of Drama

Nearly thirty years ago, Alvin B. Kernan argued that "satire always contains either an implicit or explicit set of values, which frequently takes specific form in judgments on such matters as what kind of food to eat, how to manage your wife and your household, how to dress, how to choose your friends and treat your guests, what kind of plays to frequent and what kind of books to read, how to conduct political life" (16). Readers must be able to discern these authorial "judgments"; or, as Edward A. and Lillian D. Bloom observe, "a successful satire engages its readers so that we share the satirist's point of view and his emotional strain" (34). Today this critical view still persists. George A. Test contends that "in most satires what the satirist disapproves of tends to be clear-cut because the satirist has succeeded in keeping the target in focus and in the foreground. There cannot therefore be unintentional satire" (29). Even a revisionist genre critic like John Snyder notes how satire uses "literary strategies for gaining moral, social, religious, or political ascendancy by *reasoned demonstration* [emphasis mine] that its high targets really are what they have been from the start—low" (97).

Satire's generic imperative, then, requires that the object of its attack be manifest. Even the satires of Swift, notoriously opaque, ambiguous, and self-referential, convey some sort of authorial perspective, leer as it might through trick mirrors: "From the perceived failures of human reason, Swift and his 'author'/narrators construct narratives that appear to traverse time and space, taking us with them on their pilgrimage which, we learn gradually, does not result in progress. Nevertheless, when their, and our, fictions are exposed, we then arrive not at the austere security of bare literal truth (which is nothing without a fiction to comprehend it) but at more inclusive fictions" (Zimmerman 177). Swift's author/narrators may inhabit narrative fun houses, but even that sort of metafictionality thematizes, in Zimmerman's words, "the limits of human understanding and . . . the seemingly limitless human capacity for constructing fictions that make private perversions appear to be public institutions" (177). For satire to be satire, an object—an ultimate point—of the attack must emerge, even if that object is the very opacity of satiric fictions.

As a structural device, narrative voice is essential to establishing the "ultimate point" of the satire. In some texts, the narrator makes his point by sheer *enumeratio,* if nothing else, as in Juvenal's *Third Satire,* where the speaker's complaints range from millionaires and Greeks to the "sanitary engineers and municipal architects, men/Who by swearing black is white land all the juicy contracts" (88). This tirade supposedly proves that "There's no room in this city . . . for the decent professions" (87), a sentiment the narrator seconds with his feet at the end of the poem. Satires more hortative than evidentiary in rhetorical structure also rely heavily on narration to "make a point." The speaker urges a particular proposition, one that often challenges conventional wisdom, as in Rochester's *Satyr* [Upon Mankind] where the speaker champions animal instinct over reason: "Were I . . . a Spirit free, to choose for my own share,/What Case of Flesh, and Blood, I pleas'd to weare,/I'd be a Dog, a Monkey, or a Bear,/ Or any thing but that vain Animal,/Who is so proud of being rational" (91–92). We grasp the point of the satire, quite simply, because the narrator identifies it for us.

Even when another voice appears in this sort of satire, arguing against the speaker's position (the "formal Band, and Beard," in Rochester's *Satyr,* for instance, who upholds reason), his critique does not overturn narrative point of view for this reason: dialogue within narration differs from "pure" dramatic dialogue. The latter confronts audiences *directly* with represented characters, whereas "in narrative texts they [the characters] are mediated by a more or less concrete narrative figure" (Pfister 3). Thus, dramatic characters multiply "perspectives" or possible authorial "points of view" (especially when weighted equally, as in Chekhov or Shakespeare); however, in verse and prose satire, the narrative voice mediates characters, filtering their perspectives through his own.

The speaker, then, within prose or verse satire has undue prominence by the very nature of her position: she decides what to tell us; moreover, her voice is not opposed by anything of equal weight in the text. Because the narrator occupies such an authoritative position, the temptation is great to equate her perspective with "authorial perspective" (and one might think about the elision between "authoritative" and "authorial" here). Some satirists encourage readers to draw that very equation. Pope's frequent use of autobiographical detail collapses together the normally discrete categories of "author" and "persona": who, for instance, speaks to us in *An Epistle from Mr. Pope, to Dr. Arbuthnot?* Lines like "I cough like Horace, and tho' lean, am short" (601) or "As yet a Child, nor yet a Fool to Fame,/I lisp'd in Numbers, for the Numbers came" (602) identify Pope himself as the speaker, but the verse satire is, of course, a fictional construct. And for every critic who argues that Swift's satires create a persona, a narrator who must be distinguished from the "real" author (Mack *passim*), there exists one who maintains otherwise: "*A Modest Proposal* makes sense only if we treat the voice as the author's throughout" (Ehrenpreis 35). So successfully does narration impart point of view that either we want to identify the speaker with the author, or we feel the need to argue against that very identification, which is, paradoxically, yet another manifestation of its power as a structural device.

Satires that are opaque, ironic, and self-reflexive do not as readily disclose their "ultimate point"; they nonetheless rely on narration to establish the illusion of a "truthful" or "objective" speaker, if only to allow for a deconstruction of that very objectivity (and that deconstruction eventually becomes the content of the satire). The semiotic texture of narrated language—its tendency toward *histoire* rather than *discours*—lends the narrator an air of authority, providing credence to his observations (Benveniste 237 ff.). As Keir Elam notes, "*histoire* abstracts the *énoncé*— the utterance produced—from its context" (144). In other words, while drama actively produces dialogue within a dynamic context (*discours*), narrative detaches dialogue from that context, filtering it instead through a speaker who recounts past events (*histoire*). Thus, narrative defers those questions that *discours* elicits regarding the interlocutors and their dynamic situation. Dramatic language underscores the *presence* of the interlocutors before us, making that very presence an aspect of their speechact. By contrast, a narrator recounts events and conversations that have already occurred; since we were not present at the moment of utterance (as in drama), we must perforce accept the narrator's account of things as being authoritative unless cued otherwise.

For a satirist like Pope, who speaks "in his own voice," *histoire,* or the objectified mode, linguistically sustains his textual authority, all the more important given the customarily vexed status of the satirist's own public persona (e.g., who—or what—authorizes his railing?). Even Swift, who creates patently fictional, oftentimes insane or unreliable narrators, paradoxically needs the objectified mode for his opaque, self-reflexive satires. *Histoire,* for instance, colors Gulliver's conversations with the King of Brobdingnag in Part II of *Gulliver's Travels.* By describing English political customs in the past tense, the eponymous narrator suggests their place in the natural scheme of things and himself as someone who witnessed these customs firsthand: an insider who "knows how things work." He virtually preens in the role of authoritative speaker, prefacing every description with self-important linguistic markers, such as "I began my Discourse"; "I dwelt long"; "I then spoke at large"; "I described"; "I then descended" (103–4). Not only do these statements remove us temporally from the scene of utterance (e.g., we only have Gulliver's version of what he told the King), but they also underscore his status as an unbiased observer, one who begins, dwells, speaks, and describes—all verbs of judicious impartiality.

*Histoire* also functions as one of two binary terms in a deconstruction of Gulliver's objectivity. For instance, his description of the House of Commons as "all principal Gentlemen, freely picked and culled out by the People themselves, for their great Abilities, and Love of their Country, to represent the Wisdom of the whole Nation" (104) can, of course, be taken at face value. This sentence—indeed, the entirety of Gulliver's account to the King—claims to be *about* English political culture, rather than a subjective interpretation of that culture, a claim that the objective mode grounds ontologically. The past tense in this sentence and others (e.g., "these were the Ornament and Bulwark of the Kingdom" or "to these were joined several holy Persons") shifts the grammatical emphasis from Gulliver as active interpreter to the "thing" itself, predicating his culture as unmediated presence. And it is only as unmediated presence that England can be conveyed "accurately" to the King of Brobdingnag. Moreover, Gulliver's vivid and profuse language—the doubling of verbs, the abundance of adjectives and adverbs—secures the impression of someone who knows whereof he speaks: this is simply how things *are,* he tells the King (and, by extension, us).

That same linguistic excess, though, unravels Gulliver's narrative authority and produces the irony so characteristic of Swift's writing. What, exactly, are "principal" gentlemen? And the politicians are not only "picked" by the people (as in "chosen") but "culled out," a phrase also evocative of a "cull" (an animal, according to the *OED,* removed from the flock when inferior or too old for breeding), the process of "culling," or a "cully" (a dupe). Are candidates, then, "picked and culled out" from humanity, like so many decrepit sheep from an otherwise hardy flock, to serve in the House of Commons when they are no good for anything else? If they are obsolete or nonproductive human beings, then how can Gulliver praise their "great Abilities" or claim they "represent the Wisdom of the whole Nation," especially when common experience suggests that politicians are known for neither attribute? How do we trust someone so sublimely oblivious to his own language?

Gulliver's figures also prove untrustworthy. Politicians ("Principal Gentlemen") are not described metaphorically, as might be expected from an essentialist like Gulliver, but metonymically: they were "picked and culled out" in order "to represent the Wisdom of the whole Nation." Metonymy, based on association, rather than metaphor, based on substitution, reveals the very difference Gulliver represses in his "objectified" account of English political culture as unmediated presence. English politicians are not the "Wisdom of the whole Nation"; rather, they are "culled" (like decrepit livestock?) in the hope they will prove worthy to *represent* this external attribute. Metonymy tacitly discloses a gap between "Principal Gentlemen" and "the Wisdom of the whole Nation." This figural gap, of course, functions as part of a thematic and semiotic network that structures the entire satire. *Gulliver's Travels* is pitted by such lacunae.

The objective mode characteristic of narration, then, is essential to conveying Swift's satiric perspective. As argued above, *histoire* grammatically constitutes Gulliver's authority and accuracy (the literal reading); however, other rhetorical elements in the sentence discussed call that authority into question, moving us to a second, ironic reading. As with any deconstruction, one reading does not replace another; rather, "none can exist in the other's absence" (De Man 12). Unless Gulliver's "objectivity" is first constituted, it cannot function as the error denounced by the second reading. Similarly, unless English culture is first posited as unmediated presence, it cannot subsequently prove to be representational, figural—the projection of subjective interpretation. In the end, Swift suggests that we cannot know the "outside" of our fictions. More important, we as readers grasp his satiric attack on Enlightenment positivism *because* of the role that narration plays in first constituting and then deconstructing it.[3]

Narration, arguably one of prose or verse satire's most important structural devices, constitutes drama's most fundamental lack: "Dramatic texts . . . lack the fictional narrator as an overriding point of orientation. Here, it is therefore the time-space continuum of the plot alone that determines the progress of the text within the individual scenic units" (Pfister 5). Several consequences for satire follow from this dramatic law. First, satiric point of view cannot be conveyed effortlessly in drama; characters unmediated by a narrator diffuse satire's argument by multiplying potential authorial perspectives. For a fiction to qualify as satire, as argued above, it must somehow communicate the idea, person, institution, or cultural practice under attack. Drama, more inclined to produce discursive structures, works against satire's need for argumentation and binarism.

Second, in narration the time scale of the speaker eclipses the time scale of the story, thus allowing easily for rearrangements in chronology, topography, narrative time, and locale. Satiric plots often progress disjunctively, "pieced together out of chaotic bits, or even logically illogical," in an effort to make the reader distinguish "between order and disorder, between genuine and debased values" (Bloom and Bloom 108). These kinds of disjunctive satires need the capacity to traverse time, space, and chronology that narration so easily affords. Moreover, satire, in order to explore epistemological issues, frequently uses "opticks" and perspectivism (e.g., Parts I and II of *Gulliver's Travels* or *A Tale of a Tub*), a structural technique once again secured by the different worlds, locales, and/or time frames so effortlessly produced by narrative. Drama, by contrast, lacks the mediating communication system of narration; indeed, as Manfred Pfister observes, the "temporal immediacy of dramatic presentation is *one* of the prerequisites for its physical enactment on stage" (5). The time-space continuum of successive scenes alone determines the progress of the plot in drama. Moreover, "real" time in the theatre corresponds to fictional time, an overlapping which also applies to every structural element of the theatrical text (e.g., associating the "real life" identity of the actor with the character portrayed). Thus, this absolute form of dramatic communication (theorized from Aristotle through Castelvetro) mitigates against the sort of shifts in time and locale natural to narration. "While theatre is certainly capable of panoramic changes (Shakespeare's history plays come immediately to mind), nonetheless each shift of locale and each jump in time actually undermines the absolute autonomy and immediate quality of the fiction presented because they cannot be related to an expressive subject in the internal communication system of the fiction" (Pfister 253–54). At the same time, because dramatic form lacks a central "expressive subject" to mediate those discontinuities, they must instead be organized through an internal communication system of contrasting and corresponding scenes. Therefore, this kind of discontinuous dramatic structure tends to produce expansive, epic plays in which playwrights explore multilayered plots, extensive dramatis personae, and the effects of conflict on all segments of society. Epic plays may very well convey complex and ambiguous issues, whether moral, social, or political (or an admixture of all three); however, that expansiveness runs counter to satire's need to stake out a position.

Finally, because dramatic communication results from a succession of scenes (the time-space continuum described above) organized into an action, it relies heavily on such devices as recognition, discovery, reversal, and denouement. In effect, drama creates meaning through conflict and change.[4] In satiric plots, however, we rarely see change of this nature:

"The visible satiric structure need not bring before the reader's eyes mutations akin to the theatrical ones of dramatic discovery or recognition leading to a reversal in action and a resolution. Nevertheless, a process of change emerges even though we do not expect it to take place within the structure itself or in the objects, things and people, satirized. The kinetic phenomenon becomes rather one of vision, initially the disapproving vision of the author and—he hopes—ultimately that of the reader" (Bloom and Bloom 106–7). In a sense, the plot of satire must remain constant for critique, whether authorial or readerly, to occur. Change resulting in resolution, typical of dramatic structures, undermines the very *raison d'être* of satire: if the problem has resolved itself, why the satiric censure? Thus, we can see that drama, lacking a narrator, relies heavily on movement—the temporal and spatial progression of scenes—for purposes of communication. That dramatic need for movement, however, counters satire's need for stasis, for nonmovement.

At this point, we might test some of these claims. Early on I argued that many Restoration plays "of the comic variety" remain uneasily poised between satire and comedy, partly for structural and, as I will argue below, partly for political and performative reasons. If we turn to a play like John Dryden's *The Kind Keeper or, Mr. Limberham,* some of the structural problems become evident. As in so many Restoration comedies, the transgressor (usually a male) not only escapes punishment but is seemingly rewarded for thumbing his nose at conventional morality. Although Van R. Baker sees "the very repulsiveness of the characters and the setting . . . as moral" (reform by negative precept?), the action careens rather gleefully from coupling to coupling for such an edifying message (374). *Limberham* tells the story of Woodall, a young man recently come to town, who takes lodging in a boardinghouse run by one Mrs. Saintly, a "Hypocritical Fanatick," as the *Personae Dramatis* informs us (Dryden 274). The ensuing action reveals that the boardinghouse is little more than a bordello, the landlady little more than a bawd, and Aldo, one of the other boarders, none other than Woodall's long-lost father. After much switching of partners and pressing of mattresses, Woodall is pledged to Mrs. Saintly's supposed daughter who turns out to be a true aristo: "she has as good blood running in her veins, as the best of you . . . besides, a Fortune of twelve hundred a year" (Dryden 91). The Limberham of the title is actually an ancillary character in a subplot involving Mrs. Tricksey, his "Termagant kept Mistress." His inability to maintain her sexual interest provides the longest-running (and most tired) joke in the play.

Dryden himself claimed in the dedicatory epistle to Lord Vaughan that the play "'twas intended for an honest Satyre against our crying sin of

Keeping," a moral the central plot does not convey (5). Woodall and his father appear to be the principal transgressors in this regard; however, they are rewarded with rich wives simply by virtue of their class origins. Limberham wants only to be with his mistress, hardly shocking behavior by Restoration standards, but his ineptitude at maintaining a whore's interest becomes the stuff of macho scorn. Is he the principal satiric object? Rumor has come down that Limberham represented Anthony Ashley Cooper, the first Earl of Shaftesbury and, by 1677/78, the increasingly embattled Lord Chancellor of England.[5] There may indeed be a pun on the character's name: "limber" in the seventeenth century designated the "shaft" of a wheel; "bury" and "ham" are both common suffixes for proper names of towns. Wordplay aside, for the principal object of a satire, Limberham takes up surprisingly little of the play's space or energy. He is too much the minor fool who can never quite keep up, sexually or otherwise, with the rest of the guys. That leaves only Aldo and Woodall, the "main" keepers, as possible satiric targets; the plot, though, rewards their libertine exploits.

Although Dryden in the dedication specifies both genre (satire) and target (the sin of "keeping"), nothing in the play fits those specifications. It is common enough for writers to disavow satiric intent, less so for them actually to claim it. Perhaps Dryden truly thought he had written a satire about keeping; we have before us, of course, only the printed play text to go on. Even if Dryden's remarks are overlooked and the play is sifted for other possible satiric targets, we come up empty-handed. As a play, *Limberham* cannot summon up the satiric devices so easily produced by narration; only the plot can manufacture the satiric "message." And *Limberham*'s plot—its internal system of communication—urges comic diffusion, not satiric concentration. Neither the characters nor the events provide a satiric focus; moreover, the concluding marriages domesticate the rakes, rendering any complaint against "keeping" redundant. Why scold (and who does scold in this play?) when marriage not only solves the moral issue but seemingly rewards the "keepers"? Thus, in *Limberham* we see how several of the structural elements of drama—characters unmediated by narration, multilayered plots, and scenic progression resulting in change—undermine whatever satiric intention Dryden may have had in writing the play.

The same can be argued of *The Man of Mode* and *The Plain Dealer*, as well as countless other plays from this period. Consider the never-ending critical debate over Dorimant in *The Man of Mode*. Is he satiric butt or charming roué? If the play satirizes Dorimant and his libertine lifestyle, then why is he depicted so glamorously? And why is he rewarded with Harriet (even as he attempts an assignation with Mrs. Loveit, his former mistress)? Even a play harsher in tone, such as *The Plain Dealer*, defies satiric categorization. Given Manly's shrill misanthropy—the sort of scolding usually manifested by a Juvenalian narrator—it would seem that he occupies something of a narrative role in the play (with the accompanying authority), observing and commenting on various social evils around him. By the third act, though, Manly moves from a subjective to an objective position within the plot; no longer the dominant voice railing about human frailty, he instead embodies jealousy, vengeance, and—worst of all—the very hypocrisy he disdains in others. This shift in character accompanies a shift in plot. During the first two acts, the "authoritative" Manly, whose perspective seems coterminous with Wycherley's, directs the satire against the hypocritical society he so despises. By the third act, Manly, implicated as a hypocrite, becomes himself part of the satire. Ultimately, what—or who—does the play satirize? The Widow Blackacre subplot further complicates matters since she too seems to function subjectively and objectively within the story.

This is not to posit the utter impossibility of satiric meaning on the stage. Although I have sketched out those structural characteristics that make drama and satire odd bedfellows, strange matches are sometimes surprisingly successful. Drama can potentially compensate for lack of narration in a variety of ways. While multiple characters in drama tend to proliferate authorial perspectives, thereby undermining satiric intent, the play text and the performance can endorse one perspective over another. Information relayed through dialogue (an unpleasant report about a character) that is secured nonverbally (the character's grotesque behavior verifies the report) clearly establishes a hierarchy of perspectives. Plot, especially the "poetic justice" meted out to villains or spoilsports, also privileges certain characters (and their viewpoints) over others.

Additionally, the deliberate violation of generic expectations can direct satire against a particular situation or character. And extratextual cues can confirm information relayed by the plot. For instance, Molière discredits Tartuffe in the title of the play as a *hypocrite* and *imposteur* and in the dramatis personae as a *faux dévot,* labels borne out by the reports of other characters, not to mention Tartuffe's own reprehensible behavior. Dedications, prologues, and epilogues all potentially underscore the author's satiric "message" as well. By the late nineteenth century, prefaces to printed plays functioned as virtual extended commentaries on the play proper; one thinks of G. B. Shaw's attempts to shape audience response through the prefatory essay.

While these techniques compensate partially for drama's lack of narration, nonetheless I would argue that plays are constituted (as are all literary forms) to perform some tasks better than others. Simply put, the structural characteristics of drama incline more towards comedy than satire. A playwright determined to use the theatre as a satiric medium must not only compensate for drama's lack of narration, but also must overcome its fundamental principle of absolute autonomy. Thus, a satire like *Volpone* (revealingly, always the lone play cited in generic studies of satire) collapses together the external and internal communication systems that drama usually holds apart; the one-dimensional humours characters function almost like the allegorical figures in a medieval morality play, interpreting themselves and their own actions in accordance with the author's evaluative schema. Volpone and Mosca, descendents of the personified "Vice" figure, spell out their depravity (and their respective plots) in direct address to the audience, thus serving as mouthpieces for Jonson. Satire triumphs but at the cost of dramatic complexity and autonomy.

Despite Thomas Shadwell's various attempts at reviving Jonsonian-style humours satire—all ridiculed by Dryden and others—this sort of aesthetic strategy did not work on the Restoration stage. As I argue below, ideological forces, as well as pragmatic considerations, rendered impossible the production of "pure" satire in the theatre. Additionally, performance conditions within the theatre made difficult the communication of satiric meaning.

### iii. Politics and Pragmatics

Many critics claim that the formal contradictions traversing *Limberham, The Man of Mode,* and *The Plain Dealer* are replicated in nearly every comedy written during the Restoration. If we assume a dialectical relationship between these texts as aesthetic phenomena and culture as explanatory context, then we can readily conclude, as several fine Marxist scholars have over the past ten years, that the divided nature of dramatic satire, as well as other literary forms ranging from tragicomedy to verse satire reflect—or attempt to resolve fictionally—contradictions within Restoration culture. Historically speaking, there is a good case to be made here. Nor does such a theoretical move necessarily oppose the structuralist approach I have taken above. As Umberto Eco notes, the semiotic structures of the work always corroborate historical and sociological hypotheses (*The Role of the Reader* 126).

Ideological readings of dramatic form are appealing in their very totalization—they account for everything. Laura Brown, for instance, collapses *all* Restoration plays into two comprehensive categories: the heroic action and the dramatic social satire. The former "embodies the royalist ideology of the reinstated aristocracy" (25); the latter represent "the fundamental moral and social contradictions of their time and place" (63).

Whether a play reflects ideological contradiction in its generic fissures or resolves contradiction into a seemingly harmonious whole (the latter inevitably doomed to failure), ultimately the result is the same: literary form always connects directly to global forces. Such a method, though, by overlooking local contexts, levels generic differences. Thus, Michael McKeon can take two dissimilar texts, the one a verse satire originally intended for coterie consumption, the other a "mixed plot" play written for public performance by the King's Company, and reach the identical conclusion about both of them. Of *Absalom and Achitophel* he says that "a historicized reading . . . shows that it, too, encloses a set of 'contradictory interests' within its ostensibly single-minded unity" ("Historicizing *Absalom and Achitophel*" 38). Of *Marriage A La Mode,* he observes that "in the end it may even appear that the only convincing demonstration of the play's unity demands candid acknowledgment that its ideological conflict never is resolved" ("Marxism and *Marriage A La Mode*" 143).

While ideological approaches are good at detecting contradiction, they are perhaps less successful at explaining differences, especially formal differences, between texts. Even if Dryden's poem is measured against *Limberham,* as mentioned, a play he himself considered to be a "satyr," the two simply *look* different. The satiric issues at stake in *Absalom and Achitophel* are fairly apparent; the same cannot be said of *Limberham.* Local context, especially a consideration of how "global forces" refract through cultural markets and mediating institutions, helps account for that difference. Verse satire circulated in manuscript; if printing caused trouble, the satirist could always disavow authorship (Swift, of course, never claimed authorship on title pages) or affect dismay about pirated copies. The dramatist had no such recourse in a medium as public and institutionalized as the theatre.

Although Annabel Patterson sees the "discourse" of censorship infiltrating the entire seventeenth century, unconsciously shaping and silencing writing, that sort of Foucaultian reading ignores distinctions between literary milieus, not to mention historical periods.[6] Censorship actually *increased* during the Restoration; the theatre in particular, came under the close scrutiny of the court. The Office of the Revels, traditionally responsible for licensing plays, was eclipsed by Charles II's use of court clients to enforce censorship. The two theatre managers, Thomas Killigrew and William Davenant, were responsible for overseeing the production of plays, the indefatigable Roger L'Estrange for the printing of plays. In 1668 Killigrew conveniently took over the Mastership of the Revels (White 12). There was good reason for the court to turn to clients, especially in the jittery aftermath of the Civil War. Both the Office of the Revels and the Stationers' Company had proven ineffectual bureaucracies; moreover, they could not rival the zeal of court clients hungry for patronage and perquisites.

That playwrights consciously and deliberately responded to fluctuations within the immediate institutional setting (rather than internalizing a "culture of censorship") is borne out by the aftermath of the Popish Plot and the Exclusion Crisis. So many playwrights jumped into the fray that between 1680 and 1683 the Lord Chamberlain silenced some seventeen productions. The sudden outpouring of political (and satirical) sentiment is usually attributed to "the times"; however, we might remember the various crises of the 1660s and 1670s that did *not* precipitate a flood of writing. Arguably, playwrights, like most people, respond pragmatically to their immediate situation when weighing risks. As Terry Eagleton observes: "[T]here is no reason to assume that . . . political docility signals some gullible, full-blooded adherence to the doctrines of their superiors. It may signal rather a coolly realistic sense that political militancy . . . might be perilous and ill-advised" (36). The Licensing Act expired in 1679; moreover, William Davenant and Thomas Killigrew, both dead, were replaced by ineffectual young sons with little interest in the theatre and less in censorship. Neither of them were clients of the king as their fathers had been. A Restoration dramatist, then, contemplating a satiric attack upon Whig complicity in the Exclusion Crisis, would have perceived few institutional controls: the law had changed and the people he dealt with firsthand, the theatre managers, were callow youths. That the Lord Chamberlain eventually had to involve himself in censorship, a task normally delegated to subordinates, during this period indicates how far the theatre managers let things slide. Clearly, a number of playwrights thought they could get around the customarily strong controls over the production of plays and took the risk. Generally, though, regulation of the stage would have discouraged the production of "pure" satire in the manner of *Absalom and Achitophel.*

### iv. Performance Conditions and Satiric Meaning

Theatre unfolds in space and time, and the spatial and temporal properties of live performance mitigate against satiric meaning. Someone reading the play text of Fielding's *Tom Thumb,* for instance, can ponder those droll Scriblerian footnotes to her heart's content; indeed, some satires, like *A Tale of a Tub,* would be virtually incomprehensible without the time to pause, reread, and flip back to earlier passages. Plays, though, cannot be stopped in mid-performance because they unfold in "real" time as well as fictional time. There is no reprieve for the viewer who misses a topical allusion, a satiric personation, a political hit; the performance moves rapidly on to the next moment. It is theatre's very temporality, of course, that has defied didactic playwrights like Brecht. While video technology has imbued film with "readability" (viewers can scan back-and-forth at will), a live performance cannot be "reread" for meaning in the same way. Arguably, the so-called "Age of Satire" coincides with the age of print for the reason that print, in its very printliness, provides the satirist with normative possibilities. Think of the attributes of print that Scriblerian writers, from Swift to Fielding, revel in: footnotes, dedications, prefaces, even typographic conventions. Part of the satiric joke derives from the stability print affords. Precisely because print manages satiric codes—in other words, the rules which assign meaning to signs—so well, these writers can play freely at violating this normative process (Elam 35). Moreover, the fixity of print allows for a greater chance of controlling (or even deconstructing) satiric meaning. By contrast, theatre, because it multiplies codes along several channels (speech, gesture, spatial and kinesic relationships, scenic design, and so forth), diffuses satiric argument: the audience takes in "the whole show." Additionally, every performance is live and therefore slightly different, once again potentially obscuring or altering the playwright's "intended" meaning.

Finally, satire, especially the highly contextualized verse and prose satire common to the Restoration and eighteenth century, depends upon reader competency to decipher meaning. *A Tale of a Tub,* for instance, assumes knowledge of politics, philosophy, theology, and the conventions of print, just to name a few. We know from market research on the habits of readers that they consume books and other cultural products, not according to the whims of "humanistic" interest, but according to socio-economic determinations: class trajectory, education, and the habitus, those unconscious dispositions structured by one's immediate environment (Bourdieu passim). Print satire in particular requires the reader to decode highly refined literary rules in addition to a host of topical issues. One does not pick up *The Dunciad* randomly.

Because theatre multiplies codes along several channels, it is far more likely to attract viewers with varying competencies than print does. Someone knowledgeable about scenic design, for instance, might see a play for the special effects alone. This is not to resurrect the hoary and misguided distinction between theatre as popular art and literature as high art but rather to suggest that the multiplication of codes in the theatre can result in the presence of some spectators who know relatively little about aesthetic form or political innuendo. *The Beggar's Opera* cannot select its audience to the same degree as verse or prose satire. Spectators coming for the familiar ballad tunes, the costumes, or the skill of particular actors might never "get" the political point, a risk writers undoubtedly weigh when deciding their literary medium.

In addition to these general impediments to satiric meaning are the more local conditions of performance during the Restoration. For over thirty years now social scientists have postulated everyday life as theatrical performance; as Umberto Eco observes, it is not simply a matter of theatre imitating life, but social life itself "that is designed as a continuous performance and, because of this, there is a link between theatre and life" ("Semiotics of Theatrical Performance" 113). Arguably, the Restoration is a particularly "theatricalized" culture, one that often blurred the line between social and dramatic performance. Richard Braverman notes how the libertine in Restoration comedy conveyed the *élan* of the court, suggesting an especially intimate relationship between courtiers in the audience and the actors upon the stage (143). J. L. Styan makes much the same point: "Everything points to this extraordinary fact about Restoration drama: that the social attitude of its audience was the narrowest in the history of the public theatre . . . its special homogeneity enabled author and audience to create a social comedy in which the performance jokes would be frankly 'in-house'" (7).

This sort of intimate dynamic, whereby the members of the audience see themselves reflected in the mirror of the stage, arguably sabotages the alienation necessary for satire. While the satirist also presents recognizable social types, she does not want the audience to identify affectionately with the characters; rather, their reaction should be sufficiently disturbed to reject or, at the very least, ponder the social grievance or idea under consideration. Playhouse design also encouraged audience identification with the spectacle. The Restoration practice of staging comedies principally on the forestage emphasized their generic connection to the audience. As Peter Holland argues, "the audience saw the actor as in a situation potentially analogous to their own, rather than in a totally fictive world" (29). In effect, playhouse conditions during the Restoration fostered comedy, not satire.

## v. Last Thoughts

In this essay I have offered explanations—structural, political, as well as performative—for the existence of that hybrid, the Restoration play poised between comedy and satire. Although I have made a particular case for late-seventeenth-century plays, outlining the historical conditions possibly affecting this generic medley, nonetheless, the structural characteristics of drama alone are powerful enough to undermine most attempts at pure satire on the stage. Like any marriage of convenience, satire and drama may put in the occasional public appearance at the theatre; however, in their most private of lives, they remain very much apart.

## Notes

1. Aubrey L. Williams notes that despite the generic slipperiness of *The Double-Dealer*—its odd suspension between tragedy, grotesque satire, and comedy—Congreve nonetheless "stamped it 'A Comedy' on its title page" (126). Dedications and title pages to plays during the Restoration were notoriously casual about generic designations.

2. "Postmodern," of course, means any number of things: a historical milieu (the period following modernism), an artistic style (as in postmodernist architecture), an attack upon Enlightenment positivism, or even, in the words of Fredric Jameson, a historical effect of the "third stage of capitalism" (400). Throughout this essay, though, I use the term in the same sense as "poststructuralist."

3. One might also think of the various twentieth-century experiments in meta-theatricality as a point of comparison: significantly, none of them function as satire. Lacking the "objectivity" provided by narration, plays by Pirandello, Beckett, Stoppard, and, more recently, Churchill, cannot establish the binary structure necessary for satire. Objectivity, of course, functions as one of two essential terms within such a satiric fiction, the thing to be deconstructed. Drama, lacking narration, cannot as easily manufacture objectivity; rather, multiple points of view and the time-space continuum of the plot diffuse satire, resulting in plays that have satiric elements but overall strike us as being "absurd," "dream-like," or "black." One could argue that these writers selected drama, rather than a narrative form, for the very reason that "objectivity," especially by the twentieth century, is no longer at stake intellectually.

4. There are, of course, static plays, such as Absurdist dramas or performance pieces; however, these tend to be registered by audiences as *departures* from a structural norm. Indeed, their very status as avant-garde art depends upon such a departure.

5. Susan Staves carefully reviews the evidence for the possible personation of Shaftesbury in the play; ultimately, she argues "that we do not know" (*Mr. Limberham* 10).

6. Patterson explains that "Michel Foucault has taught us to think of all discursive codes and practices that we take for granted in society, such as the internal codes of the professions, as forms of tyranny, rules that require our submission if we wish to participate in 'le vrai,' if we wish to have access, through discourse, to power and influence" (16).

# Works Cited

Baker, Van R. "Heroic Posturing Satirized: Dryden's *Mr. Limberham.*" *PLL* 8 (1972): 370–79.

Benveniste, Emile. *Problems of General Linguistics.* Miami: U of Miami P, 1970.

Bevis, Richard W. *English Drama: Restoration and Eighteenth Century, 1660–1789.* London: Longman, 1988.

Bloom, Edward A., and Lillian D. *Satire's Persuasive Voice.* Ithaca: Cornell UP, 1979.

Bourdieu, Pierre. *Distinction: A Social Critique of the Judgement of Taste.* Trans. Richard Nice. Cambridge: Harvard UP, 1984.

Braverman, Richard. "The Rake's Progress Revisited: Politics and Comedy in the Restoration." *Cultural Readings of Restoration and Eighteenth-Century English Theater.* Ed. J. Douglas Canfield and Deborah C. Payne. Athens: U of Georgia P, 1995. 141–68.

Brown, Laura. *English Dramatic Form, 1660–1760; An Essay in Generic History.* New Haven: Yale UP, 1981.

De Man, Paul. *Allegories of Reading: Figural Language in Rousseau, Nietzsche, Rilke, and Proust.* New Haven: Yale UP, 1979.

Derrida, Jacques. *Of Grammatology.* Trans. Gayatri Chakravorty Spivak. Baltimore: Johns Hopkins UP, 1974.

Dryden, John. *The Kind Keeper or, Mr. Limberham.* Vol. 14 of *The Works of John Dryden.* Ed. Vinton A. Dearing and Alan Roper. Berkeley: U of California P, 1992.

Eagleton, Terry. *Ideology.* London: Verso, 1991.

Eco, Umberto. "The Frames of Comic 'Freedom.'" *Carnival!* Ed. Umberto Eco, V. V. Ivanov, and Monica Rector. *Approaches to Semiotics* 64. Berlin: Mouton, 1984. 1–9.

———. *The Role of the Reader.* Bloomington: Indiana UP, 1979.

———. "Semiotics of Theatrical Performance." *The Drama Review* 21 (1977): 107–17.

Ehrenpreis, Irvin. "Personae." *Restoration and Eighteenth-Century Literature: Essays in Honor of Alan Dugald McKillop.* Ed. Carroll Camden. Chicago: U of Chicago P, 1963. 25–37.

Elam, Keir. *The Semiotics of Theatre and Drama.* London: Methuen, 1980.

Etherege, Sir George. *The Man of Mode.* Ed. W. B. Carnochan. Lincoln: U of Nebraska P, 1966.

Frye, Northrop. *Anatomy of Criticism: Four Essays.* Princeton: Princeton UP, 1957.

Fujimura, Thomas H. *The Restoration Comedy of Wit.* Princeton: Princeton UP, 1952.

Holland, Peter. *The Ornament of Action: Text and Performance in Restoration Comedy.* Cambridge: Cambridge UP, 1979.

Hume, Robert D. *The Development of English Drama in the Late Seventeenth Century.* Oxford: Clarendon, 1976.

Jameson, Fredric. *Postmodernism, or, The Cultural Logic of Late Capitalism.* Durham, NC: Duke UP, 1991.

Juvenal. *The Sixteen Satires.* Trans. Peter Green. Harmondsworth: Penguin Books, 1967.

Kern, Jean B. *Dramatic Satire in the Age of Walpole 1720–1750.* Ames, IA: Iowa State UP, 1976.

Kernan, Alvin B. *The Plot of Satire.* New Haven: Yale UP, 1965.

Loesberg, Jonathan. *Aestheticism and Deconstruction: Pater, Derrida, and De Man.* Princeton: Princeton UP, 1991.

Mack, Maynard. "The Muse of Satire." *Yale Review* 41 (1951–52): 80–92.

Markley, Robert. *Two-Edg'd Weapons: Style and Ideology in the Comedies of Etherege, Wycherley and Congreve.* Oxford: Clarendon, 1988.

McKeon, Michael. "Historicizing *Absalom and Achitophel.*" *The New Eighteenth Century.* Ed. Felicity Nussbaum and Laura Brown. New York: Routledge, 1987. 23–40.

———. "Marxist Criticism and *Marriage A La Mode.*" *The Eighteenth Century: Theory and Interpretation* 24 (1983): 141–62.

Nokes, David. *Raillery and Rage: A Study of Eighteenth Century Satire.* New York: St. Martin's P, 1987.

Patterson, Annabel. *Censorship and Interpretation.* Madison: U of Wisconsin P, 1987.

Pfister, Manfred. *The Theory and Analysis of Drama.* Trans. John Halliday. Cambridge: Cambridge UP, 1988.

Pope, Alexander. *The Poems of Alexander Pope.* Ed. John Butt. New Haven: Yale UP, 1963.

Powell, Jocelyn. "George Etherege and the Form of a Comedy." *Restoration Dramatists: A Collection of Critical Essays.* Ed. Earl Miner. Englewood Cliffs, NJ: Prentice-Hall, 1966. 63–85.

Rawson, Claude. *Satire and Sentiment 1660–1830.* Cambridge: Cambridge UP, 1994.

Rochester, John Wilmot, Earl of. *The Poems.* Ed. Keith Walker. Oxford: Basil Blackwell, 1984.

Rothstein, Eric, and Frances M. Kavenik. *The Designs of Carolean Comedy.* Carbondale: Southern Illinois UP, 1988.

Sacksteder, William. "Elements of the Dramatic Model." *Diogenes* 52 (1975): 26–54.

Snyder, John. *Prospects of Power: Tragedy, the Essay, and the Theory of Genre.* Lexington, KY: UP of Kentucky, 1991.

Staves, Susan. *Players' Scepters: Fictions of Authority in the Restoration.* Lincoln: U of Nebraska P, 1979.

———. "Why Was Dryden's *Mr. Limberham* Banned?: A Problem in Restoration Theatre History." *Restoration and 18th Century Theatre Research* 13 (1974): 1–11.

Styan, J. L. *Restoration Comedy in Performance.* Cambridge: Cambridge UP, 1986.

Swift, Jonathan. *Gulliver's Travels.* Ed. Robert A. Greenberg. 2nd ed. New York: W. W. Norton, 1970.

Test, George A. *Satire: Spirit and Art.* Tampa: U of South Florida P, 1991.

White, Arthur F. "The Office of the Revels and Dramatic Censorship during the Restoration Period." *Western Reserve University Bulletin* 34 (1931): 5–45.

Wimsatt, W. K. *The Idea of Comedy: Essays in Prose and Verse, Ben Jonson to George Meredith.* Englewood Cliffs, NJ: Prentice-Hall, 1969.

Wycherley, William. *The Plain Dealer.* Ed. Leo Hughes. Lincoln: U of Nebraska P, 1967.

Zimbardo, Rose A. "The Satiric Design in *The Plain Dealer.*" *Restoration Dramatists: A Collection of Critical Essays.* Ed. Earl Miner. Englewood Cliffs, NJ: Prentice-Hall, 1966. 123–38.

Zimmerman, Everett. *Swift's Narrative Satires: Author and Authority.* Ithaca: Cornell UP, 1983.

# The Semiotics
# of Restoration Satire

*Rose Zimbardo*

With the exception of David Vieth's pioneer work and the more recent readings of Dustin Griffin, Kevin Cope, and Barbara Everett,[1] one may safely say that the universally accepted view of Restoration satire is that expressed by Raman Selden, who says, "[I]t is significant that the leading satirists of the day (Butler, Rochester, Oldham and Dryden) all ridicule deviations from a strongly held norm in the spheres of philosophy, religion, politics, or literature. It is true that the skeptical Butler and the Hobbesian Rochester themselves depart from that Augustan norm of rationality which was to be expressed definitively by Locke in the final decade of the century. Nevertheless they acted as front-line troops in the Augustan negative criticism of the 'irrational' beliefs and 'dangerous' dogmas of the past" (73). Three hundred years of conditioning in Lockean positivist thinking have so blinded us that we cannot see beyond the eighteenth-century binary model for satire, which determines that in order to be satire a text must direct us toward a positive norm, must contain or, at least indirectly, uphold a clear *moral* "satiric antithesis." If a satirist does not fit the model then his departure from it must be explained away, and, above all, he must be considered the exception that proves the rule. Therefore Rochester, who, in direct defiance of materialism, calls upon the "great Negative" to expose all "blind Philosophies," as we have seen, is labeled a "Hobbesian." And Butler's radical unraveling of epistemic constructs that Cope so well describes—"To dodge the evils of experience and philosophy Butler creates a model of behavior which corresponds to and is anchored in nothing" (31)—is dismissed as idiosyncratic skepticism. A "strongly held norm" of rationalism *must* somehow be upheld in Restoration satire, otherwise how can we call it satire? No matter that, as Selden admits, Locke's definitive expression of rationalism did not yet exist when Rochester, Oldham, and Butler were writing.

Having cut the eighteenth-century, morally uplifting model for satire in stone, we do not allow that deviations from it call the model into question. On the contrary, we consider that exceptions confirm its rule. We ourselves are products of modernist epistemology, and in our thinking about the norms of satire we reflect eighteenth-century thinking, wherein "validity . . . is established according to the tautological procedure of the human sciences, which take the limitations inherent in empirical knowledge as the very proof of this knowledge's truth. The knowledge thus constituted claims an unimpeachable prerogative to impose its norms as the universally applicable ideal for humanity" (Racevskis 234).

And just as we cannot abandon the notion that upholding a positive norm is the determining generic function of satire, neither can we give up the idea that satiric discourse is mimetic. Even a critic as astute as Everett Zimmerman, writing on a subject as problematic as Swift's narrative strategies, cannot rid himself entirely of the assumption: "because satire assumes the prerogative of commentary on existents external and prior to itself, the interpretive strategy that it suggests is to define a historical author writing to a historical reader about historical events. In sharing, or pretending to share, a border with polemic, satire urges its reader toward a truth that appears outside the borders of its text" (62–63). Happily, the assumption of a mimetic function does not hinder Zimmerman's very intelligent and sensitive reading of the texts, but it does often hold him back from accepting the full implication of his own interpretations. For example, Zimmerman cannot altogether acknowledge that there *is no* authorial "I" either within or behind a satire like *A Tale of a Tub.* On the subject of self in Swift he says, "[W]riting is for Swift invariably an expression of self. But Swift does not, like Montaigne, use this perception to sanction the pursuit of self as the most legitimate object of writing. Instead, he attempts to counteract self by attending persistently to its deforming powers. . . . For Swift, self is a standpoint but not necessarily an enclosure" (87). I would argue, on the contrary, that Swift's early satire, *A Tale,* deliberately deconstructs "self" and explodes the idea that writing is "self-expression." The conceptions of a deep-seated internal arena, the locus of truth and font of self-expression, is the very "new scientific" notion that is the *target* of satire in *A Tale.* We have always had difficulty in trying to fit Swiftian satire to the binary, moral-emendation model. We have usually solved the problem by assuming that Swift was far in advance of his time, was, indeed, anticipating twentieth-century sensibility. Claude Rawson interestingly suggests that "Swift parodied both Sterne and Beckett in advance. . . . The fact suggests an intuitive understanding of the fragmentation of 'modern' sensibility and of the literary modes that this was to call forth" (7). Rather than Swift's being *ahead of* his times, I believe that (most especially in *A Tale*) his satire is a *throwback* to Restoration deconstructionist satire and for that very reason it resembles postmodernist works like the plays and novels of Beckett, the theoretical experiments of Derrida, and the semiological explorations of Eco.

For a deconstructionist a text "overruns all the limits assigned to it"; it is a *process,* a dubious system of signs having relation without positive terms, that can never arrive at closure, and that operates "to undermine everything that was set up in opposition to writing (speech, the world, the real, history . . .)" (Derrida, "Living on the Borderlines" 84). A semioticist recognizes no empirical "reality"; there are for him, rather, various systems of signs that simultaneously inscribe and erase conceptual frames, which, because they too are linguistic, are inherently dubious. The task of the deconstructionist, as Gayatri Spivak puts it, is to demonstrate that "a certain view of the world, of consciousness, of language has been accepted as the correct one, and if the minute particulars of that view are examined, a rather different picture (that is also a no-picture . . .) emerges" (Spivak xii). That is because the "minute particulars" of the picture which is also no-picture are signs, and "the strange 'being' of the sign" is such that "half of it is always 'not there' and the other half 'not that.' The structure of the sign is determined by the trace or track of that other which is forever absent" (Spivak xvii).

We associate these conceptions with Jacques Derrida, and because Derrida has argued that "the history of the West" depends on "the determination of Being as presence in all senses of the word" (*Writing and Difference* 279), we think of the deconstruction of signs and the discovery of the "not that/not there" component in signs as postmodern phenomena. But Derrida is wrong in asserting that Being = Presence throughout Western history. The presence of absence in the sign is a central principle in medieval language theory, the foundations of which are laid by St. Augustine.

In *On Christian Doctrine* Augustine says, "Now when I am discussing signs I wish it understood that no one should consider them for what they are but rather for their value as signs which signify something else. A sign is a thing which causes us to think of something beyond the impression the thing makes on our senses" (14). In *De Magistro,* an often playful and brilliantly ironic Socratic dialogue with his son, Adeodatus, Augustine again and again drives his demonstration of the nonidentity between sign and referent. He has Adeodatus reduce a sign from a word to a single letter to a gesture—all in order to prove that a sign and its referent *cannot* correspond if a sign is to function as sign. For Augustine a sign—a word *or* thing—is a sign precisely because it indicates to the mind the absent *other-than-itself.* A key example with which he plays is *nihil,* which is *nothing* and is also *not what it signifies* since something is meant by it: "Instead of saying *nihil* signifies something which is nothing, shall we not say that this word signifies a certain state of mind when failing to perceive a reality, the mind finds, or thinks it finds, that such a reality does not exist?" (*The Teacher* 10–11). The Scriptures themselves, because they are words/signs, cannot designate knowable truth absolutely. Once written, once filtered through the mouth and mind of man, the word of God itself enters the inevitably dubious semiotic system and therefore cannot have positive value. In Book XI of the *Confessions* Augustine speculates upon this matter:

> Moses wrote this . . . [that God created heaven and earth]. He wrote it and went away; he passed hence . . . and now is not before me. For, if he were, I should hold him, and beg him, and beseech him through Thee to throw these words open before me. I would offer the ears of my body to the sounds bursting forth from his mouth. If he were to speak in Hebrew, it would impinge upon my sense to no avail, nor would any part of it reach my mind, but, if in Latin I should know what he said. But from what source would I know whether he told the truth? And, if I did know even this, would I come to know it from him? (331–32)

Like any postmodern semioticist or deconstructionist, Augustine allows for the *real presence* only of language: "[N]othing has been found, as yet, that can be shown by means of itself, excepting language, which among other things which it signifies, signifies also itself: which yet, because itself is symbol, shows nothing that stands out clearly that can be taught without means of symbols" (*De Magistro* 192),

For the medieval philosopher, as for the postmodern philosopher, everything that is perceived is a sign; all signs refer only and inevitably to other signs; and inherent in the sign is the absent "other," the "not that" and "not there." As Derrida notes, "[T]he play of difference supposes in effect syntheses and referrals which forbid at *any* moment, or in any sense that a simple element be *present* in and of itself, referring only to itself. Whether in the order of spoken or written discourse, no element can function as a sign without referring to another element which itself is not simply present" (*Positions* 26).

The persistent and pervasive influence of Augustinian thought in late-seventeenth-century England has been so often and so amply demonstrated that it hardly needs to be reviewed here. Seventeenth-century writers knew Augustine so well that they quite often conducted their own philosophical speculations in conversation with him. And, most interestingly for our purposes here, Restoration writers frequently used Augustinian semiotics to subvert both the materialist philosophy coming to dominance in their own day and the essentialist philosophy that was their inheritance from Augustine's time, the Middle Ages. Let me give a rather complicated example of what I believe to be a three-way seventeenth-century conversation with Augustine.

In the *Confessions* Augustine, in his usual brilliantly ironic manner, speculates upon the construct time, and, in speculating upon it, erases it:

> What then is time? . . . if nothing passes away there would be no past time; if nothing were coming there would be no future time; if nothing were existing there would be no present time.
>
> Then, how do those two periods of time, the past and the future, exist, when the past is already not existing, and the future does not yet exist? And again, the present would not pass away into the past, if it were always present . . . . So, if the present, in order to be time, must be such that it passes over into the past, then how can we say that it *is*; for the sole reason for its existence is the fact that it will stop being, that is to say, can we not truly say that time *is* only because it inclines not to be. (343–44)

Hobbes responds to Augustine from a materialist's perspective: "The *present* only has being in Nature; things *past* have a being in memory only, but things *to come* have no being at all . . ." (*Leviathan* 11).

Rochester, in turn, uses the Augustinian reduction of temporality to nothing and also uses the Hobbesian idea of a *real* present to undermine the constructs—self, love, constancy—that convention, particularly the linguistic constructs of pastoral literature, has written upon our consciousness.

> All my past life is mine no more,
>     The flying hours are gone.
> Like Transitory Dreams giv'n o'er
> Whose images are kept in store
>     By Memory alone.
>
>             ii
> The Time that is to come is not;
>     How can it then be mine?
> The present Moment's all my Lot;
> And that, as fast as it is got,
>     Phillis is only thine.

iii

Then talk not of Inconstancy,
    False Hearts, and broken Vows;
If I, by Miracle, can be
This live-long Minute true to thee,
    Tis all that Heav'n allows. (*Works* 22)

Consider the valences of this "conversation." Rochester is Augustinian in that he erases the construct time. Rochester is also Hobbesian in that he centers the only possible apprehension of time in the present moment. But the confluence of Augustinian and Hobbesian lines do not mingle in Rochester's poem; rather, they cancel each other out. Rochester goes a step further than Augustine in erasure. The discourse of both Augustine and Hobbes suggests an observer, a speaking "I." With greater comic irony than Augustine, Rochester *locates* inconstancy, or, more properly speaking, locates the collapse of temporality, in an "I" who is also "not-I," since, like all other entities, it has no duration in time: "this ending makes of the lines a decisive handing over of the self to some unknown quantity, the 'present' being only a knowledge of what is unknown. And this . . . self-offering is . . . able to suggest the perpetual existence of self as in a void, created from moment to moment as a poem is from line to line. For the poet of 'Life and Love' has, by definition, nothing at all to call his own—neither past nor future, nor any present that he knows, beyond that Miracle of the poem's live-long Minute" (Everett 11). Nothing exists except writing and the reader's response to an absolutely "open text."

For Augustine there are no things, only signs out of which the imperfect human mind creates and deconstructs fragile designs that are in no way reflective of the distant realm of pure Idea. There is no present "here." For Hobbes, and the new scientists who followed him, (as in the motto of the Royal Society) there are "no Ideas but in Things." Hobbes's "present" has existence only because it exists in Nature, and is therefore empirically verifiable, for Nature—solid, material, changeless—is everything, and all that is. "The whole mass of all things that are, is corporeal, that is to say, body . . . also every part of body, is likewise body, and hath the like dimensions; and consequently every part of the universe, is body, and that which is not body, is no part of the universe: and because the universe is all, that which is no part of it is *nothing* and consequently nowhere . . ." (*Leviathan* 440). Restoration satirists made that "nothing" and "nowhere" their province. They used Augustinian semiotics to demonstrate the conventional nature of language and thereby to call all constructs, all laws, all values, all concepts—like "reason," "mind," or "truth"—into doubt.

However, for Augustine that illumination of "truth which presides over the mind itself from within" (*De Magistro* 33)—which *cannot* be captured by signs, but rather, whose existence can be inferred *only by the process of dismantling signs*—comes from God. Even the twelfth-century "radicalized sign theory" of Abelard—a theory that "relegated to the realm of the contingent, relative, and historically determined that which once partook of the necessary, absolute, and eternal" (Bloch 146)—left intact the unknowable, mysteriously centered, ordained cosmos. All signs, contingent as they are, by the very absence inherent in them, point toward that invisible, mysterious center, which alone is full. In contrast, in the Restoration period "an ordered world based on universally acknowledged laws [was] being replaced by a world based on ambiguity" in which "directional centers are missing and . . . values and dogma are constantly being placed in question" (Eco 53–54). Eco's description of twentieth-century post-structuralist thought can also describe Restoration satire as it confronts the emergence of a multivalue logics that *incorporates* "indeterminacy as a valid stepping stone in the cognitive process" (57–58). As Barbara Everett puts it, "The 1660's and the 1670's were something of a cultural no man's land, a pause in time equally out of touch with the past and the future, the medieval and the modern" (11).

Paul de Man has defined two kinds of irony that to my mind can be useful in distinguishing the two kinds of satire with which I am concerned. Both ironies arise out of a perception of difference. However, in the one case, the difference is intersubjective; that is, it occurs "in terms of the superiority of one subject over another, with all the implications of will to power, of violence, and possession which come into play when a person is laughing at someone else—including the will to educate and improve" (195–96). This, in my view, is the ironic perspective invoked by an eighteenth-century satire. The second irony which de Man discriminates differentiates the self from the world and "transforms the *self* out of the empirical world into a world constituted out of and in language" (197). That dislocated self thereby "exists only in the form of a language that asserts knowledge of [its own] inauthenticity," and "before long the entire texture of the self is unravelled" (197). This is the ironic perspective evoked by Restoration satire.

Restoration satire, which for so long was thought to be realistic, grossly physical, even pornographic, is, on the contrary, the most literary of modes. It exists nowhere but in language, for it is both *of* and *in* language. The collisions, the ruptures that it effects are among words, genres, and mental constructs to whose inauthenticity it calls constant attention. Moreover, this satire is an excellent example of what Eco calls the "open work" in that it makes complicit in its own deconstructive operations the mind and memory of the reader, and because as it does so, it calls "mind" itself into question and "brings to a crisis its relation with language."

Because we have so long believed Restoration satire to be mimetic, and have assumed in it a binary form that brings into collision an idealized antithesis and a thesis, which, however downwardly exaggerated, images the *real,* we have taken its fictional libertine personae, the grotesque goings-on in St. James's Park that it figures, or the prodigious sexual performances of King "Sardanapalus" as "real"—as exaggerated, but nonetheless reliable records of the degenerate times of Good King Charles's Golden Days. Indeed, biographers have invariably used events and images derived entirely from the literary products of their authors to construct their "lives." For example, Willard Connely's *Brawny Wycherley* is no more than a reconstituted "Plain Dealer," while the "real" Rochester is a more variously patched product, a combination of his own "Disabled Debauchee," Burnet's sinner-reclaimed, and the literary imaginings of his dramatist contemporaries—a "Count Rosidore" or "Dorimant."[2] I have no quarrel with these biographers. My interest in establishing the fictionality of the "real" and artifactuality of "truth" in Restoration satire is not aimed at discrediting work that has been done, but at demonstrating the semiotic, deconstructionist nature of Restoration satire.

The problem that such a project raises is this: after three hundred years there is no "real" that is not a fiction. Since any event or circumstance, once narrated, of necessity becomes fictionalized, and since the Restoration period especially has accrued to itself very highly colored, markedly biased imaging, it is not possible to extract a "real" representation of the times that is not tainted by literary conventions. How then to demonstrate that a Restoration satire *does not* put into collision an upwardly exaggerated fictional ideal and a downwardly exaggerated real (as in an eighteenth-century satire)? How then to prove that the oppositions effected in a Restoration satire are among *equally fictional* constructs and are designed to effect a *semiotic crisis* in the mind of the reader? An opponent of my argument might well ask, "Why isn't the extravagantly perverse sexual activity in 'A Ramble in St. James's Park' what really happened there? Why isn't the Whitehall of *The Plain Dealer* a perhaps exaggerated, but nevertheless accurate depiction of the Whitehall of 1676? Who are you to say that Oldham's 'Cunt was the Star that rul'd

[Sardanapalus's] fate' is not an exaggerated but an accurate assessment of the sensibility of the real Charles II?"

Dustin Griffin's brilliant book *Satires Against Man,* especially in its conversations with the invaluable work of David Vieth, can open a path that may enable us to deal with this problem. For instance, Griffin sees Rochester's "A Very Heroical Epistle in Answer to Ephelia" *neither* as an attack upon the "real" Mulgrave, the supposed satirical speaker of the poem, *nor* as a simple defense of the libertine philosophy espoused in it. Rather, he understands both Rochester's poem and the poem of Etherege, "Ephelia to Bajazet," to which it gives answer, in the context of the Ovidian model in which both poems exist: "When viewed in this light, as a devilishly cavalier answer to a complaining cast-off mistress, with a tradition of Ovidian love epistles in the background, the poems of Etherege and Rochester form a self-contained whole, requiring no external reference" (Griffin 60). The point is that neither poem is mimetic; neither refers to "existents external and prior to itself" nor "urges the reader to a truth that appears outside its own border," as Zimmerman would say. Rather, individually and together, they call into question the Ovidian model in the context of which both poems exist; they deconstruct a genre, a mind-set.

Elsewhere in the book Griffin argues that "on one level" Rochester's "A Ramble in St. James's Park" is image-for-image a response to Waller's "On St. James's Park as Lately Improved by His Majesty" (1661). Griffin says "on one level" only, but always and everywhere, the aim of a Restoration satire is to present violent collisions among images, genres, linguistic constructs. Their effect is much like the ending of Ionesco's *The Bald Soprano,* when conventional words and phrases jump out of narrative—almost, indeed, off the stage or page—to engage in senseless, chaotic battle. Even the very simplest "satiric antithesis" in a Restoration satire is never "real," is never mimetic. Whether Fidelia in *The Plain Dealer,* or the lines of Waller that Dorimant so often quotes, or the invisible Waller wash-tint pastoral fluttering behind "A Ramble in St. James's Park," in a Restoration satire satiric antithesis is 1) *always* literary and remote, and 2) *never* a behavioral norm from which the satiric thesis measures deviation.

Of Dryden's satire Earl Miner once said, "Between the cities of satire and those of Utopia there exists a real city; . . . Dryden [called] that reality 'nature'" (16). However, much of Dryden's later satire, and most especially his theoretical *A Discourse Concerning the Original and Progress of Satire* (1695), present a special case in an assessment of Restoration satire. Dryden's practice of the 1680s and 1690s and, most certainly, his late essay herald the new, mimetic eighteenth-century model of satire. (That is perhaps why we felt comfortable talking about "The Age of Dryden, Pope, and Swift," whereas we would be distinctly uneasy calling it "The Age of Rochester, Pope, and Swift" or "Wycherley, Pope, and Swift," even though both Wycherley and Rochester were thought by their contemporaries to be greater satirists than Dryden.)³ My argument is that in a Restoration satire "between the cities of satire and those of Utopia there exists" *Nothing.* The collisions among genres in a Restoration satire are not designed to show us "nature"; they are designed to show us that we are "whore[s] in understanding."

To demonstrate this point let me take for preliminary analysis a rather simple example, Rochester's "Song," "Fair Chloris in a pigsty lay." Antithesis is established in the very first line of the poem between the supersensuous airy realm of pastoral and the gross arena of satire by the words "Chloris" and "pigsty." The dichotomy runs in continuous contrast through the fabric of the poem. Pastoral images ("snowy arms," "ivory pails," "love-convicted swain"), pastoral rhetoric ("Fly nymph! Oh fly ere 'tis too late"), and pastoral dream vision are syntactically intertwined with "mumuring gruntlings," a lover who "throws himself upon" his mistress, a rape, and finally, among the "mumuring pigs," a masturbation. We slip from the wash-tint realm of pastoral landscape—which exists *nowhere but in our minds,* in the invisible horizon of expectation that the words "Fair Chloris" call up—into the *equally fictional* realm of libertine erotica:

> She hears a broken amorous groan
> The panting lover's fainting moan
> Just in the happy minute.

—which, again, exists *not* in the dreaming mind of Chloris, but in the literature-conditioned mind of the reader—and, finally, we fall into the pigsty with the auto-erotic swineherd. There is no nature here at all; there is simply the clash of literary stereotypes drawn from antithetical literary genres. Well, then, what is the point? Who or what is the target of this little satire? Two loaded words in the last line point the target: "She's *innocent* and *pleased.*" *We* are the targets of this little satiric song. It is the mind of the reader at which the poet has the last laugh, because that mind is exposed as a storehouse of junky stereotypes. Both our conceptions of innocence and our conceptions of pleasure have been shaped in us by empty words, by creaky literary constructs. That place in ourselves that we value so highly, the mind, is a windy, empty attic stored with nothing but whimsies spun out of words.

Michael Seidel has argued that "history covers up so that events proceed legally," while "satire creates a frenzy around points of terminus, penetrates to elaborate moments of regression where origins are ends and where all efforts to continue come to nothing" (21). This is not true of all satire; much eighteenth-century satire, like Young's *The Love of Fame* (1725), for instance, is the very handmaiden of historical cover-up. However, Seidel does here describe admirably the satire of "zero point": Imperial Rome under Nero, Caligula, and Domitian; Restoration England; and late-twentieth-century America. There is such striking similarity among these three "points of terminus" that I believe the procedure I shall adopt in demonstrating the semiotics of Restoration satire is justified, though I admit that it is highly unorthodox in a critical scholarly examination of this kind. To my mind the best way to overcome the difficulty of establishing the fictionality of what we have supposed to be the Restoration "real" from a three-hundred-years' distance is to analyze the semiotic operation of a late-twentieth-century "toward zero" satire as a preliminary exercise to analyzing a Restoration satire that employs the same methods. My examples for analysis will be Mel Brooks's *Blazing Saddles* and Rochester's "A Ramble in St. James's Park."

"Satire is all our own," Quintillian said (10:1, 93). That is because satire is a public mode, a city mode. It was invented when Rome was the center of power of the whole known world. *Blazing Saddles* was made when America came to be the modern Rome: the superpower, the guardian of Western values. And just as surely as the *Aeneid* shapes the great cultural myth of the Eternal City, won after arduous trial and pilgrimage, wrought by divine destiny and providence, so too does the American Western movie shape the American cultural myth of origins: the Nation won out of the "wilderness" by Pilgrims, in arduous trial guided by "Manifest Destiny" and the hand of God to stretch "from sea to shining sea." At the simplest level *Blazing Saddles* is simply a mock-heroic poem that laughs at our nationalistic pretensions. But it is far more than that; closer inspection reveals it to be a deconstructionist satire, which like a Restoration satire, explodes the foundational constructs that comprise our culture: mind, reality, truth. Like "A Ramble" or any other Restoration deconstructive satire, *Blazing Saddles* is a "system where the central signified, the original or transcendental signified, is never absolutely present outside a system of differences" (Derrida, "Structure, Sign, and Play" 249). There is no historical reality which it parodies; it exists in a system of differences from, and parallels and referrals to, other fictional, dubious sign systems.

We will recall that deconstruction demonstrates that "a certain view of the world, of consciousness, of language has been accepted as the correct one, and if the minute particulars of that view are examined a very different picture (that is also a no-picture . . .) emerges" (Spivak xvii). It is in its manner of examining the minute particulars of the picture that is also no-picture that *Blazing Saddles* reveals its deconstructionist intent. Let us take for example that very opening scenelet. Railroad track is being laid by a work gang of African and Asian Americans. Many are dropping in the heat of the sun, and an Asian who has fainted will be docked of his pay for sleeping on the job. On the surface the satire of this scenelet operates merely to contradict the horizon of expectation conditioned in us by the Western: 1) that the opening of the West was the heroic fulfillment of Manifest Destiny; 2) that the hardy pioneers who opened it, sons of the founding fathers, were good, heroic folk inspired by American democratic values. The equation at surface level is simple and binary: the West was opened not by homespun pioneers, but by greedy, corporation power brokers. But, because it is a deconstructionist enterprise, *Blazing Saddles* opens the "minute particulars" of this simple contrast to view. The scenelet goes further than mock-heroic parody. The white gang bosses ride up and ask the black workers why they are not singing spirituals. Stereotype 1 = the happy slave singing with joy as he works in the master's fields. Then the bosses ask the workers to sing a song composed by a white man in black dialect, "De Camptown Races," and when the workers do not know the song, the bosses demonstrate—singing, clapping, and jigging in "darky" style. Stereotype 2 = the white mental image of blacks is a white construct unknown to blacks. The black men finally agree to sing for the entertainment of their oppressors, and they render a jazz quartet version of "I Get No Kick from Champagne." Stereotype 3 = black people are more sophisticated and cool than whites. (This stereotype is re-inforced when the newly deputized Sheriff Bart appears in a Rodeo Drive outfit, complete with Gucci saddlebag.) In this small bit of business what is satiric antithesis? What is "satiric thesis?" Which is "real" or "true"? Where is the "norm of nature" here? There is none. Thesis *and* antithesis, expectation *and* the confounding of expectation, upward exaggeration (hypsos) *and* downward exaggeration (bathos) are all and equally empty stereotypes. Moreover, even among the stereotypes, binary opposition is never constant, never fixed.

Like all great satires, *Blazing Saddles* aims particularly at the pillars of culture: authority and morality. The Governor, for example, is a grotesquely exaggerated lecher, incompetent to govern because, like Sardanapalus, "Cunt [is his] sole Bus'ness and Affair of State." But the satiric treatment of the Governor is not merely a mock-heroic, King-Fool binary opposition. Rather, the movie's imaging of authority calls its own semiotic process to attention and, consequently, extends beyond the simple disequation Governor = John Wayne to expose the emptiness of the "literary" conventions involved in our representations of authority. For instance, the public relations companies that shape the American consciousness of candidates for political office invariably picture candidates with their spouses and families. In America, as in imperial Rome, the honor and reputation of a citizen depends upon his being a *paterfamilias.* (That is why Naevolus, the bisexual steward in Juvenal's *Satire Nine,* has to work so hard.) By the exaggerated fictionality of its semiosis *Blazing Saddles* mocks the fictionality of the real in American political consciousness—fictions that shape our consciousness and move us to cast our votes, or, perhaps more accurately, to choose sides—in a continuous game that has neither beginning nor ending, but rather exists in a semiotic field of difference without positive terms.

*Blazing Saddles* is designed to expose the fictionality of cultural inscriptions that are altogether empty yet are powerful enough to move us to kill one another. There is no "nature," no "reality" in such a satire. Equally fictitious, equally conventional signs collide to expose the emptiness underlying them. Inauthentic constructs erase each other in a continuous process that exists for the sole end of undoing itself. The whole satire unpeels itself to expose fiction after underlying fiction. For example, the villain in the Western is fierce and implacably evil. Here Hedley Lamar, whose name makes him a fiction-in-opposition to the romantic fictional image of the movie glamor queen Hedy Lamar, is an exaggerated sign of the corporation hatchet-man. At surface level he is a parody villain; that parodic mask is stripped to reveal a parody capitalist political operator who uses money and sex for gain; that parody falls before an effete little nasty playing with his froggie in the tub; that parody, in turn, falls to reveal an actor in the lobby of Grauman's Chinese Theater, who is shot/not shot by another actor in a scene that spills over the borders of its narrative into a parody Busby Berkeley musical set, which, in turn, spills into a fictional studio commissary where signs from every movie genre—storm troopers, chorus girls, cowboys, extraterrestrials—collide in pointless battle.

In the same way that authority is not simply overturned but semiotically eradicated, so too is morality. Maria von Schtupp is a parody of the dangerous and irresistible seductress image associated with

Marlene Dietrich. On the simplest level the counterfeit mocks the original; the sexuality of romantic obsession is reduced to "They quote Byron and Shelley/Then jump on your belly/And break your balloons." But, as in "Fair Chloris in a pig-sty lay," one generic stereotype does not simply cancel another; rather, the collision among *many,* various stereotypes (for example, the racial-erotic clichés subsumed under the clichés of sexual obsession) exposes the vacancy of the cultural consciousness shaped by them.

The climactic action of *Blazing Saddles,* if, indeed, a plotless deconstructive dramatic satire can be said to have one, consists in the exaggeratedly parodic townspeople foiling the exaggeratedly parodic villains by building a false façade replica of their town under the direction of their clever-possum sheriff. This action, itself a sign, is what Keir Elam calls "the gesture of putting on show the very process of semiotization involved in the performance" (9).

The semiotics of *Blazing Saddles* is designed not to attack "real" persons, or to ridicule "real" circumstances or behavior, but to attack our fatal tendency to believe that the empty fictions which govern and shape our consciousness are real. This is a satire entirely *in* and *of* sign, a satire that puts on show the duplicity that makes truth possible, thereby destroying "truth."

Dustin Griffin's analysis of "A Ramble in St. James's Park" reads the satire as on one level a response to Edmund Waller's panegyric "On St. James's Park as Lately Improv'd by His Majesty" (1661). Nevertheless, Griffin understands satiric thesis in the poem as realistic, a depiction of things as they were: "Rochester's anti-pastoral satire . . . measures the distance between Waller's old ideal and present reality by parodying the panegyric" (*Satires Against Man* 29). I believe, rather, that the relation between Rochester's and Waller's poems is similar to the relation that Griffin observes between Rochester's "Heroical Epistle" and Etherege's "Ephelia to Bajazet" cited earlier. That is, in "A Ramble" Waller's and Rochester's poems speak to each other in the context of the pastoral *locus amoenus* tradition and "require no external referent." That there is, indeed, a St. James's Park and that it was a fashionable meeting place in the 1670s is no more significant to Rochester's satire than the real existence of the nineteenth-century American West and the historically verifiable existence of cowboys, settlers, and sheriffs is to *Blazing Saddles.* "A Ramble in St. James's Park" is not the realistic narrative of a libertine's encounter with his faithless mistress in the sexually licentious atmosphere of the park; it is rather a loosely organized collision among a variety of generic models, literary conventions, and mind-sets which assaults both its fictional speaker and its imagined reader as fashion-conditioned, convention-conditioned "whore[s] in understanding."

The title of the poem sets an initial dichotomy that runs as an underlying thread through the fabric of the text. This ramble stands in juxtaposition to Waller's stately romantic "lovers walking in the amorous shade" of modernized pastoral landscape. However, the subversion of pastoral extends far beyond mere parody of Waller. The whole pastoral tradition of the "sacred grove"—from Virgil to Guarini to Fletcher—is deconstructed by Rochester's "all-sin-sheltering grove." Rochester's "sacred" place is "consecrate to prick and cunt." Here the priest of pastoral, who stands within his bower blessing the innocent shepherd-lovers as they pledge their platonic troths, is fiction-in-opposition, a Sullen Satyr figure who "would frig upon his mother's face." Furthermore, Rochester's "lovers" are "walking" to amorous encounters as forced, unnatural, and self-induced as that of their presiding genius.

Thomas E. Maresca has said that "satire . . . is a protean creature. . . . It is not truly a genre. It actually has no fixed form. . . . It exists in and as flux, as the breakdown of canons or the deconstruction of forms."[4] Once again, I do not believe that this description is applicable to *all* satire, but it is very illuminating indeed of Restoration satire, and it is particularly accurate as a description of the deconstructive process which constitutes "A Ramble." Rochester's poem does not measure the distance between the removed scene and style of pastoral and present reality. Rather, it is designed to fracture and subvert the constructs that the "serious" and "respectable" literary genres have written upon our consciousness. It makes chaos of genres, of conventions, of language itself.

Consider, for example, the operation of lines 10–32, which we would expect to be the opening of a narrative:

> There by a most incestuous birth,
> Strange woods spring from the teeming earth,
> For they relate how heretofore
> When ancient Pict began to whore,
> Deluded of his assignation
> (Jilting it seems was then in fashion),
> Poor pensive lover, in this place
> Would frig upon his mother's face;
> Whence rows of mandrakes tall did rise
> Whose lewd tops fucked the very skies.
> Each imitative branch does twine
> In some loved fold of Aretine,

And nightly now beneath their shade
Are buggeries, rapes, and incests made.
Unto this all-sin-sheltering grove
Whores of the bulk and the alcove,
Great ladies, chambermaids, and drudges,
The ragpicker, and heiress trudges.
Carmen, divines, great lords, and tailors,
Prentices, poets, pimps, and jailers,
Footmen, fine fops do here arrive,
And here promiscuously they swive.

The passage begins by exploding the very idea of a "tale" of mythic origins, that is, the origin of the park in the time of the ancient Picts, which is a story "they relate." The mythic ancient priest of nature—in romance a figure who fosters and tends nature's life—is monstrified into a violator of his Mother Earth. Subversion of the cultural myth of origins is succeeded by perversion of the celestial-terrestrial order. Trees fuck skies not just to parody Waller's "bold sons of earth that thrust their arms so high" but also, shockingly, to overthrow our most basic spatial sense, our sense of cosmic order and balance. Having grotesquely inverted the relation of earth and sky, the poem turns to creation of vegetable chaos. Branches grow deformedly, forcing themselves into Aretinian postures. From the convolution of vegetable nature we move to corresponding unnatural distortions in the human realm—"buggeries, rapes, and incests." Splintering the mirror of nature occurs in an explosive chain of descent: from mythic origins, to cosmos, to vegetable nature, to human nature, and finally to social chaos: the "promiscuous" mixture of "whores," "chambermaids," "ragpickers," "great lords," "pimps," "footmen," "fops." Ring by ring, circle by circle, we tread the structural design of romance-epic, shattering as we go that highest of genres' claim to truth. In the last seven lines of the passage, as figure upon figure, image after image, piles up helter-skelter, and all the world "promiscuously . . . swive[s]," language itself abandons all pretense at orderly narrative or description. Words collide with words, images with images, in random, atomistic chaos.

Having deconstructed the epic/romance vision of cosmic and earthly *harmonia*, "A Ramble" turns our attention to Cavalier lyric. "When I beheld Corinna pass" constructs in order to deconstruct a perfect miniature Caroline lyric of the kind that in the idyllic age "before the Flood" would have celebrated *precieuse* "Platonick Love" concepts of love and honor. Rochester elegantly *works* the convention before, in the last line, he demolishes it. Lines 33 to 40 are worthy of Lovelace or Suckling. Moreover, the reversal—"But mark what creatures women are:/How infinitely vile when fair"—is itself *conventional.* Think, for instance, of Book II, Canto xii, Stanza 75 of *The Faerie Queene,* wherein a perfect *carpe diem* lyric is completely inverted by the substitution of a single word, "sin," for the word expected, "love." A single word, by confounding the reader's expectation, reverses the generic thrust of the lyric. The object of satire in this passage is not some "real" person, but the mistress of Rochester, or of some other "real" libertine. What is at war is not a literary convention and a reality. Rather, whole armies of literary conventions are in dubious battle on a darkling plain.

In an almost Aristotelian progression, "A Ramble" moves from the demolition of romance modes and conventions to those of the drama. The three "Knights o' the elbow" are conventional types from Restoration comedy/dramatic satire: the courtier/not courtier; the Wit-would, who uses postures and language he learns from the stage to seduce his City land-lady; and the adolescent Pinocchio-blade, who is learning the lore of his fake mentors. As in a dramatic satire of Etherege or Wycherley, these types are not "characters," not parodies of real social types. They are, rather, linguistic signs. The blades, as well as Corinna's response to them, are signs of the mental processes "A Ramble" is designed to deconstruct, the process by which the human mind "Converts abortive imitation/To universal affectation." A contemporary example may open the function of these signs to us. Two figures, male and female, but both androgynous in appearance, execute a series of highly unlikely, highly artificial postures on a television screen. They mouth some unintelligible babble in which the word "obsession" is repeated several times. This enactment of what, in reality, would be a mental disease (obsession) is used as a seductive image of fashionably conceived sexual attractiveness to move the viewer to want to be *like* the figures on screen, empty as they are, and thereby move her to buy Calvin Klein perfume. The viewer is persuaded to this action by "neither head nor tail." Corinna's encounter with the fashionable empty signs of men is designed to expose this process whereby we are moved to act neither by generous "lust" nor by a spontaneous attraction to the Beautiful generated in understanding—neither by body nor by mind, but by empty conventions, by au courant, "in" notions of what is sexy. The process corrupts us in body, for we are moved by empty, mutable cultural inscriptions to enact mechanically and without feeling a natural act that thereby becomes unnatural. It corrupts us in mind, for we force our natures to the contours of empty images as surely as the grotesque St. James's Park trees force themselves into

Aretinian postures. The process forces us to *create* the "artifactuality of the real" and to embrace "the fictiveness of truth."

Finally, the poem exposes its libertine speaker as yet another empty shape, an artifact of literary invention. First, the speaker-libertine is revealed as a false libertine. He uses the language of libertine love lyric—

> When leaning on your faithless breast
> Wrapped in security and rest
> Soft kindness all my powers did move
> And reason lay dissolved in love—

to disguise a process as mechanical and unnatural as Corinna's when she goes off with the blades. The image of swooning lovers is false. By admission the libertine has been *forcing* to spend himself into what he considers to be a sink. What is worse, he has used a convention-designed image of the heroic love mistress to hide his compulsively mechanical action from his understanding in a veil of language.

However, even to speak of the satiric spokesman of the poem in such terms is to create a totally false impression of "characterization," of interiority and psychology in a satiric speaker that is, in fact, a linguistic sign, a wholly conventional *literary* type. The curse that ends the poem discloses the speaker as a convention centuries old in the native English satiric tradition. He is the satyr-satirist, a highly complex persona. Tradition determines that this satiric spokesman 1) is guilty of the very vice he castigates, 2) uses language as a weapon because he is impotent to act, and 3) in the act of cursing becomes what he hates. In the final curse the extravagant, lashing language of the speaker is a substitute for action. Like his enemy, he is a "whore in understanding," and he wills for the other—insatiable longing that must turn to wild despair—the essential quality of the libertinism he represents. "A Ramble in St. James's Park" ends by erasing the speaking "I," by demonstrating that the speaker exists nowhere but *in* language, is a product solely *of* language.

## Notes

1. For Vieth, see "Toward an Anti-Aristotelian Poetic," *Attribution in Restoration Poetry,* and *The Moriae Encomium as a Model for Satire in Restoration Court Literature.* For Griffin's contribution see *Satires Against Man* and especially "Satiric Closure." See also Cope, "The Conquest of Truth," and Everett's "The Sense of Nothing."

2. See, for example, Arthur R. Husboe, *Sir George Etherege,* or Willard Connely,

*Brawny Wycherley.* Eugene McCarthy in *William Wycherley* attributes Wycherley's whole personality to his relation with his father precisely because Daniel Wycherley was so litigious that court records provide a good deal of evidence about his life, while there is no data on his son's life until William reached the age of thirty and precious little after that time beyond anecdotal evidence.

3. As widely different personalities as Marvell and Voltaire thought Rochester a great satirist and genius. Charles thought Wycherley a satirist of such penetrating sense that he would be a fit tutor for kings, while most of his contemporaries, including Dryden, thought him the Restoration's Juvenal.

4. In "The *Satyricon*: No Text, Context, Pretext," a chapter in Maresca's forthcoming book on allegory which the author has graciously allowed me to read in manuscript.

# Works Cited

Augustine Aurelianus. *Confessions.* Trans. Vernon J. Burke. *Fathers of the Church.* Vol. 5. 1953. Washington: Catholic UP, 1968.

———. *De Magistro. The Philosophy of St. Augustine: Selected Readings and Commentaries.* Ed. John A. Mourant. University Park, PA: Pennsylvania State UP, 1964.

———. *On Christian Doctrine.* Trans. D. W. Robertson, Jr. Indianapolis: Bobbs-Merrill, 1958.

———. *The Teacher.* Trans. Robert B. Russel. *The Fathers of the Church.* Vol. 59. Washington: Catholic UP, 1968.

Bloch, Howard R. *Etymologies and Geneologies: A Literary Anthropology of the French Middle Ages.* Chicago: U of Chicago P, 1983.

Connely, Willard. *Brawny Wycherley.* London: Scribner's Sons, 1930.

Cope, Kevin. "The Conquest of Truth: Wycherley, Butler, Rochester, and Dryden," *Restoration* 10 (1986): 19–40.

De Man, Paul. "The Rhetoric of Temporality." *Interpretation: Theory and Practice.* Ed. Charles S. Singleton. Baltimore: Johns Hopkins UP, 1969. 173–209.

Derrida, Jacques. "Living on Borderlines." *Deconstruction and Criticism.* Ed. Harold Bloom and Others. London: Routledge and Kegan Paul, 1979. 75–176.

———. *Positions.* Trans. Alan Bass. Chicago: U of Chicago P, 1981.

———. "Structure, Sign, and Play in the Discourse of the Human Sciences." *The Languages of Criticism and the Sciences of Man: The Structuralist Controversy.* Ed. R. Macksey and E. Donato. Baltimore: Johns Hopkins UP, 1970. 247–72.

———. *Writing and Difference.* Trans. Alan Bass. Chicago: U of Chicago P, 1978.

Eco, Umberto. *The Role of the Reader: Explorations in the Semiotics of Texts.* Bloomington: Indiana UP, 1978.

Elam, Keir. *The Semiotics of Theatre and Drama.* London and New York: Methuen, 1980.

Everett, Barbara. "The Sense of Nothing." *Spirit of Wit: Reconsiderations of Rochester.* Ed. Jeremy Treglown. Hamden, CT: Archon Books, 1982. 1–41.

Griffin, Dustin. *Satires Against Man.* Berkeley and Los Angeles: U of California P, 1973.

———. "Satiric Closure." *Genre* 18 (1985): 173–89.

Hobbes, Thomas. *Leviathan.* Ed. Michael Oakeshott. Oxford: Oxford UP, 1960.

Husboe, Arthur R. *Sir George Etherege.* TEAS. Boston: G. K. Hall, 1987.

McCarthy, Eugene. *William Wycherley.* Athens, OH: Ohio UP, 1979.

Miner, Earl. "In Satire's Falling City." *The Satirist's Art.* Ed. H. J. Jensen and M. R. Zirken. Bloomington: Indiana UP, 1972. 3–27.

Quintillian. *The Institutio Oratoria of Quintillian.* Trans. H. E. Butler. 4 vols. London: Heinemann, 1921–22.

Racevskis, Karlis. "Geneological Critique: Michel Foucault." *Contemporary Literary Theory.* Ed. D. G. Atkins and L. Morrow. Amherst: U of Massachusetts P, 1989. 229–45.

Rawson, Claude. *Order from Confusion Sprung.* London: George Allen and Unwin, 1985.

Rochester, John Wilmot, Earl of. *The Works of John, Earl of Rochester.* London, 1714.

Seidel, Michael. *Satiric Inheritance: Rabelais to Sterne.* Princeton: Princeton UP, 1979.

Selden, Raman. *English Verse Satire, 1590–1765.* London: George Allen and Unwin, 1978.

Spivak, Gayatri. "Translator's Preface." Jacques Derrida, *Of Grammatology.* Baltimore: Johns Hopkins UP, 1976. ix–lxxxviii.

Vieth, David. *Attribution in Restoration Poetry.* New Haven: Yale UP, 1963.

———. "Toward an Anti-Aristotelian Poetic." *Language and Style* 5 (1972): 123–45.

———. "The *Moriae Encomium* as a Model for Satire." *Restoration Court Literature: Rochester and Others.* Los Angeles: The William Andrews Clark Memorial Library, 1988. 1–32.

Zimmerman, Everett. *Swift's Narrative Satires.* Ithaca: Cornell UP, 1983.

# Ideology, Sex, and Satire

## The Case of Thomas Shadwell

*Jean I. Marsden*

When Satyr the true medicine is declin'd,
What hope of Cure can our Corruptions find?
. . .
Instruction is an honest Poet's aim,
And not a large or wide, but a good Fame.
But he has found long since this would not do,
And therefore thought to have deserted you:
But Poets and Young Girls by no mishaps
Are warn'd, those damning fright not, nor these Claps.
Their former Itch will spite of all perswade,
And both will fall again to their old trade.
  —"Prologue," *The Lancashire Witches*
  *and Tegue O Divelly the Irish Priest* 4.102

### 1

In these opening lines to his most controversial and openly satiric play, Thomas Shadwell explains his reasons for writing satiric drama. Shadwell's words link the satiric urge to female sexual desire, implying that both "Itches" are powerful and ultimately uncontrollable. This connection between satire and female desire permeates much of Shadwell's satiric drama; Shadwell relies on women not only as objects of his social satire, but as the mouthpieces for his opposition political views. As Shadwell's drama itself suggests, however, this analogy is flawed. While satire can be seen as a corrupt society's only hope of "cure," female desire is far more dangerous. Although women are central to his satiric purpose, Shadwell finds the representation of female desire ultimately disruptive, as destablizing to his satire as his satire was to his enemies.

Despite Dryden's memorably caustic depiction of Shadwell as an inept and soporific writer, in the later seventeenth century Shadwell was not only a leading playwright, but the most prominent Whig dramatist of

his day, using his plays to attack what he saw as the excesses of a Catho-
lic-leaning monarchy. Because his drama was subject to censorship, if
Shadwell wanted his plays to succeed on the stage (and thus earn him a
share of the proceeds), his politically incorrect views had to be expressed
indirectly.[1] While Shadwell does use the fame of other writers as a shield,[2]
more often he couches his politically explosive ideas in terms of domestic
relationships and places them in the mouths of his female characters.
While eighteenth-century critics such as John Hughes found the behavior of Shadwell's women socially subversive (he complains that they outwit "those who had a Right in the Disposal of them"), in the later seventeenth century these women were a seemingly safe outlet for political
commentary. Unlike the more overt political commentary of his male
characters, the words of Shadwell's women escaped censorship. The appearance—and later disappearance—of these female mouthpieces indicates
the political utility of Shadwell's outspoken women. When Shadwell returned to writing drama after a six-year hiatus following the censorship
of *The Lancashire Witches,* his female characters rarely played this politically crucial role.[3]

The staging of female desire becomes the stumbling block in Shadwell's
otherwise idyllic picture of female political autonomy. The topic of desire is safe so long as the woman is one of the young ladies of wit and
sense who appear in most of his comedies. These young ladies stand up
for their "political" right to marry the man of their choice, but they are
never explicitly lusty; they long for marriage rather than sex. This socially acceptable representation of female desire is ultimately unthreatening
because it upholds rather than challenges the sexual status quo. More explicit expressions of desire can be tolerated only if expressed by whores,
who are by definition sexual commodities, or by the older married women
who are frequently the butts of Shadwell's social satire. But when women
step outside of their traditional roles and become the driving force behind the satire, then expressions of female desire become problematic. In
plays such as *The Woman Captain* (1680) or *The Lancashire Witches* (1681),[4]
both written during the politically volatile years of the Exclusion Crisis,
women are not only mouthpieces for Whig ideology, but are also the
means by which the satiric butts of Shadwell's comedies are ridiculed. The
implications of this representation of female authority are too destabilizing
to be sustained, and Shadwell's political and social satire collide, resulting
in the erasure of female desire, or in a blurred satiric purpose.

2

Shadwell's uneasiness with regard to female desire is clearly apparent in his careful stereotyping of female characters. The women in his plays fall into two distinct groups determined by social class and sexual experience: the romantic leads, unmarried upper-class virgins of "Wit and Vertue" (*A True Widow*) who marry the hero(es); and the older, more experienced whores and their upper-class counterparts, the "whorish" married women. The first group of women is small; aside from their often explicit endorsement of Whig ideology, they resemble the heroines of other Restoration comedies. They frequently appear in sets of two to offset the paired heroes to whom they are inevitably married or betrothed by the play's conclusion. These "women of good Humour, Wit and Beauty" (*Dramatis Personae, The Lancashire Witches*) are frequently static; while they are outspoken about their individual independence, they usually do little to effect their "right" to choose for themselves beyond refusing the absurd suitors their fathers, uncles, or guardians present to them. Indicative of their status as women of virtue, they do not engage in bawdy talk or in sexual behavior, focusing their desires on the goal of socially acceptable marriage.

The second group of women far outnumbers the first. Shadwell's plays are dominated by whores and "whorish" married women and contain the densest concentration of whores in Restoration drama. Nearly every play has at least one prostitute, and in some plays, such as *The Woman Captain,* they outnumber the other female characters three to one. (Shadwell even inserts three "wenches" into his adaptation of Molière's *The Miser,* making Frosine/Cheatly a "procurer" rather than simply a matchmaker.) These women are part of a clearly defined equation in which sex equals money and in which the terms of the equation are explicit. At the conclusion of *The Woman Captain,* Bellamy arranges a settlement with the prostitute Celia expressed in legal terminology akin to that used in signing a lease: "*Item,* it is articled and agreed between this Lady and me, that I am to use, possess and enjoy the Tenement of her Person without any lett, hinderance, or molestation whatsoever, buying a Coach and Horses, as aforesaid; and paying the annual Rent of 400 £ *per annum,* of lawful Money of *England*; half yearly by true and equal portions: The first payment to be made at the *Temple-Hall,* at the Feast of the *Annunciation,* and the next at the Feast of St. *Michael*" (4.83–84). Such settlements are couched in terms of male possession of the female object, where the male subject "uses," "possesses," and "enjoys" his property for the duration of the contract. Unless secured by an agreement such as this, Shadwell's whores are inclined to be unfaithful, but their roving desires are sanctioned because of their status as sexual commodities.

While such explicitly sexual behavior can be condoned in a whore, it comes under sharp attack when practiced by other women. There are no laudable older women in Shadwell's plays and few honorable wives. Some are affected fools, such as Lady Fantast in *Bury Fair*, but most are what Shadwell describes in the *Dramatis Personae* as "whorish." The list of such women is almost as long as the list of whores,[5] but more than the whores, these women seem possessed by insatiable desires. In *The Virtuoso*, for example, Lady Gimcrack's appetite appears voracious; she fails in one tryst but succeeds in sneaking offstage with two different men for "quickies" in the final act. (As Longvil comments, "I never knew one so free of her body, and so nice of her face before" 3.174.) Direct exposure is reserved for the wives of "citizens," such as Mrs. Bisket and Mrs. Fribble, who, unlike the wives of foolish aristocrats, are caught by their husbands *in flagrante delicto*. These "whorish" women become the objects of the satirist's scorn. They are exposed as lecherous and hypocritical, often losing ground in their power struggles with their credulous husbands. The relentless vilification of these women suggests that their enactment of desire represents potential chaos and thus deserves the satirist's lash.

Linked theoretically to national security in legal documents and social tracts, women's sexuality and its representations had important ramifications in the Restoration.[6] While Shadwell ridicules desire in middle- and upper-class women, he sanctions it on the part of a prostitute, and in general the whores fare better than the "whorish women." Sexual behavior is a necessary part of their "profession," and thus desire is by definition part of their nature—it is not an object of satire. Shadwell "rewards" these women by marrying them to fops, fools, and occasionally their keepers.[7] Because a whore is promiscuous by profession, her desire is ultimately unthreatening. She is a commodity on the open market and can be dropped by her keeper at any time with her contract voided. She cannot cuckold a man unless she marries and joins the ranks of whorish women. In contrast to the whores whose sexuality is controlled by those who possess them and who exist outside the social power structure, married women are more dangerous, and, if uncontrolled, their desires have serious ramifications. Concern over a married woman's chastity was more than a social fetish. England's network of property lines, and through them the lines of power, depended on the woman not simply as vessel of the male seed but as vessel of the proper male seed. England's sociopolitical stability thus relied on containing female desire.

Dramatic representation of transgressive desires could, it was feared, set a bad example and influence otherwise virtuous women in the theatre audience, in effect shattering national security. John Dennis, always concerned with the effect of drama upon an audience, objected to the staging of Dryden's *All for Love* for precisely these reasons, and he outlines the dangers of uncontrolled female sexuality with nationalistic zeal:

> Is not the Chastity of the Marriage Bed one of the chief Incendiaries of Publick Spirit, and the Frequency of Adulteries one of the chief Extinguishers of it? . . . For when Adultery's become so frequent, especially among Persons of Condition, upon whose Sentiments all Publick Spirit chiefly depends, that a great many Husbands begin to believe, or perhaps but to suspect, that they who are called their Children are not their own; I appeal to you, Sir, if that Belief or that Suspicion must not exceedingly cool their Zeal for the Welfare of those Children, and consequently for the Welfare of Posterity. (2.163–64)

For Dennis, as for many moralists of the Restoration and eighteenth century, married chastity represents the foundation of public spirit and ultimately of patriotism, because by being unchaste a woman can destroy the structure of inheritance ("posterity") on which the nation is built. Unlicensed desire could lead, as Dennis asserts, to the destruction of the aristocracy and through it the destruction of the state itself. In this guise, female desire becomes dangerous, and, in order to diminish and ultimately contain the threat of instability posed by uncontrolled female desire, the sexually voracious female must become the object of ridicule.

When one of the whores in *The Woman Captain* marries, a fellow prostitute reminds her "there's no Wife lives like of one of us" (4.85), and this simple statement encapsulates Shadwell's representation of female desire. There is indeed no wife who can live like a whore—sexual freedom is the whore's prerogative. As Shadwell's plays demonstrate, such freedom damns any other woman who tries to practice it. Shadwell presents only one young and virtuous woman (tellingly of middle-class origins) who yields to her desires. Lucia, the attorney's daughter in *The Squire of Alsatia,* is "debauch'd" by Belfond Junior and barely escapes being cast out of her family and marked as a whore. Belfond Junior's early promise to better her position translates not into marriage but into a cash settlement and the obliteration of her own sexuality, as she vows: "I will hereafter out live the strictest Nun" (4.276). In trying to bridge the gulf between the heroine and the whore, Lucia loses both her freedom and the man she loves. Her fate reinforces the rigid stereotypes Shadwell establishes in his other plays. In the world of Shadwell's drama, female desire can be sanctioned only if sublimated and channeled into a socially acceptable genteel marriage or in the form of the whore whose lower-class origins (and unfocused sexuality) render her essentially powerless.

### 3

Complicated by the scopic dynamics of performance, Shadwell's sexual stereotypes break down in the two plays where Shadwell depends on women as the agents of his satiric agenda. These plays, *The Woman Captain* (1680) and *The Lancashire Witches* (1681), were both written in the volatile years of the Popish plot and the Exclusion Crisis. At the time, Shadwell was actively involved in supporting the opposition party and its leader, the Earl of Shaftsbury, in their attempt to prevent the imposition of a Catholic monarch on the Protestant throne of England. Seeking to replace the Catholic heir to the throne (James, Duke of York) with Charles II's illegitimate son, the Duke of Monmouth, the Whigs opposed Tory claims of Divine Right with arguments for *"the Peoples Liberties"* (*The Lancashire Witches* 4.137). These political concerns permeate Shadwell's drama, but are rarely expressed directly, because drama explicitly expressing Whig views was frequently prohibited from the stage. Cloaking his political agenda in a feminine guise, Shadwell uses the domestic sphere to comment upon the political sphere, employing unconventional women as his mouthpieces. Mrs. Gripe (the "woman captain") and the witches dominate the action, pummeling, both literally and metaphorically, the men who surround them and thus effecting Shadwell's satiric goals. Such female vigor is refreshing, but by the end of each play it creates rifts within the social fabric of the dramas.

As the dominant satiric force in *The Woman Captain,* Mrs. Gripe fits none of Shadwell's female stereotypes. She is young and attractive (although neither trait is stressed) but married, a wife who is neither whorish nor a fool. She begins the play imprisoned by her unduly jealous husband, the miser Gripe, who not only locks his wife away to prevent others from seeing her but starves her to save money and to "keep down her Lusts" (4.27). It is her situation as an abused wife on which the play's political agenda hinges, representing as it does the abuse of power by a (domestic) monarch. Mrs. Gripe articulates her plight by placing it in the explicitly political context of unjust tyranny over a free English subject. When her husband temporarily releases her near the end of the first Act, she cries: "Will this Tyrannie never be at an end? Must I be always thus abridg'd of Liberty?" (4.27) and continues "I deserve not to be used so, I will have the liberty of a She-Subject of *England*" (4.28). The expressly political terminology ("Tyrannie," "Liberty," "Subject of *England*") links Mrs. Gripe's domestic problems with those of the English people and presents her desire for marital liberty as part of an inherently English privilege. Her vow, "I'll make you know the right of an English Woman before I have done" (4.38), not only reiterates the terms of the larger ideological problem of personal liberty, but, more important, establishes Shadwell's satiric agenda for the play. The "English" rights of liberty Mrs. Gripe plans to attain for herself are precisely those that Shadwell advocates for a larger political arena, in particular the importance of the *"People's Interest"* in government. As articulated in *The Medal of John Bayes: A Satyr Against Folly and Knavery,* Shadwell envisioned a monarch linked to the people by Parliamentary action:

> But Heaven preserve our Legal Monarchy,
> And all those Laws that keep the People free.
> Of all Mankind, for ever curst be they,
> Who would or Kings, or People's Rights betray,
> Or ought would change, but by a Legislative way. (5.261)

Personal liberty thus becomes a necessary part of "Legal Monarchy."

Mrs. Gripe effects these goals by donning male garb and becoming the "woman captain." Disguised as her twin brother, she goads her husband to enlist (he cannot resist taking the "King's shilling") and then forces him to participate in military drills and threatens to ship him over to the war in Flanders, beating him soundly when he complains.[8] She uses similar means to punish Sir Christopher Swash, Heildebrand, and Blunderbus, the bullies whose drunken behavior disturbs the peace and destroys property. She finally gains her liberty and overthrows tyranny by forcing Gripe to sign a separate maintenance agreement. Her male garb invests her with the power she lacked as a mere woman, allowing her to employ the physical violence which is both the basis for much of the play's rough humor and the means by which the satiric butts are ridiculed. In the process, Shadwell makes Mrs. Gripe the conscience of his play, investing her with moral, political, and social authority. She is the arbiter of justice and the protector of English liberty.[9]

As the active center of the play, she stands in contrast to Shadwell's only other cross-dressed woman, the lovelorn Philadelphia in *Bury Fair,* who dresses as a page to escape an unwelcome suitor and who can do no more than watch helplessly as the man she loves courts another woman. Comparing Mrs. Gripe with Philadelphia pinpoints an important feature of *The Woman Captain*—the virtual absence of female desire. Whereas Philadelphia languishes for love of her master, Mrs. Gripe expresses no desire beyond that of gaining her liberty. Other characters project their desires onto her: her husband fears cuckolding and locks her up to contain her "lusts" while the servant Richard brings her various tidbits "and something else in my Breeches—I have an honour for my Mistress, and should be loath to see her want" (4.37). Mrs. Gripe not only remains impervious to such temptations throughout the play, but even seems devoid of sexuality—at least on the printed page.[10] This erasure of female desire points to a crucial dilemma which underlies Shadwell's representation of women. In the world of Shadwell's plays, female desire and female autonomy can coexist only when directed toward—not out of—marriage. This incompatibility is heightened in *The Woman Captain* because in the play female autonomy connotes political autonomy, and to admit female desire would sabotage the basic premise of Shadwell's satire. Closer examination of the play reveals that female desire is linked to a pervasive identification of women as sexual property and suggests that women cannot be object and subject at the same time.

From the beginning of the play, women are established as sexual objects with an exact monetary value. In the opening scene, a Bawd sells Sir Humphrey "three Maiden-heads"; later Gripe hordes his wife in the same way that he hordes his money;[11] and at the end of the play Chloe and Celia accept contracts paying them each £400 "annual Rent" for the use of their bodies. Repeatedly, women appear as desired objects, but not as desiring subjects. Only the whores see desire as a fact of life, complaining bitterly that Gripe's incarceration of his wife unnaturally contains a woman's freedom of desire:

> *Chloe.* Woman was meant to go at large. Thou shame of Mankind!
> *Phillis.* Shall Woman, that's wild by Nature, be tam'd by thee base
>     Fellow? (4.41)

Although Celia, Chloe, and Phillis claim freedom of desire as a natural right for women, their claims are immediately undercut by a male interpretation of the situation as Sir Humphery explains: "He [Gripe] invades the right of Whoremasters, and 'tis not to be born; we have the right of Commonage, and he impales" (4.41). Sir Humphery's comparison of women and public grazing land redefines women's "wildness" as the whoremaster's "right" to communal property—locking a woman up ("impaling") does not infringe on her right to liberty but on the right of other men to use this piece of common property. Women's sexual freedom thus becomes the possession of men, leaving women no more than objects of male desire. Mrs. Gripe has declared herself a free subject and, in a world where female sexuality is the property of men, expressing desire would link her to the whores, jeopardizing both her freedom and the satiric import of the Shadwell's comedy. Thus, she refuses to accept this vision of woman and chooses a male role as her route to freedom.

As *The Woman Captain* demonstrates, Mrs. Gripe identifies not with her own sex, but with the political ideal of liberty, a process which renders her character essentially sexless (although, one might add, not rendering the actress who played her sexless). Not surprisingly, her only amorous sallies are directed at the whores themselves. Inherently harmless, these interludes play with the notion of female desire for a female object but threaten neither Mrs. Gripe's hard-won autonomy nor the larger male power structure. In the end, the distance between Mrs. Gripe and the whores is quietly erased when they all end up accepting the same maintenance agreement of £400 per year. Their common fate subtly but inevitably links them together,[12] and the play ends abruptly after this link is established.

While Shadwell's political argument is effective in *The Woman Captain* because he evades the issue of Mrs. Gripe's desire, in his next play, *The Lancashire Witches,* the problem of female desire threatens to derail a political agenda already complicated by partisan censorship. Written during the furor over the Popish Plot, when anti-Catholic sentiment was running high, it brazenly attacks Catholicism, French sympathizers, High-Church Anglicanism, and authoritarianism, all objects of the Whigs' scorn in their attacks on the current regime. Not surprisingly, large segments were excised by the Master of the Revels, Charles Killigrew. When Shadwell published *The Lancashire Witches,* he included the censored sections (printed in italics) and complained bitterly of his treatment in the open letter "To the Reader" published with the play.[13] As written, the play contains blunt attacks on Catholicism and on what Shadwell portrays, in the figure of Smerk, as a corrupt Anglican clergy which is itself closely tied to Catholicism. Its most explicit references to people's liberties and its most violent attacks on Smerk are voiced by male characters such as the bluff, honest Sir Edward or the two romantic heroes, Bellfort and Doubty. Cut by the censor, these protests vanished from actual performances of the play. As staged, *The Lancashire Witches* is a hodgepodge of witty, determined lovers, witch hunts, and spectacular special effects. It is also a play in which women become the dominant characters; even more than *The Woman Captain, The Lancashire Witches* is a woman-centered drama filled with aggressive, powerful, and desiring women. With Shadwell's most direct political broadsides omitted, the play in its censored form emphasizes the role played by women, and Shadwell's female characters are left to articulate his satiric agenda.

While Shadwell intended the play to begin with Sir Edward berating the corrupt Anglican chaplain Smerk, this scene was excised by the censor. Instead, as staged, the play begins with celebration of the ideal woman as Sir Edward memorializes his dead wife: "Fair, and not proud on't; witty, and not vain; . . . She was all meekness and humility" (4.109). Tellingly, none of the play's female characters approach this meek and modest ideal. Even Isabella and Theodosia, the play's two romantic heroines, violate this code of passive mildness. They, like Mrs. Gripe, are the mouthpieces for Shadwell's more abstract political ideals, championing the cause of liberty, which in their case represents the very specific issue of choosing a husband.

> *Isabella.* Well, we are resolved never to marry where we are designed, that's certain. For my part I am a free English woman, and will stand up for my Liberty, and property of Choice.
> *Theodosia.* And Faith, Girl, I'le be a mutineer on thy side; I hate the imposition of a Husband, 'tis as bad as Popery. (4.111)

Although the attack on absolutism here is as explicit as it is elsewhere in the play, these lines escaped the censor, presumably because of their feminine context. Yet the right they claim, the freedom to desire whom they please, is precisely that which John Hughes, writing thirty years later, saw as an especially dangerous "Moral" (*Spectator* 141). While for Shadwell, these words have a distinct political message regarding the imposition of an unpopular Catholic monarch (James II), for Hughes the issue—and the monarch—is dead. He sees social rather than political implications to Isabella's and Theodosia's conversation.

Although physically confined by their position as upper-class virgins, Isabella and Theodosia nonetheless get what they want. They actively discourage distasteful suitors (Isabella throws rocks at her swain) and even appropriate the trappings of satanic power, masquerading as witches in order to achieve their "property of Choice." Here female desire can coexist with political rhetoric because it is held in check by social decorum (Isabella and Theodosia are the only chaste women in the play) and because it is directed into the unthreatening confines of socially sanctioned marriage. Not only are Isabella and Theodosia's desires centered on marriage, but their choices result in marriages even more prosperous than those originally planned for them, a conclusion which pointedly eliminates any economic disadvantage caused by woman's freedom of choice. Thus fenced in and unspoken, desire becomes politically and socially safe.

The same cannot be said for the "real" witches who dominate Shadwell's comedy. These witches are the heart of *The Lancashire Witches*; their antics made the play exceptionally popular in Shadwell's day and kept it a part of the eighteenth-century theater repertoire.[14] They fly through the air, appear and disappear through trap doors, call imps and devils from the underworld, and even kiss the devil's "arse." Although the witches are seen only by the irrational (or politically suspect) characters, the audience watching the play is placed in the same position as the play's fools as it watches the witches appear and disappear. Women who exist outside of social boundaries, the witches take the place of the whores in Shadwell's cast list. (As Clod tells Mal Spencer, the two are essentially the same: "thou are a fow Queen, I tell o that, thou art a fow Witch" 4.148.) But the witches are whores with a difference. They are not only sexual but powerful and exercise their power at male expense. Their powers, as they point out, encompass most of the material world. As represented in the play, the witches enact a war of the sexes; all the overt objects of their sorcery are male, and the play's broadest humor comes from watching clever women outwit silly men. Until the final act, the witches buffet men unseen, lead them astray, and ride them like horses. Mal Spencer's bridle, which she uses to control Clod, symbolizes the witches' ability to dominate the men around them. The witches' influence extends even to Theodosia and Isabella, who are most successful in their attempts to discourage foolish suitors when they mimic witches.

The nature of this power is strongly sexual. The witches are truly women "wild by Nature," but unlike Phillis and her fellow whores, the witches control not only their own sexuality but men's as well. They are the sexual aggressors in this play, seducing priests, brewing potent love charms, and in general initiating sexual contact. Unlike the whores, they have sex on their terms, and, unlike Lady Shacklehead and Shadwell's other over-sexed older women, they are not the objects of ridicule. Instead, they are the means by which Shadwell ridicules his chief satiric objects, Smerk and the Irish priest, Tegue O'Divelly. Tegue's copulation with Mother Dickerson demonstrates his salaciousness, corruption, and fundamental stupidity: "By my Shoule I have had communication and Copulaation too vid a Succubus; Oh! phaat vill I do! Phaat vill I do!" (4.169). A more sympathetic figure than Tegue, Mother Dickerson even swears to convert the priest so that she can marry him ("Oh damn'd Protestant Vitch!" he cries, 4.175). The witches are most influential, however, in their ability to control not only their own sexuality but that of men as well. Sir Jeffery swears that they have made him impotent (although, as Sir Edward remarks, "those things will happen about five and fifty" 4.145). In contrast to Sir Jeffery's incapacity, the chambermaid, Susan, administers a witch's brew to arouse Smerk's lust, using his inability to control his desires as a means of forcing him into marriage. Here the witches invert traditional power structures, made possible by female sexuality under female control.

But such untamed female power is too destabilizing to remain unchecked, and Shadwell ultimately must establish limitations to the witches' powers. The witches are nominally under the leadership of a male devil who appears briefly in the guise of a goat in Act II. We see nothing, however, of his powers, and he remains little more than a figurehead. A more substantial check on the witches comes at the end of the play, when Tegue captures Mother Dickerson (although how this happens is unclear as the staging indicates that she "*lays hold on him*" 4.175) and the rest of the witches, in the form of cats, are rounded up by townspeople who "[beat] 'em into Witches" and thus force them to relinquish their powers (4.179). For obvious religious and moral reasons Shadwell cannot let the witches remain dominant. Proper Christianity, not satanic ritual, must triumph in the end. However, this abrupt quashing of the witches results in a confused and confusing satiric lesson. Up until this point, the witches have only appeared to the foolish or corrupt characters; intelligent and virtuous figures, such as Sir Edward, the play's representative of the ideal Englishman (Bellfort describes him as "a wise, honest, hospitable, true English man" 4.118),[15] do not believe in witches, while Tegue, the butt of much of the satire, is the most outspoken advocate for their existence. The capture and interrogation of the witches, however, vindicates the judgment of those whom Shadwell ridicules, and, in the process, the play's political message is clouded.

While *The Lancashire Witches* ends in a flurry of activity with the witches herded offstage, three surprise marriages, and the arrest of Tegue for conspiracy, these movements toward closure do not obscure the fact that in performance it was the witches who carried Shadwell's play.[16] The witches brought audiences into the theater and made the play a success in its almost yearly revivals during the early eighteenth century. While Shadwell's political argument may be obscured, the play remains effective precisely because of the theatrical magic of its witches' power. The spectacle of wild women descending from the heavens, duping a series of self-important fools, and seizing control over the material world provides a brief interlude of Bahktinian carnivalesque where gender roles are inverted and sexual decorum suspended. Female desire, unmediated by the social con-

trols of courtship and marriage, drives the play, resulting in social up-
heavals and making satire possible. Uproarious as the effects of this interplay of female power and sexuality may be, they must ultimately be
brought under control and social order reinstated; while Shadwell's politics may have been radical, his social agenda was not.

This split between Shadwell's political and social agenda redounds on
his particular mixture of women, politics, and satire. In contrast to most
Restoration playwrights, Shadwell creates women who play a politically
significant role. But at the same time, these women are more likely to
remain within the confines of sexual stereotypes than characters in the
comedies of Wycherley, Behn, or Etherege. In *The Woman Captain,* and
particularly in *The Lancashire Witches,* the combination of women and satire creates an uneasy alliance. Shadwell's use of women as the vehicle for
his political agenda works both for and against his satire. When women
simply voice political statements, the satire remains on track, but the
plays are less successful when these same women step outside of their
socially proscribed sexual roles. Ultimately, Shadwell's more conservative
social vision undercuts his political satire. When women give a voice to
Shadwell's political views and act out their sexual desires, the connection
between political rhetoric and women falls apart and the satire unravels.

The disjuncture between the political and social roles played by Shadwell's
women is indicative of the destablizing effect of female desire in a world
where male desire was sanctioned and even exalted—as long as it was
firmly under male control. When female sexuality intrudes into the world
of politics, it can only be seen as disastrous, as John Wilmot, Earl of
Rochester, complains of Charles II: "His Scepter and his Prick are of a
Length,/And she may sway the one, who plays with th'other" ("A Satire
on Charles II" 11–12). Attacks on unguarded female desire represent
more than a social double standard; they demonstrate a deeper concern
with the social and political ramifications of women's sexual behavior.
Because it threatens social order, female sexuality which eludes male control runs counter to the didactic concerns of satire, unless, as in Rochester's
poem, it also becomes the object of the satire. Shadwell's attempts to link
the two illustrate the tension between political ideology and potential
social disorder. The female "itch" is not the satirist's "itch," and, in the end,
it must be hidden away in order for satire's "true medicine" to function.

# Notes

All references to Shadwell's plays are to the *Complete Works* edited by Montague Summers and are cited by volume and page number.

1. Although official censorship was not formally introduced until the Licensing Act of 1737, the Master of the Revels exercised some control over the plays staged in the Restoration, and few overtly Whig dramas were staged uncut before the Glorious Revolution. For the problems Shadwell faced, see Slagle.

2. Most notably in his adaptation of Shakespeare's *Timon of Athens,* where he uses Alcibiades's struggle against the corrupt leadership of Athens to mirror Whig struggles against Tory powerholders.

3. The women's political commentary in the plays after 1688 is muted, limited to complaints against those who tried to take power after the Glorious Revolution or praise of the now ruling party. In *Bury Fair,* Gertrude exclaims: "I am a free Heiress of *England,* Where Arbitrary Power is at an end, and I am resolv'd to choose for my self" (3). Susan Staves seems to be the only recent critic who has commented on the political function of Shadwell's women (Staves, *Players' Scepters* 135, 169–79).

4. The dates given are those of the first publication of each play. *The Woman Captain* was first staged in autumn of 1679.

5. In *Epsom Wells* we find Mrs. Bisket, "an impertinent, imperious Strumpet"; Dorothy Fribble, "a humble, submitting wife, who Jilts her Husband that way, a very Whore"; and Mrs. Woodley, the most discreet (and most upper-class) of the lot, "Jilting, unquiet, troublesom, and very Whorish" (*Dramatis Personae*); in *The Lancashire Witches* Lady Shacklehead is described as "a notable discreet Lady, something inclined to Wantoness" (*Dramatis Personae*); and in *The Virtuoso,* Lady Gimcrack is not described in these terms but behaves in a manner which could only be described as wanton.

6. See Staves, *Players' Scepters,* on the ideological implications of marriage relations.

7. Only in *The Woman Captain* are they made the butt of the joke when the three whores, Phillis, Chloe, and Celia all pursue a woman in male garb. But even though they are ridiculed for their misdirected desire, all three end up either married or comfortably kept.

8. The motif of the husband-beating was a popular element of contemporary ballads and broadsides. See, for example, *The Woman's Victory: Or, the Conceited Cuckold Cudgel'd into good Qualities* [1690], where the young wife of an old husband beats him into submission on account of his unfounded jealousy. When the jealous husband attempts to beat his wife:

> His bitter blows I could not bear
> Therefore next morning, I declare

> While he was sleeping fast in bed,
> I with a ladle broke his head.
>
> . . .
>
> He with a cudgel ran at me,
> I took a club as well as he,
> Crying, I am resolv'd to try
> Who shall be the Master you or I.

The ballad concludes with the wife's total victory: "Pray keep your word, I then reply'd,/Or else, adsfoot, I'll thrash your hide."

9. When Thomas Odell adapted *The Woman Captain* into *The Prodigal: Or, Recruits for the Queen of Hungary* in 1744, he substantially reduced the importance of Mrs. Gripe. As the change in title suggests, the play focuses on the exploits of Sir Humphery Scattergood and the Prologue claims:

> Our Bard To-night, but with a trembling Heart,
> One play has ventur'd to reduce to Art;
> New plant the Fable, and the Plot refin'd,
> Whence strikes the instructive Moral to the Mind. (17–20)

*The Prodigal*'s "instructive Moral" lies in the near bankruptcy of Sir Humphery and in the generosity of his whore, who rescues him from bankruptcy all for love.

10. On stage, of course, the cross-dressed actress who played Mrs. Gripe presented an overt sexual spectacle. The role of Mrs. Gripe was originally played by Elizabeth Barry, one of the leading actresses of the Restoration, whose sexual exploits were famous.

11. Gripe claims: "'Tis nothing but my love, my great love. Dost thou think I do not love my Money—why I am jealous of that, and lock it up as I do thee—I know what a Treasure thou art" (4.28).

12. In *Married Women's Separate Property,* Susan Staves opens her chapter on separate maintenance contracts with a description of the popular eighteenth-century conception of separate maintenance contracts—that they allowed women to get away with adultery, i.e., to behave like whores.

13. In this "letter," Shadwell faults his political opponents rather than the official censor: *"The Master of the Revels (who I must confess used me civilly enough) Licenc'd it at first with little alteration: But there came such an Alarm to him, and a Report that it was full of dangerous reflections, that upon a Review, he expunged all that you see differently Printed, except about a dozen lines which he struck at the first reading"* (4.99).

14. Revivals of *The Lancashire Witches* were staged almost every year between 1705 and 1728.

15. For the ideological implications of Sir Edward's character and that of many of the other figures in *The Lancashire Witches,* see Canfield.

16. Downes stresses the play's theatrical spectacle, describing it as "being a kind of Opera, having several *Machines* of flyings for the Witches, and other Diverting contrivances in't." He reports that because of these elements, "it prov'd past Expectation; very Beneficial to the Poet and *Actors*" (38–39). Advertisements for later revivals of the play stressed the theatrical spectacle; the advertisement for the July 1, 1707, performance focused on the entertainment value of the witches, assuring viewers that the play would be staged "with all the Risings, Sinkings, and Flyings of the Witches, as they were Originally perform'd." Variations on this advertisement appeared regularly. See listings in *The London Stage.*

## Works Cited

Canfield, J. Douglas. "Shifting Tropes of Ideology in English Serious Drama, Late Stuart to Early Georgian." *Cultural Readings of Restoration and 18th-Century Theater.* Ed. J. Douglas Canfield and Deborah C. Payne. Athens: U of Georgia P. Forthcoming, 1995.

Dennis, John. "Letter to Sir Richard Steele," July 10, 1710. In *The Critical Works of John Dennis.* Ed. Edward Niles Hooker. Baltimore: Johns Hopkins UP, 1943.

Downes, John. *Roscius Anglicanus.* Ed. Montague Summers. London: The Fortune P, [1928].

[Hughes, John]. *Spectator* 141, Aug. 11, 1711.

*The London Stage 1660–1800: A Calendar of Plays, Entertainments and Afterpieces Together with Casts, Box-receipts and Contemporary Comment Compiled from the playbills, Newspapers and Theatrical Diaries of the Period.* Ed. Emmett L. Avery et al. Carbondale, IL: Southern Illinois UP, 1962–68.

Odell, Thomas. *The Prodigal: Or, Recruits for the Queen of Hungary.* London, 1744.

Shadwell, Thomas. *The Complete Works of Thomas Shadwell.* Ed. Montague Summers. 5 vols. London: The Fortune P, 1927.

Slagle, Judith B. "Thomas Shadwell's Censored Comedy, *The Lancashire-Witches*: An Attack on Religious Ritual or Divine Right?" *Restoration and Eighteenth-Century Theater Research.* Second Series, 7.1 (Summer 1992). 54–62.

Staves, Susan. *Married Women's Separate Property in England, 1660–1833.* Cambridge: Harvard UP, 1990.

———. *Players' Scepters: Fictions of Authority in the Restoration.* Lincoln: U of Nebraska P, 1979.

Wilmot, John, Earl of Rochester. *The Poems of John Wilmot, Earl of Rochester.* Ed. Keith Walker. Oxford: Basil Blackwell, 1984.

*The Woman's Victory: Or, the Conceited Cuckold Cudgel'd into good Qualities.* [London, 1690.]

# "The Monster Libell"

## Power, Politics, and the Press in
## Thomas Otway's *The Poet's Complaint of His Muse*

*Jessica Munns*

Thomas Otway's twenty-one stanza ode, *The Poet's Complaint of His Muse; or, a Satyr Against Libells,* was written in 1679 and published in 1680.[1] It was written at the height of the Exclusion Crisis—the movement to exclude the heir, the Roman Catholic James, Duke of York, from the royal succession—which many feared was a prelude to another civil war. Although the poem describes the contemporary political fractures and concludes with a panegyric on the Duke, the work's overt political content has been ignored. The few critical comments that have been made about *The Poet's Complaint* have tended to stress the originality of its opening, probably autobiographical, stanzas, and the work is generally referred to now only as a source of information about Otway. Apart from any gleanings *The Poet's Complaint* may offer with respect to Otway's short and troubled life, however, the poem offers compelling evidence of what Deborah C. Payne has described as the flawed "cultural machinery" of the Restoration.

As Payne notes, while aristocratic and royal patronage encouraged the "project of royalist myth-making" the gap "between professed aristocratic munificence and actual material practice was far too apparent to impoverished writers and other artists" (106). This gap is certainly apparent in the dedication of the poem to the Earl of Ossory, as the author sues for patronage promising that he will then be enabled to write a second and celebratory part to the poem (Otway 2: 403–4).[2] But by July 1680 Ossory was dead: there was no patronage and there is no celebratory second part to *The Poet's Complaint.* The materiality of the political-poetic culture of the Restoration is inescapable.

The very structure of *The Poet's Complaint* incorporates a critique of the failed structure of royal and aristocratic cultural politics. It begins with a loyal poet complaining of his failure to secure "Royall Favour" and patronage (5.121) and concludes with a depiction of the royal family torn apart by power of Libell's "dirty Rhymes" (19.621). The poem, however, not only articulates flaws within the "cultural machinery" of patronage but also exposes flaws in the "royalist myth." A broadly based popular movement is pitted against a monarchy, one of whose claims to authority rests on the fact of its popular restoration. Anti-exclusionist patrilineal descent is defended amidst images of sterility, and the sacred nature of kingship, another strut of Stuart authority-claims, is evoked by dwelling on images of regal sacrifice and exile. *The Poet's Complaint* is a poem whose margins invade its center and whose apparent center moves to a marginalized wasteland of inarticulacy. In the monstrous power the poem grants to the oppositional forces ranged against the late Stuart monarchy, we can trace the emergence of new discursive formations articulating the politics of the crowd.[3]

In the opening six stanzas the author meets a poet, a friend of his, who is raving in a desolate landscape replete with emblems of infertility and degeneration. The poet sketches in a youth of intellectual virtuosity, suddenly cut short and followed by his migration to London.[4] London is described in conventional satirical terms as the haunt of "Gay Coxcombs, Cowards, Knaves, and prating Fools,/Bullies of o're-grown Bulks, and little Souls,/Gamesters, Half-wits, and Spendthrifts" with whom the poet spends two years in "fulsome Follies" (4.90–92, 97).

The personal materials of the opening stanzas, although offering tantalizing material to the biographer, are generic. Satiric conventions authorized the shaping of an autobiographic presence, often, as in Milton's *Lycidas,* allied to pastoral conventions. Alvin Kernan, characterizing the satirist in *The Cankered Muse: Satire of the English Renaissance,* notes that "[s]omehow the satirist seems always to come from a world of pastoral innocence and kindness: he is the prophet come down from the hills to the cities of the plain; the gawky farm-boy, shepherd, or plowman come to the big city; or the scholar, nurtured at the university, abroad in the cruel world" (18). The opening stanzas manage to convey many of these thoughts with the happy childhood and precocious academic genius of the poet contrasting strongly with his subsequent life of debauchery in "our new *Sodom*" (10.310, emphasis in original), London, which he now abhors. The poet goes on to describe his development as a writer couched, conventionally, in terms of a love affair with the Muse who allured him with promises of "Royall Favour" and "endless Fame" but neglected to warn him of their brief and transitory nature (5.119, 121). Initially, the affair was happy and fertile, producing "Off-springs of the choicest kinds,/Such as have pleas'd the noblest minds" (6.144–45). At the height of his success, however, the poet's inspiration dried up, "my faithless Muse was gone . . . The more I strove, the more I fail'd," and his literary productions, "the hidious Issue of my Brains," were deformed (6.152, 155, 163). The poet, sterile as the landscape he now inhabits, swears "never [to] write agen" (6.165). At this point the poem takes another direction.

The poet calls on Reason to reveal the truth about the Muse, who is shown to be a "rampant, tawdry Quean" (7.213) with a shabby "Train" of bad poets. The processional description that follows is in the mode of the lampoon *A Session of the Poets* (ca. 1676). Indeed, the group includes the "blundering Sot" (8.224) who wrote the *Session,* as well the author of the pornographic *Sodom; or, The Quintessence of Debauchery,* and "*Lord Lampoon* and *Monsieur Song*" who promised to make the Muse "famous at Court" (8.234–36, emphasis in original).[5] The "*City Poet*" (8.237, emphasis in original), Thomas Jordan, who had just created a pageant for the Whig Lord Mayor of London, Sir Robert Clayton, is included and, bringing up the rear, comes "The Poets Scandall, and the Muses Shame," a monstrous beast called "LIBELL" (8: 245–46, emphasis in original). With the entrance of Libell, the poem really takes off as the poetamachia of the Restoration is superseded by an allegorical narrative of the genesis of Libell.

Libell's factional credentials are impeccable and are worth outlining. They represent a brief history of Restoration England, an anatomy of the Whig faction, and not only an explanation but even a justification for civil unrest. Libell's mother is a witch who used to live in the wilderness in a cottage "Built of mens Bones slaughter'd in Civill War" (9.257); her "late dead Pander" was "Old *Presbyter Rebellion,*" and her name is revealed as "THE GOOD OLD CAUSE" (9.285, 286, 288; emphasis in original)—the term associated with the civil war parliamentarians. After the plague and fire, the witch, disguised as a modest widow, makes her way to the city of London—the stronghold of the Whigs—where she sedulously ferments discontent. Her constituency as outlined here represents a broad coalition ranging from those who have been "disgusted at the Court," or have failed to find preferment, to the "Atheist" hoping for "*Toleration,*" to rebels seeking "*Pow'r,*" spendthrifts seeking royal or church lands, and, finally, the "Ungovernable, headlong Multitude" to whom she promises "strange *Liberties*" (11.337–55; emphasis in original). It is from her vigorous sexual congress with this entire multitude of social and political discontent that Libell is born.

The birth of Libell is an emphatically female event attended by "Bawd *Hypocrisy,*" "Madam *Impudence,*" "Dame *Scandall,*" Queen "*Malice,*" and, last but not least, "Midwife *Mutiny*" (12.371–78, emphasis in original). Libell is sent to nurse with a "*Sister-witch . . . of another sort*" who, from her abode in the "outcasts of a Northern factious Town," Edinburgh, can be identified as Scottish Presbyterianism (13.396, 399, emphasis in original).[6] Libell's higher education is at the hands of a "Wretche," perhaps William Petyt, the rising Whig barrister, whose *The Antient Right of the Commons of England Asserted,* published in 1680, was in circulation in late 1679.[7] Certainly, the wretche's favorite reading is "Old worn-out Statutes, and Records/Of *Commons Priviledges,* and the *Rights of Lords,*" and the "*Acts, Resolves,* and *Orders* made/By the old *Long Rump-Parliament*" (14.456–57, emphasis in original). The "*Rights of Lords*" was a major plank in the Whig platform as in *A Letter from a Person of Quality to his Friend in the Country* circulating in 1675 and warning against weakening the power of the nobility who stand between the people and the imposition of arbitrary monarchical power.[8] Thus tutored in Whig Parliamentary politics, Libell learns how to distinguish between "*Legislative,* and *Judicial* power," and how to insinuate a "*Commonwealth,*/And *Democracy*" by pretending an interest merely in a "*Well-mixt Monarchy*" (15.481–85, emphasis in original).[9] Generally, works such as Petyt's, pamphlets such as *A Letter from a Person of Quality* and *A Letter from a Parliament Man to his Friend* (1675), and polemics such as Andrew Marvell's *Account of the Growth of Popery and Arbitrary Government* (1677), had reinvigorated the debate over parliamentary rights versus the royal prerogative.[10] The issue of how to define the nature and locus of political authority and national sovereignty lay behind the contemporary crises and informs the style, organization, and topics of *The Poet's Complaint.*

Bred and schooled in the alternative radical tradition of English politics, Libell successfully enters the political arena, gains "Authority and Place," and signals his adherence to Shaftesbury's camp by the "wearing of a Mysticall green Ribband in his Hat" (15.503, 508).[11] Significantly, along with this entry into the political arena comes Libell's access to the press. The poet reveals that Libell now enjoys the embraces of his "faithless *Clio*" and is "Poetry all o're," becoming the author of a wide range of oppositional texts: "*Painter's Advices, Letanies,*/*Ballads*" (16.514, 519, 523–24; emphasis in original), as well as the "Lucius Junius Brutus" pamphlet.[12]

As the poem reaches this point, with Libell strongly placed in London and fluently denouncing the government of Charles II in a variety of literary genres, the poet, filled with despair, asks, "But from such Ills when will our wretched State/Be freed?" (16.531–32). The poem offers no answer to this question, and instead makes a transition from satire to panegyric with a portrait of Libell's latest and greatest victim, the Duke of York, forced into exile by the exclusion fever Libell has whipped up. The poem's last four stanzas review the Duke's naval career in glowing terms and depict the heroic grace with which he acquiesces to the "Mandates" from "the most *Loving* BROTHER, *Kindest* KING" (19.631, 634, emphasis in original) to leave the country. The last line of the poem describes observers watching the royal barges fade out of sight and then turning their eyes once more inland to "the hated Shore"—an England over which the monarchy has lost control.

In terms of its style, *The Poet's Complaint* is not so much innovatory as indebted to older forms of political verse: to Spenser's allegorical treatment of Britain in *The Faerie Queene,* or to the high seriousness of Abraham Cowley in his three-book poem, *The Civill Warre* (ca. 1643). The poem's use of allegory is more sustained than was usual, but allegory was also a regular feature, as in Elkanah Settle's *The Medal Reversed* (1682), which features the *Hags Sedition and Persecution* (30–45), or John Ayloffe's *Oceana and Britannia* (1681) in which Mother Britannia debates eagerly with the spirit of Republicanism over the fate of her "Daughter," Parliament.[13] The alternation from satire to panegyric was also a standard feature of satire; Antony Wood, for instance, praised John Cleveland for his "high panegyric and smart satyrs."[14] A mixture of styles was often held to be a feature of satire, as in Menippean mixtures of high and low forms, digressions, fantasy, obscenity, and obscure pedantry. *The Poet's Complaint* certainly contains Menippean elements of the grotesque; however, unlike Samuel Butler's *Hudibras,* to which the poem refers, it cannot be classified as a thoroughgoing Menippean satire.[15] *The Poet's Complaint* describes anarchic disorder, but in tone, mood, and style it does not embody anarchy. It is grimly depressed and somber and distinctly lacking in extravagant wit or, indeed, in any sort of wit. Thomas Shadwell (if he is in fact the author), commented in the satire *The Tory Poets* (1682) that Otway's style was oddly suited to his subject matter.

> Sure thou wast drunk, when in Pindarick strain,
> 'Gainst *Libels* didst thy dull Muse Complain:
> But why didst term it *Satyr? Satyr* [is] tart. (221–23)

Shadwell (or whoever) had a point. From his plays we cannot doubt but that savage humor was well within Otway's capacity, but in avoiding "tart" satire he was, surely, drawing on older models to attempt a kind of solemn satire which signaled its distance from the contemporary and degraded forms employed by Libell.

It was not unusual for the satires of the period to attack what were felt to be lowly forms of attack, the lampoon and the libel. The argument over styles of satire was often couched in terms of a comparison between the plain style and good nature of Horace and what Ramen Selden describes as Juvenal's "majestic . . . reprehension" (96). This debate antedates and postdates the years of the Popish Plot and Exclusion Crisis, but is never merely a question of style; it is also always a question of political and social site. In his *Essay on Poetry* (1682), Mulgrave gravely insisted that

> But 'tis mens *Foibles* nicely to unfold,
> Which makes a Satyr different from a Scold.
> Rage you must hide, and prejudice lay down:
> A Satyr's Smile is sharper than his Frown.
>
> (121–24, Mulgrave 2: 290)

In moving satire to the higher ground of the censure of human foibles, what is also being projected is the upper-class castration of a verse form strongly associated with popular political agitation. For the confidently aristocratic Earl of Rochester, such well-bred attacks are as pointless as venting wind: "I'd fart just as I write, for my own ease" (*An Epistolary Essay from M.G. to O.B. upon Their Mutual Poems*).[16] However, for less aristocratic writers engaged in political debate, linguistic violence needs justification if the writer is to retain the higher ground for his party.

John Oldham, for instance, defended the use of violent language and crude style in his "Prologue to *Satires Upon the Jesuits*"(1679, pub. 1681). He looks forward to drawing blood with his "stabbing pen" and remarks that "Nor need there art, or genius here to use,/When indignation can create a muse" (2: 28–29). Surgical severance, as later advocated by Dryden in his *Discourse Concerning the Original and Progress of Satire* (1693), is, perhaps, the most approved, aristocratic, and authoritative form of attack: "there is still a vast distance betwixt the slovenly butchering of a man, and the fineness of stroke that separates the head from the body, and leaves it standing in its place" (*Of Dramatic Poesy* 2: 137). Butchering, such as Oldham advocates, however, is allowable in a discourse on a subject which deserves no better. As in Oldham's and Dryden's satiric practice, alternations between urbanity and "Billingsgate" indicate a righteous moral anger held in check by a superior intellect. Either satiric form takes authority from its form: elegant ease indicates courtly confidence; scabrous attack, particularly when prefaced by explanatory justification, indicates a writing down from a position of strength.

Aristocratic disdain and the urbane sneer are not options for a poet who has opened with stanzas indicating his poverty and his marginality to the world of the court. Placed from the start in a position of weakness not strength, and specifically attacking the poetry of violence and anger, Otway endeavored to find an alternative form and voice. To select, however, a form and voice outside of the available current forms of burlesque inflation or deflation, anger and lofty contempt, as Otway has in writing *The Poet's Complaint* as an allegorical Pindaric ode, is a dangerous choice. Indeed, the poem's mixtures of modes combine to elevate the opposition and lay poetic wreaths at the feet of the monarchy. The Pindaric's strains of glory can all too easily function as an elegiac commentary on a lost cause; autobiography demonstrates the sterility of the author/s; literary lampoon indicates the success of others; allegory portrays the power of sedition, and panegyric depicts the defeat of the royal family. What Otway failed to do in *The Poet's Complaint* was to pour aristocratic disdain on the lowly form of the political libel, or to show by the raw violence of his own form that he suited his style to his lowly subject. His monster Libell is the true Tory nightmare—vital, articulate, and popular. He flourishes in the city, "A Leader in a factious Crew" (15.499), and as the Muse's new and vigorous lover is highly productive.

Libell's power is further emphasized by the recounting of a myth of defeated royalty. Libell is compared to a "Serpent's head," a "huge Dragon, sent by Fate/To lay a sinfull Kingdom wast" (16.532, 534) and duly fed virgins by a terrified city until, running out of lowly maidens, the King sacrifices his own daughter. Now, the poem asserts, the situation has called for the sacrifice of "A ROYALL BROTHER" (16.549, emphasis in original). The parallelism the poem insists on between the virgin sacrifice and the Duke's exile enables the transition from allegory to direct statement, and thus from fantastical England to "real" England. However, integrating myth and allegory with politics and people creates problems here as "this Dragon *Libell*" is elevated to an instrument of "Fate" punishing a "sinfull Kingdom," (17.550, 16.534–35, emphasis in original). If, however, the current political unrest is an instrument of fate, and if the kingdom is sinful, then the Stuarts' misery can figure as pathetic but providential.

Moreover, in emphasizing that while the King of legend sacrificed his "*Royall Daughter*" the present King sacrifices his "ROYALL BROTHER," the myth chosen as parallel also draws attention to the fact that Charles has no legitimate children (16.349, emphasis in original). Due to the failure of the royal bed, the King's brother is heir and must stand in as royal sacrifice. The topic of the exile of the Duke of York, audaciously but also almost suicidally in terms of Tory politics, concentrates on the weakest link in the royal platform. The Duke of York, who had declared himself a Roman Catholic in 1673 and had married a Catholic Princess as his second wife, was, of course, at the heart of the Exclusion Crisis as well as being implicated via members of his household in the Popish Plot. In early March 1679, seeking to lessen conflict with the newly elected Parliament about to take its seat, Charles II ordered his brother's exile, and it is with the enactment of this exile that the poem concludes, depicting, at variance to other contemporary accounts, the King's sorrow at his brother's departure.[17]

For the Whig opposition, the Duke's religion and character combined into a package threatening the imposition in England of absolutist rule along the lines of the French monarchy. J. P. Kenyon cites a report on the Duke of York drawn up for Shaftesbury before March 1679 (i.e., before the sitting of the Parliament elected in February), which is notably violent in its language. "His religion well suits with his temper; heady, violent and bloody, who easily believes the rashest and worst of counsels to be the most sincere and hearty . . . . His interest and design are to introduce a military and arbitrary government in his brother's time" (171).

The poem's attempt to refute such beliefs is evident as stanza eighteen opens with a description of the Duke's willingness to sacrifice his life for "his ungratefull Country's sake" (18.578). The stress, however, on the Duke's military (naval) prowess was unlikely to be reassuring to those who never doubted that the man was brave and, indeed, feared he might unleash that courage and military ability on the "ungratefull" nation.

Charles II followed the advice of his first minister, the Earl of Danby, in sending his brother into exile, an action which could be seen as acknowledging his brother's unsuitability and unpopularity. Kenyon describes the King's decision as "unwise" (171), and according to J. R. Jones "most people interpreted James's exile as the prelude to his abandonment" (140). Tactlessly, but in tune with the poem's mournful and defeated tone, it is this critical moment of concession, widely seen as establishing the grounds for further concessions, that is highlighted.

What is missing in the poem's allegorical structure is Perseus or any other vision or version of salvation, such as Libell turning his venom on his fellow scribblers. Such a possibility is suggested in *Absalom and Achitophel* (1682), as Dryden predicts that the viper of conspiracy will end up by consuming itself (1012–13). Dryden successfully modulates from his own mud-slinging libel and evocations of the grotesque and unruly into panegyric. The awakened David expels the forces of the grotesque, restores order, and, through that restoration, erases the need for satire and its lowlier cousins, libel and lampoon. A series of panegyric portraits sketch in the qualities of the brave and loyal men who support the throne, and their character and fidelity gives credence to the emergence of David as a just, grim, and powerful monarch. Authority is represented and enacted—just as after proroguing the Oxford Parliament of 1681, Charles II was managing to stem the Whig opposition. In *The Poet's Complaint,* however, written at a critically earlier date, the only authority the poem can call upon is the grace with which the Stuarts face defeat.

Insofar as Charles sought to remove his brother from the public gaze and to reduce that visibility that endangered the entire Stuart monarchy, the poem reverses that royal policy. Otway, in a passage that emphasizes eyes—the Duchess's weeping eyes and the "longing Eyes" and straining "sight" (21.702, 708, 710) of those who watch the embarkation—puts the Duke of York back firmly in the picture. Despite, or because of, the glowing terms used to describe Charles II as a "most *Loving* BROTHER, *Kindest* KING," filled with "*Royall Goodness*" (19.634, 21.687, emphasis in original), there is an inescapable implication that Charles is not merely an "unhappy Monarch," but a powerless monarch. The use of panegyric to articulate Tory praise for royal policy precludes the possibility of portraying the exile of the Duke of York as a short-term, if Machiavellian, policy while the King rides out the storm quietly. The alternative, however, is to portray Charles submitting passively to the all-powerful Libell as he bids farewell to those he loves. The closing stanzas' themes of royal suffering, mourning, and sacrifice elevate the monarchy with their religio-magical connotations, but also elegize it out of existence as the regal scapegoat fades from sight (21.710).

All too well this undoubtedly "loyal" poem depicts the weakness of royal authority and the power of a popular opposition movement. All too well it depicts the current unrest as the product of long-standing grievance with its roots in a civil war which the "other" side won. As represented by the poem's broad historical and social scope, Libell's power wells up from the past, embraces all the present causes for discontent, and threatens to overwhelm the future. A broad base of popular political dissent is delineated as the witch unites the free-thinking atheist and the canting puritan, the city businessmen, the disgruntled courtier, and the "Ungovernable . . . Multitude." For all these disparate groups Libell, child of the times, has a voice and the ability to incite and inscribe their anger in any and all styles and genres.

In 1679 it was plausible to see Libell as triumphant. The Licensing Act that enabled government censorship had lapsed and the period sees an enormous outpouring of satiric materials both from the press and from the manuscript houses. The production and distribution of antigovernment political materials were taken very seriously, and, in the absence of a Licensing Act, the Treason Act of 1660 served, indicting "all printing, writing, preaching, or malicious and advised speaking calculated to compass or devise the death, destruction, injury, or restraint of the sovereign or to deprive him of his style, honor, or kingly name."[18] In 1677 coffeehouses, seen as sites for the distribution of manuscripts untouched by the Licensing Act, were briefly closed down. Printers of Whig verses, such as Francis Smith, and the owners of manuscript houses, such as Robert Julien, "Secretary to the Muses," repeatedly had their premises raided and were fined and pilloried.

Despite these efforts, verse and prose libel and lampoon constantly eluded government vigilance. Historians have credited the flow of political propaganda, which intensified during the two elections of 1679, as contributing to the widespread politicization of the period. Libell could indeed be seen as contributing to the destabilization of the realm. Satires, as I have indicated, are often also literary critiques, but *The Poet's Complaint* is in many ways one of the first critiques of the media. The allegorical narrative delineates the seductive power of the media to reach mass audiences (the Muse as whore); it emphasizes the rich variety of the oppositional press (Libell as general author), and it grants that press the ability to create consensus (the mother of Libell copulates with all sects and factions). In granting such effective powers to Libell, the poem also demonstrates that the government has lost control of the media. Otway loyally responded to a period of disruption and represented the danger of the popular politics. The method he chose, however, an elaborate allegory of the varied and dynamic forces of subversion, also undermines the royal authority he wished to support.

Otway's allegory works against itself, or, in Paul de Man's terms, works as allegory must to reveal, even as it strains to reach beyond itself, that there is nothing beyond itself.[19] The royal family cannot represent any overarching fixed principle exterior to the world of the poem. They too are engulfed by the words Libell has unleashed, and by the end they are sent out into the "wider Flood" (21.711), which is not just the English Channel but also the deluge which wipes out all known signs. In contrast to the images of fading royalty, the allegorical figures take on a life and demonic energy of their own, spawning new stories and possibilities as the personifications expand, alter, and grow. Indeed, the danger, power (and attraction) of the allegorized figures and forces lie in their constantly mutating and all inclusive natures—natures which take them beyond allegory's putative power to stabilize meaning.

The Good Old Cause is an ugly witch, becomes an attractive widow, becomes the mistress of mankind, becomes a mother—Libell is a boor, a reasonably accomplished scholar and Latinist, an able politician, a skillful poet, an ardent lover, and lastly a devouring dragon. The witch, as an allegorized personification of the Good Old Cause, emerges from her marginal position in a hovel, an aberration from some normative order, perversely threatening that norm to become in all her variety and power a new norm as a principle of alteration and movement. There is a chiastic shift of styles and positions as the "real" figures of Duke and King become fabulous projections from "Ancient Legends" (16.533) and exiles and outcasts, while the vibrant and seditious personifications, identified with the Whig political press, occupy the central ground. The mutability of the personifications not only endows them with energy but also defeats the ability of the allegory (even if only briefly) to stabilize and fix meaning.

Loyalty to the Stuart cause (and it is here that the autobiographical materials matter) is situated at the social margins, articulated by a rejected poet to the shadowy figure of the listener, also an author, but one on whom Fortune "always turn'd her Back" (8.207). Marginal men, the poet and his friend are passive spectators and turn the readers into similarly passive spectators of the pageant of Libell's triumph. The loyal writers' literary impotence and sterile site represent, I suggest, an unconscious referent to Stuart political impotence, which is also figuratively embodied in the dragon myth.

As already indicated, an issue which that myth highlights is precisely that the King was *not* a father, not legitimately at least, which was why, if the political myth of male rule was to be sustained, James, Duke of York, had to inherit the throne. This failure in paternal reproduction is intimated in the first stanza. The poet's site—the position of Stuart loyalty—has reverted to a primal nothingness, "bare, and naked," like the world before

> . . . by the Word it first was made,
> E're God had said,
> Let Grass and Herbs and every green thing grow.
> (1.11–14)

The paternal "Word" has failed, and the transcendental phallic signifier is notable only by its absence. The "good," loyal poet is unable to impregnate the Muse and the voice and words of the text itself are fractured by division into two "authors," or even three, with Otway lurking behind the barren poet and his unsuccessful friend. What has taken over possession of the word is the monstrous Mother as "faithless" Muse and fertile witch, aided and abetted by all those personified bawds, madams, queens, and midwives—Hypocrisy, Impudence, Scandall, Malice, and Mutiny—who preside over the birth of Libell. Libell's wide variety of fathers, in effect, render him fatherless—child of the m/other—and place him outside the patriarchal/patrilineal patterns of orderly decent. Against defeated and ineffectual royal grace, the poem pits the unleashed power of the popular and public voice, and shows it to be victorious. The real sovereign is the popular media, Libell, who has seized and holds the word, potent, mutating and female.

Political division along lines of party and interest as opposed to family and faction was new to this period, and there was as yet no language and no political system available to domesticate such division into a patriotic two-party system. Forms of political organization were being invented during the Exclusion Crisis—from pope-burning processions and centralized electioneering to the newsletter, polemics and libels—and, as Richard Ashcraft has argued, "the emergence of new forms of political *organization* is the key indicator of intense social conflict" (7). Fully alert to the power of new political and propaganda formations, *The Poet's Complaint* recognizes that a birth of sorts has taken place in the political arena and fails either to erase or incorporate the political nature of division or the power of the press.

*The Poet's Complaint* succeeds, however, in depicting the provenance of a new source of power and new potential patrons signaling alterations in the materials of culture. Although Shaftesbury is indirectly referred to, not so much specific people as *The People* move through these stanzas. What is being depicted (with horror) is their entrance into politics and their access to the press as writers and as readers of Libell's various and fluent productions. The "discontented Vermin of ill Times" (19.619) have seized the time: royalty bows down before them, and loyal poets, denied patronage, denied access to the press, are mute or, as in this poem, given voice only to despair.

The Filmer-recycling option, indicating the "absolute dominion" inherited by all kings directly from Adam, is not attempted (*Patriarcha* 7), nor, as has been indicated, are there any signs of an effective counter-press, a probable cessation to Libell's outpourings, or the disillusion of his constituency.[20] Instead, it is the inherent contractions in patriarchal-monarchical ideology that become visible. Susan J. Owen has argued with respect to Tory dramatizations of the period that they tend "to bring out the fragility of and contradictions within late Stuart ideology" (71). A similar process can be discerned as *The Poet's Complaint* comprehensively demonstrates the literal and political senses in which the monarch is not the father of his people, reveals that the restoration of the monarchy was not universally popular, and allows the illegitimate myth of Libell to supersede and erase the weaker myth of royal sovereignty.

As Robert Markley has pointed out, however, the visibility of ideological fracture can support the need for vigilant repression: "ideology foregrounds contradictions to demonstrate the need for continuing vigilance, censorship, and repression" (72). As a warning text and, indeed, as a self-interested text, *The Poet's Complaint* points to the dangers of an uncensored press attacking a weak monarchy and surely seeks censorship for Libell and patronage for Loyalty. However, as it pits "dirty Rhymes" against majestic sorrow (19.621), unpopular royalty against popular "democracy," masculine control against feminine anarchy, and loyalty against Libell, there is a danger that it has *too* effectively loaded the opposition's dice and *too* effectively pointed to the specific inadequacies of the embattled remnant. A fractured ideology may garner political support to shore up its cracks and repress its opponents, but a defeated ideology (as we have seen in this latter part of this century) may have to pack up shop.

Moreover, in this poem, as in many of the Tory dramas of the period, a posture of party political support is in itself self-defeating. There should be no possibility of a party against the King who by his nature, by the nature of monarchy, divine regality, and the fatherly care of his people, should be above party, beyond politics, and in no need of defense. In his dedicatory epistle, Otway expresses his hopes "to add a second part and doe all those Great and Good men Justice, that have in his Calamities stuck fast to so gallant a Friend and so good a Master" (404). That is the project Dryden carried out successfully inside a single poem, *Absalom and Achitophel*: it is not a project anyone was willing to fund Otway to carry out. This is not surprising, for even as he outlines the second part celebrating the Duke of York's supporters, the elegaic and despairing note is dominant.

In the short term, of course, Otway was wrong: the monarchy would survive the crisis and the Duke of York would (briefly) inherit the throne. In the long term he was wrong, too: the emergence of party politics led to the expression of competing but loyal interests; the press became the Fifth Estate, usually loyal, usually conservative; and the people remained safely "mute inglorious Miltons." Nevertheless, or, indeed, because Otway's visions of subversion represent our orthodox pieties—democracy and a "free" press—what the poem succeeds in presenting from the depth of its dismay is a moment of systemic disarray. This poem delineates but also refutes monarchy's authority claims and refutes but also delineates oppositional claims to authority. In its concentration on the shifting sites of textual power, *The Poet's Complaint* is a poem about processes that cannot be divorced from a specific history. The poem is also about a specific history—a moment of extreme crisis—which is being textualized under the pressure of collapsing practices and emergent formations.

## Notes

1. The poem concludes with James Duke of York's departure for the Spanish Netherlands which took place on March 3, 1679. The Duke returned to defend his accession in September 1679 after Charles II was taken seriously ill in late August. Since neither the Duke's return nor the King's sickness are mentioned, it seems probable, though not certain, that the poem was completed before September. The first reading of the Exclusion Bill was on May 11, 1679, and the poem's representation of the Whigs as busy parliamentarians and the concluding vindication of the Duke of York suggests that the poem was reacting to the Exclusion Bill. The poem was entered in the Term Catalogue for February 1680.

2. All citations from the poem are taken from *The Works of Thomas Otway: Plays, Poems, and Love-Letters,* ed. J. C. Ghosh (Oxford: Clarendon, 1968) 2 vols., vol. 2.

3. On the (various) politics of the crowd, see Tim Harris's *The London Crowd in the Reign of Charles II: Propaganda and Politics from the Restoration until the Exclusion Crisis.*

4. Much of this description of the "Poet's" life fits what we know of Otway's own life; for an outline of Otway's life, see J. C. Ghosh's introduction to his edition of Otway's works.

5. Otway seems to have been under the impression that the Whig playwright Elkanah Settle was the author of *A Session* and hence of its vicious attack on him.

6. As J. C. Ghosh, the most recent and reliable editor of Otway's works points out in his notes, the Whigs supported the Scottish Covenanters who rose in rebellion at Bothwell Brig in 1679.

7. J. G. A. Pocock notes that the work was being read as early as October 1679, which, if Otway is referring to Petyt, would indicate that the poem was completed after the Duke of York's return from exile. This is not inconceivable, but makes the poem's stress on the Duke's exile especially tactless. Pocock also notes that three of Petyt's clerks were questioned in 1676 about writing libels (*The Ancient Constitution* 186).

8. This pamphlet, ordered burned by the common hangman, emanated from the circle around the Earl of Shaftesbury and was, perhaps, drafted by John Locke.

9. The debate over the concept of a mixed monarchy—that is, a balance of power between King and Commons and people—had been current during the civil war and was revived during this period of crisis. See, for instance, Philip Hunton's *A Treatise on Monarchy* (1643, reissued in 1680), which advocated a theory of corporate monarchy. Sir Robert Filmer's *The Anarchy of a Limited or Mixed Monarchy* (1648) was largely written in response to Hunton. With regard to republicanism hiding behind theories of mixed monarchy, see J. G. A. Pocock's discussion of the mid-seventies revival of interest in the works of James Harrington, author of *Oceana*, in *The Machiavellian Moment* 401–22.

10. See also Corrine Western's essay, "Legal Sovereignty in the Brady Controversy," and Caroline Robbins's book, *The Eighteenth-Century Commonwealthmen.*

11. According to Richard Ashcraft, as early as 1677 people were sporting the green ribbons associated with Whig political clubs, see *Revolutionary Politics and Locke's "Two Treatises of Government"* 141, 143.

12. The "Advice to the Painter" genre, inaugurated by Edmund Waller's *Instructions to a Painter* (1666), which offered advice on how to portray the Duke of York heroically after his naval victory over the Dutch in 1665, had rapidly become a vehicle for satire, particularly but not solely associated with Andrew Marvell's series of "Advice" and "Instruction" poems. *The Countrey's Late Appeal: An Appeal from the Country to the City: For the Preservation of his Majesties Person, Liberty, Property, and the Protestant Religion* (1679), signed Lucius Junius Brutus and probably written by Charles Blount, a notorious free-thinker.

13. These works are reprinted in Lord 267–277; *The Medal Reversed* 304–15.

14. Cited by Ruth Nevo, *The Dial of Virtue* 6. See also Nevo's discussion of railing and raillery in ch. 8 of that work. On the classical precedent for negative and affirmative elements in satire, see Mary Claire Randolph, "The Structural Design of Formal Verse Satire."

15. *Hudibras* is cited in stanza 11 (333) in describing the witch's descent on London. See also David J. Rothman's "*Hudibras* and Menippean Satire" 23–44.

16. *Complete Poems,* 144, line 36. Rochester is responding to the earlier poem, "An Essay upon Satire" (1679), by Mulgrave and probably also Dryden.

17. As Ghosh notes, Gilbert Burnet stated that the Duke shed many tears at parting "though the King shed none" (Otway 2: 534).

18. Cited from the introduction to Lord, *Anthology of Poems on Affairs of State* xxvi.

19. Paul de Man has argued that allegory, like language itself, is always self-defeating and cannot point towards a singular truth: "Why is it that the furthest reaching truths about ourselves and the world have to be stated in such a lopsided, referentially indirect mode? Or, to be more specific, why is it that texts that attempt the articulation of epistemology with persuasion turn out to be inconclu-

sive about their own intelligibility in the same manner and for the reasons that produce allegory?" (2)

20. Sir Robert Filmer's *Patriarcha,* written in prison during the civil war, was published in 1680 in what may be seen as a rather desperate attempt to bolster a political theory of the monarchy. The ideas of patriarchal kingship, however, were widespread and were regularly preached from pulpits.

# Works Cited

Ashcraft, Richard. *Revolutionary Politics and Locke's "Two Treatises of Government."* Princeton, NJ: Princeton UP, 1986.

———— "The Language of Political Conflict in Restoration Literature." *Politics Reflected in Literature.* Los Angles: William Andrews Clark Memorial Library, U of California P, 1989.

Ayloffe, John. *Oceana and Britannia. Anthology of Poems on Affairs of State: Augustan Satirical Verse, 1660–1714.* Ed. George deF. Lord. New Haven and London: Yale UP, 1975. 268–77.

Blount, Charles (?) *The Countrey's Late Appeal: An Appeal from the Country to the City: For the Preservation of his Majesties Person, Liberty, Property, and the Protestant Religion.* London, 1679.

Cowley, Abraham. *The Civil War.* Ed. Allan Pritchard. Toronto: UP of Toronto, 1973.

De Man, Paul. "Pascal's Allegory of Persuasion." *Allegory and Representation.* Ed. Stephen J. Greenblatt, Baltimore: John Hopkins UP, 1981. 1–25.

Dryden, John. "A Discourse Concerning the Original and Progress of Satire." *Of Dramatic Poesy and Other Critical Essays.* Ed. George Watson. 2 vols. London: Dent; New York: Dutton, 1962.

Filmer, Sir Robert. *The Anarchy of a Limited or Mixed Monarchy, Patriarcha and Other Writings.* Ed. Johann P. Sommerville. Cambridge: Cambridge UP, 1991.

Hunton, Philip. *A Treatise on Monarchy. Divine Right and Democracy: An Anthology of Political Writing in Stuart England.* Ed. David Wootton, Harmondsworth, Middlesex: Penguin Books, 1986.

Jones, J. R. *Charles II: Royal Politician.* London: Allen and Unwin, 1987.

Kenyon, J. P. *The Popish Plot.* Harmondsworth, Middlesex: Pelican Books, 1974.

Kernan, Alan. *The Cankered Muse: Satire of the English Renaissance.* New Haven: Yale UP, 1959.

Markley, Robert. *Two-Edg'd Weapons: Style and Ideology in the Comedies of Etherege, Wycherley, and Congreve.* Oxford: Clarendon, 1988.

Marvell, Andrew, *Account of the Growth of Popery and Arbitrary Government.* [London], 1677.

Nevo, Ruth. *The Dial of Virtue: A Study of Poems on Affairs of State in the Seventeenth Century.* Princeton, NJ: Princeton UP, 1963.

Oldham, John. *The Poems of John Oldham.* Ed. Harold F. Brooks in collaboration with Ramen Selden. Oxford: Clarendon, 1987.

Otway, Thomas. *The Works of Thomas Otway: Plays, Poems, and Love-Letters.* Ed. J. C. Ghosh. 2 vols. 1932. Oxford: Clarendon, 1968.

Owen, Susan J. "Interpreting the Politics of Restoration Drama." *The Seventeenth Century.* Special Issue. *Forms of Authority in Restoration England* 8.1 (Spring 1993): 67–97.

Payne, Deborah C. "'And Poets Shall by Patron-Princes Live': Aphra Behn and Patronage." *Curtain Calls: British And American Women and the Theatre, 1660–1820.* Ed. Mary Anne Schofield and Cecilia Macheski, Athens: Ohio UP, 1991.

Pocock, J. G. A. *The Ancient Constitution and the Feudal Law: A Study in English Historical Thought in the Seventeenth Century.* Cambridge: Cambridge UP, 1957.

———. *The Machiavellian Moment: Florentine Political Thought and the Atlantic Republican Tradition.* Princeton, NJ: Princeton UP, 1975.

Randolph, Mary Claire. "The Structural Design of Formal Verse Satire." *Philological Quarterly* 21 (1942): 368–84.

Robbins, Caroline. *The English Commonwealthmen: Studies in the Transmission, Development and Circumstances of English Liberal Thought from the Restoration of Charles II to the War with the Thirteen Colonies.* Cambridge, MA: Harvard UP 1959.

Rothman, David J. "Hudibras and Menippean Satire." *The Eighteenth Century* 34 (1993): 23–44.

Selden, Ramen. *English Verse Satire, 1590–1765.* London: George Allen and Unwin, 1978.

Settle, Elkanah. *The Medal Reversed. Anthology of Poems on Affairs of State: Augustan Satirical Verse, 1660–1714.* Ed. George deF. Lord. New Haven and London: Yale UP, 1975. 304–15.

[Shadwell, Thomas]. *The Tory Poets: A Satyr.* London, 1682.

[Shaftesbury circle?]. *A Letter from a Person of Quality to his Friend in the Country.* London, 1675.

———. *A Letter from a Parliament Man to his Friend.* London, 1675.

Sheffield, John, Earl of Mulgrave. *An Essay Upon Poetry. Critical Essays of the Seventeenth Century, 1650–1685.* 3 vols. Ed. J. E. Spingarn. Bloomington: Indiana UP, 1957.

Waller, Edmund. Instructions to a Painter. *Anthology of Poems on Affairs of State: Augustan Satirical Verse, 1660–1714.* Ed. George deF. Lord. New Haven and London: Yale UP, 1975. 19–30.

Western, Corrine. "Legal Sovereignty in the Brady Controversy." *The Historical Journal* 15.3 (1972): 409–31.

Wilmot, John, Earl of Rochester. *The Complete Poems of John Wilmot, Earl of Rochester.* Ed. David M. Vieth. New Haven and London: Yale UP, 1968.

# Satiric Embodiments

## Butler, Swift, Sterne

*Richard Braverman*

Over the past decade, the study of the body and its history has mushroomed from a fledgling cottage industry into a full-blown sub-discipline. When Francis Barker's *The Tremulous Private Body* and Elaine Scarry's *The Body in Pain* appeared in the mid-eighties,[1] there were few works in literary studies that bore the now-familiar tag, "and the body." Less than a decade later, however, titles with that phrase or with words to that effect now appear with such regularity that academic forecasters are more or less unanimous that "bodywork" will continue to be a growth industry for the foreseeable future, if not beyond.

Its growth potential aside, the aim of bodywork is not only descriptive but strategic: it signals an affiliation with the new cultural history, whose theoretical bedrock is the sociohistorical construction of persons, places, and things.[2] When applied to the body, this premise has evoked a crop of studies that have revealed how cultural practices as diverse as table manners and autoeroticism constitute bodies both as sites of social relations and as physical entities. Bodyworks typically factor sociopolitical power into the equation as well; in fact, they do so with such frequency that studies "on the body" sometimes seem curiously disembodied, focusing as they do on bodies as theatrical sites rather than as corporeal entities. On that account works claiming to bridge the public and private spheres may be reproducing the classical mind-body duality upon which their own revisionism is premised, since sociopolitical authority is expressly embodied as coercive force but typically disembodied when serving as the ideological cover for it.

That contradiction—the nemesis of political legitimacy—is resolved in diverse ways. In the time frame touched upon in this essay, early modern Europe, it was typically accomplished by means of a figure that Bakhtin aptly terms the "classical body."[3] The avatar of the body politic, the classical body was the civil counterpart of the *corpus mysticum*. In that capacity, note Peter Stallybrass and Allon White, it is imbued with an aura akin to the "passive admiration" demanded by a classical sculpture viewed

from below: "We *gaze up* at the figure and wonder. We are placed by it as
spectators to an instant—frozen yet apparently universal—of epic or
tragic time" (21). Like the artwork itself, the classical body, they add, "is
in a sense disembodied for it appears indifferent to a body which is 'beautiful' but which is 'taken for granted.'" The point is well taken, though
the "indifference" they note applies in more than "a sense." It is consistent with the ideological construction of the classical body itself, which
as Peter Brooks notes, projects its physicality but deflects its corporeality
so as to sustain the aura rooted in the elevation not of just *any* body but
of the *male* body as "the public body par excellence, the measure of the
world" (16). As the measure of the world, the male body is the measure
of the public sphere, literally and figuratively. The embodiment of unity,
it reconciles the fundamental differences that constitute the social order.
However, in those scenarios when it fails to do so—whether on holidays
when social differences are temporarily suspended or in political crises
when they are dissolved—the classical body may be supplanted by its
antithesis, a figure Bakhtin calls the "grotesque body." While the concept, if not the term, has been applied with great success to revolutionary circumstances by Lynn Hunt and others,[4] Bakhtin uses it for the most
part outside the political sphere, focusing instead on festive rites in which
the grotesque comes to life in order to rekindle communal spirit. On
those occasions the social order is renewed through forms of bodily excess that transgress social boundaries. In bridging the gulf between spirit
and matter, they transmogrify the *corpus mysticum* into the *corpus materium,*
reuniting the one and the many in the process: "The body and bodily life
have here a cosmic and at the same time an all-people's character; this is
not the body and its physiology in the modern sense of these words, because it is not individualized. The material body principle is contained
not in the biological individual, not in the bourgeois ego, but in the
people, a people who are continually growing and renewed. This is why
all that is bodily becomes grandiose, exaggerated, immeasurable"
(Bakhtin 19). Transformations of this kind take place, however, only during the "unofficial time" of carnivalesque rites when the grotesque body
banishes the classical body. Beyond that, the grotesque body returns to
its lowly niche, while "the grandiose, the exaggerated, and the immeasurable" resume their former lives in "official discourse" as antithetical
words that police the boundaries between the classical body and its grotesque rivals.

The history of those boundaries is a significant, if neglected, part of
Bakhtin's project, since the fate of the grotesque body is bound up with
them. That fate is premised on the contrast between Renaissance and En-

lightenment attitudes towards the body, a contrast that historians see as a long-term result of the post-Reformation reaction,[5] but which Bakhtin explores primarily through the relationship of popular and polite culture. As he sees it, the grotesque body as represented in literature lost much of its potency during the early modern period as official culture gradually severed its organic connections with popular culture. Those connections, which ran deep in the Middle Ages, crested in the Renaissance only to undergo a slow but steady decline until the eighteenth century when—under the pressure of Enlightenment philosophy, rational religion, and neoclassical aesthetics—they atrophied to the point that the body as a site of regenerative excess was little more than a relic in high culture (Bakhtin 4–24, 33–45, 116–18). At the same time, and as part of the same process, popular culture was refigured almost without exception in the negative as elites and elite culture retreated from direct contact with the popular, "withdrawing," as Harry Payne puts it, "to a different world" (18). That is not to say that the grotesque body was banished from Enlightenment texts, only that it was no longer the source of productive excess it had once been.

Shorn of its vital signs, it was resurrected as a caricature of its former self by writers for whom it had already been reduced in status to a satiric trope. Swift and Pope come to mind here, because as "great champions of the classical body," as Stallybrass and White call them, they ventriloquized the grotesque body, adopting its terms "whilst attempting to purify the language of the tribe," namely the "body of classical writing" that required "a labour of suppression, a perpetual work of exclusion upon the grotesque body" (105). That "labour of suppression" was the battle of the ancients and moderns, a battle that Swift and Pope, despite their status as "great champions of the classical body," were far from confident of winning. As they saw it, theirs was a rearguard action against an invader that could not be turned back, and in resurrecting the grotesque body for satiric ends they recognized that the classical past could not be restored. Nor, they recognized, could the classical body be restored, whether as a "body of writing" or as the time-honored principles that sustained it, namely those principles that grounded the classical body in the metaphorics of blood.

In its place came the grotesque body, which as the revolutionary threat from below gave vent to popular desire in politics and culture alike. If to early-eighteenth-century satirists popular culture was monstrous, it was not so just because the taste of the court had become the taste of the mob but because under Walpole—the "new man" who, as England's first prime minister, "usurped" the powers of the crown—money was thicker than blood. The matter was not quite as neat and simple as that, to be sure, yet the point is that culture and politics were inexorably linked in the minds of Swift and Pope, for whom the discourse of the body was framed in political terms because in art as in politics the preeminence of blood had been abrogated.

If Swift and Pope gave the grotesque body a local habitation and a name, they also situated it within a historical continuum that did not begin and end with Walpole but harked back to an earlier crisis, the civil war, when the threat from below had dissolved the body politic. While both Crown and Lords were restored in 1660, English politics lived in the shadow of that conflict until the middle of the eighteenth century, when the scenario was finally put to rest with the Jacobite rout in the '45. Until that time, the fear that the world might again be turned upside down was a constant of political culture. The threat of the grotesque body was therefore quite real. Its reality, moreover, was political (rather than philosophical or aesthetic) at the core because the fundamental issues left unresolved by the civil war were reprised in various scenarios—the most important of them the Exclusion Crisis, the Glorious Revolution, the Hanoverian accession, and the '45—down to the middle of the eighteenth century. Only then, as Jonathan Clark has shown, did the political terrain undergo a fundamental change, and with it went the revolutionary threat that had been a subtext of political conflict for so long.

The passing of that subtext had a measurable effect on body-politics. If, as Foucault has argued, the metaphorics of both the body and the body politic were fundamentally transformed in the eighteenth century as the values of "blood" were replaced by those of "health,"[6] the process was assisted by the transformation of the political terrain. The attempt to depoliticize the body had of course begun, as Pocock shows, much earlier in the social discourse of the age, as Addison and Steele, among others, sought to convert the passions (through which men had been defined as political or religious beings) into manners (by which they were transformed into polite creatures in order to transcend the political passions that had divided the nation for so long) (37–50). An attempt to create a consensus beyond politics, "politeness" was more than social decorum: the "manners" it fostered were the signs of a new social discourse beyond politics, a discourse rooted in the reconstitution of the body as the site of social bonds grounded in sentiment rather than blood. Literature played its part in the development, in the private sphere of the novel, yet the transformation of body-politics was not simply about the privatization of experience; it was about the de-politicization of that experience, and in that regard it was not until around mid-century, when the old political terrain was finally abandoned, that a new body-politics came into its own.[7]

In her account of the rise of the novel, *Desire and Domestic Fiction*, Nancy Armstrong makes this point in an analogous way when she claims that in the second half of the eighteenth century, domestic fiction "actively sought to disentangle the language of sexual relations from the language of politics" (3). The rise of the "domestic woman" is the key to her "political history of the novel," a history which argues that not only in domestic novels but in the culture at large "a new form of political power" challenged the old body-politics. It is a compelling argument to say the least, but if the domestic novel marked the disentangling of "the language of sexual relations from the language of politics," that process was facilitated by politics to a much greater extent than Armstrong acknowledges because it was only after the agenda that had defined English politics for so long was significantly revised that the language of sexual relations was by and large de-politicized. Only, that is, when the civil war was no longer the palimpsest of political conflict—replayed as it had been in the protracted "cold war" of party politics—did the balance tip in the favor of a new body-politics.

That change did not mean that sex and politics were no longer bedfellows; that would be unthinkable. What it did mean was that politics was no longer sexual in quite the same way. With the passing of the "cold war" grounded in the civil war, the sexual-cum-political body was no longer the invasive code by which private affairs signified public ones. A cigar was likely to be just a cigar in the new sociopolitical terrain, and if a number of writers recognized the new state of affairs, Sterne sized up the situation better than anyone. While he conveyed this in a number of ways, let me briefly turn to one of Walter Shandy's political reflections to make the point. A throwback in tune with the philosophy of Robert Filmer, Walter is stuck in a mind-set wherein a body is never just a body, so that even when the body in question belongs to his pregnant wife he is predisposed to see it through the lens of a dead political analogy. Musing on the right that Mrs. Shandy reserves to remove to London to lie in, he gets stuck on the body politic:

> He was very sensible that all political writers upon the subject had unanimously agreed and lamented, from the beginning of Queen *Elizabeth*'s reign down to his own time, that the current of men and money towards the metropolis, upon one frivolous errand or another,—set in so strong,—as to become dangerous to our civil rights;—tho', by the bye,—a *current* was not the image he took most delight in,—a *distemper* was here his favourite metaphor, and he would run it down into a perfect allegory, by maintaining it was identically the same in the body national as in the body natural, where blood and spirits were driven up into the head faster than they could find their ways down;—a stoppage of circulation must ensue, which was death in both cases. (I.18)

Walter's eccentricity aside, the passage turns on terms—"distemper" and "current"—that evoke different discursive contexts. His preference for "distemper" is not simply a predilection for the dead metaphor that springs to mind (the "body national"); it is symptomatic of a partiality for the old political framework over the newer vocabulary of civil society. "Current" applies to men and money alike because together they are the economic lifeblood of a society whose health is the product of their circulation. Such circulation applies, moreover, to the action of men in private pursuits that in their totality make society "civil." Walter, however, is not part of that wider society by the simple fact that we barely see him beyond Shandy Hall. Yet even at home it is clear that he remains largely outside the "current" that makes men civil. He may be on the sympathetic wavelength of his brother Toby, but when it comes to body-politics he is still a member of the old school, putting blood before sentiment. That is a foible for which he pays a satiric price twice over, because not only is Tristram botched but Bobby predeceases him, and in a dependent clause to boot: "When my father received the letter which brought him the melancholy account of my brother Bobby's death, he was busy calculating the expense of his riding post from Calais to Paris, and so on to Lyons" (V.2).

If the future of the Shandy line is shrouded in the mock-mourning that follows, it is because in the world of the novel sentiment is thicker than blood, a point that Sterne gives wider scope in the reconstitution of the body as a site of productive—as opposed to reproductive—excess. In this respect he was part of the larger social current that reinscribed the body as a site of sentiment rather than of passion as it made virtue the product of feeling rather than of birth. That current was class bound, of course, but even as narrow in scope as it was, in transforming passion into sentiment it not only de-politicized sex, but, with sympathy as its currency, domesticated it, too. While Sterne did as much, bringing self and other together *through* the body, he took the transaction one step further, embodying sentimental transactions not only through live bodies but through textual bodies in order to parody the textual incarnation of the classical body. In the process those elements of the grotesque that Bakhtin claimed were marginalized if not banished altogether from enlightenment discourse took a step towards their recuperation. The step was a relatively small one, because even with Sterne's help the grotesque would not come close to bridging the gulf between popular and polite that would occur with the romantic resurgence to follow. Yet it was a significant one all the same because it moved body-politics beyond the long shadow of high politics.

Despite its atrophy in mid-eighteenth-century literature, the shadow of high politics lingers as a subtext for the balance of this essay, which explores the notion of grotesque embodiment in Butler and Swift not merely as a prelude to Sterne but as evidence of the historical grotesque as it works in conjunction with the political template sketched above. Given that Sterne saw himself as the heir of Swift, and in light of Swift's admiration for *Hudibras,* these three writers provide a historical context not only for mid-eighteenth-century body-politics but also for the presence of the seventeenth century in the literary imagination of the eighteenth. Of the three, only Sterne was out of the political loop, so to speak, yet in setting *Tristram Shandy* in the historical past he was fully aware that once-contested ground had been reduced to the status of background.

The same, however, did not hold for Butler or Swift, for whom the only ground was the ideological ground that had been contested since the threat from below had turned the world upside down in the civil war. To Butler in particular the grotesque was firmly anchored in the historical ferment that transformed rebellion into revolution. In 1641, when the Tudor constitution buckled under parliamentary pressure, it was unclear what the future would hold; but when Parliament put arms in the hands of the people, it was clear that it would not be the future envisioned by royalists or parliamentarians. To royalists, at least, the rise of the New Model Army meant that the great rebellion had become the mob revolt that the king's advisers had forewarned on the eve of the war: "[They will] destroy all rights and properties, all distinctions of families and merit, and by this means this splendid and excellently distinguished form of government end in a dark, equal chaos of confusion, and the long line of our many noble ancestors in a Jack Cade or a Wat Tyler" (Kenyon 28). The mantle of Tyler and Cade fell to Cromwell, who might be cast in the role of Cincinnatus by a parliamentarian like Marvell, but who was a military creature by nature rather than calling to most Englishmen. It was in that guise that Butler memorialized him in *Hudibras,* as the man with the armed heel:

> So have I seen, with armed heel,
> A Wight bestride a *Common-weal;*
> While still the more he kick'd and spurr'd,
> The less the sullen Jade has stirr'd. (I.i.917–20)

The "sullen jade," England refuses to cooperate with Cromwell astride her, his armed heel the spur that reminds the nation of the force by which he rules. While the spur is the symbol of military might, the armed heel is an Achilles heel at the same time because it is physical evidence that authority and power cannot coalesce in a man who lacks divine sanction.

The failure to legitimate coercive possession of the body politic is the narrative subtext of *Hudibras,* too, which translates the dilemma into the ill-fated exploits of the Presbyterian knight and his Independent squire, Ralpho. While the two set out to cure the ills of the world, their moral mission is only the pretext of a more significant quest, a political quest that finds narrative form in the knight's attempt to win a widow and her jointure. Just as the "sullen jade" represents England as Cromwell rides her, the lady whose hand Hudibras seeks in marriage embodies England in her "widowed" state after the dissolution of the old regime. With the future up for grabs, Hudibras would, as her husband, become master of her person and property, a goal that would fulfill a quest that is political at heart, namely the quest to legitimate *de facto* possession of the nation and the Puritan Revolution with it.

But the widow is too savvy to yield either her person or her jointure to the knight. Recognizing that her body and her property coalesce in the sexual power that Hudibras seeks to control through marriage, she refuses to be seduced. Her response is not surprising, given the knight's physical appearance. There is, to begin with, his enormous buttocks and paunch:

> . . . as *Æneas* bore his Sire
> Upon his shoulders through the fire:
> Our Knight did bear no less a Pack
> Of his own Buttocks on his back:
> Which now had almost got the upper-
> Hand of his Head, for want of Crupper.
> To poize this equally, he bore
> A *Paunch* of the same bulk before. (I.i.287–94)

Granted, Hudibras is not the widow's physical type, but that does not prevent the dogged pursuit that ensues. In it, physical debility takes a back seat to rhetorical ability because the knight's fate is bound up with his skills of persuasion. Rhetorical power is the poem's dramatic fulcrum, and on that account Hudibras seeks to simulate the authority of the sovereign word that had been put up for grabs with the dissolution of the monarchy. He ventriloquizes any and every means that might help him reach his goal, namely the political legitimacy that can be gotten only through the widow. From the first time the lady visits him in the stocks to his final bow in the long set piece, "An Heroical Epistle of Hudibras to his Lady," he tries to shed his true skin in the hope that the widow will accept what amounts to a simulacrum of the classical body. In the protracted courtship, he draws on the Bible, on cultural dogma, on patriarchal political theory, and even on Petrarchan love poetry in the attempt to make himself over. But body and text never go together. Despite his hypocrisy, however, the knight's cynicism is refreshing at times, as, for example, when he admits to the widow that he only loves her for her jointure:

> I do confess, with *goods* and *land,*
> I'd have a wife, at second-hand
> And such you are: Nor is't your person
> My stomach's set so *sharp* and *fierce* on,
> But 'tis (your better part) your *Riches,*
> That my enamour'd heart bewitches. (II.i.471–76)

The widow will be a wife only at "second-hand" because the knight's desire is fixed on the political estate that her jointure ultimately represents. While that is his real quest—what "bewitches" him—there is another point to be made here. In placing the pang in the knight's stomach ahead of the pain in his heart, Butler conjures a wider cultural context. That context is Hobbesian in the sense that Hudibras resembles the body-in-motion motored by appetite rather than reason. A materialist model of man that flew in the face of Aristotelian tradition, the body-in-motion coalesced at the same time with another Hobbesian idea, the "artificial person," insofar as such a being did not embody an anterior essence—did not, that is, observe the time-honored body-politics of blood. As the famous frontispiece of *Leviathan* portrays it, the state was such a "person" because the body politic was ultimately grounded in representation rather than correspondence. But if the state was a convenient fiction rather than a *corpus mysticum,* that left the door wide open for those who believed that government must be grounded in consent. Butler's thoughts on this matter are not entirely clear, but from the evidence of *Hudibras* it seems safe to say that, like Hobbes, he saw the body politic as a convenient artifice rather than a divine body. But he parted company when it came to the trope's dark side, since for Hobbes the idea of the "artificial person" was the prelude to an argument for authoritarian rule that banked on the pervasive fears evoked by the civil war. Butler knew those fears along with most Englishmen, yet like others of his time he also recognized the danger that lay in the principle of consensual rule. It had been the backbone of the parliamentary rebellion of 1641, but only a few years later it came back to haunt those same men when rebellion quickly turned into revolution.

That state of affairs—the dissolution of the natural order after the defeat of the monarchy in the first civil war—is the historical context for much of *Hudibras,* which begins after the collective Puritan "conscience" has turned the world upside down. While Butler debunks "conscience" as mere appetite to insinuate that the knight and his cause were driven by the will to power, beneath the satiric surface Hudibras *embodies* the threat from below as an "artificial person."[8] It is only by impersonating a true knight-errant that Hudibras will ever be able to paper over the coercive means by which the commonwealth was won. Given his incompetence he does not have a chance at winning, yet how he plays the game is important to Butler because the widow's consent turns on the knight's ability—and the ability of the Revolution with it—to produce a consensus after the fighting ends. How he plays the game is important to the widow, too, because as far as she is concerned the power of his word is as dangerous as the force of his sword. As with the sword, the authority of the word is figured as sexual potency, but there is no way in the world that Hudibras can control its seductive side. However, the fact that he attempts to manipulate it in the ways that he does suggests that the social boundaries defined by the word are no longer as "natural" as they once seemed.

Hudibras crosses those boundaries as the threat from below, but as the avatar of the grotesque body he is only symptomatic of the broader carnivalization of history that underlies the poem's body-politics. The knight may have his own overheated libido, but in the post–old regime world of *Hudibras* sex is everywhere, especially in the promiscuity of language. That goes without saying for Hudibras, whose "ordinary Rate of Speech" had "an odde promiscuous Tone,/As if he had talked three parts in one." Yet if the miracle of multiplication is the method in his madness, the unholy trinity born from his "promiscuous" ways applies beyond the babble he spews, because the unity of public discourse was itself fragmented beyond repair with the dissolution of the body politic. In its wake, words were stretched to excess in carnivalesque fashion, giving substance to the Hobbesian notion that language was no more than a form of desire. While that notion comes across clearly in the knight's quest, it is so pervasive in the poem that its trace is evident even in Butler's trademark, the witty rhymes like "philosopher" and "glossover" that continue to amuse readers for whom much of the poem's content has been lost. The rhymes are one more bit of evidence that the "promiscuity" that characterizes Hudibras's speech applies to the world-turned-upside-down at large. There, in the carnivalized sphere of the *corpus mysticum,* words breed promiscuously, having been set free from their old restraints. The "crossbreeding" that results turns language into the site of the threat from below because the body-politics of blood applies to words as much as it does to persons. In fact, as Butler sees it, the promiscuity of language is far more dangerous, because while men can be constrained by force, the radical ideas that flew out of the Pandora's box in the 1640s might never be put back in place. That is the bottom line if a new political consensus is to be reached, but given the poem's aversion to closure Butler does not seem optimistic. Not only does the knight fail to win the widow, no one from the royalist camp rides forth to do so. Moreover, when the poem moves into the time frame of the Restoration in the third canto of part two, Butler does not represent the Restoration itself; instead, he makes the angry mob that burned the Rump in effigy the instrument of historical change. Once again, excess is the engine of English history, and in that light Butler seems to be warning that the deep schism opened up in 1641 would not be healed with the restoration of the king. The fighting might be over, but the civil war was not.

Butler was right. Civil war was averted in 1681 and again in 1688, but even so both the Exclusion Crisis and the Glorious Revolution made it clear that the fundamental issues of 1641 were still unresolved. Those issues were replayed in a number of venues, though by far the most persistent for Swift was the troubled religious settlement that he felt had given too much freedom to dissenters. These were, after all, the heirs of the Saints, and, in renewing the historical threat from below, their "promiscuity" drew his recurrent satiric wrath. For Swift, that promiscuity came in other forms as well, from the dangerous innovations of modern hack writers to the ruin of political discourse by party politics, but Dissent was the main culprit because of the role it played in what to him was the historical point of no return for England, the civil war.

While there is little question that the war did not have the immediacy for Swift that it had for Butler, it is nonetheless clear that Swift thought of the seventeenth-century schism as the Pandora's box of English history. Significant traces of that crisis are scattered throughout his writings, but for the sake of argument I will direct my attention to *Gulliver's Travels,* beginning with the historical framework in which the book is set. Swift is careful to let us know that the *Travels* unfolds between 1699 and 1715, doing so, I think, to place the work within a broader historical continuum that fulfills the dark side of the civil war with the Hanoverian succession. The historical past that leads up to that defining event is first touched upon in Part I, in Gulliver's brief ethnography of Lilliput. Amid the facts and figures that he provides, Gulliver is careful to remind the reader that the Lilliputian culture he describes is not the same culture that exists at present, since what he reports refers only to "the original institutions, and not the most scandalous corruptions into which these people are fallen by the degenerate nature of man" (361). If by this we are to suppose that history follows the path of man's degenerative nature, in the next voyage we find out that the process has a more local habitation. Following the series of conversations he has about English institutions with the King of Brobdingnag, Gulliver caps off the litany of horrors with what the king no doubt takes as appropriate illustrations drawn from English history: "And I finished all with a brief historical account of affairs and events in England for about an hundred years past." Gulliver's travels, as mentioned above, are set in the first two decades of the eighteenth century, between 1699 and 1715 to be precise. While the "hundred years past" that Gulliver recounts would put the beginning of his story in the first years of the seventeenth century, I think it is likelier that the "hundred years" refers instead to the time frame of the book's publication, 1726, since it fits Swift's own view of English history. Measured from that point, the century of division and decline recounted by Gulliver begins with the reign of Charles I, who, as Swift saw it, was martyred in the deluge that followed.

Swift was a casualty of that deluge, too, at least insofar as it was replayed years later after the death of Queen Anne. As Swift saw it, the changing of the guard that brought the new dynasty to England meant more than exile for himself; it meant the fulfillment of the civil war legacy because the succession abrogated the body-politics of blood. That view is sounded with deep resonance at the end of the *Travels,* where Swift evokes the tale of the Trojan horse to mark the passing of the age. The passage he cites is from *Aeneid* II: "Nec si miserum Fortuna Sinonem/Finxit, vanum etiam, mendacemque improba finget" (lines 79–80), which Robert Fitzgerald translates: "Fortune has made a derelict/Of Sinon, but the bitch/Won't make an empty liar of him, too." Like Sinon, Gulliver is a liar, but the deeper irony of the allusion lies in the fact that the *Travels* reprises the fall of Troy because the tragic history that the horse contains has *already* escaped the belly of the beast and penetrated the walls of the city in the form of a man who thinks he is a horse. If tragic history is repeated as farce here, there is little joy in the repetition for Swift; after all, his own exile was so closely bound up with it, so that the figure of Gulliver as the Trojan horse was the envoy of a broader historical *fait accompli.* That is why the book concludes in 1715: the year of Swift's exile, it was also the year of Gulliver's homecoming, which coincided with the Hanoverian succession because to Swift that event was the historical culmination of the long descent that began with the civil war.

Like Butler, Swift registered that descent through body-politics. But if promiscuity ensued when the threat from below escaped the belly of the beast, Swift added a dimension to the matter through what might be called the autoerotic body. That figure is foreshadowed, in the *Travels,* in the famous first-chapter reference that raises most readers' eyebrows: "my good Master Bates." While the wordplay, which caps a setup that begins several paragraphs earlier, remains controversial, I believe that the onanistic joke it insinuates is the opening gambit of what we in time come to recognize as the diary of a madman who recasts the world in the image of his own desire. Swift conveys as much when he names the desired object in Part III: *Laputa*. *Laputa* is, on the one hand, the flying island, but as *la puta* it is more than a place; it is what Gulliver wishes to possess above all else, the life according to nature. Read in this light, *la puta* is his *femme fatale,* the fatal passion (madness here, not death, though it is a kind of death-in-life) that reason turns out to be. While she is her most provocative in Part III, *la puta* is in fact Gulliver's fatal passion all along, with her final incarnation bodied forth in Part IV in the form of rational animals who confirm the hero's irrational belief that reason and nature coalesce. In spite of his high hopes, however, Gulliver is banished from Houyhnhnmland because he is *lusus naturae,* the thing that is not. With that, he has no choice but to fulfill his quest in a barn, where he reminds us of the danger that lies in the axiom that man is the measure of all things. Given this final descent, Swift makes good on the onanistic imputation at the beginning of the book, because the *femme fatale* turns out to be prophetic in the sense that the desire for *la puta* that was projected onto the rational animals is nothing less than the hero's own displaced egotism. There is, of course, no sex to speak of in the *Travels,* yet Gulliver's desire is real, its object the autoerotic body that evokes the spirit of the grotesque.

While that spirit is embodied most obviously in the reports that Gulliver dutifully gives on physical bodies and their emissions, it is far more resonant in political context, because to Swift the most dangerous emissions of the autoerotic body were the misguided beliefs that had dissolved the unity in church and state. While *Gulliver* conveys as much in his descent into madness, Swift registered that fragmentation earlier, in *A Tale of a Tub,* when he drew on features of the autoerotic body that he would later return to in the *Travels.* In this regard we are told, for example, how the *Tale* was by and large "conceived": "Now, to assist the diligent reader in so delicate an affair, as far as brevity will permit, I have recollected, that the shrewdest pieces of this treatise were conceived in bed in a garret" (265). Granted, threadbare poets write in bed to keep themselves warm, but I think that Swift hints at an onanistic subtext here. The hack, we know, sends enough material (presumably of the lesser sort) out the *postulatum* to be sure, but his best "conceptions" (if not the entire text he makes out of whole cloth) are products of the autoerotic body, whose nature is underscored by the fact that he is a writing machine, his pen the instrument of creative self-stimulation.

It is not surprising that the subtext of writing as bodily excess that appears in both the *Tale* and in the *Travels* resurfaces elsewhere in Swift.

While it is mostly a satiric device it was also a problem that struck home, because as much as Swift wished to avoid the fall into modernity it was a fate that he knew he could not evade. Like Butler, he recognized that in the post-1641 world, language was promiscuous because of the maze of political desires that were so deeply embedded in it. That, of course, did not stop him from claiming the moral high ground against those who wrote in the service of political faction. In *The Battle of the Books,* for example, he set himself apart from men who turned bile into ink in the service of party: "This malignant liquor was compounded by the engineer who invented it of two ingredients, which are gall and copperas, by its bitterness and venom to suit in some degree, as well as to foment, the genius of the combatants" (351). While these "mere writers" were getting themselves as well as others dirty, he took the high road of "authorship" because it was immune from *writing*'s taint. Just as Virgil was not to be identified with "certain sheets of paper, bound up in leather, containing in print the works of the said poet," neither was he; he was an author, not a writer, and he applied that distinction to his political pieces, which were not occasional in the way that his satires were.[9] But even if he convinced himself that his ink was not gall and copperas, that he was able to keep clean in the world of party politics, he knew that he was not immune from the predicament that "mere writers" faced. Their words were embodied because they were *only* occasional. But so were Swift's, though it took the fall of the Tory ministry in 1714 to drive home the point. Just four years earlier, in the *Examiner* (7 Dec. 1710), he had welcomed the new ministry that brought him to prominence: "Why should not a *Revolution* in the Ministry be sometimes necessary, as well as a *Revolution* in the Crown?" Four years later, he was on his way to Ireland, where he would have a lot of time to learn that the luxury of authorship was contingent on the unexpected revolutions of ministry and crown alike.

If Swift's predicament lay in the fact that his words were positioned because they were imbedded in politics, in no way could he escape the condition. The situation, however, was far different at mid-century for Sterne, who, as Swift's heir, was able to take the liberties of his predecessor without incurring the same risks. In *Tristram Shandy,* for example, he moves into the historical past self-consciously aware that the double encoding that had been *de rigueur* earlier in the century—whether it was intended by the author or not—was now a relic. He makes the point implicitly in his refusal to conjure the war against France that was going on as he wrote, even though the novel so frequently touches upon the earlier conflict with France, the War of the Spanish Succession. In this regard, Walter, who seems to be as innocent politically as Toby is sexually, announces that "There was little danger . . . of losing our liberties by *French* politics or *French* invasions" (I.18). Walter would be way off the mark for, say, 1700, but he is on target for 1760, which is precisely the difference that Sterne wishes to exploit, because with the demise of the Jacobite threat in the '45 the fear of a French invasion was no longer a reality. The same political effect applied to "Lillibullero" as well, the tune that Toby whistles when he is confronted by situations he cannot deal with. "Lillibullero" conjures the civil war: used by Irish Catholics to rally against Protestants in 1641 and again in 1688, its effect, wrote Bishop Percy, was "more powerful than either the Phillipics of Demosthenes, or Cicero; and contributed not a little towards the great revolution in 1688" (I.21). After 1688 it was turned against Irish Catholics in mockery, but in the person of Toby it is wholly domesticated, by which Sterne seems to say the desire that was once political is now personal.

As I mentioned above, Sterne was instrumental in the new body-politics that recuperated the body as a site of productive excess. As men and women were redefined as polite rather than passionate beings—as sentimental rather than religious or political, that is—the grotesque body was transformed insofar as the threat of "promiscuity" that went with it was in effect domesticated. There are multiple sites of the grotesque body in *Tristram Shandy,* sites through which the "current" of civil society circulates. Sterne is no rank sentimentalist, but in this regard it is noteworthy that many eighteenth-century readers felt that his best performance was Le Fever's tale. Most modern readers take it, at least in part, as a tongue-in-cheek performance, but in using physical weakness as its strength, it was able to purge its first readers through the body, that is, through tears.

Purgation is not Sterne's usual *modus operandi,* yet the point remains that sentiment figures in the new politics of "health" that Foucault ascribes to the later eighteenth century. "Health" is not a political element here but a facet of civil society, and in that role it recuperates the grotesque body in its capacity to renew through physical excess. This is not the grotesque body of Bakhtin to be sure; the bare fact that the Shandy men have little knowledge and less luck when it comes to sex requires no further commentary. But the text recuperates the grotesque in the sense that the body is refigured in socially productive, rather than biologically reproductive, terms. The Shandy line may be curving downward, subject to satiric gravity, but it only reinforces the fact that blood has taken a back seat to sentiment.

If the recuperation of excess applies to bodies, it applies to words as well. While the promiscuity of language conjured genuine fear in Butler and Swift, the same did not hold for Sterne, for whom the unity of the word was not at stake. For that reason, he is free to be a "writer" according to Swift's distinction. However, he can have the pleasure without the guilt since he can accept the *embodied* nature of language without the political price. In *Tristram Shandy,* only Toby refuses the intercourse of the word by refusing the sex that is implicit in language. For the rest, and for Sterne in particular, words mingle because, like men and women, they are sexual creatures. While the excess they produce is a satiric current that runs through the text in the miscommunication that plagues the dysfunctional family, it is what motors the author himself. Following Swift's hack, he acknowledges that he is governed by his pen: "Ask my pen,—it governs me,—I govern it not" (VI.6). But his "ruling instrument" is not filled with gall and copperas; its ink inseminates, despite the onanistic imputation: "Lord! how different from the rash jerks, and hare-brain'd squirts thou art wont, *Tristram*! to transact it with in other humours,—dropping thy pen,—spurting thy ink about thy table and thy books,—as if thy pen and thy ink, thy books and thy furniture cost thee nothing" (III.28). The immediate context is the difficulty that Tristram has in writing his life. But the moment is only a respite from the usual *frisson* of writing; and on that account Sterne was able to wallow in the pleasure of the text in ways that even Swift could not.

## Notes

1. For a useful survey of recent works on the body with an accent on medical perspectives, see Roy Porter, "History of the Body." For provocative studies that focus on the eighteenth century, see John Wiltshire, Barbara Stafford, and Carol Houlihan Flynn.
2. The mainspring of the movement is *Representations,* but historians have begun to read cultural phenomena as texts, as *The New Cultural History* abundantly demonstrates.
3. Peter Stallybrass and Allon White give a nail-on-the-head definition in *The Politics and Poetics of Transgression*: "In Bakhtin the 'classical body' denotes the inherent *form* of the high official culture and suggests that the shape and plasticity of the human body is indissociable from the shape and plasticity of discursive material and social norm in a collectivity" (21).
4. By Hunt, most recently, in *The Family Romance of the French Revolution.* For another approach to the Revolution that likewise emphasizes changing representations of the body, see Dorinda Outram, *The Body and the French Revolution: Sex, Class and Political Culture.*
5. On the development of civility as the privatization of bodily functions in the works of the Renaissance humanists, see Norbert Elias, *The Civilizing Process,* and Elias, *Court Society.*

6. *The History of Sexuality,* particularly ch. 5, "Right of Death and Power over Life," where Foucault describes the change as one from the sovereign power to subtract by punishing the (individual and corporate) body to the administrative power to multiply by promoting conditions amenable to its growth.

7. John Sitter takes a different route but comes to the same conclusion in *Literary Loneliness in mid-Eighteenth Century Literature*: "We can best appreciate how fundamental a shift occurs here by recalling that one of the deepest connections we can find between Dryden and Pope—and many of the contemporaries of each—is the shared sense of the poet's role as historian of his own times" (82).

8. For an interesting account of the idea, see Jean-Christophe Agnew, *Worlds Apart* ch. 3.

9. On the distinction between writer and author that Swift respectively applied to his satiric and political works, see Edward Said, "Swift's Tory Anarchy," in *The World, the Text, and the Critic* 54–71.

## Works Cited

Agnew, Jean-Christophe. *World Apart: The Theater and the Market in Anglo-American Thought, 1550–1750.* Cambridge: Cambridge UP, 1986.

Armstrong, Nancy. *Desire and Domestic Fiction: A Political History of the Novel.* New York: Oxford UP, 1987.

Bakhtin, Mikhail. *Rabelais and His World.* Trans. Helene Iswolsky. Cambridge, MA: MIT P, 1968.

Barker, Francis. *The Tremulous Private Body: Essays on Subjection.* London: Methuen, 1984.

Brooks, Peter. *Body Work: Objects of Desire in Modern Narrative.* Cambridge, MA: Harvard UP, 1993.

Butler, Samuel. *Hudibras.* Ed. John Wilders. 2 Vols. Oxford: Oxford UP, 1967.

Clark, Jonathan. *The Dynamics of Change: The Crisis of the 1750s and English Party Systems.* Cambridge: Cambridge UP, 1982.

Elias, Norbert. *The Civilizing Process.* New York: Urizen, 1978.

———. *Court Society.* Oxford: Basil Blackwell, 1983.

Flynn, Carol Houlihan. *The Body in Swift and Defoe.* Cambridge: Cambridge UP, 1990.

Foucault, Michel. *The History of Sexuality.* Trans. Robert Hurley. New York: Pantheon, 1978.

Hunt, Lynn. *The Family Romance of the French Revolution.* Berkeley: U of California P, 1992.

———, ed. *The New Cultural History.* Berkeley: U of California P, 1988.

Kenyon, J. P., ed. *The Stuart Constitution, 1603–1688: Documents and Commentary.* Cambridge: Cambridge UP, 1966.

Outram, Dorinda. *The Body and the French Revolution: Sex, Class and Political Culture.* New Haven: Yale UP, 1989.

Payne, Harry C. "Elite versus Popular Mentality in the Eighteenth Century." *Studies in Eighteenth Century Culture* 8 (1979): 3–35.

Pocock, J. G. A. *Virtue, Commerce, and History.* Cambridge: Cambridge UP, 1985.

Porter, Roy. "History of the Body." *New Perspectives on Historical Writing.* Ed. Peter Burke. University Park: Pennsylvania State UP, 1992. 206–32.

Said, Edward. *The World, the Text, and the Critic.* Cambridge: Harvard UP, 1983.

Scarry, Elaine. *The Body in Pain: The Making and Unmaking of the World.* New York: Oxford UP, 1985.

Sitter, John. *Literary Loneliness in mid-Eighteenth Century Literature.* Ithaca: Cornell UP, 1982.

Stafford, Barbara. *Body Criticism: Imaging the Unseen in Enlightenment Art and Medicine.* Cambridge: MIT P, 1991.

Stallybrass, Peter, and Allon White. *The Politics and Poetics of Transgression.* London: Methuen, 1986.

Sterne, Lawrence. *Tristram Shandy.* Ed. James A. Work. New York: Odyssey, 1940.

Swift, Jonathan. *Gulliver's Travels and other Writings.* Ed. Louis Landa. Boston: Houghton Mifflin, 1960.

Wiltshire, John. *Jane Austen and the Body.* Cambridge: Cambridge UP, 1992.

# The Mechanics of Transport

## Sublimity and the Imagery of Abjection
## in Rochester, Swift, and Burke

*Allen Dunn*

Obscenity and sublimity would seem to be natural opposites, and in the poetics of Restoration England, this opposition seems to delineate contrasts in poetic temperament if not ideological commitment.[1] Those poets who present grotesque or obscene images of the human body do so, it appears, as a calculated affront to the presumption of spiritual transport that seems to inspire heroic verse. The relationship between sublimity and the sheer physicality of the grotesque is, however, much more complex than this simple opposition suggests, and in this chapter I will argue that the popularity of both the poetics of transport and the poetic imagery of defecation, copulation, disease, and decay is symptomatic of a breakdown in the epideictic rhetoric of praise and blame, a breakdown in the rhetoric of the Renaissance poetic tradition in which many of the Restoration poets were trained. At the core of this crisis in the epideictic literary tradition is an inflationary devaluation of the language of praise and a corresponding blurring of distinctions of social rank and degree.[2]

Both the imagery of abjection[3] and the rhetoric of the Burkean sublime offer a potential remedy for this crisis by re-establishing an essential difference or disadequation between the poet and the object of the poet's desire. Both offer poetic strategies for preventing the language of praise from becoming the mere projection or mirror of the epideictic poet's desires. Unlike the satiric poet, however, Burke transforms bodily abjection into a sign of sublimity itself.

Whether playing the role of lover, politician, or scholar, the epideictic poet is, of course, one of the most popular targets of Restoration satire. Here, the epideictic poet is portrayed as a shameless egotist whose literary efforts pose a clear threat to public values. From the satirist's point of view, the epideictic mode is dangerous not just because it encourages flattery or false praise. Nor is it problematic simply because the poet's praise whether justified or not is likely to be part of the poet's strategy for material or social advancement. Beyond these obvious abuses of epideictic rhetoric, the suspicion persists that the act of praising itself, the epideictic gesture, conceals a more fundamental type of egotistical presumption. That is, the epideictic stance is presumptuous because it masks a tacit act of identification in which the poet internalizes or incorporates the person and qualities that are the objects of praise. This surreptitious act of poetic identification is doubly disturbing since it not only challenges the distinctions of class or social ranking but because it also threatens to obliterate the boundaries that demarcate public and private dimensions of experience. Epideictic rhetoric tends to internalize the public arena by allowing the poet to usurp the functions of both performer and spectator.

This moment of covert identification appears most dramatically in the moment of "transport" as it is introduced in Longinus's *Peri Upsos.* In the "lightning flash" of sublimity, Longinus tells us, the boundaries of the self temporarily collapse, and the auditor shares both the glory of the poet and the great emotions and great thoughts that make up the poet's subject matter (2). According to Longinus, sublimity gives the members of the poet's audience the sense that they have written the poem to which they are listening. Longinus's numerous examples of sublimity are taken from both poetry and oratory and depend heavily upon an epideictic model. What Longinus implies but does not say is that the audience's rapt identification with the poet depends on the poet's prior identification with the heroes and lovers that exemplify the overpowering thoughts and emotions that constitute his more abstract subject matter.

If the transport of sublimity allows both the epideictic poet and his audience to share the glory of the great-souled man, to feel that they themselves are the authors of his greatness, it is not surprising that such transportation across social boundaries should become the *bête noire* of Tory satirists. Even in its less dramatic or sublime forms, epideictic rhetoric paradoxically threatens to undermine the very social distinctions that it appears to endorse and uphold. As the satirists frequently remind us, the sheer number of poets setting themselves up as arbiters of fame and honor undermines any poet's ability to confer those very distinctions.

The satirists' suspicions are further confirmed by the natural affinity between an idealized rhetoric of praise and various progressive philosophical movements of the seventeenth and eighteenth centuries. The tropes of amplification that are commonly found in epideictic poetry depend heavily upon moral abstractions such as the allegorical personifications of qualities like truth and justice, and such abstractions are featured prominently in philosophical systems of universal humanity such as Shaftesbury's and Hutcheson's. In such systems a universal humanity is affirmed by a collective identification with the ideal, by a shared attraction to beauty. This aspiration for the ideal, however, is precisely what the satirist fears, since it involves an individualistic appropriation of moral value through a process of internalization and establishes social harmony by weakening the standards of social hierarchy. Shaftesbury's description of the psychology of sympathy in "Concerning Virtue or Merit" provides a good example of this. For Shaftesbury, "a natural joy" in the contemplation of the harmony which supports universal nature "is essential in the constitution and form of every particular species or order of beings," and this shared joy in natural harmony provides the rationale for liberal democracy (I:296).

It is surprising and sometimes comical to see how difficult it is for the epideictic poet to refute the satirist's suspicions. The more the poet protests that he or she is not acting out of self-interest, is not flattering, the more she is trammeled in suspicion and the more she has shifted the focus of the poem from praise to self-justification. Litotes, understatement (which is dangerous in any case), is likely to appear as impertinent familiarity, hyperbole as flattery. Every gesture of self-effacement is simultaneously an act of self-defense and shifts the reader's attention to an internalized arena of psychic struggle. This, in turn, tends to collapse rather than to maintain the distance between the poet and the object of her praise. This predicament is probably most dramatically apparent in the language of dedications, wherein the poet performs a kind of verbal hara-kiri for her patron. Charged with the impossible tasks of asserting both the poet's worthiness and her abject humility, both the patron's good taste and the patron's charitable beneficence beyond the poet's deserts, such performances tend to collapse under the weight of pure contradiction. The preface to *Marriage A-la-Mode,* for instance, in which Dryden dedicates the play to Rochester, also thanks Rochester for championing the play without being asked to do so. Dryden cites this as an example of Rochester's exceptional generosity, but one cannot escape the suspicion that he is also stressing this fact as implicit proof of the play's exceptional worth. This suspicion persists even when Dryden claims that the meanest word that Rochester ever wrote is better than Dryden's best, and it is paradoxically amplified when Dryden ventures a simile comparing Rochester to God and himself (Dryden) to Rochester/God's creation. This simile is meant to confirm the absolute distance between Dryden and his patron but backfires by making Rochester strangely responsible for and even intimate with Dryden's creation. (Indeed, Rochester as God was too much for Dr. Johnson: Dryden's prefaces earn the wrath of Johnson who describes them as fulsome flattery [355]).

Dryden's simile illustrates the uncanny way in which epideictic rhetoric creates equivalencies (in this case, the creation as the mirror image of the creator) while insisting upon distinction (that is, while insisting upon the absolute superiority of creator to creation). Satirists such as Rochester and Swift typically attempt to expose the presumption of the epideictic poet by undermining the rhetoric of equivalence, the rhetoric of transport that allows the poet to share the glory of the person or quality that she is praising, and, I am arguing, Rochester and Swift (although they are certainly not unique in this) find the abject body, the body of farts, shits, abscesses, and menstrual blood, to be an essential tool in this satiric sabotage of epideictic presumption. In its gross physicality the abject body resists the impulse either toward pity or toward admiration; it clouds the specular language of epideictic identification and presents in its repulsive opacity a physical argument against universal humanity. In rhetorical terms, abjection is not only a denial of epideictic amplification but of mimetic representation insofar as it implies a process of generalization or the linguistic exchange of one term for another. The imagery of abjection supports a nominalist skepticism; it subverts linguistic equivalence with a deictic gesture toward a pure particularity.

Rochester's satiric personifications of the epideictic poet typically dramatize a process of inward collapse. What is supposed to be praise for another person is revealed to be self-praise. This self-praise becomes, in turn, a mere self-description that reveals at its core a blind, egotistical impulse. For instance, In "A Very Heroical Epistle in Answer to Ephelia" (Rochester's send-up of Mulgrave, Dryden's patron), Mulgrave is writing to his mistress ostensibly to make amends for his infidelity. However, what should be a letter of supplication soon turns into a hymn of self-praise:

> In my dear self I center everything:
> My servants, friends, my mistress, and my King;
> Nay, heaven and earth to that one point I bring. (7–9)

Since he is the standard by which the rest of the world is to be measured, he argues, it is impossible to accuse him of inconstancy. He then fantasizes about the joys of the happy sultan who reduces all men to his slaves and all womankind to his whores. If woman's complaining tongue wounds the sultan's sacred ears, "a nimble mute straight ties/The true love knot, and stops her foolish cries" (51–52). Thus, this reply to the complaining mistress concludes with a thinly veiled fantasy of her murder.

In "An Epistolary Essay from M.G. to O.B. upon Their Mutual Poems," Rochester again attacks Mulgrave using a similar strategy. Here Rochester has Mulgrave reverse the roles of poet and patron, writing obsequiously to the poet who is in his pay and apparently admitting that he has taken credit for a poem that Dryden has in fact written. Mulgrave protests, however, that he is indifferent to the approval of any audience since he writes only to give himself pleasure:

> And if, exposing what I take for wit,
> To my dear self a pleasure I beget,
> No matter though the censuring critic fret. (18–20)

Writing, unlike the "unsavory wind" released in farting, forces itself on no one. The inevitable metaphoric reduction follows:

> What though the excrement of my dull brain
> Runs in a costive and insipid strain,
> Whilst your rich head eases itself of wit:
> Must none but civet cats have leave to shit?
> In all I write, should sense and wit and rhyme
> Fail me at once, yet something so sublime
> Shall stamp my poem, that the world may see
> It could have been produced by none but me. (40–47)

Vieth comments in his notes to the poem that this is a surprisingly early reference to Longinus (a French translation had just made Longinus accessible to many English readers for the first time). It seems that in England the excremental imagery of the anti-sublime arrives at the same time as the sublime itself.

This metaphoric equation that reduces the divine afflatus of the epideictic poet to the flatulence and excrement of the abject body is, of course, one of the cornerstones of Swift's poetics.[4] Unlike the satires of Rochester, however, Swift's vituperative attacks upon the poetry of praise reflect his own struggle and frustration with that generic medium. The early odes of Swift are a case study in what I have described as the epideictic crisis. All of these odes proclaim the unbridgeable gap between true virtue and the fallen human language that attempts to represent that virtue. In the "Ode to the Athenian Society," for instance, the anonymous Athenian society has a wisdom that no name could represent; in the "Ode to Dr. William Sancroft," the celestial Archbishop Sancroft moves "too high/To be observ'd by vulgar eye" (149–50), and his image defies earthly representations. Elsewhere, in "Ode to Sir William Temple," Swift claims that Sir William Temple possesses the virtue and transparent innocence that his scholar enemies cannot find in "Philosophy! the Lumber of the Schools" (24). These are just a few examples of an argument that is sounded repeatedly (and, I would argue, obsessively) throughout the odes. Paradoxically, but not surprisingly, Swift uses some of his most elaborate and stilted rhetoric to represent this unrepresentability of virtue.

In these odes to a virtue that cannot be represented in language, Swift assumes a posture of humility. His authority as a poet derives from his recognition of the inability of epideictic rhetoric to represent true virtue and from his corresponding awareness of the blindness and impertinence of those who think that they possess a language that is equal to such subject matter. That is, as Swift presents himself in these poems, his major strength as a poet derives from his ability to see the epideictic presumption in other poets and to avoid such presumption in his own poems. Accordingly, Swift is constantly contrasting himself with either the critics or flatterers of the individuals whom he is praising. These others (often his poet competitors) fail to realize the chasm that separates the language that they are using from the truth to which they aspire. As Swift presents them, both flatterers and critics are guilty of using language to name and thus to appropriate fame and honor that is beyond both their deserts and their comprehension. The critics whom Swift most frequently attacks in the odes are the religious sectarians and scientific projectors who will feature so prominently in his later satires. By Swift's account, these critics debase such elevated qualities as truth and virtue by dragging them down to their own level. They appropriate truth by describing it in materialist or mechanical terms. In "Ode to the Athenian Society," this is the sin of the materialist critics of the Athenian society who reduce the world to a "*Crowd of atoms* justling in a heap" (127). The flatterers, by contrast, assume an inappropriate familiarity with those whom Swift feels are praiseworthy. In "To Mr. Congreve," for instance, the flatterers steal Congreve's language and prostitute his name. In doing so they are presuming to be Congreve's equals, but Swift compares them to the footboy who dreams he is the friend of the lord or the fresh miss who dreams she is the beauty of the town (115ff.).

Both critics and flatterers are guilty of what Swift calls leveling. In response to Sancroft's critics, he claims, "[W]hate'er theologic lev'llers dream,/There are degrees above I know/As well as here below" and goes on to imagine a paradise filled with "patrician souls dress'd heavenly gay" (230–32, 234). Swift is obviously taunting Sancroft's low-church opponents here, but leveling is precisely the impulse that he sees at work in the presumptuous language of those he criticizes.

Given Swift's attitudes toward epideictic language, it is not difficult to see why his odes enjoyed little success. Despite his earnest admiration of those whom he is praising, he is much more comfortable attacking their enemies than he is attempting to describe their virtues. When he attempts praise, his metaphors often collapse into absurdity. In "Ode to the Athenian Society," for instance, he imagines a dove attempting to grasp a sourceless sound with its beak (57–59). Furthermore, his poet persona is often trapped in the ironic gesture of asserting that he is superior because of his humility, because he can see what he cannot see. Swift stages this dilemma of self-contradiction in the ode "Occasioned by Sir William Temple's Late Illness and Recovery," perhaps his last attempt at epideictic poetry. Here Swift turns from his description of a world which he claims has been thrown into chaos by Temple's illness and savagely attacks his Muse as a "malignant goddess" who is "the universal cause of all [his] woes" (80–81). Swift claims that his muse (who is clearly the muse of epideictic poetry) has driven him mad with her impossible demands. He quotes the advice that his muse has given him. She has admonished him to "Stoop not to int'rest, flattery, or deceipt;/Nor with hir'd thoughts be thy devotion paid;/Learn to disdain their mercenary aid" (138–40). However, the muse's speech breaks off with an unfinished clause:

> "And since unhappy distance thus denies
> T'expose thy soul, clad in this poor disguise;
> Since thy few ill-presented graces seem
> To breed contempt where thou has hop'd esteem."— (143–46)

What conclusions the muse has reached about his frustrated attempts to expose his soul and to gain esteem are never specified, but the impossibility of realizing these aspirations seems to dawn upon him as he breaks off with the exclamation, "Madness like this no fancy ever seiz'd,/Still to be cheated, never to be pleas'd" (147–48). The muse's advice to avoid self-interest and mercenary aid is mad if not hypocritical, especially since it appears in a poem dedicated to a patron upon whose aid Swift was dependent. The lines about self-exposure are more surprising, however. They acknowledge that the odes have been a project for the soul's exposure and for hop'd esteem, a project frustrated by unhappy distance, rhetorical distance, one assumes, and the ill presentation of graces that were supposed to garner self-esteem. Swift's defense against this straight talk from the muse is to reduce her to a derangement of the optic nerve, a delusion of a sickly mind. Since her entire existence depends upon his breath, he dismisses her with a puff.

Not long after this exorcism of the epideictic muse, Swift began work on *A Tale of a Tub*, in which he traces the epideictic inspiration to its source in the abject bodies of the Aeolist pretenders. "The Problem," a short poem written around the same time, captures this dynamic. A lord, the lover in this poem, is pursued by ladies who have heard that sexual passion will cause a man to emit an odor but that "None but the Fav'rite Nymph can smell it" (12). After some strained comparisons between the release of flatulence and the release of Cupid's bow, Swift describes how the ladies spread their charms to catch a fart. In the heat of passion, my lord's farting and speaking become indistinguishable, and after an argument the ladies decide that they all have ample evidence of his odoriferous passion. Therefore, they conclude, he must be a universal lover. By ostensibly making flatulence the language of love, the medium of universal sympathy, and the inspiration for self-transcending identification, Swift is, of course, making the case that repulsion is much more natural and immediate than universal love. The same metaphoric logic is at work in both *A Tale of a Tub* and *The Mechanical Operation of the Spirit*. In both of these works, the inspiration that provides the very medium of sublime transport is traced to the abject body of the poet/writer wherein the grosser manifestations of the self have been mistaken for the presence of a transcendent spirit. Epideictic ecstasy appears as mere self-infatuation in the case of the Hack and as sexual aggression in the case of the Puritan Preacher. Swift is just as assiduous in attacking the objects of epideictic praise as he is in satirizing the poets who produce it. He returns continually to the medieval topos of feminine beauty as a disguise for corruption and never tires of examining the scabrous bodies of fops and whores. By modern standards, it is remarkable that he can so exhaustively catalogue the suffering and decay of the body without tempting his reader to sympathetic pity.

Thus, the natural repulsion occasioned by the imagery of abjection in the work of Rochester and Swift forecloses any possibility of subjective interiority. It implies a "natural" system of social differences and rescues social relationships from the speculative interiority of the poet's mind. These poets manage to externalize social relationships, however, only by obliterating subjective interiority. Their satiric personae establish social distance by reducing the self to a cyst or a bowel complaint. Rochester seems to delight in watching this collapse; he celebrates the nothing that is affirmed when the reasoning engine of the grandiose self collapses in the dirt. By contrast, Swift attempts to talk from beyond abjection. He offers the decayed body as homage to human limitation and the social distance that it insures but cannot resist speculation about what Prince Posterity will say when that vanity is stripped away; he cannot resist killing himself to find out what will be left, as he illustrates in "Verses on the Death of Dr. Swift."

Although, as I have been arguing, these gestures that reduce transport to a mechanics of abjection seem to strike at the very heart of the poetics of sublimity, they are surprisingly congruent with Burke's theories of the sublime. Those theorists, like Burke, who distinguish beauty from sublimity do so in order to contrast the self-dissolving social sympathy excited by beauty with the self-isolating pain stimulated by the sublime. Burke's sublimity, however, unlike the abject body of the satirists, manages to affirm a power which remains distinct from the logic of reduction. In the satirists' scheme the poet's ideals are revealed to be at odds with her material existence, but the status of the ideal, the status of greatness itself, is left in doubt. Burke's theory of the sublime also invokes the materiality of the body as proof of the essential nature of social difference and as an implicit refutation of the epideictic model of aspiration and identification.[5] Burke, however, asserts that the materiality of the body is not only proof of social difference and a block to the leveling which occurs when inferiors imitate their betters, but also a positive proof of a greatness which is itself inimical to imitation. In his treatment of the sublime, Burke rejects the testimony of poets and critics (whose reflections he claims he distrusts) and focuses instead on the mechanical chain of causes and effects which he claims produces sublimity. By far the most important of these sublime effects is the spectacle of power and vulnerability as it is presented in such figures as the criminal hanged or tortured, Milton's Satan cast down from heaven, or Job enduring the wrath of God. Each case presents palpable injury as it is inflicted on the body of the sufferer, and this palpable suffering contrasts dramatically with the ineffable power that produces it. In Burke's account of sublime spectacle, the body as it is marked by injury or even distorted by the fear of injury provides a mute testimony to a power that the suffering subject of sublimity can neither understand nor control. As the objects of satire, the diseased bodies of fops, whores, and hacks demonstrate an essential repulsiveness that is at odds with the self-images which these characters project onto the world. The mangled bodies of Job, Satan, and the hanged man also contain elements of grotesquery and repulsiveness, and, like the bodies anatomized by the satirists, they dramatize the absolute distance that separates human reality from the human aspiration, but as a token of the sublime, the broken body becomes the most potent sign of a higher power.

Thus, Burke's *Enquiry* employs the type of reductive empiricism that the satirists ridicule, but employs it for purposes that the satirists themselves might endorse. Like the reductive materialism of satire, Burke's mechanistic account of beauty and sublimity challenges the notions of judgment, reflection, and identification that support an epideictic rhetoric. By invoking the body marked by power as the emblem of sublimity, Burke dispels any notion that sublime greatness can be incorporated in an egalitarian vision of the world, that it can be shared as a kind of communal property to which all subjects aspire. The unbridgeable gap between the source of power and the physical harm that great power either threatens or produces asserts the primacy of physical differences over any shared abstract ideals, and it gives material form to the inexpressible greatness that so frustrated Swift's early efforts.

While Burke reduces both beauty and sublimity to the machinery of empirical cause and effect, he further undermines the epideictic model of imitation and aspiration by insisting that beauty and sublimity have their origins in distinct and antithetical passions: beauty derives from the social passions and sublimity from the passions of self-preservation. On the basis of this distinction, Burke attempts to demonstrate that the passions of self-preservation and not the passions of sociality are the motive forces behind human progress. Specifically, Burke is rejecting the Neoplatonic assumption that beauty is the reflection of an ideal harmony, a harmony which can be grasped and understood only through a process of rational reflection. According to Neoplatonic aesthetics, human arts aspire to this harmony and are beautiful to the extent that they succeed in imitating it; but, although the process of imitation yields progress, the perfect harmony which the arts seek to appropriate remains forever on the horizon. Such a model, of course, supports the notion (implicit in epideictic rhetoric) that imitation is aspiration and that successful imitation can facilitate the improvement of both self and society. John Dennis and other early-eighteenth-century theorists of the sublime use such a Neoplatonic framework for identifying beauty with sublimity. Dennis claims that sublimity is the highest and most incomprehensible degree of the harmonies that are represented in beauty. Sublimity represents for him an apocalyptic horizon where decay and dissonance will be banished and a prelapsarian harmony restored in what must have looked to his critics like a suspiciously egalitarian state.

Burke spends a good portion of the *Enquiry* attempting to destroy this notion that beauty might motivate a Neoplatonic progress toward perfection, and he is especially impatient of the idea that imitation might provide the means through which such perfection is grasped. Beauty is a mechanical operation of the spirit: "We must conclude," Burke insists, "that beauty is, for the greater part, some quality in bodies, acting mechanically upon the human mind by the intervention of the senses" (112). Accordingly, the cause of beauty is not to be found in such abstractions as proportion, fitness, harmony, or virtue but in such physical qualities as smallness, smoothness, and sweetness, qualities which have a relaxing effect upon the nerves, since "beauty acts by relaxing the solids of the whole [bodily] system" (149–50).

But, if beauty is mechanical, Burke insists, so are the social passions from which it derives, and so are types of mimetic behaviors which these passions inspire. This means that imitation itself must be understood as blind, mechanical repetition and not as Neoplatonic progress. As a process of blind repetition, he insists, imitation destroys distinction and produces a social stasis. This makes imitation the enemy of ambition, not its ally as the epideictic model would have it. At the conclusion of Part I of the *Enquiry,* Burke delineates the dramatic differences which he thinks distinguish imitation and ambition. Here he classifies both imitation and ambition as social passions, but notes that while imitation is a pure social passion, ambition is a complex passion which is also inspired by the sublime instinct for self-preservation. Because it is motivated by this passion of self-preservation, ambition is conducive to greatness. Burke describes imitation, by contrast, as a curiously inert, unmotivated, and even mindless activity: "For as sympathy makes us take a concern in whatever men feel, . . . we have a pleasure in imitating, and in whatever belongs to imitation merely as it is such, *without any intervention of the reasoning faculty, but solely from our natural constitution*" (49 [emphasis mine]). The *Enquiry* has little to say about the specifically social effects of imitation, but speaks instead of the arts of poetry and painting as they may produce pleasure by imitation alone without regard for the humble nature of the objects which they represent.

While Burke does admit that passion for imitation is powerful and one of the instruments used by Providence to bring order to human nature, he presents it as a positive impediment to human improvement: "if men gave themselves up to imitation entirely, and each followed the other, and so on in an eternal circle, it is easy to see that there never could be any improvement amongst them" (50). To avoid this kind of circularity and stagnation, Burke argues, God has planted a sense of ambition in men. This passion "drives men to all the ways in which we see in use of signalizing themselves, and that tends to make whatever excites in a man the idea of this distinction so very pleasant." This desire for distinction is so strong, Burke continues, that it has made "very miserable men take comfort that they were supreme in misery," and when we cannot distinguish ourselves by something excellent, it prompts us "to take a complacency in some singular infirmities, follies, or defects of one kind or other" (50).

In Burke's account, then, the desire for singularity, the desire for a pure and abstract social difference, is the driving force behind ambition. This ambition is indifferent or even hostile to the various value systems that might authorize distinction. The need for distinction allows one to find satisfaction in the singularity conferred by misery, folly, and vice, to find satisfaction in the very failure to meet evaluative standards. Burke separates the ambition for distinction from the desire to possess specific virtues or moral qualities in order to emphasize that the need for social difference exceeds any mimetic impulse to reproduce shared social values. Ambition, for Burke, is not inspired when one person witnesses the bravery, generosity, honesty, or other virtues of another and attempts to imitate those qualities because they seem inherently worthwhile. This would make imitation an integral part of ambition and lend support to the Neoplatonic model of aspiration. Rather, Burke insists, singularity or social difference is a good in and of itself, inscrutable and sublime. The self's pride in its own autonomy must come from such a sense of singularity, even if that singularity is produced by the drama of subjugation. Paradoxically, this means that what the ambitious person desires are not the qualities that distinguish a great person (these qualities only emphasize mimetic dependency) but the effects of greatness, the difference and distinction that greatness produces.

Of course, the effects of greatness, shorn of any mimetic content, any representable virtue, find their definitive expression in the sublime, and in his discussion of ambition, Burke claims that swelling of that emotion "is never more perceived, nor operates with more force, than when without danger we are conversant with terrible objects, the mind always claiming to itself some part of the dignity and importance of the things which it contemplates" (50–51). The terrible objects of the sublime spectacle demonstrate the effects of power, and, as Burke emphasizes, there is "nothing sublime which is not some modification of power" (64). Power is sublime because it is represented by distances, not by human qualities that might become the objects of admiration and imitation. *Pure power is the only form of greatness that defies the mimetic impulse.* Its terrible and destructive effect is the one thing that the powerless aspirants to greatness cannot imitate or claim as their own. The dignity and importance that the mind feels when exposed to the spectacle of sublimity derive, as Burke's discussion of ambition makes clear, from the power of distinction and singularity itself. The observer identifies not with greatness or power as positive entities but with the social difference or singularity that greatness produces as its effect.

The various spectacles of sublimity which Burke presents constantly draw our attention away from the source of power and focus it on the effects of power, and, as I have argued, chief among the "terrible objects" that are the effects of power is the abject body of the person who has been killed, tortured, or merely terrified. This focus on terrible objects, on the body reduced to a material vulnerability, contrasts dramatically with earlier notions of a mimetic sublime. Burke illustrates this contrast in the discussion of Longinus which concludes his analysis of ambition. Here Burke identifies the inward swelling produced by the "terrible objects" in the spectacle of sublimity with the "sense of inward greatness" that Longinus claims will transport those who have heard sublime poetry or oratory (50–51). Yet, although Longinus and Burke might often agree about which poems are sublime, what should impress the modern reader is the different ways in which these judgments are derived. Burke has no use for the great thoughts and emotions that facilitate identifications between the poetic subject, the poet, and the poet's audience. The sublime objects that galvanize Burke's spectators are silent about the powers they symbolize; the materiality of these objects mark their absolute difference from the power that has shaped them.[6]

Thus, the example of the execution of the "state criminal of high rank" which Burke uses in Section XV to demonstrate the superiority of "real" sublime effects over artistic representations of sublimity is as notable for what it does not mention as for what it does. Burke does not mention the character of the criminal nor comment upon his guilt. Nor does he mention powers that have condemned and sentenced him, nor the more visible powers that have carried out the execution. The "most sublime and affecting tragedy" with which Burke compares the real execution would have made much of these things, but the sublimity of this execution does not depend on any of them (47). Burke may be alluding to a specific execution, as some of his commentators suggest, but his description implies that details are not necessary to appreciate the "power" of the spectacle and that this "power" will be greater in any real event than in any imitation of that event, no matter how detailed the imitation might be. Of course, Burke insists on the separation of the objective effects of sublime power from the source of such power when he argues for the sublimity of obscurity itself. A clear idea is to Burke's reckoning necessarily a little idea, and familiarity breeds only contempt. Great powers must therefore necessarily appear as obscure, Burke argues, if they are to impress themselves upon us with sublime force. To illustrate this, he offers the example of one of the apparitions that appears to Job. The effects of Job's terror are described in graphic detail, but the vision which produced these effects remains shrouded in obscurity. The sublimity of this episode "is principally due to the terrible uncertainty of the thing described," Burke claims; "wrapt up in the shades of its own incomprehensible darkness," it is more moving than the liveliest and most accurate representation could present (63).

The ways in which Burke and the satirists use the abject body as an argument against Enlightenment universalism anticipates later anti-Enlightenment arguments. The abject body is an irreducible particular which resists universals; it is opaque, impenetrable, and as Burke's rage against clarity emphasizes, it resists the system of visual metaphors that supports the Enlightenment's vision of intellectual progress. Finally, the body is by turns repulsive, grotesque, and terrible, a barrier to a community based upon shared values, sympathy, and mimetic identification. But, as opaque, particular, and repulsive, the body becomes a symbol for the forces that define it, for forces that cannot be rationalized or internalized, that cannot be represented in human terms. That is, it becomes the symbol of a power with a scope and application that rivals reason itself.

Burke begins his discussion of the sublime with the example of the torture and execution of the regicide Damiens, the same example that Foucault will employ at the beginning of *Discipline and Punish*. Foucault, like Burke, offers the spectacle of pain as the alternative to the scopic Enlightenment regimen of internalization and universalization. Unlike Burke, Foucault is ambivalent about the effects of power, but in the body externalized, materialized, and differentiated, he finds a defense against the various self-monitoring disciplines of reflective subjectivity and their mimetic drive toward an anesthetized sameness. Yet, in theorizing the body both as a node of resistance to reflective subjectivity and as the transcript of an inhuman power, Foucault must struggle with many of the same problems confronted by Rochester, Swift, and Burke. These problems include the poverty of a language without human qualities and the need to witness the finality of the abject body while at the same time speaking from within its limitations.

## Notes

1. I would like to thank Jonathan Lamb, Jim Gill, Mary Papke, and especially Laura Mandell for reading and commenting on drafts of this essay.
2. On social rank and degree, see McKeon's chapter, "The Destabilization of Social Categories" 131-75.
3. At the outset of my discussion it will be helpful to distinguish my use of the term "abjection" from Julia Kristeva's influential treatment of this concept in *The Powers of Horror*. Kristeva describes abjection as the (non)object of primal repression, as a pervasive otherness that constantly threatens the ego's boundaries and its self-consistency. As such it inspires both fascination and horror, fascination with the possibility of a return to the plenitude of a preobjective state, horror at the threatened dissolution of the ego's boundaries. Because it threatens these

boundaries, abjection precipitates what Kristeva call a crisis of narcissism. She describes the abject as "edged with the sublime." For her, they are not the same moment but are related insofar as both lack an object and both presuppose a loss of self. Her remarks on the sublime are suggestive rather than definitive, but she seems to identify sublimity with an ecstatic self-loss, with raptures of "bottomless memories" rather than with the drama of conflict and self-affirmation which is described by Burke and Kant.

In presenting the imagery of abjection as a form of reductive materialism, I stress its rhetorical function as parodic re-description of the drama of inspiration and imitation. As a form of reductive materialism, the imagery of abjection allows conservative writers to turn progressive dogma against itself by *opposing* egalitarian notions of virtue to materialist science. Employed in this way abjection upholds distinction and becomes the metonymic effect of a power which always is assumed to be incommensurate with its cause. The loss of distinction which abjection implies is thus transformed into a paradoxical kind of proof of a more absolute distinction. Kristeva's speculations about the psychic genesis of abjection are not necessarily incompatible with my argument and may shed some light upon the ambivalent mixture of disgust and fascination that sometimes attends the imagery of the body's reduction to a broken materiality, but my argument does not require that one share her assumptions about the psychic origins of horror and disgust.

4. Of course, Rochester's libertinism should not be equated with Swift's conservatism. I am arguing, however, that Rochester's reductive materialism invites us to revise our understanding of social hierarchy but does not encourage us to challenge that hierarchy. Certainly, Rochester's view is hostile to any progressive notion of a natural sociality. For a similar argument about the conservative tendency in libertinism, see Maximillian Novak's "Margery Pinchwife's 'London Disease.'" I am indebted to Laura Mandell for calling this article to my attention.

5. See Steven Knapp's *Personification and the Sublime* for a wide-ranging discussion of the way in which the artificial nature of allegory regulates the sublime process of projective identification.

6. Several commentators have noted the way in which Burke's explanation of the sublime as a physiological instinct is contradicted by his numerous appeals to a reflective consciousness. This is especially true in his discussion of ambition. Apropos of this discussion, Knapp argues that this contradiction forced Burke to confront the "essentially figurative structure" of sublimity and that this figure brings sublime self-inflation "perilously close to ironic deflation," as when Burke admits we can take pride in misery (73). I agree that Burke's physiological description of sublimity is contradicted by his appeal to reflection, but I do not think that this contradiction is as threatening to Burke's sublime as Knapp implies. This is because the "terrible object" of the sublime is not simply "taken

to signify power in the self," as Knapp claims. The "terrible object" *is* the (a) self as it is shaped by a power that it cannot represent. See Knapp 66-74 and Ferguson's *Solitude and the Sublime* 37-53

# Works Cited

Burke, Edmund. *A Philosophical Enquiry into the Origins of our Ideas of the Sublime and Beautiful.* Ed. James T. Boulton. South Bend, IN: U of Notre Dame P, 1958.

Dennis, John. *The Critical Works of John Dennis.* Vol. I. Ed. by Edward Niles Hooker. Baltimore: John Hopkins UP, 1939.

Dryden, John. Preface to *Marriage A-la-Mode. The Works of John Dryden.* Volume XI. Ed. John Loftis and others. Berkeley: U of California P, 1978. 221–24.

Ferguson, Frances. *Solitude and the Sublime: Romanticism and the Aesthetics of Individuation.* New York: Routledge, 1992.

Foucault, Michel. *Discipline and Punishment: The Birth of the Prison.* Trans. Alan Sheridan. New York: Vintage Books, 1979.

Johnson, Samuel. *Lives of the English Poets.* Ed. George Birkbeck Hill. Oxford: Oxford UP, 1905.

Knapp, Steven. *Personification and the Sublime: Milton to Coleridge.* Cambridge: Harvard UP, 1985.

Kristeva, Julia. *The Powers of Horror: An Essay on Abjection.* New York: Columbia UP, 1982.

Longinus. *"Longinus" on Sublimity.* Trans. D. A. Russell. Oxford: Clarendon, 1965.

McKeon, Michael. *The Origins of the English Novel, 1600–1740.* Baltimore: Johns Hopkins UP, 1987.

Novak, Maximillian E. "Margery Pinchwife's 'London Disease': Restoration Comedy and the Libertine Offensive of the 1670s." *Studies in the Literary Imagination* 10.1 (1977): 1–23.

Rochester, John Wilmot, Second Earl of. *The Complete Poems of John Wilmot, Earl of Rochester.* Ed. David Vieth. New Haven: Yale UP, 1968.

Shaftesbury, Anthony Ashely Cooper, Third Earl of. *Characteristics of Men, Manners, Opinions, Times, etc.* Vol. I. Ed. John M. Robertson. Gloucester: Peter Smith, 1963.

Swift, Jonathan. *Poetical Works.* Ed. Herbert Davis. London: Oxford UP, 1967.

———. *A Tale of a Tub, To which is added The Battle of the Books and the Mechanical Operation of the Spirit.* Ed. A. C. Guthkelch and D. Nichol Smith. 2nd ed. Oxford: Clarendon, 1958.

# "Credit Exhausted"

## Satire and Scarcity in the 1690s

*Robert Markley*

> The Revolution of 1688 ushered in a decade of some of the most momentous events in the history of England. Unfortunately, both contemporaries and later commentators thought it ushered in one of the dullest decades in the history of English literature.
>
> —William J. Cameron

As Cameron's comment suggests (*Poems* vii), the literature of the 1690s traditionally gets a bad press. Critics usually either dismiss the poetry and drama of the decade as a dull, if not distasteful, body of work, mired in the controversies and calumnies of partisan politics, or try to salvage the reputation of individual writers, such as Congreve, by arguing that their work transcends its historical circumstances to achieve aesthetic coherence and moral purpose.[1] Both the period's detractors and champions, however, overlook the brutal facts which confronted every writer during the 1690s: between 1689 and 1697 England was a nation at war, committing extraordinary financial and human resources to the Continental struggle against French "tyranny." Whatever their political allegiances, then, writers were aware, and often painfully so, that to defend the revolutionary principles of 1689 and the Protestant succession, Parliament had to acquiesce, often reluctantly, to an unprecedented concentration of money and power in a centralized, increasingly sophisticated bureaucracy dedicated to managing an expensive and seemingly interminable conflict (see Brewer 144–54; Jones, *War and Economy,* and Jones, "Sequel to Revolution," 389–406). The "momentous events" of the period—the founding of the Bank of England, the machinations of the Whig Junto between 1694 and 1697, the efforts of the country interest in Parliament to ward off the King's attempts to impose a general excise tax, and the recoinage of 1696–97—are not background or context for literary works but crucial influences on and, to a greater extent than has been recognized, the subject matter of satire during the decade. In this respect, literary responses to the Nine Years War take one of two dialectically related forms: authors either retreat from the "meaningless iteration" of

politics and celebrate literature as a means to safeguard the morality of
the nation or they mobilize topical satire to accomplish what conventional politics cannot: an attack on both William's war and the corruption of traditional values that it symbolizes (Bywaters 129). If the literature of the 1690s seems "dull," it may be because critics lack a theoretical
vocabulary to describe this dialectic, to discuss the significance of the insistent efforts by poets to translate the economic problems of life during
wartime into moral and satiric terms. Rather than discussing the literature of the 1690s in the traditional critical idioms of aesthetics or morality, then, I want to explore what happens when we read the topical satire
of the decade as a contribution to, and a protest against, the practices of political economy: the efforts by the government to collect taxes, pay and provision soldiers, maintain naval superiority, and support financially strapped
allies while simultaneously trying to balance the competing demands of different segments of society for shares of increasingly scarce resources.[2]

In this essay, I shall concentrate on two minor, yet, I would argue, paradigmatic satiric poems of the 1690s—Charles Mordaunt, the Earl of
Monmouth's, "On the Last Treasury Day at Kensington" and the anonymous "Farewell to England" (both written in 1697 before the final campaign of the Nine Years War)—to examine the complex relationships
among political satire, the perception of economic hardship, and disruptions within larger structures of value exacerbated by the war. Both poems, the former by a radical Whig, the latter by an unregenerate Tory,
lay claim to a common—and contested—language of virtue and anti-
institutional resistance to "tyranny," which John Brewer identifies with the
emergence of a "country ideology" during the period (155–61). Whatever
their political differences, however, Monmouth and his Tory counterpart
share, exploit, and resist what I shall call the ideology of scarcity—the
belief that humankind has fallen from a golden age of peace, virtue, and
prosperity to a war-induced present of political corruption, social upheaval,
and economic deprivation. Confronted by the contradictions within this ideology, both poets set idealized visions of abundance against dystopian
views of scarcity; they take refuge in a moralistic rhetoric of "us" versus
"them" and reinscribe a binary logic of value.[3] Their satires become a way
to assess blame, to make the King, the Whig Junto, excisemen, and customs officers scapegoats for the brutal logic of scarcity; for both satirists,
even the need to debate how to allocate scarce resources becomes evidence
of political tyranny and moral corruption. Yet the vehemence of their satire paradoxically reveals the tenuousness of the very values—virtue, patriotism, and prosperity—they present as absolutes. In this respect, "On
the Last Treasury Day at Kensington" and "Farewell to England" reflect
crises within what Jean-Joseph Goux calls the "symbolic economies" of

money and identity, the dynamics by which values are asserted, contested, subverted, and reinscribed. These crises provoke the satirists' recognition that the ideology of scarcity binds politics, economics, and political identity to the logic of an irrevocable fall from a golden age.

1

By the end of the seventeenth century, the myth of the golden age, seemingly irrevocably, had been politicized; Dryden's translation of Virgil's Fourth Eclogue (1697), for example, occasioned a host of imitations in 1702 by Tories who saw the ascension of Anne as the dawn of a new era of prosperity and several sardonic parodies by Whigs who viewed the Tory bias of the queen with downright hostility. Although the literary fascination with the golden age has been discussed in some detail, what is less frequently noted is the crucial role this myth plays in economic thought (Levin throughout; Giamatti 15–33). For many writers, economists as well as poets, the golden age serves as a powerful image of the abundance of nature; it signifies both a specific time and an ideal condition before humankind had to contend with the specter of scarcity, the Hobbesian war of all against all, and before society was forced to consider what Charles Davenant calls the "perplex'd, tedious, and intricate" concerns of managing the economy (Davenant, *Discourses on the Publick Revenues* 126). Faced with the economic demands of war in the 1690s, writers invoke the golden age to serve as the image of a prelapsarian "bounteous Nature," when, as Behn maintains in her poem "The Golden Age" (1684), "kind increase" made competition for resources unnecessary (Behn 6: 140). But the very frequency with which writers otherwise as different as Davenant (the Whig commissioner of the excise) and Behn (the Tory apologist) invoke this mythic time suggests the extent to which it becomes the site of contested political beliefs and competing ideological investments. Precisely because the golden age is imagined as a pristine standard against which contemporary failings can be judged, it can be appropriated by radicals and conservatives alike to satirize their political adversaries and to displace onto them their own frustrations with a fallen, corrupt world.

The satire of the 1690s uses the language of politics—the lament for the lost golden age—to decry the politicizing of the economy. For the Whigs, the golden age takes the form of the Lockean myth of the consensualist origins of government, a past in which property was founded on one's labor, and, in theory, property, freedom, and social identity were inalienable.[4] This vision of the golden age, articulated in Locke's *Second Treatise of Government,* depends ultimately on the individual's ownership of land at a time before competing claims arose to challenge the integrity of one's property and, by extension, one's identity; property, in theory, becomes infinitely expandable without encroaching on others' rights. Locke captures this economic dimension of the golden age succinctly when he asserts that then "All the world was America" (Locke 2, 5: par. 49). Locke's image erases the indigenous peoples of the Americas to present the "inexhaustible" resources of the new world as either unclaimed or conquerable in a just war. This imaginary extension of property depends on the anti-ecological fiction that the resources of the natural world can be used—indefinitely, infinitely—without being used up (see Markley and Rothenberg 301–21).

For their part, Tory writers at the century's end make explicit what usually is left implicit by their Whig counterparts: the golden age is a mythic extension of an ideal aristocratic existence. Labor is unnecessary because the privilege of luxury is posited as ontologically prior to the effort needed to acquire it—use-value can be expanded infinitely to satisfy the boundless desires of the imagination and to legitimate unequal distributions of power and wealth. As Molly Rothenberg and I have argued, Behn recognizes that scarcity both produces and is produced by the repressive strategies of politics, honour, power, and property; the mechanisms of an internalized ideology of self-policing and constrained sexual desire inscribe a coercive political authority on the consciousness of the individual. But Behn's efforts to reimagine the golden age by yoking sexual freedom and the abundance of nature come up against a fundamental contradiction: her attempt to free sexual desire from ideological constraints conflicts with her recognition that scarcity and repression exist symbiotically (Markley and Rothenberg 311–12). The golden age can exist, in other words, only when conditions of abundance forestall the political conflicts and psychosexual repression occasioned by "Right and Property" (Behn 6: 140). Like Locke, Behn cannot explain precisely how or why the fall from abundance occurred. Even though she demystifies the ideology of property and links it provocatively to an anatomy of sexual repression, she, too, must refuse to acknowledge that the conditions which constitute the golden age as a symbolic whole—particularly the abundance of nature—are themselves imaginary.

In this respect, different versions of the golden age myth reinforce a common—and always self-consciously literary—idealization of use-value: in art, if not in life, nature can produce the limitless resources necessary to satisfy all desires. Yet it is precisely the fictive nature of the golden age, the obviousness of its idealizations, that makes it a powerful means of producing desire, of making us want and work for what is forever beyond our reach. Because the golden age is always and only imaginary, then, it must be defined as the *negation* of the conditions of scarcity and repression that characterize the postlapsarian world. Behn, for example, relies on strings of negative constructions to describe humankind in the golden age, acting "Not [in] fear of Gods, no fond Religious cause,/Nor in obedience to the duller Laws" (Behn 6: 141). Ironically, for Behn and for a host of other writers at the end of the seventeenth century (including Isaac Newton), corruption is figured as ontologically prior to the innocence of the golden age; the pristine world of Locke's primal property owners and Behn's lordly swains can exist only as an imaginary erasure of the conflicts brought about by scarcity.[5]

In its paradoxical commitments to idealization and the primacy of corruption, the golden age reproduces the dialectical logic of value described by Marx and elaborated by Goux. This logic is crucial to understanding the ways in which satire gives voice to the other, devalued half of the dialectic described by the golden age: the repressed awareness of scarcity. The money form of value, says Marx, is based on the symbolic guarantee of the "general equivalent," the "excluded, idealized element" that underwrites all forms of exchange as a universal standard or measure of value but that remains unaffected by these transactions (Goux 4). The idealized, absolute value of gold lies not in its "fixed" price but in the fact that it is always the means by which the prices of other commodities are negotiated. Goux extends Marx's discussion to argue that the Father in the symbolic economy of identity, the phallus in that of desire, and language in that of representation are "structurally homologous" to gold; they are the incorruptible standards by which all exchanges of value are measured (Goux 4). The logic of the general equivalent, Goux maintains, is the "centralization of value and of values" that "*magnetizes* or *funnels* towards its ideal center all value relationships, making them its tributary rays" (44, 45). But because this "centralization" depends on an originary alienation between "concrete labor, production, translinguistic productivity" and a "legislative agency" that is "abstract" and "transcendent," value originates in the "renunciation" of "the unbridled pursuit of satisfaction," in our submission to the logic of "the world of the substitute, of compensation—and thus the world of *values* implicit in 'exchange'" (53). This logic of substitution is, in effect, the logic of the fall: our allegiance to abstract and transcendent authority can be experienced only as a fundamental alienation from a lost ideal, a golden age which, as Behn implies, exists as the negation of our experience of alienated existence. If the golden age, in this respect, represents the imagined unity of fulfilled desires, unrepressed sexuality, and an Adamic language, then its existence depends on a means to project that fiction of unity and abundance from an analysis—or a mere listing—of the fragmented and corrupt conditions of the postlapsarian world. That means, the genre of "renunciation," is satire.

"On the Last Treasury Day at Kensington" and "Farewell to England" depend on the implicit invocation of the golden age as a counter to corruption; yet the poems' opposition between the golden age and a corrupt present is constantly breaking down, provoking endless negotiations between absolute and contingent values. Goux terms this process "the production and reproduction of interposition which automatically poses two terms [the ideal and the material] separated by the 'inter' of a third" (239). Satire, in effect, is a form of restless "interposition." It imposes, always imperfectly, the idealizations of the golden age on a stubbornly resistant reality, then laments the failure of this imposition. In this sense, satire is the recognition of the Imaginary in crisis; it is the corrective voice that must supplement the golden age and, paradoxically, reveal it to be a fiction. Although Monmouth and the anonymous author of "Farewell to England" invoke the imaginary vision of an England uncorrupted by war and politics, they find themselves implicated in the very evils they condemn, trapped by the logic of substitution, renunciation, and exchange—that is, by the ideology of scarcity.

## 2

"On the Last Treasury Day at Kensington" dates from March 1697, immediately before William left for his 1697 campaign on the Continent. Monmouth's poem draws on two familiar forms in seventeenth-century verse satire: multiple speakers, satirically undone by their own speeches, and a *vox ex machina* that transcends rather than resolves politically the problems of corruption and national poverty. The first three speakers voice different cynical strategies to repair the financial ravages of the war: Charles Montagu, chancellor of the Exchequer, warns "the gathering storm [is] breaking" and that bankruptcy is inevitable; Sir Stephen Fox, First Lord of the Treasury from October 1696 to April 1697, when he was replaced by Montagu, advises more bribes to placate corrupt members of Parliament; and John Smith, a commissioner of the Treasury since 1694, declares, "[W]e must supply the war/At any rate" and advocates "Seizing the Exchequer" to finance a final push for victory (Cameron 502–3). The King speaks next, mocking "the desponding Board" and reveling in his willingness to beggar his subjects in order to continue the war and maintain his power. The poem, then, becomes a satiric version of Davenant's recognition that "War is quite changed from what it was in the time of our Forefathers; when, in a hasty Expedition, and a pitch'd Field, the Matter was decided by Courage; but now the Whole Art of War is in a manner reduced to Money; and now adays that Prince, who can best find

Money to feed, cloath, and pay his Army, not he that has the most valiant Troops, is surest of Success and Conquest" (Davenant, *An Essay upon Ways and Means* 27). Focusing on the degradation of traditional values and the scramble to "find Money," Monmouth implies that penury and powerlessness rather than war are the true evils brought about by the King and the Whig junto. But, after he finishes speaking, the King is upstaged by "a new voice . . . Distinctly heard in all the rooms around" (lines 68, 70) that re-establishes the sense of patriotic virtue which the other speakers have violated and, in the case of William, gleefully corrupted. This virtue, though, is less that of an emergent "country ideology" than that of a "republican" iconoclasm; Monmouth, as satirist and former First Lord of the Treasury, remains a radical Whig, out of favor (temporarily, at least) with the King he had helped to power.[6]

Montagu, as First Lord, begins the poem by satirically condemning himself as he laments his inability to finance the war. Suffering, he says, is universal: "Dejected grief in every face appears,/A town in murmurs, and a land in tears,/Credit exhausted" (3–5). What may seem at first a familiar litany of satiric abuses—corruption, taxation, and tyranny—becomes more complex, and troubling, as the implications of "Credit" multiply. The exhaustion of credit recalls the specific measures the government took to continue the war: in addition to the spate of new taxes levied in the 1690s and schemes, like the First Million Lottery, that mortgaged future government funds to finance the war, "Credit exhausted" raises the specter of additional burdens, specifically William's efforts, led by Montagu, throughout the 1690s to impose a general excise tax (Brewer 144–49). The phrase speaks, too, to widespread anxieties about the future of England. The problems of financing the war were exacerbated by the recoinage of 1696–97, as clipped coins minted before 1663 were removed from circulation, melted down into bullion, and gradually replaced by new milled coins. The shortage of ready money, in turn, provoked a credit crunch of unprecedented dimensions that made itself felt throughout the economy. In this context, it is worth remembering that before the ascension of William and Mary, the debt was the monarch's alone, a personal obligation; one of the consequences of the Commons' restrictions on monies granted to the Crown in 1689 was that the debt to finance the war on the Continent became, with the establishment of the Bank of England, truly national. By 1697 the national debt was recognized and frequently deplored as a permanent feature of the economy. Its growth, therefore, becomes a threat to the integrity of the nation, to Monmouth's perception of England as a bastion of virtue, fiscal responsibility, and the consensual sanctity of property.

The King becomes the principal target of Monmouth's satire, I would argue, because the loss of "Credit" registers profound dislocations in the symbolic economies of value—political and personal as well as financial—that he ostensibly anchors. In his *Review* of August 9, 1711, Defoe offers an important gloss on what we might call a Whig redefinition of credit, a relocating of the authority of government from the monarch-as-father—as the guarantor of patrilineal values—to the imaginary coherence of the institutions of government and society symbolized by the "ancient Constitution": "Publick credit is no more or less, than the Satisfaction the People have in the Faith and Honour of the Government: By the Government, is here to be understood not the Ministry, not this or that Party, no, not the Queen personally—But the Constitution, the Queen or King for the Time being, and Parliament. . . . I lay it down as an undoubted Truth, That the Foundation of our Credit is the Constitution, as is above noted, and nothing else" (8, 59). By making credit an article of faith, Defoe constitutes it as both an absolute measure of value and a form of symbolic capital, a general equivalent, and a means of exchange. Although Pocock has described the feminization of credit in the works of Defoe and Addison, it is worth noting that Defoe locates credit in this passage in the realm of "faith" and "honour," an essential move in redefining the monarchy as an institution representing the collective obligations which bind together monarch, Parliament, and people under the sign of the unwritten, imagined "Constitution" (Pocock 100). "Credit exhausted," the bankruptcy of the state, in this regard, presages and embodies a more general crisis of value that encompasses and extends beyond the "perplex'd, tedious, and intricate" concerns of political economy. Monmouth locates this crisis in the degeneracy of the King, scapegoating William for the instability and anxieties that the poet associates with the fall into scarcity.

William, then, becomes the embodiment of moral, political, and economic corruption rather than a noble leader misled by his advisors, a familiar strategy in the satires of Marvell and others written during the 1660s and 1670s. The King revels in his expenditures and in the poverty of his subjects: having "beggared this insulting town," he declares, "If any hoarded stock of wealth remains,/I'll draw the utmost farthing from their veins" (44, 48–49). The familiar image of the body politic is satirically perverted: "This haughty, humorsome, rebellious brood/Must be drained low and emptied of their blood" (46–47). Figured as a ghoul, William becomes a parody of the father figure gone bad, the constitutional monarch turned tyrant; ironically, savagely, he describes his tyranny as "paternal care" (65). The corruption of the King's paternal duty contributes to the general crisis of value precisely because, as Goux sug-

gests, "the king's duty in the political sphere . . . is that of general equivalent, administering equivalences before a group of individuals who becomes his subjects" (39). To the extent that the King represents and informs the "paterialist ideology" of an essential identity elevated above
the material world, his corruption throws the dynamics of individuals'
identity formation into chaos (Goux 225). In other words, if the king-as-
father becomes corrupt, then the logic of value which he, as general
equivalent, underwrites must also erupt into crisis. Thus metamorphosed
into a Machiavellian stage tyrant, William concludes his speech by threatening the propertied basis of the Constitution:

> Those I employ
> Shall take what I will give with secret joy.
> They shall attend, and humbly sue for grace,
> I'll yoke them double to a single place.
> Land tax, a general excise, and poll
> Shall tame their courage and their pride control.
> Peace they expect, but my paternal care
> Shall give them want, and parliaments, and war. (59–66)

The orderly workings of government are corrupted by William's use of
the familiar strategies of tyranny: like the exiled James II, he subverts
Parliament's independence by secret payments, the manipulation of "place-
men" (MPs who accepted lucrative places in the Treasury or the military
and thus depended on the Crown for their sinecures), and the imposition
of new taxes. "Peace" gives way to "want," to the indefinite frustration of
legitimate desires. The country—particularly members of the gentry subject to land, excise, and poll taxes—are cast in the role of adolescents at
the mercy of the King's "paternal care." In this respect, his "control" of
their economic fortunes undermines their efforts to represent themselves,
through Parliament, as men in control of their destinies, as coherent political subjects free from "paternal" tyranny. The penury induced by the
war threatens the gentlemanly ethos of self-government, a crucial aspect
of Whiggish, and republican, notions of sociopolitical identity (Worden
241–77). The threat to the economic security of the gentry reveals as
well the tenuousness of the individual's sense of self, his dependence on a
logic of general equivalents, of renunciation, to construct an identity
modeled on and forever in rebellion against the authority of the King.

The *vox ex machina,* as Cameron notes, is identified in the Rawlinson
manuscript of the poem as "England's voice from above." In one sense,
this voice articulates the concerns of an antiwar Whig, championing the
interests of (propertied) people, as represented in Parliament, as the true

national interest: "True Englishmen in votes assert their right,/And gain
a nobler conquest than by fight" (77–78). But, in another sense, the voice
seems that of the "faith" and "honour" of the Constitution; it casts seventeenth-century England as heir to a golden-age past that can be invoked,
particularly in times of crisis, to re-create the nation as an imagined, even
Edenic stronghold of virtue and sociopolitical stability.[7] "England's voice
from above" thus retreats into the realm of a self-confirming ideal: "Our
hope's best centered in our selves alone" (76). For the satirist, the corruption of war ironically becomes the means to reassert the integrity of a
national, and mythic, identity—the ideal of fraternal unity stands as a
bulwark against the tyranny of the King.

At stake in Monmouth's satiric attack on the King, then, is an attempt
to contain the radical implications of an always incomplete revolution:
the transfer of absolute value from king-as-father to the imaginary conditions of authority-as-consensus. This attempt at containment is what
we call morality, the reassertion of metaphysical order by judging present
actions against the standards of an (absent) golden age. In this respect,
the poet's allegiance ultimately is not to a specific set of policies (the re-
peal of certain taxes, for example) but to the logic which we saw operating in Behn: a dialectic of demystification and idealization, a satiric critique that depends on the fiction of a transhistorical position from which
to condemn corruption. Soon after he wrote this poem, Charles Mordaunt
succeeded his uncle as Earl of Peterborough; by that title he is familiar to
historians for his stormy tenure as joint commander of British and allied
forces in Spain in 1705–6 and to literary historians as an intimate of the
Tory satirists. Politically, he becomes identified after 1713 with the country interest against Walpole. This tendency for Mordaunt-Monmouth-
Peterborough to remain in unregenerate opposition to those in power
suggests the extent to which his politics—radical Whiggery and later a
kind of radical Toryism—depend on his cultural nostalgia for an imaginary origin of virtue and value, a golden age which already and always
has fallen prey to a metastasizing corruption. To replace the King with
Parliament or to make gold beholden to credit does not alter the *dynamics* of the money form of value. Politics changes, but the ideology of scarcity—the presuppositions of political economy—remain an evolving but
always powerful metalanguage to describe the "perplex'd, tedious, and
intricate" operations of interposition. If, as Goux suggests, western philosophy enshrines the logic of general equivalents, then satire represents
both the failure of that logic and the reinscription of the imaginary conditions under which poems such as "On the Last Treasury Day at Kensington"
would no longer need to be written.

3

Although "Farewell to England" was published in Tom Brown's *Remains* (1720), its attribution is uncertain (Cameron 520). The poem, however, can be dated between April 1697 (the appointment of the nine regents to govern while William was on the Continent) and September (the Treaty of Ryswick which ended the war). The satiric persona, a Tory disgusted with the war and the measures needed to support it, proclaims repeatedly his intention to leave England. The poem opens with a litany of wartime deprivations and satiric evils brought about, in part, by the disruption of trade:

> Farewell false friends, farewell ill wine,
> Farewell all women with design,
> Farewell all pretty cheating pranks,
> Farewell lotteries, farewell banks;
> And England, I in leaving thee
> May say farewell to poverty.
>     Adieu! where'er I go, I'm sure to find
>     Nothing so ill as that I leave behind. (1–8)

The satirist offers what seem two registers of complaint: standard-issue satiric targets ("false friends," "women with design") and the specific hardships suffered by England in the late spring or summer of 1697— the scarcity of prohibited French wine, the lotteries offered under the directorship of William Neale, and the founding of the Whig-dominated Bank of England to finance the national debt. What unites the elements of this satiric catalogue is the poet's emphasis, reinforced by the rhyme, on "poverty" and its effects. Like "Credit exhausted" in Monmouth's poem, "poverty," as a near-personification of England in crisis, is symptomatic of larger disruptions in value and national identity. The refrain, which appears at the end of each of the first five stanzas, marks a retreat to an indefinite locale where "Nothing so ill" exists. Because "ill" has been used in line one to describe bad wine, it is tempting to read the refrain less as an overt moral condemnation than as the expression of a desire to escape from the conditions of poverty. The farewell to war and its deprivations, in this respect, is a farewell to scarcity itself.

The satiric condemnation of national impoverishment continues in the second stanza. As financial misdeeds and corruption are catalogued, the listing of evils to be left behind seems an increasingly static device:

> Farewell a nation without sense,
> Farewell exchequer without pence,
> Farewell army with bare feet,
> Farewell navy without meat,
> Farewell writing, fighting, beaux,
> And farewell useless Plenipo's. (9–14)

The subordination of logical development to satiric lists leaves the speaker suspended in a present moment of continual leave-taking. The "useless Plenipo's," the plenipotentiaries negotiating unsuccessfully (since November 1696) to end the war, become images of the inability to end a state of war-induced scarcity which has taken on a life of its own, sapping the "sense" of the nation as well as its purse. Significantly, the war is portrayed not in terms of violence and brutality, in the traditional masculinist rhetoric of conquest and valor, but in an attenuated language of cost-benefit analysis. In the fourth stanza, "gulled unthinking fops,/ Poor broken merchants, empty shops" are obvious effects of "eight years' war for England's good" (27–28, 30), but they also testify to the complicity of gulled Englishmen in their own victimization. This familiar satiric paradox—the need to reform those incapable or unwilling of reformation—takes on particular force for the antiwar persona. Rather than converting the foolish to a normative moral standard, he concedes defeat, leaving England to the "good old cause promoters" and "bribed military voters" (MPs paid to support the war) responsible for, among other indignities, the Bill of Attainder passed in January 1697 against the Jacobite plotter, Sir John Fenwick.[8] Although the speaker, in the fifth stanza, attacks familiar targets of Tory satire—the "haughty little mouse" (Charles Montagu), "long nose" (the King), and the "Reverend Oates and all his books" (the infamous Titus Oates had authored several vicious attacks on the deposed James II in 1696–97)—his ultimate indignation seems reserved for the very spirit of England that Monmouth invokes at the end of "The Last Treasury Day at Kensington":

> Adieu once more Britannia! fare thee well.
> And if all this won't mend thee,
> May the Dutch triumph in your spoil,
> May beggary run throughout your isle,
> And no one think it worth his while
> To take up to defend thee. (41–46)

The worst curse that the speaker can hurl at the nation he is abandoning is "beggary." But the force of this curse betrays the reformist tendency that underlies the satire; although the speaker has told us for six stanzas that he is leaving, his line, "If all this won't mend thee," reveals his threat to leave as a rhetorical gesture. His phrase, "all this," though, is ambiguous: is his invective supposed to cure the state of the nation or is the experience of deprivation supposed to move the reader to action? In one respect, the speaker seems to want the patriotic intentions of his poem to emerge, even as his curse condemns his country to economic servitude to the Dutch, yet his final images depict the defense of the realm as a profit-less endeavor, literally "worth [no one's] while." Victims of self-induced "beggary," the English become unable to "mend" themselves; the image suggests a domestic, almost feminized care on the part of the poet that contrasts sharply with the insensitivity brought about by poverty and war.

If the speaker's repeated farewells anticipate the stance of the Tory satirists in the early eighteenth century—the retreat to a bucolic country-side away from the corruption of politics, business, and society—they also testify to his unwillingness or inability to describe his unnamed destination. It seems appropriate that the persona is still leaving, still bidding farewell to England at the end of the poem, because his destination remains, as it must, imaginary. In a time of a general European war, there is literally nowhere for a peace-loving, tax-hating Tory to go, no ideal realm where "poverty" and "beggary"—where scarcity and debt—do not exist. The golden age remains always and necessarily out of reach, and the alienated, disgruntled Tory seems less a "subject," a psychological and moral being protesting an immoral or useless war, than an image of the poet's and the reader's resistance to having their subjectivity revealed as a function of the logic of scarcity. Trapped between satire and (an implied) golden age encomium, the persona remains suspended between leaving and not leaving, between a rejection of war, corruption, and poverty, and a desire to return to an imagined time before "writing, fighting, [and] beaux." In one sense, what he cannot escape are the conditions of scarcity, which are both the cause and the effect of the war he detests. These conditions compel the satirist to protest and to reinscribe the ongoing crises of political economy.

4

Marxist and feminist critics of eighteenth-century literature, no less than formalist critics and historians (old and new), are caught between impulses to find antecedents for their own beliefs in the works they study and to measure writers such as Monmouth ahistorically against twenti-eth-century standards of political enlightenment. The satire of the 1690s makes a poor model for critics searching for politically "progressive" foremothers or forefathers because its efforts to transcend or to banish corruption resist offering "realistic" solutions to the problems of war, re-pression, and economic deprivation. But ignoring the "minor" satire of the 1690s carries its own risks: in consigning poems such as "The Last Treasury Day at Kensington" and "Farewell to England" to the oblivion of topical ephemera, we bury yet deeper the contradictions that they para-doxically foreground and mystify, the crises of political economy in a time of war and scarcity. The next step in revamping the canon of eighteenth-century studies may be to resurrect writers such as Monmouth as a way to explore our own critical and ideological blind spots. In this respect, to read the topical poetry and the political economy of the 1690s against, and in conjunction with, the canonical works of Behn and Locke is to confront the constructed nature of our basic assumptions about scarcity, poverty, and property. As a heuristic conclusion, I would suggest that the divisions between Whig and Tory to which I have called attention may be only surface manifestations of the deeper ruptures within what we might term, after Jameson's idea of the "political unconscious," the eco-nomic unconscious: the repressed recognition that the golden age of plenty is a fiction, that humankind is always engaged in seeking to deny, ignore, or minimize the consequences of a fallen ecology.

## Notes

1. On formalist approaches to Congreve, see Holland and Williams. Recent feminist criticism has extended dramatically our understanding of the gender politics of the 1690s—see Finke, Merrens, and Lowenthal. Timothy Reiss (148) has called attention recently to the "alliance of literature and power" in the late seventeenth and early eighteenth centuries and to the constitutive role that these relations play in the development of modernity.

2. On the problems of defining political economy, see Caporaso and Levine 1–3. Political economy presupposes, as I argue below, that finite resources must be allocated, at least in part, by government action rather than by the operations of the economy. In exploring the intervention of satiric poems within the discourse of political economy, I am breaking with a tradition which assumes that modern political economy begins in the late eighteenth century with Adam Smith; as Joyce Oldham Appleby has demonstrated, the language of economics, what William Petty and Charles Davenant term "political arithmetick," emerges in the seventeenth century by developing transhistorical models to describe objective

"laws" of economic behavior. My assumption, then, is that "political economy" includes a variety of discourses concerned with the problem of scarcity (see Appleby throughout and Davenant, *Discourses on the Publick Revenues* 13–14).

3. On the economic problems of the 1690s, see Brewer 144–64. My use of "ideology" differs from Brewer's. Ideology cannot be conflated with specific political programs, platforms, or bodies of consistent philosophy. As Foucault suggests, ideology is marked by contradictions, by dialogic struggles to control common vocabularies of thought and perception. Ideology provokes dissent and disruption to justify its ongoing efforts to police, repress, or reconcile warring elements—see Foucault's description (20–22) of the operations of power. I discuss the difference between politics and ideology in *Two-Edg'd Weapons* 41–43.

4. Although pro- and anti-government Whigs share a vocabulary which celebrates consensus, liberty, and property, there are important differences between supporters of the junto and "radicals" such as Monmouth, as I suggest below. On the problem of identifying and describing a tradition of "radical" or "republican" Whigs in the late seventeenth century, see Greaves, Dickinson (63–84), and Worden (241–77).

5. On Newton, see Markley, *Fallen Languages* 145–53.

6. Charles Mordaunt (1658–1735), Earl of Monmouth (1689–1697) and then Earl of Peterborough (1697–1735), began his public career during the Exclusion Crisis as an intimate of Shaftesbury's circle; he led parliamentary opposition to James II, then fled to Holland, where he encouraged William to claim the English throne. He was rewarded in 1689 by being made a privy councillor and later First Lord of the Treasury and the Earl of Monmouth. In 1690, however, Monmouth resigned his Treasury post (taking a pension instead) and, within a year, had fallen out with the King. From the 1690s on, Monmouth's career is one of continuing controversy arising out of his actions in Spain as joint commander of the English expeditionary force. Spurned by Queen Anne on his return in 1706, Peterborough was investigated by the House of Lords in 1707–8 and acquitted of wrongdoing, ironically championed by the Tories. Monmouth's friends and associates included Locke, Algernon Sidney, and John Wildman. The significance of his radical politics has yet to be explored. For the complicated history of the period, see Holmes 229–92, and J. R. Jones, especially 258–59.

7. On the significance of "constitutionalism" for seventeenth-century radicalism, see Wood 69–75.

8. Monmouth was embroiled in the Fenwick case, first offering to intercede with the King on the prisoner's behalf if Fenwick would implicate high-ranking Whigs in plots against the monarch, then, after his offers were rebuffed, arguing vigorously for his execution. See the account in the *DNB,* which is indebted to Macaulay's *History.*

# Works Cited

Appleby, Joyce Oldham. *Economic Thought and Ideology in Seventeenth-Century England.* Princeton: Princeton UP, 1978.

Behn, Aphra. *The Works of Aphra Behn.* Ed. Montague Summers. 1915. New York: Phaeton, 1967.

Brewer, John. *The Sinews of Power: War, Money, and the English State, 1688–1783.* Cambridge, MA: Harvard UP, 1990.

Bywaters, David. *Dryden in Revolutionary England.* Berkeley and Los Angeles: U of California P, 1991.

Cameron, William J., ed. *Poems on the Affairs of State: Augustan Satirical Verse, 1660–1714.* Vol. 5: *1688–1697.* New Haven: Yale UP, 1971.

Caporaso, James A., and David P. Levine. *Theories of Political Economy.* New York: Cambridge UP, 1992.

Davenant, Charles. *An Essay upon Ways and Means of Supplying the War.* London, 1695.

———. *Discourses on the Publick Revenues and on the Trade of England.* London, 1698.

Defoe, Daniel. *A Review of the State of the British Nation.* 8, 59 (Aug. 11, 1711).

Dickinson, H. T. "The Precursors of Political Radicalism in Augustan Britain." *Britain in the First Age of Party 1680–1750: Essays Presented to Geoffrey Holmes.* London: Hambledon P, 1987. 63–84.

Finke, Laurie. "The Satire of Women in *The Female Wits.*" *Restoration* 8 (1984): 64–71.

Foucault, Michel. *The History of Sexuality.* Vol. I: *An Introduction.* Trans. Robert Hurley. New York: Pantheon, 1978.

Giamatti, A. Bartlett. *The Earthly Paradise and the Renaissance Epic.* 1966. New York: Norton, 1989.

Goux, Jean-Joseph. *Symbolic Economies After Marx and Freud.* Trans. Jennifer Curtiss Gage. Ithaca: Cornell UP, 1990.

Greaves, Richard L. *Secrets of the Kingdom: British Radicals from the Popish Plot to the Revolution of 1688–89.* Stanford: Stanford UP, 1992.

Holland, Norman. *The First Modern Comedies: The Significance of Etherege, Wycherley, and Congreve.* Cambridge: Harvard UP, 1959.

Holmes, Geoffrey. *The Making of a Great Power: Late Stuart and Early Georgian Britain 1660–1722.* New York: Longman, 1993.

Jameson, Frederic. *The Political Unconscious: Narrative as a Socially Symbolic Act.* Ithaca: Cornell UP, 1981.

Jones, D. W. *War and Economy in the Age of William III and Marlborough.* Oxford: Clarendon, 1988.

———. "Sequel to Revolution: The Economics of England Moment: The Economics of England's Emergence as a Great Power, 1688–1712." *Essays on the Glorious Revolution and Its World Impact.* Ed. Jonathan I. Israel. Cambridge: Cambridge UP, 1991. 389–406.

Jones, J. R. *Country and Court, England 1658–1714.* Cambridge, MA: Harvard UP, 1978.

Levin, Harry. *The Myth of the Golden Age in the Renaissance.* Bloomington: Indiana UP, 1969.

Locke, John. *Two Treatises of Government.* Ed. Peter Laslett. Cambridge: Cambridge UP, 1988.

Lowenthal, Cynthia. "Portraits and Spectators in the Late Restoration Playhouse: Delarivière Manley's *Royal Mischief.*" *The Eighteenth Century: Theory and Interpretation* 35 (1994): 119–34.

Markley, Robert. *Fallen Languages: Crises of Representation in Newtonian England, 1660–1740.* Ithaca: Cornell UP, 1993.

———.*Two-Edg'd Weapons: Style and Ideology in the Comedies of Etherege, Wycherley, and Congreve.* Oxford: Clarendon, 1988.

Markley, Robert, and Molly Rothenberg. "Contestations of Nature: Aphra Behn's 'The Golden Age' and the Sexualizing of Politics." *Rereading Aphra Behn: History, Theory, and Criticism.* Ed. Heidi Hunter. Charlottesville: U of Virginia P, 1993. 301–21.

Merrens, Rebecca. "'Unman[ned] with thy words': Regendering Tragedy in Manley and Trotter." *Broken Boundaries: Forms of Feminism in Restoration Drama.* Ed. Katherine Quinsey. Lexington: UP of Kentucky, forthcoming.

Pocock, J. G. A. *Virtue, Commerce, and History: Essays on Political Thought and History, Chiefly in the Eighteenth Century.* Cambridge: Cambridge UP, 1985.

Reiss, Timothy J. *The Meaning of Literature.* Ithaca: Cornell UP, 1992.

Williams, Aubrey. *An Approach to Congreve.* New Haven: Yale UP, 1979.

Wood, Ellen Meiksins. *The Pristine Culture of Capitalism: A Historical Essay on Old Regimes and Modern States.* London: Verso, 1991.

Worden, Blair. "The Revolution of 1688–9 and the English Republican Tradition." *The Anglo-Dutch Moment: Essays on the Glorious Revolution and Its World Impact.* Ed. Jonathan I. Israel. Cambridge: Cambridge UP, 1991. 241–77.

# Angry Beauties

## (Wo)Manley Satire and the Stage

*Melinda Alliker Rabb*

In 1696, Delarivier Manley staged her first play, *The Lost Lover, or the Jealous Husband.* Despite its subtitle, the play's actual dramatic focus is not on Smyrna, the jealous husband, but on the character of Belira, a betrayed mistress whose idealization of the power of love ends in frustrated rage. Belira is partly a reworking of the womanly role epitomized by Aphra Behn's Angelica Bianca, the prostitute in *The Rover* (1677). Both characters function as authorial figures positioned (liminally) outside of conventional morality, or rather as transgressors of those moral codes. Significant differences exist, however. Behn, like her predecessor Thomas Killigrew in *Thomaso* (1654, 1664), explores the ironies surrounding the "white angel," a prostitute whose selling of her body proves not very different from the marriage negotiations of respectable women. In Manley's play, the "white Angel" becomes the "angry beauty" (*bella-ira*) who curses and rails against the materialistic world of compromises. Implicit irony becomes explicit satire.

Critical assessment of Manley must contend with the relationship between gender and genre that underlies the study of satire. While novel writing has a strong association with women, satire conventionally has been a understood as the practice of men. Discussion of women and satire typically describes satires *on*, not *by*, women. Felicity Nussbaum's *The Brink of All We Hate*, for example, articulates misogynistic conventions in the work of Dryden, Oldham, Rochester, Swift, Pope, and others. Theories of satire (from the seventeenth century to the present) usually invoke figures of masculine aggression: the "blasts" of the Roman god of winter; the embattled warrior armed with "barbs," or the "piercingly" learned wit. The modern canon of criticism and theory about satire has almost always failed to question its own gendered assumptions and thus has perpetuated notions of a "masculine" genre. Northrop Frye's identification of satire with Saturn, Robert Elliott's study of the magician's ritual-murder, Maynard Mack's various male personae (the *vir bonus*, etc.), Alvin Kernan's biologically male species of writing through which "man has learned to control aggression and manage it to useful ends," David Worcester's celebration of "tragic" satire, Claude Rawson's identification of the satiric speaker with the male machismo of Norman Mailer—all assume male authorship, all yearn for conventional heroism as an ideal, expressing transcendent values and moral norms grounded in a patriarchal humanism.[1] I. D. McKillop is representative: "The Satirist in *His* Own Person" (Erskine-Hill 157). The reliance of these definitions of genre on constructions of gender has gone almost wholly unquestioned in the twentieth-century critical canon. Even Dustin Griffin's recent "re-introduction" to satire—its practice, criticism, and theories—devotes only one paragraph to the question of women as satirists. Their exclusion is asserted summarily as the inevitable consequence of their domesticity and passivity. "[T]he organization of culture has made it difficult for women to write and publish satire . . . because women were long permitted little knowledge of the world outside their own domestic domain; because until recently women have been trained not to develop or display aggressiveness." (Griffin 189–190)

In the seventeenth century, the persistent spelling "satyr" indicates the identification of the genre with a male mythical creature, whose aggressive sexuality frightens the feminine delicacy of nymphs and dryads. In the eighteenth century, Joseph Wharton complained that the potency of Pope's satire made English "depravity and corruption" seem in contrast "emasculated and debased" (*Essay Upon Pope* II.357). Even recent feminist theoretical critiques of satire often assume a male writer attacking "phallic female power" (Stanton 118–19). Yet the writers representing the period of intense satiric creativity during the late seventeenth and early eighteenth centuries included Delarivier Manley, who attempted to make satire womanly, or rather, (wo)Manley. Political and social problems are represented in her work as hinged on gender conflict. While she does not replace the male norm with a female one (to do so would have been impossible and probably inconceivable), she does repeatedly test gendered conventions. Oppositions of Whig and Tory, of aristocratic and nonaristocratic, of domestic and public, and even of moral and immoral are constructed in terms of sexual difference. Even the more strictly literary opposition of differing genres (comedy is "feminine" and tragedy is "masculine") rests on the same crux. These observations are not meant to homogenize her work: the transgressive strategies required to challenge manly writing with (wo)Manley rewriting vary in technique and in success.

Recent interest in Manley has centered on the successful *roman à clef, The New Atalantis* (1709), whose effective satire on the Whigs resulted in Manley's incarceration in the Tower of London.[2] This interest has been bound largely to theories about the rise of the novel. Yet if we compare

*The New Atalantis* as a narrative fiction to Swift's *Gulliver's Travels,* rather than to Richardson's *Pamela* or Defoe's *Moll Flanders,* the need for another theoretical context becomes clear. Manley's persistent attacks on specific political figures, her Tory journalism, and her employment by Harley and her collaboration with Swift in *The Examiner* suggest that she was no incipient lady-novelist. Yet the critical apparatus for analyzing satire is very unaccommodating to a woman writer. One of the purposes of the present essay will be to rethink generic assumptions that, unexamined, have very limited language with which to describe Manley's work. This essay also contends that her development and importance can be understood more fully by starting at the beginning of her career and examining the plays of the 1690s. Much evidence exists to suggest that she thought of herself as a satirist from her earliest efforts, that she, along with her contemporaries, saw a significant relationship between satire and drama, and that experimentation at this time shaped the role she was later to play during Queen Anne's reign.

In 1696, she produced two plays: *The Lost Lover, or the Jealous Husband,* a "Restoration-style" sex comedy that played at Dorset Gardens (Drury Lane) in March, had little success because (Manley claims) the audience knew it was by a woman; *The Royal Mischief,* a heroic tragedy that played at the new theater in Lincoln's Inn Field in April, had a great cast and more success. Manley's rapid production of comedy and tragedy is suggestive: Restoration comedy and heroic tragedy were two sides of the same cultural coin, or, to borrow a related metaphor, "much as a photographic negative stands to its developed print." Thus the plays may be understood as a single effort to determine her position as a writer. They represent her negotiation through conventions available to her; they allude fairly specifically to male and female writers against whom she defines her own authorial stance: Dryden, Rochester, Davenant, Behn, and Philips among them. Perhaps most important, writing for the theater (as opposed to tastefully circulating manuscripts of poems and translations) meant entry into a public forum. Although her plays did not have long runs, their transgressive potential did not go unnoticed. They seemed to have twinged the nerves of her male contemporaries because, within five months, *The Female Wits, or, the Triumvirate of Poets at Rehearsal* (September 1696) appeared, and Manley was embroiled in a satirical war.[3] She was "the chief Character" in this anonymous attack, "the Lady whose play is rehears'd" (preface to the 1704 edition). She became a satiric target because she had violated established dramatic conventions crucial to the reification of male autonomy. "The mere fact that a male author (or authors) felt the need to write a scathing satire against his female counterparts, particularly Delarivere [*sic*] Manley suggests something of the threat that 'female wits' like Manley, Mary Pix, and Catherine Trotter posed to the male literary establishment and, as significantly, to traditional perceptions of authorship as a male prerogative" (Finke 64). Manley had flamboyantly asserted her authorial rights by defying the theatrical management and taking her tragedy, already in rehearsal, away from the Drury Lane theater. She had it performed instead at the rival Lincoln's Inn Fields, where "an extravagantly histrionic villainess, exotic near eastern setting, and complex staging . . . would probably have attracted the veteran actors, even if they had not showed up their rivals by doing the play" (Milhous I.102). Needless to say, *The Female Wits* was written for Drury Lane, a theater with increasingly strong Whig affiliations opposed to Manley's Tory leanings. It is not necessary to overvalue her plays as brilliant stagecraft in order to understand their provocative function. One critic has explained the attack on Manley because "*The Royal Mischief* often seems deliberately overblown, an attempt to outdo heroic tragedy by celebrating its flamboyant excesses" (Finke 65). A different explanation is offered here: the excesses of Manley's first two plays are not celebrations of dramatic traditions, but parodies or ironic reworkings of them. Thus *The Female Wits* is not simply an attack, but a counterattack.

## The 1690s: Authority, Women, Satire

The decade of the 1690s has attracted scholarly attention for many reasons. Critics and historians of various priorities and perspectives independently conclude that these years were "fraught with ambiguity and confusion" and involved in "collective obsession" with respect to at least three areas of debate: political authority according to the earlier model of patriarchal family/state, the "woman controversy," and the nature of satire. These areas are independent in some senses, but very much overlapping in the case of Manley. In 1688, the Glorious Revolution briefly seemed to settle the violent power struggles of the preceding fifty years. (England had nine rulers during the course of the seventeenth century.) But faction and deal making had become permanent features of English government, while uncertainty persisted with respect to succession, religion, peace, and prosperity. The profoundly hierarchical culture of the Renaissance had been "modernized" by regicide, revolution, and economic change. Among the complex differences between Renaissance culture and post-Restoration culture is that hierarchy becomes a less clear and a more anomalous concept. Robert Filmer's *Patriarcha* (1680) desperately attempts to reassert incontrovertible patriarchal order, but even John Locke found his ideas unacceptable. Filmer's *Patriarcha* bases an entire social and moral order on the subjugation of women.[4] Like Restoration satires on women, its vehemence is more likely an indication of actual uncertainty about hierarchical stability. As Stallybrass and White point out in *The Poetics of Transgression* (100–118), the need to define the "other" (in this case, woman/lower order) increases with the need to define "self" (male/higher order). If antitheses remained intact in practice, they would be obvious and in no need of assertion. However, the terms "female," "woman," and "feminine" paradoxically both connoted and enacted change.

Women and the "feminist controversy" constitute an important dynamic during this decade. Women, as is common during times of war, had assumed new roles, and there was no turning back. Two Queens, Elizabeth I and Mary II, had occupied the center of power. Yet England's political troubles were owing partly to the inability or unwillingness of these female bodies to produce a viable heir and make succession simpler. (The mistresses of the kings were also well-known examples of feminine sexual/political power.) By the 1690s, Princess Anne, married and often pregnant, was waiting to assume power and seemed on the way to fulfilling both essential political requirements: to be an upright monarch and to supply the next generation on the throne. "Thy princes shall be nursing mothers" was the theme of her coronation speech. At her side was the ambitious Sarah Jennings Churchill. Other powerful women would soon exert their influence over the throne: principally Abigail Hill Masham and the Duchess of Somerset. Women's education had been suppressed earlier in the century because of "concern about the disturbing effects of women's learning on the family unit and on society at large" (Nussbaum 9). Yet Bathsua Makin's *An Essay to Revive the Antient Education of Gentlewomen, in Religion, Manners, Arts, and Tongues* (1673) is among several predecessors of the most influential appeals for female education in the 1690s: Mary Astell's *A Serious Proposal to the Ladies for the Advancement of their true and greatest interest* (1695) and Daniel Defoe's *Essay on Projects* (1697). Manley had a relatively good education in English and French. She also had observed firsthand the exercise of power, legitimately by her father as governor of Jersey and illegitimately by the king's mistress, Barbara Villiers, the Duchess of Cleveland, for whom Manley served as companion. Before witnessing the corruptions of court life, Manley had been seduced into a bigamous marriage by her cousin, John Manley. She had experienced pregnancy and childbirth.[5] In her life she was no stranger to the use and abuse of power as it affected women in the roles available to them: daughter, wife, mistress, and mother. She thus participated in a significant contradiction to the cultural construction of feminine domesticity in the 1690s by joining the growing number of professional women writers. Paula Backscheider points out, "[T]hat women became writers in significant numbers during this period is now well established. . . . [I]t is often forgotten how insistent the earliest professional women writers were about their stake in what has come to be called 'the public sphere'" (Backscheider 68; see also Cotton 180–212). The years 1695–1700 saw the publication of by far the largest number of works by women (96 titles) than any comparable period during the seventeenth century. And during the 1695–6 theatrical season of Manley's first plays, over one-third of the new plays were by or based on works by women (Backscheider, 71; Cotton, 81–82). Yet these years also saw intensified activity in the male authorship of and critical debate about satire. Is there a relationship?

The modern editors of the California edition of Dryden's works assert that "from the perspective of the 1690s both the word and the idea of satire were fraught with ambiguity and confusion. . . . The problem of what satire should be understood to mean began (and was not resolved) in antiquity; it was intensified, especially in England, when the word and the *genre* revived just a century before Dryden's *Discourse*. Four sorts of confusion can be distinguished. One was generic: is satire verse or drama? A second was etymological: is the word actually 'satire' or 'satyr'? A third was ethical: what is the appropriate character for the imagined speaker of a satire? And a fourth was literary: in what style should a satire be written?" (*Works* 4: 515). A fifth question not raised by Dryden's editors is gender-based: can satire be written by a woman?

Dryden assumes that what he calls "manly satire" is beyond a woman's prerogative. In 1693, he published a translation of Juvenal and Persius, prefacing it with the *Discourse Concerning . . . Satire*. Manley knew the *Discourse* and refers to it in the dedicatory remarks to Part II of *The New Atalantis*. Satire as defined by Dryden might have intimidated a woman writer. He criticizes Donne for "perplexing the Minds of the Fair Sex with nice speculations of Philosophy, when he should engage the Hearts, and entertain them with the softness of Love" (7). Manley, as will become clear, was not one to be easily intimidated; she reverses this condescension by making "the softness of Love" the central satiric metaphor for (human) social corruption.

Dryden's analysis of satire is so insistent on the link between gender and genre as to make its "manliness" seem overwrought or suspect. Feminist critics have understood the need to protect male autonomy as central to the purposes of conventional satire, with which, according to one recent critic, an "incorruptible masculine self" is neurotically affirmed "through the creation and debunking of an image of phallic female power" (Stanton 118–19; Ballaster 219). Dryden's long digression on heroic poetry in the

*Discourse . . . Concerning Satire* contributes tellingly to the same broad cultural project of asserting male autonomy and traditional gender difference. As we shall see, the relationship of heroic tragedy to satire bears directly on Manley's *The Royal Mischief.* Dryden calls tragedy "the most perfect work" of art because it is "the most united" (4: 26). Yet the "comprehend[ing] the whole Beauty . . . [of] a Hero and a Prince" suggests, from our perspective, the need to shore up the actual dissolution of faith in heroes and princes in late-seventeenth-century politics. Dryden recommends classical models for study, a typical maneuver for excluding women, most of whom were uneducated in Latin and Greek.

Dryden moves deftly from heroic to satiric, lifting attributes from the tragic and epic protagonist and applying them to the writer of ironic verbal attacks. Masculine metaphors describe the satirist's skill. The sword of wit, for example, symbolizes potency, pleasure, and control: "Yet there is still a vast difference between the slovenly butchering of a Man, and the fineness of the stroak that separates the Head from the Body, and leaves it standing in its place" (71). In the *Life of Lucian,* he writes of satiric irony as the "keen and shining weapon in [Lucian's] hand; it glitters in the Eyes of those it kills, . . . his greatest enemies are not butchered by him, but fairly slain: they must acknowledge the Hero in the Stroak" (20: 221). At times the successful satiric thrusts are metaphorized distinctly as sexual gratification. Dryden explains his preference for Juvenal over Horace in these terms: "[T]he delight which Horace gives me is but languishing. . . . He may Ravish other Men; but I am too stupid and insensible to be tickl'd" (4: 63). "[T]he Reader [of Horace] is uneasie, and unsatisfi'd; he . . . desires something which he finds not" (4: 65). In comparison, "Juvenal is of a more vigorous and Masculine Wit, he gives me as much Pleasure as I can bear: He fully satisfies my Expectation."[6] Juvenal's "impetuosity" and "lively agitation" "create in us an Appetite of Reading him." If he has a fault, "'tis that he is sometimes too luxuriant." Yet, Dryden concludes, this luxuriance will "contribute to the Pleasure of the Reader" and make "his Transports . . . the greater" (4: 64–65).

Dryden's history of satire is construed as a race between three poets who assume the roles of Virgilian hero-athletes. His favorite, Juvenal, "ride[s] first in Triumph. *Alter Amazoniam pharetem; plenamque Sagittus Treiaiis, late quom circumplecititur auro Balteus, & tereti subnestit Fibula gemma.*" He is given "the quiver of an Amazonian Dame" (surely an image of female phallic power) to "gird his manly side." More piercing weapons become his and they are explicitly taken from the woman warrior who might threaten his dominance. Dryden disapproves of anything like burlesque because it "gives . . . a boyish kind of pleasure" that is "not so proper for manley satire" (80). John Oldham writes similarly: "strait to the thrusts I go,/And pointed Satyr runs him through and through" (Oldham, *Works*, 2: 132). Dryden compares Oldham and himself to Virgil's Nisus and Eurylas (*Aeneid* v.315–39); "To the Memory of Mr. John Oldham" (2: 175). A race between heroes again becomes the metaphor for competition between satirists, echoing the competition for fame between Horace and Juvenal. Milton images the male weapon of satire which "ought . . . too strike high and adventure dangerously" (*Apology for Smectymnuus*, 1642). The Earl of Mulgrave's *Essay on Poetry* (2nd edition, 1691) also stresses the fine thrust which "Distinguishes [male] Satyr from a [female] Scold." (*Prose Works* 1: 916; Spingarn 2: 296).

We have seen that satire was in some respects a genre that did protest too much about its manliness, that was unsure of itself and consequently may have presented an open challenge to an angry and politically committed woman like Manley. Its frequent misogyny may well indicate its own vulnerability and confusion about the (male) norm. The "lexicographical array" of possibilities for the identity of satire/satyr meant (and this is a crucial qualification) that not every writer concurred with Dryden's views or principally used metaphors of male autonomy and potency to describe this problematic *genre*. Swift, a notable exception, used the now-famous figures of the bandied ball and the trick mirror—images of dispersal, randomness, refraction, and deflection—that is, images of disunity. Dryden had downplayed the idea of satire as a mirror: "For in English, to say Satire, is to mean Reflection, & we use that word in the worst sense" (48). But Manley is attracted to this metaphor, and subtitles her first narrative satire, *The History of Queen Zarah*, "a Looking-Glass for ———." This attitude begins to suggest the collegiality between Swift and Manley in 1711–14 when they collaborated as Tory satirists. Manley expresses her dissent from Dryden's ranking of classical satirists (Juvenal and Horace as best and next-best). She claims for herself the model of Varronian or Menippean satire in the preface to *The New Atalantis*, Part 2: "The New Atalantis seems, my Lord, to be written like Varronian Satyrs, on different Subjects, Tales, Stories and Characters of Invention, after the Manner of Lucian, who copy'd from Varro" (Koster 526–27). Here too she warrants comparison with Swift (and Rabelais). While it may be objected that this choice is still a male satirist, in point of fact, no surviving works of Varro or Menippus exist. It is appropriate that a woman should ally herself with the absent satirist, projecting into "his" silence, her own voice, and finding in his absence her authorial presence. The Varronian/Menippean qualities of Manley's satire become clearest in work of 1705–14. Her knowledge of Dryden's critical views on, as well as his practice of, comedy, tragedy, and satire begins earlier.

The final preparatory step to be taken before examining in detail Manley's plays will be to clarify the assumptions about the relationship between satire and the theater in the 1690s. Dryden's editors state the obvious: "The association, or confusion, of satire with drama takes two chief forms: a) satire and comedy, and b) satire and tragedy." Horace allies satire with Old Greek Comedy, exemplified by Aristophanes. Traditions of wit, laughter, exposure of vice, topicality, and local reference forget his association. Etymologically, satire was thought to have arisen out of the Greek satyr play, which Aristotle associates with (and Milton later says) was "borne out of tragedy." Both were "goat songs": the sacrificial animal of Greek ritual (trag-oidea) and the half-human creature of Roman myth (satyr) promise human transcendence of the order of nature.[7] These learned theories would not, of course, be part of a woman's education. Manley comments in the Prologue to *The Lost Lover* that men think women should "to Fringe and Tea confine their Sense." However, her allusions to Dryden, Rochester, Milton, and others document her awareness of various kinds of satiric/dramatic discourse. During the "absolutely unprecedented" 1695–96 theater season (unprecedented because of its representation of women's work), Manley's two contributions are the "negative" and "photographic print" of comedy and tragedy, and may now be considered as experiments in satiric authority. In *The Lost Lover* she rejects the model of the woman writer epitomized by Katherine Philips, the "chaste Orinda," making her the object of satire. But she allies herself with Aphra Behn, the outspoken professional. In *The Royal Mischief,* she ironically rewrites her source (Sir Charles Chardin's *Travels through Persia*) and the conventions of heroic tragedy as epitomized by Davenant's *Siege of Rhodes* and Dryden's *Conquest of Granada.* The play pushes the limits of the tragedy into a mock-heroic attack on male autonomy.

## Satire and Comedy: *The Lost Lover*

Comedy would have seemed a more congenial genre to a woman writer. English playwrights traditionally had been more willing to foreground a Beatrice, Rosalind, or Portia, rather than to allow Ophelia or Cordelia to upstage Hamlet or Lear. Comedy's apparent domesticity made it seem "lighter" and more "feminine" than the weighty griefs of tragedy. The comic heroine's transgressive behavior is associated with the marriage plot, not principally with matters of state. With its focus on weddings and its ultimate reaffirmation of the *status quo,* comedy permitted its female characters more license and more temporary independence. The comic plot complications of *The Lost Lover* involve the marriages of three women: Olivia, who is recently married; Lady Younglove, who is widowed and about to remarry; and Mariana, her daughter, who is ready for marriage. A fourth woman, Orinda, is the vehicle for satire on the writer

Katherine Philips, who was famous (here ironically so) for her long and faithful marriage. But it is a fifth woman, Belira, whose personality dominates the play. Her function is partly to place Manley in the tradition of Aphra Behn, whose character Angelica Bianca she resembles. But Belira functions beyond mere allusion and shows Manley developing a distinctive perspective as a satirist. Manley, who delighted in wordplay on names (especially on her own), changes Behn's prototype of the ironic "white angel" to a specific figure of satire: "angry beauty," or perhaps "beautiful rage," a feminized version of invective and accusation.

Manley's self-consciousness as a woman writer is evident throughout *The Lost Lover.* Yet disclaimers and apologies in the Preface, Prologue, and Epilogue are characterized by the kind of indirection and contradiction that are typical of her developing irony. "I am now convinced writing for the stage is no proper way for a Woman, to whom all Advantages but meer Nature are refused," she offers. She gestures at the conventional disclaimer of the play's origin in "some idle Hours." Yet her statement "there is a Tragedy of mine rehearsing" suggests her refusal to give up her aspiring career. (She wrote six plays, two of which have been lost.[8]) When "the curtain's drawn . . . by a lady's hand," different critical standards apply: "[I]f our play succeeds, [the men] will surely say,/Some private Lover helped her on her way." She imagines the male audience flirting in the stalls and boxes instead of paying attention to the performance on stage: "[A]sk not this Mask to sup, not that to Show/ Some Face. . . ." Even the playwright herself ultimately will be viewed as a sexual object by her begrudging male audience: "Tho' in Private would be sworn her Lover,/Scarce one the Friend in Public will discover." Irony (she is, in a sense, the "lost" lover) is a sign of tenacity. The claim of heroism refers to Behn, who similarly represents herself as writer—"the Heroin me"—in the Preface to *The Dutch Lover.*

Manley's comedy positions her in relation to the traditions of women's writing she inherited from the preceding generation. Feminist critics have described the importance of the two opposing models established in the 1660s and 1670s: first, the transgressive and sexually daring example of "Astrea" (Behn); second, the modest lyrical verse of the discreet "matchless Orinda" (Philips).[9] Both are, as Backscheider rightly cautions, "author functions" rather than knowable women, by the 1690s. In the Preface to *The Lost Lover,* Manley says: "Had I confined my Sense to some short Song of Phillis, a tender Billet, and the freedom of agreeable Conversation, I had still preserv'd the character of a witty Woman." The implicit rejection of Philips becomes entirely explicit in the play's unpleasant ridicule of Orinda. Philips had been praised for maintaining the modest privacy "appropriate" to women. For Manley's Orinda, domesticity becomes total self-absorption. It becomes an egoistic refusal to risk involvement in public or social issues. Philips had celebrated female friendship; Manly's Orinda cares only for men. The idea of circulating manuscripts instead of publishing is demeaned as dilettantism. Philips's literary advisor and mentor Cotteral is satirized as a Sir Courtall, an indiscriminate woman-izer. In this travesty of "circulating," he is eventually (and easily) seduced away from Orinda. Orinda herself makes a ridiculous exit. She rushes off in a huff of (sexual) frustration, awkward rhetoric, and bad poetry: "So slighting, she has debauch'd him from me. O I can't hold my Muse! Muse go lament the Misfortune. For to Love is Noble Frailty, but Poor Sin/ When once we fall to love, unlov'd again." In the play's final pairing-off of characters, the "matchless Orinda" is literally without a match, i.e., alone, at the end.

The spectacle of one woman attacking another is not particularly pleas-ant. Philips's reputation for virtue and marital happiness was impossible for Manley to emulate and may well have rankled the younger woman, a victim of bigamy left to write for her bread. However, Manley's uncom-promising rejection of the model of female domesticity is also under-standable in light of her public aspirations. Beyond personal animosity, the reductive portrayal of Philips seems to have been a decisive step Manley had to take on her way to becoming a satirist. She insists on reframing her lack of success as a playwright in terms that construe her heroically: "like a Hero, not contented with Applause from lesser Con-quests, I find myself . . . disappointed." She is a "fair Warrior" making her "first attack." Losing one battle for public praise will only "make [her] say with a Grecian Hero, *I had been lost, if I had not been lost.*"

Manley also works out her relationship to Behn, especially to Behn's two *Rover* plays, with their ironic analysis of courtship and marriage, frank sexuality, and cynicism about love. Against Philips/Orinda and Cotteral/Courtall, we find Behn's seductive Wilmore recurring, along with echoes of Angelica Bianca in Belira, Julia in Olivia, and Hellena in Marina. In *The Rover,* the prostitute's public sale of her body is likened both to Behn's sale of her works and to the sale of marriageable female flesh in the nuptial marketplace. The boundaries between illicit and proper are suspended. Manley takes an arguably darker view of marriage. It is "fatal," a noose, a living death: Olivia's "father buried [her] in a rich old Merchant's arms." Even outdoors, Olivia is "stifled" by the mask she is forced by her husband to wear.

Act I invokes Restoration stage conventions. Wildman (a Dorimant/ Horner figure) plots to seduce the good Olivia and thereby cuckold the jealous Smyrna. The aristocratic rake thus attempts to outwit the bour-geois merchant. Yet, significant differences manifest themselves early in the play. When the young unmarried women have their scene of feminine chatter, they forgo polite "agreeable conversation" in order to gossip about sex in the manner of Rochester's Artemisia and Chloe. The world invoked is one of promiscuous sexuality, of women "relish[ing] country sparks, after being cloy'd with Town Beaux." When "undistinguishing Night had reduc'd the Sense of Seeing, into that of Touching," various couplings occur. A footman brings information to a fine lady, and "she interrupted him in the midst, to tell him he had a Pretty Mouth, which cou'd be better employ'd than in delivering his message." Another woman is "courted . . . for awhile" but wantonly asks her suitor "if they cou'd not love without marrying." Yet another woman has "granted . . . [sexual] favours in an open Calash, whilst her Husband drove it." In this corrupt world, even an "innocent maiden" like Marina is knowing. Marina eventually will receive her fortune and marry Wilmore. She should be, but is not, the center of the plot. Significantly, the "happy" couple have very little dialogue together. The virtuous Olivia, whose marriage seems to be highlighted by the play's subtitle, is sympathetically but coolly portrayed. Her characterization raises the disturbing idea that her self-control, in the face of Wildman's youthful ardor, is really numbness or lack of sexuality. She is impervious because she is "buried" in the tomb of Smyrna's arms. She is muffled, masked, and not fully animated or alive. The most powerful role is given to the transgressive character, Belira.

Belira is an intelligent, sexually experienced woman who understands the centrality of sex and money as motives for behavior. A capacity for real passion makes her reckless. Other characters may scheme and plot for "love." Elaborate stage business revolves around comic scenes with a charlatan/conjuror and Wildman disguised as a doctor, as they conspire against the jealous Smyrna. But these deceptions leave no lasting scars and have no significant consequences. Olivia remains true to Smyrna; Smyrna remains the same unattractive stereotype of a rich old man; Wildman goes on the next pursuit. The temptation to see parallels between Wildman and Belira (he, too, is energetic, imaginative, scheming, and at risk of losing a lover) must end in difference. His words to Olivia—"Do I deserve no reward for all my unwearied hours of Love?"—ring hollow. In the preceding scene, he has castigated Wilmore for his "virtue" as a lover. Belira is an idealist, while Wildman is a cynical egoist: "What I have suffered . . . this is mortifying one" are typical utterances. He does not believe Olivia's goodness to be genuine; he can explain her resistance to adultery with him only by suspecting that she has another lover.

Belira's parallels to Angelica Bianca are more apt. Like Angelica, she seems at first a controlling figure of strength who manipulates the fates of Lady Younglove, Marina, and Wilmore until Act V. She gives herself to Wilmore (as Angelica does to Behn's Wilmore) for love that she mistakenly believes transcends typical transactions between men and women. The play's bitterest moment is the disabusement of this belief:

> Bel. [H]ow often hast thou told, thou couldst forever love me?
> Wil. I told you that I cou'd, not that I wou'd.

Belira inevitably suffers for the vulnerability incurred by her own desire for gratification, emotionally and physically. She has glimpsed an ideal, very rare in the world of the play, that reality will not sustain. Olivia, whose pragmatism has numbed her to desire, embodies central social virtues. In contrast, Belira, who is fully alive to pleasure and pain, must be marginalized.

Belira has a formidable sense of self: "Thou hast lov'd me a little, but thou knowest me less," she tells Wilmore. She is given to heroic utterance—"I would divide the world"—that jars with the comic world of love intrigue. She is too earnest for "truth, mark that word," and the crushing of her ideal unleashes her "Manl(e)y" rage. The climactic scene of her confrontation with Wilmore reverses conventional gender roles. To Wilmore's taunt of jealousy, she compares herself to Othello, whose racial "otherness" makes him an interesting choice. When Wilmore's protests, "You were not us'd to fly my arms," Belira mocks him for exhibiting "the sorry cunning of our sex": "Just so does a wife when her husband has caught her false. He gives her his sword, and she laughs at the idea that he might 'turn hero': 'Ha, ha, ha—Let me laugh . . . ; go on, I'm in the vein of an Audience; let me hear . . . how well thou canst turn Woman.'"

In Act V, which is full of disturbing speeches, Wilmore declares himself ready to sacrifice wealth for Marina, yet he tells Belira: "We live not in those Romantick constant days, where their first Mistress was their last. I lov'd you once, and still esteem you, but Vows that made in Love are writ in Sand."

The marriages all are bleak compromises: Lady Younglove and Sir Courtall are ridiculous caricatures of aging desire represented without affectionate indulgence; Marina gets her money and marries Wilmore who believes love is "writ in Sand"; Olivia remains "buried" alive in Smyrna's arms. The disappearance of love is, of course, the general theme of the play's title and ironic subtitle. The jealous husband Smyrna is, in a sense, the only character who has not lost his lover, although such love has been portrayed as death. The "lost lover" could apply to Wildman (lost to Olivia), Wilmore (lost to Belira), Sir Courtall (lost to Orinda). In the most crucial sense, the "lost lover" is the failed idea of human faithfulness and fulfillment in the play.

*The Lost Lover* is an angry, brittle play, and perhaps this is the reason why it did not succeed as a comedy. The figure of the angry beauty who curses a world of destroyed ideals, whose personal rage expands to a satiric perspective broadly judgmental of a corrupt society, strains the decorum of comedy and pushes it toward satire. Manley does not seem invested in giving depth to any of the other characters. Sympathy would undermine the satiric impulse. A work that Manley alludes to frequently is Rochester's 1679 satiric poem, "A Letter from Artemisia in the City to Chloe in the Country" (Vieth 104–12). Its jaded view of sexual relations, its caustic portrayal of knaves and fools, and its placement of the satiric voice in a female speaker clearly appealed to Manley. The poem's brief representation of Corinna seems pertinent to the play: Corinna does more bad than good, yet the moment of abandonment, when her witty lover "made his jest and went away," complicates the poem's ironies in ways that Manley emulates.

## Satire and Tragedy: *The Royal Mischief*

The Belira-figure of the transgressive woman reappears in the character Homais, the protagonist of Manley's next play. Manley's love of wordplay on names suggests several French-English puns on Homais: *homme*-ly, because Homais in part represents Man-ley the author and because she attempts to usurp the masculine domain of political power, or perhaps more sardonically, *homme-est,* because, in a patriarchal culture, man is, and woman is not. Or perhaps the name is an ironic counterpart to the famous epitome of masculine heroism, Almanzor (all-man-zor) from Dryden's *Conquest of Granada.* The angry beauty thus becomes the manly heroine whose function is to mock yet another set of conventions before meeting her inevitable demise. Like Belira's, her final scene is one of "rail[ing]," and her final speech is a curse.

Young, beautiful, rich, she married the Prince of Libardian, who is old, unattractive, and impotent. As the play begins, he is just returning from war, during which time he has imposed a strict confinement on his wife. Homais bitterly describes it:

> Yon proud pampered prelate bore the sway,
> Denied me leave to pass the castle-gates
> And suffered none to have access, but just
> My women, and my slaves. Hence 'twas I found
> My servants were his Creatures, my guards
> My gaolers, and himself the master spy.

She has become an object, relentlessly under the gaze of a possessive and controlling authority—husband or priest. The "tragic" struggle for power in which she becomes embroiled renders sex (passion) and politics (liberty) indistinguishable. She is "made passionate, by want of liberty." The suffocating restrictions of Olivia's marriage in *The Lost Lover* cannot be tolerated by Homais, for whom "resistance but augments desire." Homais's pent-up energy ricochets within the castle walls, igniting explosive emotions and ruining lives. Reckless sex (she drugs her husband so that she can make love to Levan Dadian, her husband's nephew, while promising sex to Ismael, a former lover, as a reward for political favors, etc.) affects other characters as well and begins to suggest the kind of promiscuity that later serves Manley as a metaphor for social/political disorder in *The New Atalantis.* The emotional, rhetorical, and literal explosions of *The Royal Mischief* arguably have the heroic form itself as their ultimate target. Manley avoids the (outright or implied) misogyny of conventional heroic tragedy. Instead she exposes its limitations. Some background on the relationship between tragedy, satire, and gender will place Manley's experimentation in context.

*The Lost Lover* and *The Royal Mischief* were produced within months of each other, and their composition must have been almost simultaneous. Textual evidence suggests an imaginative closeness, despite the apparent opposition between domestic comedy and heroic tragedy, the "photograph" and its "negative." Until 1696, the only English heroic tragedy produced and written by a woman was Aphra Behn's *Abdelazer* (1670). Why did women not write heroic tragedy? Traditionally, it was, like satire, a male genre. Comedy represents the domestic world of love, sexual relations, and marriage; its inverted world temporarily allows a young, intelligent woman new freedoms of self-assertion and influence. Tragedy, on the contrary, represents the public realm of war, power relations, and government dominated by kings and other patriarchal nobility. These gendered distinctions have a long history in English criticism.[10] Feminist criticism has challenged the validity of these categories, arguing, as Dympna Callaghan does, that "all tragedies are, to some degree, domestic" (Callaghan 36). "[T]he social formation of marriages and families within tragedy has been ignored in favour of more abstract themes. . . . It is indeed remarkable that although representations of marriage and kinship have invested in them the whole weight of society's attempts to inculcate moral and social order, they are not traditionally regarded by critics as fit subjects for tragedy" (35). Conventional tragic plots construct woman as both necessary yet marginal to the drama. A woman typically is involved as a crucial cause of man's misfortune/transgression, although she is not central to his (or the audience's) cathartic epiphany. She may die, but her demise is no guarantee of transcendence. Familiar Shakespearean examples include Ophelia, Lady Macbeth, Desdemona, and Gertrude. The status of tragedy has been justified by its "universal" significance. However, Catherine Belsey and others have observed that the "universal" significance of tragedy depends on a male norm and that its "universal" meanings ignore constructions of gender difference (Belsey 9). Critical respect for tragedy has been too willing to leave its assumptions unexamined. I. A. Richards claims that tragedy is "invulnerable" and "the most . . . all ordering experience known" (247). Other traditional critics similarly praise tragedy in masculinist terms as ineffably edifying, transcending the specifics of historical context, rising above socioeconomic realities, and defying even the power of rational analysis: tragedy gives "an intuition of the meaning of suffering . . . inaccessible to reason," "its perfection as the instrument by which the artist reveals a vision of man's relation to the forces of evil . . . affords a basis for renewed acceptance of life"; it is a "system of cause and effect which explains the suffering of the individual by linking it to the cosmos" and views "*him* [the hero] moving to measures played above, or outside, our normal space and time."[11] All of this, to borrow Whitehead's vague but long-respected definition of tragedy, supposedly demonstrates "the remorseless working of things . . . the inevitableness of destiny" as defined by the "pilgrim fathers" of the modern imagination, the "great tragedians of ancient Athens" (Whitehead 15–16). Such abstract critical adulation suggests its own antithesis: that acceptance of tragic convention is neither "inevitable," "inaccessible to reason," nor "invulnerable" to revisionist (feminist) thinking.

Manley's *Royal Mischief* is a satirical revision of tragedy and heroism, a female mock-heroic, limited by its historical context and framed without benefit of feminist theory. Homais's transgressions dominate the play. The possibility of her transcendence is thwarted by the play's insistence on sexuality and physicality. Its patriarchal "cosmos" intractably resists the demands of female desire. Homais is stabbed in the back by the Prince while she is embracing her lover. The conventional intimations of reborn political order that end most tragedies, embodied in figures like Fortinbras and Edmund, are denied by *The Royal Mischief*. Corpses accumulate, until Manley dismisses the remaining characters with the stage direction, "They all leave." Only the aging, impotent Prince endures, an image of sterility and oppression.

Behn's influence on Manley is instructive. Behn's *Abdelazer* draws for its source on an earlier play called *Lust's Dominion or, the Lascivious Queen: A Tragedy* (ca. 1600; London, 1657). *Lust's Dominion* is a transparently anti-Catholic and anti-Spanish work whose most interesting feature is its conflation of sexuality and politics as expressions of power. Transgressions of race and family occur while Eleazor the Moor "wade[s] to a Crown through blood" (III.iv). The Spanish monarchy is weakened by the royal family's sexual incontinence. "Blush not, my boy, be bold . . . like me thy mother" (II.vi), the Queen tells her son. The play asserts rather than analyzes its conflated categories. Love does not complicate lust. The lascivious queen commits adultery, incest, and murder, yet survives and is pardoned. This moral sleight-of-hand is accomplished by a final act of marginalization. Her sexuality (i.e., power) is simply removed: "I'll now repose myself in peaceful rest,/And flye unto some solitary residence;/Where I'll spin out the remnant of my life,/In true contrition for my past offenses" (V.ii). The interesting centrality of sexual desire to the tragic plot gives way to anti-Catholicism, xenophobia, and misogyny.

Behn rewrote *Lust's Dominion* as *Abdelazer* at a time when heroic tragedy was already on the wane, yet the play enjoyed a long-standing popularity and was revived to celebrate the opening of the new theater in Drury Lane, where *The Royal Mischief* would play a few months later. Behn's alterations of her source result in a more dramatically satisfying play: the dialogue is improved; the characters (given the incredibilities of heroic convention), more credible. But the most pertinent change is the representation of the Queen: she is still "lascivious," but her sexuality is frustrated rather than grotesquely satisfied. Behn insists on the exploitation of female desire by the Moor Abdelazer, who feels nothing for the Queen (who passionately loves him) and only wishes to use her to gain political power. Thus the potential alliance between two "others" of gender and race—woman and moor—is rendered problematic (as it is in *Oroonoko* between woman and slave). Unlike *Lust's Dominion,* both Abdelazer's and the Queen's transgressions meet violent death. As the only extant heroic tragedy by a woman before Manley's play, *Abdelazer* does not make the play a woman's tragedy. While feminine desire briefly disrupts patriarchal order, the evil Queen lusts without compelling motivation, violating conventional boundaries of marriage, motherhood, religion, and race. The spectacle of her transgressions and punishment may account significantly for the play's popularity during a period when English political stability was repeatedly threatened by monarchical incontinence. Unlike Manley, Behn does not establish an ironic perspective from which to view the "heroic" relationship between desire and power.

Manley found opportunities for ironic revision of heroic stage conventions in Dryden's plays as well. Dryden was familiar with "feminine" romances by women writers whose narratives proffered "all for love." Dryden's editors attempt to minimize the influence: "For plot materials Dryden drew largely upon several French heroic romances of Madeleine de Scudery, but masculine vigor and violence sustain and often surcharge his dramatic action" (Nettleton 7). The introduction of domestic pathos into *All for Love*, in the famous scene with Antony's children, temporarily "unmans" Antony and must be rejected. With "masculine vigor and violence" to "sustain" them, characters like Antony escape the compromises of a lasting relationship. The super hero who is "all man" is epitomized by Almanzor (All-man-zor) in the *Conquest of Granada*. Like a seventeenth-century Rocky or Rambo, he flexes his actual and metaphorical muscles through the *Conquest*, Parts 1 and 2. He and other pumped-up heroes with large egos vie and bond with other men. A princess or other "love interest" is talked of and to, but initiates little. Almahide is Boabdelin's prize in Part 1 of the *Conquest* and Almanzor's prize in Part 2. (Similarly, Orazia, the Inca's daughter, is literally the "gift" demanded by Montezuma in *The Indian Queen* I.i.) In both instances the woman is "bestowed" by someone else and submits to patriarchal notions of duty. Almahide's heroic action is to subdue herself, not others. Codes of honor entangle her in convoluted rationalizations for why Almanzor may be "commanded" to live. Passion is disembodied and de-sexualized in talk of "love which sisters may to brothers bear" (V.iii.281) and the "soul's far better part." Self-sacrifice and obedience, not the fulfillment of desire, prevail. Even in Part 2, when Almahide is widowed and all obstacles between her and Almanzor are removed, she remains without independent passion and must be required to remarry. Love proves "manhood," not feminine desire, which remains, despite the excesses of heroic utterance, unspeakable. "Bad" characters, like Lyndaraxa, coolly calculate seduction. "Good" women rest (living or dead) upon "the cold cold bed of honour." In striking contrast, when Manley's Homais warmly discusses the experience of orgasm, remembers the details of her first love-making, and goes behind an onstage screen to make love, a long tradition of representation is being altered.

In attempting to rewrite and re-politicize these conventions, Manley discovers new possibilities for the female satirist to attack not women but abuses of women. Dryden explains Aristotle's ranking of tragedy as "the most perfect Work of Poetry" in terms of male autonomy: "[I]t is the most United" (*Discourse Concerning Satire, Works* 4: 26). The true hero, emulated in Dryden's drama, can proclaim with Almanzor, "I alone am king of me" (I.i.206). Further, the heroic action is always predicated on war, the battles of which were fought "man to man" and "shield to shield" in Homeric style, without the impersonal and modern intrusion of gunpowder explosions and "limbs flying through the air" that Swift would condemn in *Gulliver's Travels* (see Rawson, *Satire and Sentiment* 48–66). Satire, on the other hand, appealed through variety more than unity— Dryden's *Discourse Concerning Satire* cites Virgil: "[W]e offer the smoking

Entrails in great Platters" (36). Manley's *Royal Mischief* seems to borrow ironically from both of these traditions: in Act V, the "heroic" Osman is shot from a cannon (so much for male autonomy and hand-to-hand combat), and his "smoking relics" are gathered up by his wife. Paralleling the confinement and destructive exaggeration of Homais's emotions in Act I, Osman's body is crammed into the narrow circumference of a cannon and physically blown apart; the play offers an alternative to Dryden's idea of "great" men "scatter[ing their] Maker's image through the land." Manley had written in similar images of disjunction of women's revisionary authorship of "serious" plays: female playwrights [Manley, Trotter, Pix, etc.] "snatch'd a Lawrel [men] thought their Prize" and "their Empire have disjoyn'd."[12] The "burning piece[s]" of Osman serve as an emblem of Manley's metaphorical disruption of male autonomy. Whereas Dryden had urged the "fine stroak" and abjured "the slovenly butchering of a man," *The Royal Mischief* insists on violent disruption.[13] Just as Dryden drew his heroic plots from the women writers of French romance, Manley would later borrow from de Scudery and D'Aulnoy in *The New Atalantis* and *Memoirs of Europe* (1709, 1710). However, the explicit source for *The Royal Mischief* is *The Travels of Sir John Chardin into Persia, through the Black Sea, and the country of Colchis*.[14] "Travels" were another predominately "male" kind of writing. Soldiers, knights, diplomats, and adventurers may undertake battles, quests, journeys, and expeditions. But women, like Homer's Penelope, were more likely to stay at home. (Romance heroines might travel, as exemplified by Madame D'Aulnoy's *Travels through Spain*. Lady Mary Wortley Montagu was a notable exception among actual women when she traveled through Turkey and wrote her famous letters a decade after Manley's play.) Manley knew only too well the confinement suffered by women and the difficulty of merely getting from London to Exeter (see Morgan, *A Woman of No Character* 70–71).

Manley may have read Chardin in the original French or in the translation published in 1686. In her play, she radically transforms the historical particulars of a passage from the travels by combining it with the fictional constructions of heroism and tragedy. The power struggles of the Persian court, narrated by Chardin, suggest ironic parallels to the hostile factions quarreling in England: "and certainly 'tis a thing equally to be observ'd and wonder'd at, That such small and inconsiderable Kingdoms should continually produce such Tragick revolutions" (*Travels* 133). The "Barbarous" behavior described by Chardin occurs between 1658 and 1680, years of revolution, political unrest, and changing leadership in England. "This happen'd in the year 1659," writes Chardin, "at what Time the Turkish Basha had no sooner turn'd his Back, but the Grandees of Imiretta, out of their natural Treachery and Inconstancy, refus'd to obey their new King . . ." (143). So did the "new [restored] King" of England, one year later, encounter continuing faction. Chardin's account of Persian civil wars, jealousies with neighboring countries, and especially problems within the royal family should have twinged some political nerves. Brothers, uncles, cousins, and illegitimate children vie for the throne of "Mingrelia" and complicate relations with the kingdom of "Imiretta." Like Whigs and Tories, "the Prime Ministers of Mingrelia and Imiretta had continual Quarrels with one another," making political stability impossible. Writing less than a decade after the "Glorious Revolution," Manley did not need to travel to find local analogues to the scandalous politics represented in her source.

Chardin's account of Persian government contains a subtext of sexual politics upon which Manley expands significantly. Love intrigues are woven into the history of power struggles between male rulers. However, for Chardin, women are merely desirable objects to be conveyed from one male possessor to another, in the traditional patriarchal manner. The implicit and explicit moral of his stories is that women are trouble: their allurements "make" men do crazy things, and their sexual/political longings end in disaster. They begin to seem interchangeable in the *Travels*. Manley's Homais draws on hints from at least two characters in Chardin (Darejan, Chilake, Chikakite—all referring to the wife of the Prince of Libardian— and Sistan Darejan—wife of Bacrat, Prince Imiretta). Manley, herself a victim of bigamy and a former companion to a king's mistress, would eventually narrate a series of transgressive relationships in the "foreign" country of Atalantis as a satire on Whig government. In Chardin, she encountered a culture in which polygamy and remarriage without widowhood occurred. To Chardin, this culture is incomprehensibly "other" and he attempts to naturalize it with orthodox Western moralizing. Manley reacts to its "otherness" by focusing on the transgressive woman, giving her depth of motivation and character.

The figures in Chardin engage in intrigue while remaining loveless and flat. Characters are easily confused with one another—several "wicked women" and several noblemen with their eyes "pull'd out" appear but have no individuating qualities or dialogue. One "barbarous" tragedy begins to look like another and Chardin writes of them "altogether": "These Barbarous Tragedies happen'd in the Year 1667, from which time till the Year 1672, there fell out a Hundred more of the same Countries, altogether as Infamous and Inhumane; and therefore I pass 'em over in silence, as being Stories rather frightful than pleasing to the Ear."

Chardin narrates with relative equanimity. Occasional exclamations against violence and corruption punctuate but do not deter his journey, which moves on to the next place and the next events. He is able to distance himself (and his implied reader) from any threatening implications of what he has witnessed by retreating to moral platitude in which "Justice" prevails "always": "I shall only add . . . that the Traytor Cotzia was himself also Treacherously slain. . . . By which we may find there is a Visible Providence in the modern Histories of these Impious People; upon whome Heav'n still inflicted such severe and speedy Justice: while the Murderers are always Assassinated, and with those Circumstances which plainly demonstrate that God hath a Hand in it, and made the one of his Instruments to punish the other" (147).

*The Royal Mischief* transforms its source. Manley departs from Chardin in many significant particulars, creating a highly ironic work. Chardin clearly frames "these Tragedies" as a man's story of a fallen hero, Levan Dadian: "The most Famous Prince that ever Mingrelia had, since it revolted from the King of the Imiretta, was *Levan Dadian.* . . . He was Valiant, Generous, a Person of great Wit, indifferently just and more happy in his Undertakings. He made War upon his Neighbours and vanquish'd em all; and no question but he would have made an excellent Prince, had he been born in a better Country. But the Custom of his Country of Marrying several Wives, and those near Relations, was that which transported him to such Excesses as render'd him unworthy of all Encomiums" (133).

In Manley's hands, the Persian conflicts become the story of a clearly individualized woman's desire for freedom and the price she pays for it. Homais transgresses the heroic code. Despite her conniving and wrongdoing, she is a surprisingly genuine and compelling character. In contrast to the traveler's movement along the open road, Homais's actions are bound by the cloying world of the guarded castle. Her isolation is "psychological" as well as physical. All of her companions misperceive her, and Manley is careful to provide background information about Homais's former girlish innocence and its loss. Unlike the "types" of evil women in most heroic plays, Homais is the "artist-figure," even if her creations end in disaster. Unlike characters who simply *are* wicked, Homais becomes wicked, or so Manley makes us believe, in response to a world that has few constructive options.

When the play begins, her relationships consist of an ineffectual former lover (Osman), a cynical seducer (Osman's brother Ismael), an impotent husband (the Prince of Libardian), and a eunuch (Acmat). Typically, the eunuch Acmat misunderstands her discontent; he assumes, in conventional heroic terms, that she imagines a "second Alexander," a "glorious busy hero" who will carry her off. Homais corrects him:

> Dull, dull, eunuch,
>
> . . .
>
> How far would'st thou extend thy busy search,
> Hunt round the world for airy heroes,
> When the reality's at home? (I.i.)

One of her distinctive functions is to debunk trite heroic rhetoric as "airy" emptiness. She also insists on the human need for actual, not metaphorical or metaphysical, satisfaction. Her beauty, intelligence, and energy prove to be a volatile combination in a world in which women are supposed to react, and not to act independently.

The intensity and recklessness of Homais's will, like Almanzor's "boundless" egoism in *The Conquest of Granada,* has liabilities. Its sexual nature privileges primal needs over abstract heroic motivations of honor and duty. She wants a man worthy of her. Until the end of Act III, Homais remains a sympathetic character, daring and successful:

> Now could one ask him [her husband] what
> Avails his prisons, spies, and jealousies?
> Would he not say a woman's wit
> Had made them fruitless all? (III.i.)

Her outspoken "truth" is discomfitingly "naked." Acmat views sex animalistically: the "royal hunter" is "upon the scent" of Homais's "charms at bay." He advises her to "play" the "game" coyly: "Let him [Levan] not find you vicious." She, however, objects to "guile":

> What? To conceal desire when every
> Atom of me trembles with it! I'll strip
> My Passion naked of such guile, lay it
> Undressed and panting at his feet.

The justifications for Homais's behavior certainly do not exist in Manley's source, nor does her representation of desire as truth.

Other salient differences between Chardin and Manley should be mentioned. Many characters in the *Royal Mischief* are complete fabrications: Acmat, the brothers Osman and Ismael, the dutiful Selima (married for political reasons to Osman), and the virtuous Bassima (married to Levan Didian but beloved by Osman) among them.[15] The Prince of Libardian is neither old nor sexually incompetent, and he ultimately tolerates his wife's indiscretions. The royal couple is mutually unfaithful: Darejan, the Homais prototype, was "a lovely Princess, and a Woman of a great Wit.

'Tis true she was tax'd with being none of the most Faithful Wives, which perhaps might be in revenge of the Foul-play which her Husband openly play'd her every Day" (134). The Prince of Libardian in Chardin's *Travels* "had a great kindness for his Wife, as much as an Adulteress, and as wicked as she was." He unsuccessfully attempts to regain her by force, "But Levan was Valiant, and had good Soldiers about him, so that George was constrain'd to retire into his Mountains, where he died from Grief and Vexation." This is very different from the rapid denouement of *The Royal Mischief* in which an enraged prince devises various deaths for Homais's single transgression and finally runs her through with his sword while she is embracing Levan. Manley sardonically makes clear, after killing off every vital character in the play, that the impotent prince will continue to rule his sterile kingdom.

Chardin's Levan Dadian is no fresh warrior/bridegroom but an accomplished womanizer who has fathered several children. In contrast to the seduction-as-work-of-art staged by Manley's Homais, Chardin's Levan initiates the relationship with his uncle's wife, who is merely "among the other women" he has desired. He has been married for several years, not newly wed to a coldly virtuous princess. His only breach, from Chardin's perspective, is of the male bond to his uncle: "Levan being Twenty Four Years of Age, Espous'd the Daughter of the Prince of Abca's, by whom he had two Sons; . . . Now among the rest of the Women with whom he fell in Love, one was the Wife of George his Uncle, who had been his Tutor, and to whom he had been so highly oblig'd (134)." In Chardin's version of the story, Darejan (Homais) and Levan live "in an incestuous league" for two years before "[h]e Marry'd her, and eight days after sent home his first Wife ignominiously . . . back to her Father, King of the Abca's, after he had caus'd her Nose, her Ears and her Hands to be cut off." He orders the cruel execution of his first wife's supposed lover by having him "stopp'd into the Mouth of a Cannon." Personal honour does not motivate him; he sacrifices the innocents to sway public opinion and to "satisfy the Hatred and Jealousie of Darejan." He dies a nonviolent death, wholly unlike the dramatic suicide in Act V.i of *The Royal Mischief,* in which a guilt-stricken Levan falls upon his sword.

Manley, in further contrast, creates the new character Homais and portrays her sympathetically. Her husband is old, impotent, and oppressively possessive, "with jealous age suspicious." The love affair with Levan Dadian becomes irresistible "true love," brief and passionate. The contrasting brothers Osman and Ismael are added to explain the shaping of Homais's desires. Homais's physical beauty is celebrated in romance terms as a power capable of moving worlds, and her will assumes "heroic" proportions, marshaling armies to follow her lead. The figurative language of the play frequently constructs images of obstruction and violent release, paralleling the pattern of Homais's experience. Act I establishes the imagistic pattern. Levan "slowly returns [from battle], with honour press'd,/As thick'ning laurels, sprung to stop his passage." Yet he quickly is swept into love, the destructive "swelling current [that] will admit no bounds" (I.i). Homais's youthful passion for Osman was once obstructed by her modesty and by his shy inhibitions. She vows never to "forgive the baulk" lest she "dash the full bowl [of pleasure] when lifted to my lips,/And all the senses eager for the tastes." Similarly, the recurrent figure of the little circle—Homais's eyes, the miniature portraits exchanged by the lovers, the implied image of female sexuality, the confining circumference of the castle walls, the fetters on Homais's arms, the mouth of the cannon into which a body may be "crammed"—metaphorize the constricted energy of the heroine.[16] A woman of spirit and talent cannot exercise her strengths on any other battlefield than "love," the "little circle," and close embrace, having been culturally barred from other means of gratification. The greatest act of bravery is to "stand the enjoyment of [one's] own desires" (240).

*The Royal Mischief*'s satiric alteration of heroic tragedy, qualities that its sources and predecessors do not explain, intensifies in the play's final acts. By the end of Act III, the political alliance/wedding between Levan and Bassima is yielding to the siege by Homais and Osman. Characters choose between reckless passion or prudent marriage at the same time that they choose between dangerous conspiracy against or practical duty to the state. Levan and Homais, now illicit lovers, instigate an illicit rebellion against the Prince of Libardian. The abstract ideas upon which heroic conventions rest receive ever-decreasing lip-service from the characters. "Honour and justice are [now] low sounds, can scarce be heard when love is named." Virtue is a "brittle toy" now "burst . . . to pieces." When Acmat urges ways to makes amorous "joys . . . lawful," Homais replies, "Impossible." In fact, desire is represented as the most powerful yet least lawful human motivation. "Woman's wishes" are "boundless" and "vast." The desires of the men who surround Homais are more specifically imaged as appetite, not of nurturance but of prey. Levan tells Homais, "I can feast on nothing but you." The sensuous feast becomes a metaphor for the kind of sexual promiscuity that Manley uses to describe political disorder as well. Ismael, the prime conspirator, envies Levan's "feasting on [Homais's] charms." He hopes to "be allowed sometimes a taste,/Some small remains" of her sexual favors. Homais's "fall" is from heroic love to sex for political power. Or perhaps it is more accurate to say that the veils and screens used onstage in the first part of the play are pulled aside, revealing the political nature of "love." In Act II, Homais plans to drug her husband to sleep while she and Levan hold an amorous tryst. In Act IV, she strikes a sexual bargain with the conspirator Ismael to "bless [his] longing arms with their first joys" if he will murder her husband, the Prince of Libardian. Cynicism undercuts heroism. Love is reduced to egoism and self-deception ("Tis one great point of Love, first to impose upon our own belief, so self-deceived/Are better fitted to deceive another"). Sexual desire spreads to involve Homais and other characters in incest, adultery, and promiscuity, much in the way that madness wins converts in Swift's satire.

> Show me but one who, tho' inconstant as
> The rising winds or flowing seas, still
> Swears not fealty to the reigning object,
> Nay, fancies he shall surely keep it, too,
> Tho' he has broke ten thousand vows before,
> Took new desires, new faith for every fair,
> And loathed as much as ever he had liked.
> 'Tis one great point of love, first to impose
> Upon our own belief, so self-deceived
> Are better fitted to deceive another. (IV.i)

But even more interestingly, the analogy between sex and politics begins to form clearly along gender lines. The virtuous Bassima seems at first Homais's opposite, her "enemy." But by end of Act III, she shares Homais's sense of "crowding" and potential explosion: "Like some prophetic priestess full of the/God that rends her, must breathe the baleful/Oracle or burst" (III.i). She also shares Homais's ability to deflate the rhetoric of the "hero" who woos her. When Osman asks, "Who would not be ten thousand years a wretch,/To be one hour a god?" Bassima replies, "You like a lover entertain your fancy, But I still have the fatal land in view." Especially, Bassima shares with Homais the fate of being principally an object of male desire. In Act V, Bassima, poisoned by Homais, lies "fainting upon a couch." Although they are political enemies, they are allied as women and suffer similar fates. Bassima is confined to an inner chamber of the castle, as Homais was formerly. Osman enters and, with an insensitivity that surpasses even Ismael's suggestion to Homais that she imagine he is Levan while they are in bed, proposes that they make love before the poison completely does poor Bassima in:

> Therefore, my Princess, since your fate and mine
> Are both so near, and there remains no means
> To save you, let us employ the time
> In kind revenge, and Heavenly joys.

Oh, do not banish me from Earth unblessed!
Send not your true adorer hence
Unrecompensed for all his constant love. (V.i)

"Oh, do not argue thus, my fair," he tells her even as they hear soldiers coming for them, "the doors I've fastened/All behind. They've five to force, before they/Can disturb us, an age if well employed." Such necrophilial fantasies conflate male lust and death. (In Act V, the Prince of Libardian similarly indulges in fantasies about how beautiful Homais will look after he has poisoned her: "[Death]" will make "the odious Homais fair.") These fantasies arguably exceed even the conniving sexual engagements of Homais, whose "boundless" desire to live and seize authority recklessly involves her in simultaneous seductions of her husband, Levan, and Ismael. At least some justification is offered for the extremes of her behavior—she is "[m]ade passionate by want of liberty"—whereas Osman's and the Prince of Libardian's ardor for near corpses has none except a perverse association of love with death. The ironic implication of the scene in which Osman seduces the dying Bassima is that, taken to its fullest expression, heroic tragedy tries to make death beautiful. But death, Homais contradicts the Prince, will not subdue her into a beautiful and controllable "form": "swelled with the fatal draught, I should have burst/These bonds that now confine me close." *The Royal Mischief* exposes the aesthetic that depends upon a relationship between dying and ecstasy, death and femininity.[17]

The idea that reckless, dangerous love serves as a metaphor for reckless, dangerous politics is central to *The Royal Mischief,* whereas in Chardin, the actions of the Persian court are simply dismissed as barbarous, as other. In Manley's play, purposeful conspiracy, rather than random misdoing, clearly reflects the problems arising out of gender difference: once Homais refuses to be an object, a prince's "treasure," she has violated the domestic tenet/paradigm upon which heroic ideals depend. By insisting that the "naked" truth about her sexuality is its active and creative potential, its ability to initiate plot, and its desire to "govern," Homais explodes the peaceful, orderly repression of the court. And implicitly, Manley rejects the conventional ideals of heroic tragedy. Osman's lust for the dying Bassima parodies absurdly "til death do us part" love. Indeed, Osman does love until death by cannon parts him into a thousand pieces. Heroic death is even more grotesquely parodied in the description of Selima, Osman's jealous wife, who "ranges the fatal plain,/Gathering the smoking relics of her lord,/Which singe her as she grasps them" (V.i). Selima represents the fate of those women who slavishly embrace patriarchalism:

> Now on the
> Horrid pile herself had heaped. I left her
> Stretched along, bestowing burning kisses
> And embraces on every fatal piece.

Homais, like Belira, becomes an angry beauty, cursing and railing at the end, hoping to "scatter unthought plagues around." Neither the content of conventional heroic drama—the celebration of male autonomy—nor its form—the unities of time, place, and action—survives intact. Within a day, Homais has enraptured Levan, poisoned Bassima, rekindled Ismael, incited revolution to overthrow her husband, and met violent death. The rush from the couch of love-making to the grave is dizzying. So much restless, unsatisfied desire goes up in smoke, like Osman in the cannon. The private fantasy of heroism in Act I disintegrates into public slaughter in Act V. There is a general failure of love to forge relationships and of heroism to renew order. The conventional ending of heroic tragedy, with its promise of rebirth and a new order, a Fortinbras to follow Hamlet, is subverted. The Prince of Libardian speaks more feelingly of his homosocial bonds with Levan than of his feelings for Homais:

> to lose thee
> Thus, after all my ardent longings,
> And mighty strivings to advance your glory,
> Unwreathed this brow to place on yours the laurel,
> Showed you to conquered nations, as my boasting
> Proved to be made your glory's foil.
> My dearness to thee urges more tears of grief
> Than anger from me.

But Levan (unlike Chardin's Levan) commits suicide. Bodies, once full of beauty and desire, are literally or metaphorically wrenched apart. The same old impotent ruler continues to govern the same self-enclosed world. Manley has literally and metaphorically exploded the heroes of her play and exposed the threat that the transgressive woman poses to the homosocial assumptions underlying political and sexual power. Homais, ever feisty, dies angry and unrepentant: "a curse on fate and my expiring strength." Manley has used the conventions of heroic tragedy to make it grotesque and self-critical, creating a female mock-heroic.

By modifying the conventions of both comedy and heroic tragedy, she regenders satire to accommodate a woman's indignation. In both *The Lost*

*Lover* and *The Royal Mischief,* the figure of the angry beauty conflates the roles of transgressive woman and satirist. She expresses frustrated idealism, articulated as the failure of "love," an absent but implied ideal. Ideal love (like "right reason" in male satirists such as Rochester, Swift, and Pope) has the potential to establish creative relationship and coherence. The plays, however, represent a world with neither. Humanity is merely *amoris capax.* Promiscuous desire for sexual gratification and uncontrolled desire for economic or political power become confused. This ironic device is central to Manley's most famous work, *The New Atalantis,* in which political satire on the Whig government is framed in amorous episodes. In this later narrative, the transgressive woman as desired object and/or desiring subject reappears. Scenes of comic deception, such as the "bed trick" scene between Germanicus and the Countess, and scenes of heroic (or even tragic) pretense, such as the tribulations of the Princess Ormia, recall the satirically revised motifs and forms enacted in 1696 by Manley's angry beauties.

## Notes

1. In general I am indebted to Robert Elliott, *The Power of Satire*; Alvin Kernan, "Aggression and Satire," and *The Cankered Muse: Satire of the English Renaissance*; Claude Rawson, *Gulliver and the Gentle Reader: Studies in Swift and Our Time*; David Worcester, *The Art of Satire*; Maynard Mack, "The Muse of Satire"; and Northrop Frye, "The Mythos of Winter: Irony and Satire" in *An Anatomy of Criticism* (1957). More recent studies of eighteenth-century satire similarly reinforce the idea that satire is a man's domain. See, for example, David Nokes, *Raillery and Rage: A Study of Eighteenth-Century Satire*; or Claude Rawson, ed., *English Satire and the Satiric Tradition*.

2. The complete modern edition of Manley's "novels" is *The Novels of Mary Delarivière Manley*, 2 vols., ed. Patricia Koster. This edition includes *The New Atalantis, Memoirs of Europe, The History of Queen Zarah*, and *The Adventures of Rivella*. A more recent edition of *The New Atalantis* has been edited by Ros Ballaster.

3. Two modern editions of the play exist. It comes as no particular surprise that modern publication of the attack on women playwrights, specifically on Manley's *The Royal Mischief,* preceded modern publication of the plays themselves (see Lucyle Hook's edition of *The Female Wits*). Citations in the current work are to the second modern edition, in which *The Female Wits* provides an ironic conclusion to Fidelis Morgan's 1984 anthology of plays by Restoration women—*The Female Wits: Women Playwrights of the Restoration, 1660–1720.*

4. Filmer writes, "If we compare the natural duties of a Father with those of a King,

we find them to be all one, without any difference at all but only in the latitude or extent of them" (63). See also Schochet throughout.

5. The best account of Manley's life is Fidelis Morgan, *A Woman of No Character: An Autobiography of Mrs. Manley.*

6. Ros Ballaster comments on the implications of the language of sexual pleasure in Dryden's *Discourse* in "Manl(e)y Forms: Sex and the Female Satirist," in Brant and Purkiss, *Women, Texts, & Histories 1575–1760*, 217–41.

7. The figure of the satyr originates earlier in Greek myth. However, the representation of the half-human, half-bestial satyr combines features of *horse* and man. Such figures occur on Greek vases, for example. The association of the horse, rather than goat, with the mythical deity of satire makes one wonder again about Swift's Houyhnhnms.

8. In addition to *The Lost Lover* and *The Royal Mischief,* Manley produced *Almyna* (1707) and *Lucius* (1717). In her will she mentions two other plays that she hopes eventually will be staged. They have never been found. PROB11/599/194–5.

9. For discussions of the choice faced by women writers between the opposing models of Behn and Philips, see Jeslyn Medoff, "The Daughters of Behn and the Problem of Reputation," and Carol Barash, "'The Native Liberty of the Subject': Configurations of Gender and Authority in the Works of Mary Chudleigh, Sarah Fyge Egerton, and Mary Astell" in Grundy and Wiseman, *Women, Writing, History 1640–1740,* 33–54; 55–71.

10. George Puttenham describes comedy as "the common behaviour and manner of life of the meaner sort of men" in *The Art of English Poesie.* The "meaner sort of men" seems to include women. Sir Philip Sydney, in contrast, describes tragedy as focused on the "higher" sort of men, those princes and kings on whose fall catharsis is predicated. For a fuller discussion of the feminist analysis of English traditions of gender and *genre* with respect to comedy and tragedy, see Callaghan 9–73.

11. R. P. Draper, ed. *Tragedy: Developments in Criticism*; Irving Ribner, *Jacobean Tragedy*; Eva Figes, *Tragedy and Social Evolution*; Maynard Mack, "The Jacobean Shakespeare: some Observations upon the Construction of the Tragedies," *Stratford Upon Avon Studies, Jacobean Theater,* Vol. I; and Laurance Michel, *The Thing Contained: Theory of the Tragic.*

12. Manley was praising Catherine Trotter's play *Agnes de Castro.* For a general discussion of "serious" plays by women, see William J. Burling, 311–24.

13. The misogynistic author(s) of *The Female Wits* make this idea part of their satire. Marsilia (Manley) explains that after considering various deaths for her hero Amorous, she "resolv'd to ram him into a great gun and scatter him o'er the sturdy plain" (III.i. page 425).

14. French and English editions appeared in the same year: *Journal du voyage du chevalier Chardin* (Londres et Amsterdam, 1686); *The Travels of Sir John Chardin into Persia* (London, 1686). References are to the latter edition.

15. Chardin mentions a scheming minister of state, a Vizier/Ismael figure, who involves "the wicked Darejan," wife of Bacrat, in a power plot and then betrays her. The pair of contrasting brothers and the sexual relations between Homais and them are entirely Manley's invention.

16. Manley's emphasis on eyes may be conventional windows-of-the-soul imagery, but it is possible that she was responding to the repeated references to eyes, especially eyes being put out, in Chardin's account.

17. For a discussion of the relationship between female beauty and death in literary and visual representations primarily of the nineteenth and twentieth centuries, see Elisabeth Bronfen's *Over Her Dead Body: Death, Femininity, and the Aesthetic.*

## Works Cited

Backscheider, Paula. *Spectacular Politics: Theatrical Power and Mass Culture in Early Modern England.* Baltimore: Johns Hopkins UP, 1993.

Behn, Aphra. *Oroonoko, The Rover, and Other Works.* Ed. Janet Todd. London: Penguin, 1992.

Belsey, Catherine. *The Subject of Tragedy: Identity and Difference in Renaissance Drama.* London and New York: Methuen, 1985.

Brant, Clare, and Purkiss, Diane, eds. *Women, Texts, and Histories: 1575–1760.* London and New York: Routledge, 1992.

Bronfen, Elisabeth. *Over Her Dead Body: Death, Femininity, and the Aesthetic.* New York: Routledge, 1992.

Burling, William J. "'Their Empire Disjoyn'd': Serious Plays by Women on the London Stage, 1660–1737." *Curtain Calls: British and American Women and the Theater, 1660–1820.* Ed. Mary Ann Schofield and Cecilia Macheski. Athens: Ohio UP, 1991. 311–24.

Callaghan, Dympna. *Woman and Gender in Renaissance Tragedy: A Study in King Lear, Othello, The Duchess of Malfi and The White Devil.* New York and London: Harvester, 1989.

Chardin, Sir John. *Travels of Sir John Chardin into Persia, through the Black-Sea, and the Country of Colchis.* London, 1686.

Cotton, Nancy. *Women Playwrights in England, c. 1363–1750.* Lewisburg: Bucknell UP, 1980.

Davenant, Sir William. *The Siege of Rhodes.* London, 1663.

Draper, Ronald P. Tragedy: Developments in Criticism, A Casebook. London: Macmillan, 1980.

Dryden, John. *The Works of John Dryden.* Ed. E. N. Hooker, Vinton Dearing, Alan Roper, and Others. 20 vols. Berkeley, Los Angeles, and London: University of California P, 1956–72.

Elliott, Robert. *The Power of Satire: Magic, Ritual, Art.* Princeton: Princeton UP, 1960.

Erskine-Hill, Howard, ed. *The Augustan Idea in English Literature.* London: E. Arnold, 1983.

*The Female Wits.* Ed. Lucyle Hook. Augustan Reprint Society, No. 124. Los Angeles: Clark Library, 1967.

Figes, Eva. *Tragedy and Social Evolution.* London: J. Calder, 1976.

Finke, Laurie A. "The Satire of Women Writers in *The Female Wits.*" *Restoration: Studies in English Literary Culture 1660–1700,* 8.2 (1984).

Frye, Northrop. "The Mythos of Winter: Irony and Satire." In *An Anatomy of Criticism.* Princeton: Princeton UP, 1957.

Griffin, Dustin. *Satire: A Critical Reintroduction.* Lexington: UP of Kentucky, 1994.

Grundy, Isobel, and Susan Wiseman, eds. *Women, Writing, History 1640–1740.* Athens, GA: U of Georgia P, 1992.

Kernan, Alvin. "Aggression and Satire: Art Considered as a Form of Biological Adaptation," *Literary Theory and Structure: Essays in Honor of William K. Wimsatt.* Ed. Frank Brady, John Palmer, and Martin Price. New Haven: Yale UP, 1973.

———. *The Cankered Muse: Satire of the English Renaissance.* Hamden, CT: Archon Books, 1959.

Killigrew, Thomas. *Comedies and Tragedies. . . .* London, 1664.

*Lust's Dominion, or The Lascivious Queen: A Tragedy.* Ca. 1600; London, 1657.

Mack, Maynard. "The Jacobean Shakespeare." *Jacobean Theatre.* Ed. John Russell Brown and Bernard Harris. *Stratford-upon-Avon Studies* 1. New York: Capricorn Books, 1967. 11–41.

———. "The Muse of Satire," reprinted in *Satire: Modern Essays in Criticism.* Ed. Ronald Paulson. Englewoood Cliffs, NJ: Prentice-Hall, 1971.

Manley, Delarivier. *The Lost Lover: or, the Jealous Husband: A Comedy.* London, 1696.

———. *The New Atalantis.* Ed. Ros Ballaster. London and New York: Penguin, 1992.

———. *The Novels of Mary Delarivier Manley.* 2 Vols. Ed. Patricia Koster. Gainesville, FL: Scholar's Facsimiles and Reprints, 1971.

———. *The Royal Mischief.* London, 1696.

Michel, Laurence Anthony. *The Thing Contained: Theory of the Tragic.* Bloomington: Indiana UP, 1970.

Milhous, Judith. *Thomas Betterton and the Management of Lincoln's Inn Fields, 1695–1708.* Carbondale and Edwardsville: Southern Illinois UP, 1979.

Milton, John. *Complete Prose Works of John Milton.* Ed. Don M. Wolfe. New Haven: Yale UP, 1953.

Morgan, Fidelis. *The Female Wits: Women Playwrights of the Restoration, 1660–1700.* London: Virago P, 1984.

———. *A Woman of No Character: An Autobiography of Mrs. Manley.* New York and London: Faber and Faber, 1986.

Nettleton, George H., and Arthur E. Case, eds. *British Dramatists from Dryden to Sheridan.* 2nd ed. Boston: Houghton Mifflin, 1969.

Nokes, David. *Raillery and Rage: A Study of Eighteenth-Century Satire.* New York: St. Martin's P, 1987.

Nussbaum, Felicity. *The Brink of All We Hate: English Satires on Women, 1660–1750.* Lexington: UP of Kentucky, 1984.

Oldham, John. *The Works of John Oldham, In Four Parts.* London, 1696.

Pearson, Jacqueline. *The Prostituted Muse: Images of Women and Women Dramatists 1642–1737.* New York and London: Harvester, 1988.

Rawson, Claude. *English Satire and the Satiric Tradition.* London: Basil Blackwell, 1984.

———. *Gulliver and the Gentle Reader: Studies in Swift and Our Time.* London and Boston: Routledge and Kegan Paul, 1973.

———. *Satire and Sentiment 1660–1830.* Cambridge: Cambridge UP, 1994.

Ribner, Irving. *Jacobean Tragedy: The Quest for Moral Order.* 1962. Reprint, New York: Barnes and Noble, 1983.

Richards, Ivor Armstrong. *Principles of Literary Criticism.* New York: Harcourt Brace, 1959.

Schochet, Gordon J. *Patriarchalism in Political Thought: The Authoritarian Family and Political Speculation and Attitudes, especially in England.* London: Basil Blackwell, 1975.

Schofield, Mary Ann, and Cecilia Macheski, eds. *Curtain Calls: British and American Women and the Theater 1660–1820.* Athens, OH: Ohio UP, 1991.

Sheffield, John, Earl of Mulgrave, Duke of Buckinghamshire. *An Essay on Poetry. Critical Essays of the Seventeenth Century,* vol. 2. Ed. Joel E. Spingarn. Oxford: Clarendon, 1908. 286–96.

Stallybrass, Peter, and Allon White. *The Politics and Poetics of Transgression.* Ithaca, NY: Cornell UP, 1986.

Stanton, Donna. "The Fiction of Preciosité and the Fear of Women," *Yale French Studies* 62 (1981).

Van Lennup, William, ed. *The London Stage, 1660–1800,* Part I, 1660–1700. Carbondale: Southern Illinois UP, 1965.

Wharton, Joseph. *Essay Upon Pope.* London, 1782.

Whitehead, Alfred North. *Science and the Modern World.* New York: Macmillan, 1948.

Wilmot, John. *Complete Poems of John Wilmot, Earl of Rochester.* Ed. David M. Vieth. New Haven and London: Yale UP, 1968.

Worcester, David. *The Art of Satire.* Cambridge: Harvard UP, 1940.

# The Persona as Pretender and the Reader as Constitutional Subject in Swift's *Tale*

*Brian A. Connery*

I . . . appeal to every one's own Experience, whether the shadow of a Man though it consists of nothing but the absence of Light (and the more the absence of Light is, the more discernible is the shadow) does not, when a Man looks on it, cause as clear and positive an *Idea* in his mind, as a Man himself, though covered with clear Sun-shine? And the Picture of a Shadow, is a positive thing. . . . And thus one may truly be said to see Darkness.
—John Locke, *Human Understanding* 2: 8.5–6, 133

It may be necessary, as well now as heretofore, for wise men to speak in parables and with a double meaning, that the enemy may be amused, and they only who have ears to hear may hear. But 'tis certainly a mean, impotent, and dull sort of wit which amuses all alike, and leaves the most sensible man, and even a friend, equally in doubt, and at a loss to understand what one's real mind is, upon any subject.

—Shaftesbury, *Freedom of Wit and Humour* 2: 45

## I. A Digression of the Modern Kind Concerning Critics— Intended Only for Themselves and Which the Modest Reader May Conveniently Overlook

Beginning with Edward Said's essay on "Swift's Tory Anarchy" in 1969 and with increasing frequency in the last fifteen years, readers of *A Tale of a Tub* have shifted the focus of attention and discussion away from the formerly much discussed problem of the boundary between the *Tale's* speaker (a.k.a. the Hack, the Modern, the Tale-teller, the *persona*) and the potentially normative author (a.k.a. Swift) and toward the *Tale's* self-conscious textuality and its purportedly consequent radical indeterminacy. It was, of course, exactly this apparent self-consciousness in the *Tale* which gave rise to the attention to *persona,* as in Robert Elliott's claim that "the commanding centre" of the *Tale* is the "consciousness of a created character, the 'I' who purports to be writing the work. . . . And it is the constant task of the reader to pin down the point of view and to make the leap from it to the standard of excellence against which the point of view—and the human values which it represents—is to be judged" (443). Early *persona* criticism, with its emphasis upon the *agon* between reader and author (evident in Elliott's wrestling metaphor) readily recognized the *Tale* as a textual site of interpretive contestation, though it did not use the political terminology that has since become commonplace.

Poststructuralist theory has convincingly demonstrated the arbitrariness of readers' attempts to "pin down" point of view, and with its demonstration of the constructedness of the modern subject by discursive practices has, in fact, eliminated exactly the "point" which is the *sine qua non* of point of view.[1] Moreover, in its complementary move of empowering the reader through the death, or at least the fragmentation, of the author, it has heightened our awareness of the complexity of the *agon* between author and reader.

Still, most readers, both earlier *persona* critics and their poststructuralist successors, agree that the speaker of the *Tale* is in many ways transparent. Ronald Paulson suggests that the *Tale*-teller's mixed metaphors and self-contradictions produce "an abstractness which tends to deny the Hack the individuality necessary if he is to be accepted as a fiction," even while it is exactly these self-contradictions which produce in the reader "moments of extraordinary intensity" (32–33). Such moments of intensity throughout Swift's works, according to Claude Rawson, are what constitute a "central Swiftian personality . . . behind the screen of indirection, ironies, and putative authors . . . which is always actively present and makes itself felt" (6). Yet the irony which implies this Swiftian presence is not simple, for as any reader of the "Digression on Madness" knows, reading the *Tale* by means of a simple irony (i.e., replacing any assertion with its opposite) leads the reader into further contradictions and consequent discomfort. Thus, as Everett Zimmerman explains, "Instead of allowing the reader to assume the existence of an authoritative author from whom the satire emanates, Swift requires the reader to search for the principle of authority that validates the satire" (13).

The tensions in Swiftian texts between the absence of the controlling author and the presence of a seemingly nonauthorized author are translated simultaneously into poststructuralist and political terms in Said's essay, and the political terms from his title (Tory/anarchy) seem to have established the poles for subsequent readings. In terms quite like those in which Roland Barthes announced the death of the author, Dustin Griffin has recently articulated the underlying "politics" of the *Tale*'s text: "The act of interpretation is political in the radical sense. Any interpreter of a text

acts within a social situation (involving the writing along with other interpreters and readers) and seeks to control the meaning of the text for
his purposes. . . . Interpretation is politics at the verbal level" (152).

Poststructuralist approaches since Said have worked primarily to de-
stabilize any principles of authority one might bring to bear upon the
*Tale* (see Atkins; Saccamano; Wyrick; Kelly; Griffin). However, in the
very process of problematizing the text of the *Tale,* contemporary critics
(excepting Saccamano) treat unproblematically the very problem which
earlier readers had recognized that the *Tale* poses, that of the concept of
the "author." Though their conclusions are often diametrically opposed,
these discussions all assume a "Swift" to whom they refer unproblematically, i.e., though they disagree about *what* the authorial intention is in
the *Tale,* they implicitly agree that there is authorial intention. Thus,
Deborah Baker Wyrick produces a conflicted Swift behind the work:
"Swift wants both the protection of absence and the effective control of
presence. He wants his targets to know when they're hit; he may wish to
disguise authorship, but he does not wish his works attributed to someone else; even as he constructs polysemic texts, he wants to be read properly. The absolutist desire for true, good, and natural meanings conflicts
with the liberal textocentric desire for infinitely open significance" (23).
Wyrick here uses for her discussion an *a priori* Swift compelled into writing by his absolutist desire, a Swift who is the product of exactly the
assumptions about the determinacy of meaning which Wyrick rejects as
she opens up the text and thereby constructs the opposition (absolutism
versus open significance) which creates the conflicted Swift she produces.
This seems frequently to be the case with poststructuralist readings of
the *Tale* in which claims of Swift's difference from himself are the result
of holding up for contrast the Tory Swift created by previous generations
of readers and the anarchic Swift produced by poststructuralism.

Griffin's reading of Swift is strikingly similar to Wyrick's and informed
by similar theoretical assumptions—but his conclusion is radically different: "To some extent, then, Swift seeks to stabilize and control interpretation. In another respect, however, Swift acts not to ensure that his
text bears a simple meaning, not to provide his reader with unambigu-
ous direction, but to embrace interpretive anarchy . . ." (160). With
Wyrick's attribution of "absolutist desire" to Swift and Griffin's attribution of an "embrace of anarchy," we are, I'm afraid, on the verge of another hard/soft controversy: Swift as absolutist versus Swift as anarchist.[2]
As with the fourth book of the *Travels,* the material in the *Tale* is sufficient to support either position; and as the "Swift" which I want to construct here would point out, the similarities between the two arguments

are certainly more important than the differences[3] Swift's binarism in the *Tale* (allegory/digression, reason/madness, judgment/wit, author/persona, knaves/fools, outside/inside), as throughout much of the rest of his writing (Ancients/Moderns, Tories/Whigs, Houyhnhnms/Yahoos), is prolific in its production of such opposed readings, and, I would argue, resembles poststructuralism in its recognition that such structures of meaning produce an indeterminacy which is most frequently negotiated by means of an arbitrary cultural privileging of one term over the other. But I would also argue that this binarism is the product of Swift's ludic handling of the fallacy of the either/or argument, and that another way to negotiate the apparent indeterminacy of such oppositions is to introduce a third term which is always excluded by the dyad.[4] Such an interpretive move is both common and commonsensical in readings of *An Argument against the Abolishing of Christianity* in which readers negotiate the apparent opposition of atheism versus "nominal Christianity" with the third term, "Christian." So, too, in readings of the fourth part of the *Travels,* some readers resolve the tension between Houyhnhnm and Yahoo by means of the third term, "Human Being." In the case of Swift's ironic works, the *Tale* being the case in point here, it is productive similarly to negotiate the oppositional structure, Author/Persona, with the third term, "Reader," or to negotiate the structure of Author/Reader with the third term, "Persona."

If absolutist critics have relied upon an *a priori,* pre-constructed "historical Swift" to produce their readings, anarchist critics have rejected that move on the basis of the inaccessibility of such a Swift, and have concluded that without the guiding authority of "Swift," no stability is possible, ignoring the processes represented and enacted by the text which assert the possibility of provisional stability and determinacy. In what follows, I hope to offer a reading of key aspects of the *Tale* which operates on a somewhat different interpretive model, one derived from the text itself as well as from the text's context and pretext. In doing so, I hope to re-introduce to the discussion of the *Tale* both the problem and the uses of *persona.* My conclusion, like Wyrick's, has the advantage of consistency with a commonly accepted characterization of the historical Swift, but, perhaps unfortunately, none of the contemporary glamour of Griffin's anarchistic Swift: the "Swift" created in the production of the *Tale* is neither absolutist nor anarchist, but, much like the Swift established by those less ludic texts attributed to him, a supporter of a limited or mixed constitutional monarchy.

The *Tale* itself is about reading, authorship, and authority, and it contains within itself representations of reading and misreading even while, as text itself, it prompts processes of reading and misreading. While the *Tale* does not—and, I think, claims that it cannot—determine meaning absolutely, it both represents and enacts a procedure by which meaning can be determined contingently. That is, in an argument that Stanley Fish has reiterated two hundred and sixty years later, it both demonstrates that meaning is provisional and urges the active construction and establishment of provisional meaning by interpretive communities. In order to explore what this argument would have meant in the early eighteenth century, I will turn first to the pretexts and contexts to which the *Tale* itself points, then look at the ways in which the text represents these issues, and finally return to a discussion of how the text enacts, in its dialectical relations with the reader, a provisional resolution of these issues.

## II. *A Tale of a Tub,* Designed for the Distraction of Critics and the End of Faction

In any reading of the *Tale,* the most inviting place to begin is with the seemingly stable allegory of the three brothers. As Richard Nash points out, in contrast to the digressions and other apparatus which require the reader to make rapid and precise judgments, this fable invites us through tropes, puns, and learned commentary to recognize an allegorical account of the history of Christianity, and particularly of the Reformation. But as most readers recognize, and as Zimmerman explicitly notes, the issues raised in the allegory are related as well to the politics of the seventeenth century and to the Ancients versus Moderns controversy which provided the occasion for the completion and publication of the *Tale.* While the father in the allegory clearly represents God, and his Will represents Divine Law, fatherhood is also a trope both for kingship and for authorship. It is, perhaps, the assumption of the identity of these three tropes which produces the absolutist/anarchist dichotomy in current readings of the *Tale.*

If we are going to attempt to read the politics of the text of the *Tale,* it behooves us to look at the politics of the period. For readers in the early eighteenth century, the allegory of the father, combining as it does the issues of genealogy, authority, and divinity, could not but resonate with echoes of the constitutional settlement of 1688, and particularly with the arguments represented by Sir Robert Filmer's *Patriarcha* and Locke's first of the *Two Treatises of Government.* Filmer, the seventeenth-century royalist champion of Divine Right, summarizes the argument of the monarch's absolute authority based on inheritance of God's gift of absolute dominion to Adam. As his title suggests, Filmer's argument relies on the analogy between God/King/Father, and is particularly forceful, if not logical, in his suggestion that the dissolution of authority at one level will precipitate a dissolution of authority at all levels; thus, he appeals to the individual male reader's fear of anarchic households as well as to the British subjects' fear of an arbitrary government at the hands of a minority (as in the Interregnum). At first glance, the allegory of the coats in the *Tale,* with its apparent implied norm of passive obedience to the father's will (by means of an objective or literal reading), would seem to support or at least to parallel Filmer's argument: Father knows best.

Moreover, Locke's argument against Filmer, which uses the analogy of the family from the bottom up, as it were, and suggests that sons are not required to submit to arbitrary or destructive fathers, seems contrary to the *Tale*'s allegorical moral (or at least it is not plainly represented within the allegory), for the father of the *Tale* is clearly benevolent and the sons' interpretive rebellion in their reading the will against its intention is revealed in the course of the narrative to be contrary to their best interest. Moreover, the brothers' rebellion against their father's will is clearly a revolution, and all revolutions, as the *Tale*-teller subsequently explains, are the results of madness. Such reasoning, of course, underlies the construction of the absolutist Swift who demands passive obedience to the text. We ought, however, at this point in the interpretation to feel a bit of uneasiness in finding ourselves relying so unproblematically upon the *Tale*-teller's equations of madness and revolution. And as readers who are involved in and implicated by a process of interpretation characterized by uncertainty, we ought to ask ourselves why we think that the problems of interpretation faced by the brothers are so much simpler than those we face.

As Martin's predicament at the close of the allegory indicates, any norm must take history into account. In this, the allegory *does* parallel Locke's rebuttal, which points out that Filmer's argument, like that of the Roman Catholic Church tracing the ecclesiastical genealogy of the pope to Peter, depends upon the faulty assumption of a single uninterrupted line of descent from Adam. Both the Reformation and the constitutional settlement are founded upon the contrary assumption, that the line of descent has been interrupted and that consequent gaps have been introduced. Similarly, while the *Tale*'s allegory represents the initial self-interested misreadings of the father's will as mistakes, it neither suggests that these mistakes can be undone nor that we should pretend that we can recover the will and then totalize its application (the mad solution of Jack). Even if Martin could determine the intention of the will and of the father, he can no longer observe it, and consequently he must interpret the will both in terms of its possible original intention and in terms of his own historically determined situation: his coat cannot be returned to its original pristine condition. On the allegorical level, we must read this to mean that in the course of dissemination and interpretation Scripture itself has been fashioned and refashioned so that we can no longer separate the original from its accretions.

Filmer's and Locke's treatises, both based upon biblical exegesis, in fact, embody the problem of determining God's will through a written text riddled with gaps, contradictions, and ambiguities, and thus are connected to the problems of hermeneutics raised and politicized by the Reformation. Like the beginning of the Reformation, the religious controversies of seventeenth-century England, as the allegory indicates, grew out of problems of interpretation of Divine Law, as represented by the Bible, a movement like that of Martin and Jack (Luther and Calvin), initiated by a rebellion against the authority of a purported misinterpreter of the text, the Catholic Church as represented by Peter, and followed by an attempt to return to fidelity to the text. Critics have amply analyzed the *Tale*'s allegory's applications to the Reformation but have commented less amply on the theological implications of the initial crisis represented in the allegory which makes the plot of misinterpretation possible and inevitable: the death of the father and the transmission of the will. Absolutist critics, those who promulgate a "Swift" whose text represents the necessity of readers submitting to the will of the father/author, tacitly assume that the *Tale* represents such submission as both possible and relatively unproblematical. Anarchist critics, on the contrary, focus upon the will's and the *Tale*'s textuality and consequent indeterminacy. In religious terms, we might characterize these polarized views as the opposition between fundamentalism (absolutism) and atheism (anarchy), neither of which seems consistent either with the representation of Martin or with "Swift" as commonly constructed.

The death of the father and the transmission of the will in the allegory represent the absence of direct and immediate revelation from God, that is, the silence of God and the encoding of God's word in writing. Within the Bible, we can identify two moments which represent this transition, the moments which establish the old and new covenants: 1) the delivery of the tablets to Moses marking the end of prophecy and the beginning of Law, and 2) the discovery of the empty tomb of Christ which at once marks the beginning of his absence and silence and thus precipitates the reconstruction of the absent God through the writing of the Gospels. Both moments mark the transition from divine presence to divine absence, from voice to writing, as God is replaced by Text.[5] The father in the *Tale* most clearly echoes God's speech as reiterated by Moses: "You will find in my Will (here it is) full Instructions in every particular concerning the Wearing and Management of your Coats; wherein you must be very exact to avoid the Penalties I have appointed for every Transgression or Neglect, upon which your future Fortunes will entirely depend" (73–74). So, Moses presenting the tablets to Israel: "If you are not careful to do all the words of this law which are written in this book . . . the Lord will bring on you and your offspring extraordinary afflictions" (Deuteronomy 28.58). As Richard Jacobsen suggests, this moment marks in the Old Testament the movement of the word of God into its written codification, the beginning of the dispensability of prophecy through which the Voice of God was heard and God became present, and the beginning of reliance upon writing in the absence and silence of God. It also marks the beginning of the rabbinical tradition of exegesis and hermeneutics.

So too, in the New Testament, Christianity finds both its central mystery and the beginnings of its codification in writing at the moment when the two women visit the tomb of the crucified Christ to discover that the stone has been rolled away and the body is gone, replaced by one (Matthew and Mark) or two (Luke and John) angels who proclaim his resurrection and thus mark the beginning once more of God's absence and silence on earth and the necessity of the beginning of writing (i.e., the Gospels) in order to preserve the new covenant. Again, the beginning of writing, induced by the silence of an absent God, is also the beginning of interpretation.

The historical passage of God into silence and the divine will into writing, thus, stands between us and our desire for a presence that confers certainty and thus absolutism. The *Tale* recognizes the consequent uncertainty and indeterminacy. In the allegory of the *Tale* both Peter and Jack attempt to revive prophecy (through claims of divine inspiration) in order to supplement the will and to fix its meaning with certainty. Peter, particularly, identifies his own voice with that of the father, confusing the roles of author and reader, but the *Tale* clearly disapproves of such posturing. With the beginning of silence and the fall into writing and so into interpretation, as Locke makes clear in his investigation of the "Imperfection of Words," we fall into confusion: "The Volumes of Interpreters, and Commentators on the Old and New Testament, are but too manifest proofs of this. Though every thing said in the Text be infallibly true, yet the Reader may be, nay cannot chuse but be very fallible in the understanding of it. Nor is it to be wondered, that the Will of GOD, when cloathed in Words, should be liable to that doubt and uncertainty, which unavoidably attends that sort of Conveyance . . ." (*Human Understanding* 3: 9.23, 489–90). Locke's insistence on the necessity of fallibility in the interpretation of writing prefigures the *Tale*'s insistence on the irretrievability of the original intention and meaning of the father's will, and it is exactly this necessity which has launched the contemporary "textocentric" readings of the *Tale*. The "absolutist" argument, thus, springs from a misreading of the allegory of the coats, assuming that what the allegory asserts is the necessity of passive obedience to the father's will—when what the allegory actually asserts is the impossibility of obeying without interpreting and the impossibility of interpreting without misreading. While the allegory does express nostalgia for the presence of God/Father/King, this yearning itself—like the plot of the allegory (and like Gulliver's yearning to be a Houyhnhnm)—is the product of the impossibility of such a return.

The problem of reading, as made manifest in the religious allegory, lies at the heart of the third context for the *Tale*, that of the Ancients versus Moderns controversy, particularly as it was being played out between Swift's patron, Sir William Temple, and his chief opponents, the Type of the Modern Critic, William Wotton and Richard Bentley. Here the question of interpretation becomes inextricably bound up with the question of how to relate authority to authorship, for the master stroke of Bentley in answering Temple's *Treatise on Ancient and Modern Learning* was the demonstration that *The Epistles of Phalaris,* to which Temple had naively referred for support of his claims, were in fact forgeries. Thus, Bentley demonstrated simultaneously 1) philology's utility, 2) Temple's lack of expertise, and 3) the reader's power over the author, represented in the allegory by the three brothers' apparently willful misreadings of the father's will.

Bentley's argument renders the text of the epistles of Phalaris unauthorized and thus unauthoritative. As Neil Saccamano argues, given the emergent modern sense that "books express the opinions of individuals who have become authors through publication" (248), Bentley seems to have discredited the text by removing the authorizing agent and thus the source of the intentionality which produces meaning. But Swift does not need Roland Barthes to demonstrate that the "death of the author," figured by the death of the father in the allegory, although it introduces indeterminacy into the text, does not thereby render the text meaningless. Nor does he need Michel Foucault to demonstrate that, in their quest for meaning and determinacy, readers will actively construct an author in order to stabilize their readings. And even as the dispute between the Ancients and Moderns unfolds, it must become apparent, as Stanley Fish has been insisting, that even though—as Locke has asserted philosophically and the *Tale*'s allegory has asserted figuratively—every reading is a misreading, the interpretive community (Peter, Martin, and Jack;

or the supporters of the Ancients or Moderns) is always negotiating and restabilizing the discursively determined meanings of texts.

As Bentley's argument here suggests, what is at issue is the dynamics *not* between the author and the text, but between the reader, the text, and the *name* of the author: the *name* of the author, as Foucault argues in "What Is an Author," *identifies* the text, context, and pretext. But because the name itself is a word and consequently, in either a Lockean or a Saussurean linguistic universe, arbitrary and subject to misreading, the very word which should stabilize the text is itself subject to misreading (see Locke's *Essay* 3.9). The very attempts by *persona* critics to identify the voices in the anonymous text of the *Tale* (as, once again, the Teller, the Hack, the Modern, Swift) are, thus, attempts to name, by means of difference, the purported author and thereby to stabilize the meaning of the text. Because these names for the persona are names for a purported author, rather than a "real" author, their consequent effect is to *de-autho-rize* the text in preparation for a *re-authorization* under the name of Swift.

The limitation, if not the fallacy, of Bentley's argument, is hinted at in the *Tale*'s comment regarding modern critics that "Town Wits . . . are in grave Dispute, whether there have been ever any Antients or no" (124–25). That is, although the name of the author of the *Epistles of Phalaris* may be in dispute, there can be no dispute that the writing indeed has an author, whether or not the identity of that author can be determined. Indeed, both the *Tale* and *The Battle of the Books* play with the idea of the interchangeability of the names of authors and assert that books them-selves—and not the originary presence of the author—are what con-structs authorship. The Bookseller at the outset of the *Battle* cautions the reader "to beware of applying to Persons what is here meant only of Books in the most literal Sense. So, when Virgil is mentioned, we are not to understand the Person of a famous Poet, call'd by that Name, but only certain Sheets of Paper, bound up in Leather, containing in Print, the Works of the said Poet, and so of the Rest" (214).[6] Typically read today as a Swiftian jab at the materialism of the age and especially of Bentleyan critics, these directions for reading do not, however, point ironically to a norm and seem in fact to concede the point to Bentley that all we have are words on a page. These words, however, are capable of gesturing to an originary presence:

> In these Books, is wonderfully instilled and preserved, the Spirit of each
> Warrier, while he is alive; and after his Death, his Soul transmigrates there,
> to inform them. This, at least, is the more common Opinion; But, I believe,
> it is with Libraries, as with other Cemeteries, where some Philosophers
> affirm, that a certain Spirit, which they call *Brutum hominis,* hovers over the

Monument, till the Body is corrupted, and turns to *Dust,* or to *Worms*, but then vanishes or dissolves: So, we may say, a restless Spirit haunts over every *Book,* till *Dust* or *Worms* have seized upon it; which to some may happen in a few Days, but to others, later. (222)

While conceding the death or the absence of the author, this passage argues for the text as an embodiment of a continuing intention and meaning (a restless Spirit), even as it concedes further the gradual disintegration of that intention and meaning over time. Indeed, it would appear that the process of dissolution is accelerated by readers and commentators, as the materialist Bentleyan critics, i.e., the consumers of the text, are figured here as "Worms."

And therein seems to lie the crux of the problem from the point of view of the *Tale* and the *Battle*: neither denies the instability or indeterminacy of the text, and neither asserts the possibility of recovering the full meaning of an originary author. Given the success of contemporary forgeries and second parts, it would be foolish for the *Tale* to insist on the determinacy of authorship.[7] In fact, at the close of the 1710 "Apology," the author appeals to Bentley to de-authorize through exposure any false claimants to authorship and authority (184). Indeed, although the comments on reading attributed to Swift elsewhere may seem to assert a metaphysics of presence, no such absolute assertion is made: "When I am reading a Book, whether wise or silly, it seemeth to me to be alive and talking to me" ("Thoughts on Various Subjects," *PW* 4: 253). This claim does *not* assert that the *author* is talking or even that the book is talking but that the book *seems* to be talking.

It is the very problem of becoming an author that the *Tale* addresses in its first section (Sect. 1, Introduction) following the prefatory apparatus: "Whoever hath an Ambition to be heard in a Crowd, must press, and squeeze, and thrust, and climb with indefatigable Pains, till he has exalted himself to a certain Degree of Altitude above them" (55). As the introduction subsequently suggests, one must first be *seen* in order to be *heard*.[8] Becoming visible is a matter of distinguishing oneself from the herd, of establishing differences, after which one's identity is achieved not solely by self-assertion but by recognition.

This is, of course, also the problem posed by the *Tale* itself. Published anonymously, it bears no name with which the reader can fix or stabilize its meaning and intention. Oftentimes ironic and frequently self-contradictory, it demands that the reader distinguish its "author" from the herd of moderns, whose opinions and views are represented throughout the *Tale* as an ironic norm. The *Tale*'s ironies produce a dialectical relation between reader and text, inducing the reader to distinguish literal from ironic meanings and, as a result, to distinguish the purported author from the "true" author. It is thus a mistake to argue absolutely that the "combination of anonymity and irony thwarts the Bentleyan critic who wishes to found meaning on author identity and intention" (Saccamano 251). One *can* have a soul without having a visible Shoulder Knot. A text *can* have an author without bearing the author's name; and, in fact, it probably does. The problem for the reader is one of inferring the nature of the "true" author by means of recognizing the false ones.

The "Apology for the, &c" inserted into the fifth edition in 1710 actively argues against naming: "He [the Author] thinks it no fair Proceeding that any Person should offer *determinately* to *fix* [my emphasis] a name upon the Author of this Discourse, who hath all along concealed himself from most of his nearest Friends" (6). Throughout the Apology, curiously, the author refers to himself, as above, in the third person, putting himself in the position of both subject and object and thereby illustrating through a curious sort of self-consciousness his difference from himself. At the close of the *Tale,* the author reveals his plans with his bookseller to promote sales of the book by changing the attribution of authorship through renaming according to literary fashion: "At length we agreed upon this Expedient; That when a Customer comes for me of these, and desires in Confidence to know the Author; he will tell him very privately, as a Friend, naming which ever of the Wits shall happen to be that Week in the Vogue . . ." (207).

The detachability of names from persons, as Veronica Kelly has pointed out, like the detachability of accidents from substances (or signifiers from signifieds), is also instanced in the Bookseller's plans to track down the signified after determining to dedicate the book with the signifier "DETUR DIGNISSIMO" (Kelly 245). And here we find a representation of an ingenious though certainly provisional and fallible means of establishing the meaning, as the Bookseller turns first to a local Curate to English the phrase and then polls the local poets to determine its reference, upon which finding them "all in the same Story . . . infallibly convinced me, that your Lordship was the Person intended by the Author" (24). The task of identification is undertaken through an interrogation of the interpretive community and successfully determines Sommers to be the signified by means of the discovery of consensus in second readings in spite of a complete anarchy of first misreadings. It is perhaps not unimportant that in the process of determining the name of Sommers (i.e., in determining the author's meaning and intention), the Bookseller, not unlike the reader of the *Tale* encountering a *persona,* must repeatedly reject the first identification and seize upon the second.

In a reverse operation, within the allegory of the *Tale,* each of the three brothers becomes named only *after* he has distinguished himself from the others through his reading of the will. Originally, it will be remembered, the three are indistinguishable, even by birth order. In the process of seeking justification for the wearing of shoulder knots, Peter begins to emerge from the trio as a distinct personality on the basis of his careful distinctions: "But the distinguishing Brother (for whom we shall hereafter find a Name) now his Hand was in, proved by a very good Argument that K was a modern illegitimate letter" (84). Peter becomes fully himself and receives his name as he assumes simultaneously the position of hero, author, father, and lord: "He told his Brothers, he would have them to know, that he was their Elder, and consequently his Father's sole Heir; Nay, a while after, he would not allow them to call Him, *Brother,* but Mr. PETER; And then he must be styl'd, *Father* PETER; and sometimes My *Lord* PETER" (105). So, too, only after they have stopped following Peter do Martin and Jack receive names ("These two Brothers began to be distinguished at this Time, by certain Names . . ." [134]). As in the case of Sommers, the process of naming here has two steps: 1) the identification of each brother emerges as a function of individuality and difference, and 2) the name or individuality is then ratified by the interpretive community. As the digression on the Aeolists makes clear in the connection to Jack, each of the three brothers, through his revolution, becomes a strong author, in Harold Bloom's sense, or a founding author in Foucault's sense: the naming of each of the brothers is simultaneously the naming of a discourse, and these namings are thus a function—not a precondition—of discourse. However, in order to read the allegory of the brothers properly, the reader of the *Tale* must exercise judgment in order to distinguish Peter's revolution from Jack's and Martin's counterrevolutions. In Fish's terms, some misreadings are better than others; and some misreadings (especially Peter's and Jack's) are simply untenable. Again, these differences will be arbitrated by the interpretive community established by the *Tale.*

Assuming then that the text of the *Tale,* as sketched out above (and as generally agreed to by both the absolutist and the anarchist textocentric critics, as well as by the *persona* critics) gives instructions for its own reading even as it shows the instability of text and the indeterminacy of reading, I want to return to the problem of the naming of the author of the text, the move which all of the above critics make in order to stabilize their meanings (even when those meanings imply their own instability), and in the process to bring the notion of *persona* to bear upon the textocentrism which has predominated in recent readings of the *Tale.* As the allegory suggests, interpretation is always based upon a leap of faith, and error is routinely the consequence of that leap. But both the interpretation and the leap are necessary if provisional meaning is to be established. In order to stabilize the text at all, it is necessary (as Barthes, Foucault, and Fish all agree) to posit an author (not such a silly assumption, really), and even arguments for the indeterminacy of the *Tale* have done so—but, excepting Zimmerman and Saccamano, they have done so tacitly and have qualified their positions, perhaps precisely because to posit the author "Swift" *is* a leap of faith—not unlike inferring a God from the Creation. Though I am not arguing for the nature of the author/God one posits, I *am* arguing that the leap is voluntary and that the leaps of individual readers are mediated by the discourse of criticism. And, finally, I am arguing that a text that self-consciously induces such a leap is neither authoritarian nor anarchistic but liberal, i.e., it is consonant with a limited monarchy as represented by the constitutional settlement of 1688.

Again let us turn to the text of the *Tale,* and the speaker's suggestions for reading his work: "Whatever Reader desires to have a thorow Comprehension of an Author's Thoughts, cannot take a better Method, than by putting himself into the Circumstances and Postures of Life, that the Writer was in, upon every important Passage as it flow'd from his Pen; For this will introduce a Parity and Strict Correspondence of Ideas between the Reader and the Author" ("Preface" 44). With its subsequent prescriptions for diet, posture, lodging, and monetary condition, this passage mocks both the materialism and the potential solipsism of Lockean epistemology and ironically questions the ability of the reader ever to identify with the author. If we reject the speaker's prescriptions, we must question some suppositions we may have made about reading in the allegory of the coats: if complete identification with the author is not possible (or even possibly desirable), how is it possible to recover the "ideas" and thus the intention and meaning of the author?

It is exactly this complete identification, this Romantic unity between an author and a reader, cohabiting the same transcendent idea, that absolutist critics claim that Swift demands of the reader, via the allegory of the coats. This view of Swift as totalizer seems untenable, either in the early eighteenth century or in the late twentieth century. Swift's remark about his own experience as reader, quoted above, makes clear that he did not experience mystical union with the authors he read, but that, just as in conversation, his ego boundaries remained intact even as he participated in the imaginary dialogue created by reading. The most simplified Hegelian analysis, which tacitly underlies most of the political poststructuralist readings of the *Tale,* of the claim that the Author plays Master to the reader's Slave suggests that even though the Author may offer the definition of the work to be done, it is the Reader/Slave who performs the work and thereby defines its actual existence, and thus the Author is recognized, defined, and in fact constituted by the Reader.[9]

The *Tale*, of course, if read literally, attempts to blur boundaries, including those between author and persona and, as the invitation to imitate the *Tale*-teller's diet indicates, between author and reader. But such blurring is, in fact, the very inducement to the reader to do the work of reading, interpretation, and particularly judgment (characterized in the eighteenth century as the faculty of making distinctions).[10] The reader who accedes passively to the author's demands, that is, who believes in an absolutist Swift who demands Passive Obedience, is a reader who, in the terms of the eighteenth century, has refused to exercise judgment, the capacity for making distinctions, the most important distinctions here being those between author, *persona,* and reader. Interpretations of the *Tale* have long emphasized the polarity between credulity and curiosity, essentially the polarity of wit and judgment. To be credulous and to withhold judgment is to confuse allegory with digression and madness with heroism, as well as to confuse authors with readers. And particularly it is to confuse author and persona.

Although satire is characterized by the representation of confusion, it is, in fact, a genre engaged in boundary keeping and as such it constantly requires the exercise of judgment on the part of the reader. Like a priest, the satirist transgresses boundaries in order to reify them. Absolutist satire, of course, would represent the transgressions committed by others and simply demand that the reader's judgment accede to those judgments explicitly made by the voice of the Father Satirist. A different type of satire, on the other hand, the type of the *Tale,* itself transgresses boundaries and thus provides opportunities for the reader to exercise judgment apparently independently (and thereby to reify those boundaries), although in a pre-established and textually defined context. By eliminating direct access to the voice of the Father Satirist, such satire forces the reader to become conscious of decisions that otherwise may be tacit. When reading satire, as Gerald Bruns points out, "one is always looking for a position to occupy" (122), and one necessarily defines that position in relation to the satirist and the object of the satire. In a satire in which direct access to the Voice of the Satirist is denied, one is also looking for a position for the author to occupy.

I am following here the lead offered by Richard Nash who argues generally that "Swift's irony . . . requires the reader to participate actively in the text's creation of meaning in a manner that conforms to the meaning being created" (431). That is, to the same extent that the author is a product of the work of the reader—but is also identifiable as separate from reader because a function of the text—so too is the *persona* a function of the text and a product of the work of the reader and also distinct, by definition, from the author. Indeed, in the *Tale* the *persona* is a necessary precondition for the reader's construction of the author.

Denied access to the voice of the Father Satirist, the reader must exercise (in fact has already exercised), by determining the absence of the Father's Voice, increasingly fine judgment. Having determined that the voice of the text is not the voice of the satirist, the reader has identified a *persona,* and thus has simultaneously constructed an author who is at once identified with and different from himself. Such a difference is simultaneously opened up within the reader, making it possible, as Bakhtin suggests, not only that the text opens up a dialogic relation with itself but that readers open dialogic relations with themselves.

Such relations are instanced in the often cited passage in which the speaker of the *Tale* explicitly articulates his self-authorization, and in so doing attempts to appropriate the authority of the reader: "I here think fit to lay hold on that great and honourable Privilege of being the *Last Writer*; I claim an absolute Authority in Right, as the *freshest* Modern, which gives me a Despotick Power over all Authors before me" (130). Here the division between Swift and *persona* opens up simultaneously as the division between the reader seeking to follow the text and the reader seeking to judge the text opens up: indeed, following the text creates a division against itself.

What happens, in effect, in the political terms which have been used throughout this essay, is that the reader, through interaction with the text, has recognized an Author as the Father of the text and thus as the purported monarch of the text. The reader recognizes also the abuses against both himself and the text committed by the Father, argues within himself between Passive Obedience and Revolution, justifies Revolution on the basis that the Author is really a Pretender to the Throne (i.e., a *persona*), and consequently conducts a readerly revolution, overthrowing the *persona* and placing in its stead the True Author. Recognizing that such readerly revolutions can lead to textual anarchy and consequent meaninglessness, the reader argues to himself that such revolutions are justified by the Law of Reading, which is founded upon the supposition of the text's constitution as a product of both Author/Father/Monarch and the Parliament of Readers, at whose pleasure the Author shall serve. In short, the reader's recognition of the *persona* within the *Tale* produces an enactment of a constitutional settlement and a mixed or limited monarchy.

Thus far, I have been arguing on the basis of the dynamics of the text of the *Tale* itself. Having now committed patricide/regicide/deicide against the *persona,* it behooves me to justify this revolution to the interpretive community by demonstrating that the new Author whom I have put in the place of the deposed *persona* is the True Author, i.e., Swift, as constituted by other readers and other texts. The political views of Swift are clearly evident elsewhere, and are consistent with the analysis which I have just offered of the reading dynamics of the *Tale*. In his *Sentiments of a Church of England Man,* the author proclaims that "Whoever argues in Defense of absolute Power in a single Person ought, in all free States, to be treated as the common Enemy of Mankind" (*PW* 2: 16). Against the analogy of Author/Monarch to God, the Church of England Man argues that the difference between God and man is also the difference between God's authority and man's authority and that this difference "directly" proves "that no Mortal Man should ever have the like" (2: 17). Indeed, regarding the doctrine of Passive Obedience, Swift argues against the identification of the monarch as Supreme Magistrate to whom such obedience is due: "By the *Supreme Magistrate* is properly understood the Legislative Power, which in all Government must be absolute and unlimited" (2: 16). And in the *Examiner* papers, Swift attacks the doctrine of Passive Obedience by creating a fictional abusive monarch (much like the abusive teller of the *Tale*): "The Doctrine of *Passive Obedience* is to believe that a King, even in a limited Monarchy holding his Power only from God is only answerable to him . . . . If a King of England should go through the Streets of London, in order to murder every Man he met, *Passive Obedience* commands them to submit . . . . The People were certainly created for him, and not he for the People" (3: 112).[11] Finally, let me gesture again to the *Sentiments of a Church of England Man* in which Swift openly avows a preference for anarchy over arbitrary power, and a preference for a limited monarchy over both:

> WHERE Security of Person and Property are preserved by Laws, which none but the *Whole* can repeal, there the great Ends of Government are provided for, whether the Administration be in the hands of *One* or *Many.* Where any one *Person* or *Body* of Men, who do not represent the *Whole* seize into their Hands the Power of the last Resort; there is proper no longer a Government but what Aristotle and his Followers call the Abuse and Corruption of one. This Distinction excludes Arbitrary Power, in whatever Numbers; which, notwithstanding all that *Hobbes, Filmer,* and others have said to its Advantage, I do look upon as a greater Evil than Anarchy itself; as much as a *Savage* is in a happier State of Life, than a *Slave* at the Oar. (2: 15)

The speaker of the *Tale,* the Pretender to the Throne, has recognized not only his own shortcomings but also the possibility of the superior power and judgment of the reader, as for instance when his own tendencies towards anarchism, evidenced in his digressions, suggest the absence of self-control in the controlling presence: "The Necessity of this Digression will easily excuse the Length; and I have chosen for it as proper a Place as I could easily find. If the *judicious* Reader [my emphasis] can assign a fitter, I do here empower him to remove it into any other Corner he pleases" (149). Like a smart monarch, he pretends to give away power when he recognizes his powerlessness.

His deference to readers of the *Tale* indicates a recognition of the dependence of his own status as Master upon the work of the reader as Slave. Such recognition is clear, for instance, as he considers the future of his book and his hope that his words "which, however scattered at random, when they light upon a fruitful Ground, will multiply far beyond either the Hopes or Imagination of the Sower" (186). In fact, the greater the work performed by the reader, the greater the recognition of the author, for writings are "*fruitful* in the Proportion they are *dark*" (186). It is on this assumption that the teller humbly proposes the "experiment" that "every Prince in Christendom will take seven of the *deepest Scholars* in his Dominions, and shut them up close for *seven* Years, in *seven* Chambers, with a Command to write *seven* ample Commentaries on this comprehensive Discourse" and proposes further that "whatever Difference may be found in their several Conjectures, they will be all, without the least Distortion, manifestly deduceable from the Text" (185). This would be textual anarchy indeed. Contradictory meanings are all admitted as equally true, and within such a fantasy the text's meaning becomes indeterminate—absolutely anarchic, one might say. But this occurs only if we assume, as the teller does in his construction of this thought problem, that each scholar is incommunicado with the others and that the charge itself is to generate seven commentaries. Here, difference is sought for its own sake.

In fact, if we refer back to the allegory of the coats, it becomes clear that the initial deviation from the will of the Father comes as a result of the emergence of one of the brothers as the despotick voice of authority, and the passive obedience of the other two brothers, as yet undistinguished, to Peter's interpretation of the will. As Paulson suggests, the dynamics here reflect the conflict between Irenaeus and the Gnostics in the early Church, with Irenaeus maintaining the position, notable for its nonrepresentation in the allegory, that "any necessary interpretation . . . should be agreed upon by a council of the bishops" (101). As Fish maintains, the interpretive community finally arbitrates and negotiates among the individual differences generated by individual readers. We do not stay locked up in our own rooms for seven years. Indeed, the provision of footnotes in the fifth edition of the *Tale* visually represents the text as a social site of contestation and negotiation.

Kevin Cope argues that "Swiftian knowledge, as Shaftesbury might say, is a forming rather than a form" (139). The text itself represents to us an indeterminacy and in so doing offers us the opportunity either to stabilize its meaning through recourse to the collective construction of an authorizing voice or to revel in or lament its indeterminacy. My reading of the *Tale* has *not* resolved the difference between those critics arguing for determinacy and those arguing for indeterminacy; it has only investigated the conditions which make that difference possible. In reading the *Tale* itself as enacting and representing the provisional determinacy of meaning, I have, I hope, demonstrated that such determinacy is not the consequence of absolutism, but of a readerly settlement with authorial authority, a settlement which itself is induced by and represented within the text, and which is consistent with "Swift's" professions of a belief in limited monarchy: "Freedom consists in a People being governed by laws made with their own Consent; and Slavery in the Contrary" ("Drapier Letters" 10: 87).

Finally, let me suggest that this mechanism points to a fundamental truth regarding the efficacy of satire, one which has been implicit in the ongoing discussion of "reader entrapment" in eighteenth-century satire and which is implicit throughout the works of Swift. The most effective satire in the modern age beginning in the eighteenth century is constitutional. Unlike Dryden's effort to authorize his satire in *Absalom and Achitophel* through the revival of the voice of God, Swift abandons the monological Voice of the Satirist Father. In the *Tale,* as in other ironic, Swiftian satires, we, as readers, are satirized by an author whom we have constructed and thus authorized to do so.

## Notes

Composition of this essay was undertaken during a Summer Seminar for College Teachers funded by the National Endowment for the Humanities and directed by Professor John Sitter. I am grateful to the NEH for its support and to Professor Sitter for his patience and assistance as I rehearsed (and re-rehearsed) the argument of the essay with him.

1. For a discussion of the implications of postmodern theory, especially that of Lacan, for analysis of the persona in late seventeenth-century satiric verse, see James E. Gill, "The Fragmented Self in Three of Rochester's Poems."

2. Nigel Wood has made a similar observation, distinguishing two fundamentally different readers of the *Tale*, "the one stressing the culpability of the Teller and the artistry of the omniscient Swift, the other seeing in the *Tale*'s desperate humour Swift's explorations of tensions otherwise inexpressible to an Anglican clergyman" (42). Wood, however, as his labels of "mimetic" critics versus

"textocentric" critics indicate, is pitting what I have called *persona* critics against what I have labeled "poststructuralists." What I am demonstrating here is that the textocentric camp itself is divided into diametrically opposed readings precisely because of differences in mimetic readings which are unacknowledged.

3. In this emphasis on the common ground between factions, I am following Daniel Eilon's lucid analysis of Swift's views on political discourse (*Faction's Fictions*). Similarly, I want to stress my recognition of the value of the analyses with which I appear to be quarreling. My selection of the works of Wyrick and Griffin is based upon their value in representing the two seemingly contrary conclusions which have come to dominate readings of Swift. Both readings are more subtle, perceptive, and instructive than my necessarily oversimplified synopses and selected quotations indicate.

4. See Swift's *Sentiments of a Church of England Man*: "And indeed when the two Parties that divide the whole Commonwealth, come once to a Rupture without any Hopes left of forming a Third with better Principles, to ballance the others; it *seems* [my emphasis] every Man's Duty to chuse one of the two Sides, although he cannot entirely approve of either" (*PW* 2: 2).

5. For a thorough poststructuralist exegesis of these moments, see Jacobsen.

6. I take the liberty here of applying the text of *The Battle* to a reading of the *Tale* on the basis of the original publication of the two texts, along with *The Mechanical Operation* under one cover.

7. The "Apology" of the 1710 edition of the *Tale* notes the ease with which one author may be mistaken for another as well as the frequency with which this situation is exploited: "THERE is in this famous Island of *Britain* a certain paultry *Scribbler*, very voluminous whose Character the Reader cannot wholly be a Stranger to. He deals in a pernicious Kind of Writings, called *Second Parts* and usually passes under the Name of *The Author of the First*. I easily foresee, that as soon as I lay down my Pen, this nimble *Operator* will have stole it . . ." (183). See also, for example, Pope's *Epistle to Dr. Arbuthnot*: "And then for mine obligingly mistakes/The first Lampoon Sir *Will* or *Bubo* makes./Poor guiltless I! and can I choose but smile,/When ev'ry *Coxcomb* knows me by my *style?*" (279–82).

8. I am grateful to Stephen C. Chastain for his thoughts on the relationship between vision and hearing, which inform this paragraph.

9. As Thomas Docherty suggests, summarizing current analyses of authority: "The reader, the critical consciousness located in history, is the position that authorizes or legitimizes the text or its reading. The author is the 'co-respondent' of the reader, and writes or transcribes the text in the face of his own critical reading, a legitimization of the provisional *lex,* or following Barthes, *lexie,* which establishes the very possibility and condition of the text itself" (10).

10. For the importance of reading with judgment, especially in the digressive matter of the *Tale,* see Nash.

11. For a lucid analysis of Swift's views of monarchy, see Michael DePorte's "Avenging Naboth." My notes here on these views, outside of the text of the *Tale*, are based on his essay.

# Works Cited

Atkins, G. Douglas. "Interpretation and Meaning in *A Tale of a Tub*." *Essays in Literature* 8.2 (1981): 233–39.

Bakhtin, M. M. *The Dialogic Imagination: Four Essays.* Trans. Caryl Emerson and Michael Holquist. Austin: U of Texas P, 1981.

Bloom, Harold. *The Anxiety of Influence: A Theory of Poetry.* New York: Oxford UP, 1973.

Bruns, Gerald L. "Allegory and Satire: A Rhetorical Meditation." *New Literary History* 11 (1979): 121–32.

Cooper, Anthony Ashley, Third Earl of Shaftesbury. "Sensus Communis: An Essay on the Freedom of Wit and Humour." *Characteristics of Men, Manners, Opinions, Times.* Ed. John M. Robertson. New York: Bobbs-Merrill, 1964.

Cope, Kevin. *Criteria of Certainty: Truth and Judgment in the English Enlightenment.* Lexington: U of Kentucky P, 1991.

DePorte, Michael V. "Avenging Naboth: Swift and Monarchy." *Philological Quarterly* 69 (1990): 419–33.

Docherty, Thomas. *On Modern Authority: The Theory and Condition of Writing 1500 to the Present Day.* New York: St. Martin's Press, 1987.

Eilon, Daniel. *Faction's Fictions: Ideological Closure in Swift's Satire.* Newark: U of Delaware P, 1991.

Elliott, Robert C. "*A Tale of a Tub*: An Essay in Problems of Structure." *PMLA* 66 (1951): 441–55.

Fabricant, Carole. "The Battle of the Ancients and (Post)Moderns: Rethinking Swift through Contemporary Perspectives." *The Eighteenth Century: Theory and Interpretation* 32.3 (1991): 256–73.

Filmer, Sir Robert. *Patriarcha and Other Writings.* Ed. Johann P. Sommerville. Cambridge: Cambridge UP, 1991.

Fish, Stanley. *Is There a Text in This Class? The Authority of Interpretive Communities.* Baltimore: Johns Hopkins UP, 1981.

Foucault, Michel. "What Is an Author?" *Language, Counter-Memory, Practice: Selected Essays and Interviews by Michel Foucault.* Ed. Donald F. Bouchard. Trans. Donald F. Bouchard and Sherry Simon. Ithaca: Cornell UP, 1977.

Gill, James E. "The Fragmented Self in Three of Rochester's Poems." *Modern Language Quarterly* 49.1 (Mar. 1988): 19–37.

Griffin, Dustin. "Interpretation and Power: Swift's *Tale of a Tub*." *The Eighteenth Century: Theory and Interpretation* 34.2 (1993): 151–68.

Jacobsen, Richard. "Absence, Authority, and the Text." *Glyph* 3 (1978): 137–47.

Kelly, Veronica. "Following the Stage Itinerant: Perception, Doubt, and Death in Swift's *Tale of a Tub*." *Studies in Eighteenth-Century Culture* 17 (1987): 239–58.

Locke, John. *An Essay concerning Human Understanding*. Ed. Peter H. Nidditch. Oxford: Clarendon, 1975.

————. *Two Treatises of Government*. Ed. Peter Laslett. Cambridge: Cambridge UP, 1960.

Nash, Richard. "Entrapment and Ironic Method in *A Tale of a Tub*." *Eighteenth-Century Studies* 24 (1991): 415–31.

Paulson, Ronald. *Theme and Structure in Swift's* A Tale of a Tub. New Haven, CT: Yale UP, 1960.

Rawson, Claude J. *Gulliver and the Gentle Reader: Studies in Swift and Our Time*. London: Routledge and Kegan Paul, 1973.

Saccamano, Neil. "Authority and Publication: The Works of 'Swift.'" *The Eighteenth Century: Theory and Interpretation* 25.3 (1984): 241–62.

Said, Edward. "Swift's Tory Anarchy." *Eighteenth-Century Studies* 3.1 (1969): 48–66.

Swift, Jonathan. *The Prose Works of Jonathan Swift*. Ed. Herbert Davis. 14 vols. Oxford: Clarendon, 1937–68.

————. *A Tale of a Tub*. Ed. A. C. Guthkelch and D. Nichol Smith. 2nd ed. Oxford: Clarendon, 1958.

Wood, Nigel. *Swift*. Sussex. Harvester, 1986.

Wyrick, Deborah Baker. *Jonathan Swift and the Vested Word*. Chapel Hill and London: U of North Carolina P, 1988.

Zimmerman, Everett. *Swift's Narrative Satires: Author and Authority*. Ithaca: Cornell UP, 1983.

# Pharmakon, Pharmakos, and Aporetic Structure in Gulliver's "Voyage to . . . the Houyhnhnms"

## James E. Gill

One approach to the problem of reading Gulliver's fourth voyage which has not, as far as I am aware, been attempted is an examination of the satire in terms of scapegoating mentalities and mechanisms, and so I would like to approach Part IV of the *Travels* in one of those admittedly partial efforts to understand the peculiar "deferring" nature of its symbolism, argument, and plot by taking a cue from both deconstructionist and "sacrificial" as well as reader-response or "entrapment" critics.[1] I especially borrow from Jacques Derrida in "Plato's Pharmacy," René Girard in *The Scapegoat,* and Andrew J. McKenna's penetrating *Violence and Difference,* a work which examines the parallels in the thought of Derrida and Girard. Rather than the mélange or succession of generic modes or contexts which Frederick N. Smith and others have recently studied in the *Travels* as decentering or "exploding" its meaning, I am concerned to deal with some of the displacements and deferrals of satiric effects in Part IV of *Gulliver* which may be said to entrap the reader through the devices and themes of pharmakon and pharmakos—the cure-poison and the physician-scapegoat—as these relate to the symbolism of Yahoo and Houyhnhnm and as they are related to Gulliver's desire to remain in and his exile from Houyhnhnmland. I hope to show how a satiric scheme—one doubtless supporting a logocentric view but also self-deconstructive—employs the radical differential devices (i.e., deferring and displacing devices) of the cure/poison and of successive scapegoatings in ways that suggest but do not always consciously embrace deconstruction of its own procedures. The resulting structure is "aporetic," one which defers closure by suggesting an ongoing "sacrificial crisis."[2]

Beginning with Girard, I wish briefly to explain what I believe to be the relevant aspects of his sacrificial theory, even as elaborated or modified by several of his critics and followers. The process of victimization, according to Girard, is complex and arises from complicated rivalries, including the "hidden" rivalry (either "imitative" or "emulative")—in which model may also become obstacle—between follower and leader as well as between equals or enemies.[3] It produces what Girard calls the "sacrificial crisis": "a crisis of distinctions . . . affecting the cultural order . . . , a regulated system of distinctions in which the differences among individuals are used to establish their 'identity' and their mutual relationships" (Girard, *Violence and the Sacred* 49). The victim of persecution or the scapegoat is not, according to Girard, collectively persecuted because she is different—most societies, as Girard observes, tolerate variant behavior; s/he is rather persecuted because s/he threatens a society's *system* of differences. No matter how weak and impotent such scapegoats may appear to be, they are credited with sinister powers if in their being and/ or actions they are seen as attacking "the very foundation of cultural order, the family, and the hierarchical differences without which a distinctive social order might not exist. In the sphere of individual being and action they correspond to the global consequences of an epidemic of the plague or of any comparable intellectual disaster (such as those imagined, for example, by the opponents of evolutionary theory). It is not enough for the social bond to be loosened; it must be totally destroyed" (Girard, *The Scapegoat* 15) or threatened with disaster. In actual persecutions, the victim—from society's point of view as victimizer—possesses certain traits: he is an outsider; it is feared that he possesses sinister powers; he is in some sense physically or morally monstrous; and the victim's expulsion rids the community of perceived dangers. But in myth and ritual the scapegoat may also be curiously innocent, may possess healing powers, and may even in some sense cause a "belief in transcendental power that is . . . double and will bring . . . both loss and health, punishment and recompense" (44). From this doubleness can arise even a belief in the curative and creative power of "generative scapegoating" (Girard, *Violence and the Sacred* 106), and texts which depict violent persecution may take the perspective of either the persecutors or the victims. The scapegoat, or *pharmakos,* combines both the capacity to endanger and, if even only in a privative way, to heal the community. As Derrida observes, the *"pharmakos* (wizard, magician, poisoner)" is both a physician and a scapegoat.[4]

> The *evil* and the *outside*, the expulsion of the evil, its exclusion out of the body (and out of) the city—these are the two major senses of the character and of the ritual. . . . The ceremony of the *pharmakos* is thus played out on the boundary line between inside and outside, which it has as its function ceaselessly to trace and retrace. *Intra muros/extra muros.* The origin of difference and division, the *pharmakos* represents evil both introjected and projected. Beneficial insofar as he cures—and for that venerated and cared for—harmful insofar as he incarnates the powers of evil—and for that, feared and treated with caution. Alarming and calming. Sacred and accursed. The conjunction, the *coincidentia oppositorum*, ceaselessly undoes itself in the

passage to decision or crisis. The expulsion of the evil or madness restores *sōphrosunē* (*Dissemination* 132–33).

Now the relevance of this general scheme to satire is most interesting since satire makes many of the same claims that the "victimary hypothesis" makes in that it records rivalries between different positions, both punishes the monstrous and presumes to cure, and both alienates and restores. The term "satiric victim" is strangely double since it may refer to the entity which is attacked within satire, whether by the satirist or by agents whom the satirist attacks (the satirist may excoriate knaves who victimize fools, for example). The satiric victim is often credited with sinister powers and is seen as threatening society in fundamental ways. On the other hand the satiric victim may be risible or pitiful because he may appear to be no match for the forces arrayed against him—she may be victimized by other satiric victims. The satirist himself may be threatened and either cowed or driven to take desperate measures—the poet in *The Epistle to Dr. Arbuthnot,* for example, at first wants only relief from the importunities of his admirers as well as enemies and from this retiring position is driven to diatribe. And the satirist, according to traditional satiric theory, may purge himself of unhealthy emotion at the same time that he purges society of polluting attitudes and agents. Even so, by curious reversals, the satirist, like the persecutor, may incur blame—may be satirized—and the victim may in some way—by cure or even by his absence from it—contribute to the re-establishment of community.

In all this there is a powerful complicity between the victim and the victimizer since scapegoating probably is possible because of the victimizer's assumption of an imaginary consubstantiality with the offending party—an interpretation of the victim's motives and beliefs in terms of desiderata and their antitypes. Victimizer and victim can achieve, in a limited sense, an understanding and sometimes even a kind of sympathy each with the other in ways which may repel either or both as well as a third party and render both culpable. Horror at real or imagined evil involves a kind of "mimetic" alienation from the self and even from one's society. What is desired or admired can be perceived and imagined in terms of what is feared and hated, and the hatred and fear of violence-as-difference, for example, can produce violent, reactive thought and behavior. Representation of the desirable through its antitypes may thus become an inherently and sometimes uncontrollably violent process in quite complex ways, and thus the victim "is not a property of the system . . . but the impropriety that the system seeks to ignore in order to function." In this case the victim stands for "sacrificial, exclusionary mechanisms that are blind to their own violence, which is ever imputed to the element they expel" (McKenna 189–190).

Yet another aspect of the "sacrificial paradigm" or theme is compression of the functions of the pharmakos into the pharmakon, the cure-poison—sometimes represented as a potion which relieves pain by deadening the senses and the memory. As Girard observes in connection with the Platonic critique of writing as a pharmakon—a topic which Derrida has treated extensively—"the Platonic *pharmakon* functions like the human pharmakos and leads to similar results" (Girard, *Violence and the Sacred* 296). That is, as a drug which can injure or kill as well as promote forgetfulness, forgiveness, and/or health, the pharmakon is possessed of a doubleness analogous to that of the mythic scapegoat. A classic example of the pharmakon is the potion Helen administers to Telemakos and his Spartan hosts to make them forget past griefs in *Odyssey* IV.219–32 (47–48).

These powers are, as I have noted, the subject of Jacques Derrida's brilliant critique of Socrates's scapegoating of writing in Plato's *Phaedrus* and of the "violent" inception of philosophy itself as a result of that sacrificial crisis. Writing is threatening not because of writing's difference from origin, "the selfsame presence of the idea (*eidos*)," but because of "its indifference to origins [presence], whence its paradoxical likeness to the origin it supplants" (McKenna 28–29). Writing becomes a surrogate for or supplement to "the selfsame presence of the idea." "It is not, so to speak, dangerous in itself, in that aspect of it that presents itself as a thing, as a being present. In that case it would be reassuring. But the supplement is not, is not a being (*on*). It is nevertheless not a simple nonbeing (*mē on*) either. Its sliding slips it out of the simple alternative presence/absence. *That* is the danger. And that is what enables the types always to pass for the original. As soon as the supplementary outside is opened, its structure implies that the supplement can itself be 'typed,' replaced by its double, and that a supplement to the supplement, a surrogate for the surrogate, is possible and necessary. Necessary because this movement is not a sensible, 'empirical' accident: it is linked to the ideality of *eidos* as the possibility of the repetition of the same" (Derrida 109).

Writing brings into existence the chain of signifiers whereby meaning can be distorted and displaced away from its clear springs of sense. Writing includes the possibility that it is not itself, and it bears all the subversive, monstrous traits, as well as the meliorative ones, typical of the scapegoat. In the Platonic critique, according to Derrida, writing "is insubordinate in principle and, more importantly, of principle as such. As such it must be repressed much as the scapegoat is sacrificed. The emergence of the logos as the condition of truth, of the presence of the idea to itself, is thus traced to the expulsion of an otherness in which it originates" (McKenna 32). But its trace remains, and there is not, nor can there be, a harmless remedy, a remedy that is not a pharmakon, a cure-poison that does not bear the trace of its "violent" origins. In the suppression of insubordinate writing, according Derrida, Socratic-Platonic philosophy is born.

Keeping in mind that I am not arguing that Swift specifically follows Plato's deeply abstract and deeply nested argument in the *Phaedrus,* much less the analytical schemes of any twentieth-century critics, the reader must understand that I perceive in the later seventeenth century an argument analogous to that we have been following—one that privileged a kind of quick, clear induction over the "rotten weed of putation" or chains of reasoning. And I think there was connected with confidence in this "rational intuition" a deep distrust of abstraction, hypostatized entities, and chains of reasonings, especially as these appear in complicated written arguments. This kind of thought was deeply conscious of the "deferring" nature of "the rotten weed of mere putation" and of what today we might call the supplement, of "excesses" in figuration, say in metaphor and other tropes, which in the hands of satirists like the Scriblerians could lead to the development of the literalization of metaphor and other devices in the "art of sinking" employed in many of their satires.[5] The kind of thought which I am attributing to Swift is, of course, deeply logocentric even while it is also deeply suspicious of much philosophical writing. And thus, as I have said, while Swift's devices and practices are not the same as Derrida's concepts and strategies, the latter may have considerable power in the explanation of the former because both are, in radically different ways, acutely aware of a similar problems—the violence of representation, the scapegoating tendencies of "systematic" thought, and hence the omnipresence of a kind of sacrificial crisis of the intellect.

Let us then examine "The Voyage . . . the Houyhnhnms" for pharmakon- and pharmakos-like devices and structures, marked as they are by substitution, awareness or traces of intellectual violence, and deferral. Discussion of such devices and deferring structures can be perhaps effectively initiated by commenting on the very clear appearance of a quite literal pharmakon in Chapter VII of Part IV, where it appears as both narrative fact and as metaphor. In the midst of a devastating comparison of relatively simple Yahoo versions and very complicated civilized versions of human infirmities and evils, of diseases and their possible cures, the pharmakon signals the problematic of outside and inside and of physical/moral disease and cure. Here there is a description of the chief illness of the Yahoos, "the only animals in this Country subject to any Diseases; which however, were much fewer than Horses [and men] have among us, and contracted not by any ill Treatment they meet with, but by the Nastiness and Greediness of that sordid Brute." The cure for this mélange of diseases arising from surfeit, "*Hnea Yahoo, or the Yahoo's-Evil,*" as it is earlier described by the Master horse to Gulliver, is a "Mixture of *their own Dung and Urine,* forcibly put down the Yahoo's Throat. This I have since often known to have been taken with success: And do here freely recommend it to my Countrymen, for the publick Good, as an admirable Specifick against all Diseases produced by Repletion" (246).

One aspect of this micro-allegory of the Houyhnhnms' medicinal remedy for Yahoo's-Evil is that a common structure of feeling in the *Travels* —alimentary-excretory disgust—is again brought into play, is asserted, and then is disrupted or dissipated: a revolting animal who habitually gorges itself and has the temerity to affect "melancholy" also habitually is then readily cured of these maladies by being forced to ingest its own excrement. Suggested is a dynamic wherein excess or vice is followed by a reaction of disgust (the ingesting of the product of disgust); disgust is followed, curiously, by a "purification" or restoration of health and, it may be, a renewed indifference to moral soundness.[6] Crudely one might say, "When a creature succumbs to inactivity or 'overfeeds,' 'sh——happens'; men besh—— themselves and each other, and for a cure they must be fed their own and others' excrement. When they get fed up or when they overindulge or imagine themselves ill, a dose of their own 'dung' can sometimes do them a world of good and restore them to their normal — —— and ———— selves." Disgust, which Dr. Johnson saw as the primary emotion of the *Travels,* is here disrupted, if only for a moment, into relief, a restoration of the Yahoo to his "normal" Yahoo self chiefly because this cure is really as much a fit return for the kind of activities typical of Yahoos, a pay-off which restores a kind of balance to the Yahoo's excesses (Johnson II: 204). The passage perhaps alludes to scraps of popular wisdom such as "it has to get worse before it can get better" and "if it doesn't taste bad it can't do any good" and certainly "slackers and wrongdoers deserve a dose of their own 'medicine.'"

Thus one aspect of the package is that of cure-as-patterned-disruption (or even reversal), the *pharmakon,* the "poison" which is also the remedy exploited, for example, by Helen in the *Odyssey* and critiqued by Socrates in the *Phaedrus* and which, as we have noted above in Derrida, is there associated with the idea of the scapegoating of writing as a supplement always threatening to supplant living speech even as it seeks to avoid and thereby remedy its evanescence. As vile products of their misshapen bodies, the Yahoo's ordure is clearly the product of their gluttonous excesses, and hence it symbolizes their filthy habits, their hatreds, sloth, and vile dispositions, which must be ingested by their producer in order to neutralize them or at least to distract from the imaginary evils of "the spleen." But the "medicine" may also be seen as being like satire itself, a form of writing, in a way the record and the product of filthy living tainted by its subject, yet so much dead matter or externalized or abstracted knowledge. It is a form of knowledge distanced from the living being and living lore—a "poison," an evil concoction, which in a manner the satirist crams down the satiric victim's throat as an unpleasant remedy or a punishment—the abstracted product/knowledge of his own sordid behavior. And it results even in an attendant self- and species-hatred on the one hand (one of the peculiar marks of man-Yahoo) or in a transient revulsion and forgetfulness on the other. Such satiric hatred recalls not merely a satirist's hatred of vice but a general theme of the alienation of man from man and from nature which figures prominently in the early response of Gulliver to the Yahoos and theirs to Gulliver when they "discharge their Excrements on [Gulliver's] Head" (208).

In reading the passage describing this "cure" the question arises whether indeed the action of the pharmakon on the Yahoo is merely physical and as spectacle, sacrificial—a punishment the aftermath of which is mere "comic" relief—or whether it is curative and remedies, if only temporarily, the Yahoo's condition. In other words, is the idea of satire presented as merely punitive or as corrective? Here is a question indeed calculated to entrap the reader reflexively, for it draws him beneath the surface of the narrative to ponder the effect of satire on himself. Is satire, as Swift ironically states in the *Tale,* a futile kick vainly expended on, or felt only for a moment by, the world's insensate posteriors (48)? Does the violence in and behind the so-called cure victimize or sacrifice the satiric victim to the reader's need to see and to experience punishment and purification of others? Is satire a "violent" concoction now become a punitive and/or purgative end in itself? In this instance the Yahoo is forced to ingest the pharmakon and the reader forced into the readerly crisis of ironic entrapment. The reader can ignore the demand to interpret the micro-allegory, or he can explore its doublenesses. In the latter case, satire will seem to be both violently punitive and possibly curative, vile and corrective; for the allegorical and thematic thrust of the passage cannot quite obscure or displace the cruelty of the cure any more than the cruelty of the cure can forcefully dislodge the reader's need to rationalize and apply it. Indeed, the thetic dimension (or thematics) of the passage may not, indeed must not, entirely displace the ontic dimension or the mimetic effects of the vile and violent remedy, for surely there is considerable figural play between them.[7] The techniques and problematic of satire seem to be reflexively encapsulated here inasmuch as the uses of cruelty are at issue; and such play can be seen as aporetic inasmuch as it is disruptive or deferring—it effectively interrupts the narrative with an undecidable problem.

Hence the function of the pharmakon in *Gulliver* is suggested to the modern reader by, but is not identical with, Derrida's description of the irony of the "book and the drug," the "grapheme" and the "cure," and the "myth itself"; in this case something like the "myth of satire" (that is, the traditional narrative strategies, ironies, and aims of satire) is itself a pharmakon, the poison and a kind of "heart's ease" whose embodiment and condemnation of excess and violence fails to obscure entirely its own excess and violence. It becomes the ambiguous supplement—in a way like the *figure* of the Yahoo, which is itself deeply ambiguous, as we shall see, because it both symbolizes human evil and is paradoxically superior to civilized man. It corresponds to those doubts about the efficacy and morality of satire which Swift registered elsewhere in several places. It becomes, like Plato's view of the pharmakon, the destabilized signifier inevitably arising from, but not inevitably pointing to, an easily problematized version of a living truth. In short, it describes aporetically and reflexively its own technique and its own problematic—a violent effort to expel vice not entirely consistent with its moral purpose. It is ingested and experienced not so much to perceive truth decisively as to experience revulsion and dialectical reaction—violent reaction to a violent representation, and perhaps then followed by a measured reaction in a reflexive process. The distance between these two kinds of reaction defines the satire's aporetic structure. The displacing effects of the cure—the vile "drug" to purge vice, the "dead letter" of satire—and the scapegoating of the Yahoo point toward a need for, but stand against, the vital internalization of satiric "truth." Sometimes forgetful of its effort to create moral knowledge, punitive satire can become an end in itself—the supplement. Satire then both can remain the stuff of the supplement, an "excretion" which must be voided, and yet can also be re-ingested to become either more "excrement" on the one hand, or on the other, perhaps, a provocation to a deeper kind of knowledge.

In short, both the purge as supplement and the purging of the supplement are related to and here are figured forth by the pharmakon which emulates and accompanies the appearance of the pharmakos, the one being the externalized version of the other. On one level the cure is a punitive dose of one's own excrement—one's own evil or poison. The diseased Yahoo who partakes of this disgusting concoction may be (temporarily) restored to health but is not necessarily transformed by it beyond Yahooness any more than man is permanently lifted from the hidden sordidness of his condition by forcing upon him the knowledge of his vileness. Rather the Yahoo is confirmed as consisting in the vile concoction. The mixture of dung and urine is then both metonymic synecdoche and metaphoric synecdoche—that "excrement" which is displaced from humanity and a violent condensation in and of it—both of and outside its source.[8]

The appearance and function of the pharmakon here then is like many of those aporetic offsets of meaning in the work, especially in Part IV. The attempt to eliminate excess, as it turns out, generates it own excess. The term "pharmakon" may well be used to describe those self-decon-structing techniques and strategies of Part IV which generate the entrapping aporia which have so perplexed its many readers.

As Derrida observes (critically) of Socratic dialectic, "good remedy . . . comes to disturb the intestinal organization of self-complacency. The purity of the inside can then only be restored if the charges are brought home against exteriority as supplement, inessential yet harmful to the essence, a surplus that ought never to have come to be added to the un-touched plenitude of the inside" (128). If then one were to attempt to apply this concept to the case at hand, one could argue that only the Houyhnhnms seem to preserve their "essence" untainted and that if the Yahoo can, for a time, "remedy" some of mankind's principal evils by achieving a strange, dialectical superiority to civilized men, as in fact they do (Gill, "Man and Yahoo" 80–82), then this internal economy is repli-cated at the social level in Houyhnhnmland since there is also a further displacement of the sordid onto the figure of the Yahoo, of the "animal-in-the-human" onto the human animal.

Let me adumbrate this contention. A retrospective view of the development of the dialectic in chapters III–IV and a brief commentary on several other aspects and devices in Part IV can contribute vital support to my argument. In brief, as the dialogue/dialectic of the Master Houyhnhnm and Gulliver begins in chapter III to develop around the question of the relationship of Gulliver and the Yahoo of Houyhnhnmland, the noxious Yahoo grows into a figure or symbol of human vice and folly, associated with at least six of the seven deadly sins and violations of all of the cardinal virtues. But in the theriophilic dialectic of these chapters the Yahoo also becomes the beast somehow superior to civilized man. For while the Yahoo is loaded with the opprobrium of vice and folly in the work's symbolism, in contrast, Gulliver, in accord with the Master Houyhnhnm's dialectic, finds that civilized man, though cleaner than the Yahoo, is not only physically weaker ("he thought in point of real advantage I differed for the worse") but also somehow morally worse than the natural Yahoo. He finds, in short, that those traits which had hitherto been seen to his advantage—his cleanliness, his capacity for speech, and his "rudiments of reason"—come in fact to count against him because the Master horse discovers in civilized man's reason chiefly a means to "aggravate our *natural* corruptions" [i.e., the corruptions shared with the natural Yahoo] and to acquire new ones "which Nature had not given us" (243). Similarly, human speech becomes the medium of lying. And Gulliver's clothes and clean skin, the external mask and "sign" of the inner being, become signs of weakness, not strength. These last, however, possess some of the same ambiguity as the pharmakon—their "being" is "problematic," and they are external to Gulliver yet are the mark of civilized man. Even human reason and speech come to have a similar ambiguousness. They signal, "remedy," and conceal man's condition as well as "aggravate" it and hence partake of all the ambiguity of the supplementary.

Human reason is especially ambiguous. "Reason" for the Houyhnhnms consists in clear and distinct intuitions, not chains of inferences and conclusions remote from the clear springs of sense—it is not "problematic as among us, where one can argue on both sides of the question with some plausibility." Their reason then is not a chain of reasoning based on a succession of displaced signifiers but an immediate, present perception of what is: it is "fiduciary cognition." Stemming in part from Baconian hostility to rationalism and in part from the Cynic-Stoic/Skeptic distinction between *logos prophorikos* ("uttered reason") and *logos endiathetos* (the reason in and of nature), the reason of the horses consists of simple, immediate ends-means intuitions whereas that of man is characterized by complex, "remote" chains of inferences (Gill, "Theriophily in Antiquity" 404–8). For man, reason is bound to a chain of representative but misleading substitutes just as clothes represent but disguise man's "inner" nature. The operations of aporia in the text complicate the issue of mediating between our world and Houyhnhnmland because of their disruptions of the systems of differentiation of both Houyhnhnmland and Europe and indeed because of the depiction of the various subspecies of mankind as more and more remote from the world of reasonable and natural creatures. The question of the model of mankind is raised in an amusing but ultimately frightful way as the Master Houyhnhnm begins to understand European civilization through his understanding of the Yahoos and not, as hitherto, explaining the Yahoos to Gulliver as strange, alien beings somewhat like men.

Now as we have noted, the natural Yahoo—an alien being whom the Master Houyhnhnm, in accord with a theriophilic stratagem, has seen as superior in a privative way to civilized man—becomes both a condensation of human evil (metaphor) and the figure on whom and from whom human evil is displaced (metonym); the figure of the Yahoo in fact functions as the pharmakon/pharmakos—both as the representation and the displacement of human evil, as warning sign of evil, and as the means of its avoidance and expulsion—and thus it becomes doubly a scapegoat for Gulliver and civilized man. This fact can be seen after Gulliver has been convinced of his close kinship with the Yahoo by his Master's comparison of civilized man with them and by his own observations of those animals. For Gulliver and his Master also constitute that aspect of self which is the observer—in this case the pharmakos as recognizer, physician, and diagnostician—the potential cure or curer of human evil.

Now one can say that the terms "pharmakon" and "pharmakos" might well be used to describe the peculiar kind of metaphoric/metonymic figuration peculiar to Part IV as well as to denote the complex strategies of scapegoating, for one can be seen as a figure and pattern of the other's aporetic structure and supplementarity.

This complexity is seen most clearly, for example, in the simultaneous recognition-avoidance pattern—the precise pattern of the pharmakon—of Gulliver's seeing his own reflection: "When I happened to behold the Reflection of my own Form in a Lake or Fountain, I turned away my Face in Horror and detestation of my self; and could better endure the Sight of a common *Yahoo,* than of my own person." The sight of the Yahoo as Pharmakos has become like the Pharmakon itself, the medicine that both poisons with a sense of human ordure and, by repulsing, "distancing," and thereby encouraging a kind of forgetfulness, "cures." Its action is now again double in that it meliorates in one way by reminding Gulliver of human evil and his own weakness, and in another way by again displacing it, as it were, from one's self onto the figure of the Yahoo. But still, the passage implicitly preserves the Master's judgment of civilized man as being worse than the natural Yahoo—the sight of the Yahoo is more endurable than the sight of one's self; also it embodies the return of humanity's hatred of the ~~human~~—humanity's alienation from itself; and, finally, by implication it suggests also the satiric critique of its satiric vision in addition to all the previous implicit satiric critiques of earlier satiric visions that occur in the *Travels.* Gulliver as Yahoo and Gulliver as satirist, in a key aporetic passage, come together in Gulliver as pharmakos, as the doctor or surgeon/scapegoat—the embodier/hater/(a)voider of human vice and folly. His condition in Houyhnhnmland replicates the pharmakon/pharmakos invagination as he becomes for the Houyhnhnms the means whereby they, through his adulation and advice, may find the logos confirmed for them; yet by exiling him they can expel—as *he* becomes the pharmakos as victim—the supplement which he represents in their world. In short, the patterned displacements of the pharmakon/pharmakos of the later chapters of Part IV differ from but coalesce with the displacements in the earlier Cynic-Stoic-Pyrrhonist dialectic, imagery, and language of its first seven and half chapters in which the Yahoo is both better and worse than civilized man and in which clothes are both a sign of physical and moral weakness and of a saving modesty (Gill, "Beast over Man" 540–42, and Gill, "Man and Yahoo" 72–73); and these aporia lead readers to question their implicitly conflicting critical assertions, and by their off-setting or aporetic strategies they thus complicate the already complex problems of interpretation and mediation in the work.

As a mixed creature (a "gentle Yahoo"), as the subject who in his polysemous capacity to inhabit (even if only fitfully) and to disrupt radically different universes of discourse, Gulliver is both more acceptable to his Master than the natural Yahoo and also eventually more intolerable among the Houyhnhnms not despite his admiration of them but because of it—his pretensions to Houyhnhnm-ity are what enable the horses to "bring home the supplement" and hence are as responsible as his Yahoo-like qualities for provoking his exile. Gulliver is scapegoated because in a classic sense he threatens to disrupt the differential system of his hosts' world. Yet his self-hatred is such that he "could not blame the Assembly's *Exhortation* [to exile him], or the Urgency of his [Master's] Friends; yet in my weak and corrupt Judgment, I thought it might consist with Reason to have been less rigorous" (264), Houyhnhnm reason is more rigorous, consistent, and exclusive than human reason; because Houyhnhnm thought cannot tolerate mixed categories or undistributed means, because supplementarity only provokes the dialectical response restoring the logos, the horses cannot tolerate in their society even a gentle Yahoo. But to Gulliver such reasoning is bound to seem almost arbitrary, and indeed the language of Gulliver's response just quoted echoes with few differences the language of his earlier response to the arbitrary "lenient" sentence of blinding which the Lilliputian council passes on him for imaginary crimes: as he says in Part I, "I was so ill a Judge of Things, that I could not discover the *Lenity* and Favour of this Sentence; but conceived it (perhaps erroneously) rather to be rigorous than gentle. I sometimes thought of standing my Tryal; for although I could not deny the Facts alledged in the several Articles, yet I hoped they would admit of some Extenuations" (56–57). This parallel suggests the slender but real difference between narrow, hardened Lilliputian hatred and rigorous Houyhnhnm logic—between persecution on the one hand and purification on the other. In both cases Gulliver is alienated, forced out, scapegoated as it were, in the interests of ideological unity as well as political control and stability; and this stability and the admiration for it that implicates Gulliver and his "masters" in such "ideology" provide the bond of mutual admiration and emulation which leads to the emulation/idealization/scapegoating mechanism which René Girard and Paisley Livingston have so ably explained and which McKenna views as Girard's thematizing "the moral impulse of deconstruction in its ever more subtle detections of unconscious violence—the double bond and necessary complicity of admired and admirer as definers and distinguishers of each other.[9] This bond is, of course, the inverse of the disruption called scapegoating, and yet it is related to it inasmuch as it becomes the basis of rivalries.

Scapegoating, it must be remembered, requires at least two parties in a profoundly ambiguous relationship inasmuch as it requires (in one form at least) deeply ambiguous collusion between superior and inferior, between those casting out evil and those who embody it and bear it away. Both are in a sense physicians, and their bond is admiration of essential purity or at least what Girard calls "mimetic desire," the desire in some sense to emulate and/or be emulated. And it is common for the victim of a scapegoating relationship, in one or more of his avatars, to become the one who also demands sacrifices from and of others—"'Desire is always using for its own ends the knowledge that it has acquired of itself. . . . [It] bears light, but puts that light at the service of its own darkness'" (Livingston 77). Moreover, as Girard points out in his remarks on historical episodes of persecution, it is not difference which provokes scapegoating but threatened disruption of a crucial system of differentiation (Girard, *The Scapegoat* 20–21): it is not merely that Gulliver differs from Houyhnhnm and Yahoo but that he threatens the system of differentiation whereby they are separated.[10] Later, Gulliver performs the same favor for his countrymen: as misanthrope and lover of the horses, Gulliver, exiled from his Master, scapegoats all mankind as Yahoos and is himself (with Swift) duly scapegoated by the critics who cannot tolerate his disruption of their own systems of differentiation.

In this instance, and perhaps in others too, the capacity of deconstructive/sacrificial theory to adumbrate the satiric enterprise develops out of its awareness of the profound ambiguities of language, and the ironic negotiations of the critical mind with itself as it grows sensitive to the peculiar characteristics of differential systems, including the violence on which they are based or by which they preserve themselves. Most satirists are aware that they are liable to charges of "bad faith"—that their condemnation of certain kinds of violence displays its own violence, and that their violent enterprise borders on being futile or even counterproductive. Finally, I believe, some of them become aware that eventually they are seen as confounding the distinctions which they so insistently demand, and so they themselves become subject to scapegoating.

In Part I of *Gulliver*, Swift, through the big/little symbolism, has mimicked the power of "ideology" to cut into and pervert structures of feeling and yet to mask its own violence. Gulliver very nearly becomes its victim and is lucky to escape the little people's attempt to sacrifice him on the altar of its sense of "purity." In Lilliput "sizing" serves the power structure just as in Houyhnhnmland a stable "nature" and a rigorous "reason" serve a society from which civilized man is alienated through a violence of representation at once comic and mordantly ironic. It is comic because the Houyhnhnms imagine Gulliver capable of such trivial mischief. In a passage that sounds like a parody of country gentry complaining of unruly servants, poachers, and outlanders, the horses fear that a Yahoo "with some Rudiments of Reason, added to the natural Pravity of those Animals, . . . might be able to seduce them into the woody and mountainous Parts of the Country, and bring them in Troops by Night to destroy the Houyhnhnms Cattle, as being naturally of the ravenous Kind, and averse from Labour." And it is ironic because despite his adulation of the horses, Gulliver as a civilized man is capable of much worse, as well as much better deeds: neither the Houyhnhnms nor Yahoos have been offered the secret of gunpowder as was the King of Brobdingnag.[11]

Still, the double bond of mimetic desire is apparent in the relationship of Gulliver and his Master when the latter entertains the idea of castrating, i.e., denaturing, Yahoos as potential cure, a kind of negative supplement, or at least (like a dose of Yahoo dung and urine) as yet another "melioration" of the Yahoos' evil. Indeed, this "cure" suggests both the role of the pharmakos as physician and the rite of the pharmakos, of scapegoating as practiced by the ancient Athenians who attacked specifically the pudenda of the pharmakoi ejected from the city in rituals of purification since "once the *pharmakoi* were cut off from the space of the city, the blows were designed to chase away or draw out the evil from their bodies" (Derrida 131–32). This passage coheres with the earlier device of the pharmakon in establishing the successive scapegoatings of the last chapters of *Gulliver.*

We are now perhaps able to assess the complications and the ambiguities implicit in the devices of pharmakon and pharmakos, for they constantly refer the reader to efforts to restore primitive purity, or to renew the social order, and of the impure or compromised nature of those efforts. By penetrating to and evoking the "originary" violence at the heart of social differentiation and by disrupting the effort of myth and social codes to transform the violence of sacrifice into social altruism, such efforts are themselves compromised. As Michael Seidel, on the basis of Girardian analysis, reasons in his fine study of satire, the satirist's penetration of even the most innocuous patterns of behavior can involve a kind of regressive complicity in a moment of profound disorder that has become the foundation of ordered behavior (17–21). It becomes possible under this view to see—with the Marxists and Nietzsche, among others—a kind of entropic "spiritualization and deification of cruelty" as permeating, through sacrificial patterns, the history and structure of "higher culture" (19). The pharmakon/pharmakos as problematization of the relation of inside to outside, of efforts at "purification," is but a version of this larger moral/social problematic.

Gulliver as pharmakos is clearly marked in his exile from Houyhnhnmland. His admiration and imitations of the Houyhnhnms are, of course, purifying just as his exile from Houyhnhnmland purifies, in another sense, the land from the contamination of the "civilized." The goal of Houyhnhnm society in the exile of Gulliver is stable-ity, if one may be excused a poor pun, and for purity; and that demand for stability and purity—in which the Houyhnhnm, following the pattern of symbol as both metaphor and metonym, becomes "horsier" and "horsier" as the narrative moves away from describing the Yahoos and concentrates on describing the Houyhnhnms—is threatened by the doublenesses, the instability of mixed categories, an awareness of which Gulliver's presence provokes in Houyhnhnm society. In terms of the Platonic formulation in the *Phaedrus*— and perhaps as well as in their Cynic-Stoic lineages (Gill, "Theriophily in Antiquity" 401–12)—the Houyhnhnms embody a logocentric, presence-centered view of "pure" meaning, whereas Gulliver releases in his ambiguous participation in the varied "orders" of Houyhnhnmland a range of "distanced," problematic meanings, a play of appearances identified with "writing" in the Platonic text, and an attraction-repulsion relationship to the "elements" of Houyhnhnmland in himself—an attraction-repulsion or cure-poison of the sort which typifies the pharmakon-pharmakos and typifies the dialectic and the other aporetic structures in Part IV. The expulsion of a kind of "writing as cure/poison" from Houyhnhnmland through the exile of Gulliver purifies that world not only because Gulliver as a mixed creature is exiled but because as a mixed creature he belongs to the world of writing—a world of polysemous and problematic, "deferred-differed," rivalrous meanings in which "reason is problematic" and one can "argue on both sides of a question" with some plausibility. The horses' world is also one which Gulliver's appearance has complicated since now the "natural" Yahoo is both superior and inferior to civilized man, the figure functioning now as both metaphor and metonym. The world to which Gulliver returns is one in which satire is both necessary and culpable, impossible not to write and yet short-lived and relatively useless; it is a world in which he as scapegoat is a passive bearer of impurity and contagion and is both superior and inferior to the groups whose evil he bears. His double function as pharmakos—as contaminant and healer—is seen not only in his passive purification of Houyhnhnmland by his absence but also in his role as a healer—as the sometimes unwilling mediator between the natural and reasonable world of the horses and the ordinary world of Europe. After the avoidance patterns of the earlier reflection imagery in Part IV, it is something—it is not clear what—that Gulliver in England can finally gaze at himself naked in a full-length mirror. The ambiguities of reflection in the work—narcissistic self-love and pride, avoidance of unpleasant truths, distortion and magnification of evils and disabilities, the subject as knower and as the known, as lover and hater of the self (the satirist-subject and satirist as satirical object), and crucial self-knowledge—are all finally asserted in this image.[12]

These ambiguities are figured in Part IV through aporetic structure and through pharmakon and pharmakos—in complex displacements and catharses which recall the medical basis of the neoclassic theory of satire, according to which there is nearly always a double catharsis—the attempted exorcism of vice from society by identifying and scourging it and the purging of the satirist's anger through railling and irony (Randolph 125ff.). But the ambiguity also is like the Derridean description of the Socratic "cure by *logos,* exorcism, and catharsis" which eliminates (or attempts to eliminate) the excess of supplementarity. "But this elimination, being therapeutic in nature, must call upon the very thing it is expelling, the very surplus it is *putting out.* The pharmacological operation must therefore *exclude itself from itself* " (129). Human vice is identified by hypostatizing it in vicious man, but the hypostatizing must be excluded as being itself vicious.

Gulliver's exile—Gulliver as pharmakos—exorcizes the possibility of this double evil from the land of the Houyhnhnms and relieves it of an undignified and embattled struggle to win meaning through complexity and the need to cross-check and cross-bias its critical contentions or satiric visions even though the simpler and more direct evil of the Yahoos remains to trouble the horses; and as a consequence Gulliver becomes a guarantor and adjunct of their world, necessary through his absence; in his admiration of the horses and through their capacity to exclude him—through his separateness—he, like the Yahoo, becomes essential to their admiration of themselves just as his admiration of them and avoidance of his own image owes to his disdain and rejection of the Yahoos, although that superiority is, according to the Houyhnhnms at least, quite ambiguous. Without Gulliver the horses' logocentric world remains a relatively uncomplicated utopia of clearly defined honesty and duty in the Houyhnhnms, and of similarly uncomplicated nastiness and wickedness in the Yahoo. Yet the complicating bond between Gulliver and his Master is seen in the latter's projected adaptation of the European practice of castrating horses as a "final solution" of the Yahoo problem, yet another form of scapegoating. The importation of so "unnatural" and (initially) horrifying a kind of scapegoating custom (in this context) into the natural world of the Houyhnhnms marks indelibly Girard's "triangular desire" and its permutations—the complex relationship between the admirer, the admired, and the ideal—and the relationship of the sacrificer and the sacrificial victim; in another discourse, it marks again the presence of the supplement and the attempt to be rid of it. From Houyhnhnmland to Conrad's Trading Company's headquarters in Belgium in *Heart of Darkness,* from the Master Houyhnhnm's proposal to castrate all male Yahoos to the marginal exclamation of Mr. Kurtz (the erstwhile idealist), "Exterminate the brutes!" (66), there is a great distance since Kurtz's complicity in the savagery of his native followers is clear and direct. But that distance need not obscure the irony, the outlines of the beginning of a scapegoating and sacrificial crisis in Houyhnhnmland. Castration becomes the pharmakon (its scars are the script) and the aporia in which various meanings of key terms like "nature," "reason," "savagery," and "civilization" are brought into conflict. A brutal cure to Gulliver's Master when practiced by civilized men on their horses is now proposed and entertained as an acceptable cure "for the only problem" among the Houyhnhnms.

The same complex scapegoating—which includes inculcating an awareness of the ironies and vanities of the process yet still embraces a self-purification based on internalizing the healing power and saving grace of an almost total rejection of self as other—characterizes Gulliver's return to Europe and to his family. The exile and reassimilation of the satire/supplement is not, therefore, a single event in the fourth voyage any more than it is in Gulliver's previous travels. Rather, it is an ongoing aporetic process seen in the fact that the scapegoating continues as Gulliver is torn "between hatred and fear" at the sight of "honest Portugueze" sailors, treats Don Pedro de Mendez, his mild-mannered rescuer, as if he were a Yahoo, exiles his family and his neighbors from his company, and indeed exiles himself to his stables and the company of somewhat degenerate horses. What is the reader to make of this regression of scapegoatings except to see in them simultaneous assertions and displacements of meanings in an almost endless regression-progression—satirical images, statements, and visions which are reflexively self-criticizing and which in part answer to Swift's view of satire as "a glass in which every man sees his neighbor but not himself" and as a kicking of the world's indifferent posterior? But surely there is more to the matter than just that, for the satiric visions of the *Travels* are not simply undone by its reflexive strategies—who can forget these bizarre worlds and their quotidian vices and follies?—as their meanings are asserted, questioned, qualified, fragmented, and redoubled by their ceaseless repetitions, inversions, and dispersals even as we come to question the techniques and processes whereby they have developed. The process of conveying and aporetically deferring the satiric message relays and re-creates over and over again the conditions of scapegoating as demands for "purification" recur over and over and eventuate in successive scapegoatings—of Don Pedro de Mendez, of Gulliver's family, of mankind and the reader—which, as it were, repeatedly "internalize" them—attempt to bring home the "external" to the living present. Gulliver's gradualism—his suffering his family eventually to sit at the other end of a long table and his plan to admit a few neighbors to his company—are only continuations of this complex process of dialectical play, of satiric scapegoatings, and of stressful attempts at mediation which constantly seek to revivify the dying letter of the satire and to encourage the reader to separate from it the living truth.

The foregoing analysis suggests how Swift reflexively deconstructs his own narratives and allegories to avoid the kind of simplistic fable and naive prosopopoeia which he so stringently criticizes as belonging to the moderns in *A Tale of a Tub*. In place of these "modern" productions, Swift presents us with a complex intellectual exercise consisting of self-deconstructing allegories and successive ironic scapegoatings to suggest an aporetic conclusion and a living response beyond wooden allegorical devices, mechanical ironies, and rigid satirical proscriptions. Yet these complex procedures suggest why readers have always had trouble reading the *Travels* and why postmodern critics might have great difficulty in deconstructing the work: Swift himself has exposed the aporias of narrative and allegory, whereas the aporias which the text conceals from the reader are analogous to the aporia of the supplement with which Socratic dialectic only obliquely deals in the *Phaedrus* in the discussion of the function of dialectic itself: for, like the ongoing displacement of the supplement of writing in and through dialectic, the complex functions of symbols, the successive partial scapegoatings, the repeated and successive displacements of pharmakon and pharmakos in the *Travels* both suggest and defer beyond the work the assimilation of the problem of the poison/cure of satire into "living" knowledge—the growing integration of the practical and the abstract into a whole comprehension. It is as though by successive doses of the pharmakon—the cure/poison of satire—and by successive partial scapegoatings, the Mithridates-like reader could confront "the supplement," the excess of satire, the "other," and exclude it or render it harmless "at home" as it is assimilated into "living knowledge."[13] But this process also suggests an opposite "conclusion" not entirely out of keeping with some strands of its background: also possible is the view that "A Voyage to . . . the Houyhnhnms" is a work in which the mediation between "ideal" creatures and their admirer, between outside and inside, between satiric knowledge and living truth, though not conclusively forestalled, is, as its innate violence is revealed, constantly deferred and hence unwittingly delivered over into the play of *differance* and undecidability; and in this way it continues to question the easier differential systems which Swift's society valorized and on which we would still depend if indeed we could.

We can reason in this way because Swift at the end of Part IV finally brings these exfoliations of doubt explicitly to bear on European societies and their colonial policies, intent as they were to subjugate brutal natives in far-off places and their own brutalized lower classes to a ruling class's more sophisticated brutalities. Even the pastoral aristocracy of the Houyhnhnms—no doubt a minimalist version of the neo-Harringtonian "humanist" aristocracy praised by Charles Davenant and Harley and Swift himself in the later reign of Queen Anne (Pocock 423–505)—is seen as maintaining its logocentric purity and integrity not by coming to grips with the problems of European societies but by partially insulating itself from their increasingly complicated forms of inhumanity. In this sense, the discriminations of Part IV (and their "violence") are regressive and point toward what Girard calls the "originary violence" of discriminations (to Derrida it is the "violence" of *differance*) out of which society (or the multiplicity of writing) has grown. The "degenerate" horses in Gulliver's stable may represent or at least suggest an old order of favored aristocratic or Tory conversationalists in whom neither Gulliver nor we can place much real hope—the tired devotees of a higher and more remote order. For hope we must, with great doubts, look to our families and neighbors, as Gulliver someday hopes to tolerate his wife and to find his neighbors (279–80), humbled but not utterly humiliated by deferring their final condemnation (and the prospect of the extermination of the Yahoos), as it must be deferred, according to a conservative view, as many times as possible, until the unspecifiable end.

In Swift's practice, then, according to this view, satire points back to the violence of origins through its own violence; and that same satiric violence prompts the reader to hold in abeyance but at the ready the satirist's condemnation of folly and vice and its apocalyptic consequences. Satire is a poison and a cure just as the satirist sacrifices his victims and is sacrificed, vainly it often may seem, for the common good.

## Notes

At the outset I would like to express my appreciation to my friends and colleagues Allen Dunn, Jack Wilson, and John Zomchick for their patient readings of this essay in various versions.
1. Efforts to "deconstruct" *Gulliver* (and especially Part IV) are now fairly numerous

and include Terry Castle's "Why the Houyhnhnms Don't Write: Swift, Satire, and Fear of the Text," *Essays in Literature* 7 (1980): 31-44, and Carole Fabricant, "The Battle of the Ancients and (Post) Moderns: Rethinking Swift Through Contemporary Perspectives," *The Eighteenth Century* 32 (1991): 256-73. The great difficulty with most of these efforts is that they pay very little attention to the actual text—its structure and the development of the "action"—of the *Travels*. Castle's discussion is, for example, devoted mostly to a discussion of "Writing" and *A Tale of a Tub* . See also William Bowman Piper, "Gulliver's Account of Houyhnhnmland as a Philosophical Treatise" in Smith 179–202, and Louise K. Barnett, "Deconstructing *Gulliver's Travels*: Modern Readers and the Problematic of Genre" in Smith 230–45.

2. Much recent writing about the *Travels* has concentrated on its "mixed" nature, on its blend of types and genres (Smith), and on the many directions from which it can be approached (Reilly). I am indebted to Michael Seidel's fine study, *Satiric Inheritance: Rabelais to Sterne,* for his insight into the power of Girard's theory to explain certain aspects of satiric practice (17–21). The term "aporetic" as descriptive of a structure frustrating closure can be applied, among others, to the structure of those Socratic dialogues which resist closure. Cf. Derrida: "In a word, we do not believe that there exists, in all rigor, a Platonic text, closed upon itself, complete with its inside and its outside" (130). For a more conventional account of Socrates's opposition to writing and to "the book," see Nussbaum 122–35, where she emphasizes the intellectual drama of the dialogues—"the Platonic *elenchos* . . . teaches by appeal to intellect alone; learning takes place when the interlocutor is enmeshed in logical contradiction" (133). I hope that if and when the reader reaches the end of this essay, she will see that my use of the term "aporetic structure" is related both to a deconstructionist "liberation" into responsibility and to a reader-response view of reader empowerment.
Hinnant's structuralist study of the issue of purity and defilement in the *Travels* anticipates some of my concerns, but in my view it does not adequately treat the dynamics —i.e., the sacrificial schematics and dualities—of the matter.

3. Of greatest interest to students of the novel, this aspect of Girard's views was developed in *Deceit, Desire and the Novel* (1965). Here desire is always triangular and intersubjective; the object of desire becomes the desideratum of the desirer because of the "intervention" of a mediator. In *Don Quixote,* for example, the objects of desire change, but the mediator—Amadis and his fellow ideal knights—remains the same; a rivalry between desirer and mediator may develop, and Romantic works may be characterized by whether there is contact between the "spheres of possibilities of which the mediator and the subject occupy the respective centers" ("external mediation") or "whether this same distance is sufficiently reduced to allow these two spheres to penetrate each other more or less profoundly" ("internal mediation") (9).

4. On the satirist as physician and patient and on satire as medicine or cure, see Randolph throughout; and on the satirist-satirized theme see Elliott 130–222.

5. I am paraphrasing the words of Walter Charleton, Dryden's friend, in his Gassendian/Baconian criticism of rationalistic (i.e., Aristotelian and Cartesian) thought in his Introduction to his translation of J. B. Van Helmont's *A Ternary of Paradoxes.* Charleton (sigs. f2–f4v) praises the "Clarity of Abstracted and Intuitive Intellection"—clear perception and solid induction—but condemns "Reason . . . as a caduce, spurious Faculty, accidentally Advenient upon the Degradation of our Nature. . . ." Similarly he argues that "the Science of the Praemises, is always more certain then the Science of the Conclusion . . . and that Science is radically seated in the Intellect, with the concurrence of *Reason,* because we find it older then the Demonstration." Truth, therefore, is well-founded fact, and the product of "the rotten reed of Putation" is mere opinion: one is *"ens reale, verum"* whereas the other is only *ens mentale, problematicum."* I believe that what the Houyhnhnms call "Reason" is in fact very much like Charleton's "Fiduciary Induction," although Swift's version of the causes of error includes "Passion" and "Interest" as well as elaborate "putation." As Gulliver says of the Houyhnhnms, "Neither is *Reason* among them a Point problematical as with us, where Men can argue with Plausibility on both Sides of a Question; but strikes you with immediate Conviction; as it must needs do where it is not mingled, obscured, or discoloured by Passion and Interest" (251). Here Swift has given to "Baconian" skepticism a stoical slant. On Cynic-Stoic-anti-Stoic background of theriophilic arguments see Gill, "Theriophily in Antiquity" throughout.

6. Excrement is seen in Part IV as the product of natural antipathy and species hatred, as when the Yahoos in their first encounter with Gulliver climb trees "from whence they began to discharge their Excrements upon my Head" (208) and is hence linked with satire.

7. On the distinction between thetic and ontic, see Gill, "The Fragmented Self" 24ff., and Kristeva 43–45 and throughout.

8. Although his distinction is more subtle than mine since he is dealing with entire modes of representation, J. Hillis Miller's differentiation between metonymic and metaphoric synecdoche, and that differentiation's systemic implications, in his discussion of Conrad's symbolism in *Heart of Darkness* (212–13) is analogous to my distinction: "Thus, the figure does double duty, both as a figure for the way Marlow's stories express their meaning and as a figure for itself, so to speak; that is, as a figure for its own mode of working. This is according to a mind-twisting torsion of the figure back on itself that is a regular feature of such figures of figuration. . . . The figure both illuminates its own workings and at the same time obscures or undermines it. . . ." I believe there is a similar "mind-twisting torsion of the figure back on itself" in the pharmakon inasmuch as it describes both human evil and, through the vehicle of the satiric object, the action of satire

through and on itself. Cf. Girard's statement: "The discovery of the scapegoat as the mechanism of symbolicity itself justifies the discourse of deconstruction at the same time that it completes it" (Girard, *Things Hidden* 63).

9. According to Girard, above the "straight line" connecting desirer and desideratum is the model and mediator of desire, and desire is thus almost always "Desire according to the Other" (Girard, *Deceit, Desire and the Novel* 1–3). In the case of Gulliver, the object of the ship's surgeon's desires changes from managing the honor of his own kind to becoming a Houyhnhnm, but the mediator of those desires is the Master Houyhnhnm and above him, the norms of "reasonable" and "natural behavior." Of course, the mediator of desire may range from "one throned in an inaccessible heaven" to the "despicably vain" (4), and, in the case of the scapegoat, is profoundly ambiguous, representing variously the ideal, the persecutor, and the persecuted (Girard, *The Scapegoat* 198–212). For exhaustive descriptions of patterns of "mimetic interaction," see Livingston 60–102.

10. On the multiple perspectives generated by the Houyhnhnms' ignorance of the harm which Gulliver as a European might really foment and by Gulliver's expulsion, see Girard, *The Scapegoat* 55: "A detached observer who is present at, but does not participate in, an episode of collective violence, only sees a helpless victim mistreated by a hysterical crowd. But if he asks the members of that crowd what is happening he will scarcely recognize what he has seen with his own eyes. He will be told about the extraordinary power of the victim, the occult influence he exercised and possibly still exercises on the community. . . ." The same might be said of solemn persecutions and purges. Narratives arising from persecution rituals, according to Girard, almost always give attenuated versions whose violence is difficult to perceive. The blend of the ridiculous and brutal, of the comic and the nasty, in the Yahoos is no doubt related to varying perceptions of the kind Girard notes.

11. McKenna 174–76, 189. In addition Girard notes that "the juxtaposition of more than one stereotype within a single [historical] document indicates persecution." These "stereotypes" include the following: "the generalized loss of differences"; "crimes that 'eliminate differences'"; marks of victimization in the authors of these "crimes," including marginalization of various kinds; and "violence itself" such as expulsion or death (Girard, *The Scapegoat* 24). Of course Girard has in mind both actual situations and realistic fiction (chiefly of the nineteenth century) in these comments, but adapting them to eighteenth-century satire would be easy enough: consider treating other Swiftian satires under this rubric—for example the great Irish satires, *The Drapier's Letters* and *A Modest Proposal*—not to mention some earlier works.

12. The moral ambiguities of the classic Narcissus myth as they apply to Gulliver have perhaps been obscured by Christopher Fox's sensational emphasis on Swift's onanistic puns in *Gulliver*. For some implications of this fascinating topic, see Di Salvo, who studies the myth as a fecund source of reflexive themes. From a

Girardian perspective, see also the study by Mikkel Borch-Jacobsen. On the reciprocal violences intrinsic to the accounts of the new world, see Giard 317: according to Giard, in early European *accounts* of America, Michel de Certeau saw "a single narrative of the same *destructive violence* that Europe inflicted on the American Indian societies. Underneath the sound and fury of this violence, de Certeau heard the rumor of another one, more secret but equally important, the *transformative violence* of the meeting with the Other whose shock waves had finally reached Europe to undermine its old certainties. He often remarked that no one returns unchanged from an encounter with the Other." Here we have a hint of an inevitability of a complex reciprocal scapegoating under the guise of encounters with other, which, I am arguing, was surely one of Swift's most profound insights into the nature of complex satire.

13. See Gulliver's statement (251–52) that the Houyhnhnms are "socratic-platonic" in their contempt for systems of natural philosophy. In other words, it is the skeptical side of Socratic philosophy with which the Houyhnhnms agree. The "Girardian" or "sacrificial" analysis which Girard and McKenna after him explore sees violence as the essence of "origin" and finds remediating hope (in Girard's case, at least) only in the understanding, derived from the Gospels, that the victim of mimetic violence out of which society grows *is not guilty*: "rather, a return to truth is made possible by a process which, in our lack of understanding, we consider primitive simply because it reproduces the violent origin once more, this time in order to reveal it and thus make it inoperative. . . . By revealing that mechanism [of sacrifice] and the surrounding mimeticism, the Gospels set in motion the only textual mechanism that can put an end to humanity's imprisonment in the system of mythological representation based on the false transcendence of a victim who is made sacred because of a unanimous verdict of guilt" (Girard, *The Scapegoat* 166). McKenna's study of the homologous relationships of Derrida's and Girard's analyses is designed to remedy the social and ethical sterility of Derrida's grammatological critiques by applying to them the ethical implications of Girard's "anthropological" approach to the problem of origin and difference. McKenna, however, also attempts to rethink critically Girard's heuristic and finds in Scripture the seeds of deconstruction of the "law."

# Works Cited

Barnett, Louise K. "Deconstructing *Gulliver's Travels*." *The Genres of Gulliver's Travels*. Ed. Frederick N. Smith. Newark: U of Delaware P, 1990. 230–45

Borch-Jacobsen, Mikkel. *The Freudian Subject*. Trans. Catherine Porter. Stanford: Stanford UP, 1988.

Castle, Terry. "Why the Houyhnhnms Don't Write: Swift, Satire, and Fear of the Text," *Essays in Literature* 7 (1980): 31-44.

Charleton, Walter, trans. J. B. Van Helmont. *A Ternary of Paradoxes.* London, 1650.

Conrad, Joseph. *Heart of Darkness: A Case Study in Contemporary Criticism.* Ed. Ross C. Murfin. New York: St. Martin's, 1989.

Derrida, Jacques. *Dissemination.* Trans. Barbara Johnson. Chicago: U of Chicago P, 1981.

Di Salvo, Marilyn. "The Myth of Narcissus." *Signs about Signs: the Semiotics of Self-Reference.* Ed. Barbara A. Babcock. *Semiotica* 30.1–2 (1986): 1–14.

Elliott, Robert C. *The Power of Satire: Magic Ritual, Art.* Princeton: Princeton UP, 1960.

Fox, Christopher. "The Myth of Narcissus in Swift's Travels." *Eighteenth-Century Studies* 20.1 (1986): 17–33.

Giard, Luce. "Epilogue: Michel de Certeau's Heterology and the New World." *New World Encounters.* Ed. Stephen J. Greenblatt. Berkeley and Los Angeles: U of California P, 1993. 313–22.

Gill, James E. "Beast over Man: Theriophilic Topics in Gulliver's 'Voyage to the Country of the Houyhnhnms,'" *Studies in Philology* 67.4 (1970): 532–49.

———. "The Fragmented Self in Three of Rochester's Poems," *Modern Language Quarterly* 49.1 (1988): 19–37.

———. "Man and Yahoo: Dialectic and Symbolism in Gulliver's 'Voyage to the Country of the Houyhnhnms.'" *The Dress of Words: Essays on Restoration and Eighteenth-Century Literature in Honor of Richmond P. Bond.* Ed. Robert B. White. Lawrence, KS: U of Kansas Publications, Library Series, 42 (1978). 67–90.

———. "Theriophily in Antiquity: A Supplementary Account." *Journal of the History of Ideas* 30 (1969): 401–12.

Girard, René. *Deceit, Desire and the Novel: Self and Other in Literary Structure.* Trans. Yvonne Freccero. Baltimore: Johns Hopkins UP, 1965.

———. *The Scapegoat.* Trans. Yvonne Freccero. Baltimore: Johns Hopkins UP, 1986.

———. *Things Hidden since the Foundations of the World.* Trans. Stephen Bann and Michael Metteer. Stanford: Stanford UP, 1987.

———. *Violence and the Sacred.* Trans. Patrick Gregory. Baltimore: Johns Hopkins UP, 1972.

Hinnant, Charles H. *Purity and Defilement in Gulliver's Travels.* Houndmills and London: Macmillan, 1987.

Homer. *Homer: The Odyssey.* Trans. Albert Cook. Norton Critical Edition. New York: Norton, 1974.

Johnson, Samuel. *Lives of the English Poets.* 2 vols. London: Oxford UP, 1959.

Kristeva, Julia. *Revolution in Poetic Language.* Trans. Margaret Waller. New York: Columbia UP, 1984.

Livingston, Paisley. *Models of Desire: René Girard and the Psychology of Mimesis.* Baltimore: Johns Hopkins UP, 1992.

McKenna, Andrew J. *Violence and Difference: Girard, Derrida, and Deconstruction.* Urbana and Chicago: U of Illinois P, 1992

Miller, J. Hillis. "*Heart of Darkness* Revisited." *Heart of Darkness: A Case Study in Contemporary Criticism.* Ed. Ross Murfin. New York: St. Martin's, 1989. 209–224.

Nussbaum, Martha C. *The Fragility of Goodness: Luck and Ethics in Greek Tragedy and Philosophy.* Cambridge: Cambridge UP, 1986.

Piper, William Bowman. "Gulliver's Account of Houyhnhnmland as a Philosophical Treatise." *The Genres of Gulliver's Travels.* Ed. Frederick N. Smith. Newark: U of Delaware P, 1990. 179–202.

Pocock, J. G. A. *The Machiavellian Moment: Florentine Political Thought and the Atlantic Republican Tradition.* Princeton: Princeton UP, 1975.

Randolph, Mary Claire. "The Medical Concept in English Renaissance Satiric Theory," *Studies in Philology* 38 (1941): 125–57.

Reilly, Edward J., ed. *Approaches to Teaching Swift's Gulliver's Travels.* New York: Modern Language Association, 1988.

Seidel, Michael. *Satiric Inheritance: Rabelais to Sterne.* Princeton: Princeton UP, 1979.

Suzuki, Mihoko. *Metamorphoses of Helen: Authority, Difference, and the Epic.* Ithaca: Cornell UP, 1989.

Swift, Jonathan. *A Tale of a Tub &c.* Ed. A. C. Guthkech and D. Nichol Smith. 2nd Ed. Oxford: Clarendon, 1957.

———. *The Prose Works of Jonathan Swift.* Ed. Herbert Davis. Vol. 11: *Gulliver's Travels, 1726.* Oxford: Basil Blackwell, 1941.

# Mary Davys's Satiric Novel *Familiar Letters*

## Refusing Patriarchal Inscription of Women

*Lindy Riley*

Satire has generally been perceived to have a corrective function: that is, when the guardians of social order fail to maintain it, the satirist considers it his or her duty to expose corruption and point the way to reform. As Michael McKeon notes, "[T]he origins of the English novel entail the positing of a 'new' generic category as a dialectical negation of a 'traditional' dominance. . . ." He points out that eighteenth-century writers perceived the importance of writing as an instrument of social change: "this is nowhere more obvious than in the commonplace insistence that the function of literature, and of satire in particular, is to correct and reform humankind" (68). Although satire was typically a male form in the eighteenth century, women writers learned to appropriate it to their uses. Mary Davys, for example, made subtle use of the genre in her *Familiar Letters Betwixt a Gentleman and a Lady* (1725). Many eighteenth-century male epistolary writers had assumed the pose of the angry or indignant letter writer in order to attack what they perceived as social ills; indeed, many of them had wielded their pens/swords against women, both individually and generically. Davys, however, perhaps mindful of her precarious financial status and the necessity for relying on income from her writing—and perhaps aware of the fragility of her social status as a female writer and unwilling to risk virulent attacks like those heaped on Manley and Heywood when they invaded the male realm—avoided the more vehement Juvenalian satiric forms. Her work, rather than hurling abuse at individuals, questions the authority and rightness of the patriarchal order, the source of the conventions that governed female behavior, marginalizing and trivializing it.

Mary Davys was one of a multitude of females in the eighteenth century compelled to earn a living when the social support system intended to protect women failed them. Born in Dublin in 1674, she married Rev. Peter Davys, a college contemporary of Jonathan Swift and presumably familiar with the satiric voice of his more famous friend. How much contact Davys herself might have had with Swift during this period is unknown, however, so it is impossible to assess his influence on her work.

When her husband died in 1698, he left her no money, and Davys turned to writing to support herself. She began her literary career in the theatre, writing *The Northern Heiress: Or the Humours of York* (1716), which was produced successfully at the New Theatre in Lincoln's Inn Fields. Her second play, however, was not produced. Apparently despairing of supporting herself with her pen, she opened a coffeehouse in Cambridge, where, isolated from the literary mainstream in London, she began her fiction-writing career (McBurney 348–50). Her isolated location was advantageous, for, on the one hand, it prevented contact with other women writers and thus avoided the influences of current writing trends; on the other hand, it gave her access to the conversation of educated men in her coffeehouse (where newspapers were read and where, like all other coffeehouses, women did not go). In addition, her experience writing for the theatre introduced her to the satiric tone which worked successfully on the stage. Nevertheless, her early attempts at the pen were not remunerative: she sold her first novel for only three guineas (*The Accomplished Rake* 236), and she periodically applied to Swift for financial aid, which he reluctantly supplied (Spencer 11). She could not express openly her disaffection with the patriarchy which, rather than protecting and supporting her, had forced her to rely on her own resources and suffer indigence for much of her life, but she could write satiric novels which called into question the unjust codes which marginalized women and relegated them to a life of serfdom.

*Familiar Letters Betwixt a Gentleman and a Lady* (1725) is at once a manifesto against the illusions nurtured by romantic fiction of the time, a parody of the letter models prevalent at the time, and an anticipation of Richardson's *Pamela* (1740), which developed, interestingly, out of a piece Richardson had tentatively named *Familiar Letters* (McKeon 357). Coming to writing as a necessary result of the loss of her husband, her protector and provider, Davys speaks from experience when she demonstrates the precariousness of the life of a woman who has to survive on her own. The message in the novel is an admonition that women must protect themselves, for they can expect men to prey on them, not protect them. In addition to warning women of the risks inherent in their positions as females, Davys uses the novel as a kind of subversive conduct book to instruct women how to survive in a world where their gender ensures their exploitation.

Present-day critics, particularly Armstrong, Langbauer, Miller, Perry, Poovey, Schofield, Spacks, and Todd, describe the position of women writers in the eighteenth century as an uneasy one: when they embarked upon authorship, it was an intrusion into a world traditionally dominated by men. In "masculine" systems of representation, the role of femininity had been imposed on women by the narcissistic and basically antifeminist logic of such masculine systems. Women writers struggled to submit to these conventions, but inconsistencies in their writing reveal the extent to which such repression failed. As a result, their writings are unstable; the writers' discomfort with the culturally imposed role of femininity turns against the system that allows them to exist. Also, as Poovey points out, women discovered that they could maintain the pose of a "proper" woman but still express themselves indirectly (28). Davys's work demonstrates her attempts to expose the sexual politics at work in culturally imposed codes of behavior as, working from within the "masculine" system of representation, she subverts the system.

Davys's personal experience had revealed to her the inadequacy of the social safety net which was supposed to preserve and protect society's "weaker" members. Poovey traces the effect of burgeoning capitalism and the shift of the "basic middle-class economic unit" from the cooperative household to the individual male in the eighteenth century. Women were displaced as producers and transformed into consumers and the visible signs of affluence. In addition, because men feared female sexuality as a threat to the legitimacy of progeny and the ownership of property, they equated chastity with virtue. Women were required to suppress their sexual appetites and to embody their virtue in a "communicative but decorous silence" (24). Thus the social code constrained women from speaking or acting to provide for themselves. Davys's novel, by satirizing romance conventions and by exposing the workings of sexual politics governing women, rejects the illusions that "masculine" representation of women had fostered. Instead, her novel emphasizes that real human beings are nothing like characters described in courtly romance; indeed, it sees through the ideology that depicts marriage as "natural" to expose it as what Tanner calls "the all-subsuming, all-organizing, all-containing contract. It is the structure that maintains the Structure" (15). In other words, marriage is a social construction that plays a central role in sustaining the patriarchal social order that inscribes women.

The dishonesty of the patriarchal view of women is that it offers them only wishful thinking; it depicts women as able to inspire noble action in men while simultaneously keeping men at a chaste distance. It promises women that love will bring them to their rightful position in society, protected and supported, financially and socially. The truth that the masculine lie withholds from women is that love will lead women to relinquish their independent state and to submit to an ideology that renders them powerless. In fact, to accept patriarchal ideology is "not to know one's self as a woman" (Schofield 132). Davys's novel attempts to enlighten women whose vision has been corrupted by reading novels dominated by the "masculine" view—to shock readers out of their complacent, romantic expectations. Remembering her own bitter experience, Davys argues that women must not depend on the romantic notion of perfect love and happy marriage.

Although women's limited education stressed self-mastery rather than self-knowledge, women writers during the eighteenth century repeatedly repudiated the culturally constructed idea that women were incapable of reason. Hunt asserts that the Evangelical movement had promulgated a view of women as moral beings responsible for themselves and responsible to society. Women began to realize that by de-emphasizing their sexuality and developing their moral and intellectual powers they could attain power in society (11). Davys is one of the female writers who tackles the traditional antifeminist argument that associates women with ungoverned passion and men with reason. By opposing a female character who refuses to play the part of the adored goddess to a male character who wholeheartedly embraces the role of lovesick swain, Davys undermines the social fiction that women are incapable of thought and action.

Davys also argues that it is possible for women to bring about changes in the oppressive moral order. Her point is that desire cannot be purged from men—and since it governs their actions, order in the community must depend on the passions being regulated. She adds: "If the Reformation would once begin from our Sex, the Men would follow it in spite of their Hearts" (*Accomplished* 236). The fundamentally misogynistic outlook of aristocracy proposes only two roles for men in their dealings with women: that of exploiter and that of protector. Davys proposes a third option—that of companion and equal.

*Familiar Letters* undermines the conventional male plot in order to present a critique of contemporary social structures and mores. Mocking and parodying the falsely idealized romance mode, Davys's female character, Berina, reveals a clear perception of how dangerous romance ideology is to women: she resists the system which insistently devalues and exploits women, not only the actual social system, but the covert system disguised by the codes of romance. For example, Berina is willing to accept a man as her friend, but she argues for her right to refuse a suitor and, by extension, marriage, and she also blasts the notion of contemporary men as suitors. Knowing how men are socialized to view women, she regards suitors as insincere in matters of courtship and scorns the notion that men in the real world treat women as the idealized lovers in romance do. She insists that women must learn how to resist the illusions of romance, perceive more clearly the pitfalls that await impulsive and ungoverned women, and begin to inculcate a system of control, first of their own desires and then of the desires of men.

To sum up, Davys deliberately exposes the dangers of the patriarchal system of representation and reveals how the idealized conventions of the romance genre support and perpetuate the patriarchal inscription of women. Rather than creating the "feminine," unbelievably good female character, she depicts a woman who is intelligent, able to plot and to manipulate others within her limited sphere of influence. In addition, Davys motivates her protagonist to raise the consciousness of her male correspondent so that he can evolve into a companion, not a "protector." Finally, she causes her female character to be outspoken about the joylessness of marriage and about the dangerous power of love to entrap. *Familiar Letters* offers conscious criticism of the place to which women were relegated in the eighteenth-century world by revealing in an epistolary exchange between man and woman how each struggles for independence in a relationship that patriarchal ideology dictates cannot be equal.

Superficially, the letters resemble other copybook models in which the content is less important than the style and decorum with which the letters are written. But these letters are revelatory: an examination of the content reveals that each writer has a political agenda and that the letters are more than just a friendly exchange—they are really sallies in the arena of sexual politics. Although attracted to each other, the protagonists feint and maneuver, each attempting to preserve his or her liberty and individuality within the context of their relationship. Thus *Familiar Letters* has a running subtext in which the conflict results from the male's unconscious conditioning and the female's conscious repudiation of that cultural conditioning and her attempts to awaken him to the inconsistencies of the ideology which he has unquestioningly accepted.

An important theme in the novel is the satiric attack on romance language and conventions. *Familiar Letters*'s plot traces the growth of emotional bonds between the male correspondent and his female friend. The development of the plot depends upon the female correspondent's refusal to be blinded by the illusions of romance. Despite the fact that the protagonists' names, Artander and Berina, come from romance, the characters profess to reject the romantic view of love and scoff at love and marriage. Berina espouses city values that eventually clash with Artander's conservative, aristocratic views. Berina's letters emphasize her rejection of romance idealism; his responses suggest that his scoffing is merely a pose assumed to conceal his fear of public derision. He initiates the correspondence; from his country seat he writes to Berina in town: "Thought is now my only Companion, and it often diverts me with the pleasing Remembrance of your Promise of an eternal Friendship, but, as human Nature is very frail, it may possibly want the Support of Correspondence to keep it up: I therefore earnestly sue for a speedy Answer to every Letter I write" (265). The words Davys let flow from his pen reveal his masculine conviction of her inconstancy (because female) and his desire to control her discourse. He also sets the agenda by reporting: "the only Pleasure I have had since I left you, was in seeing one of your Sex mortify'd." He tells a cautionary tale of a young woman who refuses the love of a wealthy man whose "Folly in every thing shew'd his Love." To punish the headstrong woman for having made him a laughingstock, the suitor leaves the now-persuaded bride-to-be standing at the church door. Artander concludes, "How happy are you and I, who have made the strongest resolves against the Follies of Love!" (266–67) He fears being made ridiculous by a woman. Berina's response reveals a much deeper fear: she writes of a "Maiden Lady of sixty-five, who has poison'd her self for Love: the Use we are to make of it, is to hug ourselves in the midst of Liberty, and thank those Stars that inclin'd us to Freedom" (269–70). Davys's ironic juxtaposition of the two stories emphasizes how much more women stand to lose in the context of love. If they fail to gain it, they become "maiden ladies," failures often subsisting in dependency; if they do love but it is not returned, they may suffer greatly; and if they win it, paradoxically, they lose their freedom. On the other hand, men lose no social status if they remain bachelors; they may lose face, however, if they are perceived to behave foolishly.

In the early letters the correspondents trade opposing political opinions and assert their advanced views and their independence by speaking slightingly of love and marriage. By the fourteenth letter, however, Artander has begun to change his views. He writes of having attended a party where he danced till breakfast. He mentions the lovely Delia, whom he describes as second only to Berina. In response to the envy of the other ladies present, "The Gentleman of the House seeing all the Ladies in disorder, and knowing nothing gives them greater pleasure than to have a fine Woman married, because then she is out of the way, and no longer taken notice of, told 'em, *Delia* was his wife. . . . I cannot but own, I think my Neighbor happy, if it be possible for Matrimony to make him so" (294–95).

Unwittingly (or perhaps callously), he presents Berina with a strong argument against marriage, which reduces women to invisible chattels. But if he hoped that hints of his attraction to Delia would discomfit Berina, he is wrong. She blasts back: "Had I ever been a Disciple of *Artemedorus,* I shou'd have been very uneasy at my last Night's Dream, which made so dreadful an Impression upon my Fancy, that I have hardly recovered it. I thought I saw *Artander* blind; and when I wou'd have led him, he pull'd out my Eyes too. Pray Heaven avert the fatality of it, if there be any depending" (296). Berina recognizes the pattern of ensnarement, and she will not be caught. Her metaphor indicates that she does not wish to be disarmed or disabled by his strategies; she resists his seductive language. Berina points out that she has long been aware that deceit is common to the male sex (268) and that she is particularly suspicious of protestations of love, which she views as blind, deceitful, and poisonous: "Love is a thing so much against my grain, that tho' it be dressed up in a disguise of Wit, I see it thro' the Mask, and hate the base imposture" (289).

She is especially concerned after he confesses that love for her has wheedled its way past his defenses and that he has been forced to dissemble or lose her friendship (298), for, on the one hand, the admission confirms his deceit, and, on the other hand, it shows how completely he is imbued with romance ideology. She establishes control over the relationship by rejecting the discourse by which courtship conventionally proceeds. Her stance demands a new way of speaking in response to a new way of feeling. Thus Davys uses Berina's refusal of courtship discourse to suggest an alternate behavior to those who are unable to accept romance illusions unquestioningly.

Another strategy that Davys employs is her careful construction of the female character as a rational person rather than one dominated by emotion or impulse. Indeed, in this satiric rebuttal of antifeminist attacks on women as irrational, it is the male who appears to be motivated by unchecked passion as the plot unfolds. For example, the initial letters between the protagonists trade opposing political views. Davys has made Artander a Tory; Berina, a Whig. He supports the patriarchal divine rights of kings theory. Berina, in contrast, writes: "You always lay a mighty stress upon the powers of a king. Methinks it is a little strange that Heaven shou'd make them so very absolute without any Reserve for the people at all. . . . When we swear Allegiance to a King, 'tis conditional; as long as he keeps his Oath, we'll keep ours" (276–77) . Her scorn of traditional authority, so ably argued, confounds Artander. The notion of a contract imposing equal obligation upon man and woman implied in her words is repugnant, and he hastens to write, somewhat petulantly: "You cannot suppose, I want matter to furnish this letter with an Answer of the same kind, but I think nothing a greater Enemy to Friendship, than Disputes: and mine is so firm for *Berina,* that I wou'd not give way to any thing that could shake it. If yours be so, as I have no reason to doubt, you will comply, when I beg of you to put a stop to this sort of Correspondence; and let your Letters for the future be fill'd with the innocent Diversions of the Town; 'tis a pity *Berina's* Temper shou'd be ruffled with Politicks" (278). Although couched in the language of a plea to appeal to reason, this is clearly a command. It is his temper that is ruffled, not hers; if the friendship is at risk, he would seem to have as much obligation as she to sacrifice for its sake. Bested by a woman, rather than capitulate, he invokes his patriarchal privilege and puts her in her "place." Although she calls him "hard" for curbing her pen, Berina acquiesces to his request for the sake of their friendship. Having been allowed to indulge in "masculine" discourse, she is reluctant to return to the topics that make female life frivolous and meaningless—fashion, gossip, and parties. Rather than sink to that level, Berina chooses other "masculine" activities. She reminds him mildly that suppressed urges find other outlets; she will become a poetess rather than a politician. Through her protagonist, Davys reminds readers that women will find a way to express their ideas; if expression of their thoughts is blocked, it will simply seek another route. Throughout this episode, Berina is passionless and reasonable; Artander is the one who pouts and childishly insists on having his way.

As the correspondence develops, it becomes clear that Artander, whose solitude in the country provides ample time for reflection, has been tormenting himself with jealous fantasies about how Berina spends her time in the city. He begins to complain that her letters arrive too infrequently. The content of the tenth letter reveals his real fear embedded in an anecdote of a nearby farmer who finds his wife asleep in the arms of a neighbor (288); Artander demands: "I grow impatient to know the Cause of your Silence. . . . I wish you do not at last play the Woman more than the Platonick, and quit your friendship for a Husband." His letter reveals his contradictory impulses: he has confined her to women's topics in her letters, yet he does not wish her to act like a woman. He continues, "Women, they say, are so like Quick-silver, a Man can never be sure of them, either as a Friend or a Mistress; but as *Berina* is an Original in every thing else, I will believe her so in Friendship too" (286). Nevertheless, his letter has revealed that he lacks the belief that he professes.

Berina's artful silence only increases his anxiety over what diversions have prevented her from writing him. When she does reply, she somewhat testily reminds him that they have agreed to remain single in order to avoid the destructive effects of enforced companionship:

> I declare I am quite tir'd with Pleasure, and the Fatigue of constant Diversion is more insupportable, than an everlasting want of it [reminding him, of course, that she maintains a busy social schedule]; but the Pleasures of this World, lose both their Name and End by being constant: we see by Experience, nothing pleases a great while; those things of which we are extravagantly fond, if once forced upon us, beget first an Indifference, and then an Abhorrence. This Consideration, with some others equivalent, has put you and I [sic] upon the Resolve of living single, lest too much of a Husband or a

> Wife shou'd turn us into such indifferent things to each other, as I am now to Dancing and Cards. (288)

The eighteenth-century reader would have recognized this argument as the very one that rakes used to escape the noose of marriage, now ironically emerging from the pen of a woman. Berina's assertion of her freedom and her desire to remain free inflame Artander's jealousy and arouse his desire to possess her.

Artander shifts into the romance mode of discourse, filling his letters with the masculine flattery that has traditionally won women over. He knows that once he secures her consent and she is bound by the marriage vows, he can dispense with the flattery and all the troublesome posturing, but until his goal is reached, he must woo her carefully. His calculating, "*Berina,* 'tis you alone have Power to break the strongest Resolution: and let the Witchcraft of your Own Eyes answer for the Faults I commit" (298), is intended both to intimate the power of her attractions and her potential power to make him happy. At the same time, it is designed to place the blame for his broken promise on her. Yet a later comment reads, "But when every Post brought fresh Alarms to Love, and every Line gave Wings to Inclination, I soon found it was impossible to secure any Tranquility of Mind without an eternal possession of the dear Author" (302), and another, "You have promis'd me Freedom and Liberty, but is it possible to enjoy either, while I am a Slave in Fetters? Or can any thing release me from that Bondage, but an everlasting Union with *Berina?*" (304–5). When he writes that he cannot be content until he "possesses" her, his unconscious slip, however, reveals his true intentions; after marriage, their roles will shift and he will be the one to be beseeched, despite his promise in the next line to submit himself to her least desire. The vacillations of his language between terms of mastery and terms of slavery indicate the distance between what his letter appears to say and what it really means.

Berina, however, is not drawn by conventional wooers' ploys. She counters each move with a logical rebuttal, shifting away from romance discourse to rational, "masculine" discourse. When Artander complains that he "dies" for love and that if she were his friend she would ease his pain, Berina disregards his emotional outburst and discloses the real issue: she offers to "make you happy against your own Will, and keep you in a State of Life, when Freedom and Liberty may be enjoy'd" (302–3) in order to demonstrate that she *is* his friend (and incidentally, though she doesn't mention it, to preserve her own freedom). Certainly she is not swayed by his promise to be her slave: satirically pointing up the paradoxical masculine mind-set, she continues: "I do assure you, the Promise you make of inverting the God of Nature's Rules, and being all Obedience, is no inducement to me to become a Wife: I shou'd despise a Husband as much as a King who wou'd give up his own Prerogative, or unman himself to make his Wife the Head" (303).

It is clearly the man who is swept away by his emotions here; the female's feelings are held in check by her fear of loss of independence. Berina is not devoid of sensibility, but she refuses to be led into an oppressive system by unrestrained emotions.

*Familiar Letters* also emphasizes a reworking of masculine and feminine roles in courtship and marriage. Berina struggles to wean Artander from his vision of himself as a romance hero "dying" of love for a merciless woman. First she has to contend with the antifeminist bias evident in his earliest letters. In his first letters Artander has offhandedly mentioned encounters with various women, only slightly veiling his contempt for the sex. Each story, without seeming to do so, points out a "female" weakness: the young woman with the "prodigious" hoop skirt represents vanity (271); the old woman represents slovenliness and filth (275–76). Though he continues to insist that Berina is different from the rest of her sex, Artander's antifeminist stance comes repeatedly to the surface. Artander recites with relish the story of an eligible bachelor who humiliates the woman who spurned his addresses (266). The subtext reveals his conviction that a woman who is so audacious as to refuse an offer in the hopes of receiving a better one deserves to be punished. Similarly, Berina's answer is revealing. She reacts sharply to Artander's story, saying, "I pity the poor disappointed Lady you writ about, tho' I think she deserv'd her Fate; and the Gentleman's Revenge was very sharp, tho' very innocent. I wou'd send you a Story something like it, but Jilting in our Sex and Deceit in yours is so very common, that I think it wou'd want Novelty to make it diverting" (268). Berina clearly resents the social code which requires women to wait passively upon the desires of men and which encourages men to use whatever means available to get what they want from women. She is especially sensitive to the plight of the woman who is condemned to public humiliation for asserting her desire, because, of course, Berina does not intend to conform to the social code.

Berina also protests Artander's imposition of restraints on her writing. One senses that she fears the loss of what sets her apart from other females in Artander's eyes—the ability to converse wittily and assertively on "masculine" topics. Berina wants to re-educate Artander, or at least to point out that she is not willing to be enslaved. Romantic novels and social convention have produced an unrealistic and pernicious script for lovers to follow; she would have him cast away his memorized lines and speak openly and forthrightly what is in his heart. The political terminology in the following passage from one of her letters emphasizes the ideological struggle taking place in their exchange: "But when once the Blind Archer with a random Shot has hit a Heart, the wounded Fool grows stupid, sighs and cries, prays, and begs for Help and Pity, but never offers to pull out the dart, which causes all his Pain: Wou'd but every body keep their Ground, and stand boldly in their own Defense, how easily might they baffle the Attempts of a Boy? But, instead of fighting for their own Liberty and Property, they tamely yield to an arbitrary Power; and, like a Dog used to a Collar, hold down their Heads to take the Yoke" (303). Satirizing his behavior, she urges him not to conform to convention but to approach her in a mature and thoughtful fashion because she will not willingly bow to the yoke. Her letter is an invitation to negotiate a new basis for their relationship.

Finally, *Familiar Letters* demonstrates that the woman governed by rationality distrusts patriarchy's promise that marriage will resolve all the problems that the unprotected woman faces in society. Throughout the correspondence Davys shows Berina asserting her independence and struggling to preserve it. As a consequence, Berina has from the beginning rejected the deceptive, seductive claims of romance discourse. When Artander finally realizes that each romantic sally increases Berina's resistance, he concludes that he can subdue her only by appearing to surrender. As a last resort, he employs the ultimate weapon: he suggests that matrimony may bring happiness after all.

Having refused to play the role of a romance heroine all along, Berina is quick to force Artander to speak plainly:

> I wou'd have all those soft-hearted Ladies that are impress'd like Wax, read
> *Quevedo's Vision of Loving-Fools*; I daresay some of 'em wou'd find their own
> Characters very fairly display'd; but then the dismal Effects of not loving, to
> be call'd Ill-Natur'd, and an old Maid, who wou'd not rather chuse to be
> undone, than lie under such scandalous Epithets? I have dwelt a little longer
> on this Subject than I shou'd have done, because I think and fear *Artander*
> seem'd in his last Letter to lean a little that way. When once we approve a
> thing, we implicitly act it, and if you be brought to think a Man happy in a
> fine Wife, the next thing will be to get one yourself; which, if you do, poor
> *Berina* may say she had a Friend; for Artander is lost past Recovery. I desire,
> in your next, you will either make a generous Confession, or give me some
> Assurance my Thoughts are ill-grounded. (287)

The passage reveals Berina's dilemma only too clearly: if she refuses to be "impress'd like Wax" as others of her sex allow themselves to be, then she faces the prospect of being derided as an "old maid"; but to accept marriage is to be "undone," that is, to lose her identity as an individual. Her demand that he declare himself disrupts the romance convention that women are to remain helpless and passive. It also suggests her horror at the notion of relinquishing her selfhood to drink the "Bitter Cup" of marriage. She concedes that there can be happiness in marriage—but only if the marriage is based on mutual respect: "The Notion I have always had of Happiness in Marriage, is, where Love causes Obedience on one Side, and Compliance in the other, with a View to the Duty incumbent on both: If any thing can sweeten the Bitter Cup, 'tis that" (303). The biblical allusion suggests that a marriage without such reciprocity results in symbolic death for women—a death of self.

Artander's next letter confirms his deceit: "I have often heard and with some Impatience, that Love and Friendship, notwithstanding the nice Distinction between, were inseparable Companions, especially between different Sexes; and 'till I knew *Berina,* and some time after, I thought all Arguments offer'd upon that Subject weak and trifling, tho' it was not long before I began feel an Inclination to the same Faith: yet was forc'd to dissemble it, lest a Confession shou'd have brought a Forfeiture of that happy Friendship along with it" (298). Berina calls his letter a *"Pandora's* box, full of Poison and Infection" (300). Having taken his letters at face value, she now wonders whether anything he has said was true. She rejects his semantic sleight-of-hand and sternly reminds him of the promise in his first letter that he "shall never desire more than Friendship" (265): "He that breaks one Promise, may break a thousand; and if you have deceiv'd me as a Friend, I have little Reason to trust you as a Lover" (301).

But it is not easy to reconstruct one's worldview, or even to recognize the ideology to which one has unconsciously subscribed. The remaining letters prove conclusively that Berina's attempts to raise Artander's consciousness have failed. In this antimasculinist satire, Davys's depiction of Artander as the suffering lover who begs for mercy from the disdainful goddess who has him in her power reveals him as unworthy of Berina. Clearly, stronger measures are required. She fires back an exasperated letter in which again she ridicules his affectations: "I'll swear, Artander, I was never so merry in my Life, as at the reading of your last Letter: I don't believe that a Man in the World, that defies Love as you do, cou'd assume the Lover like you: Why you mimick it as naturally as if you had serv'd an Apprenticeship to its God: Methinks the very Paper whines, 'tis writ in such a beseeching Style" (306). Her ironic commentary on social conventions exposes their inadequacy in real life. Nevertheless, Berina generously offers him the option of pretending that he is merely parodying the style of a lovesick swain; if he does not accept that choice, however, she strongly emphasizes the dishonesty of such a pose and urges him to be more forthright.

In his final letter, Artander chides her for belittling his real pain; her satiric barbs have hit home, but they have not achieved the desired effect. "Cruel *Berina*!" he cries. "How can you use me thus? Believe me, Madam, if you were merry over my last Letter, I have been the very Reverse over yours, and have scann'd every Line with more Concern than I dare tell *Berina,* lest it shou'd serve to make me yet more ridiculous" (307). His concern over a wounded ego seems inconsequential when measured against Berina's fears, but the point escapes Artander. He has not been conditioned to deal with a woman who refuses to submit to the system of discourse which exploits her. Assuming that her response is designed to keep him groveling, he persists in his fictional role and still intends, apparently, to fling himself at her feet. Though at first glance the relative positions of male and female in this proposed finale suggest feminine triumph, Berina has recognized that it is the only moment of feminine domination in the relationship; if she accepts his scenario, she will be transformed into chattel and slave. Nevertheless, Artander has the last words in the sequence of letters. He closes by telling her that he has given orders to leave the next morning, "since I die with Impatience for a Performance, 'till when, and always, I am *Dearest Berina's Faithful Adorer,* Artander" (308). The reader is faced with the same difficulties that plague the correspondents in the novel: lacking the face-to-face confrontation, the reader has none of the clues that gesture, intonation, and body-language provide. All that remain are words—words that represent a plethora of meanings and connotations. In this case, the ambiguity is intriguing: does Artander suggest that Berina's resistance is merely a pose? Or does he acknowledge that he is acting and playing the romantic role?

There it ends. Davys tantalizes the reader with the possibilities: will Berina prove just as dishonest as he and suddenly be transformed into a conventional lady of fashion, or will she continue to insist that a permanent relationship cannot be founded on clichéd emotions and romantic speeches? Will Artander finally be jolted into an awareness that Berina is truly different from others of her sex in that she has rejected the pose of the romantic heroine and that the only relationship she will accept is one based upon open and candid expression of the state of his mind? Will he then find himself equal to the effort of developing an honest, forthright relationship with a woman? Or will he try to bully her into submission to the role society expects her to fill? The text refuses to answer these questions: it interrupts the expected trajectory of the dangerous single woman safely into wed "lock."

Nancy Armstrong has observed that readers find satisfaction in endings that result from "repeated pressures to coax and nudge sexual desire into conformity with the norms of heterosexual monogamy" without questioning whether sexual desire preceded the "strategies devised to domesticate it." Thus readers accepted the many novels that ended in marriage without noticing the role that traditional fiction played in the shaping of social forces (6). But women who wrote novels often devised ways of expressing discontent with oppressive social standards without challenging them directly.

Joseph Boone categorizes as "counter-traditional" the novels that represent sexual conflict as an "ongoing battle that can never be resolved given the patriarchal rules and oppositional roles which society has locked partners in wedlock into place" (20). One example is the open-ended text that "refuses to bring its multiple narrative lines together in one univocal pattern, because, as Robert Adams puts it, 'unresolvedness' is part of the meaning" (146).

The open ending subverts the closure of the traditional male novel even while it may appear to affirm it. Preset expectations affect interpretation: those who have failed to detect Davys's satire will project Berina's capitulation to Artander and acquiescence to her "proper" role. Indeed, even some feminist critics read *Familiar Letters* as a failed attempt at subversion: for example, Todd complains that Davys loses courage at the end of the novel and falls in line with the male model (84). However, it is possible that Davys recognized the risk of disappointing a reading audience trained to expect a "happy" or romantic ending and that she devised the open ending as a concession to her economic need. Yet the ambiguous ending only makes the novel more interesting. Boone suggests that the degree to which a writer attempts to create the appearance of order and unity in a fiction is evidence of the degree to which the writer accepts or rejects "reigning narrative and social conventions" (146). It can be argued that Davys disguises her revolutionary ideas to keep them from being unilaterally rejected, yet the concealment is only partial so that a receptive reader may see that once the female's social mask is removed, her struggle for an authentic self can be revealed. Believing as she did that women must initiate the reformation if a new regime were to emerge, Davys creates a character who can aggressively, yet subtly, manage a correspondence in order to enlighten a male (and, at the same time, to enlighten her readers). (Can it be coincidental that Berina's name is an anagram for

Brain-e and Artander's Retardan?) It is Berina who sets the goal: she wants marriage to result, but she refuses to play the traditional courtship game or to assume traditional courtship roles in order to achieve it. Artander appears to be unsure of his real feelings at first; he disguises his intentions until Berina forces him into self-awareness and a declaration, but his language and strategies are the deceptive ones typical of the enslaving patriarchy.

Aside from the question of whether she will or not, the unresolved conclusion also underlines the point that an unmarried young woman has few options: she can marry on patriarchy's terms; she can remain unmarried and suffer the humiliations of dependence, pity, and scorn; or, if she is careful, she can "sweeten the Bitter Cup" (303) of marriage by insisting on respect as the basis of the relationship. (Female discomfort with patriarchal ideology is underlined here: Berina resists the enslavement of marriage just as vehemently as the stereotypical aristocratic male character who wishes to preserve his freedom to fulfill his desires.) Davys, refusing authorial commentary and judgment, disrupts the reader's traditional expectation of return to stability and forces the reader to draw his or her own conclusions.

By denying the reader the satisfaction of closure, the novel also suggests that a woman is not likely to find satisfaction in the choices offered by social and legal institutions. Thus, the novel allows for covert criticism of marriage but at the same time allows readers who accept social convention to believe that Berina will accept Artander when he arrives in London. The open ending makes several interpretations possible: we can read it to say that Berina prefers to remain free and suffer outside of marriage rather than in it; or, if we prefer, that Berina will achieve the re-education of Artander; or we can read the ending as an ominous warning that marriage deprives the female of a voice (for it is Artander who has the last word: he announces his intention to arrive in London and the correspondence ends); or we can interpret the abrupt cessation of letters to mean that Berina, discouraged by Artander's obtuseness, never writes to him again.

At any rate, it is clear that *Familiar Letters* represents not only Davys's repudiation of the falsely glamorized position of women as depicted by female characters in the romance genre, but also represents her satiric exposure of the dangerous and uncomfortable position of women in eighteenth-century social structure. Davys's use of the traditionally male genre, albeit gentle, exposes the double standards of patriarchy.

# Works Cited

Armstrong, Nancy. *Desire and Domestic Fiction: A Political History of the Novel.* New York: Oxford UP, 1986.

Boone, Joseph Allen. *Tradition Counter Tradition: Love and the Form of Fiction.* Chicago: U Chicago P, 1987.

Davys, Mary. *The Accomplished Rake: Or, Modern Fine Gentleman. Four Before Richardson.* Ed. William McBurney. Lincoln: U Nebraska P, 1963. 232–373.

———. *Familiar Letters Betwixt a Gentleman and a Lady.* 1725. New York: Garland, 1973.

———. *The Northern Heiress: Or the Humours of York.* London, 1716.

Gilbert, Sandra, and Susan Gubar. *The Madwoman in the Attic.* New Haven: Yale UP, 1979.

Hunt, Linda C. "A Woman's Portion: Jane Austen and the Female Character." *Fetter'd or Free: British Women Novelists, 1670–1815.* Ed. Mary Anne Schofield and Cecelia Macheski. Athens: Ohio UP, 1986. 8–28.

Langbauer, Laurie. *Women and Romance: The Consolations of Gender in the English Novel.* Ithaca: Cornell UP, 1980.

McBurney, William. "Mrs. Mary Davys, Forerunner of Fielding." *PMLA* (1959): 348–55.

McKeon, Michael. *Origins of the English Novel.* Baltimore: Johns Hopkins UP, 1987.

Miller, Nancy K. *The Heroine's Text: Readings in the French and English Novel, 1722–1782.* New York: Columbia UP, 1980.

Perry, Ruth. *Women, Letters and the Novel.* New York: AMS Press, 1980.

Poovey, Mary. *The Proper Lady and the Woman Writer: Ideology as Style in the Works of Mary Wollstonecraft, Mary Shelley, and Jane Austen.* Chicago: U Chicago P, 1984.

Schofield, Mary Anne. *Masking and Unmasking the Female Mind: Disguising Romances in Feminine Fiction, 1713–1799.* Newark: U of Delaware P, 1990.

Spacks, Patricia Meyer. *Imagining a Self: Autobiography and Novel in Eighteenth Century England.* Cambridge, MA: Harvard UP, 1976.

Spencer, Jane. *The Rise of the Woman Novelist: From Aphra Behn to Jane Austen.* Oxford: Basil Blackwell, 1986.

Tanner, Tony. *Adultery in the Novel: Contract and Transgression.* Baltimore: Johns Hopkins UP, 1979.

Todd, Janet. *The Sign of Angellica: Women, Writing and Fiction, 1660–1800.* New York: Columbia UP, 1960.

# Event as Text, Text as Event

## Reading *The Rape of the Lock*

*David Wheeler*

"*The Rape of the Lock,*" the student asks, "is that a funny or a serious poem?" While recognizing the lack of sophistication implicit in such a formulation of binary opposition, we also realize how unsatisfying our likely response of "both" or "that's something you'll have to determine for yourself" will be for the student intent in his or her quest for the poem's "meaning." It seems to me, in fact, that for this impossibly complex work, any attempt, by student or critic, to close the text interpretively with "the" meaning, or with *any* meaning, will produce not satisfaction, but frustration.[1] *The Rape of the Lock,* whether examined as a formal whole or as a chain of word utterances, offers only a series of contradictions. And though such contradictions render impossible a "standard" reading of the text, they offer, for the reader interested in opening the text, in actualizing a meaning for himself or herself, a situation analogous to that presented to a child who disembarks from the school bus to confront a boundless playground with an infinite variety of play apparatus. In his *Fearful Symmetry,* Northrop Frye refers to another outdoor metaphor: "It has been said of [Jacob] Boehme that his books are like a picnic to which the author brings the words and the reader the meaning. The remark may have been intended as a sneer at Boehme, but it is an exact description of all works of literary art without exception" (427).

My intention, in considering the reader's role in *The Rape of the Lock,* is to focus upon contradictions present in individual couplet structures, contradictions that must invariably inform our experience of reading and thus produce, as it were, multiple readings. As I proceed, I hope to keep in mind Wolfgang Iser's caveat: "As meaning arises out of the process of actualization," Iser suggests, "the interpreter should perhaps pay more attention to the process than to the product. His object should therefore be not to explain a work, but to reveal the conditions that bring about its various possible effects. If he clarifies the *potential* of a text, he will no longer fall into the fatal trap of trying to impose one meaning on his reader, as if it were the right, or at least the best, interpretation" (*The Act of Reading* 18). Before I engage in exploring the potential of individual couplets, however, I wish to identify quickly some larger issues that seem to me to be contradictory and, as I go, raise questions about the implications such contradictions pose for readers.

The first of these larger issues is, no doubt, the very nature of mock-heroic form. Here the name itself identifies the contradiction, and perhaps the form will always generate questions like the one above posed by my uninitiated, hypothetical student. But we initiated, especially those initiated in eighteenth-century literature where the mock-heroic is a fairly common form with a rich and clearly delineated heritage, think we know how mock-heroic works, how comic and serious are intermixed for (usually) satiric effect. Despite this confidence (or, as I would argue, because of it), questions arise, and attempts to answer them produce often-conflicting interpretations. In the mock-heroic, for instance, how does allusion, a favorite Popean device, function? Do the often-rehearsed Miltonic echoes from *Paradise Lost* elevate Pope's subject to the seriously moral, by comparison, or do they deflate it to the comically trivial, by contrast? And Clarissa's speech? Does it, as an imitation of Sarpedon's rallying oration to Homer's Greeks, signal the poem's true hero(ine), as Pope's famous note to the 1717 edition suggests, thereby providing a kind of satiric norm? Or does it illustrate in its heroic style and demonstrate in its ill success an inappropriateness, a foolish failure to differentiate the heroic world from the mock, producing as it does precisely the opposite of its intended effect?

Or we could take the large (and I think we can still use the term) thematic issue of triviality/superficiality/artificiality (in both senses of the term—artful and unnatural/manmade). It has been argued, and argued ably and often, that *The Rape of the Lock* satirizes a society that values the superficial, materialistic trappings of civilization while neglecting the substantive: that honor is reduced from real virtue to mere reputation; that Belinda prizes a transient, outward beauty rather than true merit; that her behavior reflects that of a tantrum-throwing child who makes mountains out of molehills. These are reasonable interpretations made from reading the text. Yet, it can be argued equally, I think, that Pope's poem itself manifests the very conditions it presumably satirizes. If Belinda exaggerates the trivial into the monumental, what is Pope doing? If Belinda valorizes the purer blush of the artful stroke of her makeup brush, what can be said of a poem, that among Pope's canon, is perhaps supremely adorned with the elegant, witty, or rhetorical dress that Pope subordinates to thought in the *Essay on Criticism*? Fancy's maze or not, *The Rape* is to the poems of the 1730s what Belinda is to grave Clarissa. Indeed, Pope's own references to the poem in his correspondence speak of laughter, art, triviality.[2] What can we make of a poem that is what it satirizes? Or of a poem that, as perhaps the best-known poem of the century, immensely popular among polite society even before it was published, so clearly contributes to the society it condemns?[3]

With these questions in mind, we shouldn't be surprised that critical response to the poem has varied so radically, from John Dennis, who lamented that the poem contained no moral whatsoever, to Aubrey Williams, who portrays Belinda's fall from superficial perfection to earthly imperfection, and Jeffrey Meyers, who finds the poem concerned with "the dangers and evils of vanity and pride."[4] Even one of its first readers, Arabella Fermor herself, seemed pleased or displeased with her image depending upon how the mirror was held. As evidence, we have Pope's letter to Caryll of 8 November 1712 where the poet complains that "the lady herself is offended, and, which is stranger, not at herself, but me" (*Correspondence* I: 151). This offense seemingly prompted Pope to write the dedication for the 1714 edition which so pleased Ms. Fermor that, according to Tillotson, she posed as Belinda for her formal portrait (98–99).

*The Rape of the Lock* has been disparaged for its lack of originality, its appropriation of authors, texts, whole systems, and it has been praised for its original use of familiar materials. Critics have established careers on their explanations of Pope's use of Milton, Rosicrucianism, Homer, ombre, and the mock-heroic form. Pope even presents in his prefatory letter to Arabella Fermor an explanation of the sylphs and throughout the text provides citations for his literary allusions and notes that define, identify, or explain specific passages. Pope seemingly depends on his reader's knowledge, and when he cannot depend on it, he instills a knowledge in the reader. But as he depends on this knowledge, he also uses it—by shifting the context of the allusion, by reversing the syntax of the line, by altering our frame of reference—to force reader participation in producing meaning. The situation is similar, I think, to the one in *Joseph Andrews* described by Iser: "Expectations aroused in the reader by allusions to the things he knows or thinks he knows are frustrated; through this negation, we know that the standards and models alluded to are somehow to be, as it were, things of the past; what follows cannot be stated, but has to be realized. Thus negation can be seen as the inducement to realization—which is the reader's production of the meaning of the text" (*The Implied Reader* 37).

Readers of the *Rape of the Lock,* however, have not always read the poem as this kind of text, regarding it, instead, as a straightforward (largely satirical) moral tract. In the same section of *The Implied Reader,* Iser draws the distinction: "In the past, when book and world were regarded as identical, the book formulated its own exemplary meaning, which the reader had only to contemplate; but now that the reader has to produce the meaning for himself, the novel [*Joseph Andrews*] discloses its attitudes towards degrees of negation, thwarting the reader's expectations and stimulating him to reflection. . . . Historically speaking, perhaps one of the most important differences between Richardson and Fielding lies in the fact that with *Pamela* the meaning is clearly formulated; in *Joseph Andrews* the meaning is clearly waiting to be formulated" (46). It seems to me that the *Rape of the Lock* is not exclusively a moral satire, a mere description of an event whose representation discloses social inadequacy, human imperfection, or moral vacuity, an already formulated text, a *Pamela*. Rather than regard the poem as a representational (mimetic) structure, I suggest that we consider it as a presentational (a communicative or rhetorical) one that actively engages the reader in its actualization. This engagement relies on an implicit awareness of audience and the collective consciousness of that audience with regard not only to certain social and literary norms but also to its act of reading poetry itself. An example of what I mean here is provided easily by the Cave of Spleen episode in Canto IV. Rather than describe mimetically Belinda's anger, Pope presents us with a mythic journey that draws upon the reader's familiarity with the epic (and mock-epic) convention of the journey to the underworld and, in doing so, demands from the reader an imaginative configuration of an angry Belinda. Since there exist countless possibilities for such configurations, the reader cooperates with the poet to create the character and, by extension, the poem. A similar process occurs throughout the work, and a recognition of it can help to illuminate troublesome passages.

Anyone familiar with the poem and the criticism of it probably knows that much has been made of the couplet,

> Here Files of Pins extend their shining Rows,
> Puffs, Powders, Patches, Bibles, Billet-doux. (I, 137–8)

At least since Tillotson, the "standard reading" suggests that the presence of Bibles on a dressing table creates a profane incongruity and, consequently, serves as a metaphor for Belinda's own moral disorder. Tillotson states in his note to the second of these lines that "the list with one incongruous item" signals satire and that this particular satiric formula enjoys a rich literary heritage. Support for this reading of Belinda's religious confusion and moral inadequacy can be found, I suppose, in another incongruity occurring early in the second canto where the most sacred symbol of Christianity is transformed into a sex object:

> On her white Breast a sparkling *Cross* she wore,
> Which *Jews* might kiss, and Infidels adore. (II, 7–8)

Part of the incongruity here is achieved by the inverted syntax of the first line of the couplet. Were the line "she wore a sparkling cross on her white breast," then the "which" of the second line would refer to breast, an appropriate devotional object for men of any (or no) religious persuasion. Nevertheless, because of the inversion, the referent for "which," though arguably ambiguous, is seemingly "cross," creating the incongruity of Jews and infidels kissing and adoring the Christian symbol. But the cross, because of its placement on the breast, loses its religious significance as viewers look beyond the cross to the breast itself, and the adoration is of Belinda's beauty and sexuality, which are powerful enough to apostatize the viewers.

We must be careful, however, not to ascribe to Belinda a confusion of religion and sex. The lines say nothing about her religious values, and we cannot fault her as a Christian (probably, like Arabella Fermor, a Catholic) for wearing a crucifix (even an ornamental one that sparkles) or for wearing a fashionably low-cut dress to a party at court. The incongruity lies not in Belinda's dress but in the response to the event—the reaction of the Jews and infidels. The onus is on the viewer, who overlooks the religious significance of the emblem as he is overwhelmed by the sexual significance of the breast. And we must remember that the second line of the couplet is in the subjunctive. Jews and infidels adoring are not part of the action of the poem; rather, they are the poetic speaker's vision of what *might* happen, a kind of double fantasy, existing, as it does, within the fiction of the poem. This fantasy is at once a response to an event—the sight of beautiful Belinda—and an effort to assimilate the event into the context of the speaker's world of experiences. It is an act of reading. The incongruity is in the speaker's fantasy, and the moral confusion results, I think, from the reader's participation in the fantasy, the result of a conflict between a sexual titillation and an awareness of the emblematic significance of the cross, an awareness the reader brings to the poem. To blame Belinda results from a desire to pass moral judgment as a cover-up to our own confusion: How dare she do such a thing to us! How dare she wear the cross *there!* In such a response we overlook, I think, our participation in the reading experience.

Let us now return to the line with the puffs and Bibles. Again, what does the line really tell us about Belinda's religious values? That she has

Bibles on her dressing table hardly seems a valuation. Just as in the passage discussed above, where we might be pleased that she is converting Jews, here we might be pleased that she possesses Bibles at all. Would we feel better about Belinda's moral state if the Bibles were tucked away in a drawer somewhere rather than immediately accessible, located, as they obviously are, in a place where she clearly spends considerable time? There are infinite positive explanations for their presence on the table. She could devoutly be reading as her maid does her hair, for example. And we wouldn't be surprised, let alone shocked with moral outrage, to find a Bible on a friend's kitchen table, bed, or car seat.

Yet, we cannot deny the incongruity in the line. It is not, however, an incongruity inherent in the event itself but one that exists in our act of reading the line. It's not that we're surprised to discover Bibles on a dressing table but that we are surprised to find them in this line of poetry. Our surprise occurs not only because Bibles are a different sort of object from the others in the line but also because the *word* "Bibles" interrupts the alliterative series of puffs, patches, and powders and is linked alliteratively (presumably profanely) with the suspect "Billet-doux." Perhaps more importantly, at this point in the poem, if we are readers of even average perceptiveness, we have been seduced by the description of ritualized dressing into an expectation of order, an expectation frustrated when we arrive at "Bibles." Since this incongruity, like the cross and the breast, is an act of reader response rather than any necessary moral deficiency in the heroine, we might ask how a frustrated expectation is transformed into blame of Belinda.

We return, therefore, to Tillotson's assertion that the incongruous item in the list signals satire, the assertion of a highly sophisticated, knowledgeable reader. But is Tillotson right? And is this why we read the line the way we do? Do we, as readers, bring the same body of knowledge as Tillotson to the text? Let's take an example from a lesser-known poet, one for whom we likely know less about the work and perhaps the "literary traditions" that shaped it—a poet we read differently, perhaps, from the way we read Pope. Carolyn Forché, in her series of political Nicaraguan poems, *The Country Between Us,* frequently uses the same device of the list with the incongruous element. I'll provide two examples, the first describing the revolutionary Sandinistas, the second describing participants in Samosa's military regime:

> Your women walk among the *champas*
> with baskets of live hens, grenades and fruit.
> Tonight you begin to fight
> for the most hopeless of revolutions. ("Message" 21)

> WHAT YOU HAVE HEARD is true. I was in
> his house. His wife carried a tray of coffee and
> sugar. His daughter filed her nails, his son went
> out for the night. There were daily papers, pet
> dogs, a pistol on the cushion beside him. ("The Colonel" 16)

In lines that assault our morality more directly and more seriously than any in *The Rape of the Lock,* Forché has her incongruous elements—grenades and pistol—and the incongruity calls attention to them. But I am certainly reluctant—as I'm confident most of us are—to call the lines satiric. Why? Had I included just one of the passages, we might assume a confidence that we know Forché's political perspective and assume she is satirizing the opposing political force. But with both passages, we are less certain. Unable to use our knowledge to get a foothold on perspective, we tend to take the lines at face value—flat, descriptive, matter-of-fact declarations of what is. The lines make us uncomfortable. In our desire to impose a pattern of order on such chaotic signs, we wish the grenades and pistols weren't there. But as readers we are, with such little "evidence," unsure what form that order should take.

With Pope, I suggest, we think we are more sure. We are not naive readers of Pope; we have read his poems and we have read what 250 years' worth of readers have said about them. Like Tillotson, we are experienced readers indeed. We know about Pope's century, we know the forms he used, we know his rhetorical devices, we understand his moral perspective and his irony. When we read his poems, like *The Rape of the Lock,* for the classroom, for our own work, we use this information to decipher meaning. It is precisely because we are experienced readers that our students turn to us for answers to their questions. The danger with this procedure, I think, is that we commonly read the early poems as compositions by the wasp of Twickenham, the author of *The Essay on Man, The Epistles to Several Persons,* and the Horatian poems of the thirties. We take meaning gleaned from decidedly moral works, satiric and philosophical, and impose it on a work of a different sort. We search for order, and we find it.

I cannot quarrel with searching for order; all acts of reading are, in fact, processes of ordering. But as we pursue our interpretive quests for meaning, we must recognize what Jane P. Tompkins points out so clearly in her essay "The Reader in History": "[T]here is no escape from interpretation, not because the text is undecidable, as the deconstructionists would have it, but because the institutional context within which the critic works—a context created by the doctrines of literary formalism—dictates that interpretation is the only activity that will be recognized as doing what criticism is supposed to do" (225). If literary formalists, represented in the United States by New Critics, privileged the poetic text, elevating it into the realm of the sacred, then both our interpretive enterprise and our privileged place in educational institutions have elevated critics into the high priests. The deliberate mystification of critic and text can serve only to baffle with inadequacy the student who is asked "What does it mean?" A much more useful classroom question, it seems to me, is "what is it about?" What is *The Rape of the Lock* about? Many things, no doubt, but one of them surely is the act of reading itself. We know as much about the genesis of this poem—of Lord Petre and Arabella Fermor, of the severed hair and severed engagement, of the feuding families—as about any poem I can think of. The genesis of the poem is an event, the poem Pope's response to the event, an attempt to put it in perspective, to make sense of it, to order it, to read it.

Moreover, the poem's action consists of a series of responses (or nonresponses) to events, portents, actions, speeches. A list of such events/responses is a long one, but we might begin with the poem's familiar opening lines, Pope's announced subject:

> What dire Offence from am'rous Causes springs,
> What mighty Contests rise from Trivial Things[.]

Causes and things will evoke offense and (finally) contests. And along the way, the sun will open eyes; a dream produce a blush; the view of familiar objects vanquish the dream; Belinda's beauty fixate eyes of viewers; destructive locks produce the Baron's desire. The declining sun brings about an end of work—for a hanging judge, a merchant on the exchange, Belinda herself; a card game introduces a sequence of play and response; the victory causes Belinda's exultant shouts (and the speaker's aphoristic warning); coffee vapors create new stratagems; scissors set an army of sylphs into motion; an earthly lover confuses and amazes Ariel; cut hair produces lightning and screams from Belinda and triumphant glee from the Baron; rage, resentment, and despair replace Ariel with Umbriel; Thalestris's speech evokes Sir Plume's request; the breaking of the vial produces Belinda's grief and speech; the speech melts the audience in tears (but the Baron's ears are stopped, so he doesn't respond); Clarissa's speech brings about not applause but frowns and battle. A veritable chain reaction of events and responses. As readers, we are carried along in the stream and may not recognize how often we are invited (or required) to participate actively.

In, for example, the couplet, "Smooth flow the waves, the Zephyrs gently play,/*Belinda* smiled, and all the World was gay" (II, 51–52), we're offered two possibilities as to what made the world gay. If we read just the second line, we see "Belinda smiled and all the world was gay"— simple cause and effect. If, on the other hand, we read the entire couplet, we find Belinda's smile to be part of a series—smooth-flowing waves, gently playing breezes, and smiling Belinda—the combined elements forming a peaceful pattern that produces a gay world.

Or take the more troublesome couplet,

> If to her share some Female Errors fall,
> Look on her Face, and you'll forget 'em all. (II, 17–18)

Here, as in the couplet with the cross and Jews, we discover the power of beauty to obliterate more serious concerns. And the lines likewise pose problems for readers. The first line, written in the conditional, is non-committal. We're not sure if Belinda has committed errors or not. More-over, because of the conditional construction of the first line, we tend to read the second line as if it too were conditional: *if* we look on Belinda's face, then we'll forget her errors (if she has any). But the second line, the main clause of the poetic sentence, is in the imperative; it *commands* us to look and forget. But since in the poem, we never really get a good look at that face—we get others' responses to the face and a brief glance at the mirrored reflection of it—it's a difficult command to obey, and we tend to look for the errors rather than to forget them.

Such playful speculation is fun and is related, I think, to what has been written about patterns of game and play in *The Rape of the Lock.* (I'm thinking here, of course, of the work of Murray Krieger and Martin Price—esp. 146–54—and of the treatment of the general subject of play in Huizinga's excellent *Homo Ludens.*) Let me just say in conclusion that the game in the poem is one for active participants, not mere spectators. And, as we read the poem, let us not succumb to the temptation to read it too seriously, as if the poem, as an example of the mock-heroic, were somehow a companion piece to the fourth book of *The Dunciad.* The de-finitive serious reading of the poem, we must remember, was made by Pope himself in the *Key to the Lock,* and that serious reading, dependent as it is on "the only Concession which I [Pope] desire to be made me, is, that by the *Lock* is meant *The* BARRIER TREATY" (185), was a joke. Rather, if we must teach the poem or write about the poem (as indeed we must), let us mine the text for its potential, open the text to its possibili-ties, thereby helping our students and our readers to participate in creat-ing the text for themselves.

# Notes

1  There are, of course, dozens of provocative and worthwhile critical interpretations of *The Rape of the Lock*. Recent readings that I find compelling include those of Ellen Pollak, Murray Cohen, David Fairer, Laura Brown, Howard Erskine-Hill, John Loftis, Charles Martindale, and the articles in the special issue of *New Orleans Review* devoted to the poem, vol. 15 (1988).

2. See, for instance, the letter from Pope to Mrs. Marriot, 28 February 1714: "What excuse then, can I offer the poem that attends this letter, where 'tis a chance but you are diverted from some very good action or useful reflection for more hours than one. I know it is no sin to laugh, but I had rather your laughter should be at the vain ones of your own sex than at me, and therefore would rather have you read my poem than my letter. This whimsical piece of work, as I have now brought it up to my first design, is at once the most a satire [Pope had written no satires to this point in his career], and the most inoffensive, of anything of mine" (*Correspondence* I: 211).

3. If one wishes to read *The Rape of the Lock* as a social or moral satire, I think the right track is one suggested by Clifford Siskin: "the primary object of criticism and candidate for correction . . . [is] the deviant individual, either as individual or as the representative of a type. Society, its structure and institutions, is at worst a secondary target; most often it is perceived as a necessary tool to contain deviance within safe limits. That is why eighteenth-century satire is a powerful yet profoundly conservative weapon; as a product of Uniformitarianism, its governing value is social stability" (375). While most readers would regard Belinda as the deviant individual, I think the murky and disruptive Baron is an equally viable candidate.

4. See John Dennis's "Remarks on Mr Pope's Rape of the Lock" esp. 331; Aubrey Williams 412–25; and Jeffrey Meyers 77.

# Works Cited

Brown, Laura. *Alexander Pope*. Oxford: Basil Blackwell, 1985.

Cohen, Murray. "Versions of the Lock: Readers of *The Rape of the Lock*." *ELH* 43 (1976): 53–73.

Dennis, John "Remarks on Mr Pope's Rape of the Lock." *Critical Works of John Dennis*. Ed. Edward Niles Hooker. 2 vols. Baltimore: Johns Hopkins UP, 1939, 1943. II: 322–52.

Erskine-Hill, Howard. "The Satirical Game at Cards in Pope and Wordsworth." *English Satire and Satiric Tradition*. Ed. Claude Rawson. Oxford: Oxford UP, 1984.

Fairer, David. "Imagination in *The Rape of the Lock*," *Essays in Criticism* 29 (1979): 53–74.

Forché, Carolyn. "Message" and "The Colonel." *The Country Between Us.* New York: Harper and Row, 1981.

Frye, Northrop. *Fearful Symmetry: A Study of William Blake.* Princeton: Princeton UP, 1967.

Huizinga, Johan. *Homo Ludens: A Study of the Play Element in Culture.* New York: Harper and Row, 1970.

Iser, Wolfgang. *The Act of Reading: A Theory of Aesthetic Response.* Baltimore: Johns Hopkins UP, 1978.

———. *The Implied Reader: Patterns of Communication in Prose Fiction from Bunyan to Beckett.* Baltimore: Johns Hopkins UP, 1974.

Krieger, Murray. "The 'Frail China Jar' and the Rude Hand of Chaos." *Centennial Review of Arts and Sciences* 5 (1961): 176–94.

Loftis, John. "Speech in 'The Rape of the Lock.'" *Neophilologus* 67 (1983): 149–59.

Martindale, Charles. "Sense and Sensibility: The Child and the Man in 'The Rape of the Lock.'" *MLR* 78 (1983): 273–84.

Meyers, Jeffrey. "The Personality of Belinda's Baron in Pope's *The Rape of the Lock.*" *American Imago* 26 (1969): 71–77.

Pollak, Ellen. *The Politics of Sexual Myth: Gender and Ideology in the Verse of Swift and Pope.* Chicago: U of Chicago P, 1985.

Pope, Alexander. *The Correspondence of Alexander Pope.* Ed. George Sherburn. 5 vols. Oxford: Clarendon, 1956.

———. *A Key to the Lock. Prose Works of Alexander Pope.* Ed. Norman Ault. Oxford: Blackwell, 1936.

Price, Martin. *To the Palace of Wisdom. Studies in Order and Energy from Dryden to Blake.* New York: Doubleday, 1964.

Siskin, Clifford. "Personification and Community: Literary Change in the Mid and Late Eighteenth Century." *Eighteenth-Century Studies* 15 (1982): 371–401.

Tillotson, Geoffrey, ed. *The Rape of the Lock and Other Poems.* Vol. 2 of *The Twickenham Edition of the Poems of Alexander Pope.* 10 vols. London and New Haven: Methuen and Yale UP, 1939–1967.

Tompkins, Jane P. "The Reader in History: The Changing Shape of Literary Response." *Reader-Response Criticism from Formalism to Post-Structuralism.* Ed. Jane P. Tompkins. Baltimore: Johns Hopkins UP, 1980.

Williams, Aubrey. "The Fall of China and *The Rape of the Lock.*" *Philological Quarterly* 41 (1962): 412–25.

# Mocking the Heroic?

## A Context for *The Rape of the Lock*

*Nigel Wood*

### I

"The *Rape of the Lock* is a very *empty Trifle*, without any Solidity or sensible Meaning. . . . For by placing something important in the Beginning of a Period, and making something very trifling follow it, he seems to take pains to bring something into a Conjunction Copulative with nothing, in order to beget nothing" (Dennis 2: 330; 348). It is no doubt pleasantly ironical to reflect on John Dennis's frustration with the mock-heroic in his *Remarks on Mr. Pope's Rape of the Lock* (1728), its coat-trailing bathos now usually rescued by our critical assertions that its verses are nonetheless oddly beautiful, graceful and multi-allusive, and its mercurial changes of focus much to be desired. It appears admirable in its refusal to say exactly what it means and in its use of the past so extensively in its lack of direct comment. However, Dennis may have stumbled on the humor of Pope's mock-heroic. Does the "Conjunction" between the debased present and the grand past produce a lack of semantic center, rendering the poem, as Maynard Mack has recently termed it, just a "happy poem, from a happy interlude" in Pope's life (Mack, *Alexander Pope* 248)? Merely to term this mode ironic seems evasive as there are very specific passages where a simple split between meaning and significance is the very least that occurs.

Even given that there is obvious personal animus behind the *Remarks,* Dennis's objections to the *Rape's* indecorum deserve close consideration. Whilst Pope may have "given his fine Lady *Beauty* and good *Breeding, Modesty* and *Virtue* in words," the irony secures for her "in Fact" the reputation of "*an artificial dawbing Jilt; a Tomrig, a Virago,* and a *Lady of the Lake*" (Dennis 2: 335). Pope's very words and the "facts" on which interpretation should be based are at odds. Dennis's objections were taken seriously. In Pope's own copy of the *Remarks* his annotation makes it plain that he did intend to include a moral in the poem, one that derived from the substitution of the "female sex" as his satirical target in place of

Boileau's "Popish Clergy" from *Le Lutrin*.[1] If Pope's Catholicism was as constant a touchstone for him as has recently been claimed,[2] this need not entail a high degree of bitterness on his part, especially as he was later to claim, in either 1738 or 1739, that Belinda had "rais'd [his] Strain" in "voluntary [naturally free] Vein" (*Imitations of Horace* Ep. I. vii. 49–50). What had started life as a private compliment in manuscript had to be excused and given a moral once it was given the publicity of printed material.

Most certainly Belinda's "Rites of Pride" passage (I.121–48) can be read both as a means by which the tone of the verse is elevated and also as an instance of the "trivial Things" that provoke "mighty Contests," but is the communication of her triviality any more a "fact" than the epic "words" that lend her *levée* its divine afflatus? The arming of Aeneas in *Aeneid* VIII and Achilles in *Iliad* XIX enables the deserving mortal to take on divinity. According to Pope, when Achilles dons the armor forged by the lame Vulcan, he dresses himself in "Arms divine": "Arms which the Father of the Fire bestow'd,/Forg'd on th' Eternal Anvils of the God" (*Iliad* XIX.391–93). His superhuman daring and power against the Trojans in Book Twenty, a conflict involving divine intervention, is as much, if not more, due to additives as Belinda's "purer Blush" and "keener Lightnings" (I.143–44) at Hampton Court. However, the closest equivalent is probably Juno's efforts to distract Jupiter from favoring the Trojans in *Iliad* XIV, using the magic girdle of Venus. She is still the "virtuous Juno" who has had the "Experience of a married State" (XIV.359 n.), even when her means (including the power of Venus) and aims—seductresses suborning a God's judgment by "pure cunning, and the artful Management of their Persons" (XIV.216 n.)—are questionable. The note to line 203 may take up a reassuringly ethical posture when Pope praises the "great Simplicity" of Juno's dress compared to that issuing from a "modern Toilette," yet the episode as a whole has both a charm and moral that surmount such considerations: "it is certain, that whatever may be thought of this Fable in a theological or philosophical View, it is one of the most beautiful Pieces that ever was produced by Poetry. Neither does it want its moral [the instruction as to how a wife may keep the affection of her husband]" (XIV.179 n.). Vulcan had also "form'd" her secret "Bow'r" (XIV.193) where she arms herself for her mission and the costume and ensemble of scents is topped by the "powerful *Cestus*" (XIV.256), Venus's girdle, that consummate emblem of "conqu'ring Charms,/That Pow'r, which Mortals and Immortals warms" (XIV.225–26). It is significant that "the Sons of Heav'n" as well as mere mortals are vulnerable to the "sacred Fires" of love (XIV.228), and that these desires promote peace, for it is not just the Trojan war that is on Juno's mind when she approaches Venus but the more elemental strife between Ocean and Tethys and that between Saturn and Jupiter. Love is here a form of persuasion akin to rhetoric.

> With Awe divine the Queen of Love
> Obey'd the Sister and the Wife of *Jove*:
> And from her fragrant Breast the Zone unbrac'd,
> With various Skill and high Embroidery grac'd.
> In this was ev'ry Art, and ev'ry Charm,
> To win the wisest, and the coldest warm. . . . (XIV.243–48)

Art can soothe "fatal Feuds" and re-kindle "mutual Ties" (XIV.240–41).

If Juno is equivalent to Belinda, even as the positive to a negative, then the reader may be puzzled by the apparent surplus of signification that emerges from the logic of the allusion. Belinda cannot stand as the dutiful wife, yet there are still parallels between the two passages. Firstly, both stress the potency of Art, and secondly, the peaceableness of Juno's venture seems analogous to Pope's attempt in the *Rape,* according to Spence, to "laugh [the Fermors and Petres] together again."[3] If Belinda is too much the negative example in the comparison, then the poem is vicious indeed at her expense, implying that the *"Cosmetic* Pow'rs" (I.124) are illicit faint reminders of the more sanctionable heroic eroticism of Venus. "Slight is the Subject" of his poem, Pope admits, "but not so the Praise" of Belinda (I.5). As William Empson succinctly put it, the interest here is derived from the contrast not solely between the two ironic poles of mock-heroic allusion (Ancient/Modern) but also between this "stock response" which complacently emphasizes a debased Present and "the response demanded by the author," where the references are far less mechanical and steady state (160).

I am not claiming that the poem is predominantly hedonistic, for, obviously, there is the matter of Clarissa's speech, designed, as Pope/Warburton reminds us in 1751, to "open more clearly the MORAL of the poem" (V.9–34), but even these otherwise impeccable sentiments are questionable, *official* statements, and on closer examination turn out to be circumspect and defensive—and in any case issue from one who has helped precipitate Belinda's crisis by providing the scissors for the predatory Baron. We ought also to admire the gestures towards the passage's epic source: Sarpedon's speech to Glaucus from *Iliad* XII. The 1736 note might perhaps warn us not to allow Sarpedon's glory to be reflected on Clarissa and hence the whole poem, for it there appears as a *"parody"* of the speech,[4] which could imply that it forms an inappropriate allusion. Indeed, there is surely some mismatch between the valorous exhortations of a Homeric hero and Clarissa's tactical resignation. The two could not be more unlike. Sarpedon wants Glaucus to act heroically in order to encourage the others so that they may deserve the material possessions that masculine leadership brings: "num'rous Herds that range each fruitful Field,/And Hills where Vines their Purple Harvest yield" (29–30). The passage— from Pope's contribution to Tonson's *Miscellany* (1709)—continues:

> Why on these Shores are we with Joy survey'd,
> Admired as Heroes, and as Gods obey'd? . . .
> The first in Valour, as the first in Place. . . . (33–34, 38)[5]

Clarissa commands subservience, and Sarpedon's "Valour" becomes Clarissa's "Virtue" ("Behold the first in Virtue, as in Face" [V.18]), his assertive "Admired as Heroes, and as Gods obey'd" is transmuted to the interrogative "Why Angels call'd, and Angel-like ador'd?" (V.12). The movement from Heroism to gracious and perhaps vapid compliment signals a Fall, as does the recognition that Clarissa could never aspire to such freedom of gesture because she is female. Does Clarissa question and so expose the men's clubbery of Sarpedon, or do the traces of Homer imply a degeneration in the *jeunesse dorée*? Or both? Which is the official side of the equation, which the *intended* parallel? There is often an unholy alliance between saying too much and ending up having it amount to *nothing*.

This same fruitfulness/nothingness is more often educed from the stellification of the lock at the poem's conclusion, that "sudden Star" that shoots through "liquid Air" (V.127). Is Belinda more sinned against than sinning? Or is the graceful compliment absurd burlesque, in that she is yoked both with the deification of Julius Caesar (*Metamorphosis* XV) and Romulus the founder of Rome? Does the trope allow two-way traffic? Surely the Pythagorean emphasis on the transmigration of souls from *Metamorphosis* XV needs not be taken on board along with the undoubted aestheticism of Ovidian transformation? Here is Sandys's translation (1626), describing how Venus plucks the "new fled spirit" from Caesar's body:

> To heaven, not suffer'd to resolve to aire.
> And as in her soft bosom borne, shee might
> Perceive it take a Powre and gather Light.
> When once let loose, it forth with up-ward flew;
> And after it long blazing tresses flew.

This release involves a severing from the body, where the "better Part" of Caesar mounts the skies:

> And my immortal name shall never die . . .
> And if we Prophets truly can divine,
>   I, in my living Fame, shall ever shine. (pages 325–26)

The lock, however, cannot easily be reconstituted as a spirit. That is why there is the possibility that, as Pope indicated in making it part of the motto to the 1714 and 1715 editions, Scylla's fate in *Metamorphosis* VIII is also indicated. This is a more official and instructive example, in that Scylla, thanks to blind passion, is led to cut the "purple hair" or lock of her father, Nisus, and actually kills him. In so doing, she betrays her birthright at Megara and hands the city over to her lover, Minos. Eventually she is changed into a *Ciris* (literally a cutter, or cutting) to be preyed upon by her father, who is now an osprey.

Even in the Catullus source ("The Lock of Berenice," *Poems* no. 66), which would import a graceful compliment to the poem on its own, there is a similar duality in the allusion, in that the Lock, when addressing Berenice as a newly fashioned constellation, regrets such elevation into complete spirit and glances back at its prior existence as preferable:

> I'm not so *joyful* for this Heavenly State,
> That I'm above the reach of *Chance* and *Fate,*
> As discontented that I still must be,
> Absent from my Dear *Queen,* and *she* from *me.* . . .
> Why do the *Stars* obstruct my swift descent
> Why am I not to my lov'd Mistress sent? (11.83–86, 113–14;
>   pages 125–26)

The lock harks back to Berenice's virginal status before marriage to Ptolemy and the danger of learning so much at "*Venus* Shrine" (1.108) that the Love and Concord of a successful marriage is ignored. Much as the earlier association of Belinda with Juno had emphasized evident distinctions between them whilst at the same time drawing parallels, this allusive context suggests (almost proleptically for Belinda) the responsibilities of female sexual maturity at the same time as gesturing towards the possibilities of personal loss in the transformation.

Is Belinda an Angel/God or has she had her silly head turned by a fixated *amour*? Again, both could be the case. The waters get muddier when we also reflect on yet another possible allusion, to Dido's suicide in *Aeneid* IV, another figure who could be arraigned for a passionate involvement. Duty calls Aeneas, the intended founder of Rome, but oblivion awaits Dido. Here, in Dryden's translation (1697), is how her lock of hair is rescued: Juno sends Iris down

> to free her from the Strife
> Of laboring Nature, and [to] dissolve her Life.
> For since she dy'd, not doom'd by Heav'n's Decree,
> Or her own Crime; but Human Casualty (IV.995–98),

the Fates had not time to cut her "topmost Hair" (IV.1000); she is, therefore, stayed from death since she is not "sacred to the Shades below" (IV.1002). "Downward the various Goddess took her flight;/And drew a thousand Colours from the Light" (IV.1003–4). Iris says:

> I thus devote thee to the dead.
> This Off'ring to th' Infernal Gods I bear:
> Thus while she spoke, she cut the fatal Hair;
> The strugling Soul was loos'd; and Life dissolv'd in Air.
>     (IV.1006–9; Dryden, *Poems* III: 1170)

Although at the close of the *Rape* (V.125–26) we are reminded of Romulus's deification and at III.122ff. of Scylla's fate, the passion of Dido is also evident, along with its much darker implications. After Belinda's triumph at Ombre, the narrative expatiates on fateful steel (the scissors) at III.173–74: "Steel could the Labour of the Gods destroy [Apollo and Poseidon]/And strike to Dust th'Imperial Tow'rs of Troy." In Canto V, just before Clarissa's speech, lines five to six run, "Not herself so fix'd the Trojan [Aeneas] cou'd remain,/While Anna begg'd and Dido rag'd in vain."

It is especially significant that these allusions do not allow the reader to mock the contemporary nonheroic age with any confidence. Ian Jack's definition of the mock-epic as one where "a dignified genre is turned to witty use without being cheapened in any way" (78) suggests that we can keep the implied epic context separate in our reading from Belinda's modern rituals, and that the contrast between her and either Dido or Juno upholds the same watertight division between the positive pole of classical transcendent ideals and a negative one of contingent luxury or debased morals.

## II

What we seem to have here are a series of overdetermined allusions, defying easy reduction to coherence models. Pope emerges as fully aware of

Tartarean depths and reverses Iris's action by consigning the lock to the stars, not the shades. And yet we cannot but be aware of the surrounding anxiety behind these allusions. Do we edit some of them out, or find a new frame to comprehend their variety? Those who espouse the patterns of "historicism" do need a simplified frame within which to work, and this variety of choice, for them, must be held at bay. Causes need to be uncovered in a clarified cause-and-effect logic. The most pressing problem for orthodox hermeneutics is to establish limits to allusion so as to preserve a notion of Pope's own "intention." Earl R. Wasserman, in his valuable study "The Limits of Allusion in *The Rape Of The Lock,*" bids farewell to the New Critical phase in the reading of Pope's mock-heroic by opening out a further set of questions. Although commentators were no longer much exercised by claims that they were attending to "poetry of statement," the discovery of "extraordinary subtleties" of language and allusion had drawn up a new agenda: the question is "whether only the text of Pope's allusion acts upon his poem or whether it also imports its own context. If the context is indeed relevant, what are the permissible limits in our bringing that context to bear? How allusive are Pope's allusions? and how functional?" (425). He concludes that "such literature as this is constituted not only by its own verbal texture but also by the rich interplay between the author's text and the full contexts it allusively arouses, for these allusive resonances are not peripheral but functional to the meaning of the artistic product" (444). However, the resourcefulness of Wasserman's tracing of allusion in his essay does not exhaust its declared subject, the "rich" intertextuality of the poem. As I have suggested, this can only occur once we entertain the idea that the significance of the poem is constructed out of profound contradictions, not solely of "statements" (of whatever complexity). The "full contexts" Wasserman mentions often exceed a paraphraseable "intention" until the critic is obliged to enter the frame and make a deliberate choice of a reduced network of meanings s/he believes are "functional," ignoring those deemed accidental. Thus, it is quite orthodox and coherent to emphasize the classical allusions as polite wit. Belinda is being quietly advised to heed Clarissa's good sense, avoid Dido's fate, and aspire, in the fullness of time, to Juno's wifely complaisance—that is, if we ignore several details such as that Juno avails herself of the questionable charms of Venus to accomplish her ends, that Dido dies as a victim of loving an epic hero, that Clarissa aids the Baron in procuring the lock, that, in any case, she is only given the opportunity to supply a form of ethical closure to the poem as late in its textual history as the 1717 *Works* (when, it could be argued, Pope needed less equivocal statements about women to suit the occasion), and that the poem's widespread innuendoes threaten to disturb its apparent syntactical and verbal decorum. What is more, the poem does not consistently endorse a withdrawal from the temporal sphere. Berenice's lock would dearly like to rejoin life from its enforced transcendent position, just as Dido's lock is rescued by Iris to enable her troubled spirit to enter the Shades, not the Stars.

If we accept Wasserman's point that such full "allusive resonances" are not "peripheral" but "functional," then we have to accept that the mock-heroic strategy does not always provide a metonymic reassurance whereby the subject described is clarified by likening it to an equivalent item.[6] On the contrary, we are often given too much allusive material for that equivalence to be maintained, to such a degree that the relation is more metaphorical and a complex semiotic sign is created, where Belinda "exists" no more than the Machinery, and where Dennis's sturdy belief that certain interpretative "facts" could be inversely deduced from the common denotative sense of the "words" emerges as of only partial validity. The poem might lose some of its satirical direction, but it gains a symbolic complexity. When focusing on "the dynamics of eighteenth-century sexual ideology" Ellen Pollak has recently noted that the "exclusive and rigid categories of angel and whore," standard throughout the period, "made the integration of spiritual and erotic attributes in a single woman logically impossible" (1). The emphasis should here perhaps fall on the word, "logically."

### III

There is a potent temptation to treat this indeterminacy of meaning as composed of *aporia* after *aporia* and to conclude that the only way of avoiding their accumulation is either by evasion—or by the individual critic's determination to halt the metaphorical profusion in the interests of "relevance" or even a moral higher good. Pope "must have" intended to signify a clearer and more compact meaning. Where the text does not seem to direct us towards this, close (really close) reading ceases and other criteria become operative. If, however, we here pursue a "perverse" analysis of the figurative, there still remains a problem for the critic who would still aim to make use of abundant extrinsic material when re-constructing the work's context. Does she still search for what might probably have been Pope's original intention, or the ideology that places it in a wider framework? In what way can an appeal to History aid hermeneutics? Recently these problems have become more familiar in New Historicist criticism as it attempts to provide an answer to the deconstruction of all frameworks.[7] In his debate with John Searle about J. L. Austin's speech act theory, Derrida did not, however, simply claim that the search for a context was fruitless. Whilst "no context permits saturation" (i.e., can ever be exhaustively mapped), it is also the case that "no meaning can be determined out of context": "What I am referring to here is not richness of substance, semantic fertility, but rather structure, the structure of the remnant or of iteration" (81). No statement can ever be uttered in *exactly* the same context twice, just as mock-heroic irony will disturb any notion of *surface* meaning by constantly suggesting its opposite. If we cannot provide a clear pattern to help us derive an intention from the suggestiveness of *The Rape of the Lock,* there is still the task of trying to account for the meanings of (inevitably) partial readings. The detailed illustration of *how* certain texts are "logocentric" and how certain authors negotiate with the iterability of their work and the threatening supplements to what they perceive to be their intention still involves some historical material.

Jerome McGann's recent work has placed a renewed emphasis on a "historical method" that takes account of the material changes that a particular text inevitably undergoes once it becomes public property.[8] This could take the form of accepting that even from the earliest stages of publication a printed text is often a collaboration, and that an author's "final intention," even where it is manifest, does not necessarily challenge the validity of earlier editions, presumably at the moment of *their* publication the "final intentions" of potentially different authorial "selves." A single Ur-text does not exist. *The Rape* is an umbrella term for several "organic unities," not one: the 1712 first edition (from *Miscellaneous Poems and Translations. By Several Hands* [re-issued, 1714]), the enlarged 1714 editions (three in all), the "corrected" fifth of 1715, and thereafter its inclusion in Pope's *Works* (1717, 1736, 1740, 1743, and 1751). Even this list does not fully account for the missing manuscript copy that so met with both Arabella Fermer's and Lord Petre's approval that the printed life of the work could begin. Indeed, the assumption that texts enjoy some Edenic spiritual reality before the negotiation with publisher or reading public is often just a prop for critical generalization.

In "Keats and the Historical Method in Literary Criticism" (1979), McGann claims that the existence of any text is never completely coextensive with its linguistic structure. Rather it is inescapably a "social event," and it takes part in "a dialectical relation" throughout history between its "author-intention" and its consumption by the reading public, or to give it a more materialist base, its commercial appropriation by the market and by whoever owns the printing presses. "To determine the significance of the poem at its point of origin," as he claims in a later study, entails an account of the work's "bibliography," "the study of the poem's initial manuscript and printed constitutions" (*The Beauty of Inflections* 23). More recently he has placed greater emphasis on the "performative" impact of works of literature, not only the discovery of *what* is said but also the consideration of *how* such supposed content is signified (*Social Values* 95–114). If "Belinda," for example, never consistently refers directly to the Arabella Fermors of Pope's world, but is always part of a second-order signifying system, then apparently unrelated items are yoked together in the service of myth, not mimesis.[9]

Thoroughgoing deconstructionists often posit that, as a common effect of logocentrism, the writing they choose to address seems to enjoy a prior, "innocent" state of being, a point of origin either derived from an ethereal ego or deduced by the critical community from the principle of its supposed organic unity. Something must exist, even if only temporarily, in order for it to be deconstructed and thus its status as a historical event to be questioned. However, a detailed account of *The Rape of the Lock*'s "bibliography," in McGann's more specialized sense, uncovers original significances (or "author-intentions") that are in any case far from unitary or even complementary.

## IV

In the letter to Henry Cromwell of July 15, 1711, Pope makes a first mention of what would result in the two-canto *Rape of the Locke* (1712). Cromwell is complimented on his urbanity which is attractive to "the Ladies in particular": "The Trophy you bore away from one of 'em, in your Snuffbox, will doubtless preserve her Memory, and be a Testimony of your admiration, for ever" (Pope to Cromwell, July 15, 1711; *Correspondence* I: 125). Then follows a conflated first draft of what would eventually be Canto I, lines 89–94 and 128–34 of the 1712 *Rape,* the praise of coffee drunk from "*China's* Earth" (I.94) and the Baron's exultation at winning the Lock. The point of the lines in the letter is to demonstrate Pope's own worldliness before one whom he still (erroneously) believed might be able to offer valuable introductions to literary London. The "Trophy" will keep alive his admirer's "Honour, Name, and Praise" as long as "Coffee shall to British Nymphs be dear," and, as such, it exists as witty praise of a novel social ritual. However, by 1712, the "Honour" has passed to the Baron as long as "Nymphs take Treats, or assignations give" (I.133–34), and the comment invites a new suggestion, namely, that the opportunities for such male adventures are very much a part of the full social round and felt to last, by the fashionable world, "While Fish in Streams, or Birds delight in Air" (I.127).[10] Pope never included the letter in any of his own published correspondence as knowledge of the full relationship with Cromwell from 1708–11 would have uncovered an unwelcome persona for the future arbiter of true worth: that of the foppish pretender to Wit, inviting the confidences of a failed witling. This insight we owe to Edmund Curll, who published their unauthorized correspondence in 1726.[11]

With the enlarged 1714 edition there had come a fresh opportunity to assess its meaning vis-à-vis the intended readership. As early as December 15, 1713, Pope had in any case probably decided to alter the 1712 text. "Sir Plume blusters," Pope wrote to John Caryll, not six months after the May publication date, and even the "celebrated lady herself is offended." The result is the dedication to her in the second, five-canto edition, "as a piece of justice in return to the wrong interpretations she has suffered under the score of that piece" (Pope to Caryll, November 8, 1712; Pope to Caryll, December 15, 1713; *Correspondence* I: 151; I: 203). Reparation was apparently also offered (but rejected) in the shape of a prefatory epistle that eventually made its way into the 1717 *Poems on Several Occasions*, "To Belinda on the Rape of the Lock." When considered together, both the epistle and dedication show not so much the growth of some original idea embedded in the earlier version(s) as the unplanned incursion of extrinsic considerations. The 1712 edition might have been all-sufficient as far as Pope's own manuscript intentions were concerned, yet the opportunities for revision of late 1713 were just as much required by the sense of his readership as desired by him in order to execute his full design, the view expressed in the Dedication. Frequently, Pope lets the reader know that the tangible book s/he is perusing is the effect of a strenuous battle with the anesthetizing influence of the world of Print. Whilst it may have begun as a harmless entertainment "to divert a few young Ladies" and to have been first "communicated with the Air of a Secret," this did not prevent "an imperfect Copy" from finding its way into the clutches of a Bookseller.[12] The "Preface" to the *Works* (1717) would have us regard the process of its production as an exercise in authentication: to "look upon no verses as mine that are not inserted in this collection" so as to "avoid the imputation of so many dull and immoral things, as partly by malice, and partly by ignorance, have been ascribed to me" (*Selected Prose* 150).[13] The local reference is probably to Curll's January reissue as *Pope's Miscellany* of the *Court Poems* (1716), but the possibility of piracy, not only of one's words, but also of one's very name, is pervasive. Even if we refuse to take Pope's mention of his "little poetical present" to Caryll as the 1712 *Rape,* the vulnerability he felt about his writing at that time is still manifest: this "present" he feels cannot be entrusted to the post, "for [he] is a little apprehensive of putting it into [William] Lewis's [hand]s, who is too much a bookseller to be trusted with rhyme or reputation" (Pope to Caryll, September 4, 1711; *Correspondence* I: 133–34). A writer's life, for Pope, is not only a warfare upon earth, but a constant struggle to substantiate one's "signature" or copyright—not only as part of a financial agreement, but also of the attempt to rise above history (one's determining context) and so transcend the cash nexus.

In handing over the manuscript *Rape of the Lock* to Bernard Lintot for inclusion in the 1712 *Miscellany,* Pope was not so much furthering an earlier design as bowing to what may well have seemed inevitable. Spence records that there were several copies in private circulation by this time,[14] perhaps leading Pope to the conclusion that it would be a better course to authorize the publication of a correct version and receive the credit for it, than wait for the mangled appearance of a pirated one. In the same collection, however, Lintot printed Pope's "Verses to be Prefixed before Bernard Lintot's New Miscellany," which, whilst it offers the publisher the faint praise that he provided accurate copy, also realizes that this was the age of the Bookseller. Pantin, Elzevier, or Aldus have the tact to "print their Names in Letters small,/But LINTOT stands in Capital" (lines 9–10). Lintot also has the common touch, avoiding the straitened academic market where books "are useful but to few," to concentrate on "gen'ral Use," a wise policy, "For some Folks read, but all Folks sh——" (lines 26–30).[15] Unlike the other contributions to the *Miscellany,* including Pope's own, the *Rape of the Locke* was printed as the two last gatherings of the volume with its own title page so that it could be issued separately. Indeed, despite the sentiments of the "Verses," he appears to be no cultural Luddite, yearning for a Golden Age of Stuart patronage, but rather a clearheaded judge of what the market might appreciate. The original copyright was sold to Lintot for £7, whereas by 1714 the revisions (admittedly doubling the size of the work) fetched £15, and, in including several luxury features, such as a frontispiece and five plates printed from copper engravings on separate inserted leaves, the new edition was enhanced by more than just extra poetry. This added prominence was undeniably rewarded by exactly that measure of popular success that Lintot's imprint promised. Pope wrote to Caryll just ten or so days after its publication that it had "in four days time sold to the number of three thousand" and that it was "already reprinted . . ." (Pope to Caryll, March 12, 1713/14; *Correspondence* I: 214).

To some degree, the inclusion of the machinery in 1714 both belittles and also exonerates Belinda. In emphasizing more greatly the forces, ethe-

real as well as social, that define her choices, she is rendered less account-
able for them. Of the many additions that are then introduced, there are
perhaps three that may stand for more widespread changes of emphasis.
Firstly, there is the "Morning-Dream" (I.22) that hovers over Belinda's
head and Ariel's introduction of the "light *Militia* of the lower Sky"
(I.42). Whereas the 1712 Belinda rises quickly "'midst attending Dames"
(I.19) and, after a rapid trip down the Thames, immediately accepts the
admiration of "well-drest Youths" (I.21), the private narrative that will
reach its climax in the Cave of Spleen is here prepared carefully. "When
the World imagine Women stray," it is only the Sylphs guiding them
through "mystick Mazes" (II.91–92), not quite without a plan, but rather
in order to protect all womankind against men—"Beware of all, but most
beware of Man!" (I.114).

Secondly, the 1712 Belinda possesses her own brand of *hubris*, but it is
not specifically tied to a fault of Pride. There is a small but particularly
resonant change in the last line:

> Yet graceful Ease, and Sweetness void of Pride,
> Might hide her Faults, if *Belles* had Faults to hide:
> If to her share some Female Errors fall,
> Look on her Face, and you'll forgive 'em all. (1712, I.31–34)

This is changed to "Look on her Face, and you'll forget 'em all" (1714,
II.15–18), which has a retroactive effect on the preceding lines. The earlier version weighs "Female Errors" in the balance with Beauty and finds
them lighter. Consequently, the efficacy of "graceful Ease" and "Sweetness" is less undercut by the residual irony of the mock-heroic context.
Belinda may indeed have "Faults to hide" but Pope would side with those
who would wink at them for Beauty's sake. Alternatively, to *forget* them
would be a passive dereliction of one's moral duty. The graceful compliment in 1712 becomes the anatomy of a widespread disease in 1714. The
insertion of Belinda's "sacred Rites of Pride" (I.121–48) only underscores
her more serious and self-conscious representation in the later version.
The beauty that would survive in public is an effect of careful preparation, not effortless possession.

By far the most eye-catching change, however, for Pope's contemporaries was undoubtedly the proliferation of innuendo in 1714. We have
already noted how Dennis found Belinda a jade and Tomrig in 1728. As
the reign of Ariel is supplanted by that of Umbriel in Canto IV, so the
cosmetic powers of the mock-heroic are increasingly undermined. The
textual surface of the poem, with its careful contrivances and metrical
balance, is, at the same time, ironized. Does Belinda realize the depth of

meaning when she cries out: "Oh, hadst thou, Cruel! been content to seize/Hairs less in sight, or any Hairs but these!" (IV.175–76)? The readers of 1714 are certainly meant to recognize the unwitting innocence in the remarks as well as the repressed sexuality. Perhaps they were also to trace the parody of Dido's last lament in Book IV of the *Aeneid* (11.657ff.)[16] and the potential tragedy in such naivete. When the lines appeared in 1712 they were absorbed into Thalestris's opening salvo (II.19–20), but in 1714 they become Belinda's and the last lines of the climactic Canto IV. Part of the catalogue of fanciful transformations in the Cave of Spleen introduces pregnant men and "Maids turn'd Bottels" who "call aloud for Corks" (IV.54), a detail that now prefigures this Belinda—impotent, passive, and simultaneously demanding sexual freedoms along with the gag that would stifle such demands. Belinda's toilet ritual had performed its magic superficially, yet here there is a radical disorder. When Aeneas is permitted to venture into the Underworld in *Aeneid* VI, he is granted a preview of his destiny and a renewed purpose. In the Cave of Spleen there is no public *telos,* just a private limbo about to manifest itself obliquely in rage and confusion.

As David B. Morris has recently pointed out, Pope's revisions were not merely formal "improvements," but substantive amendments (76–102). It would seem that he could not leave his poetry well enough alone. The 1714 Dedication is surely accurate in stressing how far the poem had moved from its occasional 1712 form. The following cantos "are as Fabulous, as the Vision at the Beginning," the "Human Persons are as Fictitious as the Airy ones" and "the Character of *Belinda, as it is now managed*" (my italics), resembles the dedicatee "in nothing but in Beauty."[17] The historical event that first provoked Caryll to suggest the poem to Pope is far in the past, and the Dedication plus the revisions drive that point home.

There is an attractive editorial position, adopted by Geoffrey Tillotson in the Twickenham edition, to regard the history of the ensuing changes to the poem as "the placid one of textual improvement" (*TE* 2: 105). In a limited sense, this could be maintained in relation to the rectifying of obvious typographical errors, but if we regard as an "improvement" the inclusion of Clarissa's speech and the greater footnoting that accompanied the whole poem in both the 1717 and 1736 *Works,* then we might conclude that more text does not necessarily mean a better poem. It certainly ensures a different one. Just as he had to contend with the possible affront caused potentially influential patrons in 1712, it is probable that the reception of the five-canto edition went some way towards prompting Pope's more explicit provision of a moral framework in 1717. By the close of 1714, Pope could hardly have been innocent of the dislike felt in some quarters at little "Sawney's" effeminate French wit and the lubricious touches which gave it a meretricious air. Dapper (Pope), in Act II of Charles Gildon's *A New Rehearsal* (April 1714), held it a rule that "you must make the Ladies speak Bawdy, no matter whether they are Women of Honour or not" and cites the "Hairs less in Sight" passage as proof. What is more, the "*Machinary . . .* is admirably contrived to convey a luscious Hint to the Ladies, by letting them know, that their Nocturnal Pollutions are a Reward of their Chastity" (43–44). This same idea occurred to John Oldmixon, whose *The Catholick Poet* (May 1716) has Lintot claim that Pope "*Ravish'd a Lock* from the pretty *Belle Fermor,*/And [that he] thought with vile Smut to have charmed, the *Charmer*" (1). John Dennis was prepared to consider the poem a prurient affair as early as February 1717, when he felt that the author "could not forbear putting Bawdy into the Mouth of his own Patroness" (II: 130).

Seizing the opportunity to engage with the public's image of earlier editions is not just a feature of Pope's revisions. Swift, in adding the "Apology" to his *A Tale of a Tub* for the fifth edition of 1710, six years after the first, has ensured generations of critics the safety of finding a more or less secure ethical direction in the work, identifying the "Corruptions in Religion and Learning" (Swift 1) at the expense of the earlier illicit delights of textual play. We could claim the same about Gulliver's letter to Sympson, not added to *Gulliver's Travels* until the *Works* of 1735, or Gay's more Virgilian and manifestly less controversial *Rural Sports* of 1720, which clouds the 1713 political opposition to the City and all its works with greater allusion and the centrist, and (of course) balanced, mocking of the Country as well. John Chalker seems to take it as accepted that these "changes suggest how [Gay] wished the poem to be read" (142), just as Warburton/Pope in 1751 would have Clarissa's great (and belated) Good Sense the hallmark of the poem's whole evolution.

This is only one instance of a more widespread tendency in the work of Pope and that of several of his contemporaries. Publication did not signal the end of revision, for meaning seemed dead once it had frozen in print. A work's initial critical reception could provoke Pope to review his original design just as much as its passage from manuscript to text. The rendering of what were once private notions in a form designed to attract public notice and applause is bound to alter most writing from whatever age, yet for Pope, in early career, the realizing of just exactly the intended effect involved several potentially discontinuous stages of review, either by preface, extension, or footnote. David Foxon and Maynard Mack have both noted his fondness for substantial revision as late as the proof stage before he could allow the manuscript flexibility of both thought and its form to cease and authorial responsibility to begin (Foxon, *Pope and the Early Eighteenth-Century Book Trade* [1976], 220; Foxon, *Pope and the Early Eighteenth-Century Book Trade* [1991], 151–69; Mack, *The Last and Greatest Art*). This may account for the drastic terms in which the 1717 "Preface" is couched. The "dangerous fate of authors" means that "the agreeable power of self-amusement when a man is idle or alone" or the "freedom" of uttering "careless things," the advantages due "a Genius to Poetry," must cease and martyrdom begin. There is obviously comic hyperbole in claiming that "the life of a Wit is a warfare upon earth," yet not all of the defensiveness is an exercise in rhetorical exculpation. Published poets cannot ever be considered "idle or alone," just as the promise of infinite correction is a false one: "I confess it was want of consideration that made me an author; I writ because it amused me; I corrected because it was as pleasant to me as to write." Pope would have us consider the *Works* as merely snapshots in that they seem to be arrested action, or carefully posed set pieces. Consequently, they continually fall short of Pope's own "Ideas of Poetry," which are too fluid to be represented accurately in print. Simultaneously, however, poetry's appearance is an event, allowing it to be catalogued and priced. When Pope "collected" his poetry for the volume, it may then be no surprise that he appeared "uncertain whether to look upon [himself] as a man building a monument, or burying the dead" (Pope, *Selected Prose* 148–50).

It might be straining the evidence to conclude that the 1717 expansion of Canto V was so much an afterthought that it misrepresents some vital, initial inspiration. Indeed, when Dennis had remarked in 1728, that, unlike Pope, Boileau "seems to have given broad Hints at what was his real Meaning," the central meaning of the poem was located by the marginal note in "Clarissas Speach" (noted by Tillotson at *TE* 2: 370–71).[18] However, it would be just as negligent to overlook the fact that there are several "final intentions" that make up a fully collated edition. Is there a "mature" 1717 Pope somewhere, guiding the editor's hand? Or are we simply adjudicating between a series of "organic unities," the revisions, like Eliot's Individual Talent, simply creating Tradition anew with the fabric still intact? In that case it would therefore seem to be advisable to choose as late an edition as possible as a guide to the most reliable intention—when presumably the author had had longer to think about things. Alternatively, the inclusion of Clarissa's speech could just as easily be attributed to Pope's nervousness that the ambiguity of the poem was earning it some powerful enemies and thus queering his pitch with Catholic patrons. When Warburton included the note in 1751 that placed such emphasis on the insertion, he claimed that Clarissa was "a new Character."[19] Such a mistake may give us pause if we were to interpret the whole poem according to his advice. Given the definition of the poetic impulse in the 1717 Preface, the gradual accretion of footnotes might seem, in any case, to signal the victory of Pope-as-editor over Pope-as-author. Certainly, some of the later annotation can be read as mocking itself. Belinda's *"Toilet,"* for example, was glossed from 1736 onwards as reminiscent of some "ancient Traditions of the *Rabbi's*" which record the fact that "several of the fallen Angels became amorous of Women, and particularize some; among the rest *Asael,* who lay with *Naamah,* the wife of *Noah,* or of *Ham*: and who continuing impenitent, still presides over the Women's Toilets" (see *TE* 2: 156). At the very least we may have to conclude that Pope's Final Intention can never be wholly his own.

## V

The attraction of the mock-heroic for Pope can be explained by its elusiveness. He found in mock-forms and their ironies that he could exploit contradiction, even make an art of it, and yet maintain the view at the same time that ethical choice needed clarity and positive definitions. If Virgil could find Homer and Nature the same, according to *An Essay on Criticism* (1711), then we would be misled in demanding a "Homer" identical with the ink and paper in which he would now appear. Dionysius of Halicarnassus could still *"Homer's* Thoughts refine,/And call new Beauties forth from ev'ry Line!" (*TE* 2: 665–66). "Longinus" could be *"himself* that great *Sublime* he draws" (680) in the treatise that would seem to lay down laws on how to accomplish that end.[20] Authors are never completely identical for Pope with their written texts.

Pope's most extensive discussion of the mock-heroic occurs in the Postscript to his *Odyssey* (1726). Homer, as has often been claimed, was for Pope not only the same as Nature for the aspiring author/critic, but also an outstanding example of order in variety. The section on Style stresses both the mercurial alternation of register yet also the maintenance of epic dignity throughout: "The diction is to follow the images and to take its colour from the complexion of the thoughts. Accordingly, the Odyssey is not always cloath'd in the majesty of verse proper to Tragedy, but sometimes descends into the plainer Narrative, and sometimes even to that familiar dialogue essential to Comedy." "Dignity" however, "or at least a propriety", is always supported. Furthermore, a "real beauty" emerges from the "easy, pure, perspicuous description even of a *low action.*" These "clear, plain, and natural words" are to be differentiated from bogus figures, or *"little circumstances,"* which "clog" the overall effect. Mock-heroic writing cannot see the wood for the trees. It also obscures the divide-

and-rule tactics of the neoclassical separation of styles, for it deploys sounding metaphors for low persons, and preserves "a painful equality of fustian" (the true cause of all bombast) by swelling the language indiscriminately, no matter who is the referent (Pope, *Selected Prose* 123–25). It is for Pope Homer's most valuable quality, a subtle equipoise which can shine through a potentially bewildering array of surface effects. In the preface to the *Iliad* (1715) that work is described as "a wild Paradise, where if we cannot see all the Beauties so distinctly as in an ordered Garden, it is only because the Number of them is infinitely greater" (Pope, *Selected Prose* 90). This is Pope's answer to the prevailing critical orthodoxy, recently fostered by Dryden but operative from Servius and Scaliger onwards, that epic art only truly reached its zenith with Virgil. Homer, on the other hand, was gloriously untutored; his manifest excellence lay in his talent for confronting fanciful extravagance with natural profusion, a potential indecorum with order that could not be codified. Indeed, as "A Receipt to Make an Epic Poem" (1713) testifies, Pope had early in his career little regard for generic laws. The last sentence of the "Receipt" carries the advice that it is not the discovery of "similes and metaphors" which is the most difficult element in epic descriptions, but their application ("For this advise with your *Bookseller*") (Pope, *Selected Prose* 208). Mock-heroic writing, therefore, is not merely the "use of pompous expressions for low actions or thoughts" (his definition in the Postscript [Pope, *Selected Prose* 124]), but also more generally the negative image of Homer's whole example, in that it apes his gestures and tropes without providing any new examples *in that vein.*

In the opening section, where I attempted to illustrate the intricacy of Pope's mock-heroic allusions, it might have been possible thereafter to rest content with the conclusion that, whilst Pope might have had certain conscious aims in the writing of each version of the poem, any determined tracing of allusion would throw up such potentially contradictory signs that the identification of a global "intention" is rather beside the point. This also has consequences for our reading as well. As Wolfgang Iser has pointed out, most memorably in *The Implied Reader,* what is at stake is the "gestalt" of the text, some consistency not just of discoverable "intention" but rather of readerly perspective, as if the very dynamics of "making sense" of the work actually works to defeat such a purpose: that of mastery over the work and the production of a global explanation. Iser's examples are often those of narrative, however, where, he stresses, "the process of anticipation and retrospection, the consequent unfolding of a text as a living event" (Iser 290). Where this concerns *The Rape Of the Lock,* I would venture, is that this "unfolding" cannot only (or, indeed, significantly) occur within a narrative framework. The text's allusions "unfold" as a consequence of the necessary attention to each allusive instance, providing more synchronic satisfactions.

It would seem that a historical criticism would eventually have to draw distinctions between those influences on Pope which we deem accidental (and so discountable) and those which are personal and operative (and so part of the path to maturity). On the other hand, if we take McGann's observations in *A Critique of Modern Textual Criticism* to heart, then such drawing of lines would seem to follow merely a common Romantic obsession with the supposed authority of the autonomous creative artist. A full account of a text's suggestiveness need not be confined just to its supposedly immanent features. Even if we were to agree that there is nothing outside the text, we would still have to consider the multiple traces, from print or elsewhere, that stem from how "author-figures" negotiate with their immediate circumstances: "[A]uthority is a social nexus, not a personal possession; and if the authority for specific literary works is initiated anew for each new work by some specific artist, its initiation takes place in a necessary and integral historical environment of great complexity. Most immediately . . . it takes place within the conventions and enabling limits that are accepted by the prevailing institutions of literary production . . ." (McGann. *A Critique* 48). Any proceeding that takes the term "text" on trust may itself seem to be involved in adopting an enabling fiction.

## Notes

1. The annotations are summarized in the Twickenham edition (*TE* ) of Pope's poetry, vol. 2: 368–75. In his *A Key to the Lock* (1715) Pope reduces this allegory hunting to absurdity by taking Belinda to represent "the Popish Religion, or the Whore of Babylon" (Pope, *Selected Prose* 87).
2. See Bruckmann 3–20.
3. "A common acquaintance and well-wisher to both desired me to write a poem to make a jest of it, and laugh them together again" (Pope, June 1739, in Spence 1: 44).
4. Whilst Johnson finds the word to carry no pejorative associations in the first edition of the *Dictionary* (1755)—"A kind of writing, in which the words of an author or his thoughts are taken, and by a slight change adapted to some new purpose"—the *OED* notes its satirical edge as in use in 1598, 1607, and in Dryden's *Discourse concerning the Original and Progress of Satire* (1693): "Thus in *Timon's Silli* the words are generally those of Homer, and the Tragick Poets; but he applies them Satyrically, to some Customs and Kinds of Philosophy, which he arraigns. But the Romans not using any of these Parodies in their Satyres . . ." (Dryden 2: 627).
5. Pope was apparently much influenced by Sir John Denham's version, entitled "*Sarpedon's* Speech to *Glaucus* in the *12th* of *Homer*" (1668), 11.10–22. In his note

to the *Iliad* XII.387, he admitted that "if [he] had done it with any spirit, it is partly owing to him" (*TE* VIII: 96).

6. See also Rudat.

7. In eighteenth-century studies there have been few attempts to answer such questions as opposed to avoiding them. Felicity Nussbaum and Laura Brown in "Revising Critical Practices," in Nussbaum and Brown, embrace a revivified (and unscientistic) Marxism and attempt to define what is new about the approach. For a more direct engagement with Derrida and De Man, see Montrose and Neely. The central problems are described in Fabricant, Brean S. Hammond, "'Guard the Sure Barrier': Pope and the Partitioning of Culture," in Fairer 225–40, and Hume where a nice distinction is made between context affecting meaning as opposed to determining it (74–75; 80–85).

8. See especially "The Text, the Poem, and the Problem of Historical Method" (1981), collected in McGann, *The Beauty of Inflections* 111–32: "Facing the poem and its texts, . . . historical criticism tries to define what is most peculiar and distinctive in specific poetical works. Moreover, in specifying these unique features and sets of relationships, it transcends the concept of the-poem-as-verbal-object to reveal the poem as a special sort of communication event" (131).

9. The vocabulary is Structuralist in general and Roland Barthes's in particular. Barthes makes a similar distinction between reading the same image as a *signifier* and as a weighted *signified* which is transformed into a *sign* (111–23).

10. For a fuller review of Pope's early revisions, see Robin Grove's study.

11. In Volume 1 ("Familiar Letters written to Henry Cromwell, Esq. by Mr. Pope") of *Miscellanea, In Two Volumes*.

12. The most complete account is still Tillotson's (*TE* 2: 85–99).

13. The occasion of the writing of the "Preface" has been comprehensively described by Maynard Mack, "Pope's 1717 Preface with a Transcription of the Manuscript Text."

14. Pope, June 1739, Spence 1: 44: "Copies of it [the *Rape of the Lock*] got about, and 'twas like to be printed. . . ." The most authoritative analysis can be found in Rumbold 73–82, a model of directed yet tactful historical investigation.

15. Pope obviously took on a substantial share of the editorial work for the *Miscellany*—see Ault 27–48.

16. "felix heu! nimium litora tantum/numquam Dardaniae tetigissent notra carinae!" ("[I would have been] happy, oh, but all too happy had the Dardan prows never touched our shores!").

17. For a searching analysis of this passage and the implications for an analysis of Pope's preconceptions about gender, see Pollak 102–7.

18. For a sophisticated and unsympathetic reading of Clarissa's speech, see Morris 97–102.

19. Recently Andrew Varney has provided a trenchant defense of the speech as an ingredient intended by Pope from the first: "[T]he speech was clearly the product of deliberation and not simply an afterthought, and meant to be congruous with an already existing poem and its story, attitudes, values, and manner. If it seems out of keeping we are probably misreading it" (17). The argument is ingenious and always sensitive, yet is to my mind vitiated by its exclusion of any consideration of the poem's textual history. Why did Pope not include the speech earlier? By 1728 he may well have regarded the speech as the moral center, yet that merely illustrates the fact that he felt then that it ought to have been, not that the sentiments were implied by its earlier forms. In any case, the speech is not placed advantageously when one considers the very last (unClarissa-like) lines.

20. A fuller discussion of this passage can be found in Spacks.

## Works Cited

Ault, Norman. *New Light on Pope, with some Additions to his Poetry hitherto unknown.* 1949. Hamden, CT: Archon, 1967.

Barthes, Roland. *Mythologies.* Trans. Annette Lavers. New York: Farrar, Straus, and Giroux, 1972.

Bruckmann, Patricia. "Virgins Visited by Angel Powers: *The Rape of the Lock,* Platonick Love, Sylphs and Some Mystics." *The Enduring Legacy: Alexander Pope Tercentenary Essays.* Ed. G. S. Rousseau and Pat Rogers. Cambridge: Cambridge UP, 1988. 3–20.

Catullus. *The Adventures of Catullus, and History of His Amours with Lesbia . . . Done from the French.* Anon. London, 1707.

Chalker, John. *The English Georgic: A Study in the Development of a Form.* Baltimore: Johns Hopkins UP, 1969.

Dennis, John. *The Critical Works of John Dennis.* Ed. Edward Niles Hooker, 2 vols. Baltimore: Johns Hopkins UP, 1943.

Derrida, Jacques. "Living On: Borderlines." *Deconstruction and Criticism.* Ed. Harold Bloom and others. New York: Seabury, 1979.

Dryden, John. *Poems.* Ed. James Kinsley. 4 vols. Oxford: Oxford UP, 1958.

Empson, William. *Seven Types of Ambiguity.* London: Chatto and Windus, 1930.

Fabricant, Carole. "The Battle of the Ancients and the (Post)Moderns: Rethinking Swift through Contemporary Perspectives." *The Eighteenth Century* 32 (1991): 256–73.

Fairer, David, ed. *Pope: New Contexts.* London: Harvester Wheatsheaf, 1990.

Foxon, David. *Pope and the Early Eighteenth-Century Book Trade.* Rev. and ed. Francis McLaverty. Oxford: Clarendon, 1991.

———. *Pope and the Eighteenth-Century Book Trade.* The Lyell Lectures, 1976. Working notes held in the Beinecke Library, New Haven: Yale U [MS Vault Shelves 13].

Gildon, Charles. *A New Rehearsal*. London, 1714.

Grove, Robin. "Uniting Airy Substance: *The Rape of the Lock,* 1712–36." *The Art of Alexander Pope*. Ed. Howard Erskine-Hill and Ann Smith. London: Vision, 1979.

Hume, Robert D. "Texts with Contexts: Notes towards a Historical Method." *Philological Quarterly* 71 (1992): 69–100.

Iser, Wolfgang. *The Implied Reader: Patterns of Communication in Prose Fiction from Bunyan to Beckett*. Baltimore: Johns Hopkins UP, 1974.

Jack, Ian. *Augustan Satire: Intention and Idiom in English Poetry, 1660–1750*. Oxford: Oxford UP, 1952.

McGann, Jerome. *The Beauty of Inflections: Literary Investigations in Historical Method and Theory*. Oxford: Oxford UP, 1988.

———. *A Critique of Modern Textual Criticism*. Chicago: U of Chicago P, 1983.

———. *Social Values and Poetic Acts: The Historical Judgment of Literary Work*. Cambridge: Harvard UP, 1988.

Mack, Maynard. *Alexander Pope: A Life*. New Haven: Yale UP, 1985.

———. *"The Last Greatest Art": Some Unpublished Poetical Manuscripts of Alexander Pope*. Newark: U of Delaware P, 1984.

———. "Pope's 1717 Preface with a Transcription of the Manuscript Text." *Augustan Worlds*. Ed. J. C. M. Hilson, M. B. Jones and J. R. Watson. New York: Barnes and Noble, 1978.

Montrose, Louis. "Renaissance Studies and the Subject of History." *English Literary Renaissance* 16 (1986): 5–12.

Morris, David B. *Alexander Pope, The Genius of Sense*. Cambridge, MA: Harvard UP, 1984.

Neely, Carol Thomas. "Constructing the Subject: Feminist Practice and the New Renaissance Discourses." *English Literary Renaissance* 18 (1988): 5–18.

Nussbaum, Felicity, and Laura Brown, eds. *The New 18th Century: Theory, Politics, English Literature*. New York: Methuen, 1987.

Oldmixon, John. *The Catholic Poet*. London, 1716.

*Ovid's Metamorphoses Englished by G{eorge} S{andys}*. London, 1626.

Pollak, Ellen. *The Poetics of Sexual Myth: Gender and Ideology in the Verse of Swift and Pope*. Chicago: U of Chicago P, 1985.

Pope, Alexander. *The Correspondence of Alexander Pope*. Ed. George Sherburn. 5 vols. Oxford: Oxford U P, 1956.

———. *The Poems of Alexander Pope*. Ed. John Butt, et al. 11 vols. London: Methuen, 1939–69.

———. *Selected Prose of Alexander Pope*. Ed. Paul Hammond. Cambridge: Cambridge U P, 1987.

Rudat, Wolfgang. "Another Look at the Limits of Allusion: Pope's *Rape of the Lock* and the Virgilian Tradition." *Durham University Journal* 71 (1978): 27–34.

Rumbold, Valerie. *Woman's Place in Pope's World*. Cambridge: Cambridge UP, 1989.

Spacks, Patricia. "Imagery and Method in *An Essay in Criticism.*" *PMLA* 85 (1970): 97–106.

Spence, Joseph, ed. *Observations, Anecdotes and Character of Books and Men.* Ed. James M. Osborn. 2 vols. Oxford: Clarendon, 1966.

Swift, Jonathan. *A Tale of a Tub, with other Early Works, 1696–1707.* Ed. Herbert Davis. Oxford: Basil Blackwell, 1939.

Varney, Andrew. "Clarissa's Moral in *The Rape of the Lock.*" *Essays in Criticism* 43 (1993): 17–32.

Wasserman, Earl. "The Limits of Allusion in *The Rape of the Lock.*" *Journal of English and Germanic Philology* 65 (1966): 425–44.

# Augustan Semiosis

*Charles H. Hinnant*

In John Dryden's *Mac Flecknoe,* the throne that Flecknoe is described as preparing for the unfortunate Shadwell is located in the "low" section of London, near a nursery for the training of young actors. Dryden employs a mock-archaic Spenserian diction to portray the sexually corrupt and effeminate character of this nursery:

> Close to the Walls which fair *Augusta* bind,
> (The fair Augusta much to fears inclin'd)
> An ancient fabrick, rais'd t'inform the sight,
> There stood of yore, and *Barbican* it hight:
> A watch Tower once; but now, so Fate ordains,
> Of all the Pile an empty name remains.
> From its old Ruins Brothel-houses rise,
> Scenes of lewd loves, and of polluted joys.
> Where their vast Courts the Mother-Strumpets keep,
> And, undisturb'd by Watch, in silence sleep.
> Near these a Nursery erects its head,
> Where Queens are form'd, and future Hero's bred;
> Where unfledg'd Actors learn to laugh and cry,
> Where infant Punks their tender Voices try,
> And little *Maximins* the Gods defy.
> Great *Fletcher* never treads in Buskins here,
> Nor greater *Johnson* dares in socks appear.
> But gentle *Simkin* just reception finds
> Amidst this Monument of vanisht minds:
> Pure Clinches, the suburbian Muse affords;
> And *Panton* waging harmless War with words.
> Here *Fleckno,* as a place to Fame well known,
> Ambitious design'd his *Sh——'s* Throne.
> For ancient Decker prophesi'd long since
> That in this Pile should reign a mighty Prince,
> Born for a scourge of Wit, and flayle of Sense. (Dryden 239–40,
>     lines 64–89)

This feminization of dulness, exemplified in the subversion of traditional models of heroic upbringing, is linked to a "maternal" realm of mindless, infantile instinct that is opposed to the laws of number, division, grammar, and discrete sense. In *Mac Flecknoe,* dulness is seen as ineffectual yet militant, for it attracts terms drawn from politics and combat: "Panton" is seen "waging harmless War with words." This suggests that if wit conforms to classical and aristocratic canons of poetry, then dulness, according to a dualism that informs much Augustan satire, especially the mock-heroic, represents a materiality and opacity, the war of a speechless, maternal sound against an implicitly masculine "sense."

Although this opposition may appear to be a relatively minor matter when compared with the immense gulf that separates wit from dulness, it nevertheless has important implications for our understanding of the mock-heroic, since it points to linguistic assumptions that lie at the heart of the Augustan satirical project. Perhaps the best means of tracking down these assumptions is to begin with Dryden's starting point—the notion that dulness is a "scourge of Wit, and flayle of Sense." In examining the full implications of this phrase, one can usefully begin with certain aspects of contemporary linguistic thought, particularly elements in Julia Kristeva's unorthodox revision of semiotic theory.

From very early in her career, especially in *Revolution in Poetic Language* (1974), Kristeva has argued that the domain of linguistics should not be confined to a unitary signifying process, abstracted from considerations of passion and instinct. For Kristeva, language is not a monolithic verbal identity but consists of two distinct realms: a nonverbal, "semiotic" impulse well before logical articulation and a "symbolic" realm governed by the rules of syntax and semantics. Furthermore, for Kristeva, the interaction between these two realms is not limited to a straightforward account of the genesis of the mind from a lower to a higher stage of linguistic development. Indeed, what is particularly striking about the "semiotic," which she depicts as "nourishing and maternal," is that it continually threatens to break through into the "symbolic" and return discourse back into that roiling phonetic source which language seeks to regiment (26). Pope's well-known claim that he "lisp'd in Numbers, for the Numbers came" is directly pertinent to this argument.[1] Although it is meant to testify to his status as a child prodigy, a natural genius, it also prefigures one aspect of Kristeva's theory. An unlettered tongue, not yet given over to syllables, words, phrases, or sentences, but content with the uncoded signs of rhythm, is linked to the maternal by its infantile attributes. The mature poet is, of course, seen as moving well beyond the unfallen prattle of infancy, but—in Kristeva's argument—the infantile state continues to generate a tremulous destabilization, by means of which, well after the acquisition of language, instinctual energies may erupt into discourse and dismantle it.

Kristeva's theory is valuable precisely to the extent that it enables us to recover something "lost" or overlooked in Augustan satire. A return—via Kristeva—to Pope's allusions to Dryden's *Alexander's Feast* in *An Essay on Criticism* (lines 374–83) may disclose Pope's own awareness of a prelinguistic, preverbal dimension of language. These allusions suggest that Pope, like Kristeva, assumes that music is "a non-verbal signifying system constructed exclusively on the semiotic" (24). In order to illustrate this aspect of language, Pope cites the example of Dryden's poem in which Alexander—the *"World's Victor"*—is portrayed as being "subdu'd by Sound" (line 381), by a power that renders him helpless; the basic drives (i.e., the passions), instead of being repressed by the constraints of rationality and language, are generated and mediated through the various forms of music. Pope (like Dryden) grants a primacy—or at least a primitive character—to perceptual sound: the phonetic basis of language is in a sense more rudimentary and more forceful than speech; the fundamental terms of linguistic meaning prove powerless in the end before the spell of musical pulsions. To be sure, the identification of Dryden with the Greek musician Timotheus marks the triumph of craftsmanship over nature. Yet the autonomy of the heroic hero is exposed as a charade—an insight that contains an emancipatory moment in its recognition that heroic identity is constructed and hence alterable. At the same time, Alexander's vulnerability to the powers of music points, as I hope to show, to a potential threat to the aristocratic and rationalistic norms of Augustan satire.

The more specifically linguistic manifestation of this threat to rational mastery accompanies or approximates the familiar doctrine that "the *Sound* must seem an *Eccho* to the *Sense*" (line 365). The premorphemic sound draws off this anxiety insofar as it is an *"Eccho"* to what, in figurative terms, is a masculine sense: in much the same way that Echo is only a pale reflection of Narcissus, so the voicing of sound is permissible only via the sense, understood here as the meaning conveyed by the words. In this economy, the sound is allotted the underside of language—the side of a purely material (wholly phonic or kinetic) aspect of discourse. Yet Pope's contention that the sound must appear to be an echo to the sense does not erase the distinction between music and meaning; indeed, the very fact that he uses the word "seem" calls into question the relation between the two. With imitative harmony revealed as artifice and rendered indeterminate and unstable, any notion of a natural union of sound and sense is undermined. On the contrary, there appears to be an implicit conflict—even before the regularizing provided by onomatopoeia—

between sound as a moment of extraneous pulsation and its assimilation to meaning. This pulsation is not engendered by an infantile innocence babbling through the text, but it can lead to a certain kind of regression. It does so, not by refocusing the verse as a kind of verbal play, a freedom from the given, the prescribed, the normal constraints of poetic discourse. Rather, the pulsation transmits a dwindling textual energy along the momentarily nonsignifying body of a line without character, a line whose chiming familiarity threatens the reader "(not in vain) with *Sleep*" (line 353). In effect, the repetitive text transforms the signbound operations of the reading subject into the *"pleasing Murmurs"* (line 352) of pure melody, and in this manner allows an implicitly maternal sound to appropriate the power of a virile masculine sense. In *An Essay on Criticism,* the appeal of this positioning is enhanced by an excessive preoccupation with the underside of poetic language—the purely phonetic side—which, Pope argues, is the fallacy of one group of false critics: "In the bright Muse tho' thousand *Charms* conspire,/Her *Voice* is all these tuneful Fools admire" (lines 339–40). These "tuneful Fools" display the same susceptibility, on a Lilliputian scale, as Alexander: "Not for the *Doctrine,*" they "to Church repair . . . but for the Musick there" (lines 342–43). Pope's use of the term "Doctrine" here is analogous, we should note, to Kristeva's employment of the word "theological" to characterize the attempt by the symbolic to repress the semiotic process that produces it (Kristeva, *Revolution in Poetic Language* 58–59).

In *An Essay on Criticism,* the phonetic dimension of language is never allowed to become a major threat to sense since Pope is concerned with the normative bases of critical evaluation. Yet in the famous passage on "Numbers" (lines 337–83), Pope contends that the "Poet's Song" (line 337), with its deference to normative signification, can emerge only if armed against the temptations posed by pure *"Musick"* (line 342)—on guard, in Kristeva's vocabulary, against the irruption of the semiotic into the scene of writing. Topologically, the borderline between the two is where the sovereignty of the sign is endangered and where something irreducible to language emerges. In an extended survey of Augustan versification, the "rules" most bearing on the phenomenon of "Numbers" are enumerated by Walter Jackson Bate under the headings of "looseness and languor" and "metrical monotony," including such subcategories as vowel gaping, monosyllabism, misplaced caesuras, Alexandrines, and repetitive rhymes (8, 11). Poetic diction, it seems, induces its own aural (if silent) response, not necessarily to install itself at the level of sense but—unless handled with the utmost tact—to pull poetry back down into areas of emotive and, in particular, musical response situated well below signification and meaning. In the kind of metaphonetic criticism advocated by

Pope and brilliantly analyzed by Bate, what is read is the material texture of the poem, its phonemic rhythms and sound patterns, not just its specific semantic manifestation. In terms of Kristeva's semiotic, such a reading engages the genotext as much as the phenotext—in particular the rhythms and musicality subtending all poetry. Yet we undertake this reading with an awareness that the language of poetry is never entirely subject to the control of meaning. This is because the dictum that "the *Sound* must seem an Eccho to the *Sense*" is based, as we have seen, on an illusion and hence is subject to reversal: the sense can all too easily become a pallid echo to the sound. When that occurs—when we move from semantic to phonetic word processing, we encounter a disposition that appears to dissolve the formal play of signifying units back into an undifferentiated flow in which both phonemic and semantic differences threaten to disappear.

If Pope's injunction that the sound must seem an echo to the sense signals his effort to contain the subversive aspects of the genotext, it is clear that other writers confronted the issue of sound and sense in a similar way. This dualistic conception of language finds, as it happens, a striking parallel in the field of contemporaneous English philosophy. The contingencies of lexical definition—in particular its semantic instability—make it prone to erosions in meaning in the same manner that poetry is prey to mindless repetitions in a given context. John Locke's *An Essay Concerning Human Understanding* (1698) contrasts the semantic procedures of the adult with the phonetic practices of the child as the desired agency of precise and settled usage. Yet in chapters on the "Imperfection" and "Abuse" of words, Locke warns of an all-too-human propensity to revert back to a childish state in which words seem more important than things: "not only children, but men, speak several words no otherwise than parrots do, only because they have learned them, and have been accustomed to those sounds" (2: 12). Locke is of course warning against the power of habit, against the danger of relying on custom in place of thinking, but the implication is that this practice is a disturbance at the threshold of sense, activated through a mode of speaking that passively invokes words without even engaging the lexical apparatus through which they are transformed from an "insignificant noise" into determinate and meaningful terms.

This is the unarguable common ground of a Lockean critique of imprecise usage and an Augustan satire directed against dulness, false wit, and bathos. Both are related to the attack that Addison mounted against Italian opera in the early numbers of *The Spectator*. In Addison's account, English adaptations of Italian opera have a decided semiotic dimension, originating as they do in an attempt to make the English words conform to the underlying rhythms and melodies of the music. Demarcated thereby is an indeterminate zone halfway between sound and sense:

> I remember an *Italian* Verse that ran thus Word for Word,
>> *And turn'd my Rage into Pity;*
> which the *English* for Rhime sake translated,
>> *And into Pity turn'd my Rage.*

> By this means the soft Notes that were adapted to *Pity* in the *Italian*, fell upon the Word *Rage* in the *English*; and the angry Sounds that were turned to *Rage* in the Original, were made to express *Pity* in the Translation. It oftentimes happen'd likewise, that the finest Notes in the Air fell upon the most insignificant Words in the Sentence. I have known the Word *And* pursu'd through the whole Gamut, have been entertain'd with many a melodious *The,* and have heard the most beautiful Graces, Quavers and Divisions bestow'd upon *Then, For,* and *From*; to the eternal Honour of our English Particles. (No. 18; 1: 80)

What Addison is objecting to in these adaptations is a clearly perceived tendency to certain unpredictable and unregimented switches in metrical stress, to a preferred emphasis on the signifier over the signified. These are the delights of the ear that, in Kristeva's terms, threaten to take priority over the delights of the mind, interfering with its cognitive activities, encouraging it to begin an intensely pleasurable but regressive descent back into a state of infancy.

To insist on the primacy of sense is, therefore, to challenge any text, poetic or musical, that seeks to shift the mind away from its fascination with language and toward operations that are prelinguistic and prelexical. Within this larger, ongoing project, *Peri Bathous: or, Martinus Scriblerus, His Treatise of the Art of Sinking in Poetry* (1728) embodies Pope's satire on what he views as an overemphasis, in current poetic theory and practice, on what is ineffable and archaic, on what is more primordial than language. Pope thus focuses not only on the lofty and the failure to fly high but also on the low, on the cult of natural simplicity. It is this cult that Pope ridicules when he makes his speaker derisively ask, "Do I express myself as simply as Ambrose Philips? or flow my numbers with the quiet thoughtlessness of Mr. Welsted?" What Pope is mocking is the mystification of poetry as transcribed "Voice," as the encoded expression of an author's feelings. As something completely different from communication and dialogue, which are for Pope the locus of social exchange, emotive expression belongs to the genotext rather than the phenotext; it is animated by non-knowledge and hence appears, in Pope's derisive characterization, as "a natural or morbid Secretion from the Brain" (189). As Pope's reductive and materialistic image suggests, its true locus is the imagination of the fantasizing subject, resulting in the dreamlike logic of childhood and the earliest cultures. An expressive poetry's formulaic style, its reliance on cliché and mindless repetition, causes language to become opaque and unreal and hence to undermine any putative communicative dimension.

Accordingly, it can be argued that the topos of the infantile serves a specific function in Pope's characterization of "our celebrated modern Poems" (216). Poised on the verge of fully mastered articulation, aware of the relation between words and thoughts, but not yet in control of vocabulary, the "Infantine" (214), in Pope's argument, provides the norm for a poetry of simple feelings. Within the rhetoric that Pope sets out to chart, the "Infantine" occurs "when a Poet grows so very simple as to think and talk like a child." Stigmatizing Ambrose Philips as a notorious example of this kind of poet, Pope asks his readers to "hear how he fondles, like a meer Stammerer" (214). In Julia Kristeva's psychoanalytic terms, what is glimpsed here is a condition of instinctive motility that corresponds to the position of the *infans* before the mirror stage permits the formation of the ego. Within Pope's inverted rhetoric, the figures of speech thus take priority over the figures of thought, obscuring their position in the creation of unified and comprehensible texts.

Of course it may well be objected at this point that there is really no comparing Pope's "Infantine" with Kristeva's semiotic since Pope's category is an isolated figure of speech, while Kristeva rests her claims on the existence of a comprehensive, though fragmented and chaotic, foundation. But this objection carries less weight once it is recognized that something akin to the "Infantine" governs the entire range of tropes, figures, and styles in *Peri Bathous*. It is precisely at the point where Pope draws a contrast between "the superfluity of words and vacuity of sense" (216) that he recognizes the essential role of the signifier as the sole means by which "Bathos" (196) can readily be defined. When Pope affirms that "a Genuine Writer of the Profund will take care never to *magnify* any Object without *clouding* it at the same time," he foreshadows Kristeva by imagining the range of such figures (in Pope's words) from "The HYPERBOLE, or Impossible" (210–11) to "The INANITY, or NOTHINGNESS" (215). Hence even though these figures seem animated by effects that involve the presence of bathos and therefore seem irreducible to significance, they remain rhetorical tropes; bathos, like the semiotic, exists and can only reappear and be detected through language. Given its obscure and shadowy "Nature," bathos, like the semiotic, can only be reconstructed or inferred from the existence of cleavages, incongruities, periphrases, and lapses in taste—within a publicly accredited discourse.

The conjunction between Pope's bathos and Kristeva's semiotic might be undercut from a second point of view. While Kristeva posits the semiotic as maternal, Pope in *Peri Bathous* describes Sir Richard Blackmore as "the Father of Bathos, and indeed the Homer of it" (196). Yet in his early "On Silence [In Imitation of the Earl of Rochester]," Pope's speaker addresses an implicitly maternal figure, confessing to her that even though "Rebel Wit deserts thee oft in vain;/Lost in the Maze of Words, he turns again,/And seeks a surer State, and courts thy gentle Reign" (13–15). And the most vivid embodiment of the prelinguistic in Pope's poetry can be found in the maternal image of dulness in the *Dunciad*. The figure of Pope's "Mighty Mother" (I.1) is easily appropriated to the cause of Kristeva's semiotic, confirming the perception of a primal flow, an energy glimpsed elsewhere under constraint or erasure. In Kristeva's terms, one could say that the Goddess of Dulness has from the earliest version of the *Dunciad* been intimately involved with language; in a sense, Dulness is preoccupied, as Kristeva puts it, with "various deviations from the rules of language; articulatory effects which shift the phonematic system back towards its articulatory, phonetic base, and consequently toward the drive-governed bases of sound production" (Kristeva, *The Kristeva Reader* 28). For Pope, Dulness has always exemplified what Kristeva terms the "semiotic disposition," not only because of its potential for deviation but also because it is a power which, as Aubrey Williams aptly puts it, "deranges order in literature, in society, and in the whole world" (98). In a note on line 15 of Book I, Pope describes Dulness in terms that resembles Kristeva's semiotic: "Dulness here is not to be taken contractedly for mere Stupidity, but in the enlarged sense of the word, for all slowness of Apprehension, Shortness of Sight, or imperfect Sense of Things. It includes . . . Labour, Industry, and some degree of Activity and Boldness: a ruling principle not inert, but turning topsy-turvy the Understanding, and including an Anarchy or confused State of Mind" (721). In this respect, it corresponds to what Kristeva termed the *chora*—"an invisible and amorphous being" that precedes and underlines figuration and thus specularization and is analogous to vocal and kinetic rhythm. Toril Moi characterizes Kristeva's *chora* as "a rhythmic pulsion rather than a new language." According to Moi, "it constitutes the heterogeneous, disruptive dimension of language, that which can never be caught up in the closure of traditional linguistic theory" (*The Kristeva Reader* 13). A term that Kristeva adapted from Plato's *Timaeus*, the *chora* is associated with the mother's body and is, in her words, "on the path of destruction, negativity, and death" (Kristeva,

*Revolution in Poetic Language* 95). Pope's mock-heroic celebration of Dulness in the *Dunciad* depicts a playfully grotesque image of the maternal body; it equates destruction, negativity, and death with sleep, through which Dulness displays an immanent power appropriate to the poem's seriocomic mode.

It should be stressed, however, that the opposition between dulness and wit, like the opposition between the semiotic and the symbolic, should not be understood in a naturalistic and biological sense. Although Dulness is designated as maternal, it has no particular relation to women or to the female body; on the contrary, it appears to represent an enveloping ground of identity that threatens members of both sexes. This point might not appear to be particularly important, yet if it is not kept in mind, one could well argue, like Catherine Ingrassia, that for Pope "the cause of such moral, social, and literary degeneration [is] specifically female—Dulness herself . . . Dulness the woman symbolizes Pope's escalating fear of a pervasive 'feminization' that threatens to permeate nearly every aspect of English culture" (40). In a similar way, Thomas McGeary links the criticism of Italian opera in early-eighteenth-century criticism and in the *Dunciad* with the view that opera is inherently effeminate, positing a threat to traditional manly virtues. Castration, real or imagined (e.g., the amputation of the warbling castrati), was the most vivid form, McGeary holds, of the alienation of masculinity, the loss of wholeness, that seemed to be embodied in Italian opera.[2] Yet one can debate the assumption—shared by both critics—that Pope's appropriation of maternal metaphors of femininity was aligned with an overtly androcentric project or prejudice. There is no doubt that Pope's cultural context enshrines gendered bifurcations and steadily pulls in the direction of gendered accounts. Nevertheless, when Pope speaks of the Goddess in relation to language, he is using maternal metaphors to stand for an infantile experience of dulness, not for actual women (or women's experience of themselves). Thus if what Kristeva characterizes as "rhythmic, unfettered, irreducible to . . . intelligible verbal translation" is an essential aspect of Pope's dulness, then the argument for a purely literal understanding of gender in the *Dunciad* appears to be undermined.[3]

The point is also that Dulness's destructiveness, as exemplified in her power to disrupt, permits no stable identification with a single sex; indeed, it is related to Kristeva's much broader emphasis upon anality. Kristeva gives special point to "the importance of anal rejection or anality, which precedes the establishment of the symbolic and is both its precondition and its repressed element" (Kristeva, *Revolution in Poetic Language* 149). The return of a repressed anality is particularly evident in *Mac Flecknoe* where it is associated with the proliferation of bad poetry:

> No *Persian* carpets spread th'Imperial way,
> But scatter'd Limbs of mangled Poets lay:
> From dusty shops neglected Authors come,
> Martyrs of Pies and Reliques of the Bum.
> Much *Heywood, Shirly, Ogilby* there lay,
> But loads of *Sh*—— almost choakt the way. (98–103)

In the *Dunciad,* the obsessive fixation on excrement, the ritualized representation of the funeral games in Book II, is clearly related to the maternal side of dulness; the scatological materials serve as an imaginative manifestation of what Kristeva, in *Powers of Horror,* calls the abject—in this case, the "falling back" of the dunces, whether male or female, "under the sway of a power as securing as it is stifling" (Kristeva, *Powers of Horror* 13). These materials—a return of the repressed—are congruent with a discourse produced on the borders of language; anality, "when combined with oral pleasure," Kristeva holds, can "disturb, indeed, dismantle the symbolic function" (Kristeva, *Revolution in Poetic Language* 149).

It is Dryden, Pope's self-proclaimed predecessor in the mock-heroic, who first associated the assault upon the heroic poem with what Kristeva calls "the pulverization" of discursive language. In acknowledging the dispersive, decentering practice of bad poets, Flecknoe informs Shadwell that inasmuch as

> Thy Genius calls thee not to purchase fame
> In keen Iambicks, but mild Anagram:
> Leave writing Plays, and chuse for thy command
> Some peacefull Province in Acrostick Land.
> There thou maist wings display and Altars raise,
> And torture one poor word Ten thousand ways.
> Or if you woud'st thy diff'rent talents suit,
> Set thy own Songs, and sing them to thy lute. (203–10)

The role that semiotic considerations play in the activities of Pope's Goddess appears to be quite similar: the emergence of the productions of Grub-Street hacks from a state of prelinguistic anarchy is presented as a threat to the symbolic. This we discover early in the opening book when Dulness "beholds the Chaos dark and deep":

> Where nameless Somethings in their causes sleep,
> 'Till genial Jacob, or a warm Third day,
> Call forth each mass, a Poem, or a Play:

How hints, like spawn, scarce quick in embryo lie,
How new-born nonsense first is taught to cry,
Maggots half-form'd in rhyme exactly meet,
And learn to crawl upon poetic feet.
Here one poor word an hundred clenches makes,
And ductile dulness new meanders takes;
There motley Images her fancy strike,
Figures ill pair'd, and Similies unlike.
She sees a Mob of Metaphors advance,
Pleas'd with the madness of the mazy dance. (I.55–68)

In this parodic mimesis of semiosis in embryo, Dulness reaches into the realm of the symbolic, the realm of propriety, laws, and articulate language. Yet far from contributing, in an orderly way, to the establishment of a universe based upon the categories of syntax and speech, Dulness brings to light the incoherence, reversals, and asymmetries of Kristeva's semiotic.

In many ways, of course, the view of Augustan culture embodied in the mock-heroic poems of Dryden and Pope needs to be seen as directly opposed to Kristeva's celebration of modern semiotic disruption. For Kristeva, the *chora* makes possible the revolutionary subversion of the symbolic order that she associates with avant-garde modernist poetry; for Dryden and Pope, dulness is seen as presiding over an empire that encompasses mediocre poets, pedantic scholars, and disreputable booksellers. In the world of Pope's goddess, "instinct" becomes manifest as poetry but only in so far as it pulls the latter down from its high epic horse, away from considerations of form and genre, joining opposites like tragedy and comedy in an amorous (or murderous?) "embrace" (I.69). Indeed, the rewriting of the original poetic conventions emphasizes the violence that Dulness perpetrates on the body of the written word, forcing it into a realm of semantic corruption and decay. Dulness is as profoundly antipoetic as it is antirational. Poetry is suffered only to the extent that it appears unpremeditated and infiltrated by the mind-numbing impulses (e.g., the liquid repetitions of Ambrose Philips's namby-pamby pastorals) that art had failed to repress. There is a clear difference between this configuration of associations and the later eighteenth-century identification of artless song with simplicity and natural passion. Whereas in sentimental and early Romantic poetry, the natural is linked with an expressive aesthetic, providing a vehicle for the spontaneous overflow of powerful feelings, in the *Dunciad,* it becomes associated with the regression to a prelinguistic state of mindless babble.

For Kristeva, this state would exemplify a virtual definition of the poetic element of literary language, the irruption of the underlying semiotic (in Kristeva's special sense) into a symbolic system constructed to contain and repress it. Such an irruption is the breaching of the sign by phonetic play, the breaking and entering of the text by the subversive laxities of a sublexical music. But from the point of view of Dryden and Pope, these are the characteristics of a degenerate, subliterary culture. Hence they would probably agree with Calvin Bedient's recent contention—affirmed in a polemic against Kristeva—"that poetry is highly artificial, or at least the product of a formal instinct acting on the sound qualities of words under the example and restraints of a tradition (or a number of traditions)" (Bedient, "Kristeva and Poetry" 815).[4] In contrast to Kristeva's view that poetry—especially modernist poetry—is the *chora's* guerrilla war against culture, Bedient locates poetry in a highly self-conscious "simulation" of desire. To the extent that the narrator of *The Dunciad in Four Books* (1743) is able to escape from the mesmerizing power that he invokes, he is participating in a "discourse of representation" that is understood, in some sense, to transcend the workings of Dulness. Accordingly, his work is that of a *homo faber,* momentarily subjugating the Goddess through the creation of a textual fantasy, investing journals, odes, and pamphlets with animation, and transforming stage machinery into a created universe. In a sense, the text is like a descriptive catalogue; it imitates, and indeed becomes, a construction that reveals through its mass of allusions, notes, and prefatory materials the hand of a master poet. The poet becomes the *virtuoso* of a corporeal rhetoric which conveys the sublime joy of an invented universe, generating a series of verbal monuments dedicated to resisting the lexical decomposition it records.

The means that Pope employs to represent the activities of this "ancient" goddess are quite numerous. They range from interpolated monologues like the "quaint Recitativo" (IV.52) of the "Harlot form" (IV.45): "O *Cara! Cara!*" (IV.53) to lines whose assonantal and consonantal clusters seem to dominate, if not quite overwhelm, their sense, like the epic simile that concludes the paragraph on "Fame's posterior trumpet": "Not closer, orb in orb, conglob'd are seen/The buzzing Bees about their dusky Queen" (IV.79–80). Pope is elsewhere capable not just of insistent phonetic iteration but of an unrestrained cacophony:

> Now thousand tongues are heard in one loud din:
> The Monkey-mimics rush discordant in;
> 'Twas chatt'ring, grinning, mouthing, jabb'ring all,
> And Noise and Norton, Brangling and Breval,

Dennis and Dissonance, and captious Art,
And Snip-snap short, and Interruptions smart. (II.235–40)

Such vocalized simulation taps the semiotic noise beneath the symbolic regimentation of the couplet without enfolding itself into it; its sheer phonic confusion is recuperated by the phonemic and syntagmatic patterning of the line. The dissociation of sound from sense is also captured in Pope's transposition of the pastoral convention of the echoing landscape to London at the conclusion of Book I:

She ceas'd, Then swells the Chapel-royal throat:
'God save king Cibber!' mounts in ev'ry note.
Familiar White's, 'God save King Colley!' cries;
'God save king Colley!' Drury-lane replies:
To Needham's quick the voice triumphal rode,
But pious Needham dropt the name of God;
Back to the Devil the last echoes roll,
And 'Coll!' each Butcher roars at Hockley-hole.
So when Jove's block descended from on high
(As sings thy great forefather Ogilby)
Loud thunder to its bottom shook the bog,
And the hoarse nation croak'd, 'God save King Log!' (I.319–30).

Unlike signifying language, this swelling, pulsional roar in a sense satisfies its own desire, not by naming it, but by the act of uttering itself, the vocal play being infused with a kind of prelinguistic euphoria.

If we provisionally attend in the *Dunciad* to this dialectic between discursive speech and the undulations of semiotic pulsion, we can better understand how Dulness's long monologue in Book IV is much more than a distillation of Pope's own syllabic fluencies:

'Leave not a foot of verse, a foot of stone,
A Page, a Grave, that they can call their own;
But spread, my sons, your glory thin or thick,
On passive paper, or on solid brick.
So by each Bard an Alderman shall sit,
A heavy Lord shall hang at ev'ry Wit,
And while on Fame's triumphal Car they ride,
Some Slave of mind be pinion'd to their side.' (IV.126–34)

In specifying what we might characterize as the poetry of Dulness, we can turn to the play on "mine" and "mind" in the last line. It is part of what we might call a phonemic ponderousness that links the image of lexical degeneration and false wit to the poem's central character. Out of the epic format as well as the narrative sequence of the fourth book, this heavy, ponderous poetry breaks free, the voice of an ancient "Empress," not only roiling up amid the busy noises of the London commercial world but welling up within the symbolic monopoly of epic verse. Alvin Kernan vividly evokes the movement of this poetry in *The Plot of Satire* when he describes how Dulness "in the many forms and shapes it assumes, pours, spreads, sluices, creeps, drawls on, stretches, spawns, crawls, meanders, ekes out, flounders on, slips, rolls, extends, waddles, involves, gushes, swells, loiters, decays, slides, wafts, lumbers, blots, o'erflows, trickles" (106). My sense is that the latent energy of this monotonous, funereal movement is meant to churn, not at the level of plot, but below, in the crevices and seams of Pope's narrative. John Dennis complained that the *Dunciad* lacks action, but this lack only serves to accentuate the semiotic energies of its central figure, since it is, above all, in narrative that the before-and-after movement of syntax is most effectively captured.[5]

What such an argument suggests, therefore, is that this irruption of semiotic chaos into the rational conventions of epic discourse manifests itself formally in a verse through which poetry becomes an "Emblem of Music caus'd by Emptiness" (I.36). Description takes precedence over narration; movement and action give way at times to an almost paralyzing sense of immobility and stasis; and the text details the efforts of the dunces to dwell in a purely verbal or even phonetic world. The transformation of articulate speech into vocalized melody is symbolized by Italian opera, which "prepares the way" for the "gentle sway" of Dulness (III.301–2); enclosed within a spectacular frame which effectively separates it from meaning, Italian opera epitomizes the collapse of the major neoclassical genres—epic and tragedy—into a music that teeters on the threshold of referential or symbolic language. Pope associates this music with the "mincing steps" of a harlot, a deviant female figure whose inability to "stand" upright on her own enacts the deconstructive logic of its signifying slippages (I.46, 50). Such a stance is itself close to, yet not identical with, an older tradition of antifeminist satire. It is like the conventions of antifeminist satire in its association of what we might call a phonemic lubriciousness with a depraved female figure. It is unlike antifeminist satire in that Pope's focus on the feminine cannot be understood as a simple reduction to the natural order of biology. Thus an excessive preoccupation with "Words alone" also characterizes the pedantic headmaster, causing him to "ply the Memory, . . . load the Brain,/Bind rebel Wit, and double chain on chain,/Confine the thought, to exercise the breath;/And keep them in the pale of Words till death" (IV.157–60).

Without thought, the mind will drift, descending toward pure sound—a "jingling padlock" (IV.162)—that is not even a word, only an empty musical phrase. In Pope's daring reinterpretation, the harsh, patriarchalist figure of the schoolmaster turns out in the end to be a representative of the Goddess of Dulness. For all his sadistic energies, for all his willingness to exercise the birchen rod, the schoolmaster leaves unexamined and unchallenged the crucial terms of an evacuated, semiotic flux, and he leaves in place the defining structures and privileged forms of what is still seen as an essentially maternal oppression.

As the locus of the maternal in the *Dunciad,* the Goddess of Dulness displays a power marked by uncensored energies and sublexical excess, and in the engulfing nocturnal passage it articulates, proprieties disappear and proper names retreat into asterisks. Yet the comic apocalypse with which the *Dunciad* concludes is not meant to be understood as the basis for a matriarchal politics; throughout the poem, the zone of dulness is contrasted with the luminous realm of another female deity, Pallas (I.9), the goddess of wisdom who issued from the head of Jove. What Dulness is meant to symbolize is the broader destabilization of values within a society whose cultural expressions are increasingly shaped by weekly journalism and the logic of the popular press. The preoccupation of her offspring, the Dunces, with words and style underlines the degeneration of everyday life, the mediation of experience and identity through the consumption of cheaply produced texts and commodities that render any appeal to genuine poetry only another fiction. This energy thus not only figures the threatening uprush of popular entertainment but also uproots traditional distinctions of gender and class. For the power of Dulness acts to dislocate and displace any single system of control, including the authority of woman's language and power. As the conclusion of the *Dunciad* shows, the effect of Pope's mock-heroic technique is to deauthorize its speakers, transgress the boundaries of articulate speech, and endanger the principles that would govern any hierarchy: plenitude, order, degree, continuity. Ultimately, his seriocomic practice explodes the very concept of gender—gender as a stable, individuating cultural essence to be suppressed, deployed, or simply affirmed.

In venturing this reading, one should not minimize Pope's preoccupation with sexual difference, his willingness to stage a spectacle generated by the ludic possibilities of a narrative foregrounded in a maternal myth of origin. Certainly, Dulness's "maternal" presence looms large even in the earlier versions of the *Dunciad*—versions that articulate in their informing structures the complex dynamic of maternal adulation and mother-son kinship. Thus Dulness appears as the regal queen whose "clouded Majesty" demands the absolute obedience of Divine Right theory; as the motheranointer of the new laureate poet; as the tutelary spirit of the public games; as the mother-muse of the predominantly male dunces. The rich metaphoric associations suggested by this matriarchal mythologizing introduce fantasies of destruction reflecting Pope's unwillingness to depict the maternal body otherwise than through its association with a pervasive corruption and decay. Replaying the drama by which the (male) poet constructs an idealized genealogy—Homer, Virgil, Shakespeare, Milton, Dryden—Dulness dreams her ennobling matrilineage—a line that runs from Heywood, Shirley, and Flecknoe through Cibber, Theobald, and Ozell (I.285). Moreover, just as the semiotic—in Kristeva's argument—can only appear *through* the symbolic, so Dulness makes her presence felt in a region of Dunces populated (in the early eighteenth century) primarily by men. If actual women writers like Eliza Haywood are linked to the empire of dulness, it is not because they have any essential alignment—as women—with the Goddess. For Pope, as for Kristeva, there is no determinate or specific relation between the semiotic and some necessary attribute of woman as such.

This argument is also meant to draw attention to the difficulty of any naive attempt to characterize Pope's poem as misogynist or antifeminist in any literal sense. Inasmuch as dulness, like the semiotic *chora,* is a category and construct, one can argue that Dulness is maternal, not because Pope seeks to deny women a place in the empire of wit, or because he wishes to exclude the feminine from poetry and the arts, but rather because the categories of wit and dulness are not to be understood directly in this way. Even though both are female, both are constitutive of the subject of either sex. And when Italian opera is seen as unmanly and linked to castration, it is because opera is viewed not so much as "feminine" as desexualized and infantile; Italian opera is linked to the maternal because of the infant's dependency on the mother. This is not to say that Pope assumes that men and women are the same, or that he might not have harbored private reservations about the capacities of certain contemporary women poets. It is simply to distinguish between the term "woman" and the category of dulness or bathos. Pope published poems—most notably "Epistle II. To a Lady"—that embody categorical statements about "the Characters of *Women* (consider'd only as contradistinguished from the other Sex)" (559), but there is nothing in these statements which suggests that the question of sexual difference can be answered by an appeal to a distinction that links women to a maternal and pre-linguistic domain while locating "men" in an opposite symbolic realm. To affirm these identifications (feminine, maternal, women, preverbal) would be to ignore, at the very least, the positions that Pope is willing to assign an exceptional woman like Lady Mary Wortley Montagu or Martha Blount. And when the speaker of *An*

*Essay on Man* characterizes "Man" as "reasoning but to err" (II.10) and as "a Chaos of Thought and Passion all confus'd" (II.13), he is describing a problematic that is meant to be understood as common to both sexes.

I do not, therefore, believe that it is in this literal identification of the feminine and dulness that we should seek, in Pope or his contemporaries, for an understanding of the aims of their satire. On the other hand, the same does not hold true if we turn to a different, less subject-centered aspect of Augustan satire. This is the aspect that is preoccupied with the breakdowns, lapses, and transgressive breaches of symbolic coherence in contemporary texts. The Augustan satirists were necessarily conservative, defining their identities in opposition to the linguistic discontinuities and ruptures that contributed to defining a world of popular entertainment and bad poetry. In their desire to contain the disruptions of the semiotic, they demonstrated an underlying nostalgia for the paternal language of the Ancients, with whom they aligned themselves. Indeed, it is only from such a position within the symbolic that the cleavages and transgressions of the semiotic can be discovered and contained. It is only those who, like the satirist, occupy the position of a speaking/representing subject who can undermine or subvert the lexical excesses and corruptions of the semiotic. Call the satirist's access to such a language a defense of the symbolic order or not, in any case it is precisely the perceived regime of lexical breaks and incongruities that the satirist's irony, around its edges, resists. The poet's paradoxical fate in the *Dunciad* is that he can neither simply maintain this resistance nor can he survive without it.

While the familiar gendered connotations of Augustan satire should probably not be taken too literally, the question thus arises as to whether poems, like the *Dunciad,* participate in the energies they seek to contain. Pope's mock-epic, like other Augustan satirical poems, displays characteristics—laughter, figures of speech, reflexivity, transgressive parody— that Kristeva described as typical of modernist avant-garde texts (Kristeva, *Revolution in Poetic Language* 225). Moreover, if all poetry partakes of both the semiotic and the symbolic, then the mix of these two signifying dispositions will determine the kind of poetry produced. Augustan satire may attempt to minimize and to hide the ambiguous semiotic within it, but this maternal dimension cannot finally be extirpated. Indeed, this may be why the seriocomic conclusion of the *Dunciad* uncovers a mood not of pure pessimism, but one that is uneasily suspended between subversiveness and resignation, between acquiescence in and resistance to the dominant discursive modes of Pope's culture. But this uneasy mood points to Pope's predicament, to the reinscription of drives that always threaten his acts of ridicule and resistance. Crossing out and crossing over its own discourse, the *Dunciad* refuses to answer the question it continually prompts: Who or what is actually triumphing? Without denying the force of Pope's exposure of the cleavages and contradictions in contemporary commercial culture, the answer to this question might qualify the adversarial status of Augustan texts by revealing that their models of symbolic dominance are inevitably connected to, rather than at odds with, the semiotic energies they contest.

## Notes

I would like to express my gratitude to Charles Shepherdson and Doug Canfield for their valuable suggestions about this essay.

1. *Epistle to Dr. Arbuthnot,* line 128, in Pope, *Poems . . . One Volume Edition of the Twickenham Text* 602. All citations to Pope's poetry here are to this edition.
2. McGeary throughout and Ness throughout.
3. Kristeva, *Revolution in Poetic Language* 29. It should be noted that Kristeva's gendered conception of the relationship between the symbolic and semiotic has come under some criticism. See for example, the studies of Gross, Meyers, and Butler. For sympathetic accounts, see Lechte and Barzilai.
4. See Bedient, "Kristeva and Poetry" 815, and the exchange between Toril Moi, "Reading Kristeva," and Bedient, "How I Slugged It Out."
5. John Dennis, Remarks upon . . . the Dunciad, 1729, 19, cited in Pope, *Dunciad* xli.

## Works Cited

Addison, Joseph, Richard Steele, and others. *The Spectator.* Ed. Donald F. Bond. 5 vols. Oxford: Clarendon, 1965.

Barzilai, Shuli. "Borders of Language: Kristeva's Critique of Lacan," *PMLA* 106 (1991): 294–305.

Bate, Walter Jackson. *The Stylistic Development of Keats.* 1945. New York: Humanities P, 1962.

Bedient, Calvin. "How I Slugged It Out with Toril Moi and Stayed Awake," *Critical Inquiry* 17 (1991): 644–49.

———. "Kristeva and Poetry as Shattered Signification." *Critical Inquiry* 16 (1990): 807–29.

Butler, Judith. "The Body Politics of Julia Kristeva." *Revaluing French Feminism: Critical Essays on Difference, Agency, and Culture.* Ed. Nancy Faser and Sandra Lee Battky. Bloomington: Indiana UP, 1992. 163–76.

Dryden, John. *The Poems and Fables of John Dryden.* Ed. James Kinsley. London: Oxford UP, 1958.

Gross, Elizabeth. "Philosophy, Subjectivity, and the Body: *Kristeva and Irigaray.*" *Feminist Challenges: Social and Political Theory.* Ed. Carol Pateman and Elizabeth Gross. Boston: Northeastern UP, 1987. 125–43.

Ingrassia, Catharine. "Women Writing/Writing Women: Pope, Dullness and 'Feminization' in the *Dunciad.*" *Eighteenth-Century Life* 14.3 (1990): 40–58.

Kernan, Alvin B. *The Plot of Satire.* New Haven: Yale UP, 1965.

Kristeva, Julia. *The Kristeva Reader.* Ed. Toril Moi. New York: Columbia UP, 1986.

———. *Powers of Horror: An Essay on Abjection.* Trans. Leon S. Roudiez. New York: Columbia UP, 1982.

———. *Revolution in Poetic Language.* Trans. Margaret Waller. Intro. Leon Roudiez. New York: Columbia UP, 1974.

Lechte, John. *Julia Kristeva.* London: Routledge, 1990.

Locke, John. *An Essay Concerning Human Understanding.* Ed. Alexander Campbell Fraser. 2 vols. Oxford: Oxford UP, 1989.

McGeary, Thomas. "'Warbling Eunuchs': Opera, Gender, and Sexuality on the London Stage, 1705-1742." *Restoration and Eighteenth-Century Theatre Research* 2nd ser. 7 (1992): 1-22.

Meyers, Diana T. "The Subversion of Women's Agency in Psychoanalytic Criticism." *Revaluing French Feminism,* 145-161.

Moi, Toril. "Reading Kristeva: A Response to Calvin Bedient." *Critical Inquiry* 17 (1991): 634-43.

Ness, Robert. "*The Dunciad* and Italian Opera in England." *Eighteenth-Century Studies* 20 (1986): 173-94.

Pope, Alexander. *The Dunciad.* Ed. James Sutherland. 3rd ed. rev. London: Methuen, 1963.

———. *Peri Bathous: or Martinus Scriblerus, His Treatise of the Art of Sinking in Poetry.* In *The Prose Works of Alexander Pope,* Vol. 2: *The Major Works, 1725-1744.* Ed. Rosemary Cowler. Oxford: Basil Blackwell, 1986.

———. *The Poems of Alexander Pope: A One Volume Edition of the Twickenham Text.* Ed. John Butt. New Haven: Yale UP, 1963.

Williams, Aubrey L. *Pope's Dunciad: A Study of Its Meaning.* London: Methuen, 1955.

# Pope and His *Dunciad* Adversaries

## Skirmishes on the Borders of Gentility

*Claudia Thomas*

> The modern model of profession undoubtedly incorporates pre-industrial
> criteria of status and pre-industrial ideological orientations. . . . The collective
> project of professionalization, furthermore, has its roots in a time of radical and
> rapid change: the men involved in this project were the "carriers of social
> structure" and they carried the imprint of changing historical circumstances.
> Their product, however, was an innovation. . . .
> —Magali Sarfatti Larson, *The Rise of Professionalism* 15

1

In *The Rise of Professionalism: A Sociological Analysis,* Magali Sarfatti Larson
discerned the origins of British professionalism in the "great transformation" of Britain's economy in the eighteenth century (2). Professions such
as law and medicine succeeded in developing markets for their "products"; they standardized their services as well as an educational process
that perpetuated the "production of producers" (14–15). By the late nineteenth century, such professions were recognized as "occupations with
special power and prestige," granted for "special competence in esoteric
bodies of knowledge linked to central needs and values of the social system, and because professions are devoted to the service of the public" (x).
In this chapter, I will examine the troubled origins of the British literary
profession, an occupation that curiously failed to keep pace with its legal and
medical counterparts, as exemplified by the controversy over Alexander
Pope's *Dunciad* (1728–44).

Paid writers were literate, had access to print technology, and conveyed
information of all kinds to a burgeoning market. They even had an advantage in that universities were producing the producers of much published writing before law and medicine achieved effective university cur-
ricula. Yet writers were slow to achieve the "special power and prestige"
of professionalism. I will locate some of the causes of this failure in a web
of political and social problems that confronted Britons writing for their

livelihoods before 1750. Alexander Pope, often touted as the first truly professional British writer, was nevertheless at least partly responsible for retarding his occupation's rise to full professional status. By promoting a model that resembled the traditional elite, learned branches of law and medicine rather than their more common but rising competitors, Pope insured his own role as anomalous "carrier of social structure" rather than advancing literature's "collective project of professionalization."

## 2

Two hundred and fifty years after Colley Cibber's installation as King of Dulness, Alexander Pope's *Dunciad* inspires commentary more voluminous, at times more contentious, than the disputes that greeted the laureate's enthronement. One debate involves the nature of Pope's professionalism, and his role in promoting the literary profession.[1] Another centers on Pope's character, and whether accumulated provocations, as well as his philosophical and aesthetic intentions in the mock-epic, justified Pope's treatment of Cibber and other victims. A third inquiry concerns the so-called dunces, and whether their pamphlet replies to Pope's poem merely confirm their collective Dulness or contain any valuable insight into the mock-epic. Although each of these topics merits individual discussion, analysis guided by reader-response theory and informed by recent social-historical scholarship suggests their close relationship. Pope's enemies' responses may not indicate failure to appreciate his satire so much as recognition of a satiric goal manifest to competitors, if apparently obscure today. Due to space limitations, this essay will focus on Pope's *Dunciad* commentary and his enemies' replies rather than on the poem. Attention to these peripheral, even liminal, texts seems appropriate, however, due to the fear of social marginality betrayed by both Pope's commentary and the replies. Awareness of these skirmishes on the borders of Pope's mock-epic—skirmishes over the nature and status of literary professionalism—illuminates yet another aspect of Pope's multileveled satire. In fact, the *Dunciad* and its ensuing pamphlet warfare contributed not only to the Ancient-Modern debate and to contemporary political rivalry, but also to a social climate that resisted acknowledging writing as a profession until much later in the century. Hurling insults designed to tarnish opponents' claims to public attention, writers succeeded instead in damaging the reputation and status of their emergent profession.[2]

Pope's motives for seeking to damage his opponents' reputations cannot, of course, be neatly divided into categories such as social, professional, or political. In Pope's era, as in ours, these dimensions of individual identity were usually conjoined—often confused—for the purpose of satire. One attacked a writer's politics by attacking his or her morals, or literary style, or social status. The particular nature of contemporary political debate inevitably conflated participants' social status with their worthiness to comment on civic affairs. In *The Machiavellian Moment,* J. G. A. Pocock has argued that the *Dunciad* reflects the Augustan debate whether landed or moneyed interests best served the nation. In his opinion, credit and its attendant instability, so often condemned by Tory polemicists such as Swift, "is part of Pope's Great Anarch" (457). Pope's attacks on professional competitors would have reminded contemporaries of conservative inquiry, earlier in the century, whether the man of trade was capable of civic virtue despite the fact that commerce depended on imagination and desire rather than on landed stability. Tory political economists, such as Dr. Charles Davenant, determined that a merchant exemplified civic virtue only to the extent that his practices, such as frugality, demonstrated concern for public welfare rather than for personal gain.[3] According to Davenant, the merchant approximated virtue by promoting an environment of confidence and trust (456). While Pope's dedicatee, Swift, remained dubious about merchants' capacity for disinterested behavior (witness his condescending rhetoric in *The Drapier's Letters*), Pope's position was necessarily more complex.

Pope's difficulty lay partly in the still nebulous identity of the literary profession. As we shall see, Pope made every effort to define the ideal professional writer as a conservative gentleman. But his was one of many competing definitions. Among these, an analogy was often made between the writer and the merchant, the former dealing in words instead of more tangible goods. Like merchants, writers depended on willing consumers of their productions. Both appealed to fickle tastes, and bankruptcy followed the loss of popularity or reputation. Writers, like merchants, suffered from the suspicion that they labored purely for individual gain. Professional writers were therefore precarious speakers for political parties vying to create the impression of superior stability, not to mention of civic-minded probity. Both sides exchanged insults designed to wreck the "credit" or reputations of opposed writers. Each side wished to rob the other of its pretension to represent the moral high ground. Throughout the *Dunciad,* Pope's portrayal of Dulness's votaries as a hysterical mob accuses the Whigs of promoting social instability, which Davenant had condemned as inimical to trade and, hence, to national prosperity. Ideological conflict thus encouraged Pope's adoption of a familiar tactic when he misrepresented the status of his enemies.

For his part, Pope conducted his career in a manner calculated to unite the prosperity of a merchant with the stability of a landed gentleman.

He maintained and refined his poetic "property" as if it were real estate, and he cultivated a stable, national reputation.[4] But despite these efforts, Pope was attacked for presuming to write as a cultural arbiter. While most previous scholarship has concentrated on the omnipresent political motives for these attacks, I intend to emphasize the social, or class, consequences of Pope's "paper war." The debate over which party best exemplified civic morality was just one, albeit crucial, factor in his profession's tortuous gestation.

Critics and historians frequently attest to Pope's singular accomplishment as the first professional writer to earn a fortune through the sale of his work.[5] Until and throughout Pope's lifetime, most paid writers pieced together precarious careers, combining translating and other "writing to order" for booksellers with political journalism and patronage. Geoffrey Holmes has discussed the particular difficulty with which writers achieved professional status. Although licensing laws lapsed at the end of the seventeenth century, loosening censorship and thus encouraging a wide range of publications, writers' prestige did not keep pace with their growing numbers. Writers' status also remained low despite the relatively high literacy rate, and despite the growing public demand supplemented by patronage (31–43). The reasons for this difficulty are not immediately apparent, particularly when compared with the progress made by the traditionally subordinate branches of both law and medicine.

Due to their greater accessibility and more practical training, as well as increasing demand for their services, attorneys and solicitors, apothecaries and surgeons gradually rose to near-equal social status with barristers and physicians (Holmes chs. 5–6). Certain parallels would seem to have made possible an analogous rise in status for professional writers. As in the other professions, members of a more "middling" group sought to earn their livelihoods by appropriating what had traditionally been a privileged role, the man of letters. As in the legal and medical models, professional writers were often better trained than most aristocrats, many having been educated at Oxford or Cambridge. Similar too was the writers' growing audience—as in the case of the other professions, largely composed of merchants and professionals and their families. Both John Dunton and Daniel Defoe, for example, addressed much of their writing specifically toward Dissenters, a flourishing segment of the merchant community.

Nevertheless, the process of social assimilation that occurred in other professions did not yet materialize for writers. Perhaps the most important reason was that many writers depended on political journalism to earn their livings. Much of the "crime" that scholars such as Pat Rogers have associated with contemporary writers involved arrests for politically motivated libel.[6] Another reason was the paid writers' identification with cheap, scandalous publications. While apothecaries responded to men's and women's growing determination to free themselves from pain, and solicitors untangled the legal affairs of prosperous merchants, writers produced both edifying classical translations and titillating pamphlets. Although London booksellers sponsored a wide range of popular literature, from conduct books to political newspapers, professional writers were invariably portrayed as Grub Street Hacks, churning out reams of invective in order to stave off their creditors. By Pope's lifetime, Grub Street was both a locale and a flourishing myth, well-established since its Restoration genesis.[7] And while some writers resented this version of their livelihood, others capitalized on the colorful Grub Street image to attract readers. This maneuver associated most writers with low social status until the reading public multiplied and yielded the financial rewards that led more easily to gentility.

Pope's role as a pioneer in his profession was complex. Even the precise nature of his professionalism remains debatable. Among many ambiguities, however, questions about character—particularly in relation to Pope's treatment of competitors in the *Dunciad*—evoke perhaps the most passionate response. To sympathetic scholars such as Maynard Mack or Pat Rogers, Pope's satire was justified by the poet's contempt for his enemies' principles as well as by the cruelty of their repeated attacks. As Rogers accepts and paraphrases Pope's rationale, "the social grievance of the Dunces is the strong antipathy of bad for good" (*Hacks and Dunces* 107). On the other hand, it is difficult to read either Helene Koon's biography of Colley Cibber (1986) or Peter Seary's study of Lewis Theobald (1990), among other recent scholarship, without questioning Pope's motives for nominating each King of the Dunces. In each case, Pope's vengefulness compounded by political antipathy resulted in attacks disproportionate to either man's offense. Seary and Koon demonstrate that Pope's satiric representations eclipsed Theobald's and Cibber's genuine accomplishments, delaying recognition of their important contributions—Theobald's to Renaissance English scholarship, and Cibber's to the development of English drama. Although both Theobald and Cibber were professionals with claims to eminence in their fields, Pope minimizes any resemblance between their careers and his. Pope's failure to express professional solidarity with Theobald, Cibber, or any of his enemies was often observed by contemporary critics of the *Dunciad,* and accounts for many descriptions of the poet as envious, invidious, ungrateful, and unjust.

In 1728, Pope had yet to compose poems such as the "Epistle to Dr. Arbuthnot," in which he asserts his proud independence and manly professionalism. Having concluded his duties as translator of Homer and editor of Shakespeare, Pope could either identify with or distinguish himself from his fellow professional writers. Many contemporary enemies assumed his Grub Street solidarity. Pope's friendship with Tories such as Swift and Bolingbroke had already made him a popular target for Whig pamphleteers. His penchant for composing burlesque, even obscene, parodies, as well as farcical drama and libelous pamphlets, marked Pope as master of all the "low" genres of his age, although he rarely claimed authorship of his least edifying work. But rather than express sympathy for struggling writers, which might have hastened the rise of the entire profession, Pope disdained any affiliation with "hacks."[8] On the contrary, between 1728 and 1743, Pope issued no fewer than seventeen editions of the *Dunciad,* vehemently denying his similarity to other paid writers. In both the *Dunciad* and his Horatian imitations, Pope compares his status to that of a barrister or physician, viewing with dismay the incipient rise to respectability of the solicitors and apothecaries. Having established himself despite liabilities ranging from his faith to his physical frame, Pope was not tempted to jeopardize his status by admitting any relationship to writers desperate for a wage. As a result, Pope's poetic references to money betray the ambivalence of a man proud of his financial independence but eager to disassociate himself from the very pursuit of money which achieved his status (Bell 62–64).

In the *Dunciad,* Pope created a version of English society in which hired writers, their publishers, and their patrons were not struggling to develop a new, professional approach to writing appropriate to England's evolving economy and society. Rather, they were portrayed as regressing from the new ideal of urbane refinement. From the poem's outset, Pope established himself and his conservative friends—Swift, for example—as more worthy of the sophisticated reader's respect and attention than such "modern" (Whig) writers as Theobald and Cibber. Pope's narrow view of these writers reflects the extent to which political ideology influenced his critical judgment. But Pope's pains to diminish the perceived status of others whose livelihood was writing, despite his unquestioned literary preeminence, suggests more than political animosity. It suggests Pope both shared and exploited the insecurity that vexed professional writers throughout the first half of the eighteenth century. By emphasizing his classical orientation and financial independence, Pope aligned himself with the gentry—or rather with those prestigious professions traditionally associated with the gentry and landed elite.[9] To confirm his superior status, he derived his representations of enemies from seventeenth-century caricatures of paid writers as lower-middle-class artisans. The *Dunciad's* paper war corroborates twentieth-century assertions that a capacious middle class had not only arrived but was subdividing itself during Pope's lifetime.

Pope liked to construe his career not as a modest rise in status, but as confirmation of his gentility. By mystifying both his status and his business acumen, Pope antagonized competitors struggling to maintain their pretension to the middling station. He then bred enmity by tailoring their biographies to fit the fictional image of the "Grub Street Hack." The early part of the century was aware of upward social mobility as a possibility if not as a significant reality. By the time the *Dunciad* appeared, however, progress from either poverty to middling status, or from the middle station to the gentry, was becoming increasingly difficult.[10] In these circumstances, it is not surprising that those on the borders responded vehemently when their status was misrepresented. In the *Dunciad Variorum* (1729), for example, Pope dismissed "Tibbald"'s writings, along with Edward Ward's, to "visit alehouse where ye first did grow" (1.202).[11] In his note identifying Ward, Pope altered a description in *The Poetical Register* to state that Ward "kept a publick house in the City . . . and with his wit, humour, and good liquor [Ale] afforded his guests a pleasurable entertainment" (5: 87n. 200).

In a postscript to his rejoinder, entitled "Apollo's Maggot in his Cups," Ward replied vehemently to Pope's assertion that he kept an alehouse:

> Suppose, Edward Ward should say, in an Index under the Letter P, that *Pope Alexander* keeps a House of Intrigue at Twickenham, in order to curry favour with the Quality, and that's the Reason why so many Gentlemen and Ladies are his constant Subscribers. All this is as true, as that Ward keeps an Alehouse in Moorfields, tho' he lives there. But what makes the insincerity of Pope the more provoking is, . . . that Pope has drank wine at Ward's House, and knows it to be a Tavern; yet . . . he could not forbear translating it into an Ale-house; insinuating thereby, that Ward is possess'd of no other Qualifications than what are directly suitable to so humble a Station. (37–38)

This exchange permitted Pope to augment his next edition with a note cheerfully conceding Ward's claim. "He selleth *Port*; neither is his Publick House in the *City,* but in *Moor-fields*" (5: 198). Not only was Pope's social superiority reinforced by this adjustment, but the vintner was further damned by association with a less reputable neighborhood.

From Pope's point of view, or from that of the scholar elucidating Pope's intention, Ward's protest is ludicrous. In his recent study of Pope's rhetorical art, for example, Ruben Quintero understandably concludes that Pope's victims were "myopic" readers because they took his satire personally, failing to grasp the poem's irony (122). Michael Rosenblum has also ascribed to poor reading skill the dunces' failure to appreciate Pope's deliberate displacement of history. "Ned Ward claims that it is not true that he keeps a public house in the City—rather he keeps Port in Moor-Fields. . . . What the wise reader sees . . . is that the dunces are only raw material for a poem" (670). The correct perspective from which to view the poem is not that of mundane, current detail such as which liquor was sold by Edward Ward, but that of the timeless temple Pope erected on the ruins of his enemies' reputations (676). On the other hand, as a member of Pope's original, intended audience, Ward might be pardoned for failing to appreciate Pope's timeless vision. Peter Earle has reminded us of the importance of occupation as a "factor defining the degree of one's genteelness" in the early eighteenth century: "[T]here were many . . . distinctions which could override an individual's actual wealth in determining his social position. There seems little doubt that it was smarter to be a Levant merchant than a Baltic merchant, to keep a mercer's shop rather than to be a haberdasher, to own a tavern rather than an alehouse. Such subtle differences in degree of genteelness affected behaviour and choice of friends and marriage partners; they also affected consumption . . ." (333). In other words, Pope sought to impose on Ward a status significantly lower than that to which his occupation entitled him. In an era when readers' horizon of expectations included awareness that social mobility was difficult and reputation crucial not only to an individual but also to his or her family and connections, Pope's insult threatened Ward to an extent hardly appreciated by today's literary scholar.

### 3

While knowledge of the social circumstances that conditioned their replies redeems the "dunces" who replied to Pope from the critical assumption that they were merely obtuse, it now remains to be seen why Pope attacked such previously inoffensive writers as Ward, and how replies such as his help to elucidate the poem. Pope's enemies constituted his first intended audience, and, through their replies, the *Dunciad* emerges as a poem about the narrow and increasingly subtle border between status and non-status, a border that Pope seemed to have crossed definitively after the appearance of his Homeric translations. John Dennis observed the irony of Pope's characterizations in the *Dunciad*: "[f]or this little Gentleman to strut and be conceited upon his having a Hundred a Year, to pretend to look down upon those whom he never had the Capacity to look up to . . . to say he will answer what they urge against him when he is as much *in Debt* as they are, at the same time that he owes his little Substance to a *vile Translation* of a *poor* but *excellent* Poet. . . . To do all this, entertains the publick with the most ridiculous Farce in the

World" (xv). By shrinking Pope's income and employing social snobbery to combat Pope's assumption of intellectual superiority, Dennis merely turns the tables on his enemy. In "Durgen" (1729), Edward Ward reminds Pope that despite his current vogue, his reputation is no more stable than any other writer's. Ward predicts that Pope will soon reside in a garret; "Nor will the utmost Arts your Wit can use,/Redeem the Credit of your sinking Muse" ("Durgen" 7, lines 114–15). Ward's mercantile imagery implicitly rebukes Pope's claim to speak as civic-minded poet. Such techniques, redolent of Pope's own methods, characterize most of the counterattacks.

Not surprisingly, none of the "dunces" perceived the appropriateness of Pope's strategy in creating from the poverty of some of their members a symbol of artistic and spiritual shabbiness. Many of their replies express disbelief that a fellow scribbler who had happened to strike it rich had then stooped to berate his peers for not faring as well. Considering Pat Rogers's argument that Pope transformed Grub Street itself into a metaphor linking his enemies' artistic failures with the poverty, madness, and crime associated with local landmarks, their protests seem remarkably focused. The chief complaint of many, like Ward's, is that Pope has misrepresented their respectable status. Such is the grievance of one anonymous author, who declared that "Mr. *Theobald* would give me no Thanks for assuring the World that he sits as seldom Supperless as the Author."[12] Thomas Cooke argued that "if flushed with his Success, and deceived into a Belief of his having . . . extraordinary Desert, such a Person [as Pope] should, without Bounds, transgress all the Rules of Decency and good Sense, it becomes almost a Duty in every one . . . to make him sensible how undeserving he has been of the Applause which he has gained, and how indiscreet to have forfeited all by attacking a Number of Men, some of which are the most shining Ornaments of the Age" (109). Rogers has explained that the Scriblerians' sense of themselves as moral and artistic guardians provided Pope with ample self-justification for his masterpiece. Yet the urgency of both poem and responses suggests that Pope had more particular reasons for combating "the rise of a scribbling gentry" (Rogers, *Hacks and Dunces* 166).

By 1728, the English middle class was already becoming subdivided into upper, middle, and lower strata, distinguished according to the genteelness, wealth, and skills of its members (Earle 328–29). Teachers, clergy, and government bureaucrats usually achieved only lower-middle-class status, as an oversupply of university graduates rendered jobs scarce and salaries low (Earle 62, 68–69, 328–29). Some educated men, as well as women who needed to support themselves, turned to writing, especially journalism, to supplement their incomes. Not surprisingly, the

Whig ministry proved these writers' most reliable resource. Among the writers ridiculed in "Settle's" vision, *Dunciad 3,* Barnham Goode was a Master at Eton College, while William Popple and Philip Horneck were solicitors with government positions. In Pope's *Dunciad in Four Books* (1742), however, Popple and Horneck are reduced to synecdoche—"Lo P-p-le's brow, tremendous to the town,/Horneck's fierce eye" (3.151–52)—while Goode becomes a "Fiend in glee" (3.154). Pope chiefly despised such men for engaging in ministerial journalism, either in addition to more stable careers, or to earn money for the leisure to pursue literature or scholarship. Writers such as Cooke, in turn, reminded Pope that no professional writer's position was sufficiently secure to warrant the assumption of moral authority.

Pope's career had prospered through subscriptions, a compromise between the old patronage system and the not yet feasible method of payment based on sales. Based on his experience as well as changes in society and in the economy, Pope envisioned a market in which poets dedicated to their craft—as physicians, for example, were engaged in healing—might prosper. This concept of the profession remains latent in the first *Dunciad,* but Pope developed it throughout his Horatian imitations. Writing, according to Pope's definition, may no longer have been the preserve of leisured men, but it was very much an upper-middle-class profession, closely allied, as were law and medicine, to the elite. In such writers as Popple and Horneck, as well as Lewis Theobald, Pope viewed the evolution of a new kind of writing career: a lower-middle-class resort from poverty. Pope did not perceive himself as a transitional figure or as an anomaly; a poet who rose to prominence encouraged by the literary arbiters of his youth, but whose business acumen enabled him to profit by his genius. He feared that readers would not distinguish the professional writer from the professional who also wrote, not to mention the successful from the unsuccessful professional writer. Either mistake threatened Pope's status both as literary authority and as man of letters. To inculcate his conservative professional ideal, Pope fictionalized the literal and intellectual poverty of his competitors. In this way, he could present an apparent compromise between exaggerated types: the writer removed from considerations of the marketplace, and the writer as Bartholomew Fair huckster.

Among Pope's victims in *Dunciad 3,* Leonard Welsted offers a clear example of his motivation and technique. Like Philip Horneck, Welsted was a clergyman's son. He attended Westminster School and matriculated at Trinity College.[13] Solidly middle class, he enjoyed a successful career in government service, aided by Whig patrons who admired the "noble Simplicity" of the verses he composed in their praise.[14] In Welsted's career, Pope detected one pole of his professional antitype: the poet incapable of earning independence through his poetry, and consequently condemned to flatter patrons. Instead of being admirably simple, Pope thought Welsted's verse was more like small beer, and immortalized his impression in the *Dunciad*'s parody of "Cooper's Hill": "Flow, Welsted, flow! like thine inspirer, Beer" (3.163).

James Sutherland, in his note to the Twickenham edition, finds puzzling Pope's insinuation of Welsted's intemperance. He suggests that Pope may allude to "Oikographia," in which Welsted describes his new house—a perquisite of his government employment—to the Duke of Dorset. In the poem, Welsted lingers mournfully over his empty wine cellar (n. 163). Pope refers to "Oikographia" in a note to Book 2, as a poem "in praise either of a *Cellar* or a *Garret*" (*Works* 5: 138n. 293), insinuating that these would be the only regions of a house familiar to Welsted. In fact, "Oikographia" perfectly illustrates Earle's discussion of prosperous middle-class houses, from the sash-lit entry to the three-roomer-floor plan, prints and portraits, maps, china cups, buffet, and comfortable couch of Welsted's new home. Pope would have been annoyed by Welsted's frank acknowledgment of the Duke's patronage as the ultimate source of his new dwelling, not to mention by his wish "[t]o hail great George in Bourdeaux wine" (1.259). Pope may also have read "The Invitation" (1719), in which Welsted appropriates Horace's characterization of Ofellus while planning to celebrate George I's birthday:

> What virtue does not generous Wine impart?
> It gives a winning frankness to the heart;
> With sprightly hope the drooping spirits arms . . .
> Expect superfluous splendour from the Great;
> Ragousts, and costly follies served in plate . . .
> In foreign arts of luxury untaught,
> I give you only lamb from Uxbridge fields,
> And add the choicest herb the garden yields.[15]

Pope could not permit a Whig poet to characterize himself, let alone his royal birthday celebration, as Horatian. In the *Dunciad*, Welsted's frank praise of wine in "The Invitation" becomes an attachment to beer. From a punctilious host ("Already is my little sideboard grac'd/The glasses marshall'd, the decanters plac'd" 11–12), Welsted is transubstantiated into a plebeian mug of beer, victim of a masterful if inaccurate stroke of metonymy.

Pope's parody suggests that while a poet such as Welsted may associate with patrons such as the Dukes of Dorset and Chandos ("Characters" 23), his status remains low because of his dependence on government patronage. By borrowing the most frequently imitated of seventeenth-century couplets, Pope guaranteed that even unlearned readers would recall his damning assessment. What reader aspiring to refinement could hereafter take seriously the verse of beer-guzzling Welsted?

Another of Pope's targets illustrates the opposite pole of his aversion, the poet who aspires to independence by appeal to the lowest common denominator of public taste. Pope devotes one of his most scathing passages to a description of "Orator" John Henley as a kind of Bartholomew Fair huckster:

> Imbrown'd with native Bronze, lo Henley stands,
> Tuning his voice, and balancing his hands.
> How fluent nonsense trickles from his tongue! . . .
> Preacher at once, and Zany of thy Age!
> Oh worthy thou of Ægypt's wise abodes,
> A decent Priest, where monkeys were the Gods! (3.195–97, 202–4)

At first glance, Henley seems to justify Pope's claim that the authors he attacks were made for the *Dunciad* (*Works* 5: 205). Among contemporaries, Henley was notorious for his blend of religion, politics, and theatrics. He was despised by the genteel, whom he further outraged by running his Oratory as a business. Because his life and opinions were so well known, Henley further illuminates Pope's enemies' reception of his poem.

Pat Rogers has outlined the typical pattern of a so-called dunce's life. According to his data, most writers did not engage in hack writing as part of an upward-moving career, but "came into the occupation as their social and financial circumstances *were declining*" (*Grub Street* 208). Henley certainly fits this pattern; he became entangled with Edmund Curll in an attempt to earn his living while, as a young Cambridge graduate, he still hoped for engagements as a London preacher. Failing to win preferment in town, he gave up his living in Suffolk, then broke with the Church of England. Registering as a dissenter, he established the Oratory, "a Social Institution of an Universal extent," in 1726 (Midgley 91). Henley's eccentric opinions, and the stream of pamphlets he issued to publicize the Oratory, soon transformed him into an object of satire. His vulnerability was compounded by authorship of *The Hyp-Doctor,* a weekly ministerial newspaper, from 1730 to 1741 (Midgley 216). But by 1728, Henley was already a popular butt of the Tory wits. Henley appears to fulfill Rogers's criteria for Duncehood: "The truth is that a Dunce only becomes a social pariah as a result of his misadventures in the literary profession" (*Grub Street* 211).

Henley understandably refused to interpret the pattern of his life in this way. As Earle has observed, an oversupply of clergy meant that many aspiring clerics had to scramble for subsistence while competing for the scarce and highly coveted London lectureships. Rather than consider himself banished to the countryside when his hopes of orthodox success collapsed, Henley had taken the enterprising step of separating himself from the main body of his faith and founding his Oratory in the bustling Newport meat market. What Rogers perceives as the downward arc of a career was, from Henley's standpoint, an advance in terms of independence and public recognition. His enemies persisted in portraying him as a fairground exhibit, claiming "He drew the Dregs of the Multitude after him by his Ribaldry, and cracking Jokes, like a *Jack Pudding* in *Bartholomew Fair*, at the same Time that he was clad in the venerable Vestments of the sacred order."[16] Today, Henley's activities appear to have resembled those of the more egregious televangelists, and so were understandably distasteful to refined sensibilities. But no matter how vigorously his critics protested, Henley maintained his right to preach and to publish his opinions, and to construe his as a respectable career.

Henley apparently intuited the growing importance of publicity in a consumer society. His attention-getting pamphlets applied the principles of advertising to attract congregants, an early example of what would soon become a widespread tactic in relation to other products.[17] Henley's campaign, from this point of view prophetic, was unfortunately conceived for a public not fully accustomed to such promotion, and in any case unprepared to accept such broadsides on behalf of a religious institution. Undismayed, Henley claimed to find his career, if anything, more genteel than Pope's. After years of sniping at the poet for his inclusion in the *Dunciad*, Henley compared their careers in "Why How Now, Gossip Pope?" (1736): "in the Fling, that I wrote for Booksellers, is imply'd an Imputation on my Fortune, as to which, my Education was better than your's and not . . . *on Subscription*, which is the *Basis* of your *Toy-Shop* at *Twickenham*; I took my Degrees and Orders at my own Expense, voluntarily quitted 150 £. a Year in the Country, on an Invitation to Town, whither I brought some Hundreds of Pounds, was never extravagant, was soon retain'd here by the Rev. Dr. *Burscough*, with a handsome Salary . . ." (7–8). And so on. By the painstaking record of his education, financial resources, and polite connections, Henley attempted to place himself beyond the criticism of one whose fortune was "gained by *writing for Booksellers*" (8). From Henley's perspective, Pope is merely another entrepreneur in the literary marketplace, whose methods are in fact less genteel than his own. Amidst a flood of invective, Henley nevertheless manages to expose certain of Pope's devices, such as misrepresentation of his sources (11–12) and oversimplification of his enemies' activities in order to relegate them to social oblivion.

As Henley indicated, Pope had also earned his living and had done so without the Orator's university education. The *Dunciad* mirrors the painful evolution of England's market economy, as Pope attempts to reconcile his conservative ideal of authorship with the realities of London's literary scene. Pope found it impossible to accept Henley's behavior as an enterprising, if tasteless, attempt to attract a congregation in a society increasingly swayed by advertising. Just two years after publishing the *Dunciad,* Pope composed his "Epistle to Lord Burlington," asserting that a man's taste mirrors his morals. The vulgarity of Henley's broadsides, and his meat-market location, "proved" by contrast the Orator's immorality. Attacks such as Henley's implying Pope's kinship in his appeal to popular taste—"The World loves *Romance,* and Mr. Pope can hit that just Taste at the Expence of any Man's or Family's Reputation, with the Art of a Pick-Pocket" (10)—sufficiently accounts for the vehemence with which, in successive editions of the *Dunciad,* Pope reiterated his abhorrence of the Orator's activities.

In his "Epistle to Dr. Arbuthnot" (written 1731–34), Pope interpreted his autobiography as a cross between the older, leisure-class model of the writer and the contemporary, professional money-maker: "I left no Calling for this idle Trade" (129). In "Epistle II ii of Horace" (written ca. 1736), he described his vocation as one for which he was suited not only by ability, but by years of study and reading: "[F]ull early I begun/To read in Greek" (52–53). In contrast, the conditions endured by many paid writers made it appear that, in Roy Porter's words, "they were manufacturing a product—literature—which in the past had largely been the preserve of the learned, the leisured and the secure." In place of the gentleman's study, Porter concludes, "'Grub Street' became literature's conveyor belt" (259). In fact, most contemporary writers were from origins similar to Pope's, or slightly better in that like Henley they had acquired university educations. Adding to the *Dunciad*'s confusion, Pope includes among his dunces writers such as Sir Richard Blackmore, an eminent physician who wrote epic poems. Educated at Oxford and Padua, physician to King William and to Queen Anne, Blackmore could hardly be accused of poverty or illiteracy.[18] But to emphasize his own dignity, Pope created the perception that all of his professional opponents belonged in a different, lower class.

Peter Laslett has remarked that "Social mobility is always most pronounced at the frontiers . . . between the minority which rule[s] and the mass which [does] not rule" (35). Grub Street, center of the bookselling trade, resembled such a frontier, set at the border between city and country, "the disreputable suburb of a reputable metropolis" (Porter, 291). Roy Porter has defined the locale's significance as an emblem of the writer's interstitial status: "On the borders of social and literary respectability—Parnassus, Westminster—are set the ramshackle mansions of Grub street" (291). And, a bit farther out, the villas of Twickenham. Today we are not distressed by the similarity of Pope's career to that of a merchant; his rented estate, for example, was typical of those "used by prosperous members of the 'middling sort' as a rural retreat from the noise and stench and stress of London" (Stone and Stone 404). But Pope preferred to identify himself with the elite, occupied as seldom as possible with the details of business. From this position, he spoke as an affiliate of the landed gentry. In the *Dunciad,* he attempted to define irrevocably the border between his own work and that of a "hireling"; between his social status and that of his enemies. The responses of those he attacked indicate that Pope's intention was well understood by contemporaries.

4

Pope's successive enthronements of Lewis Theobald and Colley Cibber, as well as his decision to add Book 4 to the *Dunciad,* indicate the problematic nature of his enterprise. Theobald's criticism of Pope's edition of Shakespeare had earned him the crown, but Theobald also represented the industrious but impoverished authors from whom Pope wished to distance himself. For all his learning, Theobald found it difficult to remain solvent, and had indeed been obliged to supply his bookseller "in the worst of days,/Notes to . . . books, and prologues to . . . plays" (1.167–68). In his mock-coronation of Theobald, Pope first suggested the relationship between poverty and Dulness that provided so much fuel for his enemies' retaliation. Pope's "Tibbald," pining in his garret, asks himself whether he should "take up th'Attorney's, (once my better) Guide?" (1.190), implying that he should have remained in the inferior legal profession for which he was trained. "For men are not bunglers because they are poor, but they are poor because they are bunglers," concludes "Cleland" in his "Letter to the Publisher" (15).

Such derision incensed Pope's enemies; witness John Dennis's retort that Pope had earned his fortune translating "a *poor* but *excellent* Poet." And, Dennis might have added, by satirizing a poor but excellent editor.[19] Pope evidently realized that Theobald's enthronement drew attention to the most problematic element of his satire. A particularly ironic note glosses the *Dunciad*'s lines extolling Dulness's care of those "Who hunger, and who thirst, for scribling sake": "I must not here omit a Reflection, which will occur perpetually through this Poem, and cannot but endear the Author to every attentive Observer of it: I mean that *Candour* and *Humanity* which every where appears in him, to those unhappy Objects of the Ridicule of all mankind, the bad Poets. He here imputes all scandalous rhimes, scurrilous weekly papers, lying news . . . not so much to Malice or Servility as to Dulness; and not so much to Dulness, as to Necessity" (*Works* 5: 65n. 41). Stripped of irony, this note claims that necessity depresses talent, leading to poor writing and public opprobrium. Leisure, on the other hand, conduces to genius, which produces good writing and leads to fame. Although Pope retained this note throughout all his editions, its logic is palpably false. Pope himself frequently regretted the undeservedly obscure deaths of poets such as Dryden and, later, Gay. The note claims that only leisure-class writers possess genius, a statement abundantly refuted by the works of all the Scriblerians. Finally, the note stresses the popular ridicule attendant upon writing for pay, implying that public acclaim invariably accompanies genius. If that were so—and this sentiment pervades Pope's commentary on the dunces—how could these writers threaten Pope, and why must they be so cruelly brought to public attention from their current oblivion?

Many of Pope's victims themselves asked these questions, and the answer can only be that these writers did pose a perceived threat to Pope, if not to his genius and fortune, to his reputation as both professional writer and man of letters. By impugning Pope's editorial ability, Theobald had attacked Pope as a scholar. A largely self-taught man, deprived by his faith of a university education, Pope was particularly proud of the critical skills that aligned him with icons of gentlemanly learning like Sir William Temple (Levine 192–93). Pope's enemies, moreover, persisted in claiming that his motive in editing Shakespeare had been mercenary, the very Grub Street hallmark with which he lashed his opponents. By pointing to his wealth, Pope demonstrated that he was, according to his note's logic, both a genius and a gentleman. In other words, Theobald represented all the professional miseries from which Pope wished to remain completely disassociated, yet his had been the most convincing attempt to strip Pope of his pretension to superiority. In practice, however, Theobald failed to materialize as a real threat. Although he persevered with his superior edition of Shakespeare (1734), Theobald responded to the *Dunciad* in a good-humored manner, and he probably altered some features of his Shakespeare commentary to avoid further occasion of ridicule (Seary 99–100, 128). In portraying Theobald as his rival for prestige, Pope may have satisfied his need for an antihero of Whig political, and "modern" intellectual, principles. But he also provided justification for his enemies' charges of mean-spiritedness and insecurity. In 1743, he attempted to resolve this dilemma by elevating Colley Cibber to the throne of Dulness.

At the conclusion of the 1729 *Dunciad Variorum,* the narrator reveals that Tibbald's "raptur'd" glimpse of Dulness triumphant is, fortunately, imaginary, as "thro' the Ivory Gate the Vision flies" (3.358). In 1730, Colley Cibber defeated Theobald of his modest hope for preferment and was proclaimed laureate. Pope waited until 1743 to capitalize on this phenomenon, which enabled him to construe "Settle's prophecy" as something more than mere vision. Before Pope published this final version, rumors had reached Cibber of his intention, provoking the laureate to write two open letters of vigorous, sometimes scurrilous, self-defense, and prompting a flurry of attacks on each adversary. At least one of Cibber's letters caused Pope to grimace in anguish, while Cibber's attacks were evidently motivated by distress at the prospect of Pope's affront.[20] Pope's representation of Cibber may well reflect anger over both Cibber's and his supporters' pamphlets, but he cites his successive heroes' status as sufficient cause for the new edition. Defending his choice to dethrone Theobald, Pope observes that "Tibbald could not be the person, who was never an Author in fashion, or caressed by the Great; whereas this single characteristic is sufficient to point out the true Hero; who, above all other Poets of his time, was the *Peculiar Delight* and *Chosen Companion* of the Nobility of England" (*Works* 5: 269). In distorting Cibber's refutation of previous Popean insults in *A Letter from Mr. Cibber to Mr. Pope* (1742), Pope assumes the absurdity of Cibber's claim to genteel status, as well as the deterioration of a nobility that would choose him for a companion.[21] Such ironies characterize Pope's technique throughout the expanded *Dunciad,* reiterating and clarifying the intention of Pope's earlier version. Instead of independent professionals, Pope's enemies, as well as their wealthy or aristocratic supporters, are made to appear adherents to traditional, unhealthy patron-client relationships. Pope recalls that Cibber "wrote, as he himself tells us, certain of his Works at the *earnest Desire of Persons of Quality*" (*Works* 5: 269). In fact, the work in question is Cibber's *Letter;* the italicized phrase was the playwright's witty excuse ("as the Puff in the Play-Bills says") for stooping to answer Pope's repeated insults (Cibber, *Letter* 1). Cibber's *Letter* questions Pope's pretension, comparing the poet to a bear-garden bully (8). In turn, Pope represents Cibber as a typical hack. Only he and his dedicatee, Swift, exiled in an Ireland from which Dulness "retires" (1.25), appear sufficiently independent to resist contamination.

Book 1 of *The Dunciad in Four Books* finds Cibber in Theobald's vacated garret, "Swearing and supperless" after "an ill Run at Play/. . . and a thin Third day" (113–15). Although Theobald was dogged by poverty and could credibly be portrayed as starving in a garret, this image did not fit the poet laureate, retired after a highly successful career as playwright, theater manager, and comic actor. In fact, having commenced by observing that Cibber is beloved of the nobility, Pope asserts the identification of the aristocracy with Grub Street that increasingly characterizes the new *Dunciad.* He further distorts reality by identifying Cibber as a hack, hastily compiling works from other writers' plays:

> Next, o'er his Books his eyes began to roll,
> In pleasing memory of all he stole,
> How here he sipp'd, how there he plunder'd snug
> And suck'd all o'er, like an industrious Bug.
> Here lay poor Fletcher's half-eat scenes, and there
> The frippery of crucify'd Molière;
> There hapless Shakespeare, yet of Tibbald sore,
> Wish'd he had blotted for himself before. (127–34)

Like most playwrights, including Shakespeare, Cibber had borrowed plots and speeches from his predecessors.[22] As a dramatist, however, Cibber was best known for his astute response to public preoccupation with refinement. His near-invention of sentimental comedy had helped replace Restoration wit with more didactic humor, and clever rakes with virtuous heroines. Hard-pressed to refute this phenomenon, Pope grudgingly refers to Cibber's masterpiece, *The Careless Husband,* by making his hero beg Dulness's pardon: "Some Daemon stole my pen (forgive th'offence)/ And once betray'd me into common sense" (187–88). Except for that lapse, however, his "Prose and Verse were much the same,/This, prose on stilts; that, poetry fall'n lame" (189–90).

Pope hoped to convince readers that Cibber's entire career was of a piece with the Birthday Odes, which the laureate himself had described as "halting Rhimes" (*Apology* 20). Instead of with his role as a proponent of refinement, Cibber was identified merely with the swearing, gambling, and other minor vices to which he cheerfully admitted in his *Apology.*[23] That identification established, Cibber in his Grub Street garret, endowed with the real-life Cibber's aristocratic entrée, becomes Dulness's consort. Together, they will

> Fatten the Courtier, starve the learned band,
> And suckle Armies, and dry-nurse the land:
> 'Till Senates nod to Lullabies divine,
> And all be Sleep, as at an Ode of thine. (315–18)

In real life, Cibber's status as laureate had won him the friendship and hospitality of the great. It did not follow that, as Pope implies in this passage, he would infect the aristocracy with Dulness. More plausibly, as in the tale of Sir Balaam in Pope's "Epistle to Lord Bathurst," a corrupt aristocracy had encouraged Cibber's entertaining, if dissipated, proclivities. But Pope aimed his opprobrium at the laureate—a man who had described the admission of domestic servants to the upper gallery as "the most disgraceful Nuisance, that ever depreciated the Theatre" (*Apology* 135). By blaming Cibber, Pope confined himself to an oblique attack on the Whig grandees, whom he really held responsible for cultural deterioration. But he also created a powerful, although inaccurate, image of a beer-swilling, howling, bench-breaking crowd of writers, storming St. James at the heels of Colley Cibber, inspired to riot by a Drury Lane pantomime more appropriate for a fair booth. That these writers were also engaged in a struggle for survival in a budding profession did not concern Pope. He did not wish to compete in the version of the writing profession they presaged. His audience had to be convinced that the Whig ministry cultivated artists too mean for the regard of a fastidious reader.

Disparaging his chief rival for poetic supremacy (if in title only) by portraying him as a starving hack was an outrageous insult. That Pope intended to puncture the laureate's respectability was not lost on Cibber. Shortly after the poem's publication, he wrote a second public letter to Pope that attempted to reduce his adversary to the same status. Cibber's earlier letter on the *Dunciad Variorum* had been one of the reasons for his enthronement; there he had retailed the story of his "rescue" of Pope just as the poet was scrambling upon a prostitute. In the new letter, Cibber professes surprise that Pope has featured him in his new version:

> [B]ut at your peril be it, little Gentleman, for I shall have t'other Frisk with you, and don't despair that the very Notice I am now taking of you, will once more make your Fame fly, like a yelping Cur with a Bottle at his Tail, the Jest and Joy of every Bookseller's Prentice between Wapping and Westminster! This, you will say, is Language not fit to be us'd to a Gentleman: I grant it— but, like other general Rules, this too may have its Exceptions . . . it is at least as Gentle, as what your Oyster-mouth'd Muse has bestow'd upon your humble-Servant. (15)

Cibber employs an even more vulgar metaphor than those Pope featured in his epic parody. While the booksellers' race for a phantom poet is hardly dignified, Pope's metamorphosis into a dog racing its own tail and pursued by jeering apprentices is intended to mortify.[24] As in his earlier comparison of Pope to a bear-garden boxer, Cibber implies that the poet's "sport" with his fellow writers will entertain none but the lowliest readers. Pope has proven himself no gentleman through his use of ugly language, and has thus lowered himself beneath any of the writers he execrates. Cibber also accuses Pope of sharing the hack's motive for writing. Pope has reissued the *Dunciad* "with an eye to your getting off another Edition of your Book, by making more ample mention of Me, in it" (*Another Letter* 15).

5

Today, the logic of Cibber's responses appears circular. He could do no more than protest the scurrility of Pope's language and retaliate with even more brutal imagery of his own. Pope incorporated the cycle into his ever-growing commentary, attracting fresh accusations each time he edited and appended his enemies' replies. But the very circularity of their exchanges reveals an impasse in the capacity of either side to define satisfactorily the status of their emerging profession. Pope's enemies continued to claim that while fame and prosperity had gained him familiarity with the great, his status remained that of an upper-middle-class merchant. Hence, according to their finely tuned social perceptions, Pope had failed to reach his self-proclaimed identity with barristers and physicians.[25] Their arguments never progressed far beyond those expressed by an anonymous opponent in "The New Metamorphosis" (1728):

> Sure he might have rested, and let down his Anchor,
> And smil'd when the Bard was as rich as a Banker.
> Rejoic'd that his Eye-sight had even beholden,
> An *Age* so obliging, *Subscriptions* so Golden. (45, lines 64–67)

Inventing for Pope's mercantile family a history of distress, the same author laments his persecution of indigent competitors, since Pope's "Father was no Stranger to a *Statute* of *Bankrupt*" (48). Such slurs impelled Pope, in turn, to rescue himself by creating, in effect, two social classes of writers. He established himself securely in the genteel category, while casting his enemies as the buffoons, harlequins, and ignorant crowds at Bartholomew Fair.[26] But the ongoing struggle failed to achieve Pope's goal of disabling the literary pretensions of all who failed to conform to his conservative model.

The "paper war" also failed to elevate the prestige of those whom Pope maligned. Confined within the boundaries of middle-class status, Pope's war against Dulness remained a skirmish on the borders of gentility, a battle royal with no aristocratic pretensions. Scholars who place Pope either among the heroes of a new profession, or among its resisters, ignore the extent to which Pope and his contemporaries participated in its birth as a respectable, middle-class occupation. Pope can appear to espouse either side of the struggle because he incorporated aspects of competing models into his personal conception. Moreover, many writers engaged in invidious polemic because political journalism offered them employment. When conservative political theory admitted only gentlemen to full participation in civic deliberation, and liberal theory had no effective model to oppose it, writers invariably attacked each other's social status as the prime qualification for public discourse. As we have seen, this insistent dimension of so many publications exploited, and ultimately exacerbated, professional writers' liminal social identity. Those who ignore its contemporary social context risk vitiating the *Dunciad* of some of its urgency, not to mention one of the chief dimensions of its satire. Those who find in the poem merely evidence of Pope's bad faith are equally ignoring the very real stakes for which he felt himself contending, as he and his competitors debated the social status that would be accorded this new phenomenon compounded of man of letters, literary merchant, and word-cobbler. Only by attending to the responses of his first intended readers—his literary rivals—can we appreciate the extent to which the *Dunciad* promoted conceptions of the literary profession in which "serious" artists are distinguished from the descendents of those underemployed clerics who wrote for booksellers.

Pope's efforts to polarize the emerging profession dismayed writers in an era when middling status was becoming difficult to sustain, let alone to improve. By emphasizing distinctions among writers, Pope echoed the increasing division of middle-class status characteristic of his lifetime. Because he associated an overwhelming number of competitors with lower-middling status, Pope retarded rather than aided the rise to professional status of authors who published for their livelihoods. But his enemies reminded him that his own status remained well within the bounds of middling aspiration. Perhaps the increasing futility of this internecine warfare influenced Pope's decision to add Book 4 to the *Dunciad*. There, he extricated himself from combat with his "brother scribblers" and directly accused the elite educational system of perpetrating England's cultural decline. By denigrating the system that "produced the producers" as well as sponsors of much published writing, Pope further damaged the credibility of his literary competitors. Meanwhile, Pope had found in Horace a more congenial model for his professional identity, which he defined and aggrandized throughout his imitations.

## Notes

1. Foxon establishes beyond all doubt Pope's business acumen and his desire to set the fashion in book production. On the other hand, Colin Ward describes Pope's tragic sense of England's change from a landed to a mercantile economy. Ian A.

Bell persuasively argues Pope's ambivalence as he tried to reconcile "an image of the dignified satirist" with "his steady accumulation of cash" (66). In my view, Bell's conclusion is justified by Pope's attempts to reconcile the old-fashioned model of the man of letters with the emerging concept of professionalism, particularly in his Horatian poems.

2. Paul Monod argues that English artists were not free to develop a "diverse, partisan, and commercial sphere of art"—to emerge as a strong profession—until after the collapse of "Whig dreams of cultural hegemony" after 1730 (370), followed by the decay of Toryism in the 1750s (396). Although its effects were quite different—English writers were highly politicized, while painters were stifled by their attempts to appear neutral—writers were similarly hampered in the establishment of their profession by the intense political divisions of this period.

3. Pocock examines at length the writings of political economist Dr. Charles Davenant, whose essays from 1695–1710 exemplify Tory attempts to reconcile civic morality with new modes of exchange (436–46).

4. Susan Staves describes Pope's contribution to the "heightened consciousness that poetic texts could be owned, like other forms of property, and that they could be revised or 'improved,' just as landed property might be improved to the owner's benefit" (156). Matthew Hodgart argues that the presence of not only Walpole's name but also those of the King, Prince, and Princess Caroline on Pope's *Odyssey* subscription list signaled that Pope "was not only politically safe but had even become a national monument" (34).

5. Among these writers are Philip Pinkus, who remarks that "there was only one Pope" (260); Terry Belanger, who refers to Pope as "the watershed figure" (21); and Roy Porter in his assessment of Pope's fortune (263).

6. Pat Rogers states that Whitefriars epitomized "the classic set of duncely circumstances—crime, debtors, prostitutes, street affrays, the book trade, minor authors and the rest" (*Hacks and Dunces* 152).

7. On the Restoration fascination with Grub Street, see the studies of Emrys Jones and Kathy MacDermott.

8. Joseph M. Levine (181–263) has thoroughly demonstrated Pope's allegiance to the "Ancient" ideal of the leisured man of letters, contrary both to the new notion of professionalism and to some aspects of his own experience.

9. Stone and Stone observe that among landed families "no social stigma had ever been attached to . . . entirely genteel pursuits" such as "government service and the professions, mostly law and the army," but also including the Church. The Stones note a rise in professional involvement among the elite from 1700 to 1800 (225).

10. Stone and Stone conclude that upward social mobility was largely a myth until the late nineteenth century: "By and large, the power, wealth, and even status of the landed elite survived more or less intact until 1880" (402). Peter Earle claims that by 1730, the barriers between poverty and middling status, as well as between the middle station and the gentry, were increasingly difficult to surmount (331–32).

11. Alexander Pope, *The Dunciad*, ed. James Sutherland, in the Twickenham edition, ed. John Butt et al. 10 vols., 5: 87. All further citations of Pope's poems will refer to this edition. I will distinguish within the text between the *Dunciad Variorum* (1729–42) and the *Dunciad, In Four Books* (1742–51).

12. "A Complete Collection of all the Verses, Essays, Letters and Advertisements, . . . by Pope and Swift" xiii.

13. For details of Welsted's career, I consulted the *Dictionary of National Biography* 20: 1151–52.

14. "Characters of the Times" 24. This account also provides the basis of Pope's note on Welsted (*Works* 5:166n. 163). Rogers (*Grub Street*) notes Welsted's middle-class status (201).

15. *Works,* 64–67, lines 31–33, 37–38, 40–42. Of particular interest is Ambrose Phillips's introduction commending the moderation of such middle-class festivities as Welsted's poem promotes. "The Invitation" is also reprinted in Lonsdale 147–48.

16. "A comparison between Orator H— and Orator P— etc.," quoted in Midgley 143.

17. Neil McKendrick (187) describes how commercial advertising, evident by the turn of the eighteenth century, became an established feature of periodicals such as the *Daily Advertizer* and the *London Advertizer* of 1731, and was ubiquitous by the end of the century.

18. Harry Solomon reviews Blackmore's career as a progressive physician and pious Whig poet, opposed by Tory wits for both his political principles and "Modern" literary adherence.

19. Peter Seary argues persuasively for recognition of "the fundamental importance and novelty of Theobald's methods of elucidating [Shakespeare's] texts" (207).

20. Mack (774–81) and Koon (157–64) contain complementary, persuasive accounts of the events preceding Cibber's enthronement.

21. See, for example, Cibber, *Another Letter* 45–46 for his argument that he is as much entitled as Pope to the companionship of lords.

22. Cibber replied that of those plays he had altered "many . . . have liv'd the longer for my meddling with them" (32). Koon (37) allows the justice of Cibber's claim in relation to *Richard III*. Another reason for the unfairness of Pope's charge is his reference, in the preface to the *Works of Shakespeare,* to Shakespeare's borrowing of plots and speeches from classical and English predecessors as proof of his sufficient learning. See Goldgar, *Literary Criticism of Alexander Pope* 166–67.

23. Koon (163) discusses the effect of Pope's characterization, "a grotesque caricature of Foppington," on Cibber's reputation.

24. Hogarth depicts boys tormenting a dog by tying a bone to its tail in *The First Stage of Cruelty* (1751). Derek Jarrett reproduces the plate and discusses Hogarth's aversion to such pastimes (152–53).

25. Earle (331) quotes a Swiss observer who wrote that "Every Englishman constantly

holds a pair of scales wherein he exactly weighs the birth, rank and especially the fortune of those he is in company with, in order to regulate his behavior accordingly."

26. Stallybrass and White (112) discuss the ubiquitous recourse to Bartholomew Fair imagery throughout Pope's era, symptomatic of professional-class flight from contamination by popular culture. They observe the ultimate futility of Pope's accusations: the poet "was no more able than those whom he attacked to climb outside or above the marketplace" (118).

# Works Cited

Belanger, Terry. "Publishers and Writers in Eighteenth-Century England." *Books and their Readers in Eighteenth-Century England.* Ed. Isabel Rivers. New York: St. Martin's, 1982. 5–26.

Bell, Ian A. "'Not Lucre's Madman': Pope, Money, and Independence." *Alexander Pope: Essays for the Tercentenary.* Ed. Colin Nicholson. Aberdeen: Aberdeen UP, 1988. 53–67.

"Characters of the Times; or An Impartial Account of the Writings, Characters, Education &c. of Several Noblemen and Gentlemen, libell'd in a Preface to a late Miscellany Publish'd by P——pe and S——ft." *Popeiana* VII: *The Dunciad II, 1728.* New York: Garland, 1975.

Cibber, Colley. *A Critical Edition of An Apology for the Life of Mr. Colley Cibber, Comedian.* Ed. John Maurice Evans. 1740. New York: Garland, 1987.

———. *A Letter from Mr. Cibber to Mr. Pope. Popeiana* XV: *Cibber and the Dunciad, 1740–1744.* 1742. New York: Garland, 1975. 1–65.

———. *Another Occasional Letter from Mr. Cibber to Mr. Pope* (1744). *Popeiana* XV. 15.

Cleland, William. "Letter to the Publisher, Occasioned by the Present Edition of the *Dunciad.*" 1743. *The Poems of Alexander Pope.* Vol. 5. Ed. James Sutherland. London: Methuen, 1963. 11–21.

"A Compleat Collection of all the Verses, Essays, Letters and Advertisements, which have been occasioned by the Publication of Three Volumes of Miscellanies, by Pope and Swift." *Popeiana* VI: *The Dunciad I, 1728.* New York: Garland, 1975.

Cooke, Thomas. Preface to "The Battel of the Poets. In two cantos." *Popeiana* IX: *Tales, Epistles, Odes, Fables, &c. 1729, by Thomas Cooke.* 1729. New York: Garland, 1974.

Dennis, John. *"Remarks on Mr. Pope's Rape of the Lock." Popeiana* VII: *The Dunciad II. 1728.* 1728. New York: Garland, 1975.

Earle, Peter. *The Making of the English Middle Class: Business, Society and Family Life in London, 1660–1730.* Berkeley: U of California P, 1989.

Foxon, David. *Pope and the Early Eighteenth-Century Book Trade.* Ed. James McLaverty. Oxford: Clarendon, 1991.

Goldgar, Bertram, ed. *Literary Criticism of Alexander Pope.* Lincoln: U of Nebraska P, 1965.

Henley, John. "Why How Now, Gossip Pope?" *Popeiana XVI: The Dunciad, 1742–50.* 1736. New York: Garland, 1975. 7–8.

Hodgart, Matthew. "The Subscription List for Pope's *Iliad.*" *The Dress of Words: Essays on Restoration and Eighteenth Century Literature in Honor of Richmond P. Bond.* Ed. Robert B. White, Jr. Lawrence: U of Kansas Libraries, 1978.

Holmes, Geoffrey. *Augustan England: Professions, State and Society, 1680–1730.* London: Allen and Unwin, 1982.

Jarrett, Derek. *England in the Age of Hogarth.* New Haven: Yale UP, 1986.

Jones, Emrys. "Pope and Dullness." *Pope: Recent Essays by Several Hands.* Ed. Maynard Mack and James Winn. Hamden, CT: Archon, 1980. 632–34.

Koon, Helen. *Colley Cibber: A Biography.* Lexington: UP of Kentucky, 1986.

Larson, Magali Sarfatti. *The Rise of Professionalism: A Sociological Analysis.* Berkeley: U of California P, 1977.

Laslett, Peter. *The World We Have Lost: England Before the Industrial Age.* 2nd ed. 1965. New York: Scribner's, 1971.

Levine, Joseph M. *The Battle of the Books: History and Literature in the Augustan Age.* Ithaca: Cornell UP, 1991.

Lonsdale, Roger, ed. *The New Oxford Book of Eighteenth-Century Verse.* New York: Oxford UP, 1984.

MacDermott, Kathy. "Literature and the Grub Street Myth." *Literature and History* 8.2 (1982): 159–69.

McKendrick, Neil. "George Packwood and the Commercialization of Shaving: The Art of Eighteenth-Century Advertising or 'The Way to Get Money and be Happy.'" *The Birth of a Consumer Society: The Commercialization of Eighteenth-Century England.* Ed. Neil McKendrick, John Brewer, and J. H. Plumb. Bloomington: Indiana UP, 1982. 146–94.

Mack, Maynard. *Alexander Pope: A Life.* New York: Norton, 1985.

Midgely, Graham. *The Life of Orator Henley.* Oxford: Clarendon, 1973.

Monod, Paul. "Painters and Party Politics in England, 1714–1760." *Eighteenth-Century Studies* 26 (1993): 367–98.

"The New Metamorphosis. Being a Familiar Letter from a Gentleman in Town to a Lady in the Country: Occasion'd by the *Dunciad.*" *Popeiana VII.*

Pinkus, Philip. *Grub Street Stripped Bare.* Hamden, CT: Archon, 1968.

Pocock, J. G. A. *The Machiavellian Moment: Florentine Political Thought and the Atlantic Republican Tradition.* Princeton: Princeton UP, 1975.

Pope, Alexander. *The Poems of Alexander Pope.* Ed. John Butt et al. 10 Vols. London: Methuen, 1953.

Porter, Roy. *English Society in the Eighteenth Century.* 1982. Harmondsworth, Middlesex: Penguin, 1983.

Quintero, Ruben. *Literate Culture: Pope's Rhetorical Art.* Newark: U of Delaware P, 1992.

Rogers, Pat. *Grub Street: Studies in a Subculture.* London: Methuen, 1972.

———. *Hacks and Dunces: Pope, Swift and Grub Street.* 1972. London: Methuen, 1980.

Rosenblum, Michael. "Pope's Illusive Temple of Infamy." *Pope: Recent Essays by Several Hands.* Ed. Maynard Mack and James Winn. Hamden, CT: Archon, 1980. 652–77.

Seary, Peter. *Lewis Theobald and the Editing of Shakespeare.* Oxford: Clarendon, 1990.

Solomon, Harry. *Sir Richard Blackmore.* Boston: Twayne, 1980.

Stallybrass, Peter, and Allon White. *The Politics and Poetics of Transgression.* Ithaca: Cornell UP, 1986.

Staves, Susan. "Pope's Refinement." *Eighteenth-Century Theory and Interpretation* 29 (1988): 145–62.

Stone, Lawrence and Jeanne C. Fawtier Stone. *An Open Elite? England 1540–1880.* Oxford: Clarendon, 1984.

Ward, Colin. "Figuring Out Credit in the *Dunciad.*" *Alexander Pope: Essays for the Tercentenary.* Ed. Colin Nicholson. Aberdeen: Aberdeen UP, 1988. 68–82.

Ward, Edward. "Apollo's Maggot in his Cups; or, the Whimsical Creation of a Little Satirical Poet. A Lyrick Ode." *Popeiana VIII: The Dunciad III, 1729.* New York: Garland, 1975. 37–38.

———. "Durgen; or, a Plain Satyr Upon a Pompous Satyrist." *Popeiana VIII.* 7.

"Welsted, Leonard." *The Dictionary of National Biography.* Ed. Sir Leslie Stephen and Sir Sidney Lee. 22 vols. 1882. London: Oxford UP, 1949–50. 20: 1151–52.

Welsted, Leonard. *The Works, in Verse and Prose, of Leonard Welsted, Esq.* Ed. John Nichols. London, 1787.

# The Invention of the Countryside

## Pope, the "Idiocy of Rural Life," and the Intellectual View from the Suburbs

*Donna Landry*

This essay attempts to capture Alexander Pope's contribution to the invention of the countryside, that "favourite word of descriptive writers," as the *Oxford English Dictionary* puts it. By countryside, I mean to distinguish the irrefutable existence of "the country" itself, rural spaces and inhabitants, from representations of it and from notions about it that could only come from a distinctly unrural perspective, that indeed are produced by an urban or, in Pope's case, more precisely suburban, point of view. Sometime during the long eighteenth century, between the 1660s and the 1830s, the countryside began to cease to refer to a specific side, e.g., east or west, north or south, of a bit of country, or a river valley, or a range of hills, and became "the countryside," an imaginary, generalized space connoting not specific, local but aesthetic, global "natural unity" (*OED*).

The ideology of the countryside insists that everything in the country is lovely, and when it isn't, it ought to be. This is where the suburban impulse to tidy, purify, regulate, and decorporealize rural life and its often messy practices comes in. Nothing nasty, brutish, or short on urbane aesthetic appeal will be tolerated. The countryside exists in the imaginations of suburban intellectuals as an idyllic retreat, but the facts and the experiential textures of country life often appall and usually bore them. Always there hovers the prejudice of the town dweller towards the country man or woman, the sense of urbanity as cultural superiority, a stance which Marx and Engels share and epitomize in their famous formulation of 1848, "the idiocy of rural life" (Tucker 477).

To see Pope as historically central, even crucial, to this way of thinking about the rural may not seem entirely quixotic if we notice how his satires in particular conflate the ideology of proper stewardship with that of the moral superiority of the self-denying intellectual. Especially, that is, the self-denying intellectual in search of a rural retreat within which to practice the simple life, the antithesis of exhibitionistic or unthinking consumption. For the ideology of proper stewardship, read a managerial proprietorship of landed estates, and a certain identification with his aristocratic friends, like Bathurst and Burlington and Cobham, whose wealth wrought self-congratulatory, hardly inconspicuous or utilitarian improvements in their bit of country.

My thinking on these issues is obviously indebted to Raymond Williams's *The Country and the City* (1973). The historical sweep of that study allows Williams to pose such crucial general questions as whether or not the pastoral and the counter-pastoral have ever not been in antithetical counterpoint, and whether there has ever been an era that did not posit a vanished golden age of pastoral harmony through which to criticize the contemporary moment as inevitably a time of civil disaffection, if not outright civil strife. My much more modest project is aimed at locating the historical specificity of changes in England's rural landscape and its representation as countryside in the course of the eighteenth century. What, if anything, distinguishes the production of particular notions of the rural and of Englishness, during the century of slavery and colonial expansion as well as large-scale capitalization of agriculture? In this respect I hope the larger study of which this essay is a part might eventually extend *The Politics of Landscape,* James Turner's subtle and distinguished work on rural scenery and society in seventeenth-century English poetry (1979).

Following in this tradition, though more detached from neo-Marxist ideology critique than either Williams or Turner, Malcolm Kelsall, in *The Great Good Place,* his recent book on literary representations of the country house, points admirably to the polyvalence of Pope's satire on Timonesque consumption in the vast country estate. What, in fact, distinguishes a Timon, for which we conventionally read a Chandos or a Walpole, from a Bathurst or a Burlington or a Cobham, except that the latter were Pope's friends (Kelsall 66)?

Now, my argument is not that Pope is simply contradictory on these matters. It isn't so much that in spite of harboring residually mercantile resentments against aristocratic prerogatives, he wishes to compliment his rich and titled friends and thus sometimes seems to be having it both ways in his anti-Timon satire. Rather, I wish to argue that there is a certain coherence to his views, once we recognize the extent to which both the ideology of stewardship, especially its managerial relation to the rural and the natural world, and the suburban desire to substitute the country of the mind for the country as it is, depend upon a relation to the rural that is at once "other," primarily instrumental, and even coercively regulatory in its attitude. This attitude is also, apparently, reconcilable with a sensitivity toward animal sensibilities that consists largely of projecting human attitudes onto them, and thus makes one peculiarly likely to find things in the country less than lovely and to seek to manage and regulate them.

As Turner observes, "[R]ural poetry is always partly satirical" (117). Pope's satires, especially *To Burlington, The Second Satire of the Second Book of Horace Paraphrased, The Sixth Epistle of the First Book* and *The Second Epistle of the Second Book of Horace Imitated,* lead us to congratulate tasteful improvers of the countryside, who, like suburban intellectuals, can easily be distinguished from more barbaric country folk, including the backward hunting gentry. In fact the traditional rural as such, whether represented by agricultural labor, hunting practices, vernacular architecture, wildlife, wilderness, or uncultivated land, scarcely appears in Pope. The suburban intellectual sensibility is one that leaves little room for the rural even in the form of ancient, as opposed to new and properly Palladian, human habitation.

The only glimpse of vernacular architecture we are given in Pope's satires is a sneering dismissal of trying to do up such a place as an old farm or manor house in the modern fashion. "[S]ome patch'd dog-hole ek'd with ends of wall" (*To Burlington* 32, in Butt 589) suggests nothing so much as a low-roofed long house to which, over the years, rooms have been added, and whose central inhabited block is connected to, "eked out with," the walls of outbuildings, for housing livestock and equipment, to form a partially enclosed farmyard. Such an example of vernacular architecture, of course, looks absurd when modernized with newfangled Palladian ornaments, especially because, from Pope's tidy suburban point of view, such a dwelling was completely lacking in aesthetic or useful virtues in the first place.

I find Pope's attitude towards the rural here reminiscent of what I shall call a suburban sensibility, despite the fact that, given the choice, Pope might not have elected a suburban existence rather than an urban one; he may well have thought of himself as a Londoner unwillingly displaced. After all, he seems to have found himself taking his friend Lord Bathurst's advice and leasing the Twickenham villa with five acres rather than building a *palozzotto* (Bathurst's term) in London as he had earlier intended, at least partly to save the expense of building in town (Sherburn, *Early Career* 215, 271; Mack, *The Garden and the City* 9). Perhaps he settled on Twickenham partly because it lay beyond the legal ten-mile radius that supposedly kept Catholics a safe distance from London and Westminster, according to a statute of 1688 (I Wm & M, c. 9; Rogers, "Pope and the Social Scene" 102). As Sherburn comments, "This law like most of the other anti-Catholic laws was not generally enforced, but like all such laws it kept Catholics uneasy and fearful" (*Early Career* 35).

In the customizing of the house at Twickenham, however, and the subsequent publicizing of this private domain, Pope seems to have warmed to his task as beautifying suburbanite. As, in Morris Brownell's phrase, the "extraordinarily varied iconography" of the villa testifies, Pope was his own most energetic publicist, featuring the villa in his poetry of the 1730s as a miniature country house of the right, not the wrong, sort, complete with fashionably serpentine garden and underground grotto for receiving vatic inspiration in, and perhaps even commissioning paintings of it (15–17). Eventually, the reproduction and dissemination of images of his villa succeeded in marketing him for popular consumption predominantly as a man and poet at home in his own miniaturized, convenient-to-town, artfully artless version of rural retirement. And in retrospect, Pope himself can be read as articulating an early instance of a peculiarly suburban configuration of ideas regarding gardens, grounds, bucolic retreats, and what to eat and do for pleasure in the so-called country.

As Kelsall observes, "Twickenham provides the first major instance of the suburbanisation of the country house in England, the transfer of the ideals of the great estate to the small garden, the spread of what Wells called the 'Bladesover system' into the life style of the lower classes" (78). Pope's villa at Twickenham "is only a symbolic country house," his "few acres of garden are only the sign of an estate; his box-like dwelling the suburban retreat of a man of letters," whose "skilled marketing" (59) of his edition of Homer provided the capital for the lease and improvements. Yet appropriation of the country for urban, suburban, and commercial interests has a long history, as Kelsall demonstrates, tracing the English country house ideal back to its Roman origins, not in working farms, but in villas to which politicians, merchants, and soldiers could retreat and recreate themselves before their next enterprising ventures. "The literature of the country house in the Roman world has its roots in the myth of the original virtuous yeomanry," Kelsall observes. "That literature is written, however, by the citizens of a sophisticated, metropolitan centred, empire" (11).

Hence the English inherit the paradox of the "typical Roman country gentleman" who is a commuter to and from the city, though "the city is not his true home," and "he longs for the virtue of a country life" (13). Following Columella, generations of writers, including Pope, have argued against absentee landlords, a position that presents problems for the ambitious upper gentry and aristocracy, for whom politics is often a necessary concern. Columella's solution is Pope's Twickenham compromise, but also Burlington's (Chiswick Villa) and Bolingbroke's (Dawley Farm, near Uxbridge in Middlesex): "since 'political ambition keeps most of us away from our estates,' it is best to have an estate near town, so that we can visit it every day'" (13).

The rewards of such a commuter-belt compromise are health and intellectual tranquillity for the possessors of these properties. Robert Castell's 1728 translation of Pliny's letters as *The Villas of the Ancients Illustrated,* transposing Pliny simultaneously into an "ancient" and a contemporary Englishman, represents Pliny as writing, "I . . . enjoy a perfect health of mind and body, for I exercise my mind with study, and my body with hunting" (93; quoted in Kelsall 19). Now Pliny was a lawyer during the Emperor Domitian's tyrannical rule—a public servant, but also a man with a specific kind of knowledge, a skilled professional man, not an agriculturally minded country gent, let alone a yeoman farmer.

It is easy, perhaps too easy, for Kelsall to make a connection between Pliny and the studious Englishmen who succeed and, consciously or not, imitate him, whose notion of life in the country is "only remotely, even symbolically, agricultural." For Pliny's tastes, according to Kelsall, "are those of the most sophisticated urban civilisation: books for the library, fine pictures, statuary and bronzes" (19). But what, we might ask, has just happened in this move to catalogue the pleasures of rural retirement entirely in terms of acquisitive connoisseurship? What has become, through a significant, even symptomatic omission, of the life of the body exercised by hunting?

Hunting would seem to be Pliny's one connection to the rural as a way of life organized around reproducing the means of subsistence, his one engagement with practices that could be said to be in some sense agricultural, involving direct ecological intervention and management of the natural world for human satisfaction, however purely symbolic or ritualistic hunting may have become once agriculture has been introduced as the dominant mode of production. But Kelsall will have none of that hunting nonsense because it does not fit his notion of the country house as "the great good place," in Henry James's phrase (40). This formulation by an American visitor typifies for Kelsall the paradox or even contradiction that the ideal signification of the English country house tradition "is originated by, and belongs to, outsiders," by those who do not belong to "the patrician order," the social class which the country house itself ostensibly represents (40). Would it be going too far to say that hunting is the one practice of that patrician order in which the (sub)urban middle-class intellectual is least likely to acquiesce, the one he does not envy, whose rewards he neither covets nor finds imaginable through literary representation?

It is significant that Kelsall does not deal much with another version of the rural tradition in literature, the sporting tradition, from the poetry of William Shenstone and William Somervile, through the fiction of Anthony Trollope and R. S. Surtees and Somerville and Ross, to the memoirs of Siegfried Sassoon. Sassoon's title, *Memoirs of a Fox-Hunting Man,* could serve as title for countless other hunting reminiscences and guides for the novice member of the field that still clutter the bookshelves of many English country residences, large and small, when they haven't found their way into the more or less permanent displays of secondhand bookshops in country towns. If the country house as "the great good place" is largely a literary creation, through which the English reading public is encouraged to identify Englishness and civility with an imaginary, rural, landowning past, then hunting presents something of a difficulty in that textual transmission, just as it presented something of a difficulty for Pope.

The literary line that Kelsall traces from Pliny through Ben Jonson, Pope, and Henry James, to H. G. Wells and new suburban Barratt houses is a line of thinking in which an idea of ancient, rural tradition supports social practices convenient for metropolitan and imperial commerce. For the literary intellectual doing the representing, bookishness and the pleasures of reading, or contemplating beautiful objects and prospects, consume all one's time. For the man of business and public affairs, a bit of blood sport on one's own turf might not be quite so beside the point. And this view can carry up and down the social scale from members of the royal family and the Dukes of Beaufort, with their eponymous pack of hounds, to those rather more common members of the field signified by Surtees's Bloomsbury grocer and Master of Foxhounds, Mr. Jorrocks.

Even Pope, despite his lower-mercantile provenance as the son of a linen merchant, characterized his attraction to the rural in terms much closer to Pliny's than Kelsall can bring himself to recognize. As Maynard Mack shows by devoting several pages of his compendious biography of Pope to hunting and field sports, from the age of sixteen or seventeen Pope took to riding regularly for his health with the elderly Sir William Trumbull, official verderer of Easthamstead Walk in Windsor Forest (*Alexander Pope* 72). Writing to Martha and Teresa Blount from Bathurst's estate at Circencester in October of 1718, just five months before he settled on his Twickenham compromise, Pope represents how lovely everything is in the country, at least partly because hunting on horseback takes up a major portion of the day: "I write an hour or two every morning, then ride out a hunting upon the Downes, eat heartily, talk tender sentiments with Lord B. or draw Plans for Houses and Gardens, open Avenues, cut Glades, plant Firrs, contrive water works, all very fine and beautiful in our own imagination" (Sherburn, *Correspondence* I: 515). The writing, we notice, only occupies "an hour or two"; the hunting takes up most of the day, til that mid- to late-afternoon dinner, during and after which Pope and Bathurst exchange intimate confidences which seem inextricable from fantasies of vast improvements to the estate.

"The outside of a horse is good for the inside of a man." This horsemasters' adage accounts for Pope's good appetite and sanguine temperament, his portrayal of a life lived in fruitful cultivation of the aesthetic impulses through plenty of fresh air and exercise. And this exercise takes place in rural Gloucestershire, a part of the country to this day fashionable for equestrian pursuits, and favored by those who like to spy on the royals and their friends at play. We might notice that Pope's version of "riding out a hunting on the Downes" tells us nothing about the hunting per se. What sort of sport did they have? Either he has no idea, and just went along for the ride, or he does not care to dwell on the events, or he does not wish to write about them to the Blount sisters; we cannot tell. There is also the possibility, of course, that he and Bathurst just went riding, and that Pope, writing a letter to women he wished to impress, added "a hunting" because it sounded poetical, traditional, and suitably countrified. In any of these cases, we have a letter-writing Pope for whom riding is to be unreservedly celebrated, but hunting is muted, whether played down deliberately or rendered indistinct by lack of knowledge and interest on his part. If he goes "riding out a hunting," he hunts to ride, he does not ride to hunt; he is no Mr. Jorrocks, and there is no hound music to be heard.

This silence corroborates other evidence in Pope's oeuvre that he was less than keen on field sports, though he could hardly afford to ignore them, as a modern literary historian and critic like Kelsall can afford to do. It would be hard to discuss certain kinds of text, such as *Windsor-Forest* (1713), for instance, without attending to hunting, fishing, shooting, sex, and death, as T. R. Henn found in his reading of Shakespeare. And throughout that poem there is a tension between celebrating Queen Anne's reign, her enthusiastic pursuit of the chase and vigorous use of the Forest for royal pleasure, and regretting the unfortunate effects of these pleasures on the creatures pursued and killed. As Mack opines, in *Windsor-Forest* field sports are regarded from the point of view of the pathos of the animal victim, but as preferable to war (*Alexander Pope* 73–75). Mack considers the dominant theme of the poem to be the hunter hunted, turning attention to questions of sensibility towards animals as sentient beings. He thus shifts his focus away from the emphases of earlier, more conventionally political readings that sought parallels between William I and his forest law, and William III and his wars abroad, with possible Jacobite parallels to be drawn between the two Williams as conquerors and slaughterers of the innocent (see Wasserman, Erskine-Hill, and Rogers, "The Enamelled Ground").

Mack's reading accords well with the evidence of Pope's contribution to *The Guardian*, No. 61, "Against Barbarity to Animals" (May 21, 1713) in which we find Pope making a plea for animal welfare. Practices such as bear baiting, cockfighting, and the torture or destruction of cats, owls, and frogs are singled out for condemnation as thoughtlessly cruel and barbaric. And Pope has nothing good to say about the huntsman's practice of inviting ladies of quality to slit the throat of a captured stag, whom he describes dramatically as "a helpless, trembling and weeping Creature" (Ault 110). Yet blood sports are not his primary target in the essay, for he goes on immediately to argue that "if our *Sports* are destructive, our *Glottony* is more so, and in a more inhuman Manner" (110). Pope reserves the right to kill animals who are "Mortal or Noxious" to human beings—presumably predators of livestock, including foxes, come into this category—but he concludes with an emphasis upon the need for compassion in the care of domestic animals, particularly when their working lives are over: "there is certainly a Degree of Gratitude owing to those Animals that serve us; as for such as are Mortal or Noxious, we have a Right to destroy them; and for those that are neither of Advantage or Prejudice to us, the common Enjoyment of Life is what I cannot think we ought to deprive them of " (113).

The advice of the essay seems to be along the lines of much modern middle-of-the-road animal welfare discourse, regarding the boundary between human and animal as a permeable one, with sensibility shared on both sides. Yet Pope's discourse never directly attacks anthropocentrism, the philosophical assumption that humans are necessarily superior to and more important than other species. Today's deep ecologists, such as Earth First!'s Dave Foreman, would see this as a real sticking point or limit to Pope's thinking about the animal world. Like the contemporary social ecologist Murray Bookchin, however, Pope stresses that the difference between humans and animals that counts most is humankind's greater power over other species, the human animal's superior technology in relation to non-human animals. "Human beings can play an appallingly destructive role for non-human life-forms, or by the same token, they can play a profoundly constructive role," Bookchin writes. "They can create an ecological society, or they can easily destroy their own tenure on the planet" (Bookchin and Foreman 126). Several consequences follow from this assumption: 1) people should take responsibility for their greater power to intervene in the animal world; 2) the killing of animals should be regarded with suspicion; 3) if one must take an animal's life, let it be done as kindly as possible.

It is not difficult to connect these sentiments with the argument offered in passing in Epistle III of the *Essay on Man* (lines 152–68 and 241–68) that the fall into tyranny and superstition, or what Marx and Engels would call class society, happened with the first killing and eating of meat. Once "Man walk'd with beast, joint tenant of the shade" (152), not needing to murder for either clothing or food (154), but the eventual human consumption of blood has led to human savagery, and now mankind is "Of half that live the butcher and the tomb!" (162). It is not that

Pope makes an explicit case for vegetarianism, but that vegetarianism emerges as an attractive ideal within his philosophy. The gardener takes precedence over the hunter; the suburban connoisseur of exotic vegetables and fruits is morally superior to the countryman, of whatever social standing, who likes his bit of sport and dining on his own game.

Pope's views on hunting thus seem not entirely free from paradox or contradiction, but for that very reason they provide a guide to the distinctly suburban cast of his attitude towards the rural in general. And by understanding that attitude, we might be able to begin to crack the difference between a Timon and a Burlington or a Bathurst, and between a Lord Russel or the Wortley Montagus and a Hugh Bethel or a Colonel Anthony Browne.[1]

Like the suburban view of life, the suburban view of hunting is typically intolerant of passions or pleasures not its own. The suburban intellectual above all fancies himself as thinking broadly and deeply about philosophies for living, based on knowledge derived from books, especially the sort of gentlemanly maxims derivable from antiquity, from men of affairs such as Columella and Pliny. And he fancies that such thinking is precisely what cannot occur in the benighted country, where peasants and peers alike live not to think, but to perform, in mud and muck, unthinking tasks and sometimes bloody rituals. Thus, what distinguishes Hugh Bethel's praise of hunting as an activity stimulating appetite from Lord Russel's devotion to it for the same reason is Bethel's well-articulated attitude, phrased in terms of a philosophy of moderation and Pliny's "perfect health of mind and body":

> Go work, hunt, exercise! (he thus began)
> Then scorn a homely dinner, if you can. (*Sat.* II.ii.11–12)

Alluding in his praise of hunting to a presumably shared background in the gentlemanly classics, Bethel could be described here as a member of what the British press in the 1990s sometimes satirically calls the "chattering classes." The bookish and articulate, who always have something to say about what matters, and whose opinions are taken to be influential with the general public, who are in turn assumed to be too busy eking out a living to have been properly educated or to have formed their own opinions independently: these middle-class chatterers and professional opinion formers represent precisely the category to which Pope himself belongs, and to which he assigns his friend Bethel. And like sensible people, Pope and Bethel figure themselves as moderate, even modestly self-denying in their way of life. Not a luxurious feast but "a homely dinner" is represented as their idea of desirable fare.

Lord Russel, on the other hand, in *The Sixth Epistle of the First Book of Horace Imitated,* cloddishly goes hunting for an appetite, at the mercy of his stomach, devoid of philosophy, and incapable of formulating, let alone delivering, a rationale for his actions:

> With hounds and horns go hunt an Appetite—
> So Russel did, but could not eat at night,
> Call'd happy Dog! the Beggar at his door,
> And envy'd Thirst and Hunger to the poor. (*Ep.* I.vi.114–17)

Spence records the following anecdote, which the Twickenham editors use to gloss this passage about Russel:

> There was a Lord Russell who, by living too luxuriously, had quite spoiled his constitution. He did not love sport, but used to go out with his dogs every day, only to hunt for an appetite. If he felt anything of that, he would cry out, "Oh, I have found it!" turn short round and ride home again, though they were in the midst of the finest chase.—It was this Lord, who when he met a beggar, and was intreated by him to give him something because he was almost famished by hunger, called him "a happy dog!" and envied him too much to relieve him.— P (Spence 291; Butt 633)

The only language of which Russel is capable is thus quite literally body language, and this elicits some strange political effects. Only by attending to the semiotics of the stomach can he give any rationale to his actions, so corporeal has become the object of his desire. Having indulged himself brutishly in excessive gluttony in the past, he now devotes himself single-mindedly to pleasing, or appeasing, his digestion at the expense even of the hunting through which he hopes to recover a sounder, happier stomach. In contrast to that philosophical suburban gent, Bethel, who, when he is not hunting just enough to stay in shape, reads books and has conversations, Russel could stand as the type of backward and uncultivated country gentry who give the country a bad name. And that sort of backwardness can also be condemned by Pope as being insufficiently improving, as far as rural poverty and homelessness are concerned. Russel cannot spare a thought, let alone sympathy or food or money, for the beggar he encounters. He can recognize in the beggar's plight only the paradise lost of real hunger and appetite.

The irony here, of course, is that Russel is too solipsistic an ex-glutton even to be a sportsman. He cannot appreciate the "finest chase," but heads home instead, hoping to enjoy his dinner. In this respect, he is not unlike many other so-called riders to hounds, who, even to this day, having shown up at a meet to see and be seen, may well head home at the earliest opportunity to elaborate euphorically, over food and drink, on what great sport they have (not) had. Might there not be a sense in which Pope's Russel could be read here as a figure of fun precisely because he "has no stomach for" the chase, and goes home nervously, out of self-preservation, just as things are getting exciting? In modern horsey circles, this attitude is still often described as being "windy," or "having the wind up."

The dangers of windiness in another, but related, sense help secure the contrast between Bethel and Russel as rather different exponents of riding to hounds for one's health. Bethel extols controlling one's diet as well as taking exercise, implying that eating too much flesh of any sort spoils the digestion:

> Now hear what blessings Temperance can bring:
> (Thus said our Friend, and what he said I sing.)
> First Health: The stomach (cram'd from ev'ry dish,
> A Tomb of boil'd, and roast, and flesh, and fish,
> Where Bile, and wind, and phlegm, and acid jar,
> And all the Man is one intestine war)
> Remembers oft the School-boy's simple fare,
> The temperate sleeps, and spirits light as air! (*Sat.* II.ii.67–74)

Thus the notoriously meager rations of boarding schools recreate some of the arcadian simplicity of antique cultures extolled by Pope in Epistle III of the *Essay on Man*. Abstemiousness and even vegetarian tendencies provide the sharpest contrast between the thinking and the unthinking, the suburban and the backward rural diets. If you would not be as "windy" as Lord Russel, by implication, avoid gluttony at all costs. Go Russel one better and actually follow hounds. Don't ride home to the dinner table at the first sign of excitement like a booby lord going to his trough. Be temperate in your hunting—no need to invite ladies to engage in bloodthirsty practices like cutting stags' throats. Hunt in moderation. All things in moderation. Hunt foxes; they're noxious. But don't make hunting the sole purpose of your being or social life, for therein lies material for caricature.

If we look at the evidence of sporting art and the discourse about it, this set of attitudes can be confirmed as typical of the mixed views on hunting emerging by the 1730s. According to Stephen Deuchar, in *Sporting Art in Eighteenth-Century England,* by this decade the association of hunting with health and fitness was commonplace (40), but its association with royalty—celebrated by Pope in *Windsor-Forest* in 1713—was beginning to wane. A certain association of hunting with social and political backwardness was taking over. Not the fashionable, but the laughable and unsophisticated, might well comprise the sporting crowd, increasingly figured as drawn from the gentry's lower or at least less-well-educated ranks. Deuchar observes, "Accompanying and perhaps encouraged by the fading royal connection was a perceptible weakening in the class base of sport: rural sports were becoming accessible to more people in reality . . . as well as in theory" (62). From Sir Roger De Coverly's "remarkable enmity towards foxes," lampooned by the *Spectator,* to Defoe's broader ridicule of the backwardness of the landed interest, "They're born, they liv, they laugh, they know not why;/They sleep, eat, drink, get heirs, grow fat, and dye," Deuchar argues, "In sum, 'country squires', in their various guises, were viewed as well-meaning and patriotic but often dimwitted and reactionary opponents of prevailing political and social movements. . . . Thus even sport could now be held up as an example of the very luxury to which, traditionally, it purported to be an antidote" (63, 65).

If we search for a general antidote to luxury in Pope's satires, including an antidote to the kind of social backwardness increasingly associated with hunting and gluttony, it would seem to be, not surprisingly, an aesthetic sense connected with books and print culture generally, especially verse. *The Second Epistle of the Second Book of Horace Imitated* distinguishes its addressee, Colonel Anthony Browne, from the mass of people by his soldierly patriotism and his friendship with Sir Richard Temple, Viscount Cobham, leader of the Opposition Whigs, but also by his liking for poetry:

> Dear Col'nel! Cobham's and your Country's Friend!
> You love a Verse, take such as I can send. (*Ep.* II.ii.1–2)

Some two hundred lines later, the poem distinguishes Browne from Sir Edward Wortley Montagu on the basis that Browne's use of his small leasehold farm is far superior to Wortley's use of his vast freehold:

> If there be truth in Law, and *Use* can give
> A *Property,* that's yours on which you live.
> Delightful *Abs-court,* if its Fields afford
> Their Fruits to you, confesses you its Lord:
> All Worldly's Hens, nay Partridge, sold to town,
> His Ven'son too, a Guinea makes your own:
> He bought at thousands, what with better wit
> You purchase as you want, and bit by bit . . . . (*Ep.* II.ii.230–37)

Pope doesn't hesitate to use one of the oldest pastoral tropes by which a landowner's exploitation of his property's resources may be magically justified. Here, as in Jonson's *To Penshurst,* a poem in which fish leap, eager to be eaten by their lord and master, Abs-court yields up its produce reverently. Although Apps-Court, near Walton-on-Thames, was merely leased to Browne by its owner, Lord Halifax, Browne's use of its "Fruits" constitutes the proper landlordly relation to it.

Again, as with Pope's five acres taken to be exemplary of rural land management, we are confronted with a distinctly suburban prejudice and even the sneaking suspicion that *decent* country living might perhaps only be practicable just outside London. Browne's consuming of his leased farm's produce reveals Wortley's selling of his vast estate's produce, including such presentation gifts from tenants as partridges and venison, as reprehensible. Browne becomes, in effect, the proper representative of the landed interest, and Wortley, by contrast, a mere commercially minded interloper. Indeed, the poem argues, once Wortley has sold his landlordly privileges, his game, to town, Browne can buy and eat those partridges or that venison much more cheaply than Wortley can, if we take account of what Wortley's entire estate has cost, and continues to cost him. Here Pope neatly reverts to the position of canny suburban consumer rather than landed producer. Thus his and, by association, the Colonel's superiority to Wortley extends to their commercial sense and consumer prowess as well as landlordly entitlement.

Yet what has this contrast between Browne and Wortley Montagu to do with aesthetic sensibility, print culture, or poetry? Here we return to a preoccupation of *Satire* II.ii, the contrast between Hugh Bethel and the Wortley Montagus, both Edward and his literary wife, Lady Mary, so often satirized by Pope as Sappho once their friendship had ended acrimoniously in the 1720s. If Bethel, with his call for moderation, steers a properly gentlemanly middle course between excess and abstemiousness, the Wortley Montagus personify frugality gone mad. Their notion of country life consists in a self-congratulatory routine of self-denial, a reveling in meanness that Pope portrays as both smug and squalid. The possession of a title and considerable wealth is no guarantee of aesthetic sensibility in their case, according to Pope; far from it:

> Between Excess and Famine lies a mean,
> Plain, but not sordid, tho' not splendid, clean.
> *Avidien* or his Wife (no Matter which,
> For him you'll call a dog, and her a bitch)
> Sell their presented Partridges, and Fruits,
> And humbly live on rabbits and on roots:
> One half-pint bottle serves them both to dine,
> And is at once their vinegar and wine. (*Sat.* II.ii.47–54)

Alluding to Denham's famous couplet on the Thames in *Coopers Hill*— "Though deep, yet clear, though gentle, yet not dull,/Strong without rage, without o'erflowing full"—Pope appeals to his audience's sense of hard-won Augustan taste and cultivation. So plainly sordid and splendidly unclean are the Wortley Montagus, by contrast with this ideal, that they might as well be a hound couple, not a human one. One should not push this pun too far, however, for in traditional hunting parlance, the term "hound couple" is never taken to mean a doghound and a bitch; it is just a convenient way of counting hounds, and "couple" classes at hound shows are for same-sex pairs.

Thus without actually claiming that they are risible because they live to hunt, like caricatures of the backward hunting gentry—a charge that would be, so far as we know, unfounded in this case—Pope manages to insinuate this very association while being conventionally rude about Lady Mary's temperament. A few lines later we are told outright that the Wortley Montagus have so little idea of how to conduct themselves in a tasteful fashion, and so little sense of hygiene in particular, that they have ceased to belong to polite society. "He knows how to live, who keeps the middle state" (61), and that does not include sparing expense to such an extent that one lives immersed in country filth, overlooking, as do people like the Wortley Montagus, "The musty wine, foul cloth, or greasy glass" (66).

Pope's repertoire of revenge tactics on Lady Mary thus includes maligning her as exemplary of unaesthetic, even by extension illiterate, rusticity. Living humbly on rabbits and root vegetables is about as close to common country practices as Pope deigns to get—and then the mention is a sneer. Who will take seriously a titled woman of letters if she keeps this sort of a table? No praise of traditional frugality here, no romanticization of the simple life or of meager schoolboy fare that is easy on the digestion. Arcadian sentiment has been replaced by a decidedly suburban sense of creature comforts, including the cleanliness that is next to godliness. This is not the only place in Pope's oeuvre or in eighteenth-century poetry of the middle decades in which "the country proper," as opposed to the newly invented countryside, is reviled as a scene of perpetual incontinence. Even the Wortley Montagus are shown to overcome their habitual meanness only when they "sowse the Cabbidge with a bounteous heart" (60).

Thus those who improve the country, who render it picturesque and aesthetically pleasing enough to serve as a place of recreation for civilized folk, in effect reinvent the country to suit themselves. Those whom Pope classifies as belonging to this group recruit their members mainly from the ranks of the professional and commercially successful who also happen to have been born into the landed interest, especially as the two categories of landed capital and other capital become increasingly hard to separate in the course of the century. City money continues to legitimate itself socially by investing in landed estates and marrying into landed families, and Pope's wealthy, titled friends are no slackers when it comes to finance and business ventures. Some of the more forward-looking members of the landed interest, like Sir Robert Walpole's brother-in-law, Viscount Townshend, get involved in the technologizing and commercialization of agriculture in a big way; Pope notices Townshend's promotion of the turnip as an aid to increased agricultural productivity ("All *Townshend's* Turnips," *Ep.* II.ii.273).[2]

But Pope's favorite lords, we might notice, treat their vast estates as he does his five acres at Twickenham, as a scene of perpetual improvement of an aesthetically minded, highly inventive, sometimes downright literary sort (see Martin throughout). This is one thing that links Bolingbroke (Dawley Farm), Burlington (Chiswick Villa), Bathurst (Cirencester Park, Gloucestershire, and Richings Park, Buckinghamshire, near Slough), Cobham (Stowe), and Peterborow (Bevis Mount) as landed proprietors. They improve their estates as if they were suburban gardens, and they read and subsidize the production of verse, sometimes encouraging the verse to be written in the garden, pleased that the garden should be figured in the verse. The list of such memorials to Pope, including Pope's walk at Lord Peterborow's estate, Bevis Mount, Pope's Seat at Cirencester Park, and Pope's bust in the Temple of British Worthies at Stowe, suggests that the owners of these properties were delighted that their gardens and Pope's verse should be closely associated.

Timon, on the other hand, is notoriously not a member of the chattering classes; he collects books only for their valuable bindings, and his sole idea as a property owner is showing off by spending money for the sake of spending money, not with any ulterior design, whether of the *dulce* or *utile* sort. In terms of hospitality and sociability, he is as backward as Lord Russel, though a certain vanity keeps him from actually starving his tenants: "What his hard Heart denies,/His charitable Vanity supplies" (*To Burlington* 171–72). His table disgusts as a monument to luxury and an inducement to vegetarianism: "Is this a dinner? this a Genial room?/ No, 'tis a Temple, and a Hecatomb" (155–56). And this kind of spending, Pope insinuates, can and should be distinguished from the vast sums his wealthy, titled friends, who also *read,* spend on their properties: "I curse such lavish cost, and little skill,/And swear no Day was ever past so ill" (167–68); this from the poet whose ramblings took him from one great house to another year after year, presumably because he could bask in the hospitable skills on offer:

Who then shall grace, or who improve the Soil?
Who plants like BATHURST, or who builds like BOYLE.
'Tis Use alone that sanctifies Expence. (177–79)

In terms of the making of the countryside, that worked-over, highly produced rural space envisaged in Pope's verse, we might notice two other things about Pope's marking of difference between Timon and his own friends. Timon offends by making a display of uselessness, rather than an ornamental use of his land. And he seems to have an insufficiently nationalistic and imperial sense of his role as a large landowner. Even in these discriminations, Pope maintains a tidy, suburban view of the uses to which the rural prospect should be put. Timon sins by making his "parterre a Down" (106), but this is because the resulting parterre is too big, not because the downland should have been preserved in its natural state. Conservation in the age of Pope does not mean preserving wilderness or wetlands, moor or fen. Even the fact that Timon likes a big, empty prospect is suspect. The land should be put to use, as arable or pasture land, and Pope's revenge is to imagine a future in which some subsequent owner ploughs it up, with "the golden Ear" imbrowning the slope and nodding on the parterre, "Deep Harvests" burying all Timon's pride has planned, and "laughing Ceres" reassuming the land (173-76). Similarly, grasslands are for feeding domestic animals, "The milky heifer and deserving steed" (186). And "rising Forests" are not for preserving ecological balance—lending oxygen to the air and providing wildlife habitats—but for making buildings and building ships for his majesty's navy to rule the waves from: "future Buildings, future Navies grow" (187–88).

Applying the terms of Andrew Dobson, who usefully classifies late-twentieth-century attitudes towards ecology by means of shades of green, we could describe Pope's attitude towards the rural here as "light-green" and "'managerial,'" since it assumes that humans remain anthropocentrically in charge of the environment, using the natural world instrumentally for their own purposes (13). Modern "'green'" consumers, who usually embrace this attitude, want to buy ecologically sound products, recycle as much as possible, and maintain their current standards of consumption in a less polluting and wasteful way, frequently take up vegetarianism as the diet of the future and the crucial node of controversy within a general discourse of animal welfare, while occasionally going so far as to espouse animal rights. "Dark-Green" or capital-G "Green" radical attitudes towards ecology, by contrast, presuppose "radical changes" in our relationship with the environment, "and thus in our mode of social and political life" (13). From this "deep ecological" point of view, not "improving" the environment instrumentally for human satisfaction, nor promoting animal rights and vegetarianism, but preserving as much wilderness as possible and eventually attempting to return to gathering and hunting as a mode of production, are the primary aims.

The countryside, for Pope, is all about signs of human cultivation and intervention, human management, if not exploitation, of the environment, though we do not, we notice, hear much about any actual human laborers. The most celebrated worker in *To Burlington* is, not surprisingly, Richard Boyle, Earl of Burlington, who shows up the king himself by out-building and out-improving him. If good works constituted one's right to rule, then Burlington, not George II, ought to be king. According to Pope, Boyle's contributions to architecture through his dissemination of Vitruvian ideas and the superintending of the construction of Westminster Bridge "are Imperial Works, and worthy Kings" (204). Pope's notion of how the nation, like the countryside, ought to be managed, is a matter of identity politics, in this case the politics of proper Englishness, as opposed to foreignness, especially Hanoverian ineptitude. As in the 1730s, so also in the 1990s: back-bench Tory rhetoric remains anti-European and xenophobic.

What emerges most remarkably from reading Pope's satires in the light of recent ecological debates is how certain mid-eighteenth-century materials lend themselves to analysis within late-twentieth-century terms, suggesting that Pope occupies a space within developments in the intellectualizing of the rural with which many of the chattering classes are still continuous, still in touch, or which they have failed to go beyond. That combination of anticruelty to animals, incipient if not thoroughgoing vegetarianism, and uneasiness at blood sports, all based on anthropocentric and anthropomorphic identification and projection, along with that drive to aestheticize and improve the country into an acceptable countryside for a suburbanized intellect to contemplate, all find an origin in Pope's writings.

And this history of town and country, of intellectual and less-than-bookish differences on these matters, continues to exert its effects on contemporary notions of Britishness or, more parochially, Englishness, as recent controversies over blood sports and animal rights amply demonstrate. In terms of modern national identities, chances are that the gardener will take precedence over the hunter; the suburban connoisseur of exotic fruits and vegetables, in the tradition of Pope growing pineapples, broccoli, fennel, and asparagus in his Twickenham garden (Mack, *Alexander Pope* 361), will be seen to be morally superior to the country man, of whatever social standing, who likes his bit of sport and dining on his own game. It would seem that increasing numbers of contemporary Britons identify with the fox, the stag, or the dying pheasant of *Windsor-Forest,* rather than with the sporting gentry and country folk who pursue them. And Pope has contributed something important intellectually both to that sentiment and to the attitude that usually accompanies it, of assuming, from his vantage point of five acres at Twickenham, that he possesses all the necessary knowledge to regulate the countryside as it should be.

## Notes

1. In reading *The Second Epistle of the Second Book of Horace,* I follow the annotations of the Twickenham editors, who think the poem is addressed to Colonel Anthony Browne of Apps-Court, near Walton-on-Thames. In his biography of Pope (680), Maynard Mack takes the poem's addressee to be General James Dormer of Rousham and speculates that Pope may be in 1737 offering an early celebration of Dormer's acquisition of a second colonelcy in 1738. As a friend whom Pope visited regularly on his rambles, and one with an extensive estate and gardens, Dormer is an attractive addressee for my argument, but unfortunately Mack's attribution does not account for the poem's discussion of Apps-court Farm, as do the Twickenham editors when they choose Browne.

2. Townshend's reputation as an agricultural innovator seems to have been somewhat inflated in his own day, a misperception repeated in the work of some early agricultural historians (see Beckett 3–4, 12–18).

## Works Cited

Ault, Norman, ed. *The Prose Works of Alexander Pope.* Vol. I. *The Earlier Works, 1711–1720.* Oxford: Shakespeare Head Press and Basil Blackwell, 1936. New York: Barnes and Noble, 1968.

Beckett, J. V. *The Agricultural Revolution.* Oxford: Basil Blackwell, 1990.

Bookchin, Murray, and Dave Foreman. *Defending the Earth: A Dialogue Between Murray Bookchin and Dave Foreman.* Boston: South End P, 1991.

Brownell, Morris R. "Introduction." *Alexander Pope's Villa: Views of Pope's Villa. Grotto and Garden: A Microcosm of English Landscape.* London: Greater London Council, 1980.

Butt, John, ed. *The Poems of Alexander Pope: A One-Volume Edition of the Twickenham Text with Selected Annotations.* London: Methuen, 1963. Cited as *Poems.*

Castell, Robert. *The Villas of the Ancients Illustrated.* 1728. New York: Garland, 1982.

Deuchar, Stephen. *Sporting Art in Eighteenth-Century England: A Social and Political History.* New Haven and London: Yale UP, 1988.

Dobson, Andrew. *Green Political Thought: An Introduction.* London: Unwin Hyman, 1990.

Erskine-Hill, Howard. "Literature and the Jacobite Cause: Was There a Rhetoric of Jacobitism?" *Ideology and Conspiracy: Aspects of Jacobitism, 1689–1759.* Ed. Eveline Cruickshanks. Edinburgh: John Donald, 1982. 49–69.

Henn, T. R. *The Living Image.* London: Methuen, 1971.

Kelsall, Malcolm. *The Great Good Place: The Country House and English Literature.* New York: Columbia UP, 1993.

Mack, Maynard. *Alexander Pope: A Life.* New Haven: Yale UP, 1985.

———. *The Garden and the City: Retirement and Politics in the Later Poetry of Pope, 1731–1743.* Toronto: U of Toronto P, 1969.

Martin, Peter. *Pursuing Innocent Pleasures: The Gardening World of Alexander Pope.* Hamden, CT: Archon, 1984.

Rogers, Pat. "'The Enamelled Ground': The Language of Heraldry and Natural Description in *Windsor-Forest." Studia Neophilologica* 45 (1973): 356–71.

———. "Pope and the Social Scene." *Writers and Their Background: Alexander Pope.* Ed. Peter Dixon. Athens: Ohio UP, 1975. 101–42.

Sherburn, George, ed. *The Correspondence of Alexander Pope.* 5 vols. Oxford: Clarendon, 1956.

———. *The Early Career of Alexander Pope.* Oxford: Clarendon, 1934.

Spence, Joseph. *Anecdotes, Observations, and Characters, of Books and Men.* Ed. S. W. Singer. London, 1820.

Tucker, Robert C., ed. *The Marx-Engels Reader.* 2nd ed. New York and London: W. W. Norton, 1978.

Turner, James. *The Politics of Landscape: Rural Scenery and Society in English Poetry 1630–1660.* Oxford: Basil Blackwell, 1979.

Wasserman, E. R. *The Subtler Language.* Baltimore: Johns Hopkins UP, 1959.

Williams, Raymond. *The Country and the City.* Oxford and New York: Oxford UP, 1973.

# The Critique of Capitalism and the Retreat into Art in Gay's *Beggar's Opera* and Fielding's *Author's Farce*

*J. Douglas Canfield*

When at the end of *The Beggar's Opera* the Player complains to the Beggar that the intended ending of the play will violate the "Taste of the Town" (III.xvi), he sets in motion a reflexive intervention that has profound consequences for the interpretation of not only Gay's masterpiece but at least one of its imitations, Fielding's *Author's Farce*. Both plays present a strident critique of emergent Whig political economy, that is, of incipient capitalism, a critique that masquerades as "mere" or "sheer" entertainment. But the reflexivity of Gay's ending and the reflexivity of Fielding's entire third act force us to reconsider the significance of that which has lulled us into the complacency of comic catharsis.

## I

Gay's seriousness is questionable: everything is undercut so playfully and rapidly that the targets blend and the barbs fuse into a general, seemingly tongue-in-cheek cynicism.
> —Richard Bevis, *English Drama* (1988) 168

A satisfactory account of *The Beggar's Opera* is not to be had from examination of its satiric targets.
> —Robert Hume, "World" (1983) 253

It is a fine thing that the play is still popular, however stupidly it is enjoyed.
> —William Empson, *Some Versions of Pastoral* (1938) 240

*The world is all alike!* That is the final lesson of Gay's satire. . . . We are all cheats, paying lip service to one set of principles and motivated in actual truth by another.
> —Bertrand Bronson, *"The Beggar's Opera"* (1941) 324

[T]he moral problem of the play becomes a political one. For the gang is not just a party, a conspiracy, a set of evil individuals; it is the new system, the mercantile commercial capitalism.
> —Michael Denning, "Beggars and Thieves" (1982) 47

[E]ach member of the audience becomes the potential victim of Gay's satiric critique of the misdemeanours and vices portrayed. The spectator who overlooks the mock-heroic and ironic-satiric artistic principles of *The Beggar's Opera* may indeed have only himself to blame[.]
> —Wolfgang Zach, "Fascination and Scandal" (1988) 227

The morality of *The Beggar's Opera*, labored over by critics with such tedious care, is the morality of comedy, which is designed to laugh us out of our follies and vice.
> —Calhoun Winton, *John Gay* (1993) 127

As these juxtaposed quotations from twentieth-century criticism suggest, critics have had a difficult time sorting out their response to Gay's *Beggar's Opera*. Its enduring entertainment value perennially threatens to obscure or even efface its satiric intent, even among an audience so sharp eyed as professional academics. As Deborah Payne argues in her contribution to this collection of studies, the problem may be inherent in dramatic satire's absence of controlling narrative voice. But whatever the cause, Empson's puckish comment seems to imply that the play contains a satiric intentionality within its very medium that seduces the smart into the gullibility of the stupid, that involves even the critic in complicity with the complacency engendered by the fun of the form. Nevertheless, to my mind the best critics of the play—from Empson himself to Bronson and more recently to Kramnick and Denning[1]—have insisted that it is about something as serious as human bestiality and corruption in general and capitalism's evil potential in particular.

Audiences over the centuries seem to have fallen in love with Gay's popular airs and burlesque lyrics. Original audiences would especially have enjoyed the contrast between original and parody in music as well as lyrics, an enjoyment now all but lost on modern ears, except perhaps for Air lxvii, based upon the still recognizable "Greensleeves." But part of the fun, of the entertainment, of the very joke is the *cognitive* element, the mind's instantaneous recognition of the contrast between form and content. As I have argued with regard to Boileau's *Le Lutrin*, the effect is not so much to deflate the significance of the content as it is, at the same time, to inflate its significance by apparently trivializing what is not trivial at all.

Audiences over the centuries seem also to have fallen in love with Polly and Macheath. Even after Brecht's sharkish redaction, the American public could in the early sixties so delight in Bobby Darrin's rendition of "Mack the Knife" as to send it to the top of the popular music charts. Macheath, like the Restoration rake or the continental Don Juan upon whom he is based, is a figure of enormously attractive sexual energy, and the audience's expectation that the Beggar's intended ending really threatens is the typical Restoration socialization of the rake through marriage to the eminently desirable heroine. Macheath is similar to Etherege's Dorimant: he plights his troth to any woman he desires; such trothplight is the price of admission. He says of the Lucy he has impregnated, "But I promis'd the Wench Marriage.—What signifies a Promise to a Woman? Does not Man in Marriage itself promise a hundred things that he never means to perform? Do all we can, Women will believe us; for they look upon a Promise as an Excuse for following their own Inclinations" (II.viii). Like Etherege's Mrs. Loveit, Lucy upbraids the "*perjur'd* " Macheath for laying on her a "load of Infamy," and he, in typical rakish fashion, insists that he is her "Husband" in all but the "Form," for "From a Man of Honour, his Word is as good as his Bond" (II.ix). Yet we have already heard his acknowledgment that such rhetoric is merely performative,[2] and we have earlier heard him expound on his Libertine ethic: "I love the Sex. And a Man who loves Money, might as well be contented with one Guinea, as I with one Woman" (II.iii). Macheath and Lucy sneak off to find an "Ordinary" that she might "try" if he "will be as good as" his "Word" (II.ix)—a word we know he has already plighted to Polly. Perhaps nothing in the play is so delightful as this mock-Alexander besieged by both "wives," especially in the wonderful duet between them, "*I'm bubbled*" (II.xiii). Part of the joke, however, is on the (male) audience for bonding in complicity with the rake and his fundamental misogyny.[3]

This audience expects the typical curve of Restoration comedy: that the sowing of wild oats by the attractive youth shall be forgiven and that he, like Dorimant or Aphra Behn's Willmore, shall be socialized into monogamy at last, no longer a threat to patriarchal, patrilineal genealogy—no longer a threat to *our* wives and daughters.[4] So the Player speaks for us when he interrupts the impending tragic catastrophe, begging the Beggar for the catastrophe of romance, that comic closure that puts the world back together in a way that appeases anxiety. The "Taste of the Town" is not just the decadent desire of the beau monde; it is *our* desire for "absurdly" (the Beggar's own word, III.xvi) bringing things about in wish-fulfillment. Like Polly, we have been reading too many of those "cursed Play-books" (I.x). As she says to the protesting Macheath, "I have no Reason to doubt you, for I find in the Romance you lent me, none of the great Heroes were ever false in Love" (I.xiii). So the Beggar gives us our sop and reprieves Macheath from the gallows of poetical justice that he may publicly "take" Polly "for mine" as a dancing partner while privately assuring her, "And for Life, you Slut,—for we were really marry'd.—As for the rest.—But at present keep your own Secret" (III.xvii). Now we know why Gay, at least, if not the Beggar who had another ending in mind, portrayed the apparently gratuitous detail of Macheath and Lucy missing the ordinary and therefore the benefit of fulfilling Macheath's promised word: Macheath is married only to Polly, and they are going to live happily ever after.

And if you believe that, I've got some ocean-front property for you down in Arizona. By reflexively calling attention to the wish-fulfillment quality of the new ending, Gay undercuts it. Moreover, he has Macheath conclude the opera with an aria that celebrates *"Inconstancy"* and promises those with whom he is not dancing tonight that *"The Wretch of To-day, may be happy Tomorrow"* (III.xvii). Gay's reflexivity here forces a reinterpretation of the entire play, a realization that it has appealed to certain expectations obscuring what has been happening all along. Art has been a trickster and sold us pairs of dark glasses. We are forced to remember that Macheath has left himself vulnerable to capture twice in the play precisely because he couldn't keep his codpiece tied. Surrounded as he is at the end by six wives and several bastards, he is not a convincing candidate for reformation. Lucy has uttered the wisdom of the love-plot of the play: "Love is so very whimsical in both Sexes, that it is impossible to be lasting.—But my Heart is particular, and contradicts my own Observation" (III.viii). We are all caught between desire and reality.

We want to believe that Macheath and Polly are special,[5] but when Lucy says, "The Coquets of both Sexes are Self-Lovers, and that is a Love no other whatever can dispossess" (III.viii), we are sent scurrying back through the text to Jenny Diver's comment to Macheath that it is his own "Choice" not her lack of fondness that causes the diminishing of their relationship, a choice that her romantic fiction predicts will "determine" him, put an end to his inconstancy (II.iv), an ending even our vicarious intervention in endings never allows us to witness. Moreover, we are forced to interpret Jenny's comment in the light of her calculated action to help Peachum terminate Macheath. We are sent back to Macheath's assertion that women who are apparently seduced by false promises are really only following their inclinations, glazed by rhetoric. What is worst of all, given our desire to interpret Polly as at least one innocent in this dog-eat-dog world, the reflexivity of the ending causes us to suspect that this desire is also a self-deluding wish-fulfillment. We are sent back to Polly's statement to her father, a statement the implications of which we have been trying to ignore: "I know as well as any of the fine Ladies how to make the most of my self and of my Man too. A Woman knows how to be mercenary, though she hath never been in a Court or at an Assembly. We have it in our Natures, Papa" (I.vii). Is her apparent innocence in all else just another of the pleasing fictions of the play?[6] But if we have to conclude that sexual relations are self-interested, surely Macheath's code of honor, his aristocratic generosity, his and his gang's project for the Robin Hood–like redistribution of wealth, surely these values transcend the world of self-interest. Indeed, critics as well as audiences have tried to make them heroes (Empson; Armens ch. 2). But then why did Gay include another apparently gratuitous detail? Since Peachum and Lockit know from Diana Trapes where Macheath is and therefore can have him apprehended and impeached themselves, why have Macheath say, "That *Jemmy Twitcher* should peach me, I own surpriz'd me"? He himself reads the lesson that, despite all their posturing as men of honor and trust and courage and stoic philosophy and their own brand of social morality, "'Tis a plain Proof that the World is all alike, and that even our Gang can no more trust one another than other People" (III.xiv). And Macheath himself is no exception: he too is a troth-breaking predator, and his boasted courage comes out of a bottle. As Bronson especially has demonstrated, despite our desire, there really are no moral differences in the world of the play. And as Kramnick has argued (227–29), the old feudal, aristocratic value of mutual trust has yielded entirely to the "mutual Interest" enunciated by Peachum and Lockit (II.x), a mutual interest that, despite all the talk of credit and reputation, is at base no more than enlightened self-interest. Lockit articulates to Lucy the fundamental principle: "If you would not be look'd upon as a Fool, you should never do any thing but upon the Foot of Interest. Those that act otherwise are their own Bubbles" (III.i). Despite all their rhetoric, Macheath and his gang are motivated by this principle, as, despite their ladylike pretensions, are all the whores. And, of course, the major satirical implication of the play is that, despite all their pretensions, so are the government, the clergy, the lawyers, the merchants—all of British society, all of the bourgeois audiences of the play.[7] But Gay's satire is not some vague, humanistic diatribe against human nature, as most of even those critics who view Gay's play as satiric treat it. The repeated metaphors of being *bubbled* or *hanged* subtly remind us that *The Beggar's Opera* takes place at the end of a decade marked by the first great stock market crash, the South Sea Bubble, and by the passage of the Black Act, the first great legitimation of the bourgeois notion of crimes—especially capital crimes—against property (see Denning and also Thompson). The play is specifically a satire against the new system that has taken over Gay's world: incipient capitalism. Kramnick interprets the gang of thieves as a nostalgic allegory for a gentry that has been rendered by the new system irrelevant and anachronistic, and there is a kind of nostalgia in Kramnick's interpretation that is characteristic of critics of the period, who tend, despite their own twentieth-century liberalism, to identify with late Stuart Tory ideology. It seems to me that the world-is-all-alike motif will not allow us nostalgically to privilege the supplanted order. But there is perhaps a profounder sense of anachronism in the play than the one Kramnick has identified: Macheath as Cavalier, libertine rake is a living anachronism; he is no longer the Town Wit, the representation of a dominant class such a figure had been in Restoration comedy. The expectations of such comedy themselves are out of place here. Macheath is no match for the real figures of power in the play, Peachum and Lockit. They are the brokers of the new order, an order Gay portrays as brutally predatory—a system he portrays a century before Herbert Spencer as a social Darwinism whose fundamental principle is the unlimited acquisition of wealth by whatever means necessary.

Gay's Underworld is proffered as the mirror image of the new bourgeois Upperworld, an Upperworld we can recognize as essentially still our own. Peachum and Mrs. Trapes are just business people, providing essential services, keeping accounts, analyzing the market, getting rid of inefficient employees, keeping the rest happy—enslaved, of course, by their pimps, fences, and bawds, but minimally happy, like most workers before and even after unions. Lockit is their link to the complicit criminal justice system, a system of selective enforcement, plea-bargaining, minimum security prisons for privileged criminals, presidential co-conspirators who remain nevertheless unindicted, and so on. And Gay portrays money as the key to the entire capitalist system, as Macheath himself acknowledges, for "Money well tim'd, and properly apply'd, will do any thing" (II.xii)—bribe officials, buy offices, control markets and information and education and legislation, and so on *ad infinitum.* Gay's world is the one Foucault describes in *Discipline and Punish* where, in the eighteenth century, "the economy of illegalities was restructured with the development of capitalist society. The illegality of property was separated from the illegality of rights." That is, crimes against property by criminal subgroups were separated from a previously tolerated area of crimes and subjected to "a constant policing" (87). Howbeit displaced into a comic Underworld, Peachum represents the new order of surveillance, one functioning through informers and intended to internalize discipline. Lockit represents a new order of punishment for the masses, one privileging the new masters by creating a new area of tolerance. Foucault writes, "The bourgeoisie was to resume to itself the illegality of rights: the possibility of getting around its own regulations and its own laws"

(87). Crime doesn't pay for the lower, only for the rising middle class and its lawyers.

Thus the Beggar's original ending had nothing to do with imitating divine justice, with punishing Macheath for breaking his word and the others for breaking the law, as some recent editors, appropriating Aubrey Williams, assert (Loughrey and Treadwell 29; cf. Zach). Instead, the Beggar insists, "[I]t would have carried a most excellent Moral. 'Twould have shown that the lower Sort of People have their Vices in a degree as well as the Rich: And that they are punish'd for them" (III.xvi). If Kramnick is right (and I think he is) that Gay's play also represents "gentry discontent, an attack on law and lawyers as agents of the new artificial world brought by finance capitalism" (228), *The Beggar's Opera* portrays a world where the rising middle class is in the historical act of squeezing both lower *and* upper classes out of power, where the master trope of word as bond has been supplanted by a bourgeois master trope of self-reliance (as I have argued in *Word as Bond* in the "Afterword"), the negative side of which is a self-interest that leads not to anarchy but to a system where a tiny percentage of the population succeeds in amassing wealth and devising its own system of self-protection. Lest that moral hit too close to home, the Beggar accedes to our desire for a wish-fulfillment ending, as he has all along yielded to our desire to be entertained rather than vexed. Through humor and song and music and voice—oh, yes, exquisite voice—he has allowed us to retain our bourgeois complacency.

## II

*The Author's Farce* . . . turns out finally to be a good-natured romp. The play's satirical intentions are mild, and ultimately somewhat muddled.

—Ian Donaldson, *The World Turned Upside-Down* (1970) 194

*The Author's Farce* [ends] in a shower of self-consciousness. The play seems to raise serious philosophical questions—about illusion and reality, about the nature of drama and its application as ritual or play, about the making of metaphors for fictional worlds, about how reality is distorted by custom, tradition, and convention, and about how reality refuses to surrender to representation but equally refuses to be divorced from it. But if these issues are raised, they are never really addressed, for Fielding is content to tease us out of thought rather than guide us into it.

—J. Paul Hunter, *Occasional Form* (1975) 55

Fielding, it will appear, protests the conception of literature as a commodity with a marketable value, suggesting that this conception (held in the play by both the bookseller and the theater managers) is a cause for the prevailing literary degeneracy.

—John Loftis, *Comedy and Society* (1959) 40

Murdertext's protestations of the immorality of the puppet show reveal that he has missed its point, for the whole emblematic entertainment is a moral protest against the mercantile ethic whose commercialism has promoted and sustained the very "pleasures of the town" that Murdertext hypocritically claims to despise.

—Valerie Rudolph, "People and Puppets" (1975) 35

Scrappy and cheerful as *The Author's Farce* is, it conveys with zest its author's caustic view of the profession of writing and the state of English culture. . . . But grumpy as Fielding was about Cibber and Drury Lane, the play fairly bubbles with high spirits.

—Robert Hume, *Henry Fielding* (1988) 66

Like Gay's Beggar, Fielding's author, appropriately named Luckless, is impoverished but is determined to make a living by writing. The old aristocratic system of patronage, to which Luckless appeals with no luck, was yielding to a bourgeois system of publish or perish. One might make a living off the receipts of a successful play—if one could produce such a play per year (Hume, *Henry Fielding* 21–28)—or perhaps off such receipts coupled with publication, though the remuneration was not at all commensurate with the artist's labor. As with academic publishing today, authors were alienated from their labor with a vengeance. Like Diana Trapes's whores, as the poet in hell describes it, "authors starve and booksellers grow fat" (III.205): those who produce get no fair market value for their goods, the products of their bodies or their minds; instead, the bawd or the publisher takes the lion's share. Luckless first tries to get an advance from a publisher—a decent advance, one he could live on. But Bookweight protests that the play has not yet been accepted for performance, and like paper money (or perhaps an academic monograph), "A play . . . is of no value before it is accepted, nor indeed when it is, very often" (I.vi.8–9). Perhaps if Luckless had "a great reputation" Bookweight might hazard an advance, a system that, as he acknowledges, works to have plays applauded even against the "senses" of audience and readers (I.vi.38–43), just because of the name of the author (from Cibber to Neil Simon). The real question is who can judge the "value" of a work of art: publisher, producer, actor, audience? Fielding harshly satirizes Marplay and Sparkish, figures for the theater managers Colley Cibber and Robert Wilks, two of the triumvirate at Drury Lane. Luckless reads to them from a tragedy, trying to alter it according to their boorish, ignorant suggestions. When Luckless employs Latin to make a point, Marplay demonstrates his lack of education and therefore, at least according to Fielding's values, his lack of a right to judge: "I don't understand you[r] hard words, sir. But I think it is very hard if a man who has been so long in a trade as I have should not understand the value of his merchandise, should not know what goods will best please the town" (II.i.46–49). An additional point of the exchange is that the two last phrases are not necessarily congruent: the taste of the town is no accurate measure of the value of art either. So Luckless decides to pander to the taste of the town by producing a farce, entitled *The Pleasures of the Town,* performed by puppets and complete with pantomime, dancing, and operatic singing. Yet of course, the author's farce is a parody, a rhapsody of apparent meaninglessness, which at the same time satirizes degenerate British culture from its art to its professions and especially to the consumers that perpetuate the system. Brought to the Court of Nonsense in hell are the bombastic Don Tragedio, the absurd Sir Farcical Comic, the sound-without-sensical Signior Opera, the mute, inglorious Monsieur Pantomime, and the salacious Mrs. Novel. But like Swift's and Pope's satire, Fielding's extends beyond the Smithfield Muses to others who assault the ears of the Town. Dr. Orator is the Televangelist of his time, intoning his incantatory rhetoric, which is powerful enough to convince his audience of contradictory absurdities. Yet Orator does more than preach a meditation upon a fiddlestick; Luckless employs him to satirize the professions from soldier to physician, from usurer (read: banker) to county magistrate, from lawyer to merchant (see his "Chimes of the Times" in III.461ff.). Corruption pervades all the classes:

> The tenant doth the steward nick
> (So low this art we find),
> The steward doth his lordship trick,
> My lord tricks all mankind. (III.532–35)

And the corrupting agent is gold, which "Turns all men into knaves" (III.510).

In other words, like Gay, Fielding, though his focus is on the commodification of art, attacks what Valerie Rudolph calls the commercialism of the mercantile ethic, that is, by extension, the entire system of incipient capitalism, a system Fielding too portrays as fundamentally at odds with traditional Western humanistic values because of inherent materialism and selfishness.[8] It may be that we would characterize the values Fielding at least implicitly supports as patrician, as nostalgically aristocratic and patriarchal, although it could be argued that Fielding really supports a benevolist bourgeois ethic. But the point of the play is not just the classical lesson that money corrupts, but that the new economic system has profoundly corrupted Luckless's world, from art to the general economy. Signior Opera sings an aria in which the traditional man of wisdom, the philosopher, is displaced by the modern "wise man" who knows that "In riches is centered all human delight" (III.360–62).

Again, the satire is not some general humanistic diatribe. Like Juvenal's, Fielding's satire on greed is historically specific: Why attack greed in the middle of the eighteenth century? Because, as with Gay, of a gentrified bias against the ethos of the increasingly dominant bourgeoisie. The point is not that Fielding is right about incipient capitalism in some absolute sense. The developing system had its defenders from Locke to Adam Smith. The point is that Gay and Fielding chose to cast their lot with what Michael McKeon has characterized as the "conservative" position and to attack the "progressive" position in terms of a generalized satire against the perceived evils of an unbridled bourgeois political economy, one whose inherent principle of the unlimited individual acquisition of wealth threatened genteel codes of behavior and the art that supported them.

Again like Gay, Fielding implicates no one more than the members of his audience. When Luckless stages his puppet show at the Haymarket, we are already *in* the Haymarket; we are the audience of both the play and the play-within-the-play whom as Master he repeatedly addresses. And Fielding's reflexivity so turns inside into outside and vice-versa that reality and representation are indistinguishable. The actor Mullart plays Luckless, who plays the puppet master, who repeatedly interrupts his play not only with comments to us but with dialogue (and even disputes) with his characters (e.g., Punch). His characters are actors playing puppets who act like lords and ladies. And his play is interrupted by apparently real people representing the values of the audience. Luckless turns to Charon, who is supposed to be one of his characters, and addresses him not by the actor's name but by the name of the character over whom he ought to have control: "How now, Charon? You are not to enter yet" (III.684). Where does Luckless himself stand? And are *we* merely characters too? Charon introduces a constable and a Presbyterian minister who have come to stifle the play, for "People of quality are not to have their diversions libeled at this rate" (III.694–95). The world is so topsy-turvy that we are led to conclude with Luckless's friend Witmore, "'Sdeath! I have heard sense run down and seen idiotism, downright idiotism triumph so often, that I could almost think of wit and folly as Mr. Hobbes does of moral good and evil, that there are no such things" (II.ix.25–28). By selling out to nonsense in order to survive ("Who would not then rather eat by his nonsense than starve by his wit?" III.9–10), Luckless, despite his satire (for no one in the audience is smart enough to recognize it as anything but high spirits), has contributed to the triumph of the Goddess of Nonsense, who has been declared the "Goddess of Wit" (III.551). Distinctions between not only nonsense and wit but real person and puppet, reality and illusion have collapsed. Fielding's final gesture in the face of this collapse of distinction is his trapdoor ending, his retreat into the fantastical world of romance and wish-fulfillment. Luckless turns out to be the lost Prince of Bantam, who is now King upon his father's death; his landlady's daughter, with whom he is in constant love, turns out to be the Princess of Old Brentford; her mother turns out to be the Queen; and Punch the puppet turns out to be her brother! The couple goes off to live happily ever after in Bantam, and all the characters representing degenerate art will accompany them, "All proper servants for the King of Bantam" (III.860).[9]

Donaldson asserts that "the final rapid sequence of accidents and coincidences does not so much suggest that life is an absurd farce as that life is watched over by a benign providence which will finally set straight all confusions, bringing rewards to the innocent and luck to the luckless" (195). But the Fielding of *The Author's Farce* is not the Fielding (or at least Martin Battestin's and Aubrey Williams's Fielding) of the later novels. The absurd ending of *The Author's Farce* suggests that the only transcendence of the vicious world of capitalism is through escapist fantasy. But, of course, Bantam is utopia: it is both no place and this place at the same time. Brian McCrea is right to point out the absence of Witmore at the end of Fielding's play (62), for wit has become inextricably mixed with nonsense, and no transcendence is possible.

### III

Fielding's reflexivity may teach us reflexively how to read Gay's play better. Fielding satirizes the commodification of art in an emerging capitalist society, a commodification that he himself cannot escape. Perhaps he looked to Pope and hoped he too would become an artistic stockjobber, someone who controlled his own investments. Perhaps, like Luckless and the Beggar, Fielding himself had to sell out and turn to the novel. But the point is that he and Gay succeed in commodifying their art, Gay eminently so. He sold to audiences from his own time down to our own a delicious satire on a system of brutal but efficient production, a satire that reflects back even more deliciously upon its own consumption. And we as critics perpetuate that consumption as we commodify our own products such as this essay and all those quoted at the beginning of each section, many of which are reproduced in some Prentice-Hall or Oxford or Chelsea House enterprise to capitalize upon canonical art. At the same time, even as we applaud Fielding's—and Gay's—plays, we are trammeled up in the consequences, and to fail to understand those consequences finally makes us as anti-intellectual as Gay's Player or Fielding's Marplay or Bookweight. To pretend that the entertainment value of these satires *under-cuts* their satire—an interesting reversal of Bakhtin's *carnivalesque*—is to pretend that such notions as humor, laughter, delight, and entertainment are free from cognitive, political, ideological contamination. And yet what precisely are we laughing at when Gay's thieves imitate their supposed betters or when the high mimetic merges with the low mimetic or when an actor's voice—like Polly's or Orator's—modulates through lyrics which satirize not something so innocuous as human folly but something so vicious as human predation? If *we critics* retreat into the lulling complacencies of art, then, like Witmore, we have no place to stand, we are as inconsequential as the empty breath that is the only reward of Fielding's philosopher. Hume believes that, in contrast to Swiftian or Popean satire, the all-inclusiveness of Gay's satire, including as it does the satirist himself, leaves us no place to stand ("World" 265–69). First of all, I can think of no satirist more adept than Swift at implicating himself in the vice and folly he attacks. Pope may adopt the Hebraic, Miltonic posture of the One Just Man railing against his society, but Swift rarely does. Gay's and Fielding's procedures in these plays seem closer to Swift's. Gay as the Beggar and Fielding as Luckless give the audience its pap and implicate themselves as authors and us as auditors in the satire even as we complacently consume their humorous, delightful products. To paraphrase Pope, wretches outside the theater go homeless or die of starvation while we dine on our aesthetic opiate prepared by these gourmet playwright-chefs. But that there is no soap box of self-righteousness available for us or them to stand on outside the range of satiric attack does not preclude our understanding the satire even as we laugh at it. Indeed, such is the nature of the very complex response to satire. Perhaps our laughter at Mel Brooks's nuns singing about the Inquisition or at Slim Pickens's riding the bomb down to end the world amidst the final chorus of *Dr. Strangelove* or at the suicide song in *M\*A\*S\*H* or at the wholesale absurdity of *Catch-22* is cathartic, a safety valve that enables us to tolerate human inhumanity. But it does not *have* to dull our moral outrage. As critics, we do not *have* to dismiss serious social satire as simple romp. We *can* give a satisfactory account of the satiric targets of these plays. Even if, to paraphrase Pogo, the enemy is us, we have a professional and indeed a moral responsibility not to take refuge in our art, in either formalistic or affective criticism that obfuscates these plays'— and others'—assault upon the evils of capitalism. That we are the employees of corporate-supported private and government-supported public universities in a bourgeois state does not mean we have to be its and their unwitting and/or uncritical agents. The reflexive retreat into art in Gay's and Fielding's plays should warn all of us against being lulled into uncritical complacency—a complacency that is ultimately complicity with the internalized discipline of the controlling system.

## Notes

1. And now Colin Nicholson.
2. For a wonderful discussion of this aspect of the Don Juan figure, see Felman.
3. See my analysis of this relationship in the three best-known versions of the Don Juan story ("Defiance").
4. For a reading of Etherege's *Man of Mode* along these lines, see my *Word as Bond* 104–14.
5. The best treatment of Gay's frustration of this kind of desire is Donaldson's: "Throughout the play Gay keeps suggesting possible exceptions to the general rule of bourgeois possessiveness and self-interest, possible avenues of romantic freedom and escape, possible evidence of a primitive honestry [*sic*]; only regretfully, ironically to dismiss such possibilities, to shut off the avenues and to reject the evidence as we approach more nearly" (165–66).
6. Empson first drew our attention to Polly's duplicity, 229–30.
7. The critics who have best examined this inclusiveness are Donaldson; Bronson; Spacks ch. 6; and Hume, "World."
8. The only gestures we have toward this kind of criticism of Fielding's play remain Loftis's isolated comment quoted at the opening of this section and Rudolph's and Ahern's virtually passing references to an attack upon some vague "mercantile ethic." Coincidentally, however, at the same session of the Samuel Johnson Society of the Northwest in which an earlier version of this paper was delivered (October 1989), Brean Hammond gave a brilliant reading of *The Author's Farce* and Fielding's "cultural politics." Because I went first, Hammond joked that I had just delivered the paper he intended to. Through the vagaries of our racket, merely a later form of the one Fielding satirized, Hammond's argument has achieved priority after all by virtue—and one should ponder the etymological ironies of the term here—of having been previously *published.* I should also note that Jill Campbell has a very provocative paragraph on the politics of gender identity in *The Author's Farce*—part of a larger argument on Fielding's plays in

general (70). And although he does not deal with the sociopolitical implications of Fielding's reflexivity, Albert Rivero is sensitive to it as what he calls the "technique of double satire," a technique supposedly enabling Fielding to make sure his audience cannot miss the satire (ch. 2). Unfortunately, though, to borrow a phrase from Zach, they have only themselves to blame; they obviously still do miss it, delighting in the imitative form itself and anti-intellectually ignoring its import.

9. For provocative readings of the implications of Fielding's reflexivity in the play and particularly its ending, see Rudolph and Ahern. Following their lead, Lewis analyzes the reflexivity as breaking down the barrier between illusion and "reality" (101–6).

## Works Cited

Ahern, Susan K. "The Sense of Nonsense in Fielding's *Author's Farce.*" *Theatre Survey* 23 (1982): 45–54.

Armens, Sven M. *John Gay Social Critic.* New York: King's Crown Press, 1954.

Bevis, Richard W. *English Drama: Restoration and Eighteenth Century, 1660–1789.* Longman Literature in English Series. London: Longman, 1988.

Bronson, Bertrand H. "*The Beggar's Opera.*" 1941. *Restoration Drama: Modern Essays in Criticism.* Ed. John Loftis. New York: Oxford UP, 1966. 298–327.

Campbell, Jill. "'When Men Women Turn': Gender Reversals in Fielding's Plays." *The New Eighteenth Century: Theory, Politics, English Literature.* Ed. Felicity Nussbaum and Laura Brown. New York: Methuen, 1987. 62–83.

Canfield, J. Douglas. "The Classical Treatment of Don Juan in Tirso, Molière, and Mozart: What Cultural Work Does It Perform?" Forthcoming.

———. *Word as Bond in English Literature from the Middle Ages to the Restoration.* Philadelphia: U of Pennsylvania P, 1989.

———. "The Unity of Boileau's *Le Lutrin*: The Counter-Effect of the Mock-Heroic." *Philological Quarterly* 53 (1974): 42-57.

Denning, Michael. "Beggars and Thieves: The Ideology of the Gang." *Literature and History* 8 (1982): 41-55.

Donaldson, Ian. *The World Turned Upside-Down: Comedy from Jonson to Fielding.* Oxford: Clarendon, 1970.

Empson, William. *Some Versions of Pastoral.* 1938. Norfolk, CT: New Directions, 1960.

Felman, Shoshana. *The Literary Speech Act: Don Juan with J. L. Austin, or Seduction in Two Languages.* Trans. Catherine Porter. Ithaca: Cornell UP, 1983.

Fielding, Henry. *The Author's Farce* (Original Version). Ed. Charles B. Woods. Lincoln: Bison-U of Nebraska P, 1969.

Foucault, Michel. *Discipline and Punish: The Birth of the Prison.* Trans. Alan Sheridan. 1977. New York: Viking-Random, 1979.

Gay, John. *The Beggar's Opera. Dramatic Works.* Ed. John Fuller. 2 vols. Oxford: Clarendon, 1983. 2: 1-65.

Hammond, Brean. "*The Author's Farce* and Fielding's Cultural Politics." Paper delivered at the annual meeting of the Samuel Johnson Society of the Northwest, University of Washington, October 1989. Essentially included in Hammond, "Politics and Cultural Politics: The Case of Henry Fielding." *Studies in the Eighteenth Century* 8: Papers Presented at the Eighth David Nichol Smith Memorial Seminar (organized by Clive T. Probyn). Special issue of *Eighteenth-Century Life* n.s. 16.1 (Feb. 1992): 76-93.

Hume, Robert D. *Henry Fielding and the London Theatre 1728-1737.* Oxford: Clarendon, 1988.

————. "'The World is all Alike': Satire in *The Beggar's Opera.*" *The Rakish Stage: Studies in English Drama 1660-1800.* Carbondale: Southern Illinois UP, 1983. 245-69.

Hunter, J. Paul. *Occasional Form: Henry Fielding and the Chains of Circumstance.* Baltimore: Johns Hopkins UP, 1975.

Kramnick, Isaac. *Bolingbroke and His Circle.* Cambridge: Harvard UP, 1968.

Lewis, Peter. *Fielding's Burlesque Drama: Its Place in the Tradition.* Edinburgh: Edinburgh UP, for the University of Durham, 1987.

Loftis, John. *Comedy and Society from Congreve to Fielding.* Stanford Studies in Language and Literature 19. Stanford: Stanford UP, 1959.

Loughrey, Brian, and T. 0. Treadwell, eds. *The Beggar's Opera,* by John Gay. Harmondsworth, England: Penguin, 1986.

McCrea, Brian. *Henry Fielding and the Politics of MidEighteenth-Century England.* Athens: U of Georgia P, 1981.

McKeon, Michael. *The Origins of the English Novel.* Baltimore: Johns Hopkins UP, 1987.

Nicholson, Colin. *Writing and the Rise of Finance: Capital Satires of the Early Eighteenth Century.* Cambridge Studies in Eighteenth-Century English Literature and Thought 21. Ed. Howard Erskine-Hill and John Richetti. Cambridge: Cambridge UP, 1994.

Rivero, Albert J. *The Plays of Henry Fielding: A Critical Study of His Dramatic Career.* Charlottesville: UP of Virginia, 1989.

Rudolph, Valerie C. "People and Puppets: Fielding's Burlesque of the 'Recognition Scene' in *The Author's Farce.*" *Papers on Language and Literature* 11 (1975): 31-38.

Shershow, Scott C. *Puppets and "Popular" Culture.* Ithaca, NY: Cornell UP, 1995.

Spacks, Patricia Meyer. *John Gay.* Twayne's English Authors Series, 22. New York: Twayne, 1965.

Thompson, E. P. *Whigs and Hunters: The Origin of the Black Act.* London: Allen Lane, 1975.

Winton, Calhoun. *John Gay and the London Theatre.* Lexington: UP of Kentucky, 1993.

Zach, Wolfgang. "Fascination and Scandal: On John Gay's *Beggar's Opera* and the Doctrine of Poetic Justice." *Literature and the Art of Creation: Essays and Poems in Honour of A. Norman Jeffares.* Ed. Robert Welch and Suheil Badi Bushrui. Gerrards Cross, Buckinghamshire: Colin Smythe, 1988. 219-37.

# Blocked Observation

## Tautology and Paradox in *The Vanity of Human Wishes*

### Jonathan Lamb

In an essay on modern pedagogy published in 1756 Thomas Sheridan points out that "irreligion, immorality, and corruption are visibly increased, and daily gather new strength" (1). He points out further that satire is useless as a corrective of this ingrained depravity, for "the edge of satyr cannot prevail against men, who cloath themselves with vice, as with an armour; nor will the sting of ridicule be felt by those, who are invulnerable to shame" (3). Writing on a similar theme the following year, John Brown makes the same sad estimate of the times as he attempts to "throw a just Light on the peculiar Causes of our calamitous Situation." But he inserts the same proviso, warning the reader that "he will be mistaken, who expects to find here a Vein of undistinguishing and licentious Satire. To rail at the Times at large, can serve no good Purpose" (14–15). Both writers de-ironize Swift's disqualification of satire as that species of critique most needed when most useless: an exercise which offends no one insofar as it consists of "commonplaces equally new and eloquent" directed indiscriminately at a general public more likely to be flattered than annoyed by them (31).

If vices are daily increasing, and thriving to the detriment of the prosperity as well as the moral health of the nation, why is satire no longer an appropriate remedy? Because the problem is too great; because the inherited methods of broaching it are too threadbare; or because the problem is no longer the problem? Sheridan places his faith not in the end of reformation itself but in the means by which it might possibly (but not necessarily) be accomplished, namely the "amazing strength, and almost boundless power of oratory" (67). For his part, Brown prefers the detailed analysis of the variety of cultural activity, no matter how nearly it tends towards luxury and depravity, to any form of coercion or reproach based on moral absolutes. They both opt for information rather than indignation—information particularized, what is more, for the purposes of rhetoric or of statistical accuracy.

However, they are unable to make this choice without processing cultural information that is now problematic or otiose. They refer here to a generic difficulty in the surveying of society that extends beyond their personal disinclination to use the language of polemical commonplace and of generalized public reproach. It is evidently a difficulty encountered frequently among the writers of the mid-century. In Fielding's *Amelia* (1751) Dr. Harrison, the pillar of moral authority, unwittingly proves the futility of satire by preaching against adultery at a pleasure garden, a task equal to those fruitless discourses enumerated by Swift, such as attacking foppery in Covent Garden, pride at Whitehall, and rapine at the Inns of Court. In his trial run at novelizing the hobbyhorse, *A Political Romance* (1759), Sterne ends up satirizing not the infirmities of church politicians but the habit of reading all allegories as satires—a satire of satire he goes on to improve in *Tristram Shandy* (1759–67). The switch in emphasis involves a revaluation not only of information (now a source of pleasure rather than a trigger for moral interpretation and judgment), but also of the satiric butt, whose peculiarities are not instanced as outrages against the norm, but as singularities indicative of a difference that is in itself interesting. The satirist who wishes to govern general positions by means of commonplace judgments, aiming to disrupt the specialized tastes and pleasures of inoffensive individuals by reference to notional standards of what is just and right is, on the contrary, found tediously malapropos or even obsessive to the point of mental disturbance, as in Smollett's *Peregrine Pickle* (1751). This switch betokens a division in communicative practice that can be variously denominated as the difference between plenary judgment and particular description, between the third-person plural and the first-person singular, between the genre known as satire and new ways of ordering information, generating norms and representing society, such as political arithmetic, the travel story, the journal, the conduct book, or the novel.[1] Each of these alternative genres or discourses needs to establish, to a greater or lesser degree of explicitness, its difference from satire. This is what gives these new departures their edge and power: they recognize themselves in this difference, and they mobilize themselves by elaborating it: "The learned Smelfungus travelled from Boulogne to Paris—from Paris to Rome—and so on—but he set out with the spleen and jaundice, and every object he pass'd by was discolored or distorted—He wrote an account of them, but 'twas nothing but the account of his miserable feelings" (Sterne 116). This is how Sterne's Parson Yorick marks the difference between satiric and sentimental traveling, cultivating in himself and his reader a taste for scenes comprising contingent elements—a hand, a glove, a snuff-box—which draw their point not from the disclosure of hidden vanities and foibles, but from the panache of the arrangement. They are managed by a character whose very name is expressive of the transition from the satiric *vanitas* handled by Hamlet to an alternative system of self-exhibition that has more in common with the epitaph, insofar as it attunes the particulars of existence to an indulgent pathos rather than to warning or blame.

This is one side of the problematization of satire. The other is the contradiction that develops in satire itself as it strives to incorporate these generic anomalies and to neutralize them. Three of the four great Scriblerian satires, *A Tale of Tub, The Art of Sinking in Poetry,* and the *Dunciad,* are impelled by the need to identify and appropriate the irregularities of the sublime before the moderns cite it as a license for experiment. They preemptively occupy a dangerous zone of literary redefinition by parodying the excesses that might disturb the authority of classical standards of imitation, ordonnance, and figuration (Brown 65 and Lamb 110–43). John Barrell and Harriet Guest have examined the contradictions that emerge in the spiritual and economic theodicies of Young and Pope as a result of an illogical desire to instance certain forms of opprobrious behavior as simultaneously necessary and exorbitant to the grand design. Everything which is, in being declared both right and wrong at the same time, tangles up the work of satire with the justification of providence (121–43). This contradiction between the authority of judgment and the authority of explanation leads to a diffidence that surfaces in the work of Samuel Johnson as the impersonation or mockery of sententiousness, symptomatic of an "internal dividedness and self-contestation" that challenges the very form of authority (Bogel 205).

I want to suggest that the authority invested in the narrative voice of Johnson's *Vanity of Human Wishes* is, despite its apparent confidence in fitting modern circumstances to a branch of Roman satire, subject to the same diffidence; and that it upsets the norms which control a neoclassical exercise and destandardizes the observations which are supposed to exemplify them. I want further to suggest that this instability has a generic aspect—namely, the difference between a sinking satiric form and a rising note of complaint whose nearest genre is epitaph. And I want to assimilate the difference to the systems theory of Niklas Luhmann, in order to assess more precisely a mode of discursive uncertainty which seems, in one way or another, to be typical of the mid-century.

*The Vanity of Human Wishes* begins with a gesture of global observational competence: the whole world can be seen and judged; every species of folly and vice is recognizable, classifiable, and risible. Nothing can shock because nothing operates outside the frame defined by the work of a personified Observation, or by the third-person judgments made under the authority of Democritus's name. Insofar as everything is clearly visible, existing in a state of maximum predictability and probability which is universally evident—"All aid the farce, and all thy mirth maintain"—each example of defective behavior is assignable to a rule, such as "love ends with hope" or "rarely reason guides the stubborn choice," that reinforces its self-evidence (67, 79, 11). Although a brief attempt is made to contrast modern depravity with ancient virtue, the verisimilitude of the poem demands a continuity of bad actions and negative judgments beyond the power either of nostalgia or instruction to remedy. The effect of this reinforcement is (like its cause) tautologous: each thing is what it is, undifferentiated by an alternative possibility or by its opposite quality. This circular logic is manifest in Observation itself, whose function is, as Coleridge pointed out, "with extensive observation [to] observe mankind extensively" (I: 292). What Observation observes and performs is the double or infoliate turn of actions governed by personifications, such as Detestation ridding an already indignant wall of what is hanging on it, or Corruption loading already tainted gales, or Fear invading what is already a dire vicissitude.

At the end of the poem, however, little of this tautologous symmetry survives. It is replaced by pleonasms denoting a privation or an excess that Observation can no longer account for. Even the most modest and punctual Christian life is dogged by loss—"Year chases year, decay pursues decay" (I.305)—irreconcilable with the implied moral economy of satire. Life protracted—any life, no matter how good or bad—is protracted woe. The multiplication of like into like produces a series of sharply particularized paradoxes rather than the self-evidence Observation was invoked to reveal. Marlborough weeps with senile fear; Swift is exposed as a driveler: each behaves in manner precisely unlike himself, as opposed to Observation, who maintains consistency by always observing. The excellence which graced or dignified a notable life is exchanged for its very opposite not because bravery or wit require correction, but because of an unappeasable force of difference which supplants tautology ("whatever is, is") with antinomy ("whatever is, is not"). Faced with such paradoxes, even keen-eyed observation is thwarted by "veils of woe" which occlude the sight of private misery, at least in any form which would make it equal to the reflexive densities required by a tautology or a personified agency.

The global consistency of observational competence ceases to be referred to Democritus, the third-person authority, for endorsement; instead, a much more contracted and incomplete view, forced on Observation by intransigent or self-contradictory examples, prompts an urgent second-person query about the adequacy of personified agents ("Where then shall Hope and Fear their objects find?" [I.343]), put to an implied first-person who names its addressee as the "enquirer." The route to this particularization both of the material and the voice of the poem proceeds through a series of instances which disturb the coincidence of observation as a universal image with observation as a set of probable and indisputable judgments upon it. No instance is more disturbing than that of Archbishop Laud's execution, which, developing out of the generalized account of the disappointments of an Oxford scholar, presents a picture so powerfully expressive of the self-valuation of the poetic voice that it breaks its own illusion of imperturbable observation in the process of identifying with it. This has often been noted, ever since Mrs. Piozzi reported Johnson crying as he read out these lines (97n.). But I want to discuss the effect of this identification specifically as a traverse between the extremes of tautology and paradox, resulting in a curiously exploded pun, or what Niklas Luhmann terms an "unfolded tautology."[2]

The identification is most dramatically apparent in the transition made from the scene of Laud's decapitation ("And fatal learning leads him to the block") to the allegory of his tomb, where the personifications of Art and Genius weep. The shift ought to have been controlled by the maxims listed in the opening paragraph of the satire ("Fate wings with every wish th'afflictive dart,/Each gift of nature, and each grace of art" [15–16]), so that Laud's death might be produced as a case perfectly adapted to the rule. But the weeping figures of Art and Genius bespeak an excess of subjective pathos that is not accommodated by the formality either of the satiric project or the imagined funerary sculpture. Suddenly the poet turns to abuse his audience, shifting from the observational proprieties of the third person to a brief but agitated passage between an implied "I" and an outrageous "ye": "But hear his death, ye blockheads, hear and sleep" (I.174). The passionate interjection sacrifices both the impersonality and the assumed success of observational competence for a judgment which not only emphasizes the insensibility of what Swift, under similar provocations, terms the "World's Posteriors" (29), but which also questions the efficacy of the satire, whether it is inflected as a public, mediated, and impassive observation, or as personal and unmediated commination.

The small remainder of the mediation once supplied by Observation and Democritus is located in the two allegorical figures, whose mourning gestures are intended perhaps to dignify and modulate emotions that are threatening to get out of hand. But their eyes, filling blindly with tears, represent a grief which is observationally useless, veiled with woe, and unmoralizable in global terms. In short, they represent the obstructed view of right and wrong responsible for the impatience which the poet now manifests.

Thus far, the poem has moved from the tautology of observational competence to an interruption caused by the unprocessed paradox of fatal learning. Everything may be as it is, but brilliant scholars are wrecked by success, and intellectual eminence means not having a head on your shoulders. The unfolding of the tautology—that is, finding some point of negotiation between "distinctions that do not distinguish" and contradictions that display the absolute difference between capacity and incapacity—depends on the physical specificity of Laud's death and its punned relation to the inattentive audience (Luhmann, *Essays on Self-Reference* 36). The insulting epithet "blockheads" establishes a false or, more precisely, a reverse analogy between the theme of the verse and its readers. The story of a noble head fated to meet the block is met with the blankness of those who have blocks for heads. The grim work of the axe, which leaves only a block where the head should be, allegorizes the dangerous insensibility of those blockheads who authorize and witness such injustice. In its condensed form, then, the tautology unfolds as a maxim of the triumph of the observationally stupid over the observationally acute: "Blockheads block heads."

It is a maxim that identifies the observational failure of the poem precisely as a blockage between the text (including the fatally marked body of Laud) and its readers.[3] This obstruction is elaborated as the carved stone of the tomb, dividing the sculptured ideal readers, veiled by their woe, from the unimprovable fools apostrophized by the poet. The *ressentiment* of the punned apostrophe can be supposed to ventriloquize the tomb's reproach to public insensibility—the cause of the death of the headless scholar whom it commemorates and of the impatience of the voice which now speaks on his behalf—in an energetic version of the conventional "address" of the graveyard inscription to the reader or "viator" which, as in more hostile first-person epitaphs, emerges as a *tu quoque*: "If I have a block for a head, so have you."

The tautology unfolds over a number of differences which, unlike the sheer circularity of the tautology or the absolute contradiction of the paradox, make a difference. It is significant, for example, that the poem acquires polemic energy at the very moment it interrupts itself in this slippage from formal satire to epitaph, discovering in the very genre of funerary verse which Johnson reserved for panegyric an occasion roundly to tell someone off.[4] It achieves contingently the same switch of categories of blame and praise which Swift arranges ironically in the Preface to *A Tale of Tub*; and it does so by virtue of self-reference—by observing the effects of observation—rather than by virtue of competence in discriminating objects within the sphere of observation. In fact, the poet observes the failure of observation, whether it be conceived as the blindness afflicting those ideal readers, Art and Genius, veiled with woe over the bleak truths observation has disclosed, or the somnolence of the mob who are undisturbed by the destruction of clever men. The incompetence of observation comprehends the indifference caused by tautological self-evidence and the agonized immobility prompted by paradox. But the difference between the blockage of the block and the headless scholar is unbridgeable and productive of no outcome, hence the poet's impatience. Likewise there exists between the dumbness of the stupid second-person reader and the silence enjoined on the enquirer at the end of the poem no productive difference. Both are aspects of the same insensibility, whose outward worthiness or triviality is undifferentiated by practical effects. The operative difference lies between this inappetent or immobile response induced by satire's observations, and the passion which refuses the tautological consolation that everything is as it is, and which avoids at the same time the paralysis resulting from exposure to an unintelligible stream of paradoxical privations. As soon as satire is understood to be acquiescent and, to a degree, complicit in the injustices it impassively arrays, the limits of observation are marked by a first-person gesture of impatience with a spectacle that is only *heard* by spectators too dull to *see*. This restriction placed upon sight is all that can be observed; and when it is, satire—if the insult leveled at the blockhead reader may be classed as the residue of the enterprise of imitative satire—arises solely from the impossibility of writing satire successfully.

That the blindness of stupid spectators should reflect that of Art and Genius establishes the ground of a further difference controlled by self-reference. The situation of the poet vis-á-vis the bad readers addressed in the second person is that of *ego* facing its *alter,* rather than a disembodied voice coextensive with the unbounded third-person views of Observation and Democritus. In its *alter, ego* confronts in its most unattractive form its own attempt at unmoved scrutiny of disasters and disappointments, and it responds with a germ of the wrathful wit which informs Johnson's satire of Parnassian theodicy, his review of Soame Jenyns's *A Free Enquiry into the Nature and Origin of Evil* (1757). It locates the blockheadedness of its own enterprise in the dullness of those who see nothing out of the ordinary in the death of an extraordinary man. It anticipates the weakness of "I" and *eye* in "ye," finding in this darkened mirror the image of a rueful companionability which, in a ghostly third-person plural, voices the plaintive doubts that begin the poem's last paragraph. The silence of enquirers and the dumbness of blockheads are set against the eye which does cry, and which is sufficiently actuated by the sense of its difference from indifference noisily to attempt the mercies of the skies.

I want to try now to situate some of these self-observations within Luhmann's systems theory. In the course of the poem the information system of satire breaks down reflexively (that is to say Observation's observation of its own limits results in something like a satire of the failure of satire) until even the informational illusion of tautology is displaced by the message that there is no message which the poem is fit to convey. It comes up against the limit of Observation which, like the earlier interruption, marks a discontinuity between the system and what might be termed its environment: a rupture in what I have referred to previously as the verisimilitude of the poem. In an effort to disguise this discontinuity the last paragraph rides over all objections by insisting that human petition and divine dispensation terminate in happiness at a point in space and time not accessible to the power of representation, but certainly within the power of belief to imagine. Yet in the three cardinal points of probability this is not a credible claim, for it is made in spite of the failure to deal with the incompatibility of different minds, or with the resistance of the audience to the message, or with the failure to act upon the message even if it were understood (Luhmann, *Essays on Self-Reference* 87–88). The improbability of the third-person satire is compounded by the interruption of a personal voice which improbably (to the extent it is unprotected by the norms of the genre to which it objects[5]) draws attention to this improbability.

Unless this discontinuity can be retrieved as a difference or an event within the system, rather than as an implausible attempt to resume the gathering of information in the regions of faith, well beyond the boundaries of observation, the *autopoiesis* of the system of satire will cease. *Autopoiesis* is the system's capacity for self-reproduction, given that it is always governed by its own self-referential logic and never by the dialectic of a relation with its other, or environment. Law is always concerned with law, politics with politics, satire with satire. If autopoiesis is not to be reduced to the zero degree of circling propositions such as "everything which is, is" or "the law is valid because it is valid" (Luhmann, *Political Theory* 191), then it has to insert a difference between the apparent identity of the two parts of the affirmation that allows some room for maneuver and for renovation of the system; but not a difference so great that it merely replaces the vacuity of tautology with the flat contradiction of a paradox. Luhmann's remarks on this topic can be read as a summary of the drama of observation in *The Vanity of Human Wishes*: "An observer can realize self-referential systems are constituted in a paradoxical way. This insight itself, however, makes observation impossible, since it postulates an autopoietic system whose autopoiesis is blocked. . . . Paradox [is transferred] to observation itself." The only way of removing this dilemma is to realize "the necessity of interruption in processes of self-referential constitution" (*Essays on Self-Reference* 39).

This has already been referred to as the unfolding of tautologies, signaled in Johnson's poem by the double action of the pun on blockhead, where the semantic rupture of the circular proposition, "blockheads block

heads," allows the poet to observe the work of observation and to reca-
pitulate self-evidence as insult. He makes what seems to be a spontaneous breach in the probabilities of satiric discourse, precipitating a relationship with his audience of maximum uncertainty and complexity: a
situation, that is, when there are more possibilities to hand than can be
actualized, and where the possibilities can produce unexpected results
(Luhmann, *The Differentiation of Society* 25). Luhmann defines this as a
confrontation between a first and a second person, where resistance, con-
tingency, complexity, and improbability are all at high levels, not unlike
the confrontation imagined between the impatient sufferer and the demanding spectator in Adam Smith's *The Theory of Moral Sentiments*.[6] The
stakes are opportunities for choice that do not exist in unmodified forms
of self-reference: "*Alter* and *ego* face each other in a mode of double contingent selectivity. There is going to be direction and resistance in the
making of selections" (Luhmann, *Essays on Self-Reference* 111).

Uncertainty is eliminated from this unstable encounter only if mutual
recognitions and anticipations create the conditions for reflexive viewing—observing the effects of observations—and rerunning one's own experience as that of the other. "To understand and adopt the perspectives
of others as my possible own ones is possible only if I see others as another I. . . . At the same time, however, I have to concede that the other
person is free to vary his behavior as I am" (Luhmann, *A Sociological Theory
of Law* 26). This scene of primal sympathy dramatizes the differentiation
of identities responsible for unfolding the tautology to which observation, if not observed, limits its instruction. To look at looking is to eye
the other I as part of a scene of mutual views as yet unrealized; it is to
calculate chances and to form expectations based on particulars and contingencies; it is to play blindly for an advantage which will restore on much
more immediate terms the probability of first-person communication.

That these conditions exist and are partly exploited in Johnson's satire, I have tried to show. The reason that the poem fails to renovate more
extensively its system of communication—for example, in the way that
Swift contrives by irony to restore satire in the form of incompetent panegyric in *A Tale of Tub*—is owing to a fundamental discomfort with highly
personal communication. The bloody particulars of Laud's death are sucked
back, like the "patron" of the anonymous scholar, or the drivelings of Swift,
into a generalizing habit of speech to which personification is inseparably
joined, provoking a weakness identified both here and elsewhere by Johnson
specifically as the exclusion from agency. "The employment of allegorical
persons always excites conviction of its own absurdity: they may produce
effects, but cannot conduct actions; when the phantom is put in motion,
it dissolves."[7] That is to say, personification is apt for the description but

not the removal of woes; it is functionally involved in the tautology of identity, making sure that everything which is remains as it is. Although self-reference may seem part of the same infoliation of like with like— observing observations, selecting selections, and so on—it brings along those contingencies (particulars, improbabilities, interruptions, and blockages) which make a difference in favor of power and action, and which set "I" and "you" in a hazardous but imminently eventful relation. Clearly personification has nothing but its universalizing idiom in common with satire, while self-reference has the action and the power which satire needs but which it cannot appropriate without loss of verisimilitude.

Johnson's difficulties in making a choice between the conservatism of folded tautologies and the adventure of unfolded ones are evident in his tendency to associate particularity with violence and first-person communication with combat. In the *ego-alter* confrontations to which he does commit himself there is an excess of negative sentiment, whether considered from the side of arguing for victory, to which he was addicted and to which the roughness of the epithet "blockhead" partly belongs, or whether from the side of the vulnerable first person performing tricks for observers whose extensive view is arranged upon the same principles as the spectators' stands at Tyburn: "We know not how far their sphere of observation may extend. Perhaps now and then a merry being may place himself in such a situation as to enjoy at once all the varieties of an epidemical disease, or amuse his leisure with the tossings and contortions of every possible pain exhibited together" (Johnson 535). As Burke is to point out a few years later, the volatilities and improbabilities of "eye" and "I" contact are not at all mitigated by the fact that "we have a degree of delight, and that no small one, in the real misfortunes and pains of others" (45). Perhaps Johnson saw in the epitaph and its related modes of sympathetic exchange a more dangerous and unpleasant set of possibilities than any that could be provoked by writing formal verse-satire, whose very edgelessness guarantees its innocence in a wicked world.

## Notes

1. On the topic of generic instabilities in prose and verse in the mid-eighteenth century, see McKeon 410 and Sitter 160–72.
2. "There can be two different forms of reflecting upon the identity of a system: tautological and paradoxical forms . . . we might say that society is what it is, or, alternatively, society is what it is not. . . . In a very general sense, systems avoid tautological or paradoxical obstacles to meaningful self-descriptions by 'unfolding' self-reference. That is, the . . . circularity of self-reference is interrupted and

interpreted in a way that cannot—in the last analysis—be accounted for"
(Luhmann, *Essays on Self-Reference* 125).

3. Compare the motto of the last *Rambler* (no. 208), translated from Diogenes
   Laertius: "Be gone, ye blockheads, Heraclitus cries,/And leave my labours to the
   learned and wise;/By wit, by knowledge, studious to be read,/I scorn the multitude, alive or dead."

4. "We find no people acquainted with the use of letters that omitted to grace the
   tombs of their heroes and wise men with panegyrical inscriptions" *An Essay on
   Epitaphs* in *Samuel Johnson* 96.

5. On the improbability of highly personal communication, see Luhmann, *Love As
   Passion* 22.

6. See Luhmann, *The Differentiation of Society* 5, and Smith 9–13, 34–38.

7. *Life of Pope* in *Samuel Johnson* 743. For an excellent discussion of Johnson's
   contribution to the debate about personification and allegory in the eighteenth
   century, see Knapp 62–65.

## Works Cited

Barrell, John, and Harriet Guest. "On the Use of Contradiction: Economics and Morality." *The New Eighteenth Century.* Ed. Felicity Nussbaum and Laura Brown. London:
Methuen, 1987. 121–43.

Bogel, Fredric. "Johnson and the Role of Authority." *The New Eighteenth Century.* 189–
209.

Brown, John. *An Estimate of the Manners and Principles of the Times.* London: L. Davis and
C. Ryemers, 1757.

Brown, Laura. *Alexander Pope.* Oxford: Blackwell, 1985.

Burke, Edmund. *A Philosophical Inquiry.* Ed. J. T. Boulton. Oxford: Blackwell, 1987.

Coleridge, Samuel Taylor. *Lectures 1808–1819 on Literature.* Ed. R. A. Foakes. London:
Routledge and Kegan Paul and Princeton UP, 1987.

Johnson, Samuel. *Samuel Johnson. The Life of Pope,* and *Review of Soame Jenyns.* Ed. Donald
Greene. Oxford: Oxford UP, 1984.

———. *The Vanity of Human Wishes. Samuel Johnson: Poems.* Ed. E. L. McAdam and
George Milne. New Haven: Yale UP, 1964.

Knapp, Steven. *Personification and the Sublime.* Cambridge: Harvard UP, 1985.

Lamb, Jonathan. "The Comic Sublime and Sterne's Fiction." *English Literary History* 48
(1981): 110–43.

Luhmann, Niklas. *Essays on Self-Reference.* New York: Columbia UP, 1990.

———. *The Differentiation of Society.* Trans. Stephen Holmes and Charles Larmore. New
York: Columbia UP, 1982.

———. *Love As Passion.* Trans. Jeremy Gaines and Doris L. Jones. Cambridge: Harvard
UP, 1986.

————. *Political Theory and the Welfare State.* Trans. John Bednarz Jr. Berlin: Walter de Gruyter, 1990.

————. *A Sociological Theory of Law.* Trans. Elizabeth King and Martin Albrow. London: Routledge and Kegan Paul, 1985.

————. *Trust and Power.* Chichester: John Wiley, 1979.

McKeon, Michael. *Origins of the English Novel.* Baltimore: Johns Hopkins UP, 1987.

Sheridan, Thomas. *British Education.* Dublin: George Faulkner, 1756.

Sitter, John. *Literary Loneliness in Mid-Eighteenth Century England.* Ithaca: Cornell UP, 1982.

Smith, Adam. *The Theory of Moral Sentiments.* Ed. D. D. Raphel and A. L. Macfie. Indianapolis: Liberty P, 1982.

Sterne, Laurence. *A Sentimental Journey.* Ed. Gardner D. Stout. Berkeley: U of California P, 1967.

Swift, Jonathan. *A Tale of the Tub.* Ed. Kathleen Williams. London: Dent, 1975.

# Satire and the Bourgeois Subject
# in Frances Burney's *Evelina*

*John Zomchick*

In *The Genius of Sense* David Morris describes a difference between post-modern and neoclassical interpretations of Augustan satire. In postmodern critical practice satire is a self-referential signifying system, liberated from the burden of reference to a world outside the text. In neoclassical practice Augustan satire holds a mirror up to nature in order to make bad men feel pain (237). According to this latter mode of interpretation, satire is tethered to the events of its own time and place, committed to a recognizable referent that will specify in order to expose the timeless yet historically inflected vices and follies of an unchanging human nature. To read the satiric text as the play of signifiers within a closed textual system is to amputate its reach and falsify its matter. The postmodern reader, in other words, inhabits the blind, vicious world that the neoclassical satirist attacks.

This roughly sketched difference between neoclassical and postmodern textuality suggests that their respective readers are relegated to exclusive epistemes, which address each other, if at all, across the unbridged gulf that divides referent from signified. Can there be a postmodern reading of eighteenth-century satire without reducing the satiric text to the mere free play of signification? Conversely, is an "Augustan" reading still possible given the (justified) theoretical suspicion of its claims to a veridical representation of the phenomenal world? In a time when anti-foundationalism denies the premises for a uniformitarian universalist description of virtue and vice, can satire still be read as a true and impartial bill of indictment against social evils? Although answers to these questions may seem irrelevant—in a pluralist interpretive community, a pragmatist might argue, the only impossible readings are those which are not recognized as such rather than those which merely arouse indignation or contempt—they extend beyond literary reception to contemporary cultural debates. In fact, these very questions have themselves generated numerous parodies and some vituperative attacks analogous to the Augustan satirists' responses to their own cultural crisis. Just as the Augustans feared the loss of the classical heritage, today's partisans battle over the right to define a tradition in order either to preserve it from the dissociative forces of postmodernity or to open it up to the transformative potential of those forces.

One way of adjudicating differences in these two approaches is to construe satire's referentiality as a textual strategy, the efficacy of which is located elsewhere than in its intention to reform its objects of attack. In his fine study, *Satiric Inheritance,* Michael Seidel writes that "in satiric invective the urge to reform is literally overwhelmed by the urge to annihilate" (3–4). According to Seidel, underlying satire's corrective referentiality is a perverse, cruel will to power intent on negating the life-world, and finally implicated in the corruption that it attacks (17–19). While I am in general agreement with Seidel's interpretation of satire's negativity, in the following essay I want to suggest that such negativity can be enlisted in the service of ideological construction. In the text that I take as my example—Frances Burney's *Evelina*—satire's moment of negation enables the construction of a unified bourgeois subject, which is gradually freed from the cruel violence found in the public sphere. In other words, satire's effects can be read as formative rather than reformative or destructive, though both reformation and destruction may advance its formative ends.

Before considering the relation between satire's negating function and the novel's productive romance paradigm, however, I want to consider a possible genealogy and method for satire's will to annihilate. As one possible response to moral and cultural incoherence, the satirist negates the degenerate world through a comparison, whether implicit or explicit, of the present corrupt times to a greener, purer, gentler age, strikingly free from the vices that deform the present. In this light the satirical moment of annihilation might be described as dependent upon an always already annihilated past, a romance ideal that exists only as a phantasmatic standard of value according to which the present always falls short, whether it be the Saturnian golden age of Juvenal's Sixth Satire directed against women or the "Boyish, Blushing Time" invoked at the beginning of Charles Churchill's "The Times," a savage attack on homosexual practices in English society:

> The Time hath been, a Boyish, Blushing Time,
> When Modesty was scarcely held a crime,
> When the most Wicked had some touch of grace,
> And trembled to meet Virtue face to face,
>
>         . . .
>
> We, better bred, and than our Sires more wise,
> Such paultry narrowness of soul despise,
> To Virtue ev'ry mean pretence disclaim,
> Lay bare our crimes and glory in our shame. (1–12)

The first lines of Churchill's poem contrast boyish innocence to modern refinement, thereby establishing a value-laden opposition between nature and culture. A return to an age of modesty, however, is foreclosed by corruption, leaving the speaker with little recourse but to rail against the supposed depravity that he witnesses: "Born in such times, nor with that patience curst/Which Saints may boast of, I must speak, or burst" (679–80). The satirist's pain at his belated, untimely birth causes him to search for relief. But whereas the past serves as a standard of value, it cannot serve as a solution to the problem of his pain. His pain is lessened only when he speaks; that is, only when he seeks to inflict pain on those who are by his own admission impervious to all else: "Men, dead to pleasure, as they're dead to grace,/Against the law of Nature set their face" (551–52). But what good does it do to lash those who are incapable of accepting the grace or feeling the pleasure of reform? In the partisan battle between nature and culture, nature has already lost. Thus, debarred from a return to a Golden Age, the speaker advises flight: "Society forswear,/Fly to the desart, and seek shelter there,/Herd with the Brutes . . ." (495–97). The satirist in Churchill's poem responds to sexual corruption by wishing, somewhat impotently, for the removal of the society that serves as its breeding ground but without necessarily providing a fit replacement for that society.

Such negativity cannot stand alone without calling into question the reformative rationale of the satiric enterprise. And so in place of the restoration of a golden age the speaker supplies the restoration of sexual difference. In order to restore sexual difference to an increasingly polymorphous—thus dangerous and disordered—world, the satirist takes it upon himself to negate the negation of that difference through the textual production of his own "Manhood" and its outrageous service to the other. He declares it his intention the "sodomites'" "steps [to] track, nor yield them one retreat" (693). This intention also alleviates the speaker's fears that he has violated the very modesty that he invokes at the opening of his poem. He declares that he writes to serve "Ye Fair": "For You I—nor wish a better plan—/The Cause of Woman is most worthy Man—" (687–88). His Manhood, so bravely expressed, becomes "The Cause of Woman," a fruitful ambiguity that points to the relational nature of normative gender relations. In short, in its negation of the negation of sexual difference, the satire attempts to produce a positive alternative to its will to annihilate the social world that has transformed a phantasmatic absolute difference into a confusing continuum.[1] In this regard, the positive moment of satire acts through a productive absence, upon which rests an absolute sexual difference.

This productive absence of satire, the golden age that serves as an un-impeachable standard of value, is a bit of a scandal for those committed to the modern side in the famous debate between classical and contemporary culture because perfection is always receding like the waters that surround the bound Tantalus. The ideological imperatives associated with an expanding commercial nation demand not a longing backward glance but rather a re-reflection of that backward glance so that it encompasses the present, making presence itself out of satire's productive absence. If the satirist tries to unmake the world as a consequence of the pain of its presence, then the novelist, by contrast, might be seen as a "progressive" wielder of the imagination, the function of which Elaine Scarry defines in the following way: "[I]t is the benign, almost certainly heroic, and in any case absolute intention of all human making to distribute the facts of sentience outward onto the created realm of artifice, and it is only by doing so that men and women are themselves relieved of the privacy and problems of sentience" (288). And here is where satire differs most from the novel, for in satire the problems of sentience threaten to collapse back upon themselves, like the return to chaos in Pope's *Dunciad,* while the novel relies upon the exfoliation and specification of romance conventions to new canons of verisimilitude in order to create a modern utopia despite the prevailing corruptions, thereby also providing for the bourgeois subject a locus of final intelligibility. To satire's vicious (dis)embodiment the courtship novel adds the glorified body of the romance hero and heroine. Furthermore, by incorporating satirical elements into its own textual body, the novel metabolizes those elements by using them to break down or deconstruct the grotesque body and generate another, more continent one in its place. This I take to be the novel's dominant ideological imperative, though to be sure I do not mean to say that the novel is wholly or even predominantly determined by this moment. When I claim an ideological function for the novel, I mean to say only that the new class who writes it and for whom it is written cannot annihilate the social world that it seeks to rule. To the end of representing a new social world in harmony with the aspirations of the new class, the novelist scavenges among residual and emergent practices in order to unmake the corrupt world and recreate a different one for her readers, becoming in the process a kind of Gramscian organic intellectual, working on behalf of an emergent class by articulating, systematizing, and finally embodying its values in the continent and successful hero and heroine.

To return, then, to my original proposition before beginning a reading of Burney's *Evelina*: satire's effects lie elsewhere than in its targets. By annihilating, it seeks to create a certain kind of subjectivity (through negation). And yet this project fails because satire itself fails to create a viable space for the subject to occupy. To do so, it must be novelized, taken over, enlisted in the service of an imperial genre, which claims the right to all that lies before it. Novelization takes many forms. For example, in his early, seminal study of satire and the novel, Ronald Paulson notes that in the "novel of manners," the satirist becomes a character, thus allowing the novel to embody satire's questionable aspects in interested and ultimately blamable agents (284–85). But the form that satire's novelization takes is not as pertinent to the discussion that follows as the effect, for it is satire's negating effects that allow the novel to construct its utopian idyll. My reading is based on the premise that in *Evelina* satirical violence "unmakes" sexual and social relations so that the novel's romance register can create a utopian ideal;[2] that is, Burney must destroy the sexualized world that Evelina creates in her letters in order to prepare her idealized heroine to enter a better world where sexuality is no more a problem than any other natural relation. *Evelina's* satiric agency, however, is embodied neither in the heroine nor in her suitor, but in others— in Captain Mirvan, whose obstreperous violence negates the domestic idyll even as it eliminates a main obstacle to the establishment of that idyll; in Mrs. Selwyn, whose voluble wit disrupts superficial social harmonies (ordered according to masculine prerogative) in order to free the heroine's repressed erotic desires; and finally, in the monkey, who in puncturing the affected human body exposes its inadequacy to the demands of a continent propriety. All in all, however, the marriage between satiric and romance agency is unstable. Tensions among representation (the movement toward mastery of the world) and indignation (the movement toward annihilation of that world) and desire (the movement toward a wish-fulfillment transformation of the conditions of that world) remain, and the restored patriarchal golden age must accept the continued presence and dissonant difference of the cruel agents of its restoration. In arguing that the satirical agents' physical and verbal cruelty makes possible the creation of a sentimental and patriarchal sexuality in the romance characters, I want to suggest that such cruelty is itself expelled from the ideal bourgeois subject through a process of narrative displacement.

As I begin my analysis of scenes from *Evelina,* I want to keep the bourgeois subject (coherent, embodying universal desires) in focus. I will show that within this subject, constituted by the narrative representation of a romantic and sentimental intersubjectivity (embodied primarily in Evelina and Orville), lies hidden an effective cruelty. This cruelty is the scandal of the novel (ultimately not explained by sexism or individualism), visible in a few characters, so that it might be recognized, repudiated, and repressed. It would be mistaken to describe the formation of the bourgeois subject as a product of the simple binary opposition of cruelty and kindness in the text (Tave 17). The reader of *Evelina* is also a subject in formation, and, in the case of this particular formation, the representation of cruel or sadistic elements demands, as Laura Mulvey has argued so perceptively, a story (22). The experience of reading *Evelina* involves a double predication: it is based on giving the reader a sense of mastery over the erotic plot through the heroine's letters and the thrill of power through the cruel—satirical—narratives composed by Captain Mirvan and Mrs. Selwyn. Mastery ultimately depends upon the vicarious experience of being humiliated and then humiliating in turn, an experience that is dispersed across the narrative agents, but which has the final effect of constructing a coherent subject in the reader, who remains blind to self-division, perhaps standing as a homology to the generic divisions of satire and novel.

Before Evelina's arrival in London—before her "Entrance into the World," as the novel's subtitle puts it—there is no indication that the character possesses satiric propensities. The subsequent emergence of this propensity produces the enigma of its genesis: what is its source? If satire can be produced by pain, which it alleviates by reproducing it elsewhere, then in investigating the origin of satire in the character "Evelina" it is reasonable to examine her for evidence of pain. In his discussion of Burney's and Austen's fictional worlds, William Dowling has argued that the capacity to feel shame is a precondition of moral agency (213). If shame can be called a moment of mental pain, then not only moral but also satiric agency may be its consequence. In *Evelina,* the most blatant and cruel satiric incidents occur only after the young writer has already drawn satiric portraits in her letters. Cruelty's belated appearance suggests it is licensed by the earlier satiric portraits, which are drawn by Evelina after her sexual drives cause her to feel the mental pain of shame.

When Evelina refuses to dance with Lovel and then accepts Orville's invitation, the social misstep is variously attributed to ill manners, female inconstancy, heedlessness, and rustic simplicity. While ignorance of convention plays a role in the heroine's transgression of social codes, Evelina's letter describing the events at the ball reveals a sexual cause.[3] In short, Evelina's transgression is nothing less than her discovery of sexual difference, a discovery that deprives her of speech while it is in progress. She writes the following account of her initial interview with Orville to her guardian, Mr. Villars: "He seemed very desirous of entering into conversation with me; but I was seized with such a panic, that I could hardly speak a word. . . . He appeared to be surprised at my terror, which I believe was too apparent: however, he asked no questions, though I fear he must think it very odd; for I did not choose to tell him it was owing

to my never before dancing but with a school-girl" (30). Evelina's terrified, panic-stricken silence at the moment of discovery can be read as an
inverse index of her responsiveness to Orville's interest in her. When she
learns later from Miss Mirvan that Lord Orville seeks her hand for yet
another round of dancing, she seeks the company of Mrs. Mirvan, whom
she calls "mamma" (28). She fails to find her "mamma," however, before
Orville finds her, causing her to feel "ready to sink with shame and distress" (31). A retreat to her "mamma" denied her, Evelina is forced to
confront both her own sexual attraction and her position in the market of
sexual exchange.

While much can be said about the division of shame and indignation
between these two recognitions, I want to focus exclusively on the agency
of sexual shame in the construction of the most remarkable aspect of
*Evelina*: the heroine's powers of satiric observation and representation. In
other words, I want to argue that the satiric register in *Evelina* owes its
presence in part to a patriarchal sex/gender system, to borrow Gayle
Rubin's formulation, in which woman is compelled to occupy the contradictory position of subject and object of erotic negotiations.[4] Such a
contradiction produces shame and rage. In Burney's fiction, furthermore,
this structural determinant of the *feminine* subject is complicated—perhaps
overdetermined—by the text's implicit commitment to the normative bourgeois subject, gendered and sexualized in such a way that it is forbidden the
cruel actions that then come to be displaced onto libidinally peripheral figures
in the text.

That Evelina's initial transgression has more behind it than the violation of a social rule is evident from her disorientation after the encounter
with Orville. And yet Evelina's reaction acquires its meaning only within
the discourse of feminine modesty. With the discovery of romantic attraction to another body has come the discovery of her own sexual nature, itself a scandal according to the codes of decorum of the time.[5] Were
this a pure pastoral, Evelina's initial embarrassment would have been gently relieved by the swain proving himself something both less and more
than a man through his native gentility, as Orville in fact does through
his polished manners. Instead, Evelina finds herself in a carnival world
thronged with bodies, all making claims of one sort or another on her. Thus,
the costs of being called into a gendered body within a patriarchal and bourgeois sex/gender system—the cruel demands placed on Evelina—are in part
deferred and in part dispersed onto fitting objects throughout the narrative:
fashionable mindlessness (which includes certain stereotypical masculinities
and femininities) and mindless desires. It is appropriate that Lovel is the
first body that denies Evelina the opportunity of recovering from her
shame, for not only does his persistent harassment keep alive the effects

of the transgression, but it also foregrounds the social circumstances that make sexual knowledge the problematic element of bourgeois subjectivity. This subjectivity, predicated in part on making the right use of sexual knowledge, demands continual self-policing. Evelina's untutored reaction to Lovel's accusation—laughter—indicates, however, that the social and the sexual are not yet ordered in her own mind. That happens only upon reflection, which comes quickly enough, for she reports that her laughter is succeeded by a consciousness of her "folly," which makes her "ready to die with shame" (33). This is certainly a cruel epiphany for the young heroine. Even if her readiness to die is only a manner of speaking, it indicates an internal war between the individual drive and communal restraints. And as in any war, the actions include observation with intent to harm (Evelina) through the dispatch of troops (satirical agents) against the enemy.

The genesis of the satiric moment in *Evelina* might be described, then, in the following way: first cause of shame (sexual) is displaced by a second cause (social): the first undergoes repression and the second stands responsible for the heroine's shame. The metonymic relation between the sexual and the social has a mutually reinforcing effect on the codes that govern both domains, with the social self standing guard over the promptings of sexual drives, which in turn fuel the indignation against the codes that frustrate the realization of these drives. The repressed sexual content of Evelina's shame, then, is also responsible for the satire that is directed at those codes as well as for the text's more aggressive manifestations of the satiric will-to-power. This critical relation is absolutely determinant of the text's ideological production, for it at once reveals and hides the oscillation between aggression directed at the self and aggression directed at the social world. Because self-directed aggression is ultimately intolerable, it must be redirected to a criticism of the material world in order to prevent the destruction of the beneficiary of satiric practice. In other words, the bourgeois subject of *Evelina* needs both an object and an agent of cruelty in order to preserve itself from the potentially disintegrative effects of shame. When Evelina meets Lord Orville again on the day following the ball, he "grieves" her by giving her the impression that he thinks "ill" of her (37). A headache follows, and Evelina resolves to absent herself from the felicities of that morning's amusement, though it is a passing resolution that she quickly regrets. Evelina's headache and self-imposed seclusion are aggressive acts against a desiring body that has betrayed those desires in the violation of social codes. The aggressive act against the self, because it is an unmaking that threatens to negate the entrance which the narrative is in the process of staging, must be redirected against the civilized world. Satire—the projection of pain outward—becomes a defense against self-unmaking.

Satire in *Evelina* has two manifestations: the ridicule directed at the vulgar pretense of Evelina's relations and the much harsher attacks on the sexually motivated actions of other characters. The performance of the latter, because it touches on the repressed cause of the heroine's shame, is relegated to other agents in the text. The first important surrogate is Captain Mirvan, who, Evelina reports, "will retire to the country, and sink into a *fair-weather chap*" (39). This amphibious creature, who has been seven years at sea, finds nothing in his surroundings to engage him except the destruction of those surroundings. Captain Mirvan's relentless cruelty (taking the form of practical jokes directed at women and men he considers effeminate) is well known to the readers of *Evelina*.[6] In making him a satirist, the text associates a form of cruelty with a caricatured masculinity, one clearly ill-suited to the bourgeois romance idyll and the domestic subjectivity that the novel sets about constructing.[7] Furthermore, missing from Mirvan's character is a history of pain, such as that experienced by Evelina, that might extenuate if not justify his actions. Given such an absence, he stands in the text as an unknowing and unknowable agent of unmaking, intent on disrupting social intercourse no matter what form it takes. In effect, Captain Mirvan represents the nihilist of the text, performing a valuable ideological function even as he delegitimizes the combination of masculinity, cruelty, and satire of which he is made.

In Captain Mirvan, furthermore, the normative sexual subject is absent. It is revealing to compare Mirvan to two other "fathers" in the text: Mr. Villars and Sir John Belmont. Villars is a portrait of sexual continence, though ultimately a sterile one, for his marriage to Mrs. Villars produces no issue and his advice to his charges also fails to generate positive outcomes. At the same time, however, he is doubly implicated in sexual relations because of what might be called his wards' sexual misadventures and because of his intimate connection with Evelina. Sir John Belmont, though a reformed rake when he enters the present dramatic action of the novel, has an involved history of sexual activity. In fact, Belmont's desire is the absent cause of the plot, the real of history that cannot be known except from its effects in the social and individual imaginary. Both Villars and Belmont, then, are sexual subjects in the text, though inadequate ones, producing the complications in the plot that ultimately lead to the romance ending. In this regard they occupy a midpoint between the utopia that the novel must create and the dystopias of London and Bath. Mirvan, on the other hand, although a father, is clearly desexualized. His daughter figures not at all in the reapportionment of the text's sexual energies, and he is a husband in name only. He and his cruelty, though arguably sexual, have no place in the new world. They are made to appear destructive rather than generative and are relegated to a different order of being in order to avoid the appearance of ideological contradiction.

What identifies Mirvan as an agent of textual satire—and thus distinguishes him from a sadistic agent such as Lord Merton or Sir Clement Willoughby—are the objects upon which he practices his satire: namely, Madame Duval and Mr. Lovel.[8] Evelina, the "writer" of this world, is implicated in the satiric attacks insofar as her descriptions of these two characters make them appropriate targets. In other words, the epistolary convention produces both a narrative problem and a startling insight into the construction of the narrating subject. If Evelina herself is to escape the imputation of cruelty—and she must—then her voice must take on as far as possible a reportorial objectivity. And yet this is impossible, for the demands of verisimilitude—which includes an accurate representation of the correspondent's reaction to her world—make it inevitable that such objectivity will be compromised by *reaction* to injury by that world. And so Evelina sets up the objects that Mirvan is called upon to knock down. Burney's practice as a novelist has not yet developed to the point where the plot can serve as a vehicle of punishment.[9] This formal immaturity makes the production of satirical agents all the more necessary even as it reveals the narrative's ideological commitments. In addition to being divided by its satiric and romance registers, the novel is also divided by its diegetic and mimetic moments; the voice of the tale-teller, because she is involved in the tale as it unfolds, cannot risk violating the decorum that awaits her as a destiny by exposing the aggressive cruelty of her own drives. And so Mirvan is summoned from elsewhere, his function to unmake the bodily world that stands between Evelina and her destiny.

Both sexual and social bodies stand between Evelina and her destiny. The first is represented by Madame Duval, who is marked as a sexual being from the moment that she is introduced to the reader not by Evelina but by Mr. Villars. Villars has both the knowledge and the authority to accuse her of being "at once uneducated and unprincipled, ungentle in her temper, and unamiable in her manners." He continues his description of Madame Duval by giving his correspondent Lady Howard some particulars of her history: Duval, who began as a "waiting-girl at a tavern," is beautiful enough to overcome the judgment of Mr. Evelyn, Villars's friend. The subsequent "unhappy marriage" makes Evelyn flee England for France, where he dies in short order (13–14). Everything in Villars's description of Duval marks her as a creature of appetite.[10] Her reappearance in England does nothing to contradict Villars's impression. She has traveled to England with Monsieur Du Bois. Evelina finds it "strange that they should be so constantly together," and must listen to the Captain's suggestion that Du Bois is Duval's "*beau*" (73), which if not true in reality is true in expectation, as Evelina learns when Duval breaks in upon her at the moment when Du Bois is down on his knee professing his devotion to the young heroine (252). Duval is also more consistently associated with the physical body than most of the other characters. "She dresses very gaily, paints very high" (53); after a coach mishap, she appears "entirely covered with mud" (65); and she is associated with money through her insistence that Evelina sue her father for her inheritance (121). That Duval is a fully embodied character suggests that she serves as a displacement for the heroine's unwanted sexual feelings. In terms suggested by Peter Stallybrass and Allon White's study of the emergence of bourgeois culture, Madame Duval is the grotesque body that must be exposed and then expelled from the narrative in order to accommodate the continent body of the rising order (136, 144–47).

No social order succeeds another without struggle and pain. No "unmaking" of the old is possible without violence and cruelty, though revolutions have been called bloodless and emergent classes have claimed their rise to have been harmless and benevolent. Just so in *Evelina*: the vulgar Duval, lacking all the traits that might qualify her for admission to the new order, must be expelled by the satirist's lash. The scene in which Madame Duval is unmade is directed by the Captain and Sir Clement Willoughby, whose sexual designs on Evelina make him a willing accomplice. Acting a robbery, the men take Duval and Evelina from the coach. Evelina describes the consequences suffered by Duval:

> [S]o forlorn, so miserable a figure, I never before saw. Her head-dress had fallen off; her linen was torn; her negligee had not a pin in it; her petticoats she was obliged to hold on; and her shoes were perpetually slipping off. She was covered with dirt, weeds, and filth, and her face was really horrible, for the pomatum and powder from her head, and dust from the road, were quite *pasted* on her skin by her tears, which, with her *rouge,* made so frightful a mixture, that she hardly looked human. (148)

The unmaking of Duval at the hands of the satirist reduces her to a bare and unaccommodated animal, the body deconstructed to its elemental components of dirt and mud. The only mark of culture that is left is the mark of a false culture, which blends with the earthly elements to create a grotesque, nearly monstrous vision. The scene, rife with libidinal excess in Willoughby, Mirvan, and Duval, is a perfect rendition of an attempt to purge by means of a surfeit. And just when the reader expects the violence to have been exhausted, Madame Duval strikes Evelina, who has come to her aid.

The spurious robbery of Duval and Evelina is another instance of the complex interweaving of the sexual and the satirical in order to mark a version of sexuality not only as illicit but also as detrimental to the establishment of an ordered domestic life, including the stable subjectivity that is held out as the foundation for that domestic life. Duval's sexualized body becomes an object of ridicule, to be driven from the world by cruel laughter. Madame Duval herself testifies to the efficacy of laughter in the following revealing statement: "I'd rather be done any thing to than laugh'd at, for, to my mind, it's one or other the disagreeablest thing in the world" (154). To be or to be made a butt of ridicule is to be devalued: one is no longer self-possessed. This form of cruelty, though perhaps not the most injurious act of violation, Madame Duval cannot tolerate. Nor can many others in the narrative.[11] By subjecting Madame Duval to the carnival world of bodily laughter, the text negates her social being.

Captain Mirvan's satirical agency is directed at the disordered sexual body in the form of practical jokes. The other chief satirical agent, Mrs. Selwyn, directs her merciless wit at the false delicacy of the disordered social body that stands between Evelina and her destiny. According to Evelina, Mrs. Selwyn lacks "gentleness" and is "not a favourite with Mr. Villars, who has often been disgusted at her unmerciful propensity to satire" (269). Despite this negative evaluation, Mrs. Selwyn is an efficient agent of the plot, instrumental in moving Evelina to a public acknowledgment both of her feelings for Orville and her wish to be accepted by Sir John Belmont, her father. At the same time, however, Mrs. Selwyn wins no one's affection, with the important exception of Sir Clement Willoughby, the man whose pursuit of Evelina has been fired by a predatory sexual desire. The pairing of Mirvan and Willoughby is here repeated to the same end of casting doubt on the propriety of the satirist in the narrative. In this instance the sexual denial that may be imputed to the spinster-satirist and the sexual indulgence attributable to the rake have no place in the new generative order, whose piety is the mean between utter parsimony and profligacy.

Unlike Captain Mirvan, Mrs. Selwyn takes pleasure in mixing in the society that is the object of her "unmerciful propensity to satire." This distinction also marks the difference between satire aimed at the presocial body and that aimed at the embodied self in society; that is, the objectionable social self must be encountered and deconstructed on its own discursive field. But the satirist's pleasure is itself a mixture of delight in destruction and self-satisfaction at the palpable evidence of her superiority within that field. Her chief antagonist and most worthy opponent is Lord Merton, member of the same status group as Lord Orville and affianced to his sister. Just as Duval must be knocked down in order to create generational difference in genealogical identity, so too Lord Merton must be silenced in order to allow his peer to articulate the true values belonging to their social rank. Selwyn's silencing of Merton effectively cancels his power to master the social world.

Their first encounter begins, appropriately enough, with three men laughing and blocking Selwyn and Evelina's way. Warned by Mrs. Selwyn to clear the path, the men "all chose to laugh" again (273). When one of the men (Lord Merton) recalls that he has met Evelina at the Pantheon in London, he begins to banter her until he is interrupted by Mrs. Selwyn, "who had . . . listened [to the brief exchange] in silent contempt." There ensues a verbal battle between the two. Although Evelina is "rather surprised" by her companion's "severity," she tells Villars that he "will not wonder she [Selwyn] took so fair an opportunity of indulging her humour" (274). By the end of the encounter a frustrated Lord Merton seeks help from one of his companions: "'The devil a word can I speak for that woman' said he, in a low voice; 'do, prithee, Jack, take her in hand'" (276). But Jack refuses, and Merton fails to arrange the desired rendezvous with Evelina. Mrs. Selwyn's wit not only punishes Merton's vanity but it also effectually negates his desire. Can Evelina but be pleased at escaping Merton's harassment, even if the cost is tacitly accepting Mrs. Selwyn's "unmerciful propensity to satire"?

Evelina's understated pleasure at escaping Lord Merton's attentions prepares her for her full investiture in a transformed world. Free herself from this "unmerciful propensity" that she describes so fully, she nonetheless benefits from it. Satire, in other words, appears to work independently of the heroine's will and at one remove from the romance interests in the novel. The satire aimed at the manners of the *beau monde*, furthermore, enables Evelina to acquire the self-possession that she had temporarily lost upon her discovery of sexual difference. If the chief representative of the precious world can be silenced by Selwyn's wit, then the world itself must be nothing but a preposterous vanity. Evelina has confirmation of this world's vanity shortly after her first meeting with Merton:

> Since I, as Mr. Lovel says, am *Nobody,* I seated myself quietly on a window, and not very near to any body: Lord Merton, Mr. Coverley, and Mr. Lovel, severally passed me without notice, and surrounded the chair of Lady Louisa Larpent. I must own, I was rather piqued at the behaviour of Mr. Lovel, as he had formerly known me. It is true, I most sincerely despise his foppery, yet I should be grieved to meet with *contempt* from any body. . . . Yet, all together, I felt extremely uncomfortable in finding myself considered in a light very inferior to the rest of the company. (289)

From shame to detestation and discomfort is a major step toward mastery, an indication that Evelina has nearly succeeded in externalizing the cause of her initial embarrassment. The text has provided her with something substantial to negate.

The cruelty of foppery, disguised in the drawing room, exposes itself in the infamous footrace that is arranged by the men in order to settle a bet. Evelina describes her feelings when she sees the old women who have been enlisted for the race: "I could feel no sensation but that of pity at the sight. However, this was not the general sense of the company, for they no sooner came forward, than they were greeted with a laugh from every beholder, Lord Orville excepted, who looked very grave during the whole transaction" (311). The cruel laughter of the spectators reveals their lack of moral sensibility. At this moment Mrs. Selwyn's propensity to "unmerciful satire" appears positively benevolent in contrast to the emotional and physical brutality of the foppish men. The social world indicts itself, and the verdict on satire, at least for the moment, comes back "not guilty." Such a world deserves to be unmade, but Evelina's and Orville's failure to stop the brutal race indicates that they lack the power to unmake it. Sentimental pity has no effect; only satire's cruelty can unmake the world.

Mrs. Selwyn unmakes the foppish world by continually disrupting the veneer of sociability upon which it is founded. Sir Clement Willoughby, her erstwhile associate, complains that "she keeps alive a perpetual expectation of satire, that spreads a general uneasiness among all who are in her presence; and she talks so much, that even the best things she says, weary the attention" (343). Just as Captain Mirvan's brutality disorders social life, Mrs. Selwyn's wit disrupts empty social rituals. That she also makes Evelina uneasy, however, renders her as unsuitable for the world-in-emergence—the world of bourgeois romance—as it does for the world in the process of dissolution. Furthermore, her excess volubility is one more index of the satirist's incompatibility with the reserved and continent emergent order.

Despite that incompatibility, Mrs. Selwyn helps constitute the new Evelina by finally cutting her off from her childhood dependencies, an action that Evelina experiences as a form of cruelty. Just as she was deprived the comforts of Mrs. Mirvan's protection at the ball in London, so Evelina finds herself forced to shift for herself in Bath:

> How often do I wish, since I am absent from you, that I was under the protection of Mrs. Mirvan! It is true, Mrs. Selwyn is very obliging, and, in every respect, treats me as an equal; but she is contented with behaving well herself, and does not, with a distinguishing politeness, raise and support me with others. Yet I mean not to blame her, for I know she is sincerely my

friend; but the fact is, she is herself so much occupied in conversation, when in company, that she has neither leisure nor thought to attend to the silent. (294)

Selwyn is revealed in this passage as a double agent of historical change, for her self-absorbed indifference to Evelina's fortunes in society accords with the dominant individualism that mandates every person for herself even as her self-absorption violates the codes of feminine decorum. As a requirement of her "entrance," Evelina must experience the humiliation of neglect so that she can discover the necessity of self-assertion, but within the limits of the codes of feminine decorum. This limited self-assertion is also necessary to distinguish the old green world of Villars's Berry Hill from the new one to be ruled by Lord Orville. That old green world had little use for the recognition of sexual difference because it always held out the possibility of a narcissistic retreat. The new one is predicated upon such a difference, and to compensate for the loss of narcissistic pleasures it offers freedom from the cruel impulses that drive both Mirvan and Selwyn.

Mrs. Selwyn, then, forces Evelina to acknowledge her own sexual nature by denying her the pleasures of maternal protection and by "rallying" her about Lord Orville. Having received from Mrs. Selwyn an invitation from Lord Orville for an airing in his carriage, Evelina remarks the messenger's archness and comments that "[t]here is no possibility of escaping her discernment" (324). In the subsequent dialogue between the two women, Evelina feels tormented and then "vexed" (325–26). Still uneasy with her sexual response to Orville—especially after believing that he has betrayed his gentility by writing her a sexually suggestive letter—Evelina experiences Selwyn's discernment as unwarranted cruelty. In order to escape Selwyn's cruelty and her own propensity to self-unmaking (which again takes the form of illness), Evelina must acknowledge her desire. Acknowledging that desire, finally, will free the body from the cruel symptoms that negate it, both subjectively and intersubjectively. Once Evelina accepts both her sexual desire and the desirability that will constitute her as a subject, she will escape her narrative origins as a "Nobody" (35) and her feelings of being a "cypher" (340).

The constitution of the new golden age at the conclusion to *Evelina* requires that the incontinent and the affected be expelled from the new social circle that will form around the romantic couple. According to the argument that I have been making, it would seem likely that the satirists—Mirvan and Selwyn—should also go. In fact, however, these agents of the new class's hegemony are retained because their cruel acts have been useful. Instead, only their victims go: for Mirvan, the text produces

Duval and Lovel; for Mrs. Selwyn, Willoughby and the "innocent" Evelina. Willoughby, whose appetites drive him to lying and forgery, is the first to flee. And he exits in a particularly graceless manner. After an interview with Evelina in which he learns of her approaching marriage to Orville, Willoughby becomes so agitated that he betrays his essentially antisocial nature:

> "I met him flying down stairs, as if pursued by the Furies [Mrs. Selwyn tells the company]; and, far from repeating his compliments, or making any excuse, he did not even answer a question I asked him, but rushed past me, with the rapidity of a thief from a bailiff!"
>
> "I protest," said Mrs. Beaumont, "I can't think what he meant; such rudeness from a man of any family is quite incomprehensible." (360).

As a common thief, Willoughby is figured as the antithesis of the bourgeois subject, who respects property as he respects life. Family too is discredited, even negated, because manners are shown to be not an indefeasible inheritance.

Madame Duval's exit is just as ignominious. Hearing of Evelina's marriage, she writes to tell her granddaughter news of their London acquaintances and then continues with news of a more personal nature: "'However, that's not the worst news; *pardie*, I wish it was! but I've been used like nobody,—for Monsieur Du Bois has had the baseness to go back to France without me'" (398). Used to being the center of attention—and dressing in the way that she thinks will secure that attention—Madame Duval has temporarily become a "nobody" in her own eyes, the unpleasant condition previously experienced by her own granddaughter. One might say, in fact, that her excessive body has been negated. Both Willoughby and Duval, whose sexualities clearly have deviated from bourgeois norms, leave the text without grace and without fulfillment, exiled to a limbo without even a postscript to tell of their futures because, according to the norms that they have ignored, they have no futures.

Lord Orville is the man of the future. By espousing Evelina, he completes her initiation into the world of adult, normative sexuality, an initiation that is accomplished only after the long and painful rites that the young woman has undergone.[12] But his path has been cleared by satire, which inflicts pain, indeed to the very end of the narrative, well beyond a need for it, as a final embodiment of its unruly excess. Captain Mirvan's last satirical practical joke reinforces the link between pain, the unmaking of the social world, and the making of a new world. While much of the Bath circle is assembled at Mrs. Beaumont's residence, Captain Mirvan introduces a monkey into the assembly, "full dressed, and extravagantly *à la mode!*" (400). After pointing out the resemblance between Lovel and the monkey, the Captain baits Lovel in what appears to be an attempt to provoke the fop to violence. Instead of striking the Captain, however, Lovel strikes the monkey with his cane. The monkey retaliates by biting Lovel's ear. The restorer of order is none other than Orville: "Lord Orville: ever humane, generous, and benevolent, . . . seizing the monkey by the collar, made him loosen the ear, and then, with a sudden swing, flung him out of the room, and shut the door" (401). This final generous act by the romance hero has at least two important implications. Because the monkey is said to resemble Lovel, Orville purges the social circle of foppery. But he effects this not as a satirist but as a hero of romance, for his action lacks any hint of cruelty, either toward the monkey or its potential victims. In effect, Orville's action marks the expulsion of violent cruelty, a violence that threatens the ordered relationships that are the essential ideological elements of bourgeois subjectivity.

Orville's action, then, appears to mark the end of the need for the text's satiric agents. And yet, the monkey is introduced after the romance plot has been fulfilled. And Orville's action comes after the satiric monkey has drawn blood, has punctured the body that stands for social affectation, after, that is, the satire has accomplished its aim. Throughout Frances Burney's *Evelina,* then, we can see the way in which satire unmakes and undoes the inhibitors and antagonists of the new bourgeois romance. That Mirvan and Selwyn both escape expulsion, however, suggests that satire and cruelty are reserved a place in this new dispensation, held in reserve, as it were, when new violators or holdovers from the old order threaten its values. Cruel removals are necessary for the flourishing of domestic ideology. What cannot be tolerated is the thought that such cruelty should have a place in the exemplars of that domesticity. The ideal bourgeois subject is represented as being free from the cruel impulse, immune to the satiric itch only because it keeps in reserve agents who do its dirty work and yet do not demand either inclusion in the order or recognition for the services rendered. The vehicle of this subjectivity—the courtship novel—proves that its essential elements of sympathy and benevolence are curiously inefficacious in attaining its end. It is only through the negativity of satire that romance can establish itself. In this relation it is possible to see a homology to the ascendant bourgeois order, for it is through the negation of earlier social and sexual structures of feeling that the bourgeois order establishes itself. But in doing so, it remains blind to that which is carried over, to the cruelty that inheres in its ascendance. For cruelty it substitutes moral judgment, which will always contain an element of mercy. Satiric cruelty, having accomplished its task, like Rochester's wit and whore, like Swift's broomstick, can be kicked out of doors. And yet, satire continues to erupt into the novel, its cruel agency remaining a necessary constituent part of bourgeois subjectivity's idealized misrepresentation.

## Notes

1. For a fascinating study of the emergence of sexual difference over the course of the seventeenth and eighteenth centuries, see Laqueur: "[S]ometime in the eighteenth century, sex as we know it was invented. The reproductive organs went from being paradigmatic sites for displaying hierarchy, resonant through the cosmos, to being the foundation of incommensurable difference" (149).
2. In a perceptive essay on *Evelina,* William Dowling argues that Austen's fiction owes a large debt to Augustan values, especially as they were transmitted by Burney: "For like Burney, like Samuel Johnson, like Pope and Dryden before them, Austen devoted herself to a kind of writing that conceives of literary language as symbolic action meant to work its transformation on a world external to literature, meant, ultimately and ideally, to reconstitute the world as a moral community in its own image" (210).
3. Julia Epstein (98–100) has argued that the letter writer Evelina is actually far more canny—if not downright manipulative—than many readers have given her credit for, suggesting that one must read the text as much for its feigned innocence as for its deliberate representation of inexperience.
4. See Poovey (3–47) and Armstrong (59–95) for the literature on decorum and sexual experience.
5. Epstein has written very informatively about the function of bodies in all of Burney's writings.
6. Ronald Paulson calls him a "Smollettian sea-dog" and a "coarse lout" (285). Margaret Doody reads the practical jokes in the text as manifestations of the masculine will-to-power (56–57). Evelina's commentary—"[She] cannot imagine why the family was so rejoiced at his return. If he had spent his whole life abroad, [she] should have supposed they might rather have been thankful than sorrowful" (38)—guides the reader's reaction to Mirvan.
7. I am thinking, of course, of Lord Orville, who, according to Evelina (whose voice is the only one that matters in this regard), has an androgynous soul even if the rest is clearly marked as masculine. It is worth considering, however, whether the cruelty of satire, driven by some internal pain, does not take the form of jealousy in Orville.
8. Mirvan's attacks on his own family members or young women in general (see 109) should be read as a textual strategy marking him as a character of humors,

perfectly understandable in his irascible prejudices. It might be argued that his humor provides him with a motive, but it still does not provide the reader with an explanation of that motive. If anything, it furthers the textual strategy of ostracizing the Captain because of his manners.

9. Burney's later novels—I'm thinking of Harrel's fate in *Cecilia* and Camilla's misfortunes—are in this regard an advance over *Evelina*.

10. William Dowling sees appetite as *the* drive that causes embarrassment, which makes one capable of moral action in Burney's and Austen's fictional worlds (213).

11. See the scene in which Willoughby visits Evelina while she is staying with Madame Duval in London. Duval succeeds in turning the tables on Willoughby, raising much laughter at his expense and causing him to lose his composure (209–12).

12. It is important to note that the text betrays its own infantile wishes by having Evelina long to return to the arms of Mr. Villars after she is married. That these infantile wishes coexist with a normative erotic object, however, does not materially affect the argument that I am making here.

## Works Cited

Armstrong, Nancy. *Desire and Domestic Fiction: A Political History of the Novel.* New York: Oxford UP, 1987.

Burney, Frances. *Evelina or the History of a Young Lady's Entrance into the World.* Ed. Edward A. Bloom. London: Oxford UP, 1970.

Churchill, Charles. *The Poetical Works of Charles Churchill.* Ed. Douglas Grant. Oxford: Clarendon, 1956.

Doody, Margaret Anne. *Frances Burney: The Life in the Works.* New Brunswick: Rutgers UP, 1988.

Dowling, William C. "Evelina and the Genealogy of Literary Shame." *Eighteenth-Century Life* n.s. 16.3 (1992): 208–20.

Epstein, Julia. *The Iron Pen: Frances Burney and the Politics of Women's Writing.* Madison: U of Wisconsin P, 1989.

Laqueur, Thomas. *Making Sex: Body and Gender from the Greeks to Freud.* Cambridge, MA, and London: Harvard UP, 1990.

Morris, David B. *Alexander Pope: The Genius of Sense.* Cambridge, MA: Harvard UP, 1984.

Mulvey, Laura. "Visual Pleasure and Narrative Cinema." 1975. *Visual and Other Pleasures.* Bloomington and Indianapolis: Indiana UP, 1989. 14–26.

Paulson, Ronald. *Satire and the Novel in Eighteenth-Century England.* New Haven and London: Yale UP, 1967.

Poovey, Mary. *The Proper Lady and the Woman Writer: Ideology as Style in the Works of Mary Wollstonecraft, Mary Shelley, and Jane Austen.* Chicago and London: U of Chicago P, 1984.

Rubin, Gayle. "The Traffic in Women: Notes on the 'Political Economy' of Sex." *Toward an Anthropology of Women.* Ed. Rayna Reiter. New York: Monthly Review P, 1975. 157–210.

Scarry, Elaine. *The Body in Pain: The Making and Unmaking of the World.* New York and Oxford: Oxford UP, 1985.

Seidel, Michael. *Satiric Inheritance: Rabelais to Sterne.* Princeton: Princeton UP, 1979.

Stallybrass, Peter, and Allon White. *The Politics and Poetics of Transgression.* Ithaca: Cornell UP, 1986.

Tave, Stuart M. *The Amiable Humorist: A Study in the Comic Theory of the Eighteenth and Early Nineteenth Centuries.* Chicago: U Chicago P, 1960.

# Goring John Bull

## Maria Edgeworth's Hibernian High Jinks
## versus the Imperialist Imaginary

*Mitzi Myers*

Miss Edgeworth is . . . a little, dark, bearded, sharp, withered, active, laughing, talking, impudent, fearless, outspoken, honest, Whiggish, unchristian, good-tempered, kindly, ultra-Irish body. I like her one day, and damn her to perdition the next. She is a very queer character.

—John Gibson Lockhart, *"Christopher North"* 262

There is no harm, but sometimes a great deal of good done by laughing, especially in Ireland.—Laughing has mended . . . many things that never would have been mended otherwise.

—Maria Edgeworth, *The Rose, Thistle, and Shamrock* 266

We are backward-looking explorers and parody is the central expression of our times.

—Dwight Macdonald, *Parodies* xv

John Gibson Lockhart, Tory man of letters, Sir Walter Scott's son-in-law and long-time editor of the *Quarterly Review,* eventually became a good friend and literary advisor of the Anglo-Irish author Maria Edgeworth (1768–1849) in her later years, but his initial puzzlement about her still offers an entry into Edgeworth's "very queer" positioning in literary history. This essay rereads that location through Edgeworth's own rewritings via postmodern notions of parody and translation, and it argues for her experimental *Essay on Irish Bulls* (1802) as a parodic text that destabilizes the models of gendered authorship, literary genre, national identity, and critical pedophobia which have effected their author's canonical displacement. Edgeworth's fascination with identity as fashioned through language, her playfulness with linguistic codes and systems of representation, her foregrounding of dialogic form and domestic anecdote, and her peculiar mix of the demotic and the allusively learned are signature traits already evident in her adolescent letters. These schoolgirl letters also support a revisionary reading of late-eighteenth-century women writers' relation to linguistic, literary, and generic authorities, which moves from a model of silencing or complicity with oppression to notice their ludic transgressions of cultural borders: the cross-writing that shakes up standard hierarchies privileging masculine over feminine, adult over child, learned universalism over oral particularity, public politics over local knowledge—or English civility over the barbarous Irish and their bulls. Because Edgeworth's own account of her father's role in her writing locates *Bulls* as a prime example of the collaborative process between men's words and the woman writer's literary production, it is proper to conclude this reading of *Bulls* with a homologizing return to the revisionist notion of authorship just sketched.

As an exemplary model of a cross-dressed work juxtaposing multiple identities, nationalities, literary genres, and linguistic systems—and parodically double-coding or translating them—*Bulls* destabilizes sexed writing as well as satiric practice. As a literary term, parody has so long a history and so many familial interrelations that recounting its genealogy would obscure the story that *Bulls* can tell us about women writers and colonial identities. Rather than offer an encyclopedic definition of a specific satiric genre, I aim to align Edgeworth's sociolinguistic practice in *Bulls* with postmodern notions of parody and heteroglossia (as in the work of Mikhail Bakhtin and Linda Hutcheon). Just as "translation" offers a model of reading affiliating gender, Irishness, and collaborative authorship, "parody" names one version of Edgeworth's typical satiric technique of recycling and refunctionalizing her literary fathers.[1]

As soon as she became an established author, Maria Edgeworth received many letters from child readers, like the little boy who did not understand what *Irish Bulls* was all about, but loved the inset story of "Little Dominick," the expatriate Irish lad persecuted by his Welsh schoolmaster for Hibernian linguistic lapses. Edgeworth, who always answers juvenile inquiries with charm and tact, urges him to enjoy what he can and let the rest alone, advice pretty much followed by the odd compendium's subsequent critics. Breeders who ordered the book expecting information on animal husbandry would have been alerted by its satiric epigraph from Juvenal, although commentators still differ on whose oxen are being gored and how.[2]

*Bulls* begins as a pedantic picaresque in search of the Irish bull: it owlishly mocks philosophical definitions, scholarly genealogies, dubious etymologies, learned casuistry, a priori arguments, syllogistic reasoning, associational philosophy, and literary criticism. It cites just about everybody, from canonical cultural figures like Herodotus, Longinus, Locke, Pope, Burke, Steele, Newton, Horace, Milton, Pascal, Shakespeare, Corneille,

Chatham, Addison, Goldsmith, Johnson, Blair, Swift, Walpole, Cervantes, Molière, Voltaire, Marmontel, and Madame de Sévigné to language specialists like James Harris, Robert Lowth, Horne Tooke, and "Hortensius," the author of *Deinology: or, the Union of Reason and Elegance,* whose list of tropes used in training lawyers for public speaking launches the authors into catachresis, hyperbole, oxymoron, and all the other classical figures, which turn out to be simultaneously learned labors and recipes for concocting bulls. Few orthodox sense-making systems go unnoticed—or unlaughed at, for almost everyone, it turns out, and not just the vulgar Irish, makes bulls. Even buildings, signs, and roadside markers can enact "Practical Bulls." Not only are great men's elitist texts crammed with bulls and blunders, but sanctioned accounts of linguistic usage read as if "ancient figures of speech were invented to palliate irish blunders" (220).

Interspersed with this cacophony of allusions and authorities are other voices, who speak a very different idiom, the "illiterate hibernian orators" whose oral dialogues are periodically embedded within the discursive argument (165). Seizing the narrative midway, the racy characters of Irish popular culture run away with the story, culminating in the parable of "The Irish Incognito," a tale within another tale which literalizes the *Essay*'s revisionary argument about who talks bulls and what one sounds like. Between the spoofs of scholars and the loving mimicry of everyday Irish life, the history of English-Irish relations emerges, with special emphasis on the bloody 1798 Rebellion. "Throw[ing] off the mask" (the *Essay*'s learned labors to pin bulls on the Irish), the "friends in disguise" conclude with an ironic and, in its context, heavily political, analysis of the *Essay*'s concerns: who owns history and language and what kinds of representation count (308). Recent theorists identify postmodern obsessions with narrative forms of interpretation and understanding as compensatory responses to multiple assaults on the Eurocentric and patriarchal master narratives of western colonialist history: once hegemonic, logico-deductive models of reason and knowledge now rate as man's truth. Little anecdotes and local knowledges currently rub up against formerly privileged global linguistic and philosophical systems for making sense of the world—and they win.[3] But genre-bending forms featuring parodic juxtapositions and plurivocal voices have a history as well as a contemporary modishness. Aligning *Bulls* with recent parodic paradigms names the weird work's strategies, its jokes about masculinist "big" history, and its homely vignettes of vernacular Irishness, but the intelligibility of Edgeworth's satiric form depends on preexisting cultural and historical conditions, and to these one must turn briefly before discussing how her parodic practices "refunction" Irish bulls and thus intervene in public politics.

The editor of an 1898 reprint of *Bulls* remarks that British library records demonstrate the work's astonishing popularity; almost a century later, references to the Edgeworths' *Essay on Irish Bulls* regularly turn up in studies of everything from colonial relations and Irish culture to genealogies of Hiberno-English and Gaelic comic traditions, from the scholarly account to the cartoon chronicle of pop culture. But *Bulls* is usually mined as a source rather than considered as a literary document with a story to tell about women's writing. More concerned with the efficacy of its arguments than how it works as a text, nineteenth-century readers like Sydney Smith, who surveyed *Bulls* for the *Edinburgh Review* in 1803, and G. R. Nielson, who introduced and expanded the reprint, insist that the book's comic exuberance and verbal excess mark it as a man's work, with the daughter just tagging along for a ride on her "harlequin" father's coattails (Smith 1: 59). They fault the book for its continually deferred definition of a bull—thus missing the heuristic point that one country's bull is another's wit—and seek to supply the lack themselves; and both consider gravely whether the Edgeworths' argument succeeds in absolving the Irish of a stereotypical propensity for making bulls or verbal blunders: probably not, though the authors get high marks for good intent. Smith really does not want to give up the notion of "national characteristics," the popular conceptualization of countries as identifiable entities, as in England's own John Bull, robust, beef-eating, phlegmatic, a character *Bulls* appropriates from John Arbuthnot's allegory and contemporary caricature, exploiting the symbol's instability for its own identity politics (Surel throughout). Nielson argues that the Edgeworths cheat because they ransack every country, author, and epoch for verbal goofs to match against Irish lapses, and after all Ireland is a little island with a small literature. For example, their treatment of the joke book favorite about the Irishman caught in the act of spying caps a supposedly native bull with several foreign sources or parallels: when the letter writer tells his correspondent about the Irishman "reading over my shoulder," the culprit bursts out, "You lie," revealing himself as stereotypically mendacious and stupid (*Bulls* 29). Racial jests, the Edgeworths rightly note, shift "as it suits the demand and fashion of the day," the formerly French turning Irish or Polish, yet a bull isn't just any old Irish or "stupid native" joke (238).

Smith, a renowned wit, finally corrals wayward bulls within an abstract and unhelpful definition which, like Coleridge's later efforts, says more about the patriarchal attitudes that *Irish Bulls* parodically deconstructs than the beasts in question. The reverse of wit, which discovers real relations that are not apparent, Smith's bull is an "apparent congruity, and real incongruity, of ideas, suddenly discovered" (1: 60). We enjoy bulls because they foster a "sense of superiority": "[I]t is seldom that a man of sense and education finds any form of words by which he is conscious that he might have been deceived into a bull" (1: 60, 62). Although he has entirely missed the book's point that men of "sense and education" make bulls every day, Smith's definition is pretty close to the *OED*'s "self-contradictory proposition . . . an expression containing a manifest contradiction in terms or involving a ludicrous inconsistency unperceived by the speaker." Most collectors of bulls, including the Edgeworths, find native bulls much less naive than the *OED*; indeed, as we shall see, the subversive duplicity which bulls encode makes them a double-edged weapon in colonialist—and gendered—rhetoric and riposte. Smith's hegemonical stance is also similar to the *Biographia Literaria*'s union of "two incompatible thoughts, with the *sensation,* but without the *sense,* of their connection," which interests Coleridge mostly for its psychological and metaphysical possibilities. To explain jokes is hard, as Freud and others have since found, but Coleridge's definition and his example—"*I was a fine child, but they changed me*"—at least gesture toward the bull as the verbal enactment of a problematics of identity (72n.).

Coleridge recapitulates Horace Walpole's "King of Bulls" while simultaneously erasing its Irish origins; in Walpole's version, an angry baronet refuses his old nurse's request for charity because of the injury she has done him: "'I was a fine boy, and you changed me'" (*Walpoliana* 1: 16). Walpole's laconic comment—"even personal identity is confounded!"—elucidates neither the bull's hidden history nor the prototypical slippages of gender and nationality which Maria Edgeworth reworks in both *Irish Bulls* and *Ennui* (1809), the first of her *Tales of Fashionable Life* (1809–12). Edgeworth's refutation of Walpole's "King of Bulls" establishes the parodic double-coding *Bulls* employs throughout: first, the bull is not Irish, since it has many learned precedents and parallels, and second, it is not stupid, since Locke, who's quoted at length (22–23) also identifies personal identity with consciousness. Edgeworth adds the crucial "at nurse" in *Bulls* (21–26), and she develops the joke into a striking argument against Gaelic biological determinism with *Ennui,* wherein the supposed Anglo-Irish hero discovers that his foster nurse is really his mother, thus neatly expanding two key points adumbrated in *Bulls*: the positive one that education and cultural construction make the gentleman and the disquieting notion that Anglo-Irish identities are always problematic, papering over the colonialist indeterminacy of origin. If, as *Bulls* repeatedly shows, the English habitually equate the Irish with savages, then the Anglo-Irish can never really be sure where they belong.

Colonialist encounters with the Wild Irishman go all the way back to the twelfth century—no doubts then about who was barbaric or who owned language—but the bull or laughable blunder is a much later seventeenth-century development, a consequence of what students of national representational systems call imaginotypical amelioration: the imperialist cannot laugh benevolently at the native's inherent verbal ineptitude if he is too scared. But, as stage historians and surveyors of colonialist attitudes have documented, Restoration dramatists and joke book compilers were already starting to find the Irish funny. Early anthologies like *Bogg-Witticisms* and *Teague-land Jests* abound in "Comical Joques, called *Bulls,* that are a preposterous kind of speaking," although the Williamite editor is uncertain whether they arise from disordered war conditions and the "natural Stupidity and Simplicity of the People" producing "Mistakes of Things" or whether they are crafty "little Contrivances," knowing statements just masquerading as blunders, "when you return my meaning as by mistake."[4] Even xenophobic joke gatherers cannot tell whether the natives are muddling through in a foreign language or dexterously putting the settlers on. After all, as collectors of Irish wit, word play, punning, and parody like Vivian Mercier have noted, Irish comic traditions of tale telling and repartee go back even further than Anglo genealogies of bulls (ch. 4). In any case, Swift and Steele (who had reason to know) could soon remark that everybody Irish is a walking joke. "There is seldom any thing entertaining either in the Impudence of a *South* or *North Briton,*" *Spectator* 20 notes, "but that of an *Irishman* is always Comick" (March 23, 1711; Bond 1: 87). Provincial, city, court, and Scotch accents may be displeasing, Swift observes, "but none of these defects derive contempt to the speaker; whereas, what we call the Irish Brogue is no sooner discovered, than it makes the deliverer, in the last degree, ridiculous and despised; and from such a mouth, an Englishman expects nothing but bulls, blunders, and follies. Neither does it avail whether the censure be reasonable or not, since the fact is always so" (4: 281). By 1741, Walpole refers casually to "that unholy land, that land of bulls"; by the 1770s, bulls were as stereotypically Irish as poverty, pigs, and potatoes, besmearing the Irish Protestant's image as well as the Catholic Gael's.[5] English travelers expected them: "I landed in Ireland with an opinion that the inhabitants were addicted to drinking, given to hospitality, and apt to blunder, or *make bulls,*" records Richard Twiss. His ill-tempered *A Tour in Ireland in 1775* recounts, among other Irish deficiencies, that of linguistic inventiveness, thus inadvertently creating a market for chamber pots with his picture inside, so that outraged readers could "p—ss on lying Dick Twiss" (8–9; Harrington 165).

English playgoers applauded the Stage Irishman, provided and acted by Irishmen who wooed audiences by domesticating the Wild Man; he's usually an impulsive soldier with a good heart, whose speech is glib rather than garbled.[6] Charles Macklin's *The True-born Irishman* programmatically revaluates English stereotypes of the Irish Other in the 1760s, freshly aligning "Irishness" with Patriot politics and depicting Anglicization not as improvement, but as a fall from Gaelic grace. When Mrs. O'Dogherty apes the London *ton,* transforming her name to "Diggerty" and her brogue to hypercorrect "Veest, imminse . . . and quite teesty," Macklin inverts the normative evaluative polarities and forecasts Edgeworth's more developed Lady Clonbrony in *The Absentee* (1812) as well as her chapter on "The Brogue" in *Bulls.* The unpublished prologue Macklin added for the London version calls attention to the fictionality of English understandings of alterity, contrasting ideology's image with "Irishness" reconstrued as the natural, artless, and forthright, a counter narrative that rejects "Nonsense deck'd with Bull and Brogue" for a "homebred Character" who will "give Irish Tones a sterling Sense" and "please without a Blunder." Richard Cumberland sums up his "reconciliatory delineations" like O'Flaherty in *The West Indian* (1771) as a rejection of "gross absurdities" and vulgar bulls: "When his imagination is warmed, and his ideas rush upon him in a cluster, 'tis then the Irishman will sometimes blunder; his fancy having supplied more words than his tongue can well dispose of, it will necessarily trip. . . . he conceives rightly, though in delivery he is confused." His language must not be vulgar or absurd, but "whilst you furnish him with expressions that excite laughter, you must graft them upon sentiments that deserve applause." O'Flaherty's errors lie "on his lip": "his heart can never trip"; in fact, he makes no bulls (*Memoirs* 142–43; *West Indian* Prologue).[7] The drama's Hibernian Fortune Hunters and sentimentalized Stage Irishmen matter to Edgeworth's *Bulls* both for what they do—she draws on the revaluative stage tradition throughout, especially in her climactic tale of "The Irish Incognito"—and for what they fail to do: the rather bland and unblundering English of expatriates like Cumberland's O'Flaherty evades the multicultural confrontation between racy vernacular idioms and a whole host of learned linguistic systems which *Bulls* structurally embodies and politically engages.

As this synopsis suggests, the Irish history that Maria Edgeworth and her readers knew is a metarepresentational narrative in which the politics of representation—how the aliens are to be presented and who is to speak for them—and the representation of politics shape the dialogic plot of an ongoing story. If "Ireland" is an image invented by England, "England" is also imagined as the Other—conquering presence or civil norm— against which Ireland defines who she is. An "English" depiction of "Ireland" is also covertly a depiction of "England," and vice versa. Contrastive structures generate foils; industrious, reliable, mature, rational John Bull invokes feminized, juvenilized Paddy: the Irish "joined hands with those two other persecuted groups, women and children; and at the root of many an Englishman's suspicion of the Irish was an unease at the woman or child who lurked within himself."[8] The struggle over Ireland as a territory, a land subject to contending laws (Brehon and British), is also a struggle between the languages (Gaelic and English) used to produce and personify "Ireland," most notably embodied in Spenser's *A View of the Present State of Ireland,* which is, appropriately, formally structured as a dialogue between Eudoxius and Irenius. Eudoxius observes that "yt hath bene ever the vse of the conqueror to dispise the language of the conquered, and to force him by all meanes to learn his." Irenius's appropriation of the traditional Gaelic imagery of Ireland as a woman blames fosterage for English degeneracy, the recurrent worry that the settlers are going native: "the child that sucketh the milke of the nurse must of necessitie learne his first speach of her. . . . So that the speach beinge Irish, the harte must needes bee Irishe" (87, 88). For Spenser, the symbiosis of mother tongue and motherland also entails a dangerous slippage between gender and nationality: Gaelic milk and words unman Englishmen.[9] At their most generous, these slippages between sex and state figure national affairs in terms of family relationships, with England and Ireland as two sisters: much eighteenth-century debate addresses which is the elder and who takes sororal precedence. Political rhetoric's preoccupation with the overlap between sexual and colonial configurations of authority rubs off on the "English" inhabitants too; if Celts are womanized, juvenilized, and dispossessed of their mother tongue, their translators and apologists—the Anglo mediators between the colonized and the English—are destabilized too, feminized by their notorious gift of gab, yet missing a language that can represent their own identity as well as the Irish Other. Irish life's juxtaposition of wild romance and sordid history, surreal Gothic and gritty realism, destabilizes interpretation of Anglo-Irish genres as well.

*Bulls* embodies formally the Anglophone Irishman's and even more the Anglophone Irishwoman's ambivalent relationship to cultural master narratives of learning, language, and history. Because Ireland's history *is* a history of how it has been represented, Maria Edgeworth must critique both formally and thematically systems of representation. Her satiric parody of what has hitherto passed as cultural genealogy—her disestablishment of paternity and lines of influence—are as important in her rescue of vernacular Irish culture as her lively vignettes. The crazy etymologies which jumble together everything from papal bulls to John Bull to the *bullæ* of Roman antiquity and the constant capping of a seeming native bull with a learned parallel are as much an embodied representation of a socially typifying language (to borrow Bakhtin's phraseology) as the "city rhetorick" of "The Dublin Shoeblack," whose intensely figurative bet with his mate ends in murder: "I out's with my breadearner, and gives it him up to Lamprey in the bread basket," that is, stabbed him in the stomach with his scraping knife, up to the very hilt imprinted with the maker's name.[10] Making the Shoeblack's idiolect "intelligible to the English," Edgeworth ironically activates and recontextualizes a literary icon: "Let us follow the text, step by step, and it will afford our readers, as Lord Kames says of Blair's Dissertation on Ossian, a delicious morsel of criticism" (130). Edgeworth's point in this clever demonstration is first that "the irish nation, from the highest to the lowest, in daily conversation about the ordinary affairs of life, employ a superfluity of wit, metaphor, and ingenuity, which would be astonishing and unintelligible to a majority of the respectable body of english yeomen," who figure throughout the *Essay* as too dim-witted for ideas, much less word play (144, 137, 160). But her racy depiction of shoeblack wit is simultaneously a good joke at the solemnities of "Blair's Dissertation on Ossian." She uses Blair—the Shoeblack's ingenuities are just as amenable to analysis and just as revelatory of primitive genius as sublime bards—and she also delicately abuses this pompous savant's expatiating upon native wit; moreover, Blair's admiration for primitive metaphorics scarcely extends to the current vernacular. Edgeworth's satirically double-coded dialogue with the past brings the literary pundit and the Noble Savage down to earth. Effacing the aristocratic, bardic mythology of the Gaelic past with a vibrant plebeian present, she also anticipates the contrasting approaches to Irish history which emblematically close the book: the Celtic investment in military and heroic nostalgia as opposed to an ameliorated future for ordinary people.[11]

The long tradition of the bull is Edgeworth's pre-text, and her almost encyclopedic allusions foreground the genealogy of intertexts explaining and reinventing savage Ireland (and civil England, self-satisfied inheritor of the Western intellectual tradition). The book's intertextuality literalizes how identity is imprinted, transmitted, and recirculated, and the narrative's textual self-consciousness, playfully calling attention to its own jokes, linguistic systems, and storytelling processes, exemplifies Bakhtin's notion of social language as an "embodied representation" of unresolvable dialogues: a heteroglot linguistic cohabitation of "socio-ideological contradictions between the present and the past," with every jostling language and belief system offering a window on the world (291). In this crisscrossing of languages, styles, points of view, and speaking subjects that Bakhtin denominates "parodic" and novelistic, boundaries really count. As the intersection between different spheres which thus define the identity of each, borders are where the writer drawn to the plurality of unmerged voices and idiolects flourishes; if parodic forms cannot regenerate the social world, their border crossings can free up our interpretive choices by offering new satiric perspectives.[12] Edgeworth's dialogic virtuosity is her strong suit as a writer, and *Bulls* exhibits the cross-writing range that her border locale enables: Anglo and Irish, juvenile and adult, anecdotes of men cross-dressed by a woman writer and the demotic voices of Irishwomen who can hold their own, as in the indeterminate dialogue between a widow and her landlord. Neither has a name, but each speaks with such extraordinary vigor that the reader does not know whether she is the victim she claims to be or a canny actor "mak[ing] her poor mouth to your honor"—poor mouthing is claiming poverty to take advantage (178; Joyce 304). Edgeworth leaves the competing voices at odds, content to show the skeptical reader that even Irish cottiers "speak in trope and figure" (160). If it is important not to judge illiterate genius "under the influence of any prejudice of an aristocratic or literary nature," it is even more important to remember that "English is not the mother tongue" of indigenous culture (127, 7). The English shamelessly mangle foreign languages, but when a poor Irish haymaker, "who had but just learned a few phrases" of English by rote mistook a feminine for a masculine noun and began his speech in a court of justice with "My lord, I am a poor widow," the grave judge and jury were convulsed with laughter at his stupidity (56–57). Many distinctively Hiberno-English characteristics of vocabulary, syntax, and idiom result from direct translation of Gaelic into English, the hegemonic language of law, landlords, bureaucracy, and education; numerous solecisms in *Bulls* come from cross-cultural interchanges in such patriarchal locales and, like this one and Walpole's "King of Bulls," insinuate Irishness as a fractured and feminized identity. It is tempting to explain these blunders as the residue of a depreciated maternal heritage, mistranscriptions revaluated by a female mediator who is herself operating within a genre that is metaphorically "feminine," the conciliatory translation of Irish natives for English readers.

But English was the language of improvement as well as dispossession, and Gaelic's demise was less the result of elite decree than popular abandonment.[13] "Little Dominick," the first inset story in *Bulls* (ch. 6), transforms a contestatory scene of instruction into a textual space that both vocalizes and formally embodies Edgeworth's theme of cultural negotiation and interdependence. From this point on, *Bulls* moves away from a discursive argument preoccupied with masculine authorities toward Edgeworth's favorite domestic romance: her little stories of everyday life nested within a narrative crammed with big names and "big" history are irresistibly and positively gendered female. From this point too, "bulls" as Irish cultural markers begin to be recoded from wayward tongues to overflowing hearts, the signature of wits rather than dullards. Because "Little Dominick" is as stylistically lucid as it is ideologically complex, Edgeworth's juvenile correspondent could enjoy it as a story about a schoolboy who is transformed from butt to hero; once hooted for his brogue and his blunders (like calling himself an "orphan" when his mother still lives), the grown-up Dominick O'Reilly returns well-to-do from India just in time to buy back his family estate and, more important, to save the childhood friend who first taught him to learn and to love. It is, like many of Edgeworth's tales of generous teaching, grateful learning, and reciprocal attachment, simultaneously a daughter's self-representational story and a woman writer's politics by other means: a narrative of social community produced and sustained by affectionate instruction.

Packed off to Wales to learn "manners and grammar" at ten, poor Dominick is the perpetual victim of his master, Mr. Owen ap Davies ap Jenkins ap Jones. Ludicrously proud of his own genealogy and his learned library, Jones has a thick accent himself, but that scarcely stops him from tormenting the "little irish plockit [blockhead]." The outcast of the school, the child becomes as stupid as everyone tells him he is; only when young Edwards befriends him does Dominick discover his capabilities. Any subaltern reader would relish the story's delicate subversion of hierarchies. Laughter and linguistic authority, Dominick discovers, can be sites of resistance as well as oppression. He develops (as had the author when a schoolgirl) a gift for malicious mimicry, aping the teacher's Welsh tones to perfection. The funniest and cleverest part of the tale is Dominick's struggle to master the intricacies of "shall" and "will": just as Asians find English verb tenses and articles thorny, native Gaelic speakers notoriously came to grief with "shall" and "will" (Joyce 74–75). Repudiating rote learning forced on children is an Edgeworth trademark, and she fuses our sympathy for juvenile victims with the glee at showing up lettered absurdities which characterizes *Bulls* throughout. The choices of target are political: "shall" and "will" were a hotly contested site for late-eighteenth-century prescriptive grammarians battling to impose elite control over language communities. James Harris, who begins his *Hermes* with contempt for those who just "speak their Mother-Tongue," stands for "GRAMMAR UNIVERSAL . . . which without regarding the several Idioms of particular Languages, *only respects those Principles, that are essential to them all*" (11). *Hermes* idealizes an abstract linguistic order, uncontaminated by the materiality of everyday life, the property of a ruling hegemony who float free of the concrete particularities and local inflections which marginalize women, children, the vulgar, and the provincial. Edgeworth lets James Harris's pseudo-logical "philosophical inquiry" and Robert Lowth's grammar satirize themselves: she need only quote and cite Harris's metaphysical tangles and classical precedents.[14] No wonder that Dominick, forced to get pages by rote, finds Harris and Lowth like

"an irish bull, if I had said it." Dominick officially loses his native brogue
and masters the dominant discourse, but he keeps his Hibernian heart
and generosity, punishing the tyrant Jones and rescuing his friend from
debtors' prison; tellingly, he resumes his juvenile accent when he wants
to express affection. Edgeworth's sly educational fable shows how to manipulate the master tongue yet simultaneously affirm cultural identity
and local attachment.

Ever since Shakespeare's history plays, the dialogue among representa-
tives of England, Ireland, Scotland, and sometimes Wales had been a favorite device for embodying or imagining Great Britain's national unity.
In the two long chapters of "Bath Coach Conversation" toward the *Essay's*
close, a dramatized "British Threesome" interpret and interrogate Commonwealth community. The anecdotal arguments of the travelers conclusively model Enlightened responses to the colonialist stereotype of
Irishness as a radical alterity, a challenging otherness (chs. 14–15). It is
currently fashionable to critique the limits of Enlightenment thinking, noticing cosmopolitan urbanity less than rationalist paradigms run amuck with
disciplining and punishing, but the recognition of intercultural processes
modern readers celebrate is mandated by the Enlightenment agenda current theorists distrust; multicultural narratives of self- and social transformation derive much persuasive power from familiar Enlightenment
priorities and fables of progress.[15] Because they're well bred, well read,
and "consequently superiour to local and national prejudice," Edgeworth's
Englishman, Scotchman, and Irishman can appreciate diverse customs
and manners without "laugh[ing] at all that may differ from their own";
they cannot, however, come up with a satisfying definition of a bull, because (despite Smith and Coleridge) wit and absurdity are less opposites
than allies (208, 213, 231). Not even Steele's bull in explaining Irish
blunders satisfies—"It is the effect of climate, sir; if an Englishman were
born in Ireland, he would make as many"—because "the leviathan of English literature" himself outdoes that when he claims that Shakespeare
not only shows human nature as it really acts, but also as it would "in
trials, to which it cannot be exposed": an incongruity which passes for
critical wisdom until the reader analyzes it (*Bulls* 236–37; Johnson 265).
Given the *Essay's* predilection for the domestic, the local, the vernacular,
the anecdotal, the oral, and the affective, and its satiric reproductions of
the masculinist linguistic and cultural explanatory systems that stand for
their opposites, it is not coincidental that the doubly English "bull"
which ends the *Essay's* efforts at formal definition comes from one of
Samuel Johnson's most famous pronouncements privileging "just representations of general nature" over "particular manners."

The *Essay's* foregrounding of language, identity, and history as narratives about what Irishness is like means that the cultural repertoire can be changed; if who we are depends on the stories told about us and on the stories we tell about ourselves, then stereotyped patriarchal logics can be countered within alternative fictional spaces. "The Irish Incognito" (ch. 16), the "hibernian tale" which the Irishman produces to exemplify the liberal attitudes embodied by the Bath Coach conversationalists, is a nested narrative of the sort that postmodern analysts of metafictionality have taught us to call the *mise en abyme*: a thematizing of storytelling concerns within a fiction which mirrors and/or critiques the main narrative (Hutcheon, *Narcissistic Narrative* ch. 3). Since "Sir John Bull was a native of Ireland. . . [whose] real name was Phelim O'Mooney," it's a story within a story about an identity within an identity. The tricky technique and punning names draw attention to the point that the story is *about* representation, a comic contestation of the usual antithetical treatment of England and Ireland: the conception of the countries as polar opposites, the civilized versus the barbarians.[16]

Phelim (his name emblematizes his Irish warmth) lodges the binaries in one protean body: he simultaneously challenges essentializing generalizations that figure Irishness as inferiority and patriarchal etymologists (like James Harris and Edmund Spenser before him) who try to tie every word to one logical, unequivocal meaning.[17] Phelim's impersonation is also identity politics, a critique of the generic Englishman's phlegm, caution, and specious civility. Deconstructing the Irish bull as stupidity, Edgeworth reconstructs it as affective ebullience and verbal dexterity, and her reconstitution of Irish subjectivity embraces identity as well as words. Since representational stereotypes define who we are by how we vocalize, the Irish national characteristics that *Bulls* has erased as indices of stupidity are reinstated—and valorized—as markers of merit. But if Hibernia stands for warm hearts, vivid imaginations, and familial connections as well as agile words, then who is John Bull? As the Bath Coach Englishman remarks, "It would be well for Englishmen, if they were a little more inclined, like your open hearted countrymen, to *blurt* out their opinions freely" (230). Edgeworth's complex little fable of the London center and the Celtic fringe explores both what differentiates and what unites the national constituencies: as an earlier bull observes, "When first I saw you I thought it was you, but now I see it is your brother" (227). The protean Phelim's national cross-dressing problematizes facile binarisms of us versus them, Ireland versus England, just as his multiple identities show how subjectivity is shaped—but not contained—by where we come from.

The framing narrative which surrounds Edgeworth's vignettes of local life and speech works throughout by incorporating and ironizing all kinds of authoritative language systems, by reading the vaunted products of the great Western intellectual traditions as if *they* were the Wild Irishman's confusion of tongues, as if *they* were bulls, which—as it turns out with rigorous reading—they indeed are. Englishmen blunder freely without being branded, because sociality would be impossible if everybody were "taxed for each inaccuracy" and compelled to talk before a "star-chamber of criticism . . . surrounded by informers." Since the metropolis refuses to extend its own "conversation-license" to the margin, *Bulls* turns the tables by subjecting the canonical language to the same kind of "logical examination" the Irish face every time they open their mouths (58–59, 230). If the *Essay on Irish Bulls* is at once a political protest against Irish jokes and a commodification of Irish jokes for an English audience, it also provides a recipe for making bulls. By placing illiterate Hibernians and learned authorities in textual dialogue, *Bulls* can transform a 1798 militia executioner cursing a half-hanged rebel who falls from an improvised gallows—"You rascal, if you do that again, I'll kill you"—into a "learned casuist," it can discover that "ancient figures of speech were invented to palliate Irish blunders," and it can pull the rug from under every great man.[18] Sublimity or bombast, absurdity or wit, here only the literary marketplace determines the cultural value (101, 220, 112). Formally, *Bulls* is, among other things, itself a bull, structurally enacting every crazy logic it encounters and—like the "practical blunder" of the Bath Coach Irishman's conversation—pleading "against myself and my country," but only "on purpose to show how little could be produced" (240). The "Conclusion" opens with throwing aside the ironic mask and frankly avowing the authors as "friends in disguise" out to prove that the Irish are "an ingenious generous people," whose national blunders are really "imputable to their neighbours" or "justifiable by ancient precedents" or "produced by their habits of using figurative and witty language." Playing to the "liberal of both nations," Edgeworth congratulates the Irish for having laughed at *Castle Rackrent* ("the caricatura of their ancient foibles") and flatters the English who will happily replace stereotypes "generally entertained" with "a more just and enlarged idea of the Irish."[19]

But the absorption and satiric recontextualization of somebody else's discourse recommences almost as soon as it stops. The political crisis that erupted in the 1798 Irish Rebellion and in Emmet's Rebellion of 1803 (the year after the publication of *Bulls*) is also a crisis of representation, a bloody inquiry into national identities and a search for origins. The ghastly images, grotesque jokes, and political cant from the 1798 Rebellion which constitute a running subtext throughout *Bulls* emerge as overt politics in the "Conclusion," again in sly parody of contemporary patriarchal attitudes, this time French and Irish as well as English. The last chapter's politically coded interreferentiality grafts right into the text the interpretive wars that preoccupied contemporary writers of history: "philosophical" cosmopolitans like Voltaire and Hume versus Gaelic cultural nationalists like Sylvester O'Halloran and Charles Vallancey. But it is much too simple to label Edgeworth an Enlightened Unionist who wishes to obliterate cultural differences and fashion a homogenized new Ireland, the subsidiary of British imperial power.[20] To read Edgeworth as the advocate of the new and the English as opposed to the old and the Irish is to reinscribe the binarisms that *Bulls* works throughout to erase, the same binarisms that still trouble our understanding of "Anglo-Irish" writers like Edgeworth: the dismissals of yesterday's cultural nationalists and Gaelicists return as today's discourses of cultural imperialism, postcolonialism, and Orientalism. O'Halloran's narration of Irishness has a global twentieth-century resonance: ironically, the binarisms of us and the Other which configure his angry antiquarianism are the always returning repressed of current critical discourses, which still disempower the Anglo-Irish woman writer, particularly if she aspires to national(ist) pedagogy. More important, Edgeworth's brief satiric critique of O'Halloran and what he stands for is crucial to the gendered aesthetics and politics which produce the book's parodic frame and embedded tales: the *Essay*'s hybrid form and hyphenated articulations of cultural difference and identification direct their energies against the antagonistic construction of the nation-state which O'Halloran's Celtomania exemplifies.

The urbanely witty dismissals of masculinist historiographies and system building which close *Bulls* are thus far from trivial or digressive. Despite the successive waves of settlers, Ireland maintains a kind of ur-Irishness in O'Halloran's national myth, possessing the only history of "all the nations of Europe . . . transmitted to us pure and uninterrupted" from preclassical sources in remotest antiquity. An "unmixt race" whose people were split and whose records were destroyed by invading English, Ireland was never conquered (*A General History* 1: v; *An Introduction* i). Should any readers grow restive with his litanies of lost battles or the "exploits, and glorious death" of heroes like Brien-Boirumhe, O'Halloran reminds them that it is of the "last consequence to the honour and dignity of this antient imperial kingdom, and to the present succeeding Irish" to understand why and how Ireland has been "so unexampledly traduced, and misrepresented to all Europe" (*An Introduction* 257; *A General History* 1: xxxviii). O'Halloran discovers in the bardic poetry he takes as true an essentialized Ireland based on an ancient Gaelic race—heroic, elite, and male: women matter as maternal progenitors who bear the lineage of champions. Crammed with alphabetical lists of ancient territories, the Milesian tribes who inherited them, and the combats of the warriors who defended them, O'Halloran's history textualizes a national identity of genetics and grievance, founded on blood and defended by blood. His romantic epic embalms a protean culture and language within a patriarchal plot: the Catholic Gael's dispossession of his rightful inheritance as king of the island. An immemorial past that's always present, the Irish story is a repetitive lost battle eliding time—an Ossianic master narrative congealed into marmoreal forms, with no space for the scarred and diverse social body of the contemporary Irish populace and no voice but the author's incantatory monologue.

Nations, recent theorists claim, are "anomalous states" produced by narration: through the representations of those who write, "the impossible unity of the nation as a symbolic force" achieves its multiple cultural significations.[21] Enlightenment "objective" historiography was supposed to be philosophy teaching by example, but, the "Conclusion" of *Bulls* remarks, most "foreign pictures of Ireland" are no more reliable than Chinese pictures of lions painted from hearsay "descriptions of voyagers," ignorantly or maliciously exaggerated. Voltaire the philosophe scarcely fares much better than Gaelic enthusiasts, although he has recanted his slander that the Irish were made to be "subject to others" and can thus be forgiven by the Edgeworths, if not by the "incensed irish historian, Mr. O'Halloran."[22] Different narratives produce different stories of "nationness": Hume's philosophe principles of constant, universal human nature; O'Halloran's totalizing and exclusionary epic grandeur; Edgeworth's antisystemic impulses, demotic populism, and disjunctive little tales of vernacular life. In Bakhtin's schema, heteroglossia and dialogic interplay characterize the novelistic and the parodic space of living culture and everyday locale; against this polyphony is the monovocality of epic discourse, the reverent memorialization of a dead past.[23] With their old hostilities and solemn idealism, codified discourses, like O'Halloran's epic, call for satiric irreverence. By reproducing and recontextualizing O'Halloran's Celtophilia, the "Conclusion" of *Bulls* repudiates both his essentialized Irish identity and his sacral construction of the nation. Accepting historical Bildung and multiple micronarratives within time rather than the stasis and eternal repetition of one grand macronarrative, the Edgeworths offer an alternative *amor patriae.* The Edgeworths position themselves as intermediaries translating a traduced Ireland for a dual audience, but they romance Irish union through alternative textual constructions of national history and national identity. Writers, not warriors, make up their list of those who honor Ireland, and they include women and living authors like Burke (314–15).

Substituting bulls—vernacular synecdoches for dislocation and dispossession—for O'Halloran's romantic beatifications, the *Essay* satirically problematizes his Irish identity politics. The notion that narrative and social structures are cognate, so that changing one story implies changing the other, is implicit in the *Essay*'s representational experiments: the disjunctive mix of parodied social authority and reproduced vernacular subalternity politicizes the textual space as potentially liberating. "Impute a peculiar mental disease to a given people, show them that it incapacitates them from speaking or acting with common sense, expose their infirmities continually to public ridicule, and in time probably, this people may be subjugated to that sense of inferiority and to that acquiescence in a state of dependence, which is the necessary consequence of the conviction of imbecility" (20). Early on, the *Essay on Irish Bulls* thus lays out the etiology of the cultural and psychic disorder that it seeks to heal through parodic pedagogy (the deconstruction of misrepresentational systems) and through performative storytelling (the legitimation of local communities through vernacular embodiment). This strikingly labile passage, most likely if read in isolation to summon a woman's or a nonwestern presence, constitutes a history of (and formula for) English colonialist bull making that is also a representation of fractured Irishness—Anglo-Irish hyphenation as well as hybrid Celticism. Because the authors simultaneously belong to the "English," the "Irish," and what Burke calls the "colonial garrison," the book's authorial identity and mixed techniques turn out to be as ambiguous as the bulls it seeks (4: 272–73).[24] Like the tropes it thematizes, the *Essay* models the collision and collaboration of hybrid discourses. Janus-faced, the "Conclusion" of *Bulls* is strategic rhetoric addressed to both English and Irish audiences, like the editorial apparatus fissured by unstable, even contradictory attitudes which was layered onto *Castle Rackrent* just before its publication in 1800 (the year the Union was passed). Sometimes the Edgeworths call England "our native country," assert that they were "neither born nor bred in Ireland," and speak as "we" when they ironically celebrate English hauteur and insularity: "It is of a thousand times more consequence to have the laugh than the argument on our side," and since we do, "let us keep [the laudable practice of ridiculing the blunders, whether real or imaginary, of Irishmen] by all means" (20, 313, 57–58). Although they sometimes talk of "the English" and "the Irish" or disperse their revaluation of "Irishness" among the Irishman, Englishman, and Scotchman who embody, interpret, and critique British union in the "Bath Coach Conversation," the authors wind up aligning themselves with Hibernia: "our Irish blunders are never blunders of the heart" (88).

Historically and formally a Rebellion narrative, the *Essay on Irish Bulls* raises textuality to thematic prominence via disjunctive forms of representation and democratic textual and cultural affiliations. Maria Edgeworth's experiment in national cross-dressing fraternizes across class, cultural, and gender lines so that the structural mix of parodied patriarchal authority and homely vernacular translation stands in metonymic relation to the political message. Edgeworth's dialogic interplay between Hiberno-English and canonical authorities enacts a generous and positive agenda, a linguistic pastiche that models the multivoiced cultural discourse that can transform a legalistic Union of territories into an embodied representation of the union of hearts she desires. The inclusive textual body of *Bulls* thus mimes an inclusive social body, a hybrid nationness written into being by a woman author who privileges little local narratives over totalizing masculinist history, thereby reconstituting not only what counts as "Irishness," but also what counts as "history." Destabilizing multiple origin myths, the writing daughter shapes her father's "feminine" oral performances of vernacular Irish ways, privileges the developing modern community of the motley people-nation over O'Halloran's monovocal representation of elite dynastic heroes, and revels in yanking the rug out from under every duly constituted authority—especially John Bull. If England's discriminatory "identification of the two kingdoms" constitutes the Union as "something very like a bull," John Bull's prejudices entitle him to the fool's cap and bells: the book's concluding image is the "practical bull" of England's crowning her "own imperial head" with the fool's regalia (262–63, 316). Re-viewed from the perspective of postmodern parody and translation theory, literary history's "Maria Edgeworth"—patriarchal England's spokeswoman for an unproblematic Unionism—similarly looks a lot like a bull. That portrait of the Anglo-Irish periphery travesties Maria Edgeworth, the sophisticated satirist whose experimental narrative structures are cognate with Ireland's evolving social realities.

## Notes

I'd like to thank the American Council of Learned Societies, the National Endowment for the Humanities, the John Simon Guggenheim Memorial Foundation, and the Huntington Library for their support of my work on Edgeworth. HM refers to a Huntington Library manuscript.

1. In her valuable discussions of postmodernism and parody, Linda Hutcheon defines the former as a politicized awareness that we can only know the world through a network of socially established meaning systems and locates the quintessential postmodernist "confrontation . . . where documentary historical actuality meets formalist self-reflexivity and parody" (*Politics* 7). *A Theory of Parody: The Teachings of Twentieth-Century Art Forms,* as the title indicates, privileges the didactic function of recent cultural productions (from novels to architecture) which

displace a Romantic aesthetic valuing individuality, originality, and genius with double-voiced parodic forms contesting the singularity of cultural production. Interpreting this refunctioning of older forms to new needs as a positive way of dealing with cultural patrimonies by overthrowing past masters through incorporation and ironic inversion, she defines "parody" as a "form of imitation," a "repetition with critical distance, which marks difference rather than similarity" (6). Since Georgian women writers, many of them adept at parodically recycling their literary fathers, are still being stigmatized for being didactic, it's important to notice how their practices often anticipate the allusive layerings and self-reflexive intertextuality that Hutcheon values as "postmodern." The notions of parodic imitation that Hutcheon explores are anticipated by Maria Edgeworth both practically and theoretically. Her work abounds in transformative rewritings of parent texts, and she also theorizes parody as a feminized and domesticated artistic and critical practice in the Edgeworths' *Readings on Poetry* (1816); "On Parody" is the only chapter in the book which analyzes a literary kind rather than a specific poem (194–213). The French work on parodic imitation to which Edgeworth refers the reader may be "Parodie" in the *Encyclopédie Méthodique: Grammaire et Littérature* (1784), which is especially interesting because it, like *Bulls,* links parody as "maxime triviale ou proverbe populaire," oral and colloquial, with parody as classical literary form: the best parody's merit and aim is "de faire sentire entre les plus grandes choses & les plus petites, un raport" and it traffics in complex "raprochement" (2: 763–65). Of particular relevance to Edgeworth's playful interweave of alternative language and belief systems are Bakhtin's discussions of heteroglossia, "socially typifying languages," and parody; see *The Dialogic Imagination* 291, 60–67, 288–96, 76, 308–14, and 358–66.

2. Edgeworth writes that she isn't "surprised that you could not understand the essay on bulls . . . that book was not written for young people and many old people find it difficult to understand & do not like it" (ca. 1804 Huntington Library HM28593). The very few critics who've commented on *Bulls* praise it for valuing the common Irish, but no one seems to have noticed that Edgeworth's parodies of patriarchal culture are crucial to her reconstitution of Irish national identity.

3. Much of the interest in oppressive metanarratives versus regenerative micronarratives goes back to Jean-François Lyotard's *The Postmodern Condition.* For a helpful multidisciplinary overview of current contestations of metanarratives, see Martin Kreiswirth's "Trusting the Tale: The Narrativist Turn in the Human Sciences."

4. For the historical contextualization of bulls, see W. J. Lawrence; J. O. Bartley's essay and ch. 11 of *Teague, Shenkin, and Sawney*; Kathleen Rabl; Annelise Truninger; D. W. Hayton's "From Barbarian to Burlesque: English Images of the Irish c. 1660–1750"; Cóilín Owens; and ch. 3 of Joseph Th. Leerssen's book. The Edgeworths culled numerous books of Irish jokes for their survey.

5. Walpole's letters are full of Irishisms (Feb. 16, 1741, OS, 37: 93).

6. Sometimes he's a servant more clever than his betters, as is Thady O'Blarney in *Botheration,* Walley Chamberlain Oulton's popular farce published in the Rebellion year of 1798; he sings the unity of the "dear sweet sisters, England and Ireland" while, like Edgeworth's Thady in *Castle Rackrent* (1800), overreaching everybody in his guise of humble servant, "[w]hose tongue may blunder, but whose heart ne'er can" (28, 46). Edgeworth's comically pedantic notes and etymologies for Mary Leadbeater's *Cottage Dialogues Among the Irish Peasantry* (1811) explain "botheration" as a vulgar Hibernicism become fashionable English because "extremes meet in language," but the English *ton* will never "equal the wit and humour of the Irish native, whether of high or low degree" (273–74).

7. For the quotations, see Macklin's *Four Comedies,* ed. J. O. Bartley, 94; Macklin's Prologue is available as Larpent 274; I am grateful to the Huntington Library for the Fellowship which enabled my access to this unpublished manuscript and many other works I've consulted.

8. For the struggle between representational systems that underwrites Irish history, see Declan Kiberd's "Anglo-Irish Attitudes" (quoted at 87); Andrew Hadfield and Willy Maley's "Irish Representations and English Alternatives"; David Cairns and Shaun Richards's *Writing Ireland: Colonialism, Nationalism, and Culture*; and Joseph Th. Leerssen's valuable survey, *Mere Irish and Fíor-Ghael: Studies in the Idea of Irish Nationality, Its Development, and Literary Expression Prior to the Nineteenth Century.*

9. Edgeworth first read Spenser's *View* in 1782, and she revises his key notions in several of her Irish tales. As *Bulls* demonstrates, she's especially interested in the possibilities of the dialogue. For useful views of Spenser's sexualization of Anglo-Irish relations, see Ann Rosalind Jones and Peter Stallybrass's "Dismantling Irena." Spenser's colonization of language and his dialogic structure are discussed in Patricia Coughlan's collection, *Spenser and Ireland.*

10. The folk culture collection *Ireland Sixty Years Ago* (ca. 1860) cites Edgeworth's *Bulls* as "so generally known" for its accurate analysis of tropes and metaphors in shoeblack speech that the editor reproduces a sketch of the knife to offer one trivial correction (ch. 7).

11. Blair's several dissertations are reprinted in the 1839 Philadelphia edition of James Macpherson's *The Poems of Ossian.* For the link between the noble savage and "picturesque and figurative speech," see "A Critical Dissertation on the Poems of Ossian" 63–64. Blair's argument that rhetorical figures are primitive rather than elegant is very much to Edgeworth's purpose; she appropriates his insights while deromanticizing the untutored speaker. As Clare O'Halloran's "Irish Re-Creations of the Gaelic Past" points out, Celtic antiquarians wanted both to reclaim Macpherson's theft of originally Irish material and to repudiate the cult of the noble savage, because (unlike Edgeworth's) their rescue of "Irishness" depended on a chivalric and ultra-civilized heritage: Scotch notions of Ossianic primitivism like Blair's jarred with aristocratic Celtic culticism.

12. For a useful approach to Bakhtin's work emphasizing the novel *as* culture, a "dense network of cross-referenced and cross-fertilized ideas" where borders matter most, see Maria Shevtsova's "Dialogism in the Novel and Bakhtin's Theory of Culture" (quote at 749). In their study of Bakhtin, Gary Saul Morson and Caryl Emerson nicely sum up the distanciation parodic borders afford: "Laughter becomes the sound outsideness makes" (435).

13. For education and the decline of Gaelic, see the essays by Gerald O'Brien and by Richard B. Walsh; Victor Edward Durkacz's book and Brian O'Cuív's ch. 13; and the collections edited by Mary Daly and David Dickson; and by Diarmaid O'Muirithe. It's easy to romanticize the loss of a mother tongue, but for an eye-opening account of child victimization under the twentieth-century regime of mandatory Gaelic, see "The Politics of Gaelic" (ch. 7) in Oliver MacDonagh's *States of Mind.*

14. The late-eighteenth-century linguistic and political struggle between thinkers (like Locke and Joseph Priestley) who interpret language as convention and elitists like Harris, who use classical precedents to derive universal grammars beyond common speech, is surveyed by Olivia Smith (ch. 1); John Barrell (ch. 2, "The Language Properly So-Called: The Authority of Common Usage," *English Literature in History*); and Stanley Andrus Leonard (73–74, 179; ch. 4). Edgeworth parodies the metaphysical pomposities of Lowth and Harris on "shall" and "will" at even greater length in her notes for Mary Leadbeater's *Cottage Dialogues,* again to contrast English men's *ipse dixit* pronouncements with Irish children's unpremeditated feeling (325–29). See Lowth 70, 78–79; Harris, bk. 1, ch. 7.

15. See Susan Stewart's "The State of Cultural Theory and the Future of Literary Form" for a thoughtful revaluation of the relationship between multicultural pedagogy and Enlightenment thinking.

16. For the deployment of this enduring motif within contemporary Irish politics, see Seamus Deane's "Civilians and Barbarians."

17. An obsessive interest in genealogies and etymologies similarly links opposing sides in earlier Irish history, as with Gaelic scholars and Spenser's Irish dialogue. The recurrent jokes about explanations based on etymology in *Bulls* have a historical resonance and a contemporary edge we may miss. Because they were interested in reforming language teaching, developing texts for Irish illiterates, and inventing telegraphic communication, the Edgeworths were well versed in linguistic theories and controversies. For the background, see Olivia Smith; John Barrell; Hans Aarsleff's *The Study of Language in England, 1780–1860*; and Nancy Struever's reading of etymologies as "Fables of Power."

18. E.g., Sir Isaac Newton's bull: after he had made "a large hole in his study door for his cat to creep through, [he] made a small hole beside it, for the kitten" (240).

19. Not all of the Irish did laugh; see the discussion in Butler's literary biography (359–60). Edgeworth's description of *Castle Rackrent,* like the depiction of

stereotypical Irish customs in *Bulls* (211) as "*tales of other times,*" is a tactical move, a fiction about the "pastness" of her own tale's verisimilitude: the Editor's assertion that "these are 'tales of other times': that the manners depicted in the following pages are not those of the present age" is rhetoric deployed to assuage the differing anxieties of English and Irish readers (*Castle Rackrent*, ed. Watson 4).

20. This rather common reading is exemplified in Ian Topliss's "Maria Edgeworth: The Novelist and the Union" (a distillation of his earlier dissertation) in *Ireland and Irish-Australia: Studies in Cultural and Political History,* ed. Oliver MacDonagh and W. F. Mandle.

21. For the interrelation between cultural constructions of nationness and narrative strategy, see David Lloyd's *Anomalous States*; and *Nation and Narration,* ed. Homi K. Bhabha, especially Simon During's "Literature—Nationalism's Other? The Case for Revision" and Bhabha's "DissemiNation: Time, Narrative, and the Margins of the Modern Nation": the quotation in the text is from Bhabha's "Introduction: Narrating the Nation" (1). This emphasis on the political signifi-cance of representation is indebted to Benedict Anderson's insight that communi-ties are distinguishable "by the style in which they are imagined" (6).

22. For an overview of the universalist strain in Enlightenment historiography, see ch. 3, "The New History: Philosophy Teaching by Example," in Carl Becker's *The Heavenly City of the Eighteenth-Century Philosophers*; for eighteenth-century writers' reconciliation of their assumptions about common humanity (the uniformity of human nature) with national differences, see John G. Hayman's "Notions on National Characters in the Eighteenth Century."

23. Whether Edgeworth satirizes or idealizes O'Halloran characters, she always associates them with origin-legends. Sylvester O'Halloran was a bourgeois eye surgeon of some repute, who published on medicine as well as antiquarian topics. In *The Absentee* (1812), Edgeworth gives O'Halloran's name and some of his traits to the noble and lovable old Gaelic soldier who brings about the marriage of the Anglo-Irish hero with Grace Nugent, whose lineage includes Gaelic and Catholic forebears. Unlike the real O'Halloran, who was in the minority of middle-class Catholics opposing the Union, the Count is an aristocrat who's pro-Union, and the marked copy of Pasley on military policy which the Count and the hero share in *The Absentee* surely relates to Edgeworth's ongoing theme, the reconstitution of Irish cultural identity: contemporary readers familiar with Ireland (like the traveler Edward Wakefield) decoded Pasley's message about the salutary intermin-gling of the Romans and their provincials in local terms, "to unite rather than to divide" (*Account of Ireland* 2: 634). Lord Colambre's encounter with the allegorized O'Halloran is in ch. 8 of the Oxford *The Absentee,* originally published as the last tale in the second three-volume set of *Tales of Fashionable Life* (1812).

24. For theoretic approaches to the gendering of translation, see Lori Chamberlain's "Gender and the Metaphorics of Translation"; Douglas Robinson's *The Translator's*

*Turn* sums up revisionist translation theory, which replaces an intellectual construct with an empathetic "somantics." Robert Welch's "Translation and Irish Poetry in English" and *A History of Verse Translation from the Irish 1789–1897* emphasize the mediatory role of translation in Brooke's work. Leith Davis's justified anxiety to rescue Charlotte Brooke's patriotic artistry from condescension risks effacing important insights on the gendered metaphorics of translation. It's right to notice Brooke's empowerment of herself in her own poem through invocation of a male muse, but that need not negate the Anglo-Irish woman writer's personal and cultural affinity with mediatory translation. Multiply marginal herself, the translator, like the parodist, is also multiply equipped to negotiate disparate discourses.

# Works Cited

Aarsleff, Hans. *The Study of Language in England, 1780–1860.* 1967. Minneapolis: U of Minnesota P, 1983.

Anderson, Benedict. *Imagined Communities: Reflections on the Origin and Spread of Nationalism.* 1983. rev. ed. London: Verso, 1991.

Bakhtin, M[ikhail] M. *The Dialogic Imagination: Four Essays.* Ed. Michael Holquist. Trans. Caryl Emerson and Michael Holquist. U of Texas P Slavic Series 1. Austin: U of Texas P, 1982.

Barrell, John. *English Literature in History 1730–80: An Equal, Wide Survey.* London: Hutchinson, 1983.

Bartley, J. O. "Bulls and Bog Witticisms." *Irish Book Lover* 30 (Nov. 1947): 59–62.

————. *Teague, Shenkin, and Sawney: Being an Historical Study of the Earliest Irish, Welsh, and Scottish Characters in English Plays.* Cork: Cork UP, 1954.

Becker, Carl. *The Heavenly City of the Eighteenth-Century Philosophers.* 1932. New Haven: Yale UP, 1968.

Bhabha, Homi K. "Introduction: Narrating the Nation"; "DissemiNation: Time, Narrative, and the Margins of the Modern Nation." *Nation and Narration.* Ed. Homi K. Bhabha. London and New York: Routledge, 1990. 1–7; 291–322.

Bond, Donald F., ed. *The Spectator.* 2 vols. Oxford: Clarendon, 1965.

Brooke, Charlotte. *Reliques of Irish Poetry (1789) and A Memoir of Miss Brooke (1816) by Aaron Crossley Hobart Seymour.* Ed. Leonard R. N. Ashley. Gainesville, FL: Scholars' Facsimiles and Reprints, 1970.

Burke, Edmund. *The Writings and Speeches of the Right Honorable Edmund Burke.* Beaconsfield ed. 12 vols. New York: Taylor, 1901. Vol. 4: "Letter to Sir Hercules Langrishe" (1792).

Butler, Marilyn. *Maria Edgeworth: A Literary Biography.* Oxford: Clarendon, 1972.

Cairns, David, and Shaun Richards. *Writing Ireland: Colonialism, Nationalism, and Culture*. Manchester: Manchester UP; New York: St. Martin's P, 1988.

Coleridge, Samuel Taylor. *Biographia Literaria Or Biographical Sketches of My Literary Life and Opinions. The Collected Works of Samuel Taylor Coleridge.* Vol. 7, pt. 1. Ed. James Engell and W. Jackson Bate. Bollingen Series 75. London: Routledge and Kegan Paul; Princeton: Princeton UP, 1983.

Coughlan, Patricia, ed. *Spenser and Ireland: An Interdisciplinary Perspective.* Cork: Cork UP, 1989.

Cumberland, Richard. *Memoirs of Richard Cumberland, Written by Himself.* Ed. Henry Flanders. Philadelphia: Parry and McMillan, 1856.

———. *The West Indian: A Comedy.* 1771. *The Plays of Richard Cumberland.* Ed. Roberta F. S. Borkat. Vol. 1. New York and London: Garland, 1982.

Daly, Mary, and David Dickson, eds. *The Origins of Popular Literacy in Ireland: Language Change and Educational Development 1700–1920.* Dublin: Trinity College; University College, 1990.

Davis, Leith. "Birth of the Nation: Gender and Writing in the Work of Henry and Charlotte Brooke." *Eighteenth-Century Life* 18.1 (Feb. 1994): 27–47.

Deane, Seamus. "Civilians and Barbarians." *Ireland's Field Day.* Ed. Field Day Theatre Company. Notre Dame: U of Notre Dame P, 1986. 31–42.

During, Simon. "Literature—Nationalism's Other? The Case for Revision." 138–53. *Nation and Narration.* Ed. Homi K. Bhabha. London and New York: Routledge, 1990.

Durkacz, Victor Edward. *The Decline of the Celtic Languages: A Study of Linguistic and Cultural Conflict in Scotland, Wales, and Ireland from the Reformation to the Twentieth Century.* Edinburgh: John Donald, 1983.

Edgeworth, Maria. *The Absentee.* 1812. Ed. W. J. McCormack and Kim Walker. Oxford: Oxford UP, 1988.

———. *Castle Rackrent: An Hibernian Tale Taken from Facts, and from the Manners of the Irish Squires, before the Year 1782.* Ed. George Watson. 1800. The World's Classics. Oxford: Oxford UP, 1981.

———. *Castle Rackrent and Ennui.* 1800; 1809. Ed. Marilyn Butler. London: Penguin, 1992.

———. *Readings on Poetry.* London: R. Hunter, 1816.

———. *The Rose, Thistle, and Shamrock. Comic Dramas, In Three Acts.* London: R. Hunter and Baldwin, Cradock, and Joy, 1817.

———, ed. *Cottage Dialogues Among the Irish Peasantry.* By Mary Leadbeater. London: J. Johnson, 1811.

Edgeworth, Maria, and Richard Lovell Edgeworth. *Essay on Irish Bulls.* London: J. Johnson, 1802.

*Encyclopédie Méthodique: Grammaire et Littérature.* 3 vols. Paris: Panckoucke, 1784. "Parodie," 2: 763-65.

Gordon, Mrs., ed. *"Christopher North": A Memoir of John Wilson.* 1862. New York: W. J. Widdleton, 1880.

Hadfield, Andrew, and Willy Maley. "Introduction: Irish Representations and English Alternatives." *Representing Ireland: Literature and the Origins of Conflict.* Ed. Brendan Bradshaw, Andrew Hadfield, and Willy Maley. Cambridge: Cambridge UP, 1993. 1-23.

Harrington, John P., ed. *The English Traveller in Ireland: Accounts of Ireland and the Irish Through Five Centuries.* Dublin: Wolfhound P, 1991.

Harris, James. *Hermes: Or, A Philosophical Inquiry Concerning Language and Universal Grammar.* 1752. Menston, ENG: Scolar P, 1968.

Hayden, Mary, and Marcus Hartog. "The Irish Dialect of English: Its Origins and Vocabulary"; "The Irish Dialect of English: Syntax and Idioms." *Fortnightly Review* 85 n.s. (1909): 775-85; 933-47.

Hayman, John G. "Notions on National Characters in the Eighteenth Century." *Huntington Library Quarterly* 35.1 (Nov. 1971): 1-17.

Hayton, David. "From Barbarian to Burlesque: English Images of the Irish c. 1660-1750." *Journal of Economic and Social History* 15 (1988): 5-31.

Hortensius. *Deinology: or, the Union of Reason and Elegance, Being Instructions to A Young Barrister.* London: Robinson, 1784.

Hutcheon, Linda. *Narcissistic Narrative: The Metafictional Paradox.* 1980. London: Routledge, 1991.

———. *The Politics of Postmodernism.* London and New York: Routledge, 1989.

———. *A Theory of Parody: The Teachings of Twentieth-Century Art Forms.* 1985. New York and London: Methuen, 1986.

*Ireland: Her Wit, Peculiarities, and Popular Superstitions: With Anecdotes, Legendary and Characteristic . . . Originally Published in the "Dublin University Magazine."* Dublin: McGlashan and Gill, n.d. [1860?].

Johnson, Samuel. *Samuel Johnson: Rasselas, Poems, and Selected Prose.* Ed. Bertrand H. Bronson. 3rd ed. San Francisco: Rinehart P, 1971.

Jones, Ann Rosalind, and Peter Stallybrass. "Dismantling Irena: The Sexualizing of Ireland in Early Modern England." *Nationalisms and Sexualities.* Ed. Andrew Parker, Mary Russo, Doris Sommer, and Patricia Yaeger. New York and London: Routledge, 1992. 157-71.

Joyce, P[atrick] W[eston]. *English As We Speak It in Ireland.* Introd. Terence Dolan. 1910. Dublin: Wolfhound P, 1991.

Kiberd, Declan. "Anglo-Irish Attitudes." *Ireland's Field Day.* Ed. Field Day Theatre Company. Notre Dame: U of Notre Dame P, 1986. 83-105.

Kreiswirth, Martin. "Trusting the Tale: The Narrativist Turn in the Human Sciences." *New Literary History* 23.3 (Summer 1992): 629-57.

Lawrence, W. J. *Speeding Up Shakespeare: Studies of the Bygone Theatre and Drama.* London: Argonaut P, 1937.

Leerssen, Joseph Th. *Mere Irish and Fíor-Ghael: Studies in the Idea of Irish Nationality, Its Development, and Literary Expression Prior to the Nineteenth Century.* Utrecht Publications in General and Comparative Literature vol. 22. Amsterdam: John Benjamins, 1986.

Leonard, Sterling Andrus. *The Doctrine of Correctness in English Usage 1700-1800.* 1929. New York: Russell and Russell, 1962.

Lloyd, David. *Anomalous States: Irish Writing and the Post-Colonial Moment.* Durham: Duke UP, 1993.

Lowth, Robert. *A Short Introduction to English Grammar: with Critical Notes.* New ed. London: Dodsley and Cadell, 1783.

Lyotard, Jean-François. *The Postmodern Condition: A Report on Knowledge.* Trans. Geoff Bennington and Brian Massumi. Theory and History of Literature vol. 10. 1979. Minneapolis: U of Minnesota P, 1989.

MacDonagh, Oliver. *States of Mind: A Study of Anglo-Irish Conflict 1780-1980.* London: Allen and Unwin, 1983.

Macdonald, Dwight, ed. *Parodies: An Anthology from Chaucer to Beerbohm—And After.* New York: Random House, 1960.

Macklin, Charles. *Four Comedies by Charles Macklin.* Ed. J. O. Bartley. London: Sidgwick and Jackson; Hamden, CT: Archon Books, 1968.

Macpherson, James, trans. *The Poems of Ossian To Which Are Prefixed . . . Dissertations on the Era and Poems of Ossian.* Philadelphia: Thomas, Cowperthwait, 1839.

Mercier, Vivian. *The Irish Comic Tradition.* Oxford: Clarendon, 1962.

Morson, Gary Saul, and Caryl Emerson. *Mikhail Bakhtin: Creation of a Prosaics.* Stanford: Stanford UP, 1990.

Neilson, G. R., ed. *The Book of Bulls: Being A Very Complete and Entertaining Essay on the Evolution of the Irish and Other Bulls, inc. Essay on Irish Bulls.* London: Simpkin, Marshall, Hamilton, Kent, and Tucker, [1898?].

O'Brien, Gerald. "The Strange Death of the Irish Language, 1780-1800." *Parliament, Politics, and People: Essays in Eighteenth-Century Irish History.* Dublin: Irish Academic P, 1989. 149-70.

O'Cuív, Brian. "Irish Language and Literature, 1691-1845." *Eighteenth-Century Ireland 1691-1800.* Vol. 4 of *A New History of Ireland.* Ed. T. W. Moody and W. E. Vaughan. Oxford: Clarendon, 1986. 374-423.

O'Halloran, Clare. "Irish Re-Creations of the Gaelic Past: The Challenge of Macpherson's Ossian." *Past and Present* 124 (Aug. 1989): 69-95.

O'Halloran, Sylvester. *A General History of Ireland from the Earliest Accounts to the Close of the Twelfth Century, Collected from the Most Authentic Records: In Which New and Interesting Lights Are Thrown on the Remote Histories of Other Nations as well as of Both Britains.* 2 vols. London: G. Robinson et al., 1778.

———. *An Introduction to the Study of the History and Antiquities of Ireland: In which the Assertions of Mr. Hume and Other Writers Are Occasionally Considered.* Dublin: Thomas Ewing, 1772.

O'Muirithe, Diarmaid, ed. *The English Language in Ireland.* Thomas Davis Lecture Series. Dublin: Mercier P, 1977.

Oulton, Walley Chamberlain. *Botheration; or, A Ten Year's Blunder: A Farce, in Two Acts.* London: George Cawthorn/British Library, 1798.

Owens, Cóilín. "Irish Bulls in *Castle Rackrent." Family Chronicles: Maria Edgeworth's Castle Rackrent.* Ed. Cóilín Owens. Dublin: Wolfhound P; Totowa, NJ: Barnes and Noble, 1987. 70-78.

Rabl, Kathleen. "Taming the 'Wild Irish' in English Renaissance Drama." *Literary Interrelations: Ireland, England, and the World.* Vol. 3: *National Images and Stereotypes.* Ed. Wolfgang Zach and Heinz Kosok. Tübingen: Narr, 1987. 47-75.

Robinson, Douglas. *The Translator's Turn.* Baltimore: Johns Hopkins UP, 1991.

Shevtsova, Maria. "Dialogism in the Novel and Bakhtin's Theory of Culture." *New Literary History* 23.3 (Summer 1992): 747-63.

Smith, Olivia. *The Politics of Language 1791-1819.* 1984. Oxford: Clarendon, 1986.

Smith, Sydney. "Edgeworth on Bulls (*Edinburgh Review* 1803)." *The Works of the Rev. Sydney Smith.* 2nd ed. 3 vols. London: Longman, Orme, Brown, Green, and Longmans, 1840. 1: 59-64.

Spenser, Edmund. *A View of the Present State of Ireland.* Ed. W. L. Renwick. London: Partridge/Scholartis P, 1934.

Stewart, Susan. "The State of Cultural Theory and the Future of Literary Form." *Profession 93.* New York: Modern Language Association, 1993. 12-15.

Struever, Nancy. "Fables of Power." *Representations* 4 (Fall 1983): 108-27.

Surel, Jeannine. "John Bull." Trans. Kathy Hodgkin. *Patriotism: The Making and Unmaking of British National Identity.* Vol. 3: *National Fictions.* Ed. Raphael Samuel. London: Routledge, 1989. 3-25.

Swift, Jonathan. "On Barbarous Denominations in Ireland." *The Prose Works of Jonathan Swift.* Ed. Herbert Davis. Vol. 4. Oxford: Blackwell, 1957.

Topliss, Ian. "Maria Edgeworth: The Novelist and the Union." *Ireland and Irish-Australia: Studies in Cultural and Political History.* Ed. Oliver MacDonagh and W. F. Mandle. London: Croom Helm, 1986. 270-84.

Truninger, Annelise. *Paddy and the Paycock: A Study of the Stage Irishman from Shakespeare to O'Casey.* Bern: Francke, 1976.

[Twiss, Richard]. *A Tour in Ireland in 1775.* London: Robson et al., 1776.

Vallancey, Lieut. Charles. *An Essay on the Antiquity of the Irish Language; being a Collation of the Irish with the Punic Language.* Dublin: L. L. Flin, 1781. No. 8 in vol. 2. *Collectanea de Rebus Hibernicis.* 7 vols. in 6. Dublin: R. Marchbank printer to the Antiquarian Society, 1770-1812.

Wakefield, Edward. *An Account of Ireland, Statistical, and Political.* 2 vols. London: Longman, Hurst, Rees, Orme, and Brown, 1812.

Walpole, Horace. *The Yale Edition of Horace Walpole's Correspondence.* Ed. W. S. Lewis. Vol. 37. New Haven: Yale UP, 1974.

———. *Walpoliana.* 2 vols. London: R. Philips, [1799].

Walsh, Richard B. "The Death of the Irish Language." *Milestones in Irish History.* Ed. Liam De Paor. Cork and Dublin: Mercier P, 1986. 84-94.

Welch, Robert. *A History of Verse Translation from the Irish 1989–1897. Irish Literary Studies* 24. Gerrards Cross, BUCKS [ENG]: Colin Smythe; Totowa, NJ: Barnes and Noble, 1988.

———. "Translation and Irish Poetry in English." *Literary Interrelations: Ireland, England, and the World.* Vol. 1: *Reception and Translation.* Ed. Wolfgang Zach and Heinz Kosok. Tübingen: Narr, 1987. 1-9.

# Elizabeth Hamilton's *Modern Philosophers* and the Uncertainties of Satire

*Janice Thaddeus*

Elizabeth Hamilton's *Memoirs of Modern Philosophers* (1800) was a book too intelligent for its audience. Satire requires especially proficient readers, but this need for a canny audience—especially at certain historical moments—breeds paradoxical effects. Some of the best readers deliberately reconfigure the text, ignoring whatever might hurt or change them. Satire, wrote Jonathan Swift in *A Tale of a Tub,* "'Tis but a *Ball* bandied to and fro, and every Man carries a *Racket* about Him to strike it from himself among the rest of the Company" (31), or, to change the metaphor, satire is a mirror in which a reader sees everyone but himself. Hence, when Hamilton anonymously published her second satire, she knew that she was returning to the most multifarious medium, but also the most uncertain.

## The Uncertain Medium

Many books are misunderstood, but in the 1790s, dominated by anti-Jacobin sentiment, misreadings of complex arguments were even more likely than they are at other times. In a century and a decade addicted to binary oppositions, the radical-conservative spectrum was often viewed as simple antithesis. Hence, the review of *Modern Philosophers* that appeared in the *Monthly Mirror* soon after it was published saw it as mere aggression. "This is an attempt to expose the absurdities of the modern school of philosophy, by shewing the effect of its precepts upon the conduct of its teachers and disciples," the reviewer begins, reducing the novel to its simplest terms; and then, never considering Hamilton's myriad interlocking plots, concludes: "The monster [meaning William Godwin] has already received his death-wound, but the author of these *Memoirs* seems anxious to 'make assurance double sure,' by a repetition of the blow; although, therefore, he has had no hand in the victory, he arrives time enough [*sic*] to participate in the honours of the triumph" (34). This anonymous review is—not surprisingly, considering the political climate—reductive and unfair; it reads Hamilton's novel so prejudicially that it fails to note any of the complexity of her undertaking, the intricacy of her thought. In a period when simplistic political readings are ascendant, a satiric text often suffers this fate. Earlier in the century, for example, the unmodulated irony of Daniel Defoe's *The Shortest Way with Dissenters* was so egregiously misunderstood that his intended allies threw him in jail. Reviewers are of course even at the best of times notoriously unfair, but it is the particular variety of misreading we must consider here, the sort of misreading generated by a sense of political crisis, and the desire to quell opposition. A reader bent on seeing his own face in the glass would certainly in Hamilton's novel miss most of the content. Luckily, there are readers as well as reviewers, and though all readers may not read intelligently, they sometimes read differently. Although the *Monthly Mirror* reviewer thought Hamilton was flogging a dead horse, the public did not. The public was politically more mobile. Her novel raced through three editions and was translated into French. This work was without doubt extremely popular, and, as I have shown in a previous article on Hamilton's domestic politics, its author was regarded with respect as an influential thinker in Edinburgh's intellectual circles. Indeed, *Modern Philosophers* is a skillful, multilayered, and important novel, written at the end of a decade that is one of the watersheds of British history and literature.

To capture the inattentive or resisting reader, the satirist often includes a list of beliefs that are to be interpreted directly, telling the truth and for once not telling it slant. Thus Swift suddenly intervenes in "A Modest Proposal" with the signalizing statement: "Therefore, let no man talk to me of other Expedients" (116), and he lists ten suggestions, some of which could quite naturally appear in a parliamentary debate. In most of his works, Swift maintains a persistent irony, and this is often the satiric technique adopted by eighteenth-century satirists. Fielding's *Jonathan Wild,* for instance, is particularly unremitting. Hamilton has drawn, rather, on the tradition of "satura," as defined as "Lanx Saturae," the plate of varied fruits offered to the Gods, or "farcimen," the mixed sausage to be digested by those attending the feast. Whether or not Hamilton was directly aware of this traditional definition, first methodically outlined by Diomedes in the fourth century, and carefully limned by Charles Knight in a recent article (139–42), it is certainly one of the important strands of satiric discourse, essential to the work of Rabelais, for example, or Swift's *Tale of a Tub.* Hamilton chose the most miscellaneous definition of satire. Ostensibly defining her book as Horatian, she takes as her epigraph "Ridiculum acri/Fortius et melius magnas plerumque secat res," translated as "Ridicule shall frequently prevail,/And cut the knot, when graver reasons fail." Further, she took the unusual step of mingling irony, parody, romance, and realistic narrative within one set of covers, letting each ricochet against the others. Her conscious manipulation of these genres is adept and fascinating. Her subtext, the unconscious elements, is equally intriguing. When like Swift she speaks of other expedients, chiefly a heterodox, portmanteau Christianity, her unmarried characters' independence persistently denies the humility and obedience her Christian doctrine invokes. Although Hamilton's novel was extremely popular and influential in its own day, and has been reprinted in ours, few readers have been shrewd enough or patient enough to listen to all of these voices or taste all of these fruits.

Indeed, there has been a tendency willfully to ignore a large segment of Hamilton's novel. The review in the *Monthly Mirror* is only a paragraph; the fourteen-page discussion in the *Anti-Jacobin Review* is of course much more detailed, but obviously this magazine, founded in 1797 as a government mouthpiece, is interested only in the attack on Godwin, and not in the rest of the novel. Of the many other characters in *Modern Philosophers,* then, the *Anti-Jacobin Review* says: "Among the rest of the characters all due poetical justice is distributed; but as they are not *immediately* concerned in the *main* design of the work, they necessarily excite not that interest which is produced by the philosophical portraits" (375). The *Anti-Jacobin Review* whets readers' appetites, defining this fiction chiefly as a roman à clef and then coyly refusing to provide the key: "[W]e shall leave it to each to discover his, or her own face, in the glass" (375). In the half of the novel ignored by the *Anti-Jacobin,* Hamilton includes a multiplicity of voices, some to be heard straight, some to be heard slant, with a number of modulations in between.

This is not satire that deconstructs itself entirely, consigning us ultimately to what Swift in *A Tale of a Tub* called "The Serene Peaceful State of being a Fool among Knaves" (110). Revolution is denied: Hamilton is liberal, but she does not wish to be radical. One conservative solution is a beneficent patriarchal government, but this would require politicians who were capable of imagining people's needs, which, as Hamilton knows, politicians do not understand. One of Hamilton's characters, for instance, argues that aristocrats, people with money and position, cannot clearly see how lesser people live: "[I]t is the peculiar misfortune of those who move in a certain sphere, to have their worst propensities so flattered as to render it almost impossible for them to escape the snare of self delusion. The possessors of rank and fortune are every one surrounded by a sort of atmosphere of their own, which not only distorts and obstructs the view of external objects, but which renders it difficult for them to penetrate the motives of their own hearts" (2: 303–4).

To change them was Hamilton's later project. She wished to work within the system, to re-educate the minds and hearts of those with rank and fortune, and to this end she published *Letters on The Elementary Principles of Education* in 1801 and *Letters Addressed to the Daughter of a Nobleman on the Formation of Religious and Moral Principle* in 1806. In 1808, she changed her tactic somewhat by publishing *The Cottagers of Glenburnie,* a novel about independent cottagers, suggesting ways in which they could make their labor profitable. Still, even in the case of this novel, Hamilton wanted those of rank and fortune to read it, to emphasize to them that they have no right to think that "the great mass of the people are . . . as so many teeth in the wheels of a piece of machinery" (ix). She continued writing treatises on education, each time directing her remarks at a slightly different audience, convinced as was Godwin that people can be molded.

To separate all of the voices in Hamilton's *Modern Philosophers,* to read it adequately, three contemporary critical concepts are the most helpful: discourse and heteroglossia, as defined by Michel Foucault and Mikhail Bakhtin, and ventriloquism, as applied by Margaret Doody to eighteenth-century poetry. Foucault and Bakhtin's terms are as familiar as they are useful, and do not require definition here. Doody's term is less well known, and demands some exegesis. Ventriloquism is important in this case, because Bakhtin's double-voiced discourse becomes, in ventriloquism, a conversation, and this sort of conversation appears in Hamilton. According to Doody, in this technique "the voice of the 'real' speaker (speaking for the poet, and his audience) is momentarily cast into the personification of the Opposite or Other; a dummy or puppet-speaker is given a strange voice. When the poet wishes, the whole piece can be carried on as a kind of dialogue between a ventriloquist's dummy and the ventriloquist as personal speaker" (44). Occasionally, Doody continues, "even mixed characters who are not enemies are treated rather as if they were, and we know that it is part of our job as readers . . . to catch the style out, to shoot the folly as it flies and recognize the source of the ventriloquy—even when we're not quite sure where exactly the ventriloquist would stand if he became personal speaker" (45). What Doody has noted in poetry also applies to the gallimaufry of voices and styles that constitute *Modern Philosophers.*

The parodic plot has captured the most attention in criticism of *Modern Philosophers,* both in contemporary and modern studies, and a canny reader must begin there, but unlike the *Anti-Jacobin Review,* must not stop there. What happens in *Modern Philosophers* is that the parodic figures and the "realistic" figures share philosophies that at first appear to oppose one another, and that ultimately the women seem to be the most effective philosophers. The author, who at first glance appears to be conservative, becomes in the discursive interchange a liberal, if not a radical, presence.

## Backgrounds: Publications, Attitudes, and Critical Responses

The debate Hamilton was joining in 1800, the debate the *Monthly Mirror* defines as finished, was a particularly vicious and widespread attack on Godwin's *An Enquiry Concerning Political Justice.* Since the first two editions of *Modern Philosophers* were anonymous, and the putative author was male, reviewers did not realize that they were dealing once more with the writer who had been one of the first to attack Godwin, in her good-humored *Translation of the Letters of a Hindoo Rajah* (1796). Hence, the statement that she "had no hand in the victory" (*Monthly Mirror* 34) was disingenuous. Her hand was there right from the start. Illness had hindered the writing of *Modern Philosophers,* and Hamilton herself realized that she was entering the lists rather later than she wanted to, after a crowd of other works on the subject, but, she said in the preface to the third edition, to which she added her name as author, "she did not find her own ideas so much anticipated by any of them, as to induce her to suppress the present work, or even to make the smallest alteration in its contents" (1: vi). The *Monthly Mirror* and the *Anti-Jacobin Review* stressed the resemblance between Hamilton and her contemporaries. Hamilton focused on the differences. Her book not only sold, but also raised her reputation in knowledgeable circles. After she moved to Edinburgh in 1804, according to Hamilton's friend and biographer Elizabeth O. Benger, she became an intellectual force, and her "private *levee* was attended by the most brilliant persons in Edinburgh, and commonly protracted till a late hour" (1: 174).

Hamilton knew what it was like to be a dependent, and it was this memory and this knowledge which drove her to sympathize with other classes and other lives. At the age of nine, Hamilton had been sent by her widowed mother to live with her aunt, and her aunt lived humbly, married to the "son of a peasant" (1: 20). Hamilton's family had had pretensions, and it was only with difficulty that her aunt, Mrs. Marshall, had reached the "true Christian humility" (1: 19) that allowed her to accept her position. She learned at last to ignore "the mortifications to which she was . . . exposed" (1: 18). Her husband, Mr. Marshall, had, however, "received the advantage of an education superior to his birth" (1: 20), so that Hamilton and her aunt suffered social but not intellectual deracination. For Hamilton, as I have argued elsewhere, this childhood meant that she understood poverty and deprivation with an awareness beyond benevolent condescension, a kind of intimate knowledge she never lost.

Hamilton's first attack on Godwin was light-hearted and not very clearly thought through. Along the lines of Oliver Goldsmith's *Citizen of the World* and Montesquieu's *Lettres Persanes,* the *Hindoo Rajah* was a playful satiric rendering of the opinions of Seeta Juin Zåårmilla, who writes to his friend Kisheen Neêay Mååndååra and receives a few replies. At this period, Hamilton was heavily influenced by her brother, who had died four years before. He had spent fourteen years in India, and through his letters he had provided his sister with what Benger calls "a *second* education" (1: 47). Hamilton admired her brother perhaps more than anyone else she was ever to meet, and the *Hindoo Rajah* was in some ways a memorial to him.

Her political views in this book, as Isobel Grundy and Susan Taylor have pointed out, squarely (and unsurprisingly) support the imperialist project. The satire of the philosophers has been generally designated as "conservative." Zåårmilla meets not just one philosopher, but a whole passel of them, including Mr. Puzzledorf, Mr. Axiom, Dr. Sceptick, Mr. Vapour, and Miss Ardent. The Rajah discovers that "to involve the simplest question in perplexity, and to veil the plain dictates of common sense, in the thick mist of obscurity and doubt, is an easy matter with metaphysical Philosophers" (2: 165). Zåårmilla tells us that Mr. Vapour thinks "the age of reason . . . to be very near at hand. Nothing, he says, is so easy as to bring it about immediately" (2: 184). The Rajah is skeptical of this "credulous philosopher" (2: 184), and so are we. Miss Ardent, unlike Mr. Vapour, believes that in the age of reason women will be valued for their minds, rather than their youth and their beauty. Peter Marshall and a number of other critics see Miss Ardent as ironically presented; her mind is masculine and her manner aggressive (214). Still, regarding women's minds, this ventriloquist's dummy has certainly here expressed an opinion Hamilton would later agree with. She has also educated a very sensible girl, Olivia, who knows how to respond to emergencies. Zåårmilla does not like Miss Ardent, and he thinks it is foolish that she "pants" for the era when men will be attracted to older women for the qualities of their minds, rather than younger women for their beauty, but Zåårmilla is not merely the author's puppet (1: 188). The contradictions spar with one another. The male philosophers clearly represent Godwin, with his imitators and followers gathered round, while Miss Ardent seems more generalized as the aggressive, masculine woman. She makes a number of extremely sensible remarks, and if she represents Wollstonecraft, the portrait is not undermining. Although its feminism is remarkable, there is no evidence that Hamilton intended this book to be taken very seriously.

Godwin's treatise, *Enquiry Concerning Political Justice and Its Influence on General Virtue and Happiness,* had come out three years before the publication of Hamilton's *Hindoo Rajah.* In the charged radical atmosphere of 1793, Godwin's anarchist book had been a stirring tonic. Hazlitt in *The*

*Spirit of the Age* described its popularity: "No work in our time gave such a blow to the philosophical mind of the country as the celebrated *Enquiry concerning Political Justice.* Tom Paine was considered for the time as a Tom Fool to him; Paley an old woman; Edmund Burke a flashy sophist. Truth, moral truth, it was supposed, had here taken up its abode. . . . 'Throw aside your books of chemistry,' said Wordsworth to a young man, a student in the Temple, 'and read Godwin on Necessity'" (33). Godwin's arguments were bold and particularly flattering to strong minds. He claimed that mankind's perfectible nature is inhibited by social and political institutions, and that marriage, government, even the mutual obligations of parenthood and childhood—indeed even gluttony and lust—would appropriately wither away in a free, truthful, and democratic world.

This was an important debate about ideas that had briefly fascinated myriad liberal as well as radical thinkers, both men and women. Hazlitt claimed that Godwin "carried with him all the most sanguine and fearless understandings of the time" (37). In spite of the three-guinea price *Political Justice* was widely read. An anonymous contemporary wrote that "in many places, perhaps some hundred, in England and Scotland, copies were bought by subscription, and read aloud in meetings of the subscribers" (Allen 57n. 2). However, the clamor of support was soon overwhelmed by a horde of attackers. Besides Hamilton's own characterization of Godwin and Mary Hays in the *Hindoo Rajah,* there were at least a score of others. For example, in Isaac D'Israeli's *Vaurien; or, Sketches of the Times* (1797), Godwin is Mr. Subtile, Holcroft perhaps Mr. Reverberator, and Thelwall Mr. Rant Subtile: "coldest-blooded metaphysician of the age" (Marshall 214). In 1798, John Ferriar satirized Godwin in a Lucianic *Dialogue in the Shades.* This was followed in the next year by Sophia King's passionate fiction, *Waldorf; or The Dangers of Philosophy,* showing how women could be undermined by sweet-talking theory; Jane West's similar tale of seduction and death, *Tale of the Times*; and George Walker's *The Vagabond,* where Godwin is Stupeo, and, as in Hamilton, Godwin's actual text is often quoted and misinterpreted. For a new twist, in 1800 Mary Anne Burges used a Bunyan imitation as a vehicle for an attack on Godwin, including characters called Mr. Hate-Controul, Mr. False-Reasoning, Mr. Credulity, Mr. Philosophy, Mr. Mental-Energy, and Mrs. Sensibility. Hence, by 1800, according to the *Monthly Mirror,* Hamilton was supposed to be hooting over an issue already written to death.

From our greater hindsight, we should not read Hamilton's *Modern Philosophers* as narrowly as did the *Monthly Mirror* or the *Anti-Jacobin Review.* The Jacobins, after all, were associated with a revolution clearly gone bloody, and many besides benighted conservatives feared the specter of the guillotine in their city squares. The weight of current, twentieth-century discussion of the period is moving toward a more nuanced reading of the works once easily docketed as antirevolutionary. Hamilton has not always been included, although J. M. S. Tompkins long ago—and more recently Katharine Rogers and Janet Todd (among others)—noted her liberal tendencies.

On the other hand, Claudia Johnson, most notably, sees Hamilton as sweepingly conservative. Johnson, in spite of her subtle rendering of Austen's politics, still presents Hamilton's *Modern Philosophers* under the rubric of "Conservative novelists" who "minimize the necessity for reflection" (14). Later on, Johnson modifies this argument, observing that both Edgeworth and Hamilton "sneak moderately feminist suggestions" into their works by burlesquing a feminist character. "As a rhetorical device, the freakish feminist exemplifies the effort of sceptical novelists to subvert the anti-Jacobin novel from within, as it were, to use its own conventions against itself, to establish an alternative tradition by working within an existing one in a different way and to a different end" (21). Here, Johnson exactly hits the mark; her earlier effort to generalize through binary contrast does not truly reflect the complexity of her reading. I would question, however, her implication that Edgeworth and Hamilton were only half aware of what they were doing. The one full-length article on *Modern Philosophers,* by Eleanor Ty, argues that Hamilton, and many other women writers in the 1790s, "learned to circumvent criticism by employing more indirect means of examining the legitimacy of masculine authority" (114). Ty further argues that Hamilton often "inadvertently" supported Godwin—and Mary Hays—even as she undermined them, chiefly by including their own words as part of her parody and not wholly denying them.

I disagree with all three of these critics. Hamilton's *Modern Philosophers* is full of reflection and rarely inadvertent. Her liberalism is not so much a reaction to Godwin as indigenous: her childhood had sensitized her. One of her favorite poets and the source of many of her epigraphs was Robert Burns, and she shared many of his experiences and preoccupations. Hamilton is one of the most self-analytical authors I have discovered in the eighteenth century, and though the object of her analysis is mainly women, their social construction, and their proper response to it, she does not neglect politics and class, or the interrelations among these elements. Her one blind spot is race.

So far as I can tell, Hamilton never really questions the imperialist project from the point of view of the native peoples. In *Modern Philosophers,* when the tragic heroine's father Captain Delmond in order to support his family goes to fight in Africa, the native peoples are never mentioned—only the fact that Delmond's health is ruined by the climate. Hamilton does not defend imperialism here; there is no statement countervailing Delmond's loss of health with a reference to the justness of his cause. But she never undermines imperialism, never directly attacks it. The foolish philosophers in *Modern Philosophers* intend to migrate to Africa and live with the Hottentots, whom they picture as an ideal race, a people who avoid marriage, and who live free. Hamilton implies that the misguided philosophers have not informed themselves about the destructive climate, but she never gives the Hottentots a voice of their own, and their idealization is ironically presented. The philosophers simply describe them, and no realistic ventriloquist's voice enters the conversation. It is clear that their idealization is misplaced; the Hottentots are merely a metaphor for noble savages, not a realistically presented alternative to British life. Nor do they ever obtain a voice sufficient to subvert the author's presentation of them. Hamilton's stereotypical Africa may be in part simply the product of her own ignorance; it is not clear how much she knew about Africa. She was certainly familiar with India. She had studied, through her brother's researches, Hindu beliefs and practices, but her brother was never critical of his own enterprise, and she remained loyal to him. Although regarding her own country her subversive faculties were very well developed, she inflexibly assumed throughout her career that although Englishmen will invariably lose their health in far tropic places, they are without doubt helping to civilize the people they find there. Suppressed native peoples, however, are the only notable absence from her liberal chorus.

## Ventriloquism: The Author

To discuss ventriloquism, one must begin with the ventriloquist, and in *Modern Philosophers* Hamilton veiled the author in many layers. As described by Benger, Hamilton herself was a very proper woman, always practicing "that delicacy which was her peculiar characteristic" (1: 128). Benger ascribes the anonymity of *Modern Philosophers* to "female diffidence" (1: 131). The forceful expressions that appear in all of Hamilton's works seem to belie or at any rate to mitigate this description, although one will never find in Hamilton what Donna Landry calls in Mary Wollstonecraft "the discourse of sexual pleasure" (269). In fact, one of Hamilton's messages appears to be that women who avoid sexual pleasure, even those who avoid marriage, are in a much stronger and ultimately more pleasurable position than their married counterparts. Hamilton was, in her own poetic summary written at the age of twenty-five to foreshadow herself at fifty-five, "one cheerful, pleased, old maid" (Benger 1: 95). She also, in Scots dialect, wrote a poem confronting old age ("Is that Auld Age that's tirling at the pin?") and was the first to celebrate in poetry the joys of her own single hearth: "My ain fireside, my ain fireside,/O cheery's the blink o' my ain fireside" (Keddie 322, 327). She was certainly less aggressive toward men than Mary Astell, but like Astell one of her most persistent ideals was the unmarried intellectual woman who was every man's equal and was cheerful as well as pleased. In keeping with her view that sexuality should be controlled, she regretted that Burns had "sunk into vice" (Benger 2: 3), but blamed his failures on his lack of an independent position. She and Burns shared a sense of humor, strong feelings, and a satiric twist of mind: "Even the strong light in which he saw the ridiculous, was, I fear, too agreeable to me" (Benger 2: 3). Hence it was clearly for more complicated motives than Benger ascribes to her that Hamilton adopted a male persona for *Modern Philosophers.* The veil was useful as well as protective. Speaking of Scottish society in the 1820s, Henry Mackenzie, who had printed Hamilton's earliest publications in his periodical the *Lounger,* could describe women authors in his *Anecdotes and Egotisms* as "ladies, most of whom are known or shrewdly guessed at; but, like the beauties of Spain, come out veiled" (in Murdoch and Sher 133). For the purposes of Hamilton's novel, a male dummy-voice could condescendingly address sentimental readers as "the dear boarding-school angels" (2: 169) in a way Hamilton would never choose to do in her own voice. That voice could also ironically imagine the philosophers weighing or measuring tears without implicating Hamilton herself, as author. Thus Hamilton can continue to sympathize with the people who really cry. A male voice can presume to be above gender, superior to the "kind reader, of whatever age or gender thou mayest haply chance to be" (2: 216). Hamilton has not, then, chosen the Fielding puppet-voice, but rather the ventriloquist's dummy, who can assume a discourse quite different from the author's, though occasionally reassuming the author's voice. The message here is that the reader of "whatever" gender should question always whether or not he or she has understood the motives of another person. Hamilton herself is nearly always aware of "the other" and conjures her readers to be equally aware.

Hamilton's putative author, besides being male, is rendered completely anonymous and thrust into critical controversy. His character and history are quite obliterated. An anonymous lodger in an unnamed inn, he has rather decorously died, bequeathing his manuscript to the landlady to pay his bill. The landlady has judged the manuscript worthless and has already burned the first fifty pages. Another lodger hears about the manuscript, admires it, and sends it to a group of critics, both male and female, who disagree profoundly about its merits. At last, "a gentleman of great worth and knowledge" (1: xiii) named Geoffry Jarvis argues for publication, confidently claiming "that in publishing this work, you will deserve the thanks of society" (1: xvi). This passel of mixed opinion immediately unsettles us. The ventriloquist is anonymous; the dummy is not even the author, but a critic, and yet of course the author controls the dummy. As Donna Landry invokes this ventriloquist technique first outlined by Doody, the emphasis is on the "subversive twist," where the dummy independently begins "to challenge the master by altering the master's texts" (6). Hamilton's text often requires to be read against the grain, but one must begin by analyzing her intentions in the ventriloquist segments. As ventriloquist, she speaks through double voices; the characters are not her own dummies, but another's. In the introduction, this extra author is critic Geoffry Jarvis; in the text the dead male lodger occasionally comments; other voices erupt into the text through the parodic renderings of Godwin's and Mary Hays's words. In addition, the reader cannot ignore the characters whom the *Anti-Jacobin Review* dismissed as those "not *immediately* concerned in the *main* design of the work" (375). Many of these apparently secondary characters speak in various ways for the author. As much as the more apparently philosophical characters, they reflect her philosophy, and Godwin's. To understand this book, a reader must first listen to all of the ventriloquist's dummies—the romantic dummies, the anarchist dummies, the ironically undermined dummies, the dummies of each gender and every persuasion. Sometimes the ventriloquist is in full control; occasionally the dummy unsettles the text.

In the Introduction to the first edition of *Modern Philosophers* Geoffry Jarvis, the critic who recommends the publication of the newly discovered manuscript, says about *Political Justice* that the lodger-author does not mean to "pass an indiscriminate censure on that ingenious, and in many parts admirable, performance; but to expose the dangerous tendency of those parts of his theory which might, by a bad man, be converted into an engine of mischief, and be made the means of ensnaring innocence and virtue" (1: xiv). Hence, right at the beginning, Hamilton the ventriloquist-author has said through one of her dummies that she is attacking only abuses of Godwin's ideas—not the ideas themselves—adding that those ideas are in part, admirable. This is hardly inadvertent. Is it ironic? Is Hamilton the author differing from Jarvis, her dummy-critic? As I hope to show, there is enough evidence within the novel to prove that here at the beginning the ventriloquist has sufficient control over this particular dummy.

The anonymous author occasionally abandons his humorous condescension and attacks an offending institution with blistering accuracy, and, at points like these, Hamilton drops the ventriloquist's stance and speaks out as ironic manipulator. The best example of this kind of attack is a segment on war. Here, we must turn to Bakhtin, applying through italics the technique he uses in analyzing Dickens, to discover the "hybrid construction" of the heteroglossia in the prose (304). In the Index to the fifth volume of the *Anti-Jacobin Review,* Godwin is condemned for "common-place cant against war in general," and even the most casual reader of Godwin will agree that he does not support the idea of war, which in his perfect society will no longer exist. Hamilton may in some instances be anti-Godwin, but she is also certainly antiwar. Consider, for instance, this statement from *Memoirs of Modern Philosophers*:

> The two nations then at war, having at length sacrificed such a quantity of human blood, and expended such a portion of treasure, as was deemed sufficient for the *amusement* of the governing powers on either side, thought proper to make a peace; and after a few preliminaries, in which the original cause of dispute was *not once* mentioned, and things were put as nearly as possible into the *same state* in which they were at the commencement of hostilities, its ratification was formally announced.

> The *wretched* remains of those numerous armies which in the beginning of the contest had marched forth, elate with health and vigour, were now returned to their respective countries; some *to languish out their lives in hospitals, in the agony of wounds that were pronounced incurable*; some to a *wretched dependance* [*sic*] *on the bounty of their families, or the alms of strangers*; and the few whose good fortune it was to escape unhurt, according to the seniority of their regiments, either disbanded to spread *habits of idleness and profligacy* among their fellow-citizens, or sent into country quarters to be *fattened* for fields of future glory. (1: 119–20)

Here, Hamilton has juxtaposed the discourse of battle and the language of ironic subversion. We can see in the first paragraph especially how deftly Hamilton subverts the official language, how few words she needs. The renegade language draws a number of motives and assumptions into the political dialogue here. The rulers are distant, unnoticing—and hence amused. They know the uses of silence and omission. And under them nothing changes. Their "wretched" employees endure bodily pain, poverty, or a descent into vice. We should pause over the word "wretched," which later in the Godwinian parody is misapplied to proud and hard-working laborers. There, the word is seen by the laborers as an insult, but here it is accurate. These are the wretched crew who people Burns's rousing anarchist cantata *The Jolly Beggars.* Here, as there, they have not been treated by their employers as human beings. Swelling to epic alliteration, the prose indicates that only the lucky few will be "fattened for fields of future glory," with the implication that their leaders will finally devour these men who have been degraded into animals. Surely the *Anti-Jacobin* reviewer could have accused Hamilton as well as Godwin of "common cant against war."

After *Modern Philosophers,* Hamilton's antiwar stance actually increased in intensity. In the *Cottagers of Glenburnie,* published in 1808, Hamilton attacks especially the "war-contriving sage," who simply ignores the feelings and moral capacities of his fellow citizens "at the time he coolly calculates how many of his countrymen may, without national inconvenience, be spared for slaughter" (x).

## Double Discourse: Parody and Tragedy

Within the novel itself, we must first consider the main plot, which is a sentimental story of the tragic destruction of Julia Delmond. Interinvolved with that plot is the parodic presence of a group of Godwinian philosophers, and it is this presence which reviewers then and now have mainly dwelt upon, and which is the chief element by which *Modern Philosophers* takes its place in a discussion of satire. These fictional characters are, however, not alone. They inhabit a more realistically presented world filled with people who in various ways speak and represent Godwinian ideas.

In form, Hamilton's novel is a parody of the romantic marriage plot. Her quadruple heroines are Bridgetina Botherim whom she names as "the ostensible heroine of these Memoirs" (3: 332), Harriet and Maria Orwell, and Julia Delmond. Harriet and Maria are realistic figures and as is proper in a romantic plot, they both marry at the end. Bridgetina is a farcical Godwinian extremist: her fate is to become ordinary, but, because she is ugly, to remain unmarried. Julia is romantic and idealistic, hence doomed of course to tragedy. Both Harriet and Bridgetina are in love with Henry Sydney, a doctor, a triangle that is responsible for a number of comic misunderstandings. Bridgetina, in this roman à clef, is a portrait of Mary Hays, and in some ways a cruel portrait. Mary Hays, author of *The Memoirs of Emma Courtney,* was evidently not tall, but Bridgetina is so short as to be dwarf-like, and she squints so badly that she cannot quite look at the person she intends to talk to and often engages the wrong person in conversation. For these unfortunate characteristics, sympathetic characters are drawn to her, though of course unthinking people and nasty people make fun of her. It is difficult for the reader to like Bridgetina, however, in spite of the physical defects she can have no control over. She frequently draws "up her long craggy neck so as to put the shrivelled parchment-like skin which covered it upon the full stretch," and in this rooster-posture is likely to intone, "Beauty . . . is a consideration beneath notice of a philosopher" (1: 195). She is self-centered to the point of sole-cism; the one person she truly talks to is her mother, to whom she is unrelievedly caustic. She has memorized Godwin's works, and spouts them whenever they are even faintly relevant, with the interesting result that Godwin's words—nearly always footnoted and printed in italics—invade Hamilton's text. When Hamilton includes Godwin's words, she usually alters them slightly, showing in Bridgetina's case that although Bridgetina can mimic Godwin's words, she does not really understand his ideas. If she did, she would not, for instance, cherish her passion for Henry Sydney, the sort of passion Godwin claimed would wither away. Hamilton has read her Godwin widely and carefully. She distinguishes, for instance, between the editions of *Political Justice,* and quotes as well from *The Enquirer.* She has also clearly read some of his novels and his memoir of his wife, Mary Wollstonecraft.

Bridgetina, the "ostensible heroine" (3: 332), has also read novels, and when she thinks about Henry, though still as usual "stretching her craggy neck" (2: 82), she switches away from Godwin's rhetorical flourishes to the language of romance: "O Julia! Julia! what a heart-moving history is mine" (2: 81). The autobiography that follows this exclamation addition-ally mixes the language of romance with the standard mock-heroic his-tory of a powerful male. Bridgetina begins at birth, where she antici-pated the midwife with "energetic impetuosity which scorned to wait for her arrival, and generated a noble spirit of independence, which brought me into the world without assistance" (2: 83). Hamilton does not men-tion the absent mother, though she is implied. This kind of reality can-not enter this kind of discourse. By a footnote, however, she leads us to Mary Hays's novel *Emma Courtney,* "a philosophical novel; to which Miss Botherim seems indebted for some of her finest thoughts" (2: 85). Hays's Emma gives a standard romantic-novel history of herself, which Hamilton evidently intends to reverberate with her mock-heroic version.

Hamilton's portrait of Hays was a palpable hit, and according to Maria Edgeworth "the name, the character of Bridgetina Botheram [*sic*] passed into every company, and became a standing jest, a proverbial point in conversation" (623). The portrait of Bridgetina is so vivid, filled as it is with the ironies of Bridgetina's willful misunderstandings of her hoped-for lover's statements, that it magnifies her insensitivity, dwelling as well on the ugliness which alone saves her from being seduced and abandoned. The physical characteristics attributed to Bridgetina have no counterpart in the Godwin portraits. Hamilton could have made good use of Godwin's "snorting laugh" (St. Clair 65) or even his long nose, but chose not to do so. Why was Hamilton, usually so sympathetic to women, so unremitting in Hays's case? Hamilton seems to agree that Bridgetina's and Hays's in-

sistence that women are free to pursue men as they wish is, in the ventriloquist Geoffry Jarvis's word, true "poison" (1: xv). Bridgetina is calculated by
ridicule both to scare young women who think they can pursue recalcitrant
men, and to save them from treacherous seducers.

To strengthen the point about the dangers women undergo, Hamilton
has intermingled her parody with tragedy. Julia's innocence and thoughtfulness represent an even more dangerous combination than Bridgetina's.
Her innocence is a familiar presence in many novels of this period, though
her thoughtfulness is not. When Bridgetina apostrophizes, "O Julia,"
Julia cannot resist a laugh, failing to notice (though Hamilton alerts the
reader) that she is using the same flawed discourse. Julia has invented an
orphan babyhood for her lover Alphonso Vallaton and even assumes that
she has located his parents. In reality, Vallaton is the child of a prostitute
(though she never owned him), called by his neighbors "the *funny vagabond*" (1: 44). He has also worked as a hair-dresser; he has always been
perfidious. Incidentally, wide as Hamilton's sympathies are, they do not
cross over into the discourse of Vallaton's rogue history and soften the
portrait of Vallaton's hanged mother. When Vallaton, a "bad man" (1:
xiv) of the sort mentioned by Geoffry Jarvis in the introduction, deftly
manipulates Julia with Godwin's arguments about free love, he succeeds
in seducing her. In Hamilton's didactic world, if not in her moral world,
a seduced woman must be punished. Julia eventually attempts suicide
by taking poison, and although the poison does not immediately kill her,
and she regrets her action, she dies from its effects.

In this roman à clef, the character who represents Mary Hays is very
obvious. But where is Mary Wollstonecraft? The answer is not obvious. One
of the Godwin figures, the philosopher Myope, travels with a companion
called "the goddess of Reason" (passim). She is certainly not Wollstonecraft,
though it has been claimed that she is (Ty 116). This Goddess has a very
heavy French accent, keeps a pug dog, and is interested mainly in fashion.
Later she proves to be named Emmeline; Emmeline runs off with Myope's
friend Vallaton, and when Vallaton proves inconvenient, she betrays him to
the guillotine. Although Godwin's companion would by a simple parallel
seem to be Wollstonecraft, the target here is rather the French Revolution
itself, represented by the woman the *Anti-Jacobin Review* calls "the strumpet who officiated at Paris as the Goddess of Reason" (41). Readers of
*Modern Philosophers* must always be wary of simple parallels.

There is one direct reference to Wollstonecraft during a discussion between Henry Sydney and Bridgetina about Rousseau. Bridgetina claims
that Rousseau was "a stranger to the rights of women," and Henry replies that "The inconsistency and folly of his system . . . was, perhaps,
never better exposed than in the very ingenious publication which takes

the Rights of Women for its title. Pity that the very sensible authoress has sometimes permitted her zeal to hurry her into expressions which have raised a prejudice against the whole. To superficial readers it appears to be her intention to unsex women entirely. But—" and Bridgetina interrupts him, insisting that there should be no distinctions between the sexes at all. Hamilton must here be denying Thomas J. Mathias's statement in his poem *The Pursuits of Literature* that "Our unsex'd female writers now instruct, or confuse, us and themselves, in the labyrinth of politics, or turn us wild with Gallic frenzy." Richard Polwhele had popularized this view by borrowing the words for the title of his poem *The Unsex'd Females* (1798 [3] n.), including a particularly sleazy attack on Wollstonecraft. Henry, who is a trustworthy speaker, shows that Polwhele's attack is unfounded in the case of Wollstonecraft. Bridgetina's response shows that in her case, Polwhele's attack is more nearly justified. Bridgetina—who claims to be a philosopher, and yet foolishly believes, as so many eighteenth-century *men* believed, that you can *force* someone else to love you—suffers from high-decibel confusion about sexuality.

Though interrupted, Henry clearly reads Wollstonecraft sympathetically and not superficially. Godwin, Wollstonecraft, and Hamilton had all suffered particularly from superficial readership, and were sensitive to reader-resistance. The implication, of course, from a speaker we can mostly trust, is that Hamilton reads Wollstonecraft in full recognition that her "zeal" is not the whole story. Thus she aligns herself with Godwin, who felt that Wollstonecraft had humanized him.

I would argue that the Wollstonecraft figure in *Modern Philosophers* is the second romance heroine, Julia Delmond, the woman who is seduced by Vallaton. Like Wollstonecraft, Julia chooses to cohabit with a lover without marrying him; like Wollstonecraft, she attempts suicide. The ironies of Julia's life are more terrible than those in the life of her original: Julia dies eventually from the lingering effects of the poison she has taken; she is never happily married as Wollstonecraft briefly was. This is parody, but it is tragic rather than comic parody, another fruit of the satura. Julia is fictional, overwrought, unnatural—and hence gains power even though she is a parodic figure. This power is reinforced by the fact that in this novel there are many other women who, through no fault of their own, find themselves in similar positions, and these women are realistically portrayed. Hamilton includes a homeless woman who is just about to sink into prostitution, and mentions the House of Industry, a haven for the seduced and abandoned. Unnamed hordes in the real world share Julia's story. Julia certainly suffers for her belief in Godwinianism, but she is also commended for these same beliefs. She is frank, brave, and open; she refuses to hide her pregnancy and abandonment—she will not skulk in the country until her baby is born.

## Ventriloquism: Godwin as the Other; Godwin as the Self

The perpetrator of Julia's seduction and abandonment, Vallaton, is a follower of Myope-Godwin and his shopkeeper hanger-on, Mr. Glib; he is a Godwin-dummy, forever quoting the master's words, or rather slightly misquoting them. The power of this flawed discourse is partly that it appeals to Julia's best qualities. Vallaton caters to Julia's pride in her energy and independence. Marriage is not his object, so he attacks it in Godwinian terms. Vallaton says, for instance, of Julia's father's relationship with her mother: *"in the hateful spirit of monopoly, he chose by despotic and artificial means to engross a pretty woman to himself "* (1: 165). The dummy is not saying what the author thinks, or even what Godwin thinks. Vallaton, like Bridgetina, misuses Godwin, with the difference that she is an inaccurate imitator and he is a designing hypocrite. What happens here is that the dummy heightens and changes the meaning of the original, with the effect that the original endures, to some degree, unscathed. "So long as I seek to engross one woman to myself," Godwin argues in *Political Justice,* failing to stress that the woman might be pretty, "and to prohibit my neighbour from proving his superior desert and reaping the fruits of it, I am guilty of the most odious of all monopolies." Godwin suggests the abolition of marriage, saying, "The abolition of marriage will be attended with no evils" (850), and further arguing that men will cease to be jealous when there is no marriage, and that relationships between the sexes, like all relationships, must be guided by "the unforced consent of either party" (851). "Unforced consent" is the argument Bridgetina so woefully misunderstands. Godwin minimizes the power of sensuality, arguing that inhibition can only "irritate and multiply" our tendency toward "lust and depravity" (851). In his idealistic view, the best women will be available to all, and sex will lose its importance: "We may all enjoy her conversation; and we shall all be wise enough to consider the sensual intercourse as a very trivial object" (851). Hamilton's point is not so much to scuttle these views as to argue that in the world as constructed in 1800, a sensual and predatory man would use these arguments about marriage to his advantage, wantonly seducing all the "pretty" women.

The ventriloquist's Godwin-dummy in *Modern Philosophers* speaks in many forms and many voices, complicating the reader's perceptions of the limitations of those who hold Godwinian concepts. Mr. Myope the philosopher is mentally nearsighted; he spouts his views, barely noticing their effects on those around him; he is a particularly dangerous kind of dummy, dangerous because so insouciant. Mr. Glib the shopkeeper parrots not Godwin, but Myope. The "author" remarks that the Godwinian characters persist in misunderstanding the world around them, "translating every sentence into their own language" (2: 234), and each does this in his special way—Bridgetina in various styles, depending on her mood; Vallaton in rhetoric borrowed from Gothic villains; Myope in a high philosophical vein; and Glib in a staccato form like the one Dickens will later use for Mr. Micawber. Although no one physically resembles Godwin, Glib is fond of double negatives, as was Godwin. Glib is apt to give advice like "Live with no one one does not like. Love no one but for what is in them" (2: 255). Glib is less dangerous than Vallaton or Myope, and as a lowly shopkeeper, more vulnerable. For his metaphysical innocence, he is betrayed into jail by the villainous Vallaton.

I have already noted that in a number of instances, untangling Hamilton from Godwin is more difficult than at first appears. Godwin inveighs against war; Hamilton does the same. Godwin decries poverty; Hamilton agrees with him. Godwin supports energy and independence; Hamilton supports them as well. Besides the characters already discussed, there are others—especially Martha Goodwin, Maria Fielding, and Mr. Sydney—who in some way represent Godwin—and Hamilton. They are not ventriloquist's dummies, because they do not actually borrow Godwin's words. But their ideas are certainly involved with Godwin's, and the separate discourses often cross. Hamilton divides herself as author among these characters, and she also divides Godwin among them.

Two women, Mr. Sydney's sister-in-law, Martha Goodwin, and Mr. Sydney's first love, Maria Fielding, speak the wise woman's version of the Godwinian system. Mrs. Goodwin, Godwin with an extra "o," is independent and strong; she faces death with an equanimity worthy of Hume, though supported by religion. One of the most important points she makes to her niece Harriet Orwell is that she has conquered passion. Thomas Laqueur remarks, following Barbara Taylor, that "Wollstonecraft shares with early socialist feminists a commitment to 'passionlessness,' whether out of some sense of its political possibilities, an acute awareness of passion's dangers, or a belief in the special undesiring qualities of the female body" (24). Certainly Hamilton nowhere discusses an undesiring female body, but she is acutely aware of passion's dangers, and of both the personal and political possibilities of celibacy. Like Hamilton, Mrs. Goodwin is a "cheerful, pleased old maid," but she emphasizes that she achieved this condition with difficulty. "By struggling with passion, I invigorated my virtue; by subduing it, I exalted the empire of reason in my breast. I learned to take a different view of life and its pursuits. I no longer cherished the idea, that all happiness was comprised in prosperous love; and that the lives of such as were united by the tender bonds of mutual affection, must inevitably be crowned with *unclouded felicity*" (2: 134). Public opinion was not helpful, and she had to steel herself against it: "[T]he forlorn state of celibacy, the neglect, the ridicule to which it is exposed, threw at times a temporary damp upon my spirits" (2: 134–35). Her remedy for these moments of discontent was to attempt to increase the happiness of others. In addition, the act of subduing her passion strengthened her reason, and this, too, has added to her happiness. "In the approbation of my own conscience; in the endearments of friendship; in the gratitude of those I have endeavoured to serve, or to comfort; and in that undisturbed peace which is the exclusive privilege of the unmarried; I have found an ample recompence [*sic*] for the mortification of hearing myself called *Mrs. Martha*" (2: 135–36). This speaker is certainly not the Godwin of *Political Justice,* but she shares some beliefs with Godwin and with Wollstonecraft. She feels that passion can be subdued, that eventually it will wither away.

Also unmarried, Mrs. Fielding has nurtured her passion for a man, even known that it was requited, though he—inveigled into thinking she had deserted him—has been rather happily married to someone else. Even so, she too is happy in her single life. When her lover's wife dies, she refuses to marry him. As Godwin would have had her do, all these years she has enjoyed her lover's conversation—his words rather than his body. She has also helped to raise his son. And she has spent much of her time aiding women who have been victimized by men, working in a place she calls the Asylum of the Destitute. It is here that Julia comes to die. And Mrs. Fielding is the character who commends Julia for her bravery in wanting to state publicly that she is about to bear an illegitimate child. Even Bridgetina begins to interpret her Godwin more effectively, to obey the ventriloquist. She begins at last to respect what Martha Goodwin called the "endearments of friendship" (2: 136). At Julia's deathbed Bridgetina sees that if she had not been ugly, she too might have died as Julia dies, seduced and abandoned. Hays was present at Wollstonecraft's deathbed, but the implication of this scene is that Hays did not learn to love and to care for others as Wollstonecraft did and as Bridgetina does. Eventually, Bridgetina values even her mother.

To replace Godwin's philosophy, Hamilton offers an enlightened Christianity. This belief, she feels, might have saved Julia. Hamilton attempts to leach the patriarchalism out of her version of Christianity, but still it is two men in particular, Dr. Orwell and Mr. Sydney, who represent the religion she presents as so supportive of women. Dr. Orwell is the local rector, and Mr. Sydney a dissenting minister, and yet their doctrinal differences do not separate them. The religion Hamilton is defining in *Modern Philosophers* is, to begin with, a religion of equality. Men and women are equal, since Jesus did not distinguish between them: "His morality was addressed to the judgment without distinction of sex" (1: 200). In

addition to sexual equality, Martha Goodwin suggests resuscitating the
creed that "I believe it is my duty to love my neighbour as myself, and to do
to others as I would have others do to me on the like occasion" (1: 203). Mr.
Sydney defines this idea as revolutionary: "The confession of charity and
brotherly love would be justly deemed an innovation big with alarm, and
quite inimical to the spirit of party zeal" (1: 204). Yet this "innovation big
with alarm" in many ways bears comparison to Godwinian schemes. Godwin
assumes that once his ideal society has been created, poverty and profusion
will be replaced by equality. In the current economic world of mutual envy
and exploitation, he sees little to commend. In one scene, Bridgetina, in her
role as a parodic surrogate for Godwin, speaking to a group of men scything
some hay, calls them "wretches" and sympathizes with their presumed misery. Unlike the suppressed native peoples—the Hindus and Hottentots—
the hay makers have a voice. When Bridgetina calls them wretches, an
old man replies, "What should make me wretched?" (1: 208). These hay
makers are not overworked. Indeed, more of them are hired than are
needed, and the profit motive is apparently not the only or even the first
motive for their hiring. Indeed, "many found employment there who
would have been rejected by more scientific farmers" (1: 206). By their
lights they live well. This laborer is happy—he is independent and well
paid. But other classes do suffer, and in the subsequent conversation in this
scene and others, it becomes clear that Hamilton agrees with Godwin that
the system itself, the nascent capitalist system, is at fault. Mr. Sydney's son
Henry feelingly describes the squalor he saw in city after city. The new
luxuries, the new manufacturing towns, have created the worst inequali-
ties in society.

"A monopoly of wealth and power," Mr. Sydney argues, is "an evil of
mighty magnitude" (3: 240). He and Dr. Orwell agree that their children, who are about to marry, do not need "a splendid establishment" (3:
240). "To the mind of Mr. Sydney, a monopoly of wealth and power appeared an evil of mighty magnitude; and far from wishing his children
to become accessaries [sic] in continuing a system, to which, in his opinion, might be fairly attributed the greater part of the miseries that have
scourged the human race, he had labored to impress their minds with a
sense of its turpitude and injustice" (3: 240). Mr. Sydney has written a
tract suggesting that all landed proprietors should make "an equal division of their property among their children, to begin that gradual and
rational reform, which would ultimately be productive of an increase of
public happiness and virtue" (3: 241). Many economic analysts, including Lord Kames and Adam Smith, had queried the process of entail, particularly in Scotland, by which the great landowners were further con-
solidating their fortunes and their power. Paradoxically, the growth of

manufacturing was strengthening this element in the Scottish economy (Campbell 94). Hamilton's suggestion did not prevail and might not have helped if it had. Given the consolidation of wealth in Scotland, Mr. Sydney agrees theoretically but not practically with Mr. Myope.

> But while he applauded the abstract notions entertained of each of these noble principles, he plainly demonstrated their inutility in the direction Mr. Myope had given them; and proved that to these, as well as to every other virtue, the principles of Christianity were the best, the only support. "I do indeed admire and applaud the zeal with which you espouse the cause of the poor and oppressed part of our species," said Mr. Sydney; "it does honour to your heart. But what does your system do for them? What does it propose to do?" (3: 290)

Myope says that by his system all people will give up their property. This, Sydney considers impractical. Carefully, Sydney argues through with Myope every portion of his philosophy, eventually showing him that "not an evil complained of could have existence in a society, where the spirit of christianity [*sic*] was the ruling principle of every heart" (3: 293). At the end, then, the Godwinians have either died or been converted. Vallaton has been guillotined, Julia perishes, Glib and Bridgetina settle down to ordinary life, and Myope seems convinced that Christianity is a better doctrine. Only Emmeline, the French Revolution, continues to pursue her destructive ways. This is the ending that the Hamilton-author would like to support, quite obviously. But how likely is it that the Godwins of this world will turn Christian?

The lodger-author ties up a different part of the plot. When all the young girls except Bridgetina find mates at the end, the male lodger archly invokes his readers: "But how could we have the heart to disappoint the Misses, by closing our narrative without a wedding? A novel without a wedding is like a tragedy without murder, which no British audience could ever be brought to relish" (3: 354–5). A couple of weddings are provided, but this ending is undercut by Mrs. Fielding's refusal to marry Mr. Sydney, by her preference for the peace of old age. Nor does Mr. Sydney indicate how he is going to put into practice the Christianity he has convinced Mr. Myope to believe in. The combined energies of all the good women and all the good men in this novel are considerable, but what will they change? Eighteen hundred years of Christianity have led to the conditions Hamilton's characters deplore. We might ask with Sydney, "But what does your system do for them? What does it propose to do?" (3: 290). Hamilton is suggesting a revolution as complete as Godwin's. And yet is it really enough that loving your neighbor is an "innovation big with alarm" (1: 205)? Hamilton does not give us an adequate answer. What will Christianity do that is different from what it has done before?

Thus Hamilton's surrogate at the end of her novel converts the Godwin figure, while agreeing with him about many of the ills in the world. Although the text does not overtly distinguish between Godwin and Hamilton except as theorists, it may be that the chief distinction between Godwin and Hamilton is not that Hamilton occasionally and inadvertently agrees with Godwin, or that Hamilton by art or by chance would, as Claudia Johnson put it, "minimize the necessity for reflection" (14), but that Godwin theorizes and Hamilton generalizes, and that Hamilton values human connection more than Godwin does. Godwin was known for being a rather remote person. This essential remoteness was what bothered Hamilton the most. She gently shows that Mr. Sydney suffers from it somewhat, for when he is seized by a botanical interest or an idea, he fails to notice his son's preoccupations. Perhaps by ridiculing Mr. Sydney in this way she intends to show that as a male he does not really study his fellow human beings in the detailed way Mrs. Goodwin or Mrs. Fielding would do. For Hamilton, every abstraction about human beings was embodied in a group of persons. She did not abstract. She generalized, and before she generalized she considered her group of persons, one by one. Godwin, in his famous conundrum about whether you would rescue Fénelon or the chambermaid from a burning building, chose Fénelon. He says he would choose Fénelon, even if the chambermaid was his wife, his mother, or his benefactor. Hamilton, I would hazard, would have chosen the chambermaid.

Throughout this essay I have stressed the difficulties of reading Hamilton and shown that eighteenth- and twentieth-century readers alike misread or half-read her work. Her particular satiric mix is an extremely effective experiment. Certainly, too, she needs to be doubly read, and the contradictions in her text must not be ignored. I wish to stress, however, that the liberal Hamilton is not merely a modern invention. Hamilton did have at least one reader, one person among the untrustworthy reviewers and the superficial public, who found in her work the energies I have been discussing. The writer of her obituary in the *Scots Magazine* said of *Modern Philosophers* that Hamilton "was far from displaying here that violent spirit of *Anti Jacobinism,* conspicuous in many similar works, and which arose from the reaction of the too violent tendency to innovation which had preceded. There breathed through it, on the contrary, a very liberal spirit, and a zeal, within certain limits, for the freedom of philosophical inquiry" (564).

# Works Cited

Allen, B. Sprague. "The Reaction Against William Godwin." *Modern Philology* 16.5 (Sept. 1918): 57–75.

*The Anti-Jacobin Review; or Monthly Political and Literary Censor* 7 (Dec. 1800) 39–46; 369–376.

Bakhtin, M. M. *The Dialogic Imagination*. 1975. Trans. Caryl Emerson and Michael Holquist. Austin: U of Texas P, 1981.

Benger, E. O. *Memoirs of Mrs. Elizabeth Hamilton*. 2 vols. London: Longman, 1818.

"Biographical Notice of Mrs. Elizabeth Hamilton." *The Scots Magazine and Edinburgh Literary Miscellany*. 78 (Aug. 1816): 563–65.

Campbell, R. H. "The Landed Classes." *People and Society in Scotland*. Vol. I: *1760–1830*. Ed. T. M. Devin and Rosalind Mitchison. Edinburgh: John Donald, in association with the Economic and Social History Society of Scotland, 1988. 91–108.

Doody, Margaret. *The Daring Muse: Augustan Poetry Reconsidered*. Cambridge: Cambridge UP, 1985.

Edgeworth, Maria. "Character and Writings of Mrs. Elizabeth Hamilton." *Gentleman's Magazine* 86 (July–Dec. 1816): 623–24.

Foucault, Michel. *The History of Sexuality*. Vol. I: *An Introduction*. Trans. Robert Hurley. New York: Vintage, 1980.

Godwin, William. *The Enquirer, Reflections on Education, Manners and Literature*. 1797. New York: Augustus M. Kelly, 1965

———. *An Enquiry Concerning Political Justice and Its Influence on General Virtue and Happiness*. 2 vols. 1793. Oxford and New York: Woodstock Books, 1992.

Grundy, Isobel. "'The barbarous character we give them': White Women Travellers Report on Other Races." *Studies in Eighteenth-Century Culture* 22 (1992): 73–86.

Hamilton, Elizabeth. 1808: *The Cottagers of Glenburnie, a Tale for the Farmer's Ingle-nook*. Ed. Gina Luria. 1808. New York: Garland, 1974.

———. *Memoirs of Modern Philosophers*. 3 vols. 3rd ed. London: G. G. and J. Robinson, 1801.

———. *Translation of the Letters of a Hindoo Rajah, with a preliminary dissertation on the History of the Hindoos*. 2 vols. 1796. Boston: Wells and Lilly, 1819.

Hazlitt, William. *The Spirit of the Age*. 1825. Menston, Yorkshire: Scholar P, 1971.

Johnson, Claudia L. *Jane Austen: Women, Politics, and the Novel*. Chicago and London: U of Chicago P, 1988.

Keddie, Henrietta (Sarah Tytler), and Jean L. Watson. "Mrs. Elizabeth Hamilton." *The Songstresses of Scotland*. 2 vols. London: Strahan, 1871. 1: 307–28.

Knight, Charles. "Imagination's Cerberus: Satire and the Metaphor of Genre." *Philological Quarterly* 69.2 (1990): 131–51.

Landry, Donna. *The Muses of Resistance: Laboring-Class Women's Poetry in Britain, 1739–1796*. Cambridge: Cambridge UP, 1990.

Laqueur, Thomas. "Orgasm, Generation, and the Politics of Reproductive Biology." *The Making of the Modern Body: Sexuality and Society in the Nineteenth Century*. Ed. Catherine Gallagher and Thomas Laqueur. Berkeley and Los Angeles: U of California P, 1987. 1–42.

Marshall, Peter H. *William Godwin*. New Haven: Yale UP, 1984.

*The Monthly Mirror* 10 (July 1800): 34.

Murdoch, Alexander, and Richard B. Sher. "Literary and Learned Culture." *People and Society in Scotland. 1: 1760–1830*. Edinburgh: John Donald, in association with the Economic and Social History Society of Scotland, 1988. 127–43.

[Polwhele, Richard.] *The Unsex'd Females: A Poem, Addressed To The Author Of The Pursuits of Literature*. London: Cadell and Davies, 1798.

Rogers, Katharine M. *Feminism in Eighteenth-Century England*. Brighton: Harvester Press, 1982.

St. Clair, William. *The Godwins and the Shelleys: The Biography of a Family*. New York: W. W. Norton, 1989.

Swift, Jonathan. *Irish Tracts 1728–1733*. Ed. Herbert Davis. Oxford: Blackwell, 1955.

———. *A Tale of a Tub*. Ed. Herbert Davis. 1710. Oxford: Blackwell, 1957.

Taylor, Susan. "The Empire Ventriloquized: Speaking of the English, Speaking through the Hindus in Elizabeth Hamilton's *Translation of the Letters of a Hindoo Rajah*." Paper presented to the American Society for Eighteenth-Century Studies. Providence, RI, Apr. 22, 1993.

Thaddeus, Janice. "Elizabeth Hamilton's Domestic Politics." *Studies in Eighteenth-Century Culture* 23 (1994): 264–84.

Tompkins, J. M. S. *The Popular Novel in England 1770–1800*. 1932. Lincoln, Nebraska: U of Nebraska P, 1967.

Todd, Janet. *The Sign of Angellica*. New York: Columbia UP, 1989.

Ty, Eleanor. "Female Philosophy Refunctioned: Elizabeth Hamilton's Parodic Novel." *Ariel* 22.4 (1991): 111–29.

# Contributors

RICHARD BRAVERMAN is Associate Professor of English and comparative literature at Columbia University. He is author of *Plots and Counterplots: Sexual Politics and the Body Politic in English Literature, 1660–1730* (Cambridge, 1993), as well as articles in *ELH, SEL, Studies in Philology, Philological Quarterly, The Age of Johnson, Studies in the Novel, Clio,* and elsewhere.

J. DOUGLAS CANFIELD is Regents' Professor of English at the University of Arizona. He is author of *Nicholas Rowe and Christian Tragedy* (Florida, 1977) and *Word as Bond in English Literature from the Middle Ages to the Restoration* (Pennsylvania, 1989); he is editor (with J. Paul Hunter) of *Rhetorics of Order/Ordering Rhetorics in English NeoClassical Literature* (Delaware, 1989) and (with Deborah Payne) of *Cultural Readings of Restoration and Eighteenth-Century Theater* (Georgia, 1995); he has published numerous articles on Restoration and eighteenth-century literature.

BRIAN A. CONNERY is Associate Professor of English at Oakland University, is co-editor of *Theorizing Satire: Essays in Criticism* (St. Martins, 1995), founding editor of *Writing on the Edge,* and author of essays on Swift, twentieth-century satire, and rhetoric.

ALLEN DUNN is Associate Professor of English at the University of Tennessee, Knoxville. He has published articles in *Boundary 2, Southern Humanities Review, Shakespeare Studies,* and *The Journal of Modern Literature.* He is currently at work on a book, *The Spectacle of Suffering,* which analyzes the dramatic representation of moral dilemmas in literature and philosophy.

JAMES E. GILL is Associate Professor of English at the University of Tennessee, Knoxville. His articles, published in *The Journal of the History of Ideas, Studies in Philology, Modern Language Quarterly, Restoration,* and *Texas Studies in Language and Literature,* among others, include studies of theriophily, Swift, Rochester, Vanbrugh, and Goldsmith.

CHARLES H. HINNANT is Professor of English at the University of Missouri—Columbia. He is the author of six books—*Thomas Hobbes* (Twayne, 1977), *Thomas Hobbes: A Reference Guide* (G. K. Hall, 1980), *Purity and Defilement in Gulliver's Travels* (St. Martin's, 1987), *Samuel Johnson: An Analysis* (St. Martin's, 1988), *The Poetry of Anne Finch* (Delaware, 1994), and *"Steel for the Mind": Samuel Johnson and Critical Discourse* (Delaware, 1994). His articles on seventeenth- and eighteenth-century subjects have appeared in a variety of professional journals.

JONATHAN LAMB is Professor of English at Princeton University. He has published *Sterne's Fiction and the Double Principle* (Cambridge, 1989) and *The Rhetoric of Suffering: Reading the Book of Job in the Eighteenth Century* (Oxford, 1995). He has edited essays from the ninth David Nichol Smith Seminar—*Voyages and Beaches: Cultural Exchange in the Pacific, 1700–1840*—for *Eighteenth-Century Life.*

DONNA LANDRY, Professor of English at Wayne State University, is the author of *The Muses of Resistance: Laboring-Class Women's Poetry in Britain, 1739–1796* (Cambridge, 1990) and she co-wrote, with Gerald MacLean, *Materialist Feminisms* (Blackwell, 1993). Her essays and reviews have appeared in a variety of major journals, and she is currently writing a book on the eighteenth-century countryside and its relation to suburban intellectuals.

ROBERT MARKLEY is Professor of English and holds the Jackson Chair of British Literature at West Virginia University. He is author of *Fallen Languages: Crises of Representation in Newtonian England, 1660–1740* (Cornell, 1993) and of *Two Edg'd Weapons: Style and Ideology in the Comedies of Etherege, Wycherly, and Congreve* (Clarendon, 1988); he has published numerous articles on eighteenth-century literature and culture, cultural theory, and the social studies of science; and he has edited three collections of essays, including *Virtual Realities and Their Discontents.* Since 1981 he has been editor of *The Eighteenth-Century: Theory and Interpretation.*

JEAN I. MARSDEN is Associate Professor of English at the University of Connecticut. She is author of *The Re-Imagined Text: Shakespeare, Adaptation and Eighteenth-Century Literary Theory* (Kentucky, 1995) and editor of *The Appropriation of Shakespeare: Post-Renaissance Reconstruction of the Works and the Myth* (Harvester, 1991; St. Martin's, 1992). She has also published articles on the representation of women on the Restoration stage.

JESSICA MUNNS is Associate Professor of English at the University of New Orleans. She has published articles on Behn and Otway and has two books in press: *Cultural Studies: An American-British Reader* (with Gita Rajan) and *Restoration Politics and Drama: The Plays of Thomas Otway, 1675-1683.*

MITZI MYERS teaches at UCLA. She has published extensively on historical children's literature and on eighteenth- and nineteenth-century women writers, including Mary Wollstonecraft, Hannah More, Harriet Martineau, and Maria Edgeworth. She is currently completing *Romancing the Family: Maria Edgeworth and the Scene of Instruction.*

DEBORAH C. PAYNE is Associate Professor of literature at American University. She is co-editor (with J. D. Canfield) of *Cultural Readings of Restoration and Eighteenth-Century Theater* (Georgia, 1995) and is now finishing a book-length study, *Patronage, Professionalism, and the Marketplace of Restoration Drama, 1660–1685.* Her articles and reviews have appeared in many journals and collections of essays.

MELINDA ALLIKER RABB is Associate Professor of English at Brown University and is currently writing a critical study of Mary Delariviére Manley. She edited *Making and Rethinking the Canon,* an MLS special issue. Her articles and reviews on eighteenth-century writers, including Swift, Pope, Richardson, Sterne, Godwin, Fielding and Scott, have appeared in numerous journals and collections of essays.

LINDY RILEY recently finished her doctorate and is a member of the extended faculty of East Tennessee State University. She has published an essay on Gwyn Jones.

JANICE THADDEUS, Senior Lecturer on history and literature at Harvard University, has published articles on Swift, Eva Maria Garrick, Mary Delany, Hester Thrale Piozzi, Frances Burney, and other English and American writers. Her article "Elizabeth Hamilton's Domestic Politics" recently appeared in *Studies in Eighteenth-Century Culture,* and she is presently working on *Frances Burney: A Literary Life* to be published by Macmillan (England).

CLAUDIA THOMAS is Associate Professor of English at Wake Forest University. Her first book, *Alexander Pope and His Eighteenth-Century Women Readers* (Southern Illinois, 1994), has just been published. She has also published articles on Pope, Johnson, and Elizabeth Carter.

DAVID WHEELER is Professor and Chairperson of the English department at the University of Southern Mississippi. He has published books on Johnson's biographies of Shakespeare and Shakespeare's *Coriolanus*, as well as numerous essays on the eighteenth century. His essay here is a part of a larger project on Pope's early poems.

NIGEL WOOD is Lecturer in English at The University of Birmingham, England. He has published essays on Romantic and modern authors, as well as on the eighteenth century. He is author of *Swift* (Harvester, 1986), co-editor of *John Gay and the Scriblerians* (St. Martin's, 1989), and editor of *Dr. Johnson and Fanny Burney: The Diaries, 1777–95.* He compiles the "General," "Drama," and "Prose" sections for *The Year's Work in English Studies* and is general editor of the *Theory in Practice* series for Open University Press, for which he acted as volume editor in the series for *The Prelude, Don Juan,* and *Mansfield Park,* as well as co-editor of *A Passage to India.*

ROSE ZIMBARDO is a State of New York Distinguished Professor at SUNY—Stony Brook. She is author of *Wycherley's Drama: A Link in the Development of English Satire* (Yale, 1965), *A Mirror to Nature: Transformations in Drama and Aesthetics* (Kentucky, 1986), and *At Zero Point: Politics, Discourse, and Satire* (under review). In addition to publishing extensively in her primary area of study, Restoration and eighteenth-century literature, she has also published articles in a wide variety of other areas: Shakespeare, Chaucer, Modern European Drama.

JOHN ZOMCHICK, Associate Professor of English at the University of Tennessee, Knoxville, is author of *Family and the Law in Eighteenth-Century Fiction: The Public Conscience in the Private Sphere* (Cambridge, 1993) and of a number of articles on the eighteenth-century novel.

# Index

Aarsleff, Hans, 387, 389
abjection, imagery of, 94–109
*Absalom and Achitophel*, 15, 16, 66–67, 71, 177
absurdist drama, 19
Addison, Joseph, 79, 117, 260–61, 273, 312, 368
Adeodatus, 25
Agnew, Jean-Christophe, 92
Ahern, Susan K., 332, 333
Allen, B. Sprague, 417
*An Argument Against Abolishing Christianity*, 161
Anderson, Benedict, 388, 389
animals, cruelty to and use of, 307–9
Anne, Queen of England, 87, 124, 131, 199, 288
*Anti-Jacobin Review*, 397, 398, 399, 401, 405, 406, 409, 417
Appleby, Joyce Oldham, 123, 124, 125
Arbuthnot, John, 370
Aristophanes, 135
Aristotle, 135
Armens, Sven, 324, 333
Armstrong, Nancy, 79–80, 92, 207, 219, 364, 365
Ashcraft, Richard, 70, 73, 74
Astell, Mary, 131, 404
Atkins, G. Douglas, 160, 161, 179
Augustine Aurelianus, St., 25, 28ff, 41
—Works: *Confessions*, 26, 27; *De Magistro*, 25, 26, 29; *On Christian Doctrine*, 25; *The Teacher*, 26
Ault, Norman, 252, 253, 308, 318
Austen, Jane, 364, 365, 402
Austin, J. L., 241
*The Author's Farce*, 320, 326–33

Avery, Emmett L., 58
Ayloffe, John, 74; *Oceana and Britannia*, 63

Bachscheider, Paula, 132, 136, 156
Baker, Van R., 11, 20
Bakhtin, Mikail, 77–78, 81, 90, 91, 92, 174, 179, 331, 368, 374, 375, 382, 385, 386, 389, 398, 405–6, 417
Ballaster, Ros, 132, 155
Bank of England, 110, 116, 120
Barash, Carol, 155
Barker, Francis, 76, 92
Barnet, Louise K., 200, 203
Barrell, John, 337, 345, 387, 389
Barthes, Roland, 160, 167, 172, 178, 252, 253
Bartley, J. O., 385, 389
Barzilai, Shuli, 273
Bate, Walter Jackson, 273
Bathurst, Allen, Lord, 302, 303, 306, 307, 309, 315, 316
Battestin, Martin, 330
Becker, Carl, 388, 389
Beckett, J. V., 318
Beckett, Samuel, 19, 24, 25
Bedient, Calvin, 267, 273
*The Beggar's Opera*, 17, 320–34
Behn, Aphra, 112–14, 118, 125, 129, 135, 136, 137, 156
—Works: *Abdelazer*, 141, 142, 143; *The Rover*, 127, 138–39, 322
Belanger, Terry, 296, 298
Bell, Ian A., 280, 295–96, 298
Belsey, Catherine, 142, 156
Benger, Elizabeth O., 399, 403, 404, 417
Bentley, Richard, 167, 168, 169, 170